T0326451

TURKEY AND THE WEST

From Neutrality to Commitment

Yusuf Turan Çetiner

University Press of America,® Inc.
Lanham · Boulder · New York · Toronto · Plymouth, UK

University Press of America,® Inc.
4501 Forbes Boulevard
Suite 200
Lanham, Maryland 20706
UPA Acquisitions Department (301) 459-3366

Unit A, Whitacre Mews, 26-34 Stannery Street,
London SE11 4AB, United Kingdom

Library of Congress Control Number: 2014951772
ISBN: 978-0-7618-6189-8 (clothbound : alk. paper)
eISBN: 978-0-7618-6190-4

Cover image: Special Session of the Assembly Convened for the
Purpose of Considering the Request of the Kingdom of Egypt for
Admission to the League of Nations, President Tevfik Rüştü Aras (Turkey).
Geneva, 1937. ©UNOG Library, League of Nations Archives.

Contents

Abbreviations

DP	Democrat Party (in Turkey)
DPRK	Democratic People's Republic of Korea (North Korea)
ECA	Economic Co-operation Administration
ERP	European Recovery Program
IBRD	International Bank for Reconstruction and Development
IMF	International Money Fund
JCS	Joint Chiefs of Staff (US)
JUSMMAT	Joint United States Military Mission for Aid to Turkey
MEC	Middle Eastern Command
MEDO	Middle Eastern Defence Organization
MFA	Ministry of Foreign Affairs (in Turkey)
MP	Member of Parliament
NAT	North Atlantic Treaty
NATO	North Atlantic Treaty Organization
NEA	Near Eastern and African Affairs (in the US Dept. of State)
OEEC	Organisation for European Economic Commission
PCC	Palestine Conciliation Commission
PRC	People's Republic of China
ROK	Republic of Korea

RPP	Republican People's Party (in Turkey)
SU	Soviet Union
SWNCC	State–War–Navy Coordination Committee (US)
TGNA	Turkish Grand National Assembly
TGS	Turkish General Staff
UNRRA	United Nations Relief and Reconstruction Agency
UNCOK	United Nations Commission on Korea
UNCURK	Unification and Rehabilitation of Korea
UNTCOK	United Nations Temporary Commission on Korea
US	United States
WEU	Western European Union

Turkish Pronunciation Guide

The Latin Turkish alphabet and its grammar introduced on November 1, 1928, has a systematic and consistent character. In Turkish, every letter is pronounced and each letter has only one sound. Importantly, two or more letters are not combined to make a new or different sound which the English speakers look for although they don't exist.

Most of the Turkish letters sound similar to their English equivalents with a few exceptions (when two or more letters combined to represent one sound):

A, a   short "a," as in "art" or "car"

Â, â   faint and longer "a," as in "parry"

C, c   "j," as in "join"

Ç, ç   "ch," as in "chest"

E, e   "eh," as in "send" or "tell"

I, ı   [undotted i] "uh," or the vowel sound in "clue" and "plus"

İ, i   [dotted i] "ee" in "see"

O, o   same as in English "phone"

Ö, ö   same as in German, or as in English "fur"

U, u   "oo," as in "blue" and "true"

Ü, ü   same as in German, or French "tu"

C, c   pronounced like English "j," as in "jet" and "John"

Ç, ç   "ch," as in "chess" and "change"

G, g   always hard, as in "go," never soft, as in "gentle"

Ğ, ğ   a "g" with a little curved line over it: not pronounced; lengthens preceding vowel slightly

H, h   never silent, as in "house" and "h"; there are no silent "h"s in Turkish, like "hour"

J, j   like French "j," English "zh," or the "z" in "closure"

S, s   always unvoiced, as in "stress," not "zz," as in "tease"

Ş, ş   "sh," as in "shout" and "should"

V, v   a soft "v" sound, half-way to "w"

W, w   same as Turkish "v"; found only in foreign words

X, x   as in English; found only in foreign words; Turkish words use "ks" instead

Foreword

Atatürk and the War of Independence rightfully dominate historical writing on Turkey. One of the chief benefits of that successful struggle was the establishment of the right of the new Turkish State to exercise a foreign policy. In fact, the ability to exercise an independent foreign policy in the world is perhaps the major product of the effective establishment of sovereignty and independence. The exercising of a successful foreign policy is thereafter very important because what is costly to win the right to exercise can all too easily be lost in the actual exercising of it.

What Atatürk and the Turkish Nation achieved in the liberation war was nothing short of extraordinary. However, in the years following the establishment of the Turkish State extraordinary circumstances and events in the world put the accomplishment of independent nationhood in the balance again. It could be said that foreign policy became all important to the extent that the achievements of Atatürk and the very life of the independent Turkish State depended upon it.

Turkey and the West: From Neutrality to Commitment is a study of the key developments in Turkish foreign policy from the second half of the 1930s to the end of 1950s. It represents an important contribution to our understanding of this pivotal period which, in terms of the Turkish role in European and Middle Eastern contemporary history, is yet to be fully explored.

An objective and detached analysis of Turkish foreign policy during this often neglected period is very much required in order to fully understand the development of Turkey's orientation in the world today.

Western academics and political commentators tend to view matters during this historical period from the Churchillian and Cold War perspectives in which states are judged according to their perceived useful-

ness, or otherwise, to the war against the Axis Powers and afterwards in
the conflict with the Soviet Union. They also tend to telescope the past
from the present, assuming that progress toward the prevalence of liberal democracy today was inevitable, when this was simply not the case.

After Atatürk's victory over the Imperialist Powers he sought to ori-
entate the new Turkish State toward the West and its democratic model.
However, as a result of the catastrophic effects of the Great War it was
far from clear if democracy had much of a future in Europe. The growth
of the Bolshevik State in Russia, as a result of the Czarist collapse, and
the coming to power of Fascists and National Socialists in circumstances
of economic crisis and elemental conflict between Left and Right across
the European continent suggested that democracy may well have become
inadequate to the problem of order and stability. Perhaps its time was up.

During this period between the two world wars even Britain, the
hold-out of parliamentary democracy, resorted to national government
and a suspension of party conflict in order to ward off political instability. But at the same time the British Empire failed to defend the political
order it had established as a result of its victory in the Great War. Britain's
vacillating foreign policy created great uncertainty in the world as to
how political affairs were to progress in the future. As a result all states
had the difficulty of navigating through treacherous waters to an unknown destination.

This was a particularly serious problem for Turkey which should not
be underestimated. At the moment when it lost its great statesman and
leader Turkey faced the growing power of the Soviet State to its North
and East. From the West loomed the expansionist aggressions of National Socialist Germany and Fascist Italy. And it saw the western democracies of Britain and France, which Turkey was most disposed toward, first appease the totalitarian states and then fail to protect the buffer
state democracies that had been created as part of the Great War settlement at Versailles.

To deal with this volatile and threatening situation took a great deal
of skill in the conducting of foreign affairs on the part of the Turkish
Government. And the survival of the Turkish State was not accomplished
through the exercise of doctrinaire principle but through improvisation
and political weaving, in the manner of a boxer who finds himself against
the ropes.

The alliance of convenience built up to destroy Hitler was an unnatural one and a new political conflict began emerging in the world even

before the one between Allied and Axis Powers had concluded. Turkey had to deal with this new situation as the Allied powers became enemies again and a new world order emerged in 1945.

Dr. Çetiner shows that Turkey's decision to choose sides and to reject neutrality in the Cold War had profound implications for the country that went far beyond its procurement as an active ally of the western democracies. This decision also had a direct impact on shaping the vision of Turkey right across the spectrum of its domestic to foreign affairs. The West has tended to give inadequate attention to this fact both at the time and even today. However, any understanding of Turkey today should be predicated upon this fact.

Throughout the period concerned Turkey was largely perceived by the West to be at the margins of the conflict between the rival blocs. In fact, Turkey had a vital role to play in the Cold War, given its proximity to the Soviet Union and its strategic importance in the Mediterranean and the Middle East. In these decades, Turkey made its transition from benevolent neutrality to full commitment in the formation of the democratic grouping of states despite the uncertainties and dangers of a troubled international situation.

This work unravels the complexities of the period from the threatening war years in which Turkish vulnerability was manifestly obvious to the outbreak of the Korean War and the revolutions in the Middle East.

By paying attention to Turkey's domestic politics the author introduces a wider and unique perspective on the subject. Dr. Çetiner's range of contacts with Turkish diplomats and his archival work in the Turkish Ministry of Foreign Affairs, which is still closed to public scrutiny, brings to his analysis both a first hand knowledge of diplomatic processes, together with a scholarly ability to explore complex and multi-dimensional issues with clarity, and without any over-simplification.

Study of this book will provide the reader with a greater appreciation of the complex issues of the period and of the difficult evaluations and choices that were made by Turkish leaders within a volatile and ever-changing political situation. It will be greatly rewarding both for those who already have a good knowledge and understanding of Turkish political history and for anyone who wishes to understand the period in a richer and more varied way than standard accounts provide.

Dr. Pat Walsh

Acknowledgments

Every scholar of international relations knows that research and writing would be impaossible without the friendly help of many people. In my research, above all, I had the good fortune to enjoy the support of Dr. Bilge Criss who also allowed me to use her private library and furnished me with countless memoirs, precious first hand sources and numerous out of print books. I would like to gratefully and sincerely thank Dr. Criss for her patience and guidance.

I profoundly thank Dr. Pat Walsh for reading my manuscript. His help came in at a stage this work was drawing closer to publication with prevailing difficulties as I was determined to maintain the content and style. Any author knows the meaning and value of this. He also gave me the honour of writing a foreword to this book.

I acknowledge with much appreciation the generosity of Prof. Yüksel İnan with his time and ideas to comment on the manuscript.

I am pleased to state my sincere thanks to my former adviser, Dr. Martin Kolinsky since the second chapter of this book carries the traces of my time in the University of Birmingham.

Ambassador Mr. Altay Cengizer's insightful remarks on the problems of interpreting history greatly enhanced this work wherever the longstanding issues such as the Balkans' role in Turkish politics were brought under discussion.

Ambassadors Mr. Halil Akıncı, Mrs. Serpil Alpman, Mr. Mehmet Taşer, Mr. Süphan Erkula and Mr. Mehmet Dönmez encouraged me to pursue my researches while continuing my service in the Turkish Ministry of Foreign Affairs in the most efficient way and provided me with their analytic view on the working of the diplomatic mechanism of MFA both today and in the past. With that said, the opinions expressed in the book are solely my own and do not reflect the views of the Turkish MFA or anyone else.

I'd like to thank the senior officials of the MFA, Deputy Minister Mr. Naci Koru, Deputy Undersecretary Ambassador Mr. Ali Kemal Aydın and Ambassador Mrs. Lale Ülker and Mrs. Şebnem İncesu who've encouraged my writing in its various forms and have generously helped each new project on its way.

Since the beginning of my studies and working life, our family friend, Lawyer Mr. Selçuk Ömerbaş and Mrs. Seçil Ömerbaş were always with us to provide help whenever we needed. I am honored to record our deepest appreciation for all the support and encouragement they generously extended to us on countless occasions.

Throughout the years of my work, my grandmother Şadan Aral, my parents Baykan and Kayhan Çetiner, especially my mother Baykan and my wife Melek Umay constantly supported me. If this work is a success, I would like to dedicate it to them as the nearest representatives of female forces of advancement in our society in Turkey and elsewhere.

Yusuf Turan Çetiner
Ankara, 2014

Chapter 1

Scope and the Contention

Before any army starts or any sword is drawn, there remain to be made the decisive move in the most dramatic and fascinating campaign of modern diplomacy. Skill more than might is likely to control the game.[1]

On the Need for a Re-Interpretation of Turkey's Move from Neutrality to the Western Alliance

As is generally agreed, political scientists are expected to search for answers regarding the making of policy in specific cases rather than approving or disapproving of what happened in history. The distant past becomes clearer with correct approaches in this regard whilst even the recent past remains as something of a haze of clichés when void of this. It is also undeniable that the approaches one takes are shaped by the available resources too.

In this context, a few words need to be said on the nature of available Turkish resources pertaining to the subject matter of this book. The great majority of Turkish authors who wrote about the making of Turkey's Western alliance are divided into two separate camps, each excluding the viewpoint of the other. The existence of the opposite view in this work therefore, should be perceived in the framework of pointing out the counter thesis which is a part of the history and has its own peculiarities as a result of the historical process in the world in general and in Turkey specifically. Under the pressure of the Cold War, similar limitations no doubt apply to those works which are on the pro-side too. It is therefore the methodology of this book to lay the ground for a robust rethinking of historical facts without disregarding the "opposite" view—through separating it wherever it merges with propaganda—in the discussion of the said process.

To fulfill this objective, materials relevant to the present study in the archives of the MFA of the Republic of Turkey were consulted within the boundaries of working in an archive which has not yet been opened to the public. They include, press statements, extracts from correspondence between the MFA and embassies and between the MFA and foreign missions in Ankara which were utilized to present a chronological flow of events as well as new material contribution to the discussion of the subject matter.

The gaps left by the MFA archives were basically bridged with information and comments obtained from the memoirs of various statesmen, officials, soldiers and journalists, and the books written by them. The FRUS, Command and Cabinet Papers, Keesing's Contemporary Archives and Documents on International Affairs series were consulted as well which offered a complete picture of Turkey's relations with the US and Britain in particular and the West in general during the period under review. In addition to the relevant literature available, the "tip of the iceberg" part of translations of published some Russian, Chinese and Korean primary and secondary sources were also examined to point out that the researchers on the emerging relevant literature will make further contribution to the discussion at hand. In this regard, consultation of the Turkish primary and secondary sources and their introduction into the English literature on the subject are done to also serve this objective.

In order to introduce further evidence to the debate, a number of interviews with diplomats, soldiers and academicians who had witnessed the developments of the period were made. They, no doubt, provide valuable insights in this research.

On this premise, the book considers the formulation of Turkish foreign policy in the period of 1938 to 1958 and discusses Turkey's shift from neutrality to become a member of the Western Alliance. It aims to indicate that Turkey's quest for a Western alliance in the aftermath of WW II was a natural end-result of the experiences inherited from its wartime diplomacy and the inclinations of Turkish governments starting from 1939. In this framework of analysis, the book discusses that forced by the conditions of an unpredictable international environment, Turkish governments of the time opted for seeking ways to enhance the country's security; an effort which paved the way to the formation of an alliance with the West.

In 1946, facing the Soviet assertiveness in global affairs, it was increasingly felt by the makers of Turkish foreign policy that maintaining an alliance with Britain and the US was inevitable and necessary. At this juncture, Britain was pursuing a regular withdrawal policy from its globally entrenched status while simultaneously working on redefining its foreign policy. In its turn, Washington was reluctant to extend its commitments and had the opinion that as far as the coordination of security planning was concerned Turkey was in "Britain's area of responsibility." It was the Truman Doctrine that marked a complete change in the US perception of Turkey and Greece. But the international arena proved to be too eventful for the Truman Doctrine to work as originally it was designed to do.

In order to deepen the discussion in this context, this work makes a comparative study of Turkish foreign policy in the period concerned as well. Thus, attitudes of consecutive governments, mainly divided between those run under the Presidency of İsmet İnönü, and the Democrat Party era after May 14, 1950 elections towards the course of international events are explored. The period subsequent to the elections of May 1950, after which the Democrat Party Administration decided to push Turkey to its limits—through hasty attempts at times—where the reflexes of benevolent neutrality towards the Allied side inherited from WW II, was abandoned in favour of an active search for security partnership with the West is examined as the last phase in this process. Here, Turkey's proposed inclusion in a Middle Eastern Defense Organization (MEDO) and its decision to assign a combat force of brigade size in the UN Command in Korea are evaluated as the main events in this crucial period of time. Within this framework, the book also aims to elaborate the view that the continuation of politics by war, and the continuation of war by politics continued throughout 1950 and 1952 finally paving the way to the first enlargement of the Western Alliance within the framework of NATO with the inclusion of Turkey and Greece.

Meanwhile, in the Middle East, Britain was mainly concerned with consolidating its own position in Egypt and in relation to the Suez Canal, at a time when the US plannings for the "containment" of any Soviet influence through the Northern Tier (and later, the Baghdad Pact) was emerging as a major priority. The British and American governments' attempt to reorganise their positions in the Middle East vis-à-vis the So-viets eventually represented a process in which the involvement of Turkey acquired a greater importance.

A Précis of the Chapters

Throughout WW II, Turkey was a country that was known to have benevolent neutrality towards the Allied side while remaining strictly non-belligerent in the global conflict. Its status was generally agreed upon by the Allied powers particularly in the second part of 1943, when it was invited to take part in the Allied side on two occasions. Eventually, Turkey remained outside the alliance schemes during the course of the war, and the struggle did not spread to its territories. However, changing times and conditions would make it an arduous option for the Turkish policymakers to remain outside of emerging trends in international relations. Therefore, it soon felt the need for a reassessment of security concerns with regard to changes in the balance of power on the European theatre as an utmost priority.

The surprisingly fast changing political climate of the post war period culminated in the Soviet control of central and eastern Europe. In turn, the construction of the NATO alliance marked a fundamental stage in the anxieties of the Soviet and Western blocks. At this stage, Turkey found itself compelled to immediately figure out the ways in which it could assure the inviolability of its national security. The division of blocs were emerging and the fate of "Soviet liberated" nations of Europe were alarmingly falling into the hands of their "liberators." No doubt, the amazing dynamism of Soviet power in the post-war months extended itself to pronounce further desires on Turkish possessions: the Straits issue; and the demand of the return of some Turkish eastern provisions to the SU being the most cited ones.[2]

While re-interpreting these critical years, the book gives a platform to the counter-argument which pointed out that the steps taken by Western and Turkish policy makers, without thorough planning for contingency, jeopardized Turkey's security at a time the SU was getting incredibly unpredictable too. It also emphasizes that adding to the difficulties of Ankara, with their war shattered economies and crippled resources, the Western Democracies were unwilling to pay immediate attention to Turkey's efforts to draw attention to growing Soviet ambitions which no doubt required Turkey to follow an active foreign policy.

Given these premises, it is the contention of this book that:

1. Turkey's quest for a Western Alliance in the aftermath of WW II was an end-result of the experiences inherited from wartime diplomacy and the political decision of the Turkish Governments which believed this to be the only way to face increasing Soviet assertiveness;

2. Ankara's adherence to the alliance of the Western grouping of states was not a single event. It was the end-product of a variety of incidents and policies which operated towards this effect. From this perspective, in a world moving onwards a bipolar "cold" or "hot" conflict, two epic events in totally different parts of the globe played significant roles: the decision to create a Middle Eastern Defense Organization—MEDO—and the Korean War. Based on these issues, particularly the interval between 1950 to 1952, witnessed a broad conflict between Soviet/communist oriented forces and the West. The interpretation to be advanced in this context, thus, includes an analysis of the interests that diverged the Western and Soviet poles and which resulted in Turkey's remaining in the Western camp;

3. An increasing tendency in the discipline of international relations considers the existence of a third-way. This is the role of third countries in the bipolar struggle for power. Having adopted this viewpoint, in line with the assumption stated above, this in turn means that there are essentially two themes in this work: the nature of political evolution in the post WW II era, and efforts to place Turkey in the Western grouping of states, which had an undeniable effect in shaping contemporary world politics;

4. In this framework, this book aims also to shed light on a set of controversial matters, particularly, on the Turkish foreign policy of the late 1930s and of the 1950s. The discussion includes the less elaborated aspects of the Turkish foreign policy of the WW II years, i.e., Ankara's balancing act towards the developments of the war years through its bridging of domestic politics (levying of Capital tax to non-muslims; its removal; trial of nationalists etc.) with the course of international affairs in order to send proper signals to belligerent

powers; and the bringing of the activities of socialists in the country under scrutiny.

The making of a multi-tracked diplomacy has always been an exhaustive process with surprising aspects emerging such as the difficulties in foreseeing the outcomes of decisions taken. As will be discussed, the period from 1938 to 1958, clearly introduced the Turkish policy makers into more than that since the complexities of these years were accepted to be those of rapid and chaotic changes when no single event could be considered in isolation.

In accordance with the above mentioned framework, the second part focuses on Turkey's famous neutrality or—as we call based on the suggestion of the flow of evens of the time—responsive neutrality against the fluctuations in international politics which took the shape of benevolence towards the Allied side and evasiveness at times depending on the course of events. The chapter argues that Turkey's neutrality was the end-result of an anxious search for saving the country from the disasters of war. Against a background of increasing tensions stemming from the revisionists' camp in the interwar period, until 1938, Turkey actively sought a solid alliance with Britain. However, this met a positive response only after the collapse of the Munich system. On the other hand, it should be pointed out that the main actors in this episode—Britain and Turkey—looked at the diplomatic conjuncture from significantly different angles, and thus tended to pronounce the different aspects of ongoing processes.

Here, it was assessed that following the menacing destruction of the Munich system in September 1938, for Britain, it was the increasing German involvement with the Balkan region that lay behind the gradual change in its foreign policy towards Turkey from a decidedly reserved outlook to a desire for Turkey's active inclusion in the Allied side. The European alliance against Hitler was primarily a "marriage of convenience" between powers which had been diametrically opposed before Hitler's invasion of the USSR and returned to political opposition after it. It has been a traditional principle of the British Balance of Power policy to form "Grand Alliances" against continental threats with states it was opposed to ideologically.

For Turkey, since the emergence of the Italian threat in the Mediterranean which goes back to 1930s, it was the rising Italian aggression in this part of the world which was the prime Turkish consideration in

seeking of allies. The chapter concludes that these two different perceptions of threats came to a juncture on October 19, 1939 when the Tripartite Agreement between Britain, France and Turkey took place.

The third part of this work analyzes the Allied and Axis relations
with Turkey and the making of Turkish foreign policy in this period. In
this context it is explained that while Turkey's sensitivity against the bloc
strategy of world powers was increasing, the Nazi–Soviet pact of 1939
demonstrated that the danger could emerge as a collective movement.
Subsequently, it is asserted that the split in this bloc had not removed the
threat, and in an unpredictable international environment, Turkey constantly sought ways to enhance its security; an effort which eventually
paved the way to building a sui-generis crisis management/prevention
system of its own. As stated in this chapter, this was a complex system
which could not be explained in terms of neutrality or an evasive foreign
policy.

Here, it will also be elaborated that, from the early 1940s on, Soviet
military strategy was geared towards post-war goals. Despite the dramatic incidents in the summer of 1941, when the SU was attacked by
Germany, Stalin maintained his political objectives. The consistent Russian purpose was revealed when Stalin offered the British a straight sphere
of influence deal at the end of 1941. He suggested that Britain should
recognize the Soviet absorption of the Baltic states, part of Finland, eastern Poland and Besserabia in return for Russia's support for any special
British need for bases or security arrangements in Western Europe.

In this framework of analysis, the very beginning of the period of
"polarization" was considered as having its roots in the diverging attitudes of the former Allies. Indeed, the Soviet plans to grasp control of
Eastern Europe was as evident in the negotiations between Molotov and
Ribbentrop held in Berlin in 1939, as in Stalin's talks with Roosevelt and
Churchill in 1945 in Teheran and Yalta. To make this point another way,
in addition to the disconcerting approach of the Soviets, Anglo–Saxons'
plannings for the ending of the war also contributed to complicating the
post-war political picture.

In certain respects, the doctrine of Unconditional Surrender stated
by Roosevelt and Churchill and their Joint Chiefs of Staff at the Casablanca
Conference in January 1943 was among the factors which created a power
vacuum in Europe. Since, the Allies persistently operated along the lines
of this agreed principle, in a European war theatre in which the US and
British troops were not present until June 1944—despite the pressures of

Stalin who was demanding the opening of a Second Front—inevitably, the strategy of "Unconditional Surrender" worked to Stalin's advantage. The propounded doctrine meant that the Red Army, having advanced to Elbe, would have a legitimate reason for staying there and for maintaining what would amount to be occupation forces in countries through which its supply lines ran. Having understood the undelightful course of developments, for the rest of the war, the Western Allies faced a situation that the war should be fought increasingly with the dual purpose of both defeating Germany and also forestalling the emergence of the SU as a mighty power in the center of Europe.

Concerning Turkish–Allied States negotiations, the events of 1943, the talks between the Turkish President İsmet İnönü and Churchill in Adana on January 30–31, 1943; the Cairo Talks between the Turkish Minister of Foreign Affairs, Numan Menemencioğlu, and the British Foreign Minister, Anthony Eden, on November 4–6, 1943, where the Allied decision of inviting Turkey to take part on the Allied side made at the Moscow Conference of October 19, was once again expressed to the Turkish officials; and the Cairo Conference of December 5–8, 1943 between İnönü, Churchill and Roosevelt, are also discussed in the context of providing the background in which Turkey chose to continue talks with the Allied powers while adapting a benevolent neutrality in the course of events. This chapter finally examines the Turkish–Soviet talks between 1944 and 1946 which culminated in Ankara's decision that the situation could not be improved with Moscow.

The fourth part focuses on the surfacing problems of peace which were coupled with consolidating rival blocs both on the part of the Soviets and the West. Here, it is suggested that by the turn of 1946, facing the growing ambitions of the Kremlin in different parts of the continent, Ankara was more apprehensive then ever about the consequences of Soviet moves. In this period, Turkey accelerated its efforts to bring its foreign policy nearer to that of the US and tried to enhance its relations with the Western camp in Europe. In this context, this chapter discusses the US' sending of *USS Missouri* to the Turkish Straits and the ambivalence of Washington about its policy towards Ankara. Here, the Turkish–Soviet exchange of Notes in 1946 on the irredentist claims of the Kremlin is examined as well.

The fifth part concentrates on the Turkish transformation to a multiparty system and its foreign policy implications with a particular emphasis on the US' inclusion of Turkey in its foreign assistance programs—the Truman Doctrine being the most cited one.

As commonly agreed, the development of Turkish democracy, basically had its roots in Ankara's wish for joining the Western camp in Europe. However, the first elections in 1946 were not a successful attempt in this regard, since rumors of Ankara's governmental manipulation in the election results were widespread throughout the country. From then on, the İnönü administration was caught between pursuing a more liberal attitude towards the opponents of the Republican People's Party (RPP) rule in Turkey and the closing of ranks against the external threat, namely the SU. In accordance with his squared interpretation of events, İnönü felt a necessity to direct Ankara's foreign policy in line with the basic trends in the Western grouping of states and adopted a strong anti-communist policy in the country. The Turkish socialists' attempts for a greater freedom of political expression for the left were systematically suppressed from then on. Finally, against a background of hopes for having a fundamentally different opposition party, the emergence of an opposition party within the ranks of the ruling RPP are analyzed.

Indeed, there had been a visible socialist activity in the period immediately following the war in Turkey. In December 1945, the Turkish socialists' attempts for a greater freedom of political expression for the left had been decisively set back by violent demonstrations. A year later in December 1946, the small bodies of these leftist opposition were dissolved under the martial law that was maintained in Thrace and in the İstanbul region since the war. İnönü's particular policy choice was criticized especially by those who believed that Turkey's relations with the SU had some basic features which diverged with that of the West in general and the US in particular. Here, the views of the opponents of single party rule arguing that Ankara's traditional relations with Moscow dated back to the foundation years of both countries could provide them with a platform of agreement are discussed.

Subsequently, the developing crisis in international affairs and its reflections on Ankara's efforts to side with the European democracies are brought under scope. At this juncture, the most serious division between the West and the SU came in 1947 over Greece. In 1946, as a result of elections, the royalists formed a government and a plebiscite favored the return of the King. Civil war between the communist guerrillas and the royalists broke out again. In its turn, London expressed to Washington that Britain, due to its financial problems could no longer assist the Greek army. Under these circumstances, the Truman Doctrine was launched to fill the emerging "gap" after the British withdrawal.

Given this, it is explained that the Turkish foreign policy makers had accelerated their efforts to include Turkey in this assistance scheme of the US as the end-result of a series of developments and through quickly formulated attempts at times. Here, it is argued that Ankara's inclusion in the US aid program was subject to considerable difficulties and truly, the US aid was not automatically offered at all, in contrast it was first requested by Ankara. Lastly in this chapter, weaknesses in Ankara's position of negotiation which opened up a period of further bilateral agreements of an unrevealed nature with the US are brought under scope.

The sixth part discusses the Turkish role in regional defense and the creation of the MEDO between 1948 to 1950. This chapter begins with discussing the increasing tensions of the Cold War in Europe which resulted in the signing of the Brussels Pact on March 17, 1948 by Britain, France, Belgium, the Netherlands and Luxembourg to face the Soviets. It is then explained that however, the coup in Czechoslovakia and Stalin's rigidity in Eastern Europe prompted thoughts that this would not be enough.

The full scale blockade of Berlin by the Soviets in the summer of 1948 fostered this line of thinking. There was also a counter-blockade in the Russian zone by the West that made Stalin agree for a mutual lift in January 1949. Clearly, the success of airlift in breaking blockade increased Western unity and confidence. However, the division over Germany through the establishment of the German Democratic Republic re-alarmed the West. Facing the course of events in Europe, Truman immediately recommended support for the Brussels Pact, and on June 11, the Senate adopted the Vandenberg Resolution, pledging the US to associate itself with regional and other collective arrangements of this kind. The direction of negotiations for a new and expanded pact was undertaken by Secretary Marshall, then completed by the new Secretary of State Dean Acheson.

Negotiations between the US and Canada then followed on the creation of a single North Atlantic Alliance based on security guarantees and mutual commitments between Europe and North America. Denmark, Iceland, Italy, Norway and Portugal were invited to take part in this process. These negotiations culminated in the signature of the Treaty of Washington in April 1949. It was confirmed by the US Senate on July 21, 1949 by a vote of 82 to 13. Although the degree to which the members were bound to take action was unclear, the US' adherence to the treaty marked the official end of its non-entanglement policy.

On this premise, it is asserted that Turkey's plea of combining its defense with the rest of Europe received poor support. Ankara was evidently excluded from the alliance as a founding member. The Turkish non-involvement in WW II was often cited as among the most crucial reasons behind this interlude in relations with the West. As will also be discussed, the Turkish policymakers were facing the dilemma of enhancing the security of their vast lands on the cross-roads between east and west, and getting involved in the active defense schemes being launched by both London and Washington which might either ensure deterrence or provoke further aggression. For Washington, it was essential to determine whether the inclusion of Turkey in NATO would provoke or deter the Soviets. Concurrently, according to some US policymakers, from a geopolitical and strategic perspective, the neutralist option for Turkey had to be kept under review too.

Undoubtedly, more than one question arose: would the advantages that would accrue be offset by the administrative burdens that would be imposed on NATO's half-completed organizational structure? Would Turkey be reassured by the additional guarantees or frustrated by the statements that NATO lacked the capabilities to offer much concrete assistance should a hot war erupt in the near future?

The US Joint Chiefs of Staff expressed similar reservations on the "untimely" admission of Turkey and Greece into NATO since this would hamper their commitments in Western Europe. Acknowledging the importance of Turkey's regional role, they nevertheless insisted that the Europe must have top priority. The decision was to offer Turkey and Greece an associate status and when western capabilities grew, it would be desirable to include Turkey and Greece in NATO. There were no explicit promises, however. In this period of uncertainty, Washington hoped to placate Turkey and sustain the strategic advantages of cooperation.

Subsequently, increasing efforts to include Middle Eastern states in this new security umbrella (to which Turkey not only joined but also sought ways to increase members in the region) are discussed. Admittedly, Britain's regular withdrawal from its Middle Eastern possessions was followed by an appeal for US contribution to positions it had created in the Middle East. Until then, due much to the historical evaluation, the importance of the Middle East to the US was determined to a large extent by its importance to Britain. Though the US held no colonies in Africa and in Asia compared to those held by the British, the US interest in the Middle East was great because of its strategic position and control of air routes. Moreover, both the US and Britain maintained their stance towards the Middle Eastern oil in the context of ensuring this strategic asset's free and unrestricted flow to their allies in western countries. Given this, it is explained that Britain's re-acknowledgement of the 1939 Treaty with Turkey and France in the aftermath of WW II was an end-result of its considerations on the continuation of its influence in the Middle East.

In May 1950, Foreign Office Under Secretary Michael Wright, raised the possibility of establishing a Middle East defense pact, perhaps linked to NATO. The US policy makers reacted unenthusiastically to extend American facilities/resources under NATO to the Middle East. However, in view of growing anxieties on domestic political factors, Washington decided to commit itself to the maintenance of stability in the region. The security of Israel was among the main issues related to the overall process. Meanwhile, arms supply to the Middle East had been a political and diplomatic issue since the UN embargo ended. To entice Egypt to participate in a joint defense pact that would settle the base dispute, Britain resumed shipments of arms to Egypt and other Arab countries in late 1949. Israel simultaneously asked permission to purchase American military equipment. The arms deliveries soon began to destabilize the entire Middle East by encouraging the Egyptian anti-colonialists and increasing Israeli uneasiness. At this juncture, a joint American–British–French declaration was designed to prevent a Middle East arms race and intra-regional aggression. In due course, American and British officials worked out the wording of a tripartite declaration, and the US, Britain and France announced the declaration concurrently on May 25, 1950.

Meanwhile, another dispute was emerging in an entirely different part of the world in Asia, further complicating the situation. The US concern about the Middle East was heightened by reports that increasing military activity was taking place on the part of North Korea. At this stage it was considered that Moscow might start a drive in the Middle East where the prize was the greatest source of oil ever known. Against this background, the outbreak of war in Korea on June 25, 1950 prompted the belief in Washington that North Korean troops marched to the Kremlin's cadence and encouraged fears that the Soviets would initiate aggression in other regions. Officials in the State Department began to apply the "lessons" of Korea to the Middle East.

Facing the tensions in Korea and deepening Anglo–Egyptian impasse in the Middle East, officials of the State Department began to consider policy alternatives. Upon the suggestion of Britain, Washington commenced a search for the ways to integrate the US and Turkey into Middle East defense planning. Significantly, this represented a shift in London's attitude. Britain's position towards the urgent Turkish request for full NATO membership formerly was along the lines of establishing a single command over the entire Mediterranean under their control. And, until this moment, Britain had no objection to Turkey's remaining outside NATO, since this would serve its policy objective of keeping Ankara under its politico–military umbrella and leave an open door for possible joint action in the region. They had envisioned appointing a British officer to the post of Supreme Allied Commander, Middle East (SACME), and linking this to NATO. SACME would chair a planning group called the Middle East Defense Board composed of representatives from Britain, the US, France, Turkey and possibly Greece, and other NATO members. Eventually, the SACME would conduct its functions in cooperation with the Supreme Allied Commander in Europe (SACEUR), General Dwight D. Eisenhower. However, a serious drain in Britain's economic resources culminated in its inability to provide the material and financial means to lead this projection in the region.

Evidently, there were other areas of conflict to which Turkey would pay particular attention to consolidate its position within the Western camp. In this framework, the seventh part discusses another concurrent struggle on the part of Korea.

Following the surrender of the Japanese forces in Seoul, the Korean lands were divided in two. In fact, almost two years before, at Cairo in December 1943, the US, Britain, and China had joined in declaring that in due course Korea should become free and independent. This multilateral pledge was reaffirmed in the Potsdam Declaration of July 1945, and subscribed to by the SU when it entered the war against Japan following the dropping of A-Bombs by the US. In Moscow in December of 1945, the Foreign Ministers of the US, Britain and the SU concluded an agreement designed to bring about the independence of Korea. This agreement was later adhered to by China. It provided for the establishment of a joint US–Soviet Commission to meet in Korea and, through consultations with Korean democratic parties and social organizations, to decide on methods for establishing a provisional Korean government. The Joint Commission was then to consult with that provisional government on methods of giving assistance to Korea, any agreement reached being submitted for approval to the four powers adhering to the Moscow Agreement. Two years later, the independence of Korea was no further advanced. In the end Korea remained divided.

In fact, the demarcation line of the 38th Parallel had no basis in Korean history, geography or anything else. It had been settled on hastily in the last week of WW II, as a temporary measure to facilitate the surrender of Japanese troops, and those north of the line had surrendered to the Soviets, those south, to US forces. Consecutively, the US continued to support that the best interests of the Korean people would be served by the withdrawal of all occupying forces from Korea at the earliest practicable date. This same view was also embodied in the UN General Assembly Resolution of November 14, 1947, in which provision was made for such withdrawal as soon as practicable after the establishment of the Korean Government which it was the intention of that resolution to bring into being. The SU, in turn, remained reluctant to cooperate in carrying out the provisions of the resolution of November 14.

Throughout 1949, the North Korean leadership continued its efforts to receive aid to incorporate the south. Receiving the North Korean leader, Kim Il Sung in the Kremlin on March 5, 1949, Stalin showed obvious concern about the plea of his interlocutor. In the beginning Stalin considered that it would be wise to wait for the maturation of the attacks from the south which Kim mentioned. He stated that only if the adversary attacked P'yongyang could they try military reunification by launching a counter-attack.

In the subsequent months, P'yongyang continued to try to persuade Kremlin that the Korean people wanted liberation and peaceful unification was impossible. Besides, it was alleged that Northern armed forces were superior to the southern army after the withdrawal of American troops. When, finally, Stalin ordered a new appraisal of the situation in Korea, sending on September 11, 1949, instructions to the Soviet embassy in P'yongyang to study the military, political, and international aspects of a possible attack on the South, the scene was set for war in Korea.

Mutual allegations of provocation followed this. By the beginning of 1949, the Soviet embassy in P'yongyang began to alert Kremlin to the growing number of violations of the 38th Parallel by South Korean forces.

The attack by North Korea came as a total surprise to the West. There had been incidents along the 38th Parallel, and Korea had been seen as a potential trouble point, but it was only one of numerous conflict points around the world and had never figured high on anyone's list. Indeed, among the manifold uncertainties at the moment was whether the invasion of South Korea was only a feint, a preliminary to a larger attack elsewhere, on Yugoslavia, Formosa or Iran.

As will also be discussed, in October 1950, one year after the establishment of the People's Republic of China, Mao Tse-tung and the Beijing leadership sent "Chinese People's Volunteers" to Korea to fight against the UN forces. In addition to the standard interpretation of China's reasons for engaging in the Korean War,[3] this chapter of the book also briefly discusses the reasons behind the blatant decision of China, a poorly developing country with a crippled economy, to enter into war. Ultimately, although China's intervention saved Kim Il Sung's regime from imminent collapse, it was unable to fulfill Beijing's aspirations of overwhelming the UN forces.

In the 1950s, Western scholars, strongly influenced by the intensifying Cold War, generally viewed China's entrance into the Korean War as a reflection of a well-coordinated communist plot of global expansion, considering that the entire international communist advance was under Kremlin's control, and that neither Beijing nor P'yongyang had the freedom to make their own policy decisions. The Korean conflict, therefore, was seen as an essential part of a serious confrontation between the Soviets on the one hand, and the Western camp on the other.

From the recognition of the Korean Government to the involvement in war over Korea, Turkey's attitude around the developments over this far eastern country gradually moved onwards combining its policy with that of the US. The UN Security Council's call of June 27, 1950, upon the members of UN for taking a stand against aggression in Korea received a positive response from the Turkish Government as well. The Turkish Government informed the UN Secretary General that a brigade of 4,500 soldiers would be assigned to UN Command. No doubt, this policy démarche later became subject to debated developments in Turkey, paradoxically creating a favourable climate for a renewed application for membership in NATO as well.

At this stage, Ankara's renewal of its application for membership in NATO in August 1951, following the Menderes Government's decision of contributing troops to the UN Command in Korea was declined by the

Council of NAT on the grounds of its smaller members' unwillingness to make commitments for the defense of Turkey.

In order to analyze the situation mentioned above, it is explained that in view of the stalemate in Korea and the course of events in the Middle East, the US policymakers maintained their suspicion that Turkey could still reappraise its attitude in the Cold War. This in turn, prompted Ankara's When Ambassador George McGhee visited Turkey in February 1951, President Celal Bayar stated his personal displeasure with the existing partnership. Why should they assent to the desires of the US Navy to mine the Straits in peacetime and why should they make commitments to allow US forces to use their airbases in war time if they lacked a guarantee of defence cooperation in return? Why should they accept to be left in a vulnerable position?

A practicable solution was apparently reached soon after the new British Foreign Secretary Herbert Morrison's public announcement of UK's support for the admittance of Turkey and Greece to NATO. Subsequently, the idea of creating a common Middle Eastern Defense Board including the US, UK, France and Turkey was welcomed. Consequently, the Middle Eastern Defence Organization (MEDO) and the Middle Eastern Command (MEC) were established. On October 13, 1951, the Four-Power proposals to incorporate Egypt into the MEC was forwarded. But the turning point came about when the Egyptian Prime Minister, Nahas Pasha, rejected the suggestions for Egypt's agreement with Four-Power statements. To some extent, Egypt's policy towards the West and Israel would become the model to be emulated by all other Arab states.

From then on, the conditions of the Cold War soon dictated its own requirements in Turkish–NATO relations. Here, it is explained that through its participation in the Korean War and in the military/diplomatic efforts in the Middle East, Ankara had demonstrated its willingness to combine its security with that of the NATO. It is finally expressed that, backed by the US' evaluation that Turkey's geostrategic position was of tremendous value for the alliance, the resistance of the European allies did not prevail.

The eight part begins with explaining the Anglo–American and the regional actors' attitudes to Middle Eastern security, Ankara being examined firstly. In this section, a reappraisal of Britain's Middle East policy in the post WW II situation is firstly analysed. Consecutively, the start of the Cold War which prompted a major turn in Anglo–American policy making is explained. This is followed by analysing the Tripartite Declaration, the Four Power Treaty and the formation of the Middle Eastern Defense Organisation (MEDO). Followingly, Committee of the Free Officers Movement's military takeover of July 1952 in Egypt is evaluated. Consecutively, the shift by the Anglo–American policy makers to the Northern Tier project of the US is discussed.

Subsequently, the formation of the Baghdad Pact is scrutinised. Here, Gamal Abd'el Nasser's arms deal with Soviets is also investigated in the context of increasing anxieties of the West at a time of formation of the Baghdad Pact. Lastly, the discussion focuses on the mounting tensions towards the precipitation of the Suez Crisis which followed Nasser's nationalization of the Suez Canal. In this context, the British policy shifted to military intervention in the Suez and the US opposition to this is analyzed. This conflict of interest is investigated in the context of differences of perception of these powers to achieve, in fact, concurrent objectives. This part also discusses Turkey's adoption of a strategy more in line with the UK and the US and its display of a reserved attitude towards the anti-status quo challenges in the Middle East posed by the nationalisms and supported by the Soviets—despite the expectations of these emerging national powers for the contrary. The chapter concludes with stating the reasons behind the poor support the Baghdad Pact could generate among the regional countries.

The last part includes the conclusions which briefly include the following:

1. Despite the existence of the Treaty of Mutual Assistance Between Turkey, Britain and France of October 19, 1939 Ankara's balancing attitude was also being shaped by the course of international affairs. It was not the signing of the tripartite agreement, but, Ankara's increased responsiveness against the fluctuations in international politics which represented a clear change from the former Atatürk era. Thus, in a comparison to the Atatürk era, the İnönü administration was in favour of maintaining a more flexible foreign policy.

2. During WW II, President İnönü's conviction never wavered that the Western nations would sooner or later win the war.[4] It was only a matter of time to save Turkey from the damages of the global conflict. Then, following the chromite

deliveries of 1941 and the signing of the Turco–German treaty of friendship in the same year, İnönü's second balancing attitude towards the Axis took stage.

In 1942, when the German armies were concentrating their strongholds throughout Europe and being deployed in key areas, Ankara had shifted to implement the "capital tax" on the revenues of non-muslims. Consecutively, an undiscriminatory wave affected the Turkish citizens of Christian and Jewish origin and some of them were sentenced to serve years in working camps since they could not meet the immense amounts of tax imposed by the Turkish authorities. A wave of propaganda which included anti-Semitist undertones accompanied by the claims on the non-Muslims were also increasingly tolerated in the press, radio and elsewhere. In this move, clearly, İnönü had planned to divert the attention of the Axis war machine to somewhere else. Meanwhile, this action of the Turkish administration as result of which no tragedy or a misbehavior were reported let alone a systemic cruelty, did not trigger a reaction of the Allies which were getting increasingly busy with the global conflict.

Although the issue of labour camps represented an episode which is hard to not to regret, another aspect of it is the fact that this decision of Ankara was taken at a time the breath of the German armies were felt and the rumours of distribution of German to Turkish dictionaries to the German troops in Bulgaria were heard. Besides, as shortly afterwards Bulgaria was brought under Hitler's pressure to send its people of Jewish origin to Poland in 1943, it prove that Ankara's choice for working camps, Van/Ashkale was among the most secure and out of sight places thanks to its proximity to Turco–Soviet border.

Within a year, when he saw that the course of the global conflict was gradually removing Turkey out of the scope of belligerent powers, this time İnönü shifted to lift the pressures on non-muslims in the country to the extent of abolishing the working camps. As a continuation of the same policy, in 1944, when the Soviet armies were gaining victories Ankara then turned against the Pan-Turanists, who were found guilty of racist activities. This represented a message to the

Kremlin which expressed that Turkey would not allow ultra-nationalist activities in the country.

3. The prelude to the post WW II period was marked by Ankara's suspicions of the Kremlin's intentions and in 1945, the Soviet demands on Turkish territories and over the Turkish Straits culminated in Ankara's search for a definitive alliance with the West. Despite the fact that some Turkish intellectuals, statesmen and ex-military officials proposed that an understanding between Ankara and the Kremlin should be reached—similar to the first Turco–Soviet rapprochement which took place during the Turkish War of Liberation—events proved that the conditions in 1917 and in 1945 were dramatically different, making any agreement almost impossible.

4. At this juncture, Turkey's embarking upon democracy was closely associated with its wish for joining the Western grouping of states. The first elections in 1946, however, were not a successful attempt in this respect. The rumours of Ankara's manipulation of elections were widespread in the country which no doubt put the credibility of the elections in question. From then on, the post-election government was at odds between adapting a more liberal attitude towards its opponents and closing of ranks against the socialist advance. In his final analysis, having seen that the opposition was mainly formed by some dissident members of the ruling Republican Peoples' Party into another party and no socialist would actually be embodied in this, President İnönü felt a necessity to direct Ankara's foreign policy once again in line with the Western camp and shifted to implement a softer policy towards the rising opposition to allow them compete the RPP in a more normal way.

5. In accordance with his perception of international affairs, İnönü thought that in the aftermath of the war, maintaining an alliance with Britain and the US was of tremendous importance. On the other hand, until the Truman Doctrine, Washington had thought that Turkey was in Britain's "area of responsibility." It was the Truman Doctrine that marked a complete change in the US' perception of Turkey and of course, Greece. Against this background, the elections of

May 1950 after which the Democrat Party administration decided to push Turkish foreign policy to its limits remarked a turning point. Subsequently, the efforts around the MEDO and the concurrent war effort in Korea, in both of which Turkey had major roles took place. The first enlargement of NATO by the inclusion of Turkey and Greece coincided with this period. The Soviet moves towards escalating the Cold War continued in the same interval and a bipolar search for balance of power was pursued, which was indeed a contradiction in the original concept of balance.

Notes

1. "After the Turk, Who?" in *The Sun,* May 17, 1903, p. 2, img. 34, Library of Congress, http://chroniclingamerica.loc.gov/lccn/sn83030272/1903-05-17/ed-1/seq-34/#date1 = 183&sort = &date2 = 1922&words = Empire + Ottoman&sequence = 0&lccn = &index = 8&state = &rows = 20&ortext = &proxtext = ottoman + empire&year = &phrasetext = &andtext = &prox Value = &dateFilterType = yearRange&page = 378

2. Many authors shaped the perception of the Soviets' image in the West through discussing the reckless ouvertures of the Kremlin, such as Kenneth W. Thomson. Thomson maintained that Stalin's military strategy from the early 1940s was geared to his post-war ambitions and despite the dramatic incidents in the summer of 1941, when the SU was attacked by Germany, Stalin never lost sight of political objectives. Kenneth W. Thomson, Cold War Theories Vol. I: World Polarization 1943-1953, (Baton Rouge: Louisiana State University Press, 1981), p. 28.

3. This selection of consulted files were edited in The Cold War International History Project Bulletin, (Washington D.C: Woodrow Wilson Center, Winter 1995/1996) and in the appendices of Sergei Goncharov, John W. Lewis, and Xue Litai's, Uncertain Partners: Stalin, Mao and the Korean War, (Stanford: Stanford University Press, 1993), pp. 226–291.

4. As will be examined in the relevant parts of the book, this conviction of İnönü was emphasized by many of his aides, regardless of their individual pro-Western or socialist views i.e. Mahmut Dikerdem who was an official of the MFA who had carried the de-ciphered cables between the MFA and Presidential Palace Çankaya during these years. In order to maintain objectivity and ensure the readers' comprehension of analytic prisms of actors, it needs to be stated that Dikerdem was a Turkish diplomat who had a declared socialist world view which became more apparent in his senior years of service.

Chapter 2

A Challenged Neutrality: Turkey Under the Pressure of Emerging Rivals (1938–1940)

Anyone who doubts the role of the individual in history should reconsider in the light of Atatürk. The nation's recovery and its achievement of establishing a functional state in the teeth of Imperialist aggression was due in large measure to producing a leader of exceptional military and political ability at the vital hour. [1]

In a period of rapid and chaotic changes, having achieved her realistic peace, it was obvious that the newly established Turkish Republic[2] would not take its place among the revisionist states. Although it thought that the Versailles treaty was an inadequate settlement, it had no reason to join the revisionist front. As regards the foreign policy, the founder of the Turkish Republic, Mustafa Kemal, commonly known as Atatürk,[3] had adopted a policy of maintaining the dialogue even with a possible enemy.

As regards the Anglo–Turkish relations, following the settlement of the Mosul dispute with the border and Good Neighbourhood Agreement with Britain and Iraq on 5 June 1926, the basis for the improvement of bilateral relations had emerged.[4] Subsequently, over the next couple of years, considering the strong possibility of an aggressive revisionism, particularly on the part of Italy, Turkey desired to improve its relations with the United Kingdom and the Western democracies.

In the second half of the 1920s, Turkey showed interest in international collaboration. It was a signatory of the Briand-Kellogg Pact of

August 27, 1928 which outlawed the war. A few years later, at its sixth plenary meeting of July 1, 1932, the League of Nations Assembly decided to place on the agenda of its special session a draft resolution submitted by the Spanish delegation and supported by the representatives of the 28 member states including Britain, France, Germany, Italy and Japan for the invitation of Turkey to join the League.

In reality, the League had completely failed to stop an orchestrated attack on Turkey, despite the fact that the Great War had ended. The League had clearly turned a blind eye to the Lloyd George instigated Greek Army's invasion of Turkey which started on 19 May 1919 and lasted until October 1922. Even at the conclusion of Greek onslaught with a certain defeat,

> the British had not lost all their hopes of bringing the Turks to heel. At the Conference of Lausanne, called to negotiate a new treaty with the Turks, the British first attempted to recognize both the İstanbul and the Ankara governments as representatives of the Turks, with a seat at the table for each. The Nationalists refused, claiming that they were the sole representatives of the Turkish people . . . the French and Italians had already decided to curry favour with the new Turkish government, and the Turks knew that the British had found military action against them to be politically impossible. The British public was sick of war and could see little profit in fighting yet another battle in the Near East. The Turks, therefore, could demand much, as long as they did not touch the new order that the British and French were creating in the Arab world. . . . Even Mosul Province, which the Turks viewed as part of Anatolia, and thus theirs, was not allowed to be a sticking point. Both sides agreed to let the Council of the League of Nations decide the point. (It later gave Mosul to Iraq.) The Straits were naturalized, control only returning to the Turks in 1936.[5]

Turkey however was not looking back, although it never applied to the League for membership. The admission of Turkey was discussed at the seventh plenary meeting of the League of Nations Assembly on July 6, where all delegates spoke favourably. Subsequently, the invitation conveyed in a letter by the Secretary General Eric Drummond was unanimously approved of in the Turkish Grand National Assembly on July 9, 1932. The Turkish Republic was with one voice admitted a full member of the League of Nations on July 18, at a special sitting of the Assembly of the League, at which 43 states were represented.[6]

Mustafa Kemal's desire was clearly to collaborate with the leaders of the western camp. On various occasions, he expressed his dislike of totalitarian regimes and their leaders. On June 17, 1934, Atatürk made clear to British Ambassador to Ankara, Percy Loraine that Turkey desired closer relations with Britain. Loraine's impression was that the Turkish President had reached the conclusion that closer friendship with Britain was not only desirable, but possible as well. Given this, in view of the imminent threat posed by the revisionists, according to some analysts, Turkey's aim was to have a partnership with Britain and the democratic front in Europe.[7] No doubt, what Atatürk had considered was to adopt a balancing attitude to prevent Turkey's remaining on its own in view of the perils of the contemporary affairs. His conviction on the necessity to permanently disassociate Turkey from the imperial politics of either Britain or any other power, however, remained unwavered.

Turkey's Measured Response Against the Emerging Threat in the Mediterranean

The emergence of revisionist Italy as a threat in the Eastern Mediterranean had greatly disturbed Atatürk. He therefore took the initiative with Greek Prime Minister Panayiotis Tsaldaris to form the Balkan Pact. On February 9, 1934, following the step taken by Turkey and Greece, with the adherence of Yugoslavia and Roumania, the Balkan Entente was established to face the Italian threat. Besides, Roumania and Yugoslavia were the Allies of France within the Little Entente.

In 1936, Turkey resolved the Straits question through international cooperation by coordinating the efforts to conlude the Montreux Convention, one of the longest lived international conventions to date. The British Ambassador, Hughe Knatchbull-Hugessen stated that, Mustafa Kemal's straightforward approach to the powers in 1935 was in pursuance of his policy of seeking the support and sympathy of others rather than by intriguing against them.[8]

In the Straits issue, Turkey was subject to unacceptable pressure. In 1936, Italy demanded in return for support of the Turkish thesis, the recognition of her annexation of Abyssinia in the League. In the same year in June, right after the opening of the negotiations of Montreux, the Soviets made a disturbing proposal to Turkey. The Soviet Minister of Foreign Affairs Maxim Litvinov, suggested to his Turkish counterpart, Tevfik Rüştü Aras,[9] Soviet partnership for the defense of the Straits.

In October 1936, Turkey rejected the Soviet proposals, but, reaffirmed the existence of good relations between the two countries. Significantly, Aras negotiated on the Soviet demands with British Foreign Minister Sir Anthony Eden. Britain's official reply was given to the Turkish Ambassador in London, Fethi Okyar. It was emphasized that the Soviet proposal would represent a military alliance between Turkey and the Soviets, and eventually embrace Turkey in one of the emerging blocs in Europe. Moreover, the British reply underlined that Turkey's power was due to her impartiality in the Mediterranean and it was making her contribution to the peace and stability through this position.[10] The Italian and Russian proposals were always remembered as distasteful incidents. Therefore, Turkey accelerated her efforts to side with the democratic powers in Europe and counterbalance the threat posed by the revisionists while upholding its neutral stance.

Meanwhile, the British Ambassador in Ankara, Percy Loraine, interpreting the current disposition in Ankara, cabled the sympathies of the Turkish Government to Britain, especially following King Edward VIII's visit to İstanbul in September 1936. In his note to a Minister of State in Ankara on December 1, 1936, Loraine emphasized Turkey's decision to transfer the building of her Karabük steel complex which was a contract of three million pounds, to a British company, Brassert, and considered this as a consequence of firm and mutually confident relations which remarkably increased in the last two years. Indeed, the German Krupp's proposal was rejected, although Mustafa Kemal had an apparent interest in obtaining weaponry from this company in defence of the Straits. In this issue, as desired by the Foreign Office, the ultimate Turkish decision was to leave her vital industry's control to Britain, not to Germany.[11]

Again in 1936, Turkey proposed an alliance to Britain[12] the boundaries of which would be drawn in accordance with her perception of the escalating tensions in international affairs as well as Britain's conceptualization of the ways in which the revisionists could be tackled. In their turn, the War Office and the Admiralty drafted a joint memorandum for submission to the Foreign Office. This urged the British Government to realize an alliance with Turkey. It emphasized that an Anglo–Turkish alliance would serve as a *counterpoise* against Italian aggression in the Mediterranean and at the same time would prevent Soviet expansion into this area. Anthony Eden and his Near Eastern experts accepted all the strategic considerations raised by the military, but rejected the recommendation for alliance with Turkey. The Foreign Office concluded that "any unilateral approch to Turkey would be interpreted by the other powers as conspiratorial."[13] It would also create negative reactions on the part of the French Government which had objected to being left out of the Anglo–German Naval Agreement in 1935.

Ultimately, the British Government choose to improve its relations with Italy through the *Gentleman's Agreement*, the Anglo–Italian Agreement which was signed on January 2, 1937. The parties to the agreement recognized "the freedom of entry into, exit from, and transit through the Mediterranean" as a vital interest to both, which was "in no way inconsistent with each other."[14] In essence, the aim of the agreement was to avoid confrontation in the Mediterranean. Moreover, Anthony Eden stated in the House of Commons on January 19, 1937 that, this mutual understanding was neither a treaty nor a pact, and did not require Britain to make any concession.[15] In fact, Britain was more interested in avoiding the Italian hostility in the Mediterranean which would require her fleet to be diverted to face this. Ironically, Britain attempted to counter Italian propaganda in the Middle East, which was based on reminding Arab states how they had been "betrayed" by Britain and Colonel Lawrence, by courting the very power which the British had used the Arabs to undermine.

Britain, in attempting to procure Italy as an ally against Germany, was acting in the spirit of her traditional Balance of Power policy. Churchill himself had made several statements like, "I have always said that if Great Britain were defeated in war I hoped we should find a Hitler to lead us back to our rightful position among the nations"[16] which were often accepted as quoted out of context in praise of Hitler—and Mussolini— while this suggests that Britain's antagonism to Germany was a Balance of Power rather than an ideological one. Although it is beyond the discussion here, the Gentleman's Agreement was among the greatest errors of the British diplomacy prior to the *Appeasement* in Munich.

On February 2-3, the Turkish Foreign Minister of Foreign Affairs, Aras met with his Italian counterpart, Count Galeazzo Ciano, in Milan. An official Communique was issued on 4 February. Here, Aras was assured of Italy's commitment to the Gentleman's Agreement. However, Ciano also drew the attention of Aras to the situation that Turkey had not yet accorded *de jure* recognition to the Abyssinian Empire, while the other member states of the League had done so. In his reply, Aras told Ciano that he would attempt to settle the question on his return.[17]

For the time being, a phony settlement was achieved in Europe. Shortly after, Britain would seek the active collaboration of Turkey in another strategic part of the world, in the Middle East.

Meanwhile, in September 1935, on the initiative of Iran, preparatory conversations were opened at Geneva for the conclusion of a Middle Eastern Pact. Turkey who had been disturbed by Italy's ambitions in the Eastern Mediterranean, joined the Iranian efforts to promote a regional security pact.

Considering the necessity of establishing a security organisation in the Middle East, Britain actively supported Turco–Iranian efforts for a Middle Eastern pact. According to London, in addition to Italian aspirations in the Eastern Mediterranean, this region was also subject to threats from the Soviets for ideological penetration. Besides, Britain had to control the Arab nationalism, which could weaken its imperial position in an era of unpredictable and rapid changes.

Turkey, having also re-considered the deterioration in her relations with the Soviets, favoured the British policy of backing a Turco–Iranian pact. With the inclusion of Iraq and Afghanistan, on July 8, 1937, the Middle Eastern or as commonly known, Saadabad Pact was signed in Teheran. Following the precedent of the Little and Balkan Ententes, by a protocol signed on the same day, a Permanent Council was established which was to meet at least once a year. The Pact was to run in the first instance for five years and provided for consultation, non-interference, non-aggression and a mutual guarantee of common frontiers. Shortly afterwards, Aras made a visit to Moscow, aiming to relieve the Soviet scepticism on this pact.[18]

On November 1, 1938, in his message to the Turkish Grand National Assembly, Mustafa Kemal Atatürk stated that, ". . . the states which signed the Saadabad Pact, vigorously freeing themselves from the myths of the past, have established their relations on a sound and fruitful basis."[19]

By this pact, it was considered that the direct or indirect interference of other Powers in the Middle East would be eliminated, and stability in this region would be achieved through solidarity between the four States. Through Turkey, the new grouping of states was linked with the Balkan Entente. As a result, an area from the Balkans to India was covered with a network of interlocking pacts and treaties.

Turning back to the mounting crisis in Europe, following Germany's annexation of Austria on March 11, 1938, Britain aimed to counter the impact of this incident in Turkey. Previously, on January 20, the Turkish Prime Minister Celal Bayar had stated that, it was unthinkable that any other political system of foreign origin could ever be imported into Turkey.[20] Indeed, on 18 January, the German Ambassador to Ankara, Keller, in his cable to the Foreign Ministry, explained the prohibition of the Turkish Government on propagandistic activities. He stated that ". . . Turkish law forbids foreigners to form political and other associations founded on the basis of race. Some of the Turks as well as foreigners settled in Turkey are forbidden to wear the dress or insignia of foreign political or military organizations."[21]

Given this fact, as it will also be discussed under the subsequent title, the British Ambassador, Loraine, suggested a visit by a member of the British Cabinet to Ankara together with the Foreign Office's reconsideration of Turkey's demands for a Mediterranean pact.[22] Subsequently, the Foreign Office concluded that the best policy would be to make a credit agreement with Turkey. Against the opposition of the Treasury, Lord Halifax pointed out that in the event of German expansion into Hungary, British lines of communication to India and the Far East would be fatally compromised "should Turkey be next to fall."[23]

On May 27, 1938, three arrangements with Turkey were concluded. Among these, the Anglo–Turkish Export Credits Guarantee Agreement was signed for the export to Turkey of goods manufactured in Britain. Besides, an agreement between the two countries which was supplementary to the Agreement of September 2, 1936, on Trade and Clearing, provided for the export of Turkish goods to the United Kingdom.[24] With these Agreements, Turkey was provided in total with a loan of £10 million. Lastly as part of the armaments credit, an additional sum of £6 million was given to Turkey. The Agreement was favourable to Turkey as this loan was payable by the Turkish Government "under any contracts concluded by that Government by the approval of the United Kingdom for the purchase in the United Kingdom of material necessary for the defence of Turkey."[25]

In their turn, Germans claimed that their trade offers would be more advantageous to Turkey. The German Foreign Minister, Joachim Ribbentrop, invited a Turkish delegation to Berlin, apparently to demonstrate the might of Germany. A delegation led by the Secretary-General of the Ministry for Foreign Affairs, Ambassador Numan Menemencioğlu, left for Berlin on June 30, 1938. Though he was interested to see what the Germans could offer to Turkey, at the end, he thought the presentation of a few old-fashioned tanks could in no respect be an alternative to the courtesy of Britain.[26] When Menemencioğlu observed that these tanks and few long-range guns presented to the Turkish Government were not up to the highest standard, Ribbentrop suggested that Turkish technical experts might like to observe and supervise German manufacturing processes. As to the non-aggression pact proposed by Ribbentrop, Menemencioğlu stated that Turkey signed them only with neighboring states, such as the Soviet Union or France, a 'neighbour' by virtue of her Syrian possessions. He also told Ribbentrop that Turkey was not considering such a treaty with Britain as no part of the British empire bordered with Turkey.[27]

In his subsequent meetings with the German officials, Menemencioğlu also declined the German proposal on the revision of the Montreux, with Germany joining the contracting parties of this Convention. To add to the increasing anxieties of Germany, Turkey concluded the Franco–Turkish Friendship Agreement on 4 July, whilst Menemencioğlu was still in Berlin.

Turning back to the repercussions of the Anglo–Turkish Credit Agreement, the outcomes of this agreement were quite positive for British policy. On July 20, 1938, Aras stated Turkey's opinion on Britain's loans as follows:

> No matter what happens, never will we be found in a camp opposing Britain. . . . I dont like the word 'alliance.' Our friendship with Britain is one of confidence and solidarity. . . Here is a country granting us a loan of £16,000,000, most of it for armaments, without asking anything in return. . . . Britain showed she has faith in us. We will show her that this faith is not misplaced. . . .[28]

According to London, the conclusion of Anglo–Turkish Agreements of 27 May 1938 was a prelude to further agreements. For the time being, Britain considered that, such an understanding uncommitted on paper had many advantages over an agreement forming a joint front which could easily provoke accusations or attacks of the revisionist powers.

Atatürk was a strategist of unmatchable perception and his assessments in the late 30s were to the effect that a war in Europe would soon break out which required Turkey to challenge the ambitions of imminent aggressors. His conviction was that this could not be done by remaining outside the democratic grouping of states. Under these circumstances, on November 1st 1937, Percy Loraine informed Eden that, during the celebrations of the fourteenth anniversary of the Turkish Republic, Mustafa Kemal, "by the unmistakable marks of personal regard, wished to emphasize to him, the excellence of Turkish relations with the United Kingdom, and the great value which he attached to those relations."[29] Having seen the Turkish Government's decision to ally herself with Britain, Loraine took further steps. On April 3, 1938, Loraine sent a messsage to Lord Halifax, the new British Foreign Secretary, following Anthony Eden's departure from the Foreign Office on February 27, 1938.[30] He suggested that a British Cabinet Minister to visit Turkey to "offset" the visit by Ciano, the son-in-law of Mussolini and Italian Foreign Minister, and by Ribbentrop, the German Foreign Minister. He also asked Halifax to give some personal attention to Mustafa Kemal.

Despite these relations between the two countries, in overall terms, because of the Gentleman's Agreement, and under the existing trends of appeasement towards the fascist regimes, whilst trying to ally Turkey to itself, Britain avoided making definite commitments in its relations with Turkey. In its turn, the Turkish attitude did not remain static either. The alarming situation, particularly following the Munich Conference, increased Turkey's leanings toward the forming of its neutrality. Britain's upredictable and haphazard relations with Germany was confusing countries attempting to understand the British position. At Munich, Britain seemed to be facilitating Hitler's success after for years preventing Weimar Germany from revising the Versailles arrangements. Then soon after an unconditional guarantee was given to Poland. Such fluctuations of policy made it very difficult for powers which opposed Germany and Italy to feel any confidence in their relations with Britain.

Following the death of Atatürk in November 1938, General İsmet İnönü succeeded him as the Provisional President and was subsequently elected as the President of the Republic by the unanimous vote of the Turkish Grand National Assembly on April 3, 1939.

As the Provisional President, İnönü made a statement which proved Turkish policy would remain along the existing line. He stated that ". . . Turkey's foreign policy will continue to be governed by faithful attachment to the cause of peace, by the spirit of understanding and cooperation which has inspired the successive Governments of the Kemalist regime up to now, by loyalty and fidelity to her friendships and alliances."[31]

In the meantime, Bayar left the Premiership (January 1939). In the course of a reshuffling of the Turkish Cabinet, Dr. Refik Saydam headed

the new Government. The Minister of Foreign Affairs, Aras was succeeded by Şükrü Saraçoğlu. The Secretary-General of the Ministry for
Foreign Affairs, Ambassador Menemencioğlu was still in office. In some
respects, the Germans were satisfied with his remaining in office.[32] With
the increasing German pressure, in January, Germano–Turkish talks for
an economic agreement similar to that of Anglo–Turkish Credit Agreement took place. In an attempt to demonstrate the impartiality of the
Turkish Government, Menemencioğlu told the German Minister Clodius
that Turkey was prepared at any time to conclude such an agreement
with Germany, "but for political reasons, she would even be eager to do
so."[33] He stated that Turkey's capital goods were such that Germany still
had a good market even after the agreement with Britain. Turkey was
trying to avoid an excessively one-sided orientation of Turkish trade.[34]

On January 16, 1939, the Germano–Turkish credit agreement negotiated between Minister Clodius and Menemencioğlu, was signed. By
this agreement, Germany gave Turkey a credit of 150 million marks for
the payment of industrial orders which Turkey was to place in Germany.
The orders were to be completed before December 31, 1941. The time
limit of the credit was 10 years and the interest rate was 5 percent. With
a confidential protocol annexed to the agreement, a corresponding increase in the export of Turkish products to Germany was agreed upon.
Additionally, Menemencioğlu's complaints on the deliveries of merchant
ships were also settled.[35]

On the other hand, Menemencioğlu came to this agreement under
German pressure. Prior to Turco–German credit agreement, the implicit
German coerciveness can be seen in a Memorandum by the Deputy Director of the Economic Policy Department, stating that "I then spoke to
M. Numan about the latest Anglo–Turkish credit agreement . . . in view
of the especially close German–Turkish economic relations we could not
permit Germany to be forced into a secondary position. . . . So far M.
Numan has not made any request for credit."[36] Shortly afterwards, Turkish
acceptance of German loans followed. This credit was to a great extent to
finance the second five-year plan. But, as the Turks were re-orienting
their economic policy towards Britain, the Germano–Turkish economic
agreement did not fully come into effect. As it will be mentioned later,
following the Nazi–Soviet pact of August 1939, Turkey aimed to cease
the chromite deliveries to Germany and sought the ways to sell this product to Britain. Given this, the export of chromite to Germany was gradu-

ally decreased. By the beginning of 1940, Turkey was selling this significant raw material of the war industry to Britain.[37]

On the part of the international powers, in the aftermath of Atatürk's death, change in the Turkish leadership had paved the way to a new calculation in politics. It was a new era in the eyes of many foreign statesmen and Turkey was seen as might be embarking upon a different path in handling its foreign affairs. İnönü was an experienced soldier and statesman and one of the masterminds of the Lausanne Treaty of 24 July 1923 which had secured the frontiers of the emerging Republic of Turkey. Atatürk and his comrades, İnönü being in the first place, had saved Turkey from a bitter fate not only with their triumphs on the war theaters, but at the negotiation table as well. Expanding on a tradition of not believing in lasting alliances but convergence of interests to allow Turkey to remain out of the conflicts, İnönü was ready to pursue a neutral stance within a delicate balance of power, Turkey would engineer around itself.

As such, İnönü was appreciated in the SU since the Kremlin had perceived his replacement as Prime Minister on October 25, 1937 by Celal Bayar prompted by his increasing Soviet inclination. The Soviet Vice-Commissar for Foreign Affairs, Vladimir Potemkin had been the last foreign representative to leave Ankara after Atatürk's funeral and this had not escaped attention.

In the tradition of the Russian state, the SU was interested in having a greater influence over the control of the Turkish Straits. The Montreux Convention was a noticeable success for the SU in that it prevented a potential attack on it by an enemy fleet through the Black Sea and granted its capital ships free access to the Mediterranean. But according to the Kremlin, Turkey's right to impede these passages in time of war, or of an imminent threat of war, represented a serious problem still needing to be addressed. The Soviets' perception of security of the Straits was closely associated with her political relations with Turkey and with Turkey's relations with the Kremlin's rivals. This was a known fact, which had started to fuel the rumours of a Turco–Soviet Black Sea / mutual assistance pact as early as 1938.

Secretary-General Menemencioğlu, instructed by İnönü, would not lose time to attempt to dispel the anxieties of Berlin on this and on February 10, 1939, he called on his German counterpart Weizsäcker. Although he firmly assured Weizsäcker of Turkey's decision to not to proceed with any arrangement contrary to Germany's interests,

Menemencioğlu received the German State Secretary's cool warning on the Turco–Russian intimacy.[38]

The Collapse of the Munich System and the Start of the British Policy of Seeking Alliance with Turkey

On March 15, 1939, German troops seized Prague. Czechoslovakia was wiped off the map and replaced by the protectorate of Bohemia–Moravia. Following the occupation of Czechoslovakia, the alarming international situation and the pressure of opposition forced Chamberlain to condemn Hitler's action. In his speech on March 17 at the Conservative Party's meeting in Birmingham, Chamberlain declared that there must be no doubt that Britain would do everything in her power to resist Germany's attempts to win world domination.

Immediately after the occupation of Prague, Hitler gave an ultimatum to Lithuania and occupied Memelland. On March 17, Roumanian Ambassador in London, Tilea, informed Lord Halifax that Germany had demanded controlling rights over his country's exports and industry. Justifying Tilea's fears, on March 23, a German–Roumanian economic treaty was concluded.

This was followed by Halifax's enquiry on the attitude of the Governments of the Balkan Entente states. The Turkish Government stated that though it had not heard anything from Roumania, Turkey was ready to consider Britain's suggestions. Regarding the immediate tension between Roumania and Bulgaria, emerging from the former's possession of Southern Dobruja, Saraçoğlu stated that Balkan Entente would come into force if Bulgaria, alone or with the help of an external state were to attack a member of the Entente. If a non-Balkan country attacked a member of the Balkan Entente and Bulgaria remained neutral, the Balkan Pact could not compel its members to come to the aid of this country. Subsequently, on March 25, Saraçoğlu told French Ambassador in Ankara that it was expected by his government that Britain and France to explicitly state their policy to resist German aggression in this part of the world.[39]

In this political atmosphere, the Italian invasion of Albania on April 7, made explicit the Axis challenge to the Versailles status quo. In reality, by the beginning of January 1939, the Italian dictator had decided to take over the control in Albania and had been designing further aggressions in the Balkans. In a secret letter from Ciano to Ribbentrop, Ciano draw up the Axis policy that "the Axis will be able to stand up to any coalition if it has within its orbit and bound up with its destiny those European countries which can furnish it with raw materials—that is to say in the first place, Yugoslavia, Hungary and Roumania."[40] Obviously, the visit by Chamberlain and Halifax to Italy in mid January did not alter the previously determined Axis policy.

Following the Italian aggression in Albania, on April 10, Knatchbull-Hugessen cabled the Foreign Office that Saraçoğlu was not completely re-assured as to the firmness of the British attitude.[41] Besides, Saraçoğlu mentioned to him rumours of Italian designs on Crete. Considering Saraçoğlu's anxiety, Knatchbull-Hugessen asked authorization for giving the Turkish Government concrete proof of Britain's intention to cooperate with Turkey. In his subsequent cable on the same day, Knatchbull-Hugessen mentioned his secret letter to the Permanent Secretary of Foreign Affairs, Sir Alexander Cadogan, in which he expressed that it was not prudent to count simply on Turkish goodwill. Therefore it was necessary to decide what Britain could offer. He said:

> We must reckon with the tremendous pressure the other side will exert and we must decide in the light of these considerations whether, if the Turks do not join us of their own accord, we can safely press for alliance or only for neutrality.[42]

On April 12, 1939, concerning the lines of approach to be made to the Turkish Government, in order to deal with the immediate menace to Greece arising out of the Italian action in Albania, Lord Halifax stated to Ambassador Knatchbull-Hugessen that the Italian action in Albania could be only one step in a wider movement of Axis expansionism. Halifax stressed that the ultimate aim of the Axis powers would be joint domination of Europe by Germany and Italy. He said, "Whichever of these two powers it is that launches the attack, it is almost certain that the other will be involved."[43] Halifax stated that Britain was prepared in principle to come to the help of Turkey in the event of any threat by Italy, direct or indirect, to the independence of Turkey in the Mediterranean area, "which is actively resisted by the Turkish Government, provided that the Turkish Government are prepared to come to the help of His Majesty's Government being involved in a war with Italy."[44] Additionally, Halifax emphasized that Britain considered it of the first importance that the Turkish Government should collaborate in any project of common defence. A day later, in his telegram to Knatchbull-Hugessen, Halifax pointed out that if Britain was to guarantee Turkey against Germany, Britain should naturally expect Turkey to reciprocate by guaranteeing the UK against Germany.[45]

Within the framework of consolidating a popular resistance in the Balkans against the Axis menace, Britain wanted to understand Turkey's policy on probable extension of Italian aggression to Greece. In his note to Knatchbull-Hugessen on April 11, 1939, Halifax urged him to interview with Saraçoğlu to ascertain whether Turkey would extend her existing obligations to Greece so that Greece might be assured of full Turkish assistance in the event of any Italian threat.[46] Halifax added that, if the Turkish reply was favourable, British Government would announce together with France a specific assurance to Greece by adding the following:

> His Majesty's Government have consulted the Turkish Government, who have intimated that they concur and are prepared to adopt the same attitude.[47]

However, in his note to Halifax, Knatchbull-Hugessen stated that the reply of Turkish Government was to the effect that it did not feel able at present to commit herself to public statement for two reasons, first constitutional questions would arise, and the Chamber's approval would be necessary, and secondly, it felt unable to agree to a statement which would place herself irretrievably on one side in present international conflict without some more definite guarantee of her own security.[48] On the other hand, it was understood that this issue was under intense consideration in Turkish political circles. A few hours later Knatchbull-Hugessen sent another telegram to the Foreign Office that the Turkish Government agreed to the inclusion of the following:

> The Turkish Government, whose close relations with the Greek Government are known, were informed on this declaration on April 12.[49]

On April 13, 1939, Britain gave guarantees to Greece and Roumania, in the context of "avoiding the disturbance by force or threats of force of the status quo in the Mediterranean and the Balkan Peninsula."[50] The above mentioned statement of the Turkish Government was also included in the text of this guarantee. Britain considered that, if Turkey were to side with the Allied Powers, it would add its weight to their position in the Balkans. Therefore, the Foreign Office aimed to extend this guarantee to Turkey and kept her informed about the progress of talks with these governments.

On April 21, Aras, now the Turkish Ambassador in London, expressed the Turkish Government's satisfaction with the treaty arrangements being made. Upon the calls for Turkey's definitive alliance with Britain, Aras raised two points before the Turkish departure from its neutrality. He asked in case Turkey was attacked in the Mediterranean if it would have the benefit of direct British assistance, and "if they would have Great Britain with them."[51] Ten days later, with regard to Britain's proposal on Turkey's inclusion in a Balkan front against the Axis aggression, Aras pointed out in his conversation with Cadogan that under the Turco–Soviet Treaty of Neutrality and Non-Aggression of December 17, 1925, neither party to this treaty was at liberty to conclude another agreement with any neighbour of the other party without its consent.

On April 25, in a meeting with Gafencu at which Chamberlain was also present, Halifax explained Britain's interest in realizing an understanding between Roumania and Bulgaria. He told the Roumanian Foreign Minister that Britain had some right to discuss this question since it had given guarantee to Roumania together with Greece. Halifax concluded that British Government had certainly no intention to force the Roumanian Government to make decisions which they might think inconvenient.[52]

Woodward pointed out that Roumania was equally nervous of Russia, and Yugoslavia, as Greece was nervous of Italy. Making the agreements impossible for a joint front, Hungary and Bulgaria had territorial claims against their neighbours.[53]

Anglo–Franco–Turkish Negotiations for the Treaties of Mutual Assistance

On April 23, 1939, Saraçoğlu spoke to Knatchbull-Hugessen of the conclusion of a treaty of alliance for fifteen years as the ultimate goal to be aimed at. At this moment, the Turkish Government seemed surprisingly ready to go beyond the limits of its previous reservations. Saraçoğlu's statement was regarded by the Foreign Office as creating the basis of an arrangement which would result in an alliance. By the end of April, Britain proposed that the negotiations to this end should be conducted through certain stages. It was firstly suggested that a Joint Declaration should be issued, announcing the intention of the two Governments to enter into a permanent agreement of mutual assistance and significantly, giving assurances of reciprocal support in the event of war breaking out, before the formal agreement was ratified. Again, it was decided that in the meantime, negotiations of Anglo–Turkish military, economic and financial experts would take place. These were not formally accepted by the Turkish Government until May 10.

On April 28, Soviet Vice-Commissar for Foreign Affairs, Vladimir Potemkin made a visit to Ankara, after Sofia. In his talks with Saraçoğlu, Potemkin stated that Soviet influence would be used in Sofia to promote a conciliation between Bulgaria and Roumania. But the persisting idea that Roumania should leave Southern Dobruja to Bulgaria, as an inducement for the latter's inclusion in the Balkan Entente, was still disliked by Roumania. In the meantime, Saraçoğlu told Knatchbull-Hugessen that Potemkin had positively regarded Turkey's understanding with Britain, and added that Turkey could also always count on material help from the Soviets.[54] However, Soviet promises remained weak to acquire a nature upon which Turkey could rely.

In order not to hamper the Turkish Government's position in its negotiations with the Soviet Government, the British intention of linking the Balkans and the Mediterranean was abandoned in the first draft of the Declaration which was sent to Ankara on April 29. On May 6, having seen the futility of Turco–Soviet talks and to avoid giving the impression that Britain was disinteresting itself in the Balkans, the British Government included in the final draft a reference to the Balkans.[55] A day later, in order to explain the progress of Anglo–Turkish negotiations towards a Joint Declaration, Saraçoğlu summoned a meeting of representatives of the Balkan Entente states and of states signatory to the Saadabad Pact.

As for the Axis, after several months of vacancy at the German Embassy in Ankara, Franz von Papen took this post on April 27. Ribbentrop had nominated von Papen as the Ambassador to Ankara on April 7, 1939, the same day with the Italian invasion of Albania. The previous year, on April 13, 1938, Tevfik Rüştü Aras had refused to accept the news on the nomination of Papen. Mustafa Kemal's rejection of Papen's appointment to Ankara was also known.[56] British Ambassador to Ankara, Knatchbull-Hugessen stated that the German Government had pressed Ankara for nearly a year to accept Papen. He also pointed out the reputation of Papen since the Great War. He said, "His record as German Chancellor, as the supposed godfather of the Hitler regime, and as Ambassador in Austria had further depressed his stock in world opinion."[57]

On the first day of his arrival, Papen met Saraçoğlu. Not surprisingly, the German Ambassador immediately asked Saraçoğlu about the truth behind the reports he was receiving on the Anglo–Turkish negotiations. He claimed that any Turkish agreement with Britain and the Soviets would amount to an attempt to encircle Germany. In his subsequent talks with the Turkish officials, Papen assured them that Germany would never start a war in the Balkans and in the Mediterranean. On May 6, von Papen told Saraçoğlu that very soon Germany would give effective guarantees to Turkey, whereas Saraçoğlu declined the German offer.

Having regarded the further reports about negotiations between Turkey and Britain, on 8 May, this time, Papen informed Secretary-General Menemencioğlu that Turkey should wait for the offers of the German Government before concluding any agreement. He told Menemencioğlu that Turkey's signing an alliance with Britain would increase the risk of war.[58] As his last effort, two days before the approval of the Declaration at the meeting of the ruling Republican People's Party, Papen urged Menemencioğlu to delay, as Germany was preparing proposals to put before the Turkish Government to ensure the Italian and Bulgarian entry to the Balkan Entente as well. In his turn, Menemencioğlu replied to Papen that for Turkey, it was the Italian entry into Albania which necessitated an understanding with Britain and France, and the admission of Italy into the Balkan Entente "would be the last straw."[59]

At the outset of the Declaration, the Turkish Government suggested the inclusion of the statement of their neutrality unless the Axis committed an act of aggression in the Mediterranean or the Balkans. This seemed to the Foreign Office as an escape clause which would be a negative way of expressing Turkish intentions. Besides, the Turkish suggestion meant that the obligation of assistance would not apply in a war which would start in Western Europe.[60] Ultimately, a compromise was reached that Turkey would abandon her neutrality in case of an act of aggression leading to war in the Mediterranean. Additionally, a joint recognition of the necessity of ensuring the security in the Balkans was included in the Declaration.[61] Subsequently, it was decided that the Declaration would be made on 12 May by the British Prime Minister in the House of Commons and by the Turkish Prime Minister in the Grand National Assembly. Among other things, the statement made by Chamberlain announced that:

> Pending the completion of the definitive agreement, His Majesty's Government and the Turkish Government declare that in the event of an aggression leading to war in the Mediterranean area they would be prepared to co-operate effectively and to lend each other all aid and assistance in their power.[62]

A few days later, replying to a question in a debate in the House of Commons, Chamberlain stated that the terms of the declaration did not preclude the cooperation of both Governments with other Mediterranean Powers in the event of an act of aggression leading to war in the Mediterranean area.[63]

Three days later the announcement of the Anglo–Turkish Declaration, Knatchbull-Hugessen talked to von Papen at a ceremony in Ankara. Here, showing his disturbance, Papen told Knatchbull-Hugessen that he was off to Berlin at once, he said, "To report on the situation which you have created."[64] Additionally, in explaining the goals of the Anglo–Turkish Declaration, Knatchbull-Hugessen stated the two principal tasks of this agreement, as the conclusion of a long-term security Pact and ultimately, the establishment of the Balkan security. He said that the first of these goals was reached when the Anglo–Franco–Turkish Alliance was signed on October 19, but the second was a "conspicuous failure."[65]

Around the same issue, on May 22, in a debate in the House of Commons, Mr. Henderson asked the Prime Minister if he would give an assurance that the Anglo–Turkish Declaration under which Britain and Turkey would seek to achieve the establishment of security in the Balkans did not preclude the Turkish Government from fulfilling its obligations as a member of the Balkan Entente. Replying to this, Chamberlain stated that the question of Turkey's obligations under the Balkan Pact was primarily a matter for the Turkish Government, but he said, "the Anglo–Turkish Declaration can not interpreted as precluding the Turkish Government from fulfilling their obligations under that pact."[66]

Previously, on March 30, the British Government had given a guarantee to Poland that was to become automatically effective in the event of an aggression directed against Poland's independence. With the launch of the British policy to extend this guarantee to Greece and Roumania, these defensive steps led to the verbal attacks of the Axis powers. In his turn, Hitler interpreted these guarantees as measures aiming at Germany's encirclement. Together with Mussolini, Hitler used this interpretation to speed up the realization of the Germano–Italian military alliance. Shortly after, at their meeting in Milan on May 6 and 7, Ciano and Ribbentrop announced the imminent conclusion of the "Pact of Steel."[67]

Although Britain had considered that separate bilateral declarations by her and Turkey, and by France and Turkey respectively, might also be evaluated by the Axis front as sign of dissension between these states, as it will be discussed under the following title, the Foreign Office concluded that this was a quicker way to realize the arrangements.

At the beginning of May, the French Government had stated that the agreement to be conducted should be a tripartite one. In reality, the negotiations had not been carried on a joint Anglo–French basis. Besides, the Franco–Turkish talks had given rise to a major difficulty which ultimately led to the absence of France in the Anglo–Turkish Declaration. Like many others, Woodward explained the reason for this as the prevailing dispute on the Hatay Sanjak between France and Turkey, emerging from the former's mandatory rule in Syria.[68] Although the Turkish Government at first raised no objection emerging from this problem, when it came to the Declaration, on May 8, it made clear that it would not consent to a tripartite agreement without the satisfactory settlement of the Hatay question.

Previously, the Germans had stated that their interest in Hatay dispute was only on academic basis.[69] However, especially towards the conclusion of the Anglo–Turkish Declaration, aiming to force Turkey to re-consider her position in the Hatay question at the expense of proceeding with the negotiations with the Allied Powers, Germany shifted to active involvement in this question. In his first note from Ankara, von Papen had suggested that Germany should intercede with Italy. Afterwards, Germany made some efforts to convince Italy to declare her peaceful intentions towards Turkey.

Again, when he was in Berlin, at the signing of Germano–Italian Treaty, von Papen emphasized the strategic importance of Turkey to Germany and advised Ciano that Italy should return the Dodecanese islands to Turkey. To impress Turkish opinion to sign an alliance with Germany, Papen would have returned to Turkey some of the Dodecanese islands taken by Italy from the Ottoman Empire in 1911. He especially called Ernst von Weizsäcker's attention to the island of Castelrosso (Meis), within three miles of the Anatolian coast. He told Weizsäcker that the Italian occupation of this island was not indispensable to Italian security and that Italian possession of it was an insult to Turkey's security. Papen also questioned whether the Italian alliance was really worthwhile. Papen's suggestion met with angry Italian replies. Ciano claimed that the island was a vantage point from which to assault the Suez Canal or blockade the Straits. But, Papen thought that the war would not be won in the eastern Mediterranean, rather on Britain's land bridge to India through Transjordan and Iraq.[70]

On March 15, the German Charge d'Affaires Kroll had been reporting from Ankara that the French were negotiating with the Turks over uniting Hatay to Turkey in return for a pact of mutual assistance. Kroll also stated that the French Ambassador, René Massigli had been saying to diplomats in Ankara that the Germans had intimated to the Turkish Government that they would support the Italian aspirations on Syria, if Turkey deviated from her neutrality towards the Great Powers.[71]

In its turn, since any delay in reaching an agreement with Turkey would apparently give rise to Axis intrigues, the British Government also put pressure on French Government to compromise on Hatay. As a result, on June 23, 1939, after the session had been arranged in favour of the Turkish thesis, a Franco–Turkish Declaration was announced in terms similar to those agreed between Britain and Turkey.[72]

In relation to the conclusion of an Anglo–Franco–Turkish Treaty, the Turkish Government was insisting that such an agreement should be preceded by substantial aid. Apparently, in the months after the Franco–Turkish Declaration, the Turkish Government was anxious to immediately free itself from the German pressure for trade. Given this, Turkey wanted to obtain loans for buying weaponry and for other economic purposes as well as finding new markets for her goods.

In the early hours of September 1, Danzig's incorporation into the Reich was declared and the Nazi armies invaded Poland. Once the war started in Europe, following the Anglo–French Declaration of war against the German invasion of Poland, by virtue of the guarantee given to Poland, the inability of the Allies to supply Turkey on a large scale hampered the negotiations for the conclusion of a tripartite agreement.

Indeed, the resources of Britain and France were being strained to provide for their own armament programmes and also with the urgent requests for help from other countries that were under Anglo–French guarantees. Moreover, it was not possible for Britain to offer Turkey markets for all the exports that Turkey had been sending to Germany.[73]

At the second meeting of the Supreme War Council on September 22, the French delegation introduced proposals for establishing an Allied force at Salonika or İstanbul. The British replied that in addition to the drain on Allied resources, such a decision would undermine the neutrality of the Balkan Bloc. When the French representatives repeated their suggestions of an intensified diplomatic approach to Turkey, Greece and Yugoslavia with economic and military assistance, Chamberlain pointed out that the Balkan countries were differently positioned, and unlikely to agree to form a bloc with a mere promise of material support. He stated that certainly the French had in mind the ninety divisions which the Balkan countries could put into the Allied side,[74] but before all, it was necessary to secure at least the benevolent neutrality of Rome.[75]

Meanwhile, the Soviet Union, which had come to an agreement with Germany following the conclusion of a secret protocol in August 23, had adopted a drastically different attitude in relation to her policy towards the Allies and Turkey. In September, the Soviets invited the Turkish Minister of Foreign Affairs to Moscow to discuss a mutual assistance pact, this time to offset or replace the one still under discussion between Turkey and the Allied Powers.[76] When Saraçoğlu was in Moscow, the new Soviet Commissar for Foreign Affairs Molotov[77] presented the Russian proposal on the closure of the Dardanelles to the non-Black Sea Powers, whether Russia was belligerent or not, despite the fact that this was contrary to the Montreux Convention. The Soviets also promised to help Turkey in defense of the Straits should Turkey become involved in war.

In the same days, after the conclusion of the Protocol on August 23, Ribbentrop arrived in the Soviet capital for the second time, to initial the Nazi–Soviet Pact. Thus, the attention of Kremlin shifted to negotiations with Germany.[78]

In fact, Hitler expected that the Nazi–Soviet pact would frighten the Turkish Government to the extent of cancelling the Friendship Declarations, therefore he sent Ribbentrop with this goal in mind too.

On October 2, following a four-hour conference between Stalin, Molotov and Saraçoğlu, the latter informed Ankara about the course of the talks, and subsequently he stated his Government's rejection of any initiative without consulting London and Paris.[79] On October 9, 1939, the German Ambassador in Moscow, Schulenburg stated that Molotov was pursuing the aim of inducing Turkey to adopt full-neutrality, and under all circumstances "the interests of Germany and the special nature of German–Soviet relations would be taken into account."[80]

On October 16, Molotov received Saraçoğlu for the last time. Much to the surprise of Saraçoğlu, Molotov once more put forward the Straits issue and also demanded that Turkey should commit herself not to make war on Germany on behalf of the Western Powers. To the disappointment of the partners of the notorious Nazi–Soviet Pact, Saraçoğlu decided to leave Moscow for Ankara without engaging in further negotiations. The official Communiqué issued by Moscow merely emphasized the existence of friendly relations between the two countries. On October 17, 1939, Schulenburg reported to Berlin that before the departure of Saraçoğlu, Molotov was unable to obtain an assistance pact.[81]

Dallin maintains that the policies of Turkey and Russia were at odds, and that Turkey had entered firmly into the alliance with the Allied Powers whilst Russia sought to maintain a neutrality which was clearly to the advantage of Berlin. In many respects, Nazi–Soviet Pact became a pretext to joint aggression of these powers as regards the immediate partition of Poland between them in October.

Following the failure of Nazi–Soviet policy towards Turkey, Papen tried to minimize the repercussions of the Nazi–Soviet pact. He told the Turkish officials that it was an attempt by Hitler to assure uninterrupted delivery of raw materials from Eastern Europe. To Knatchbull-Hugessen's astonishment, Papen told him that he regretted that the British were not able to sign an accord with the Russians before Germany did. He claimed that had the British successfully concluded their talks in Moscow "the position would be more favourable for discussions between Great Britain and Germany."[82]

Turning back to the Anglo–Franco–Turkish talks, in response to Turkish demands, Halifax had already authorized Knatcbull-Hugessen to promise Turkey a sum of £10 million, depending on the conclusion of a political agreement with Turkey. Whereas, the Turkish Government demanded a credit of £35 million for weaponry, a loan of £15 million for economic recovery, and approximately £2 million for the liquidation of the clearing deficit.[83] Despite Knatchbull-Hugessen's suggestion that the Treasury should provide the sum, it was not possible for Britain to allocate this credit at once. To make the allocation of this sum to Turkey more difficult, the French Government showed a reluctance to contribute.

An official of the French Ministry of Finance told Sir Frederick Leith-Ross of the British Treasury that the French Government had considered in view of the cession of Hatay that France ought not to be called upon to make financial assistance to Turkey.[84] Considering the economic help as it might have the strongest effect on Turkish adherence to a treaty with France and Britain, the British Government urged the Treasury to meet with the Turkish demands. "In the psychological atmosphere of the first weeks of war the financial arguments which had hitherto carried so much weight in London were outbalanced by political considerations."[85] At this stage, the French Government also showed willingness to supply Turkey with armaments credit.

Following the allocation of a credit of £25 million for armaments, and £31/2 million for the transfer of commercial credits in clearing accounts with a Special Agreement on Financial and Economic Questions on October 19, 1939, the Treaty of Mutual Assistance was signed on the same day. It was agreed in Article 2 (1) that, in the event of an act of aggression by a European power leading to war in the Mediterranean area in which France and Britain involved, Turkey would collaborate effectively with France and the United Kingdom. In the event of Turkey being involved in hostility in the Mediterranean, France and Britain would lend her all aid and assistance in their power. With Article 4 , Turkish benovelent neutrality towards Britain and France, in case they were attacked by a European Power, was agreed upon.[86] Subsequently, it was decided that, an Anglo–Franco–Turkish Commission would meet to draw up the programme for the transfer of war material and to decide on urgent supplies to Turkey. The Commission would also have a regard to the immediate possibilities of the British and French Governments.

By Article 6 of the Treaty, a suspensive clause which was to be kept secret was included. Accordingly, this Treaty would not come into force until Turkey had been supplied with the war material that it demanded for the defence of its Thracian border.[87] As another matter of significance, a 'Protocol Number Two' was added to the original Treaty to the effect that the undertakings of Turkey emerging from this agreement were not to have the effect of compelling her to go to war with the Soviet Union. It was intended to keep this protocol secret, however, the Turkish Government announced its existence.[88]

The Italian Entry into War (10 June 1940), the Fall of France and the Consequent Acceptance of Turkish Neutrality

On October 24, 1939, on the assumption that Italy was an assured neutral, it was agreed by the Bitish War Cabinet that the main body of the Mediterranean fleet which was in Alexandra, would be immediately available to sail for Turkish waters if required. Additionally, it was planned to strengthen the Turkish defence at Chanak[kale] (the Dardanelles) against the passage of Russian submarines as well. In case of a war with Russia, the aim was to lock up the Russian fleet in the Black Sea, by the closing of the Dardanelles and Bosphorus. In the same meeting, it was underlined that an attack on Turkey would almost certainly be combined with attacks upon British interests in the Middle East.[89] A few days later, on October 29, Viscount Halifax stated that:

> A year ago we had undertaken no specific commitments on the Continent of Europe. . . . Today we are bound by new agreements for mutual defence with Poland and Turkey; we have guaranteed assistance to Greece and Roumania against aggression, and we are now engaged with the Soviet Government in a negotiation . . . with a view to associating them with us for the defence of States in Europe.[90]

Ankara's decision to lean on the Franco–British support to counterbalance the potential threats, though with a careful attitude, did not help Moscow to refrain from taking further actions. On October 31, Molotov claimed that Turkey had rejected the cautious policy of neutrality, and decided to enter the orbit of the spreading war in Europe in conformity with the Anglo–French expectations, since they aimed "to drag into the war as many neutral countries as they can." Molotov continued saying that, "It is not, however, for us to guess whether Turkey will not regret her action."[91] The Russian negotiators had followed German instructions to put the Allies and Turkey's positions into difficulty.

In November, Russians took to another offensive and attacked Finland. As regards the Soviet move, Chamberlain and Churchill were entirely at one in believing that Stalin's action was in the Russian perception of national interest as neither could believe that it would suit Russia to see Germany supreme in Europe. Therefore, Chamberlain did not choose to add Russia to the list of Britain's enemies.[92]

As regards German reactions to the Anglo–Franco–Turkish Agreement, in a talk with the Turkish Ambassador in Berlin, R. Hüsrev Gerede, Ribbentrop intimidated that Turkey could share the destiny of Poland.[93] On November 3, 1939, von Papen was instructed to make a statement to Saraçoğlu to the effect that Germany considered Turkey's treaty with the Western Powers an intentional affront and reserved the right to take appropriate measures if it should lead to practical consequences affecting Germany.[94] On 11 November, in a conversation with Gerede, Ribbentrop again severely criticized Turkish policy and stated that it had taken a predominantly anti-German line. Aiming to perpetuate Nazi–Soviet designs, he said, "If the reports I had received were correct, Turkey had rejected the Russian reservation with respect to Germany, and had insisted that she would conclude a mutual-assistance pact with the Soviet Union only if it was also directed against Germany."[95]

Despite the Russian and German threatening statements, a Turkish delegation left for London in the same month to discuss the economic and political questions for a closer alliance.[96] During Menemencioğlu's visit in London, on December 5, it was stated in a report of the Chiefs of Staff Committee that one of the objectives of the Turkish Secretary-General's visit was to negotiate on the removal of the suspensive clause in the special Agreement between Britain, France and Turkey.[97] Shortly afterwards, in accordance with the desire of Allies, this clause was removed on January 8, 1940, by a Protocol signed in Paris.

Berlin's anxiety over Turkey was not confined to foreign policy. Germany needed Turkish raw materials as well. Chrome was the most important, being absolutely essential for the manufacture of steel for armaments. Towards the end of October 1939, Turkey's cutting of chromium ore deliveries led to a crisis in German–Turkish economic relations. Germany's chromium need was estimated 12,000 tons a month and the Germans had planned to obtain some part (40,000 tons at once) of this essential raw material from Turkey, through Hungary.[98] In an unsigned memorandum, it was suggested that Germany agree to negotiate agreements on trade of chromium together with other goods since the Turks "were not likely to yield to German economic pressure."[99] Papen urged his Foreign Ministry for the speedy acceptance of Turkish demands as an agreement had been seemed probable.[100] Despite the tremendous German pressure, it was not before June 13 that an economic treaty was signed between Germany and Turkey. On the same day, Papen reported that the agreement which had been signed did not provide for chromium and therefore it was also exclusive of German armament deliveries.

In May 1940, Churchill, who had been an outspoken critic of Britain's pre-war foreign policy, formed his coalition Government. With the start of the Churchill Government, Anthony Eden was brought to the War Office (May 11, 1940) where he served until his return to the Foreign Office on December 23.[101]

Following the intensification of the war in Europe with the German invasion of Holland and Belgium, the British expeditionary force crossed into Belgium. However, the military situation could not be improved and between May 27 and June 4, British and some Allied forces were evacuated from Dunkirk to Britain.

Having been encouraged by the initial success of Germany, on June 10, 1940, Italy entered into war. Mussolini, deciding that the situation was favourable, invaded southern France. The French Prime Minister, Paul Reynaud urged his Cabinet to continue the fighting. But the peace party in the French Cabinet became dominant particularly after the retreat of their British allies across the English Channel. Reynaud resigned and was replaced by Marshal Petain, who signed an armistice with Germany.

In this international situation, Britain considered supporting Turkey's position against the immediate threat arising from the Soviet Union would best to suit her. At the end of June 1940, the Soviets annexed the Baltic states and took Bessarabia and northern Bukovina from Roumania. The Soviets also tried to bring pressure upon Turkey on the Straits issue and on the possession of the two Caucasian provinces of Kars and Ardahan. Russian designs were a matter of concern for the Germans as well. On July 23, 1940, the Turkish Counsellor Alkend told his German counterpart Ripken that he had spoken to a well informed official of the Turkish Ministry of Foreign Affairs, and asked if it was true that, Russia had demanded of Turkey that it return the two provinces and that it cede two military bases at the Dardanelles. He said the official had answered the question in the affirmative. In reply to the Soviet demands, President İnönü had stated that, as far as the Straits were concerned, the Montreux Convention was decisive, and Russia had seen no enemy warship penetrating into the Straits. However, if Russia insisted on her demands, the only thing left was war.[102]

On October 7, German troops entered into Roumania. In this case, with the operationalization of the Article 3 of the Mutual Assistance

Treaty, if Britain had to implement her guarantee to Roumania, Turkey was expected to co-operate with Britain. On the other hand, Knatchbull-Hugessen cabled the Foreign Office on October 12 that it would be preferable not to involve the Turks in the Roumanian conflict because it might ask for further support. The British Government decided that it was best to maintain Turkish benevolent neutrality rather than trying to force unwilling belligerency of her.[103]

Following the Italian attack on Greece on October 28, this time, the Turkish Government informed Bulgaria that Turkey would declare war if it attacked Greece. On the same day, Knatchbull-Hugessen reported that Saraçoğlu had informed the Greek Ambassador in Ankara that Greece could count on Turkey in the event of a Bulgarian attack.[104]

On the German side, the assumption that if Turkey were to enter into war the only side it could join was the Allied one led to Berlin's ultimate decision to keep Turkey out of the conflict. On November 25, in a talk with Menemencioğlu, von Papen told him that Germany would prefer Turkey to remain neutral. Menemencioğlu replied that in case the Germans invaded the Balkans, Turkey would act accordingly to whether it felt threatened or not. Papen assured Menemencioğlu that Germany would keep Turkey out of the war, if himself was given sufficient time for diplomatic preparation in each case that might arise.[105]

Meanwhile, Hitler was becoming increasingly preoccupied with Russia. On November 24, Hitler's Chief of Staff Halder wrote in his diary that "we have to see clearly that the possibilities against Russia disappear if we decide for Turkey."[106] Hitler and his staff considered that operations against the Soviets or the invasion of Turkey were mutually exclusive projects. Halder concluded, "We have come to the considered decision to avoid conflict with Turkey at all possible cost."[107]

Churchill considered that assistance to Greece would also have an important effect on the Turkish Government. On November 26, he cabled the Commander in Chief in Middle East (in Cairo) that:

It might be that 'COMPASS' [Operation Of Aid To Greece] would in itself determine action of Yugoslavia and Turkey. . . One may indeed see the possibility of centre of gravity in Middle East shifting suddenly from Egypt to the Balkans and from Cairo to Istanbul.[108]

In November 1940, the Turkish Government finally took full mobilization. On November 23, Papen asked Menemencioğlu the reasons behind the Turkish state of alert. Menemencioğlu attributed this to the Italo–Greek conflict and the likelihood of German intervention. In his turn, Papen told him that Turkey's frontiers could be guaranteed if the İnönü administration declared its acceptance of the Axis new order. On November 29, Papen interviewed İnönü. The Turkish President turned to the subject of Albania and asked whether German troops would be sent there. Papen assured İnönü that Hitler would not dispatch troops to that country which was "irrelevant to the succesful outcome of the war."[109] İnönü questioned Papen as regards the re-organisation of the Balkans in the event that Germany won the war. According to Weber, he wanted Papen to formulate a non-aggression pact between the two countries.

Papen immediately drafted a treaty consisted of four main articles. In the first article, Turkey would declare herself sympathetic to the new Axis order and prompt to take an active part in regulating the Balkan Peninsula and the Middle East. The second article required Turkey not to become involved with any British action against Germany. The third article stated that the Axis would respect Turkey's territorial integrity and not attack her. The last article stated that Turkish delegations would be invited to all conferences on Balkan re-organisation. Weber argued that Saraçoğlu perused this draft before its dispatch to Berlin, amending the territorial guarantee to include an undefined Turkish zone of interest. In his turn, Ribbentrop declined the suggestion of Papen. He considered that Papen was undermining Italy's privileges as Germany's ally. Moreover, Ribbentrop was dubious about the reactions of Molotov who had recently been in Berlin.[110]

On the other hand, "Molotov's visit led to a quick maturing of Hitler's plans against the Soviet Union. . . . What he said about the need to expand southwards to the warm seas, and about the need for bases in the Turkish Straits, was traditional Russian policy . . . more questionable in the situation that existed at that time was Molotov's demand to exercise a similar right of guarantee to Bulgaria as Hitler exercised for Rumania . . . one could make no impression on him at all with nebulous hopes of what he might get from British possessions in the future, when Britain was defeated."[111] When Molotov became *less tractable*, Ribbentrop authorized Papen to conduct further talks to conclude a treaty with Turkey. To impress the Turkish Government, Ribbentrop sent his brother-in-law, Albert Jencke, too. He also raised no objection to the inclusion of an "undefined Turkish zone of interest" to the proposed pact and aimed to revitalize Turkey's imperialistic policies. But all German efforts were in vain.[112] To the disappointment of German officials, Turkish negotiators did not commit themselves to an alliance with Germany.

The German position in Central Europe after the Anschluss and occupation of Czechoslovakia, as well as the increase in its economic and political pressure on the East European states, led to Britain's active involvement with Turkey. This firstly came in the economic field. Britain calculated that Turkey could lead in forming a Balkan front. Subsequently, Joint Declarations and finally, the Anglo–Franco–Turkish Treaty was concluded. In the meantime, Germany sent a highly skilled diplomat, von Papen to draw Turkey to its side. Shortly afterwards, Ankara became an important political center in which Allied and Axis diplomacy were trying to counter-balance each other. Following the Nazi–Soviet Pact, the Soviets also joined Germany in an attempt to pull Turkey out of the Allied front.

Against this background, joint Anglo–Franco–Turkish talks were held in early 1940 to realize the Allied objective of building up bases in Turkey. However, the effectiveness of the Anglo–Franco–Turkish Treaty turned upon the transfer of the Anglo–French subsidies to Turkey which were already very weak. Ultimately, the increased difficulty of Britain and France to supply Turkey in weaponry and credits became one of the factors which prompted Turkey to retain her neutrality. Lord Halifax told the Military Chiefs in the War Cabinet that increased pressure on the Turkish Government "would only bring a demand for increased munitions which Britain was hard put to meet."[113]

Eventually, the war did not spread to Thrace and the Straits as the German military had been preparing a major offensive in a different direction towards the Soviet Union. In this case, for the Allies, no immediate necessity arose to include Turkey in its prime military considerations.

In essence, the Italian entry into war and attack on Greece had given Great Britain the right to demand Turkish belligerency in accordance with the terms of the Joint Declarations and the Treaty of Mutual Assistance. The war in the Mediterranean had broken out. However, this time Turkey responded with the 'Protocol Number Two' which was annexed to the Anglo–Franco–Turkish Treaty. The Turkish Government stated that belligerency might cause her to become involved in war with the Soviets. For this reason, Turkey choose to remain out of the hostilities, in its own interest. This represented a major step towards the country's consolidation of her neutral status. Turkey had demanded the inclusion

of the 'Protocol Number Two' according to which "the obligations undertaken by Turkey . . . can not compel the country to take action having, as its consequence, entry into armed conflict with the U.S.S.R.,"[114]
to this effect.

At this time, Greece was ruled by Ioannis Metaxas who did everything he would to refuse British offers of help against the Italians. Metaxas
knew that a British intervention in Greece would draw in the Germans
and Greek forces were doing well by themselves against the Italian in-
vaders. Unfortunately, however, Metaxas died and British pressure was
exerted upon the new Greek Government which ceded to the British
ouvertures. The British intervention brought a German intervention, as
Metaxas feared. Interestingly, Metaxas, as Chief of Staff of the Greek
Army in 1915 had opposed Greek involvement in the Great War and
supported the Greek King against Prime Minister Eleftherios Venizelos.
He had also been against the Greek invasion of Anatolia in 1922.[115]

To some experts, the Nazi invasion of Soviets which began with the
Operation Barbarossa, removed the basis of Turkish rejection to enter
the war on the Allied side. A stronger reason behind the acceptance of
Turkish neutrality, however could and should be found in the belligerent
powers' interest in non-expanding of the global conflict.

The following chapter concentrates on the war time diplomacy of
Turkey until the start of a period of controlled tension between Turkey
and the Soviets, following the Turkish declaration of war against Germany and Japan on February 23, 1945 and the Soviet Note on March 15,
1945, denouncing the Turco–Soviet Treaty of Neutrality and Non-aggression (signed in Paris on December 17, 1925) that was given to the
Turkish Government. At this stage, Turkey's reservations against the
Soviets proved to be right given the Soviet advances.

Notes

1. Pat Walsh, *Britain's Great War on Turkey, An Irish Perspective,* (Belfast:
Athol Books, 2009), p. 138.
2. Turkish Republic was proclaimed on October 29, 1923.
3. Gazi (Ghazi—a salutation which means veteran) Mustafa Kemal Atatürk,
1881–1938, served in the Libyan and Balkan campaigns, 1911–13; Military
Attaché in Sofia, 1913–1914; served at Gallipoli, 1915; in the Caucasus, 1916;

and in Syria, 1917. Assumed command of the Turkish national movement in 1919. First president of the Turkish Republic from 1923 until his death.

4. Ömer Kürkçüoğlu, "Türk-İngiliz İlişkileri 1920'lerden 1950'lere" (Anglo-Turkish Relations From 1920s to 1950s), in *Türk-İngiliz İlişkileri 1583-1984, 400. Yıldönümü* (Anglo-Turkish Relations 1583-1984, 400th Anniversary), note (1) on p. 79. From the interview of the author with Lord Kinross, the author of the biography of Atatürk.

5. Justin McCarthy, *The Ottoman Peoples and the End of Empire*, (NY: Oxford University Press, 2001), p. 147.

6. For a comprehensive account of this episode in the history of League of Nations, see, Güçlü, Yücel, "Turkey's Entrance into the League of Nations", in Middle Eastern Studies, Volume 39, Number 1, Cambridge: Routledge, part of the Taylor&Francis Group, January 2003, pp. 186-206, *passim*.

7. Gordon Waterfield, *Sir Percy Loraine*, London: Murray, 1973, pp. 207-208.

8. H. M. Knatchbull-Hugessen, *Memoirs*, (London: Murray, 1949), p. 135.

9. Tevfik Rüştü Aras, Minister for Foreign Affairs from March 1925 to November 1938; from January 1939 to February 1942 he was Ambassador to London.

10. Osman Okyar, *Fethi Okyar'ın 1922 ve 1934-39 Yıllarında Londra'da ulk Kez Görevlendirilmesinin Işığında, Türk-İngiliz Ticaret İlişkilerinin İki Savaş Arası Dönemdeki Gelişimi* (The Development of Anglo-Turkish Commercial Relations in Interwar Period in the Light of the First Nomination of Fethi Okyar in London in 1922 And in the Years 1934-39), in *Türk-İngiliz İlişkileri 1583-1984* (Anglo-Turkish Relations 1583-1984), Ankara: Başbakanlık Basın Yayın ve Enformasyon Müdürlüğü, 1985, pp. 73-74.

11. Selim Deringil, *Turkish Foreign Policy During The Second World War*, (Cambridge: Cambridge University Press, 1989) 25; Waterfield, *Sir Percy Loraine*, p. 210.

12. According to Okyar, Britain's response to Turkey's proposal for alliance would ultimately be the Anglo-Turkish Joint Declaration (May 12, 1939), and Franco-Turkish Joint Declaration (June 13, 1939). See, Okyar, *Fethi Okyar'ın 1922 ve 1934-39 Yıllarında, . . .* p. 74. Concerning France, Turkey's relations were not good, because of this country's involvement as mandatory power in Turkey's dispute with Syria on the Hatay Sanjak. Additionally, in comparison to Britain, Turkey was doubtful about France's economic power. Therefore, to ally with Britain was her principal choice. Ludmila Zhivkova, *Anglo-Turkish Relations 1933-1939*, p. 54.

13. Cited in Frank G. Weber, *The Evasive Neutral*, (Missouri: University of Missouri Press, 1979), pp. 5-6.

14. "Anglo-Italian [Gentleman's] Agreement, 2 January 1937," in *Documents on International Affairs 1937*, ed. by Stephen Heald, (London: Oxford University Press, 1937), p. 87.

15. As an instance of her good intentions, previously in July 1936, Britain had recalled her fleet from the Mediterranean. See, Zhivkova, *Anglo-Turkish Relations 1933-1939*, note (23) on p. 37.

16. Richard Langworth (ed.), Churchill by Himself: The Definitive Collection of Quotations, (London: Public Affairs, 2008), p. 346.

17. *Ibid.*, p. 58. For an account of Ciano's conversation with Aras, see also, *Ciano's Diplomatic Papers*, ed. by Malcolm Muggeridge, (London: Odhams Press Ltd., 1948), pp. 93-95.

18. *Documents on International Affairs*, 1937, pp. 530-531.

19. For the message of Mustafa Kemal to the TGNA, See, "Message of Kemal Atatürk to the National Assembly, 1 November 1938," in *Documents on International Affairs*, 1938, Vol. I., p. 300.

20. In his statement to the press, Bayar also rejected the existence of anti-Semitism in Turkey. He stated that, *"There is no anti-Jewish feeling in Turkey, and if a few people are trying to create one they are only imitating what is done elsewhere."* Statement by Turkish Prime Minister, Celal Bayar, on January 26, 1938, in, *ibid.*, pp. 298-299.

21. "The Ambassador In Turkey (Keller) to the Foreign Ministry, Ankara, January 18, 1938, Subject: Organization of the NSDAP Abroad," in *Documents on German Foreign Policy*, Series D, Vol. V, p. 714.

22. Salahi Sonyel, *Atatürk—The Founder of Modern Turkey*, (Ankara: Publications of Turkish Historical Society, 1989), pp. 175-177.

23. Andrew Roberts, *The Holy Fox*, (London: Weidenfeld And Nicolson, 1991), p. 136.

24. From the "Answer by British Premier Mr. Chamberlain to Mr. Attlee in House of Commons on May 27, 1938," in *House of Commons Parliamentary Debates*, 5th Series, Volume 336, p. 1565.

25. See, "Agreement Between His Majesty's Government In the United Kingdom And the Government of the Turkish Republic Regarding An Armaments Credit For Turkey, May 27 1938," *Command Papers Cmd. 5755*, Article 1.

26. Cüneyt Arcayürek, *Şeytan Üçgeninde Türkiye* (Turkey in the Bermuda Triangle), (Ankara: Bilgi Yayınevi, 1987), p. 49.

27. Weber, *The Evasive Neutral*, pp. 23-25.

28. Aras made this statement in his interview with a representative of the *New York Times*. See, "Statement By Turkish Prime Minister of Foreign Affairs, Tevfik Rüştü Aras, on 20 July 1938," in *Documents on International Affairs*, 1938, Vol. I, p. 299.

29. Cited in, Sonyel, *Atatürk—The Founder of Modern Turkey*, pp. 177-178.

30. Regarding this change, Harvey (editor) stated that, with Eden's departure, Chamberlain was free to pursue his policy of appeasement. See, John Harvey, *Diplomatic Diaries of Oliver Harvey 1937–1940*, (London: Collins Clear-Type Press, 1970), pp. 102,105.

31. "Statement By Turkish President İnönü, on 22 November 1938," in *Documents on International Affairs*, 1938, Vol. I, p. 300.

32. Arcayürek, *Bermuda Şeytan Üçgeninde Türkiye*, p. 47.

33. Cited in, Deringil, *Turkish Foreign Policy During the Second World War*, p. 26.

34. *Ibid.*

35. "Memorandum By the Head of Economic Policy Division III, Berlin, 20 January 1939," in *Documents on German Foreign Policy*, Series D, Vol. V, pp. 742–743.

36. "Memorandum By the Deputy Director of the Economic Policy Department (Clodius), Berlin, 5 July 1938," *ibid.*, pp. 727–728.

37. Cemil Koçak, *Türk–Alman İlişkileri 1923–1939*, pp. 230–231.

38. "Memorandum by the State Secretary, February 10, 1939," in *Documents on German Foreign Policy*, V, p. 560.

39. Zhivkova, *Anglo–Turkish Relations 1933–1939*, 78. Following the creation of the Balkan Pact on February 9, 1934, a secret protocol which became common knowledge guaranteed the existing frontiers and stipulated that in the event of aggression by a non-Balkan Power, in which a Balkan state also took part, the military aspects of the Pact would apply only against the Balkan aggressor. John O. Iatrides (ed.), *Ambassador MacVeagh Reports Greece, 1933–1947*, (Princeton: Princeton University Press, 1980), p. 27.

40. Muggeridge, *Ciano's Diplomatic Papers*, p. 259.

41. "Sir H. Knatchbull-Hugessen to Viscount Halifax, Ankara, 10 April 1939, 8:40 P.M.," in *Documents on British Foreign Policy*, Third Series, Vol. V, p. 162. Knatchbull-Hugessen arrived in Ankara late in February 1939 replacing Percy Loraine after Loraine was nominated in Rome.

42. "Sir H. Knatchbull-Hugessen to Viscount Halifax, Ankara, 10 April 1939, 12:20 P.M.," in *Documents on British Foreign Policy*, Third Series Vol. V, p. 165.

43. From, "Viscount Halifax To Sir H. Knatchbull-Hugessen (Ankara), Foreign Office, 12 April 1939," in *ibid.*, p. 180.

44. *Ibid.*

45. From, "Viscount Halifax To Sir H. Knatchbull-Hugessen (Ankara), Foreign Office, 13 April 1939," in, *ibid.*, p. 190.

46. "Viscount Halifax To Sir H. Knatchbull-Hugessen, Foreign Office, 11 April 1939," in *ibid.*, p. 167.

47. *Ibid.*, p. 168.

48. "Sir H. Knatchbull-Hugessen To Viscount Halifax, Ankara, 13 April 1939," in, *ibid.*, p. 187.

49. *Ibid.*, p. 188.

50. See, "Extract From Statement By The British Prime Minister, 13 April 1939 on the Guarantee To Greece And Roumania," in *Documents on International Affairs*, Vol. I (March–September 1939), pp. 201–202.

51. *Survey of International Affairs, The Eve of War,* 1939, p. 113.

52. *Ibid.*, p. 126.

53. Sir Llewllyn Woodward, *British Foreign Policy in The Second World War*, (London: HMSO, 1962), p. 15.

54. *Survey of International Affairs, The Eve of War,* 1939, note 5, on p. 118.

55. *Ibid.*, p. 119.

56. Koçak, *Türk-Alman İlişkileri 1923–1939*, note (78) on p. 139. Indeed, the post of German Ambassador in Ankara was vacant for several months. See, "The Charge d'Affaires in Turkey (Kroll) to the Foreign Ministry, Ankara, 15 March 1939," in *Documents on German Foreign Policy*, Series D Vol. V, p. 744.

57. Knatchbull-Hugessen, *Memoirs*, pp. 146; 150–151.

58. Weber, *The Evasive Neutral*, pp. 29–30.

59. Cited in, *Survey of International Affairs, The Eve of War*, 1939, p. 127.

60. *Ibid.*, p. 119.

61. From, "Statement By the British Prime Minister Mr. Chamberlain in the House of Commons," in *House of Commons, Deb.*, 5th Ser., Vol. 347, col. 953.

62. *Ibid.*

63. From, "Answer By the British Prime Minister, on 17 May 1939," in *ibid.*, p. 1375.

64. Knatchbull-Hugessen, *Memoirs*, p. 149.

65. *Ibid.*, p. 153.

66. From the "Answer By the British Prime Minister in House of Commons, on 22 May 1939," in *House of Commons Parliamentary Debates*, 5th Series Vol. 347, p. 1892.

67. Muggeridge, *Ciano's Diplomatic Papers*, 282. See also, "Conversation With the Reich Foreign Minister, von Ribbentrop, Milan, 6–7 May 1939," *ibid.*, pp. 284–285.

68. On the Sanjak of Hatay (where the main city and bay is Alexandra-İskenderun) which had acquired a special regime of local autonomy under the French Mandate for Syria, various agreements between Turkey and France had previously been made, the most recent being in July 1938, with the Franco-Turkish Treaty of Friendship. See also, Woodward, *British Foreign Policy in The Second World War*, p. 15.

69. Koçak, *Türk-Alman İlişkileri 1923–1939*, pp. 172–173.

70. Weber, *The Evasive Neutral*, pp. 35–36.

71. "The Charge d'Affaires in Turkey (Kroll) to the Foreign Ministry, Ankara, 15 March 1939," in *Documents on German Foreign Policy*, Third Series Vol. VI, p. 5.

72. *Survey of International Affairs The Eve of War*, 1939, pp. 121–122; "The Text of Franco-Turkish Declaration," in *Documents on International Affairs*, Vol I., ed. by Arnold J. Toynbee, (London: Oxford University Press, 1951), pp. 203–204.

73. *Survey of International Affairs The Eve of War, 1939*, pp. 146–147.

74. Later on, as regards the possible constitution of a Balkan Front, the following were estimated as the available strengths of the Balkan countries concerned: Roumania 31 Divisions; Yugoslavia 26 Divisions; Greece 17 Divisions; Turkey 37 Divisions. See, "The Balkan Problem, Record of A Meeting Held At the Headquarters of General Gamelin, on 11 December 1939," *Cabinet Papers*, Cab. 66/4.

75. Woodward, *British Foreign Policy in The Second World War*, pp. 14–15.

76. Annette Baker Fox, *The Power of Small States*, (Chicago: Chicago University Press, 1959), p. 14.

77. Litvinov who favoured an understanding with Britain and France was dismissed in favour of Molotov in May. As soon as Molotov was handed over the Secretariat, he engaged in the Russo-German talks which resulted in Nazi-Soviet Pact of 23 August.

78. David Dallin, *Soviet Russia's Foreign Policy 1939–1942*, (New Haven: Yale University Press, 1944), p. 108. Concerning the visits of Ribbentrop to Moscow in August and subsequently, in September, see, Isaac Deutscher, *Stalin*, (London: Oxford University Press, 1966), pp. 428–433 *passim*. See also, Weber, *The Evasive Neutral*, p. 39.

79. Dallin, *Soviet Russia's Foreign Policy 1939–1942*, p. 109.

80. "The Ambassador in the Soviet Union (Schulenburg) to the Foreign Ministry, Moscow, 9 October 1939," in *Documents on German Foreign Policy*, Series D Vol. VIII, p. 244.

81. "The Ambassador in Moscow (Schulenburg) to the Foreign Ministry, Moscow, 17 October 1939," in *ibid.*, p. 306.

82. Weber, *The Evasive Neutral*, p. 39.

83. Zhivkova, *Anglo-Turkish Relations 1933–1939*, p. 109.

84. See, *Survey of International Affairs, The Eve of War*, 1939, note (6) on p. 148.

85. *Ibid.*, p. 149.

86. "Treaty of Mutual Assistance Between His Majesty in Respect of the United Kingdom, the President of the French Republic And the President of the Turkish Republic," in the appendix of Deringil, *Turkish Foreign Policy During the Second World War*, pp. 189–190.

87. This war material consisted of, particularly, anti-aircraft and anti-tank guns. "Memorandum By the Chiefs of Staff Committee to the War Cabinet, 5

December 1939," *Cabinet Papers*, Cab. 66/4. The suspense clause which did not appear in the text of the treaty, was cancelled by a protocol signed in Paris on 8 January 1940. *Survey of International Affairs The Eve of War, 1939*, 150.

88. Deringil, *Turkish Foreign Policy During the Second World War*, p. 88.

89. These were stated as Palestine and Egypt, including the Canal Zone, and the protection of the Anglo-Iranian oil fields. Although Britain had treaty arrangements with Iraq, it was decided to attach a lower category of importance to "the defence of this country." See, "War Cabinet Chiefs of Staff Committee/ Assistance to Turkey Against German and/or Russian Aggression, 24 October 1939," Cabinet Papers, Cab. 66/3.

90. H. H. E. Craster, (ed.), *Speeches on Foreign Policy by Viscount Halifax*, (London: Royal Institute of International Affairs, 1960), p. 287.

91. Obviously, Molotov's assumption that Turkey would be involved in the war because of her agreement with Britain and France proved to be a mistake. In 1941, even the Soviet Union was in the war, Turkey was still neutral. Dallin, *Soviet Russia's Foreign Policy 1939-1942*, p. 111.

92. David Dilks, "The Twilight War And The Fall of France: Chamberlain And Churchill in 1940," in *Retreat From Power Vol. Two*, ed. by David Dilks, (London: Macmillan Press, 1981), p. 46.

93. Hüsrev Gerede was nominated to this post on September 27, 1939, in replacement of Hamdi Arpağ. On the same day Hitler received the new Turkish Ambassador and told him that good political relations between Germany and Turkey were advisable and offered rich prospects. See, "Memorandum By The State Secretary (Weizsäcker), Berlin, 27 September 1939," in *Documents on German Foreign Policy*, Series D Vol.VIII, p. 151. For the intimidation of Ribbentrop, see, Arcayürek, *Bermuda Şeytan Üçgeninde Türkiye*, pp. 56-57.

94. "The Foreign Minister to the Ambassador in Turkey on 3 November 1939," in *Documents on German Foreign Policy*, Series D Vol. VIII, pp. 371-372.

95. See, "Memorandum By the Foreign Service, Berlin, 11 November 1939," in, *ibid.*, pp. 398-399.

96. From the "Statement By Mr. Butler in House of Commons on 30 November 1939," in, *House of Commons Parliamentary Debates*, Fifth Series Vol. 355, p. 307.

97. "Memorandum By the Chiefs of Staff Committee / Policy in the Balkans And Middle East, on 5 December 1939," *Cabinet Papers*, Cab. 66/4.

98. From, "Memorandum By An Official of the Economic Policy Department, Berlin, 9 January 1940," in *Documents on German Foreign Policy*, Series D Vol. VIII, p. 635.

99. "Unsigned Memorandum," in *ibid.*, pp. 452-455.

100. "The Ambassador in Turkey (Papen) to the Foreign Ministry, Ankara, 6 January 1940," in *Documents on German Foreign Policy*, Series D Vol VIII, p. 628.

101. Lewis Broad, *Sir Anthony Eden*, (London: Hutchinson, 1955), p. 140.

102. "Memorandum By the Director of Political Division (Melchers), Berlin, on 23 July 1940," in *Documents on German Foreign Policy*, Series D Vol. X, p. 281.

103. Deringil, *Turkish Foreign Policy During the Second World War*, p. 112.

104. *Ibid.,* pp. 112–113.

105. "The Ambassador in Turkey (Papen) to the Foreign Ministry, Ankara, 25 November 1920," in *Documents on German Foreign Policy*, Series D Vol. XI, p. 703.

106. Cited in, Deringil, *Turkish Foreign Policy During the Second World War*, p. 116.

107. *Ibid.*

108. Cited in, *ibid.*, p. 113.

109. Weber, *The Evasive Neutral,* p. 63.

110. *Ibid.,* p. 64.

111. Ernst von Weizsäcker, *Memoirs*, (London: Victor Gollanz, 1951), pp. 245–246.

112. Weber, *The Evasive Neutral*, pp. 64–65.

113. Cited in, Deringil, *Turkish Foreign Policy During the Second World War*, p. 114.

114. Dallin, *Soviet Russia's Foreign Policy 1939–1942*, 110–111; Arcayürek, *Bermuda Şeytan Üçgeninde Türkiye*, p. 57.

115. The author thanks Pat Walsh, the author of *Britain's Great War on Turkey An Irish Perspective*, for his insightful remarks on the subject.

Chapter 3

The War and Neutral Obligations: Turkish Foreign Policy Vis-à-Vis the Shifting Sands of Wartime Diplomacy (1941–1945)

One thing is certain, that before Turkey will give up another slice of territory she will fight any armies that may be allied against her to the bitter end.[1]

Admittedly, many of the underlying motives of the post-war Turkish foreign policy were inherited from the years of the world war. Throughout the war, Ankara remained outside of the conflict, but the Turkish foreign policy makers always perceived a threat of being dragged into it. In war years, Ankara's threat perceptions were almost equally associated with Berlin and the Kremlin. Besides, the period between the Nazi–Soviet pact of August 1939 and Berlin's declaration of war on Russia on June 22, 1941 dramatically increased Ankara's suspicions of these totalitarian regimes. Hitler's onslaught on Russia could merely introduce a limited change in these assessments. In the eyes of the Turkish statesmen, either allied with Germany or on its own, Moscow was not reliable at all and was considered as another potential enemy at times.

Indeed, Ankara was at odds between the Nazi–Soviet aggression and the British insistence on Turkish belligerency in accordance with its undertakings as set forth in the October 19, 1939 Anglo–Franco–Turkish Mutual Assistance Treaty as well. In an international arena which was dominated by the relentless attacks of the aggressors which took over Turkey's neighbours and allies within the Balkan Entente one by one, eventually, Ankara chose to continue its policy of benevolent neutrality towards the Allied side.

This being the case, Turkish foreign policy makers' decision to build a strategy to deal with the aggressive totalitarian regimes while maintaining an alliance with the Western countries had its roots in these years. Undoubtedly, experiences of the war helped them to quickly adapt in the post war era which was dominated by Soviet expansionism. However, concurrently, Ankara's independent attitude in pursuing a calculated policy was hampered by these kind of reflexes wearing down its neutral outlook. Given this, the German and Nazi–Soviet position vis-à-vis Turkey and their economic and political pressure and finally, Ankara's emergence as an important political center in which Allied and Axis diplomacy tried to counterbalance each other will be an appropriate starting point.

The Question of Turkish Belligerency Reviewed

By the time war broke out in Europe, Turkey was unprepared to resist any large scale aggression. The economy of the early republic was in a state of serious underdevelopment. A considerable foreign debt was hindering capital development so essential for an ailing economy. The country was predominantly agrarian and underpopulated.[2] As for foreign relations, the Kemalist tradition had laid the foundations of a policy in which affiliation with alliances of unclear objectives or similar grouping of states were regarded as a threat to the regime's security. In accordance with this policy, all revisionist attempts and conspiratory endeavours with unrevealed goals were considered as having a negative impact on the international states system.

Against this background, immediately after coming to power on January 25, 1939, the government of Dr. Refik Saydam announced the peaceful orientation of Turkish foreign policy as formulated in government's program. He had stated that the spinning developments with changes in every moment in world affairs required Turkey's foreign policy to remain more alert than usual. The contemporary world crisis, bringing the nations against each other, culminating in the removal of states within a few days, was naturally of close interest to the Republican Government.

But, all these changes, being next to quick and fundamental developments, did not indicate an alteration in Turkey's foreign policy, Saydam
said. He stated, "Turkey, loyal to its friendships, alliances and as a result to its word and signature, through its affection towards peace, has
been on its way to serve peace. Before this turmoil, I can say, Turkey
has been maintaining its friendly relations under the same sincerity and
correctness with all states either big or small and will continue to try to
do so. Our government, finds serving the cause of peace, in this honest
policy."[3]

Interestingly, Saydam's speech included a strong commitment to the
effective and timely function of the TGNA, in case necessity arose in a
period of quick changes in the international arena: "With a view towards
the general interest of peace and Turkish high interest, we will subject
new conditions to a constant examination and alert status and exercise
the necessary care with attention to the Grand National Assembly to
exert its control and right decision timely and fully."[4]

At this juncture, the disturbance of the Turkish officials about the
change and unpredictabilities of the SU is worthy of mention. As previously mentioned, on October, 19, 1939, when Turkey concluded the
Treaty of Mutual Assistance with Britain and France and entered an
alliance with Western democracies, the Soviets had expressed satisfaction with this development. However, this was merely an empty gesture.
The Nazi–Soviet Pact—which was soon to be unrevealed—was secretly
concluded on August 24 and the visit of Turkish Minister of Foreign
Affairs Şükrü Saraçoğlu in the following month, had served as a catalyst
for Turkey to immediately enter into a formal alliance with Britain and
France. In Moscow, Vyacheslav M. Molotov, the Soviet Commissar for
Foreign Affairs, had repeatedly put forward the Straits issue and also
demanded that Turkey should commit itself not to make war on Germany
on behalf of the Western powers.

In fact, Ankara was also subjected to the German allegations of conspiring with the Allies against Russia. At the beginning of July 1940, a
German "White Book" containing a number of documents alleged to
have been discovered in a railway train in France was published in Berlin. They purported to deal with various subjects which the Nazis stated,
were matters of consultation between the British and French General
Staffs regarding the prosecution of the war and attempted to justify the
German invasion of neutral countries on the pretext of "forestalling Allied plans." In particular, the Germans claimed to have found plans among

the alleged documents indicating that Turkey had conspired with Britain and France to attack Russia and that the French General Staff planned to attack the oil wells at Baku by aircraft, flown over Turkish air-space with Turkish consent.

On July 6, the official Turkish news agency, the Anatolian Agency, gave a categorical denial of these allegations and stated that the "documents" were calculated to damage Turkish–Soviet relations. The allegations were also denied by René Massigli, the French Ambassador in Ankara. Meanwhile, on July 11, an official Tass statement broadcast from Moscow denied reports that Russia had presented an ultimatum to Turkey.

At a specially convened meeting of the TGNA on July 12, Dr. R. Saydam, the Turkish Prime Minister, dealt with these documents as well as other foreign propaganda and newspaper comments, the object of which, he said was to embroil Turkey's friendly relations with Soviet Russia. In a strong attack on German intrigue, particularly the efforts of Franz von Papen, the German Ambassador, to force the resignation of Saraçoğlu, the Turkish MFA, and to disturb Turco–Russian relations, said:

> Faithful to her friendships, and resolute to defend her independence and liberty, Turkey, united like a single body, awaits events. We do not attempt either to provoke or attack our neighbours. We note with satisfaction the evident proof that the same sentiments are shared by them. The only response which the Turkish people will make to any action threatening the independence of the Turkish Republic or the integrity of its territory will consist in taking up arms and defending the country to the last. In spite of the world's unstable situation our country does not seem exposed to any imminent danger, and continues to be animated by the will to maintain good relations with all States, particularly with her neighbours.[5]

The statement of Saydam included that the first thing to remember in attempting to influence Turkey was that it was no longer the dead and gone Ottoman Empire. He said, the maintenance, departure or replacement of Turkish statesmen could only take place by the decision and approval of the TGNA and the men directing Turkey had only one programme—the security of the Turkish Republic—and alongside one that hoped the friendships appropriated to Turkish interests and security. The speech was followed by the passing of a unanimous vote of confidence in the Government. As for the mobilization of the Turkish Army, it was announced on July 11 that seventeen classes of cavalry between the ages of 22 and 38, were called up in the İstanbul area, while all soldiers who had been given leave on account of ill-health were recalled.

A few days later on July 18, it was announced that a Turco–German clearing trade agreement had been negotiated, providing for an exchange of goods to the value of about £4,000,000. Under it Germany would supply Turkey with spare parts, machinery and rolling-stock and Turkey would furnish tobacco, mohair, olive oil, dried fruits, oats, cattle-feeding cake, opium, skins, and cotton.[6] Despite tremendous German pressure, Papen reported as of June that the agreement which had been signed did not provide for chromium and therefore it was exclusive of German armament deliveries. Attempts on the part of Germany to secure a more favourable exchange rate were rejected as well.

German requests for certain minerals essential to its war industries had been refused by Turkey, particularly in the aftermath of the Nazi–Soviet Pact of August 1939. From then on, Turkey aimed to cease the chromite deliveries to Germany and sought the ways to sell this product to Britain. Significantly, Turkey produced sixteen percent of the world's chromite, from which was processed chromium, an alloy used to make steel. In 1940, the British Government negotiated an agreement contracting to receive from Turkey fifty thousand tons of chromite in 1941 and in 1942, along with agricultural produce, on the condition that no chrome would be delivered to Germany. Subsequently, German requests for certain minerals essential to its war industries were refused by Turkey, such materials being earmarked for payments due to Britain in the refunding of credits for the reconstruction of the Karabük iron and steel plant and of the industrial credits of £10,000,000 granted to Turkey in 1938.[7]

Under these circumstances, the TGNA voted on July 25, 1940 an extraordinary credit of about £12,000,000 for national defence, in addition to former credits amounting to over £19,000,000. A month later, on August 31, it was announced that in order to enhance the war fighting capabilities of the Turkish armed forces, the Turkish Air Force would henceforth include three specially trained battalions of parachute troops, as part of the modernisation programme of the Turkish defence forces.[8]

On November 1, 1940, in his statement at the opening of the TGNA, President İnönü said that during the last year a great number of erstwhile free and independent countries had had to submit to foreign invasion, but the attacks directed against Britain, following the defeat of France, had met with obstinate resistance. This fact had led the war into a new phase, which seemed to be of long duration. He stated that Turkey did not covet an inch of territory beyond its own frontiers, and it had no intention of trespassing on anyone's rights. İnönü expressed that Turkey's attitude of non-belligerency did not constitute an obstacle to normal relations with countries which showed the same measure of goodwill towards Turkey. He said:

> This attitude of non-belligerency makes absolutely impossible the use of our territory, seas or skies by the belligerents against each other, and will continue to make such use impossible so long as we take no part in the war.
>
> Fresh developments in the conduct of war, however, require close attention. Our neighbour and friend, Greece, whose territory lies in that zone the security and tranquility of which is of primary importance to Turkey, find itself dragged into war. Together with our ally, Great Britain, we are carefully studying the situation which has now ensued. We hope that the political principle which I earlier stated, and which has kept our country out of the horrors of war, will in the same manner maintain our security in the future.[9]

Here, İnönü also underscored that despite the grave crisis which the world had been facing, Turkey's relations with other states remained in their normal course. Then, he explained that Turkey's relations with the SU which dated as far back as 20 years ago, had, after experiencing difficulties, the blame for which could not be attributed either to Turkey or Russia, been restored to their normal friendship. His statement included that "amid the vicissitudes of the world Russo–Turkish relations represent a factor of intrinsic value" and the two countries meant to perpetuate this fact independent of all other influences.

In the conclusion of his speech, the Turkish President did not neglect to reiterate that while remaining sensitive to everything that effected its vital interests, Turkey would continue to be faithful to its friendships and alliances. He said, at a time when Britain was carrying on under difficult conditions "the heroic struggle for its very existence, it is my duty to proclaim that the bonds of alliance which unite us to Britain are solid and unbreakable."[10] Clearly, İnönü, finding Ankara at the doorsteps of a crisis of a gravest kind was determined to perform all the manoeuvres required by the circumstances.

At this juncture, in November 1940, Molotov's talks in Berlin once more spurred Turkish anxieties of further Germano–Russian agreement. In Berlin, the German Foreign Minister, Joachim von Ribbentrop, proposed to Molotov a plan for extending the three-power pact to include the SU, accompanying it with two secret protocols inspired by those of 1939 and including a revision of spheres of influence on certain bases which envisaged Moscow's control of the region south from Russia towards the Indian Ocean; splitting of Turkey from the western system and modification of the Montreux Convention with a view to assuring only the Black Sea states of unrestricted passage through the Straits and a permanent base for the SU in the Straits.[11]

On November 26, Molotov told the German Ambassador, Schulenburg, that his government accepted Ribbentrop's proposals under the following conditions; the immediate withdrawal of German troops from Finland; the conclusion of Soviet–Bulgarian treaty of mutual assistance; the granting of land and naval bases on the Bosphorus and the Dardanelles to the SU; recognition of the zone south of Baku and Batum toward the Persian Gulf, as a center of Soviet aspirations; and Japan's renunciation of its rights to coal and oil concessions in northern Sakalin. As Andre Fontaine put it, "four years later Stalin presented virtually the same demands to the Western Allies. What interested him was the stakes themselves; it mattered little to him from what source the promise came so long as the source could deliver."[12]

A month later, at 3.00 a.m. in the morning of October 28, the Italian Minister in Athens, Grazzi handed to General Metaxas, the Greek Prime Minister, an ultimatum in which Greece was accused of tolerating the use of its territorial waters and ports by the British Navy for the prosecution of the war against Italy. Metaxas rejected the ultimatum and told Grazzi that he regarded it as an Italian declaration of war against Greece. At 5.50 a.m., half an hour before the ultimatum was due to expire, Italian troops operating from Albania attacked Greek territory. The British War Cabinet met early the same morning and replied vigorously. The plans already made for extending to Greece all the help in Britain's power under the guarantee given on April 13, 1939 were reviewed and W. Churchill sent a message to Metaxas. The day after, the First Lord of the Admiralty A.V. Alexander declared that British naval help for Greece had already begun.[13]

Pat Walsh's contribution to the analysis in here includes his remarks to the present writer that "Britain wished to make Greece a battleground for a conflict with Germany. Metaxas was determined to resist Britain's aid in response to this. Metaxas had had bitter experience of Britain's attitude to Greek neutrality having, with King Constantine, opposed British attempts, in alliance with Venizelos, to bring Greece with the first World War—an event when successfully completed through the occupation of Salonika, led to the disastrous Greek advance in Anatolia."

On the Turkish side, the Prime Minister Saydam, broadcasting to the nation, said that the situation was becoming graver. He stressed that Turkey was sure of its power and the nation would not hesitate to defend itself. Meanwhile, the British Ambassador H. Knatchbull-Hugessen and the Greek Ambassador saw the MFA Saraçoğlu, on October 28. The Italian attack on Greece they said, had called into operation Article 2 (1) of the Anglo–Franco–Turkish Mutual Assistance Treaty of October 19, 1939 which provided for Turkey's collaboration effectively and lending the UK and France all aid and assistance in its power "in the event of an act of aggression by a European Power leading to war in the Mediterranean area in which France and the United Kingdom are involved."[14] However, Saraçoğlu responded with the "Protocol Number Two" which was annexed to the Anglo–Franco–Turkish Treaty. He stated that Turkey's belligerency might cause it to become involved in war with the Soviets. Based on this reason, he explained, Turkey would retain its neutrality. In fact, facing an unpredictable neighbour like the Soviet Union, Turkey had demanded the inclusion of the "Protocol Number Two" with a view to obtaining a general reservation clause to save itself from being dragged into the global conflict.

In this chaotic international arena, Ankara was determined to maintain its non-belligerent status. The Turkish Prime Minister Saydam declared in the TGNA on January 7 that the country would remain faithful to the alliances to which it had bound itself. The government was prepared for any eventuality and followed with the utmost vigilance political and military developments throughout the world. Foreign policy continued to follow well-recognized lines the wisdom of which had been confirmed by recent events. Not surprisingly, military preparations were simultaneously taking place. The Ankara Radio, broadcasting on January 22, declared that the Turkish Government was alive to any threat or possibility of danger and that the bulk of the Turkish Army had been concentrated in Thrace. Turkey it said "fought in the last war on eight battle fronts in four years. We leave it to the imagination of those who wish to strike as to what it is capable of doing on one front alone. But far better than arguing we say 'let them try.'"[15]

At this stage, Britain was increasing its efforts to draw Ankara's attention to the strong possibility of further German advance in the Balkans. A few days later, on January 13, Admiral Sir Howard Kelly, Lieut. Gen. Sir James Cornwall and Air-Marshal Elmhirst, representing the Middle East Command arrived in Ankara for staff conversations with Marshal Fevzi Çakmak, Chief of the Turkish General Staff and the MFA Saraçoğlu.[16]

To justify Ankara's concerns, on January 17, 1941, having regarded the occupation of these countries by German troops who were constantly being concentrated in Roumania as a threat to Russian security, the Soviet Commissar for Foreign Affairs told the German Ambassador that his government considered the Bulgarian territory and of the Straits as the security zone of the SU. Berlin paid no attention to this statement. At the end of February, King Boris of Bulgaria joined the three-power pact and agreed to the German occupation of his country.[17] Under these circumstances, during 1940–41, the issue of the Straits was more than once the subject of negotiations between Nazi and Soviet leaders.

In fact, Bulgaria's ambiguous position between Germany and the SU had already turned the Turco–Bulgarian Treaty of Friendship dated February 17, 1941 for which Ankara had felt limited trust, into an ineffective document. The Soviet Commissar for Foreign Affairs was insisting that the German troops should not enter Bulgaria and this country should be left in the Kremlin's sphere of influence. However, under the pressure of Berlin, Sofia agreed that the German forces would use the Bulgarian territory for transit passage. Facing the unpredictability of Berlin, this time the Kremlin turned to Ankara and suggested the signing of a Communiqué along the lines of 1925 non-aggression treaty between the two countries. In their turn, the President İnönü and the makers of Turkish foreign policy saw no reason to decline the Russian proposal and the Communiqué was announced in Ankara and in Moscow simultaneously on March 24.[18]

It included that after news had appeared in the foreign press to the effect that if Turkey were involved in war, the Soviets would profit by the difficulties it would have to face by attacking it. In turn, the Soviet Government informed Turkey in this connection: firstly, that such news did not in any way coincide with the attitude of the Soviet Government; secondly, that in case Turkey should resist aggression and should find itself forced into war for the defence of its territory, Turkey could then, in accordance with the non-aggression pact existing between it and the Soviets, count on the complete understanding and neutrality of Russia. In this context, the Turkish Government expressed that should Russia find itself in a similar situation, it could count on the complete understanding and neutrality of Turkey.[19]

In the meantime, Saraçoğlu met with the British Foreign Minister Anthony Eden. Eden and the Chief of the Imperial General Staff Sir John Dill had arrived at Ankara on February 26, after their visit to the Near Eastern Fronts for conferences with their counterparts. Prior to the departure of Eden and Dill from Ankara for Athens on March 1, a Communiqué was issued by the Turkish Government which stated that Eden and Dill were received by President İnönü and had conversations with Prime Minister Saydam, the MFA Saraçoğlu, and Marshal Çakmak. It stated that the two governments recorded their firm adherence to the Turco–British alliance, that the present international situation was examined in detail and special attention was given to the situation in the Balkans which closely concerned the mutual interests of Turkey and Britain. It underscored that there was complete agreement between the two governments on their policy with regard to these problems.[20]

In this chaotic international environment, and in the absence of substantial assistance from the Allies, in order to balance its international position, Ankara had shifted to consider the ways in which it could obtain a treaty of non-aggression with Germany. Obviously, the ground was not convenient for Turkey to openly pronounce its intention to this effect. Following a period of exchange of letters between İnönü and Hitler, both Turkish and German Foreign Ministries were authorized to draft a treaty which would serve towards this objective.

In fact, upon his receipt of İnönü's reply on March 17, 1941, Hitler had gone to the extent of expressing that Germany had ended its friendship with the SU in order to side with Turkey on the issue of the Straits. He said, the Germans had friendly feelings towards Turkey which was Germany's former comrade in arms, and Turkey's presence in the Straits and in İstanbul were in Germany's political interest. Besides, he narrated his talks with the Soviet Commissar for Foreign Affairs in a distorted manner and said that Molotov had demanded a base in the Black Sea Straits in order to adhere to the Tripartite pact which he had strongly rejected.

As for Bulgaria, the Nazi dictator said, Molotov had demanded to send the Russian forces to this country and in return for this, he had suggested to force the Yugoslavians to cede Macedonia to Bulgaria, a proposal which himself and the King of Bulgaria had declined. According to him, the presence of German troops in this country was serving to save this country from the emergence of Bolshevism. To assure the Turkish Ambassador to Berlin, Hüsrev Gerede, of his friendly policy towards Turkey and ultimately to increase Ankara's suspicions of the Kremlin he said, through saving Bulgaria he had assured Turkey's position as a strong and independent country safeguarding the Straits. The Nazi tyrant had basically in mind securing Germany's Balkan wing before launching the offensive against the SU. As for the Italian attack on Greece, Hitler said, Germany, like Turkey had no responsibility concerning this war. The Nazi dictator put forward one single negative issue which was about the press attacks in Turkey that were directed at both himself and the Nazi regime. Turkish Ambassador to Berlin, Gerede, particularly emphasized this point in his report. In the end, Ankara's policy of staying out of the conflict remained unaltered, while Berlin's policy to convince Ankara to continue its non-belligerent status in this circumstance appeared to be successful.[21]

Meanwhile, according to Johannes Glasneck, for Ankara, circumstances had arisen to share London's perception that Germany's attack on Russia would save them from the pressure of the fascist supremacy.[22] Glasneck evaluated from this that Turkish statesmen's negotiation with Hitler on the grounds of the Nazi dictator's anti-Soviet statements however, represented a deviation from the Kemalist foreign policy. Glasneck's assessment on this issue included that despite the fact that Turkish Government had forcefully acted in this direction to a considerable extent, through this process, representatives of the Turkish bourgeoisie and German fascist imperialists had united in their rage against the first socialist state of the workers and peasants as well. Moreover, he said, through joining the Munich policy of the Western states, the Turkish policymakers had helped the outbreak of a dangerous situation for their country.

The US Secretary of State, Cordell Hull, explained that the State Department had evaluated that when Hitler invaded Yugoslavia and Greece on April 6, the intense effort they had been making to solidify the Balkans against this eventuality had come to an end. Hull stated that since the beginning of January, from all the capitals concerned, cables had been sent to Washington reporting the probability that Hitler would attack

Greece to aid his failing partner, Mussolini. From Belgrade, the American Minister A. Bliss Lane cabled Hull on January 24–25, 1941 that he and Col. William J. Donovan who was sent by Secretary of the Navy, Frank Knox, on behalf of President Roosevelt, to the Balkans to stimulate their resistance, had been assured by the Regent, Prince Paul and by Prime Minister Cvetkovic that Yugoslavia would not permit troops or war materials to pass through its territory and would resist aggression. Lane also informed Hull that it was thought in Belgrade that if Bulgaria and Turkey would adopt a similar attitude, the three countries might successfully protect themselves. In this context, he suggested the possibility of informally pointing out to the three countries the desirability of a joint defense policy. He considered that mutual distrust among the three might prevent a joint policy and that steps would have to be taken by Washington to dispel this mistrust.

Hull cabled Lane on January 29 that while it was not the US' practice directly to initiate such action as he suggested, the State Department was losing no opportunity to bring the US position relative to the war to the attention of the Balkan representatives in Washington. He also commented that the US was placing particular emphasis on assistance to Greece and Britain. The US Secretary of State gave virtually the same answer to his British counterpart Lord Halifax when he called upon him on February 5 to request US support of the British in encouraging conversations between Turkey and Yugoslavia towards a policy of mutual defense.

As reports arrived at Washington that a movement of German troops into Bulgaria was imminent, Lane informed Hull from Belgrade on February 8 that the Regent considered Yugoslavia's situation desperate. He said that Cvetkovic and his Foreign Minister Cincar-Markovic—whom Lane thought had Axis leanings—might shortly go to Berlin at Hitler's invitation, and that the Regent was disposed to avoid war at all costs. Hull explained that after talking this situation with Roosevelt, he sent Lane in Belgrade and Ambassador John V. A. MacMurray in Ankara identical cables on February 9 to be communicated to the Yugoslav and Turkish Governments. After quoting a statement by Roosevelt that the US was planning their own defense with utmost urgency and in its vast scale they had to integrate the war needs of Britain, he said this position continued to be the cornerstone of the national defense policy of the US and this effort had been intensified by the developing situation. Reiterating the words of the US President he concluded that "we know now that a nation can have peace with the Nazis only at the price of total surrender."[23]

Five days later, Hull went personally to the Yugoslav Delegation and handed Minister Fotitch a message from Roosevelt to be transmitted to his government. The message included that the US President "desires it to be realized that the so-called Lend-Lease Bill now before Congress . . . permits . . . the President to supply the materials of war to those nations that are now the victims of aggression or which might be threatened with aggression."[24] Hull cabled MacMurray the same day, instructing him, at the President's direction, to convey to the Turkish Prime Minister Saydam an almost identical message. MacMurray informed Hull on February 18 that Saydam, without making any definite commitment, had expressed his cordial appreciation of Roosevelt's message and the wholehearted support of the ideals of the United States and Great Britain.

In his memorandum to Hull dated February 20, with specific reference to Turkey and Yugoslavia, Roosevelt said: "our type of civilization and the war in whose outcome we are definitely interested, will be definitely helped by resistance on the part of Yugoslavia and, almost automatically, resistance on the part of Turkey—even though temporarily Yugoslavia and Turkey are not successful in the military sense."[25]

On March 3, Lord Halifax and Hull discussed whether the US would supply Turkey with war materials directly or whether this should be done by or through Britain. Hull replied that it was his understanding that his government would cooperate to the fullest possible extent in supplying war materials to Turkey under appropriate circumstances. A few days later, on March 10, Churchill cabled Roosevelt that the concerted influence of Anglo-American Chiefs of Mission at Moscow, Ankara and Belgrade would be of enormous value at the moment. The British Prime Minister hoped to induce the Soviet Government to give assurances to Turkey which would assist its government in withstanding German penetration.

On March 15, Turkish Ambassador to Washington, Münir Ertegün, called on Hull to inform him of certain assurances that the Turkish President İnönü had received from Hitler relative to the German occupation of Bulgaria. In his turn, Hull told his interlocutor a commonly admitted fact that the German dictator had taken this communication out of his stock on hand of similar communications. He had been sending these to each of the dozen countries he had occupied or conquered and he seemed to contemplate sending them to countries whose seizure had in mind for the future.

Turning back to Yugoslavia, following the Regent's acceptance to adhere to the Axis pact, a coup d'etat occurred in March 27, 1941 and King Peter assumed control of the country and General Simovic became premier. However, Yugoslavia could regain its independence only for the moment. As mentioned above, ten days after the coup, the Germans launched their attack on Yugoslavia and Greece. Expectedly, the Yugoslav coup d'etat which resulted in the overthrow of the Tsvetkovitch Government and its replacement by an all-party government under General Simovitch led to an immediate worsening of relations between Yugoslavia and Germany. On April 1, von Heeren, German Minister in Belgrade, left for Berlin to report after a lenghty conversation with Nintchitch, the Yugoslav Foreign Minister, at which he had demanded an apology for the anti-German demonstrations which marked General Simovitch's coup, immediate ratification of the Tripartite Pact, and demobilization of the Yugoslav army.[26]

Simultaneously, the German press and radio opened a campaign of violent abuse against this country, alleging that horrendous atrocities had been committed on German nationals in Yugoslavia, the stories being almost identical with the propaganda launched against Poland and Czechoslovakia before the attacks on those countries. Concurrently, the German propaganda attempted to drive a wedge between the Serbs and Croats by promising the latter a leading position in the future Yugoslavia. In the meantime, on Berlin's instructions, thousands of German nationals left the country and on April 3 nearly all German officials in Belgrade left for Germany. By the first week of April, reports from all Balkan capitals spoke of the concentration of German troops and mechanized forces on the Hungarian, Rumanian and Bulgarian frontiers with Yugoslavia.

Indeed, Nazi–Soviet relationship was crystalizing around the Balkan situation. *Pravda*, in an article on April 1, contradicting rumours that the Soviet Government had cabled congratulations to General Simovitch's Government, wrote: "There would have been nothing extraordinary if congratulations had actually been sent. If they were not sent it was perhaps an omission on the part of the Soviet Government, or because the idea did not occur to anyone." On the same day, M. Gavrilovitch, Yugoslav Minister without portfolio and Minister in Moscow, had a conference in Ankara after discussions in Moscow. A few days later, on April 3, Lieutenant General Sir James Marshall-Cornwall and Air Vice-Marshal Elmhirst, representing the British Middle East Command, arrived in Ankara for defence talks with Turkish Military chiefs.[27]

On April 6, within a few hours of the German invasion of Greece and Yugoslavia, a meeting of the Turkish Cabinet was held and the British, Greek and Yugoslav Ambassadors received by the MFA Saraçoğlu. Shortly afterwards, on April 9, the Allied diplomatic representatives were informed of the decisions taken by the government on Turkey's attitude in face of the extension of the war in the Balkans. On April 11, the Ankara Radio announced that the government, following the military situation, might be obliged to take new decisions and the present attitude of non-belligerence was in keeping with Ankara's treaty obligations. It was also stated that this was an initial decision, since there was no way of foretelling future developments of the war which was being waged at a close distance. Given this, Ankara paid particular attention to the attitude of Bulgaria and it was reported that the Bulgarian Minister had denied statements by the Yugoslav Minister that Bulgarian troops were operating with the Germans.

Meanwhile, on April 8, the age limit of service in the Turkish Armed Forces reserve was extended to 65 for officers and 60 for enlisted men. Other measures were being taken on such a scale that general mobilisation, although not officialy proclaimed, existed in fact. Subsequently, martial law was proclaimed in Turkish Thrace, including İstanbul and İzmit. A British military mission, after inspecting defences in this region, left for Egypt on April 13.

The coup d'etat in Yugoslavia provoked Hitler's wrath. Twelve divisions, including four armoured divisions and overwhelming air power, were diverted to the Yugoslav war, and the country was crushed under the German onslaught by April 17. Consequently, Hitler decided to postpone the invasion of the SU for up to four weeks. While it proved to be a costly delay in the long run, narrowing the time by six weeks between the launching of the offensive against the SU and the onset of winter conditions, was to the advantage of the Russians. "At the time Hitler expected that, among the consequences of the 'lightning-like' destruction of Yugoslavia, there would be a deterrent effect on Turkey should it consider action as Britain's ally when Greece was invaded."[28]

During the same period, in the Middle East, Iraq was under considerable pressure. The political elite in this country was divided into a pro-British faction led by Nuri As-Said and supported by the regent, the Amir Abdullah, and a pro-German clique led by Rashid Ali Al-Gaylani and supported by the officers of the "Golden Square." At the beginning of April, the "Golden Square" overthrew the government, which had attempted to move against them as a preliminary to breaking off relations with Italy. Subsequenttly, Abdullah fled to a British warship at Basra. In his turn, Al-Gaylani declared that the Anglo–Iraqi treaty of 1930 did not give the British the right to introduce troops without consulting them.[29]

At this juncture, Rome stated that they thought it easier for them to supply military assistance to the Iraqi Government. Then Ribbentrop informed Hitler that Iraq was beyond the range of the Luftwaffe, and that French permission would be needed for stopovers in Syria.[30] However, İnönü had made it clear that Turkey would not permit deliveries of arms to Iraq across its territory.[31] On May 4, the British War Cabinet sent instructions to the commanders of British forces in Palestine and Trans-Jordan for operations against Baghdad. In less than a month Rashid Ali and his supporters fled Baghdad and a pro-British government was brought to power.

Meanwhile, in mid-May, Berlin was focusing its attention to Crete which it attacked on the 20th. They were also prepared to establish an air shuttle route for supplies from Athens via Syria to Baghdad. There was also an Italian squadron of fighters. However, Axis preparations were hampered by lack of aviation fuel in Syria and Iraq; and "the Iranians, following the Turkish example of cautious neutrality, refused to supply it." Concurrently, British bombing of Baghdad and Mosul airfields, prevented the Germans from establishing themselves.[32]

Against this background, on June 18, 1941, the Treaty of Friendship between Turkey and Germany was signed by the Turkish MFA Saraçoğlu and German Ambassador Papen in Ankara. Article 1 of the treaty stated that "The Republic of Turkey and the German Reich mutually undertake to respect the inviolability and territorial integrity of each other and to refrain from every action directed at directly or indirectly against each other."[33] The subsequent article included that Turkey and Germany binded themselves in the future on all questions concerning their common interests to meet in friendly contact to reach an understanding on the treatment of such questions. Thus, at least on paper, the Turkish position in war was moved a step forward towards center between the Allies and the Axis. Interestingly, the TGNA ratified this treaty on June 25, 1941 with Law No. 4072, three days after Germany's attack on Russia. The protocol pertaining to the ratification of the treaty was signed by Turkish Ambassador Gerede and the Secretary General of the MFA, Cevat Açıkalın and his German counterpart Ernst Weizsäcker on July 5, 1941, in Berlin.

As İnanç underscored, although "it seems rather paradoxical that an ally of Britain would also sign a non-aggression pact with Germany, Turkey had to find ways of ensuring its survival both politically and economically."[34] It is worth noticing however that as will be discussed afterwards, one of the engineers of this agreement on the Turkish side, Numan Menemencioğlu, Secretary-General of the MFA and later the Minister of Foreign Affairs who had gained a reputation with keeping German aggression at bay through giving credit to its demands, would be obliged to resign from his seat towards the end of the war. Menemencioğlu was accused by the Soviets of maintaining favouring approaches towards Germany and not backed by the Turkish Government as the circumstances unfolded.

Nonetheless, having concluded such an agreement Turkey was not less suspicious of either German or Soviet acts since the memory of the short-lived Nazi–Soviet pact was still in minds. After Germany's invasion on June 22, 1941, the Soviet attitude towards Turkey changed overnight. Formerly, Ankara had been blamed for not maintaining complete neutrality, now it was gradually accused of objectively serving the interests of Germany by staying neutral.

As for the German attack on Russia, by the autumn of 1941, the German war-machine had understood that the Russian defense would not allow its advance as envisaged by the Operation Barbarossa. From then on, the German concept of lightning war turned to a dead-lock and the center of gravity of the German onslaught was gradually shifted to south and north wings of the front. This brought the case of Turkey under discussion again by Germany. However, it was eventually decided to refrain from coercive methods in relations with Ankara while the option of developing an attack through Anatolia was shelved for the time being.[35] Then Ribbentrop instructed Papen firstly, to enhance Turkey's confidence to the effect that Germany had no territorial claims over Turkey and recognized it as the guardian of the Straits; to revitalize the deep seated imperialist tendencies of Turkey against Russia; and finally, to decline all the suggestions of Ankara for a conciliatory peace with Britain.[36]

On August 19, 1941, Ribbentrop told Gerede that the Red Army would be destroyed within a few weeks. In his turn, Gerede told his interlocutor that based on the information he had from American sources, he had found this information to be exaggerated. When Ribbentrop inquired as to what he had thought in regard to the people of Turkish origin in the Caucasia and in the east of Caspian Sea, Gerede told him that in line with the official policy of Turkey, Ankara had no claims beyond its frontiers. Shortly afterwards, in Ankara, Saraçoğlu communicated the content of the Ribbentrop–Gerede talk to the British Ambassador Knatchbull-Hugessen.[37]

In fact, considerable evidence suggest that as his personal choice—which no doubt had an effect on his interpretation of issues—Saraçoğlu was maintaining a strong anti-communist policy. Correspondingly, on September 30, he told Papen that he attributed utmost importance to the overthrow of Bolshevism. But, he said, the "the chauvinist circles were suggesting to their leadership to wait for the development of the military operation in silence."[38]

On July 9, 1942, Şükrü Saraçoğlu—now Prime Minister, after Dr. Saydam's death on July 8—explaining his government's foreign policy in the TGNA stated that Turkey, who had not and would not run after any adventure outside of its frontiers had searched for the ways in which it could stay out of the war and had found those ways in its march on a conscious and positive neutrality. He said, "Turkey would not and will not be able to preserve its neutrality through a negative impartiality before a tragedy which has been devastating and ruining the world for three years. Turkey's impartiality is the processed form of an international system. And our policy has a sincerity and transparency which will not drag anyone into anxiety."[39] Saraçoğlu emphasized that Turkey's alliance agreement with England would continue to serve both parties as a beneficial instrument and that the Turco–British alliance was the expression of reality brought into existence as an essential pillar of the international political system. He maintained that another clear and sincere manifestation of this policy was the Turco–German agreement which confirmed the mutual understanding and friendship between Turkey and Germany. Turkish position towards these two major opposing parties and Turkey's relations with each of these states were therefore "clear examples of this positive policy."[40]

In Time of War Prepare for Peace: Strains and Stresses of Wartime Diplomacy

In August 1941, Winston Churchill as head of British Government at war and Franklin D. Roosevelt, as the President of non-belligerent US met for their first conference at Newfoundland. The two statesmen discussed a variety of topics, but the most famous if not the most important accomplishment of the conference was the production of the document known as the Atlantic Charter. That it brought the United States nearer to war was seen by Churchill who stated: ". . . The fact that alone of the United States, still technically neutral, joining with a belligerent Power in making such a declaration was astonishing. The inclusion in it of a reference to 'final destruction of the Nazi tyranny. . .' amounted to a challenge which in ordinary times would have implied warlike action. . . ."[41]

In fact, for the United States, since the enactment of the Lend-Lease Act of March 11, 1941, to convoy British shipping carrying lend-lease defense articles would have been stretching non-belligerency to a point that Roosevelt thought inexpedient. The protection against German submarines of convoys from North American to British ports was further hardened when Germany attacked the SU on June 22, 1941 and the US decided to make SU a beneficiary of lend-lease. Shortly afterwards, these enlarged efforts of the US culminated in an undeclared naval war with German U-boats.

In the meantime, a new Japanese ministry, headed by Prince Konoye, the Japanese Premier, proclaimed on August 1, 1940 a "New Order for Greater East Asia." This enlargement of Japan's empire, also named the "Greater East Asia Co-prosperity Sphere" was chiefly the plan of the new Foreign Minister, Yosuke Matsuoka. Matsuoka had opened negotiations for an outright alliance with Germany and Italy and shortly after on September 27, 1940, representatives of the three powers had signed the Three-Power Pact in Berlin, comprising mutual recognition by the three partners of the "new orders" instituted in Europe and in Asia.

Disturbed by Japan's attacks on China's independence, its affiliation with the European Axis and its attempts to capture rich raw materials of Southeast Asia, the US had begun to exert economic pressure upon this country. Japanese Foreign Minister, believing that Japan's southward drive might bring conflict with Britain or the US or both, appreciated the opportunity of signing a five-year treaty of neutrality with his Russian counterpart Molotov. However, he did not know, though he had just returned from Berlin, that Germany was preparing to attack the SU. When that event took place on June 22, 1941, the neutrality pact was of more value to the SU than to Japan.[42]

Concurrently, revisionism and its supporters in Japan were strengthening their hand. On October 18, Gen. Tojo Hideki became Premier.

Time was now really running out. On December 7, the Japanese Ambassador to Washington, Nomura, met with the Secretary of State Cordell Hull, at 2:20, one hour after the beginning of attack on Pearl Harbor. He stated that he had been instructed to deliver a statement at 1:00 pm which he then handed the Secretary, but that he was sorry that he had been delayed owing to the need of more time to encipher the message. Hull, as soon as he finished reading the document turned to Nomura and said ". . . In all my fifty years of public service I have never seen a document that was more crowded with infamous falsehoods and distortions . . . on a scale so huge that I never imagined until today that any Government on this planet was capable of uttering them."[43] In his national radio address on December 9, Roosevelt maintained that the course that Japan had followed for the past ten years in Asia had paralleled the course of Hitler and Mussolini in Europe and Africa and from its assault and on, it was an actual collaboration so well calculated that all the continents of the world, and of all the oceans, were then considered by the Axis strategists as a gigantic battlefield.[44]

Upon entering WW II, the US considered the ways to bring allies closer and took the lead in drawing up and signing the Declaration of the United Nations on January 1, 1942. Other signatories were Britain, the SU and China, five nations of the British Commonwealth, the governments in exile of eight European countries overrun by the Axis powers, and nine states of Latin America that had followed the US into the war. The original signers numbered twenty-six and as will be discussed later, particularly with an emphasis on the Turkish Government's declaration of war on Germany and Japan and adherence to the UN, before the war's end the number had increased to forty-seven.[45]

The principles of the Atlantic Charter were, as stated above endorsed by the SU with an interpretative approach and were accepted by the governments signing the Declaration of the United Nations of January 1, 1942. Kremlin, meanwhile, was working towards ends that directly contradicted the principle of self-determination so emphasized in the Atlantic Charter. Anthony Eden, the British Foreign Minister, visiting Moscow in December 1941, was confronted with a demand that Britain recognize Russia's annexation of the Baltic States and a part of Finland. In his turn, Eden passed on Moscow's proposal to London and Washington. Washington promptly rejected the demand since it was in conflict with the Atlantic Charter. Churchill concurred at the time, however in March 1942, he admitted, "under the pressure of events, I did not feel that this moral position could be physically maintained. In a deadly struggle it is not right to assume more burdens than those who are fighting for a great cause can bear." Accordingly, he wrote Roosevelt:

> The increasing gravity of the war has led me to feel that the principles of the Atlantic Charter ought not to be construed so as to deny to Russia the frontiers she occupied when Germany attacked her. This was the basis on which Russia acceded to the Charter. . . .
>
> I hope therefore that you will be able to give us a free hand to sign the treaty which Stalin desires as soon as possible. . . .[46]

Commissar for Foreign Affairs, Molotov, visiting London in May 1942, added eastern Poland and a slice of Romania to the claims which Moscow demanded recognition. In their turn, the British and US officials declined these claims, while Molotov settled for a twenty-year treaty of alliance with Britain in which both governments agreed to act in accordance with the two principles of not seeking territorial aggrandizement for themselves and non-interference in the internal affairs of other states. For the time being, this phraseology accorded well with the Atlantic Charter.

In January 1943, Roosevelt and Churchill met at Casablanca. Stalin was invited to attend the meeting, but he informed the US President and the British Prime Minister that he was unable to leave Russia at the time of the great offensive which he himself, as Commander-in-Chief, was directing. On January 26, 1943, in his remarks to the press correspondents at the close of conference, Roosevelt informed the reporters that the Democracies' war plans were to extricate the "unconditional surrender" of the Axis.

The use of this phrase, which had been endorsed in advance by Churchill and the British War Cabinet was evidently intended to convince the Kremlin that the US and Britain were determined to fight the war to a finish. However, in the opinion of most analysts, it had the unintended and unfortunate effect of stiffening enemy resistance and postponing the day of surrender. Conducing to the complete destruction of German and Japanese military potential, it helped to ensure the collapse of the balance of power and the military ascendancy of the Soviet Union in Europe and Asia.[47]

Indeed, among the essential factors which created a power vacuum in Europe, the doctrine of "Unconditional Surrender" put forward by

Churchill and Roosevelt and their Joint Chiefs of Staff at the Casablanca Conference in January of 1943, should be given. Obviously, in certain respects the strategy of "Unconditional Surrender" worked to Stalin's advantage. It increased the "proletarianisation" of the people of Germany and Central Europe, and made them more susceptible to communist influence. Secondly, the propounded doctrine meant that the Red Army, having advanced to Elbe, would have a legitimate reason for staying there and "for maintaining what would amount to occupation forces in the countries through which its supply lines ran."[48] Having understood the undelightful course of developments, for the rest of remaining eighteen months of the war, Churchill would try to persuade the Americans that the war should be fought for the dual purpose of defeating Germany and forestalling the emergence of the SU as a mighty power in the center of Europe.

Before concluding this discussion, it should be pointed out that similarly unfortunate in its hardening effect on German resistance was the approval by Roosevelt and Churchill, in September 1944, of the "Morgenthau Plan" for the post-war relations with Germany. Within a short period of time, both the US and the British leadership were convinced that the nature of the program would have ruined most of the industry in the European economy and convert Germany into a country primarily agricultural in its character. The plan was then shelved, but not before Joseph Goebbels, Minister of Information in Berlin, could exploit its propaganda value. Indeed, nothing else could be expected since the plan was made public in the memorandum signed by Roosevelt and Churchill at Quebec, September 16, 1944.[49]

At the close of a twelve days' conference between October 19–30, 1943 in Moscow, the Foreign Ministers of the Big Three issued a Communiqué and a number of declarations concerning Italy, Greece, Yugoslavia, France and Austria. Within this framework, it was agreed to set up in London a European Advisory Commission to study and make recommendations upon questions that might arise as the war developed. China was invited to join in a Declaration of Four Nations on General Security in which the four governments pledged that the united action of wartime would be continued for the organization and maintenance of peace and security and recognized the necessity of establishing at the earliest practicable date a general international organization (the United Nations) towards this end.

Consecutively, it was agreed that the next meeting would be at Teheran. This was as far as Stalin could be induced to travel from Russia at the time. In his turn, Chinese President Chiang Kai-shek did not hesitate to fly to Cairo where he conferred with Roosevelt and Churchill as they stopped there en route to Tehran. In Cairo, the three leaders issued a declaration of significance for the post-war Far East:

It is their purpose that Japan shall be stripped of all the islands in the Pacific which she has seized or occupied since the beginning of the first World War in 1914, and that all the territory Japan has stolen from the Chinese, such as Manchuria, Formosa and the Pescadores, shall be restored to the Republic of China. Japan will also be expelled from all other territories which she has taken by violence and greed. The aforesaid three great powers, mindful of the enslavement of the people of Korea, are determined that in due course Korea shall become free and independent.[50]

As will be discussed below, Roosevelt was to meet Stalin for the first time in November 1943. A month before that, Secretary of State Hull had gone to Moscow to confer with his Russian and British counterparts. In the meantime, Italy had surrendered to Allied forces and German corps were being steadily pushed back. The Red Army had taken the offensive as well. The tide of war had evidently turned and the time was nearer to consider post-war settlements.

The tumultuous events of 1943, the talks between the Turkish President İnönü and Churchill in Adana on January 30-31, 1943, where Churchill played down any active involvement in war on Turkey's part and stressed that he would not force Turkey to that effect;[51] the Cairo Talks between the Turkish Minister of Foreign Affairs Numan Menemencioğlu and the British Foreign Minister Anthony Eden on November, 4-6, 1943, where the Allied decision of inviting Turkey to take its part on the Allied side made at the Moscow Conference of October 19 was expressed to the Turkish Officials; and finally the second Cairo Conference of December, 5-8, 1943 between Roosevelt, Churchill and İnönü constituted a background in which Turkey chose to continue the talks with the Allied powers while adopting a benevolent neutrality in the course of events.

At the second Cairo Conference, Turkish Minister of Foreign Affairs, Menemencioğlu's argument with Eden concerned improvement of Turkish aircraft facilities prior to the demanded Turkish declaration of war. British Foreign Minister wanted permission to send about seven thousand technical and military personnel into Turkey to build and service airfields to be utilized to protect İstanbul and İzmir from Axis bombardment. "Only when these facilities were complete and ready to receive British squadrons, about 15 February 1944 by military estimates, would Turkey be expected to declare war." According to Menemencioğlu however, the Germans were liable to declare war before this date. He stated that the Germans would dispatch their bombers as soon as they discovered Allied personnel's sending to Turkey. Eden claimed that Germany would not necessarily find about this co-operation and if it did, would probably not have the forces to spare for retaliatory action.

In the end, Eden's threat of stopping the supplies if Ankara refused Britain's building of air bases in last November again in Cairo still on his mind, Turkish Minister of Foreign Affairs was not agreeable to this suggestion. Menemencioğlu also pointed out the complicated issue of Turkey's border security on the part of Bulgaria while the Russian guarantee covering Bulgaria still existed.[52]

Years later, Erkin, who was the Political Assistant Undersecretary then criticized Weisband and his book *Turkish Foreign Policy 1943–1945*. His work, which was named *İkinci Dünya Savaşında İnönü'nün Dış Politikası* (İnönü's Foreign Policy During the Second World War) and serialized in the Turkish Daily, *Milliyet,* in January 1974, incorrectly assessed the nature of the Turco–British talks in 1943. He stated that in his talks with İnönü, Churchill had only concentrated on understanding the military requirements of Turkey while rightly analyzing that the Turkish military arsenal of the time was weaker than that of Bulgaria in certain respects and refrained from pushing İnönü to join the war.[53]

As for the agenda of the Conference of Foreign Ministers of the Big Three, Cordell Hull, Anthony Eden and Vyacheslav Molotov held a meeting at Moscow on October, 19, 1943, where the Soviets demanded that the three powers coerce Turkey immediately into war, and an opening of the Second Front in the spring of 1944 as scheduled. Undisputedly, it was agreed then between Britain and the Soviets to push Turkey into the war on their side in one way or another. As will be briefly discussed, eventually, for the British, the most appropriate way to do that appeared as extending military aid to Turkey, around which they made a few vain attempts (given the problems of furnishing the poorly equipped Turkish army while the global conflict was being carried on).

During the war, three other conferences were held between the heads of governments of the "Big Three." To many analysts, Turkey's entry into the war was sought as it was believed that it would have a direct effect in the form of diverting nine Bulgarian divisions and leave the Germans alone to battle in Yugoslavia and Greece. In this context, at Tehran in November 1943, Churchill assured Stalin that Britain "had no ambitious interests in the Balkans but merely wanted to pin down the German Divisions there."[54] In his turn Stalin replied to his question on if or not the Turkish negotiators should be incited to war by stating, "I am all in favour of trying again. We ought to take them by the scruff of the neck if necessary."[55] It was however, suggested that the Combined Chiefs of Staff Minutes of the first plenary meeting registered the opposite and cited Stalin as having commented that Turkey could not be brought in by force.

At Tehran, Roosevelt, Churchill and Stalin negotiated the Anglo–American plan for the Second Front as well. On November 28, at the first session of Tehran, Churchill raised the issue of Turkey's entry into war. According to him, opening the Straits would allow a free flow of supply and war equipment to the Soviets and the Allies would use the Turkish airports. He asked his counterparts as to which would be the most suitable form of Turkish belligerency in strategic terms. The questions he posed were as follows: Should Turkey first attack Bulgaria and then declare war on Germany? Should it confine its military drive to Thrace or shift to a larger offensive. If this approach was adopted, what would Bulgarians consider about Russia which was their prime liberator? And lastly, what kind of affects could be expected on the part of Roumania—a country which was at odds between surrounding Axis or Allies and striving for moving out of war—or on Hungary?

According to Valentin Berezhkov,[56] Churchill addressed these questions to Stalin and added that these were matters of specific interest on which Russians had particular views. Concurrently, Stalin gradually shifted to adopt an attitude less optimistic of Turkey's entry into war. He expressed his belief that no pressure was likely to lead to this objective. However, Churchill suggested that Turkey should be deceived or pressed hard to accept belligerency before Christmas and he was willing to undertake the mission of informing the Turkish President İnönü of the decisions reached at Tehran. Churchill also stated that he was ready to tell İnönü that in case Turkey rejected the Allies' proposal for joining the war, he would state that this could have serious implications for Turkey and could effect its rights over the Straits. Moreover, he added that Britain would not be frustrated if Turkish belligerency could not be realized. The invasion of some Turkish islands could also be considered since this could secure the way through the Dardanelles. He said, this would not bother Germany either which could continue its activities in the region On November 29, the military experts stated similar views regarding Turkish belligerency that it would have rather positive effects for the Allies.

On the last day of the conference, Harry Hopkins, special aide of Roosevelt, said that the problem of Turkish belligerency depended on how much aid could be transferred to Turkey from the US and Britain. Apart from this, it was important to harmonize Turkey's entry into war with the Allies' general strategy. When Stalin recalled that Churchill had mentioned earlier to allocate 2 to 3 divisions and some further war equipment to Turkey, Churchill denied this statement and replied that these 2 or 3 divisions were planned to be used only if that the invasion of Turkish islands was decided upon.

The military arsenal which could be allocated to Turkey could comprise 17 air squadrons deployed in Egypt under the Anglo–American joint command and three anti-aircraft regiments to cooperate in Turkey's air defense. In his turn, Roosevelt explained that he was keen on keeping the promises given to Ankara, whereas he had strong anxieties given the incomplete war preparations of the JCS for OVERLORD. He said, he would prefer if this issue did not alter the agreement reached the day before.

While these deliberations were going on, Stalin chose to advance no further argument that might endanger the plans for OVERLORD. When Churchill demanded that the US add military equipment to British offers for Turkey, Roosevelt responded that he would need to consult his military advisors first. At a later stage, when Eden suggested that Turkey might be convinced to open its airports to the Allies, Stalin said that if Turkey opened its airports to the Allies, it was fairly possible that Bulgarians would not attack Turkey. The Germans would not attack Turkey either and expect Turks to attack first. In the meantime, "The Allies would use Turkish airports and harbours and this was a very good thing."[57]

To sum up, although he was ready to take advantage of the occasion, Stalin postponed a full discussion of the Soviets' overall territorial demands, whereas he realized a preliminary agreement on the boundaries with Poland. As for Turkey, at Tehran, the US was convinced that it would inevitably get involved in the Aegean and the Straits if Turkey entered the war. Stalin also reversed the position his Commissar for Foreign Affairs had taken at the Moscow Conference, and instead of supporting the British on the question of Turkey, sided with Roosevelt. He expressed the opinion that it would be better to concentrate all efforts upon OVERLORD and to consider the other campaigns as diversionary. Stalin said that he had lost hope of Turkey's entering the war and was now certain that it would not do so, in spite of all the pressure that might be exerted upon.[58]

Nevertheless, considerable evidence suggests that the SU, together with Britain, was still interested in Turkey's entry into the war. Churchill himself, was also ready to exploit Russian ambitions since he suggested that such a large land mass as Russia deserved access to a warm-water port and this could be settled agreeably as between friends. Then Stalin inquired about the regime of the Dardanelles. He said "Since England no longer objected, it would be well to relax that regime."[59]

On United States' invitation, the US, British, Russian and Chinese representatives met between August 21–October 9, 1944 at Dumbarton Oaks, a mansion in the Georgetown area of Washington. The outcome was a charter drafted along the lines of the 4th paragraph of the Declaration of Four Nations on General Security mentioned above, similar to the Covenant of the League of Nations but, it was hoped without its faults. As will be briefly discussed later, it was accepted at the Yalta Meeting with modifications, subject to final action by a conference of all nations at war with the Axis powers.

Meanwhile, among other issues, the same questions persisted in the Moscow discussions of British Premier Winston Churchill and Foreign Minister Anthony Eden with their counterparts Stalin and Molotov between October 10–19, 1944: the demarcation between the British and Soviet areas of operations and influence in the Balkans where the Red Army was then in complete control of Roumania and Bulgaria and where the Germans, threatened with encirclement from the north, were near evacuating Greece; the provision of an effective coordination between the Red Armies in Poland and the Balkans and the US–UK armies in north-west Europe and Italy; and lastly the proposals which had been under discussion at Dumbarton Oaks for a post-war world organization.[60]

When Hitler's weakened Eastern Front allowed the Soviets to advance from the Vistula to the Oder, right before the Yalta Conference, "This strategic situation reacted directly on the diplomatic discussions of that historic conference, for Stalin, having overwhelmed his enemies in the field, was able to outmaneuver his allies at the conference table."[61]

The Yalta Meeting was held in February 1945. It has been said that at Yalta, the SU was empowered to establish its control over the liberated countries of Eastern Europe. In effect, the Soviets were already in military occupation of all Eastern Europe, except Greece, which was liberated by the British forces in 1944. In the previous meeting at Teheran, the scheme put forward by Churchill to invade Eastern Europe which would have forestalled the SU, might have altered the situation, but it had lacked the support of the US.

At Yalta, Roosevelt was anxious to ensure the SU's involvement in the war against Japan. However, Stalin appeared in the remaining months of the war, highly interested in assuring Russian domination in the heart of Europe, moving up the Danube through Bucharest and Belgrade to Budapest and Poland. Stalin persuaded General Eisenhower to hold back the Western advance to Prague and resumed the attack on Berlin only when the Americans were near the German capital. Thomson stated that, "It was military strategy in WW II and not the diplomacy of Yalta which created power vacuums on either side of Russia into which it irresistibly expanded."[62] Given this, the crucial question for the Western leaders was how much farther would the SU expand? In this political atmosphere, at Yalta, the Big Three arranged for a conference to be held at San Francisco to draft the Charter of a United Nations Organization. The date set for the conference was April 25, the place, San Francisco.

Regarding Roosevelt's concerns, agreement was reached on a matter of great importance to the US. This was the SU's undertaking to enter the war against Japan. However, Soviet policy in collaborating with US was not genuine. Within three months after the the collapse of Germany, Stalin demanded the return of Russia's 1905 losses and the recognition of Soviet interests in Manchuria.

In preparing for the conference, Roosevelt paid particular attention to a variety of issues and nuances. He chose a delegation both able and bipartisan including members of both Houses. In his turn, Stalin adopted a disconcerting approach to the project. It was not until President Truman assumed the post, that he made a direct appeal to the process at hand. It was shortly after Roosevelt's death, through US envoy in Moscow, Harry Hopkins, Stalin expressed that he appointed Commissar for Foreign Affairs Molotov to head the Russian delegation.

In June 1945, following the signing of the Charter of UN Organization at San Francisco by fifty nations, concerning the structure of the UN, divergences of opinion once more arose in the US–SU relations. The divisions between the ex-Allies grew and there developed between them a system of diplomatic and economic maneuvering designed to weaken their opponents' position and strengthen their own, without actually going to war. Particularly in relation to the control of atomic energy, the SU vetoed the plan presented by the US and countered the proposal that the US must first surrender its nuclear bombs and there should be inspection.[63]

Another diverging difference arose over Poland. The Soviets had established at Lublin, a communist dominated provisional government which rivalled the exiled Polish government in London. At Yalta, Britain and the US agreed to withdraw recognition from the Polish government in London in return for holding free elections in Poland.[64] Although the SU was allowed to retain those provinces it had acquired with Nazi collaboration in 1939, little agreement could be reached over the frontiers of Poland. It was finally agreed that Poland should be compensated in the north and west at Germany's expense.

At Yalta, in the fifth plenary meeting, Stalin used Turkey as an example in raising the issue of which states should be admitted and which should be excluded. In fact, at Yalta, each of the Big Three advocated the invitation of countries who sided with them in the course of war to the United Nations.[65] Particularly Turkish socialist intellectuals criticized the decisions and the manners in which they were adopted at Yalta. Doğan Avcıoğlu argued that, Churchill, claiming that it was obliged by the Treaty of Mutual Assistance Between Britain, France and Turkey dated 1939, had pressed Turkey hard to draw it into war while he continuously expressed his content about Egypt and Spain for remaining neutral. However, he also expressed that while each of the Big Three advocated the inclusion of nations which were close to them to the San Francisco Conference, Churchill defended Turkey for its invitation. His criticisms included the partition of influence and control over the territories of Poland, Roumania, Yugoslavia, Hungary and Greece between Britain and Russia which left the control of the Mediterranean Sea to the British.

Then Roosevelt stated a principle that only those nations that had declared war on Germany should be accepted to the status of Associated Nation and suggested March 1945 as the deadline for the as yet uncommitted to declare war on Germany. Referring to Turkey, Stalin declared that certain nations had "wavered and speculated on being on the winning side."[66] In his turn, Churchill responded that if a large group of hitherto uncommitted nations were to declare war at this time it would have an effect on Germany's morale. Churchill also added that Turkey's candidacy "would not be greeted with universal approbation." But, he concluded that Turkey had allied with them at a very difficult time and had proved both friendly and helpful.[67]

Stalin also speculated about the Montreux Convention declaring it to be outmoded and needing of revision. In the end, it was agreed that the negotiation of the issue would be included in the agenda of the first meeting of Foreign Ministers to be held in London.

As mentioned before, during the war, Turkey's suspicions were first confirmed when the Nazi–Soviet Pact was concluded. Following that, Moscow had refused to withdraw its forces from Iran, and participated in an assassination attempt against the German Ambassador to Ankara, which led to a deterioration of Russo–Turkish relations. After this incident, the Turkish Ambassador to Berlin Hüsrev Gerede sent a personal telegram to Papen to whom he expressed great sympathy calling him his old fellow-in-arms, sincere friend and valuable colleague on February, 25, 1942 and arranged another telegram to be sent by the Turkish Chamber of Commerce in Berlin on the same day. He also visited Secretary General of the German Foreign Ministry, Ernst V. Weizsäecker to convey Turkish Governments' and his personal sadness about the incident.

Though Weizsäecker warmly welcomed Gerede, a few days later on March 3, asked him for another visit to the German Ministry and to the disturbance of Gerede, conveyed German Foreign Minister Ribbentrop's message demanding his personal knowledge regarding the dark side of the assassination attempt and in case he had no further information, pass this request to the Turkish Government. When the Ankara Radio broadcasted police investigation report on March 5, to leave this unpleasant debate behind, Gerede dispatched its German translation to the Ministry.[68]

On the other hand, a rather different explanation of the issue which was put forward by the US Chargé d'affaires in Bern on March, 12, 1942 in a telegram to Washington stated that the assassination was planned by Himmler on Hitler's order. A group of Serbian and Croat dissidents were engaged by the German Intelligence and dispatched to Turkey with the supposition that they would get into contact with officials of the Russian embassy. According to the German plan, this would inevitably involve the Russians in a matter of great sensation and turn Turkey against Russia. Then, Turkey would also be easily convinced to allow German troop passage through its territory.[69] In this conjuncture, it came as no surprise when on March, 13, 1945, Moscow announced its intent to renounce the December, 17, 1925 Treaty of Friendship and Neutrality with Turkey.[70]

Soviet charges against Turkey of weakening the Allies through maintaining political and commercial relations with Germany had become more aggressive particularly after the battle of Stalingrad. For his part, President İnönü chose to repel Soviet charges through suppressing both the extreme leftist and rightist activities in Turkey.

In his speech on May 19, 1944, İnönü stated that when the Independence War of Turkey ended, Turkey was friendly with only the Soviets and in the present international arena, those who claimed that Turkey had become racist and Pan-Turanist were serving the interests of foreigners. He said, "it is for sure that those who wish to perpetuate these ideas which will only bring trouble and disaster to the Turkish nation will be of no service to the Turkish nation."[71] Then, the arrests to which the government gave wide publicity followed. As will be discussed later, a result of İnönü's manipulation of domestic policy in accordance with the trends in international affairs, less than a year later was the launch of a storming campaign against leftist groups.

Meanwhile, to the concern of Ankara, the SU persistently sought ways to bind Turkey to 'special' kind of relationship with the Soviet State. This had become repeatedly evident particularly towards the end of the war. When the Turkish Minister of Foreign Affairs, Numan Menemencioğlu interviewed Sergei Vinogradov, the Soviet Ambassador to Ankara on May 22, 1944, just two weeks before his resignation due to increasing British pressures on Turkey's chromite trade with Germany in exchange of weaponry (in terms of both political—with a view to maintaining its neutrality in the global conflict as Britain failed to purchase the chromite despite long-term payment offers—and for economic reasons) Menemencioğlu felt obliged to tell Vinogradov that Turkey considered Turco–Soviet relations as having an independent nature, and implied that relations with the SU were not under the influence of Britain and the US. He further stated that issues raised in the Soviet Commissar for Foreign Affairs, Molotov's statement to the press on April 2, 1944, regarding the situation in the Balkans in general, and Roumania in particular, might be turned into an agreement between Turkey and the SU since these countries shared the view that cooperation in the Balkans would be the first step for cooperation in European affairs.

As will be stated below, his predecessor Şükrü Saraçoğlu's fairly negative experience when he visited Moscow in September 1939 in order to conclude a mutual cooperation pact limited to the Black Sea and the Straits was still remembered. Menemencioğlu suggested that such an understanding could include the expression that the two countries would undertake political consultations in case circumstances threatening their security and interests arise. Though Vinogradov was pleased to hear Menemencioğlu, Moscow's response which came on June 5 was not in the affirmative. The Kremlin stated that before Turkey terminated its relationship with Germany through making a fundamental transformation in this respect and declare war on this country, no political agreement would likely to produce any effect.[72]

Following this unfruitful visit which coincided with German Foreign Minister J. Ribbentrop's official visit to Moscow in the same days, an incurable crisis of confidence had emerged out of this which is indispensable to understand the perpetuating strains in Turco–Russian relations throughout the 1940s and then on. Indeed, Russian delaying tactics, peremptory manners and exaggerated demands turned Saraçoğlu to a strong anti-communist during his term of office as the Minister of Foreign Affairs in Refik Saydam's second Government between April 3, 1939 and subsequently as Prime Minister after he succeeded R. Saydam on July 9, 1942.[73]

Indeed, we are able to imagine that these talks were put on the desk by Moscow when its time came. Therefore, there were various examples to indicate that the Soviets had changed as well. As will be discussed later, Memduh Tezel in his memoirs *Moskova'dan Geliyorum* (I am Coming From Moscow) narrates this atmosphere which include a series of events from the interruption of their train voyage with Ambassador Sarper to Moscow in October 1944 by the searches of Soviet troops, to courier Army Cpt. Fuat Güzaltan's "committing suicide" in train on May 30, 1949 to explain this change.

The changing nature of Turco–Soviet relations requires to mention Atatürk's keeping the Soviets in line which was the end-result of his success through acting in a great room of manoeuvre provided by a close and open policy and a sheer determination. As early as 1922, in reply to a speech delivered by the Soviet Ambassador in Ankara, S. Ivanovich Aralov, Atatürk had said that

Gentlemen, five years ago, the people who constituted today's Russian Committee brought about a great revolution. The objective of this revolution was to fight against the cruel and malefic existences convened under the name of imperialism and capitalism. All the world of the oppressed was complainant of these existences which I stated with their names and peculiarities in front of you. . . . I, now, have to confess that when this uprising and revolt took place, we had not considered the meaning of imperialism and capitalism in the way it was done in Russia. We were merely aware of the powers threatening our very existence. As the state of affairs progressed, it was understood that the powers threatened us were the same with that of the existences which caused the revolution in Russia. . . . As the objective of upheaval of both Turkey and Russia emerged as the same, naturally a strong contact and cordial relationship was born. . . .[74]

In view of the above, if we attempt to perceive the degree of divergence of opinion betwen Turkey and the SU, the available data may be of use to conclude whether these differences led to a clear and drastic change in both countries' perception of each other. It appears that the change of the SU was overwhelmed with its ideological impetuosity, sometimes with correct and mostly not so correct motives. Besides, Moscow was following a covert neighbourhood policy which was equally encountered and eviscerated by Atatürk's straightforwardness and unwavered handling of international and bilateral affairs. So, for the Kremlin, a continuity in its exigent policy was always in place with some drawbacks prompted by the changes in international fora, leaving nothing to surprise for those who watch this country closely. It can then be considered that it was more of Turkey's perception of the Soviets that gradually embarked upon a change through leaving the traditional analysis of the Kremlin aside which prevented Ankara to respond accordingly.

Obviously, what went wrong in the Turco–Soviet relations was a two-way process. To explain the anger of the Soviets directed at Ankara in the aftermath of the WWII, the telegram dated August 27, 1942, sent by F. Von Papen, the German Ambassador to Ankara, to Berlin may provide useful insights. The German Ambassador communicated the content of his first visit which he made on the same day to Turkish Prime Minister Saraçoğlu with this telegram. The talks started on Turkey's general position and when it comes to the issue of "Russian question" Papen interviewed Saraçoğlu on his opinion. According to him,

M. Saraçoğlu, said that he wanted to reply to this first as a Turk, and
then as a Prime Minister.

As a Turk, he desired the total dissolution of Russia with great enthusiasm. The endeavour of destroying Russia was among Führer's great
and a rare thing to happen one could witness only once in a century
jobs.

The destruction of Russia was the endless dream of the Turkish people.
Every Turk, including Hüseyin Cahit (Yalçın) which supported England in his column could not think otherwise.

In a last statement, Saraçoğlu pronounced his loyaty to the Turco–
Mogul idea and assured the expression of this sentiment indirectly.

As Prime Minister, he is in a position to not to give any slightest
reasoning to Russians to enable them destroy the Turco–Mogul minority. . . . In Iran, those Azerbaijanis who sympathized with Turkey
were completely annihilated with their villages. . . . As Prime Minister, Saraçoğlu is obliged to safeguard impartiality in absolute manners
in order to not to jeopardize Turkey. . . . Similar to what Numan
[Menemencioğlu, the Minister of Foreign Affairs] did, Saraçoğlu too
confirmed that he could talk with me on these practical questions in
secret or designate a third person to engage in these talks.[75]

Turning back to the Menemencioğlu's resignation, Dikerdem maintained that following Menemencioğlu's authorization of three German
auxiliary ships to pass freely from the Straits, President İnönü had forced
him to resign. According to the Montreux Convention, Turkey had no
right to inspect ships up to 100 tons, since these ships were not considered battleships or battle support ships. However, throughout the course
of war, it was observed that even vessels of 30 tons might have had
armour up to 9 mm. In this case, German officials had argued that these
non-combatant ships were armoured for purposes of self-defense.[76]

In one way or another, it was obvious that the decision was made by
Menemencioğlu in his own capacity. But, İnönü considered this latest
act as threatening to his cautious and well-balanced policy. Dikerdem
also considered that the Turkish President was from a generation that
was purely convinced of Westerners' undefeatability. He had also adopted
the Ottoman Empire's principle of trying to keep Britain and Russia from
being on the same front. Besides, for him, no friendship with Russia was

attainable without securing friendship of the West. Given this, when criticisms of the British Minister of Foreign Affairs, Anthony Eden, were directed at the acts of the Turkish Government in a speech he delivered in the House of Commons on the issue explained above, İnönü nervously told Menemencioğlu: "The Ottoman Empire survived as long as it could keep Russia and Britain on separate fronts and played them off against each other. You united them on the same front."[77]

Along the same lines, Hughe Knatchbull-Hugessen, the British Ambassador to Turkey maintained that Şükrü Saraçoğlu, the Turkish Prime Minister appeared on the whole somewhat relieved on Menemencioğlu's leave of office. Saraçoğlu was critical of his Minister of Foreign Affairs' attitude which he described as too legalistic on many points and as failing through lack of broad political vision.[78]

Güçlü, referring to the *Times* which then stated that Menemencioğlu was partly to be blamed for his juridical training, states that this "induced him to pay too much attention to legalism and to overlook the political aspects." However, he concludes that İnönü, who had endorsed the policies followed by Menemencioğlu "wanted to be seen to be making a change of course to placate the Allies. Menemencioğlu's resignation indicated a change in the political situation. The Allies had invaded Normandy less than two weeks before, and allied ascendancy required Turkey to make accommodations to new political realities."[79]

On June 15, General Secretary Cevat Açıkalın, who resumed the talks following Menemencioğlu's leave of office, interviewed Vinogradov. He told Vinogradov that the SU handled the issues of improving Turco–Soviet relations and political consultations and cooperation in the Balkans separately and regarding the latter, laid down the condition of Turkey's declaration of war on Germany. Açıkalın asked if the SU had a condition concerning the improvement of Turco–Russian relations as well. Instructed by the Kremlin, Vinogradov started a tour d'horizon, expressing a series of Russian views and expectations on the trial of the Russian citizen who attempted to assassinate von Papen, Pan-Turanist movements in Turkey directed at people of Turkish origin in the Caucasus and Central Asia, press attacks against Russia, and the negative effects of the friendship treaty which Turkey concluded with Germany three days before the German assault towards Russia.

In his turn Açıkalın stated "You were not just affiliated with Germany through a military aggression pact, but as a political partner in actual practice. On our return from Moscow a couple of months ago

[Açıkalın referred to the visit of Şükrü Saraçoğlu to Moscow in September 1939—following the Nazi–Soviet Pact of August 24 which lasted nearly a month, however, without any outcome], as an answer to our proposal for cooperation, we had a German reservation in our pocket handed over to us by yourself. . . . Do you mean it was no sin when you had laid down the condition of a German reservation for our proposal for cooperation, but it is bad of us as we concluded a non-aggression treaty with Germans through succeeding to make Germans accept our alliance when and despite German armies had reached our frontiers and there was no possibility to expect any assistance from our Allies?"[80]

In fact, what had brought Turkish apprehensions concerning the ambitions of the Kremlin "to a near fever pitch in September 1944, notwithstanding the moderate Soviet position toward Iran, Czechoslovakia, Finland and Romania, was the Russian invasion of Bulgaria."[81] On September 8, in an attempt to appease the Kremlin, the Bulgarian Government, headed by Constantine Muraviev, broke diplomatic relations with Berlin and called for an armistice with the SU. However, Soviet troops under Marshal Tolbukhin had already begun to invade Bulgaria. The next day, Kimon Georgiev, the pro-Soviet leader of the Fatherland Front assumed the Premiership and King Simeon II was forced to consent to the new regime.

From then on, the possibility of a synthesis between Bulgarian irredentism and Soviet supported Communist menace alarmed Ankara. Thus, Ankara suddenly found itself bordering a country "which had long been irredentist toward Thrace and Macedonia, had long openly coveted a port on the Aegean, and which had now become the instrument not only of Bulgarian nationalism but of Soviet expansionist aspirations as well."[82] Anxieties in Ankara grew when Tito, along with Georgiev broached the subject of Pan-Slavism in January 1945.

Concurrently, Ankara was urged to declare war on the Axis so as to pave its way to the San Francisco Conference. British Ambassador to Ankara Maurice Peterson, along the lines of the decision reached at Yalta on this condition repeated the same to Turkish Minister of Foreign Affairs Hasan Saka in February 1945. On 23 February 1945, Ruşen Eşref Ünaydın, Turkish Ambassador to London cabled Ankara explaining that Anthony Eden, the British Foreign Secretary told him that "if Turkey wanted to join this conference, she should declare war on Germany. Turkey should side with the general cause completely. Given this, she should be given the qualification and glory of being a united nation. This is what we suggested. . . . The other two big have also concurred with this."[83]

Turkey finally declared war on Germany and Japan and adhered to the Charter of the UN on February 23, 1945 through the unanimous vote of existing 401 members of parliament in the TGNA.[84] In his speech before the Assembly, Prime Minister Saraçoğlu expressed the view that Turkey had sided with the democratic nations since the threat of war had begun. He stated that Turkey had proceeded in the same direction with its Assembly and the Government and this time ". . . would like to fulfill the place that we have actually been occupying in official terms as well" and towards this objective, Turkey declared war against Germany and Japan, in accordance with the good of the world and humanity and the national interests.[85]

It was apparent that Turkey was keen on safeguarding itself in a Europe which increasingly felt intimidated by the advances of the Soviets. Thus, Ankara–Washington relations were furthered as the Turkish Government signed another agreement with Washington on the same day regarding the principles of receiving the US aid which was the subject matter of the Law dated March 11, 1941.

From then on, admittedly, Turkey approached the end of the war with its closer ties to its ally, Britain, somewhat strained. George Harris maintained that if Turkey focused its attention primarily on dealing with the British in the supply of war material rather than addressing itself to Washington with the same urgency, this was because Britain was a formal ally and in fact served as the main channel for equipment during the war.[86]

A few days later than the decision of the TGNA, on March 3, 1945, the Department of State sent a Note Verbale to the Turkish Embassy in Washington informing that the US Ambassador in Ankara was concurrently conveying the invitation to the Turkish Government to join the San Francisco Conference. As the Note expressed, the invitation was made on behalf of the US Government as well as the Governments of the Great Britain, the SU and China.[87]

Previously, right after the Turkey's declaration of war against the Axis powers, on February 24, Turkish Ambassador to Moscow Selim Sarper paid a visit to Soviet Commissar for Foreign Affairs Molotov at a time the Soviets had already turned their attention towards Turkey. During their talks, Molotov brought the subject to the revision of Montreux Convention, since he said, it was agreed in principle at Yalta. He added that the Soviet Government was examining the matter and there was a requirement to discuss with Turkey as well. Sarper told in reply that the issue in concern could be the subject matter of multilateral talks and thus required to be handled accordingly.[88]

Shortly afterwards, in order to bring pressure upon Turkey, on March 19, 1945, Moscow informed Ankara that it would terminate the Turco–Soviet Treaty of Friendship and Non-aggression of December, 17, 1925, renewed in accordance with a protocol dated November 7, 1935. According to this protocol, the treaty itself was renewed for 10 years, to be prolonged by tacit consent for further 2-year periods unless denounced 6 months before expiry. If therefore the treaty were not to remain operative until at least November 7, 1947, it would have to be denounced by one party or the other by May 7, 1945, at the latest.

It was also understood that the SU had not informed the Allies of its decision a priori. The memorandum Molotov handed the Turkish Ambassador, Selim Sarper, on the same day included that though the Soviet Government, with a view to continuation of the friendship relations of the two parties appreciated the value of this agreement, because of the deep changes emerged during WW II, had found the agreement inappropriate for the new conditions and, with its conviction that it required an amelioration in a serious manner wished to terminate the agreement in concern.[89]

On March 21, the US Ambassador in Moscow, Averell Harriman, reported to Washington that it had been anticipated in Turkish circles in Moscow that the Russians would denounce the treaty and the Turkish Ambassador had advised his government to this effect one or two months ago. Then the denunciation itself was not a surprise, but the circumstances in which it took place were unexpected. According to Harriman, Sarper had arranged to return to Ankara for a period of consultation which was expected to last several weeks. He was scheduled to depart on March 25 and on March 19 he informed the Commissariat for Foreign Affairs that before his departure to Ankara he would be glad to call on Molotov for a courtesy visit since he had nothing to discuss with him.

To Sarper's surprise, Assistant Commissar for Foreign Affairs Kavtaradze told him that he was invited to call the same day on 15.00 hrs. Harriman explained that Molotov informed the Turkish Ambassador of the denunciation of the treaty and told him that the Soviet Government had intended to take this step at a somewhat later date, but in view of his impending departure had decided to act at once, in order that he might be able to discuss Turkish–Russian relations with his government against this background. Although Molotov had used this ostensible reason as a pretext to communicate the decision of the Kremlin, at this stage Harriman choose not to alert Washington and stated his assessment that Soviet Commissar for Foreign Affairs' attitude was consistently friendly and correct, and there was no intimation on his part that the action reflected ill feeling or any tendency to bring pressure on Turkey.

According to Harriman, Sarper then inquired about Molotov's views as to the ways in which the present treaty might be "improved." However, Molotov was unwilling to commit himself on this point and said that after the Ambassador had talked with his government he would be glad to learn how the Turkish Government felt on this point. He evaluated that in denouncing the treaty the Russians had in mind the anticipated discussion of the Montreux Convention at the first meeting of the Foreign Ministers of the three Allies.

The US Ambassador, however, said the denunciation of the treaty made it possible for them to insist on the early redefinition, in a new agreement, of their relations with Turkey and thus opened up a channel of pressure on the Turkish Government, which might prove useful as the question of the Straits again came under discussion. Interestingly, he needed to emphasize that the Soviet–Bulgarian policy seemed pointed in the same direction. He stated that it was evidently Russian tactics to maneuver the Turks into coming forward first with their ideas on the redefiniton of Turkish–Russian relations. What would come after that was of course impossible to predict, but the Russians would then be free to accept or to criticize the Turkish suggestion as they liked, and issues might be raised in the course of these discussions which would provide opportunities for the exertion of strong political pressure.

Not surprisingly, this in turn, would open several possibilities. In this context, Turkey might be asked to accept in advance of any broader discussions, a given set of Soviet views with respect to the regime of the Straits, on the assumption that it would be difficult for any outside power to challenge or ignore a program advanced by the two countries most directly concerned.[90]

Implications of New Soviet Tactics
and the Turkish "Long Telegram"

Turning back to Turco–Soviet talks, on June 7, 1945, Molotov received
the Turkish Ambassador S. Sarper, as will be discussed below, to introduce a pragmatic solution to the deterioration in bilateral relations. In
this context, before he left Ankara for Moscow, Sarper was instructed to
deliver Turkey's offer of an alliance with the SU.

At this juncture, the background of this transformed policy of Turkey is worth explaining. As stated before, Turkish–Soviet relations were
gradually deteriorating towards the end of WW II, and no concrete step
was taken to diffuse this unpromising atmosphere and to improve bilateral relations. Such an improvement could be realized through a cautious
and patient policy. Dikerdem stated that "however, similar to what he
had done in the August of 1939, President İnönü tried to be quick and
conclude a new pact with the Soviets."[91]

On April 4, 1945 Hasan Saka, the Turkish Minister of Foreign Affairs invited Vinogradov, the Soviet Ambassador to Ankara and handed
over him the Turkish Note in reply. The Note, among other things stated
that the Turkish Government "had the honour to inform its acceptance of
the Soviet advise that the terminated Agreement be changed to a new one
which will suit the benefit of the Parties today through including serious
ameliorations and its readiness to examine all the proposals to be made
towards this end with utmost attention and good will."[92]

The Turkish Government was in favour of continuing the exchange
of views with the Soviets until the position of the US and the British
Governments were crystallized. The venue for this would be the San
Francisco Conference beginning on April 25, 1945.

Ambassador Sarper arrived in Moscow on June 7. He was clearly
instructed to conduct negotiations towards reaching an agreement. The
way in which Sarper received by Molotov, left nothing to imagination as
to the course of their talks. Expanding on their encounter Sarper said:

> As I have seen him not standing up when I stepped into his room, I
> walked from the door towards his desk with very slow steps. When I
> got closer to desk Molotov stood up behind his desk. He shook my
> hand as such. He showed me the armchair facing his desk and sat
> behind the writing desk. In fact, this reception style was for the Am-
> bassadors of the Soviet satellites. There were two interpreters next to

his writing desk. It was for sure that Molotov was intending to to tell me something in dictating manners. Because in our previous talks, he used to stand up at once as I entered his room. We used to held talks not sitting before the writing desk, but seated in the armchairs facing each other. However, there was a cold atmosphere in today's talks and Molotov had met me in an imperious manner. Perhaps, he wished to impress me before the talks began. Having understood this I paid special attention to sit with a more erected back. In our previous meetings, Molotov used to inquire after me, extend the cigarette box on the table, offer the Russian cigarette and paper. I used to take out the cigarette case from my pocket and offer him the Turkish cigarette. I waited for the same today as well, and waited until Molotov extended the cigarette box to take out my cigarette case. Finally, Molotov, without any small talk extended the cigarette box, I took it extremely slowly and extended the cigarette case to him to offer the Turkish cigarette. I waited for Molotov to draw his lighter to light my cigarette. When only he took out his lighter I lit my lighter too and we lit each others' cigarettes. As such, through acting slowly, I wanted to break his commanding manners.[93]

At the outset of talks, to the surprise of Sarper, Molotov first criticized the Moscow Agreement of March 16, 1921 and demanded that the injustice done by this agreement should be corrected. The point raised by Molotov was quite distasteful for Turkey since the agreement in concern had laid down the basis of bilateral relations. Now, the Soviets had declared that they no longer appreciated it, and on the contrary expressed their view that they were interested in changing it. The Soviet Commissar for Foreign Affairs' statement included that the SU had suffered immense losses during the war and it was compelled to spend much of its energy on its security in the Black Sea. The situation in this region had not become a source of threat but the Soviets had felt that "the fate of 200 million people depended on Turkey's will."[94] Molotov added that they were sure of Turkey's goodwill, but they could not rely on its capability to defend the Straits.

When it was understood that no agreement was likely, Sarper suggested leaving this issue aside and continuing the talks on other matters. Molotov stated that they might not negotiate on this issue, but this would not mean that they had settled all questions of dispute between the two countries.

Sarper's difficulty in stating Turkey's proposal for an alliance with the SU continued since Molotov insisted on inquiring as to which guarantees Ankara could give to Moscow in case two countries entered into an alliance. Sarper told his interlocutor that the joint defense of the Straits could be subject to discussions of military experts in case the necessity arose, and it was evident that Turkey would do whatever necessary to be victorious if it was left with no option but to engage in war.

Then, Molotov turned to the issue of revising the Montreux Convention and to the astonishment of Sarper, put forward the view that both countries might hold parallel negotiations for an alliance and determine a joint approach towards the regime of the Straits concurrently. Regarding the Soviet Commissar for Foreign Affairs' last statement, Sarper expressed that if talks were held for the revision of Montreux in the future, this could only be a mere exchange of views since any revision in the convention was a matter of multilateral talks in the form of a conference to be held specifically for this purpose. However, there would be a difference between pursuing these talks under existing conditions and with an alliance with the SU.

Following another futile round of talks, Sarper suggested to state the issues to be negotiated in the form of articles. However, Molotov declined this proposal and said that any agreement could only be made after the issues were settled. In the end, all the matters negotiated were left unsolved.

Right after the talks, Sarper informed Ankara by phone that the situation could not be improved with the Soviets. Decoding of Sarper's telegram was completed on June 12 and on the same day it was decided in Ankara to instruct him to communicate to Molotov that no territorial change or allocation of bases with a view to the conclusion of a treaty could be accepted and no significant outcome could be expected from the bilateral talks on the revision of Montreux as explained before.

To the distress of Turkey, following the first round of talks, it was announced through *Pravda* and *Izvestia* that the decisions regarding the territorial demands of Armenia from Turkey and a call for the return of Armenians in diaspora adopted at the Armenian Catholicos Election Congress were endorsed by Moscow. Besides, illustrations of solidarity were held between the Soviet and Armenian committee representatives in San Francisco.[95]

Meanwhile, Ankara had informed Washington and London of the Moscow talks. On June 9, before he read Sarper's complete telegram which was arriving at Ankara in parts, İnönü told the Acting Minister of Foreign Affairs, Nurullah Esat Sümer, to speak to the British and US Ambassadors in Ankara about urging their governments to react against the Russian designs at once.[96]

When Sümer interviewed the British Ambassador, Maurice Peterson, Peterson's reaction was limited to saying "Don't get excited" and expressing that he would inform his government of the situation. In his turn, the US Ambassador, Edwin G. Wilson, saw no reason to refrain from promptly stating that the US would not leave Turkey alone. However, Wilson also told Sümer that the US was not in a position to promise immediate military assistance earlier than nine months because of Stalin's high prestige in the US which could only be changed in time.

The second Molotov–Sarper meeting took place on June 18. At the opening of talks, to the astonishment of Sarper, the Soviet Commissar for Foreign Affairs continued along his previous line of maximalist debate. In his turn, Sarper held the opinion that the Soviet proposals would violate Turkey's sovereignty and might adversely affect its strategic and political position. Sarper's telegram also underlined that the talks were abruptly ended:

> When Molotov said that the Soviet Republics were a great and mighty country, but this would not be a reason for sacrificing the rights of the smaller republics of Armenia and Georgia, I said I had come to Moscow with great expectations. I had very much appreciated to have the opportunity to work in order to put an order and reform the relations between our countries. But if this can not be realized . . . it is the outcome of your leaving us before this impasse. . .' Molotov standing, said 'it will be very good if you think once more about this matter.' I replied 'let's consider together, you consider it some as well' and we left.[97]

Sarper's second telegram was received on June 20. On the day Sarper's telegram was read in Ankara, the Acting Minister of Foreign Affairs, Sümer, spoke to the Soviet Ambassador Vinogradov. Sümer told Vinogradov that "under these conditions, instead of friendship and understanding we have been pursuing, a freeze and distance will resurge."[98] Sümer observed that the Soviet Ambassador appeared complacent and uninsisting in his answers to Turkish rejections.

However, the real Soviet position was contrary as Vinogradov explained to the US Ambassador in Ankara, Wilson, towards the end of

June. Wilson stated that Vinogradov was keen on expressing Molotov's demand for certain measures necessary for the security of the Black Sea without directly referring to the allocation of bases on the Straits. He also stated that territorial demands of the SU were voiced on behalf of Armenia which needed additional lands. When Wilson asked if any Armenians were living in the eastern provinces of Turkey, he replied that there were only a few since the Turks massacred most of them. The US Ambassador noted that Vinogradov was very critical of Turkey in this matter and on other issues.[99] However, it was understood that neither the US, nor Britain were in favor of imposing a constraint for themselves and handicapping the talks through declaring a policy in regard to the Turkish case two weeks before the opening of deliberations with the SU at Potsdam.

To sum up, Sarper's telegrams appear as a turning point. There are, however, counter-arguments around this issue as well. As for the personal relations between Sarper and Molotov, according to Dikerdem—who was working then in the political department as an officer and conveying the decoded cables to Presidential House in Çankaya—to begin with, the nomination of Sarper as Ambassador to Moscow who had spent his youth in Magdeburg, Germany, carrying a German style duel scar on his face as well, proved to be unfruitful in terms of gaining mileage in Turco–Soviet relations. He argued that Sarper's telegram dated June 9 was biased and poorly reflected his talks with Molotov since the Soviet Commissar for Foreign Affairs had neither openly pronounced the return of some Turkish eastern provinces to the SU nor had he made a demand for bases in the Straits. Dikerdem maintained that no document regarding the Soviet demands could be found in the archives of the MFA except the telegram of Sarper.[100]

Despite the existence of clouds of uncertainty, if one thing was certain, it was the Anglo–American policy makers' miscalculation about the Soviet attitudes after Yalta. In late February 1945, the British Foreign Secretary Eden had told the Turkish Ambassador Ünaydın that the issue of the Straits was barely discussed at Yalta and the Russians had expressed their thought to talk over this matter at a later date. Besides, Eden had emphasized that the Russians had no plans or considerations on the issue, except repeating their view on the stance of Japan and the League of Nations vis-à-vis the Straits thus, the Turkish Government should have no anxiety at all.

Interestingly, another misinterpretation of the Allies in general and Eden in particular was pertaining to the Kremlin's attitude towards Greece. As Eden told Ünaydın, after the Yalta, the Allies were convinced that the Russians were extremely sound on this matter and he was convinced that in case the Greeks had no internal dispute, the situation in Greece would represent a case for optimism. Eden also told the Turkish Ambassador that he was informed that the Greek Communists sought support from the Soviets but to no avail.[101]

Although not technically empowered as Dikerdem was, Turkish authors of socialist orientation such as, Küçük and Avcıoğlu put forward similar arguments in their interpretation of Turco–Soviet relations sometimes to the extent of totally rejecting the Soviet demands and considering them as the misperceptions of Turkish officials or merely accepting the existence of such demands but founding the roots of Soviet–Turkish cleavage in German secret documents which revealed Saraçoğlu's unfriendly views in regard to the SU.[102]

Admittedly, these counter-arguments which pointed to the weak side of the statements on the threat generated by communism are hard to defend against an ocean of literature devoted to explain global Soviet expansionism of the late 1940s and 1950s and so on, but are still intriguing. While, in one way or another, Dikerdem's argument seems granting verbal statements or allusions of diplomats a second degree of importance, all deliberations of the Big Three during the war included strategic talks at least on the parts of the Straits and Turkey's belligerency and reflected the existence of Soviet demands over Turkey. Besides, in terms of person-to-person talks, it is unrealistic to expect all statements to be written down.

Truly, threat perceptions of the states can originate from certain gestures, expressions or manners of interlocutors towards each other. Such an analysis may also have its roots in the observation of the actions of an "aggressor" or "expansionist" state vis-à-vis other states. Additionally, when they express their observation in Notes or telegrams, the diplomats are expected to reflect the atmosphere at least as categorically—friendly, hostile, neutral etc.—around the issue at hand as well, though this interpretive analysis can many times be hardly one sided or even unbiased. Classically, this common approach can be regarded as something widely accepted at that time from the above mentioned viewpoint since it is not the business of professionals in diplomacy to reason the attitude of others given the complexities of foreign policy making—internal dynamics, opposition parties, economic power, force arsenal etc.—in a given country, i.e. the Soviet Union had the right to search for the ways in which it could ensure a secure access to warm waters. Evidently, the logic does not work that way, but more towards trying to limit the area of manoeuvres of the other preferably in legitimate ways.

Of course, the diplomatic cases of 1940s were shaped without a variety of new components indispensable to contemporary diplomacy, such as a considerable degree of "transparency" in these patterns of interaction. Understandably, this meant a more open diplomacy and a care for other states' perceptions in an environment where means of communication are widespread and interdependencies and common denominators increasingly take place.

Turning back to the nomination of Sarper to Moscow, Küçük argued that under these circumstances it would be unrealistic to expect that Sarper's term of office could be fruitful. In June 1940, Sarper had left the MFA and was appointed as the Secretary General of the Directorate of Press and Broadcasting—a much criticized governmental body which exercised tremendous censorship over the Turkish press, particularly towards anti-German publications—where he served until he was appointed Ambassador to Moscow in 1944. Then, Küçük argued that Sarper "did what he was expected to do in Moscow." He emphasized that from then on, Sarper's "service in Moscow" was never forgotten by the Turkish Government and he was nominated in distinguished posts for the rest of his career.[103] A different group of analysts, however, maintain their reservations on these explanations since interpretations of the historical events are not found right when attempted to be presented within the framework of a fully coherent 'cause and effect' explanation.

Leaving aside the issue of whether the SU was following an aggressive policy towards Turkey, it may be of use to look at the Soviet policy towards other countries and try to perceive the general attitude of the Soviets. A close example can be investigated within the communist and Kurdish nationalist separatist movement which took place from the mid 1945s to the first months of 1946 in the north of Iran. There will be room for a discussion of this issue in the following pages.

Turning back to the telegrams of Sarper, it has been understood that the content of these messages were shared by the Turkish Prime Minister Saraçoğlu with the US Ambassador in Ankara, Wilson. In his telegram to Washington dated June 12, Wilson explained that Saraçoğlu had explained him that although Moscow had still not fully expressed its views, there was a feeling of disturbance on the part of Ankara and the Turkish Prime Minister's mentioned him of some "bad smells" arising thereof.[104] Two days later, US Ambassador to London John. G. Winant cabled Washington to inform that the British Ambassador to Ankara Peterson had learnt of the three demands of Molotov. The same cable stated these as the revision of the Turco–Soviet Agreement of 1921, allocation of a base to the Soviets in the Straits, and the revision of the Montreux Convention. It also included the response of Sarper to these demands which the Turkish Government had approved.[105]

Interestingly, Winant, in his cable to Washington on June 18, mentioned "the fourth demand" of Molotov which the Soviet Commissar for Foreign Affairs said "might make the other three unnecessary." Winant, stated that the Foreign Office official informing him on the fourth demand explained that "'Molotov was coy' about this." "Turks believe the fourth demand might be the rupture of the Anglo–Turkish Alliance (which the FonOff considers highly unlikely) or a 'modification' of the Turkish political regime so that the Turkish Govnt might be 'reorientated' as have been the Govts of Rumania and Bulgaria."[106] A month later in Potsdam, the Kremlin would forward his narrative of the issue once again with intriguing allegations.

In the same cable of Winant, there was another interesting reference to Peterson's remarks on the emerging perceptions of the forces behind the Turkish MFA. Peterson had wired that he had "recently invited to dinner at the Embassy the Acting Secretary General of the FonOff and Dr. Aras, former ForMin and Ambassador in London. The Acting Secretary Gen took Peterson aside after dinner and requested that he not be invited again on the same occasion as Aras, describing the latter as 'this well known Soviet agent.'"[107]

Meanwhile, Washington tried unsuccessfully to ease the tension between Ankara and the Kremlin. Britain was not less anxious than the US to develop a policy in this regard. On June 18, John Balfour, the British Chargé, called on Acting Secretary of State, Joseph C. Grew, to discuss the situation. It was indeed surprising that Soviet Commissar for Foreign Affairs should have made a demarché at a time when Britain and the US were still awaiting the Soviet views in regard to the Straits promised at Yalta. Then, Balfour communicated the proposal of London in view of the Anglo–Turkish Treaty, to support the Turkish position particularly as the position taken by Molotov appeared to be in direct conflict with statements made by Stalin at Yalta. Subsequently, the British Chargé

d'Affaires inquired if Grew would endorse a joint Anglo–American approach and that this approach be made to the Soviet Government prior to
the meeting of the Big Three at which it might well be necessary to
discuss this whole question.

In his turn, the US Secretary of State promised the necessary attention to the suggestion explaining that it would be preferable to withhold
action until the end of the San Francisco conference and that if action
were to be taken, there would presumably be plenty of time between the
close of the conference and the meeting of the Big Three. Balfour said he
agreed with Grew, but he was further instructed to state that even if
Washington should not feel in a position to make a joint approach with
the British Government, "his Government hoped that we would at least
support the British action with some step of our own."[108] Two days
later, on June 20, Ambassador Wilson in Ankara suggested that Washington express an interest in this matter at Moscow for the reason that
"the Russian proposals to Turkey are wholly incompatible with the spirit
and principles on which we are seeking with the participation of the
Soviet Union to set up a new world organization."[109]

On July 7, the Turkish Ambassador in Washington, H. Ragıp Baydur,
called on Grew and after some preliminary talk concerning the success
of the San Francisco Conference, he turned to the conversation which
had taken place in Moscow three weeks ago between Sarper and Molotov
in which the former had stated the Soviet demand for a rectification of
the Turco–Soviet frontier; a demand for bases on the Dardanelles and a
bilateral modification of the Montreux Convention. Subsequently, Molotov
had added that there might be also certain requirements from the Balkan
states, "which the Ambassador interpreted as some sort of a territorial
demand from Bulgaria."[110] Baydur said that he had come to visit Grew
for the purpose of ascertaining the attitude of the American Government
towards this situation.

Grew told Baydur that the American Government was very definitely concerned with any threat to the peace which might fall within the
purview of the UN Organization. However, for the present, he said, they
understood that the conversations had been a friendly exchange of views
and that no concrete threats had been made.

In his turn, Baydur asked Grew if the Soviet Government should
demand that the US cede to the Soviet Union the cities of Boston and San
Francisco, it should not consider such a demand as a threat, and he also
asked whether the US felt that such a demand could be a matter for

negotiation. Grew replied definitely in the negative, but asked Baydur whether the Soviet Government had specified the nature of the frontier rectification which it desired and whether the demands were yet of such a concrete nature as to be regarded as open threats. Baydur replied that "Mr. Molotov had stated that the Treaty of 1921 had been negotiated at a time when Soviet Russia was weak and he had said, 'Now we are strong.' The obvious implication was that Soviet Russia desired the return of the Vilayets of Kars and Ardahan."[111]

Consecutively, Baydur said he wished Grew to know that Turkey would not cede one inch of territory, and that if Soviets should appropriate such Turkish territory Turkey would immediately fight. A situation would thus be created which was totally contrary to the spirit and letter of all that had been achieved at San Francisco. The Turkish Ambassador underscored that the Turkish Government firmly believed that strong representations by the United States in advance of possible trouble would have a powerful effect on Moscow. Baydur had understood that Grew had told the British Ambassador, Lord Halifax, that the American Government would support the proposed demarché of the British Government in Moscow, but later the US Ambassador at Ankara, Edwin Wilson, had informed the Turkish MFA that the matter would be further studied and had implied that the US Secretary of State had made no such statement.

To the disappointment of Baydur, Grew said that the Ambassador was quite right since he had had no conversation on this subject with Lord Halifax whom he had not seen officially since his return from San Francisco.[112] He then told Baydur that he had to know very well himself that the US had been following this situation with concern; that he hoped the subject might be discussed at the meeting of heads of government and that, for that purpose, the US President had been fully briefed on all the information in possession. Grew noted that he personally believed that much more could be accomplished by a direct talk between the US President and Stalin than could be accomplished by any formal representations made in Moscow. Grew said:

I said that this Government, as a friend of both Turkey and the Soviet Union, would naturally be glad to be of assistance in arriving at a peaceful solution of the problem. The Ambassador must understand that this was in no respect an offer of mediation but merely a statement of our general attitude in all such situations. The Ambassador said that he understood my position perfectly but he wished to repeat with all possible emphasis that Turkey would cede no territory and was prepared to fight if necessary.

My attitude in the conversation clearly indicated my sympathy with Turkey's position but no commitment of any kind was made or implied.[113]

At this stage, Washington's reluctance to respond to Ankara in the affirmative, was no doubt another blow on Turkish political circles given Turkey's narrowed sphere of action under the pressure of Russian tactics which were pushing it into coming forward first with its ideas on the redefinition of Turco–Russian relations or gradually shifting to accommodate the designs of the Kremlin.

Turning back to talks of the Big Three, the third meeting of the heads of governments took place at Potsdam, a suburb of Berlin, between 17 July–1 August 1945. Roosevelt was dead and his place was taken by Harry S. Truman. Churchill and the Foreign Secretary Anthony Eden were replaced by Clement Attlee and Ernest Bevin respectively, while the Conference was in progress, as a result of the Labour Party's victory in the general election. Stalin, who was the sole survivor from the earlier meetings, had in effect obtained the position of dominance in Eastern Europe to which "Imperial Russia had aspired in vain in the First World War."[114]

At Potsdam, Turkey and the Straits were once more in deliberations, but in different ways and on different premises. Truman had come to Potsdam with the idea that the free and equal rights of all nations to transport on the waterways of Europe, the Rhine, Danube, Dardanelles and the Kiel Canal would be advantageous if not essential to the preservation of peace in Europe. He was also prepared to make such a proposal to the conference. However, at the end of the first session on July 17, Truman had the impression that Stalin wanted the Black Sea Straits for Russia, as had all the czars before him, while the British Premier was determined that Britain should keep and even strengthen its control of the Mediterranean.

Indeed, Stalin clearly expressed that the Montreux Convention was "inimical" to the SU. Furthermore, he added that Turkey was too weak to give any effective guarantee of free passage and it was only right that the SU should have bases to defend the Straits. As stated above, in his turn, Truman declared that while the US agreed to a revision of the Montreux Convention, it believed however, "that the Straits should be a free waterway open to the whole world and guaranteed by all of us." Commenting on this interchange, Secretary of State James F. Byrnes said, "that presented the issue. The Soviets wanted the free navigation of the Straits guaranteed by the Soviets, or by the Soviets and Turkey. This meant their armed forces would be on Turkey's soil. We wanted the free navigation of the Straits guaranteed by the United Nations."[115]

On July 21, the British Delegation agreed with the Soviets to take up the issue of modification of the Montreux Convention and other aspects of Soviet–Turkish relations in the deliberations. In fact, Churchill had agreed to raise these issues at Potsdam during his Moscow talks in October 1944. Against this background, on July 22, he stated that the British Government favoured the revision of the Montreux Convention through an agreement among the signatories with the exception of Japan.

Churchill also expressed that Britain would endorse an arrangement for the free movement of Russian ships, naval or merchant, through the Black Sea and back. He pointed out the necessity of not alarming Turkey as well. However, massing of forces on the part of Bulgaria and Soviet press and radio attacks and by the turn Sarper–Molotov talks had taken, Churchill argued that the Turco–Soviet discussions had not included Soviet demands from Turkey since Turkish officials formulated an alliance option with the SU.[116]

Given this premise, the Soviet demands for war reparations, and the Commissar for Foreign Affairs, Molotov's statements that the Montreux Convention, which restricted the passage of non-Turkish vessels through the Dardanelles, should be scrapped and the Soviets together with other Black Sea countries should be allowed to use the Straits freely in the future, while a Soviet–Turkish administration should replace the international regime of the Straits, were initial steps contributing towards the Cold War. Other far-reaching demands like the restoration of the Turkish provinces of Kars and Ardahan, increased Western suspicions of the SU.[117]

As for the approaching end of the war, the drop of two atomic bombs brought a quick end to the war in the Pacific, whereas uncertainty persisted in the Western Europe, especially concerning the settlement of differences of opinion over Germany. "In Germany, America and Russia confronted each other, no longer quite allies, not yet open enemies."[118]

The Western grouping of states–SU relations further deteriorated when the Kremlin concentrated on its domestic regime which became increasingly suspicious of the Western states. In 1945, Stalin charged A. A. Zhadanov[119] with the task of enhancing the control of the Communist Party, and countering the increasing power of some influential figures [120] The internal struggles, together with Stalin's concern over relations with the US, were responsible for the cautious nature of his foreign policy, "willing to test Western positions, yet receding if he met resistance, insisting on the SU's rights, yet uncertain of how to achieve them. Molotov's stubborn behaviour at the London Conference demonstrated the Soviet Union's determination to be treated as an equal by the West, and was designed to show that she was not to be overawed by the American monopoly of the atomic bomb."[121]

Following this, Molotov accepted the proposal by J. Byrnes that the Foreign Ministers should meet in Moscow in December 1945. At Moscow, it was agreed that, a Four-Power Control Commission should be sent to Romania to ensure non-communist representation in its government, while non-communists would be given posts in the Bulgarian government. In return, the US agreed to set up an Allied Council in Tokyo to make suggestions to General MacArthur, the US Supreme Commander there, about regime in Japan. Finally, it was agreed that the Council of Foreign Ministers would meet in the spring of 1946 to draw up peace treaties with Germany's former European allies. Dockrill argued that although the Moscow Conference led to a temporary thaw in US–Soviet relations, "These mutual concessions were purely cosmetic: the Western powers would continue to have as little influence in internal political arrangements in Romania as the Allied Council would have in Tokyo."[122]

As for Turkey, optimistic expectations for the new post-war order were short-lived. This was due to an intensifying Soviet propaganda warfare which seemed to have growing ambitions to envelop additional territories in Europe, Middle East and elsewhere. Following the end of the war, the Soviet Union had emerged as a vigilant force in the midst of a devastated Europe. Being on the side of winners, it had openly launched a series of revisionist demands on the side of the Red Army occupied territories of Eastern Europe, and proved to have further ambitions in other parts of the globe.

Encouraged by the vacuum in this newly shaping international environment, the SU demanded a revision of the Montreux convention of 1936, and the transfer of Turkish provinces of Kars and Ardahan—to restore the pre-WW I status quo since these provinces were gained by Russia at the Congress of Berlin, but lost again to the Ottoman Empire after the Great War. Besides, it was demanded of Turkey to break its relations with Britain and conclude a treaty "similar to those the Soviet Union was concluding with the nations of eastern and south-eastern Europe."[123] Not surprisingly, examples of Moscow's twisted rhetoric did no cease even after Turkey declared war on Germany.

As will be discussed below, at this stage, İnönü's policy line proved to be right. Indeed, the Turkish leadership was criticised both in domestic political circles and in the international arena for its over cautious, slow—but in fact, calm and collected—policy. Turkey was in a key position in the Balkans and the Middle East and both Britain and Germany wanted the country as an active ally. Ankara's decision to ally with Britain was another fact. However, events proved that Turkey was almost obliged to confine itself with the rules of neutrality, which, under the pressure of the circumstances, it had also failed to follow as cautiously as needed at times. Then, from Berlin's standpoint "a change in Turkey's attitude to benign neutrality was regarded as an important diplomatic gain at Britain's expense."[124] This occurred in June 1941 when Ankara signed a treaty with Berlin.

The Nazi Reich had also pressed for a secret protocol allowing them deliveries of military personnel and war material across Turkey into Iraq and Syria. Facing all these challenges and a highly unpredictable and chaotic course of international events, İnönü had based his policy on the following policy calculations which prove to be mostly right. The Turkish President had also decided to fully employ these as his future foreign policy references:

1. The Western Powers and the democratic front would eventually win the war;
2. On this premise, it was rightful to adhere into an alliance with Britain and France;
3. Both Germany and Russia would try to draw Turkey into an alliance or at least into a state of benevolent neutrality towards them. However, none of these might be an alternative but a lethal entrapment for Turkey. Vis-à-vis these powers, Turkey should seek the ways it could strengthen its hand and apart from its geo-strategic assets, the only way for this was to rely on an alliance with the Western grouping of states;

4. Within the WW, the real threat for Turkey had been generated from the Soviets. So the plannings of Turkey should
   have a special emphasis on avoiding this power;
5. There would inevitably be a war between Germany and Russia. In this case, alliance with Britain and France would acquire an additional meaning in the name of Turkey's security. As will be discussed below, this new international arena
   paved the way for a rapprochement to be later institutionally
   strengthened, as Turkey on the one side, the US and Britain
   on the other.

It can be evaluated that the threat posed by the totalitarian regimes
had necessitated Ankara to constitute an uninterrupted policy of integration with the West. It was clearly understood that these regimes could
unite around their objectives and create blocs as well. With a view to this
fact, it was unthinkable that Turkey could follow an independent course
without integrating its foreign policy to that of the Western grouping of
states. As will be discussed next, Ankara's steps in this direction indicated that no alliance could be maintained through an evasive policy and
alliances could prove to be costly.

Notes

1. "War Cloud Looms Up in the East," in *The Courier,* Lincoln, Neb.,
February 28, 1903, p. 7, img. 7, Library of Congress, http://chroniclingamerica.
loc.gov/lccn/sn99066033/1903-02-28/ed-1/seq-7/#date1 = 1836&index =
10&rows = 20&words = Europe + man + sick&search Type = basic&sequence =
0&state = &date2 = 1922&proxtext = sick + man + europe&y = 0&x = 0&date
FilterType = yearRange&page = 1
2. As late as 1932, the largest portion of the budget (146,210,355 Turkish
Liras) was allocated to the repayment of the public debt while only 86,007,582
Liras were expanded on defense, finance and other public services. As for the
population, it was under 14 million according to the 1927 census, with only
16.4 percent living in urbanized areas. Feroz Ahmad, *The Making of Modern
Turkey,* (London: Routledge, 1993), pp. 94–95. A census taken on October 21,
1940 gave the population of the Republic as 17,869,901, and increase on the
last (1935) census of 1,771,883 or 18 per 1,000 per annum. *Keesing's Contemporary Archives,* Vol. No. IV, 1940–1943, p. 4369.

3. From Prime Minister Refik Saydam's speech in TGNA on his Government's programme, April, 3, 1939. Available at, http://www.tbmm. gov.tr/hukumetler/HP11.htm.

4. *Ibid.*

5. *Keesing's Contemporary Archives*, Vol. No. IV, 1940–1943, pp. 4142–4143.

6. *Ibid.*, 4181. For a discussion of Ankara's political and economic agreements with Allies and the Axis, see, Dilek Barlas, *Etatism & Diplomacy in Turkey*, (NY: Brill, 1998).

7. *Ibid.*, p. 4181. On the other hand, the agreement Turkey signed with Germany to resume chromite trading on October 9, 1941 concluded that Turkey would sell Germany 90,000 tons of chromite in 1943 and 45,000 tons in 1944, in return for military equipment. Selim Deringil, *Turkish Foreign Policy During the Second World War*, 128–129. The Turkish Government, however, stated that it would not sell chrome to Germany until 1943, as all production was promised to Britain. Papen was unwilling to wait until the beginning of 1943 and he decided to obtain illegal private consignments from Turkey. In the end, Germany gained nothing from his effort. *"But to Papen's discomfiture, the Turks found out about it."* Weber, *The Evasive Neutral*, pp. 129–130.

8. *Keesing's Contemporary Archives*, Vol. IV, pp. 4181; 4212.

9. From the President İnönü's statement on foreign policy on November 1, 1940. *Keesing's Contemporary Archives*, Vol. No. IV, 1940–1943, p. 4304.

10. *Ibid.*

11. Hitler disclosed these designs after his invasion of the SU. On this see, *Documents from the Archives of the German Foreign Office, Nazi–Soviet Relations, 1939–1941*, (Washington: US Department of State, 1948), 217–259. Ribbentrop's proposal on the revision of spheres of influence were on the following bases as well: Germany: European territorial changes to be postponed until after the conclusion of a peace treaty; Central Africa. Italy: Same reservation, North and Northeast Africa. Japan: The Far East south of the Japanese archipelago. Andre Fontaine, *History of the Cold War*, pp. 146–147.

12. *Ibid.*, p. 147.

13 As for reactions of other countries, uneasiness was expressed in Yugoslavia at the news of the Italian attack on Greece and Belgrade announced that it aimed at the preservation of its neutrality. As for Bulgaria, King Boris, speaking on October 29 at the opening of the *Sobranje*, emphasized the complete readiness of every Bulgarian to defend the independence of his country, while at the same time stressing the cordiality of Bulgarian relations with Germany and Italy as well as with Yugoslavia and Turkey. Russian comment remained reticent, however the Greek Minister in Moscow saw Vyshinsky, Vice-Commissar of Foreign Affairs, on October 28. *Keesing's Contemporary Archives*, Vol. No. IV, p. 4312.

14. *Ibid.;* For the text of this treaty, see, appendix in, Selim Deringil, *Turkish Foreign Policy During the Second World War.*

15. *Keesing's Contemporary Archives,* Vol. No. IV, 1940–1943, pp. 4402; 4420, respectively.

16. For an impression of the mobilization of the Turkish Army, see, Cemal Madanoğlu, *Anılar* (Memoirs) 1911–1933, (İstanbul: Evrim Yayınevi, 1982), pp. 293–295.

17. Upon this incident, Molotov handed the German Ambassador a memorandum "deploring" the German move and warning Berlin that it could not count on the Kremlin's support on this issue. Andre Fontaine, *History of the Cold War,* (NY: Vintage Books, 1970), pp. 147–148.

18. Şevket Süreyya Aydemir, *İkinci Adam* (Second Man) Vol. II, 1938–1950, (İstanbul: Remzi Kitabevi, 7th ed., 1999), pp. 179–180; Kamuran Gürün, *Türk-Sovyet İlişkileri* (Turco-Soviet Relations) *(1920–1953),* (Ankara: TTK Basımevi, 1991), p. 239.

19. *"Communiqué,* dated March 24, 1941." *The MFA Archives.*

20. *"Communiqué,* dated March 1, 1941." *Ibid.*

21. "The Report of Turkish Ambassador to Berlin Hüsrev Gerede dated March 17, 1941 to the MFA," in Hüsrev Gerede, *Harb İçinde Almanya* (Germany At War), (İstanbul: ABC Ajansı Yayınları, 1994), pp. 184–185. See also, Johannes Glasneck, *Türkei im Deutsch-Angloamerikanischen Spannungsfeld,* Berlin 1968, trans. Arif Gelen, *Türkiye'de Faşist Alman Propagandası,* (Ankara: Onur Yayınları, 1970), pp. 144–145.

22. *Ibid.,* pp. 145–146.

23. Cordell Hull, *The Memoirs of Cordell Hull,* Vol. II, (NY: The Macmillan Company, 1948), p. 929. Subsequently, Hull asked the Bulgarian Minister in Washington to come to the State Department, where he was given the substance of the cables to the Turkish and Yugoslav Governments. As mentioned above, however, a few weeks later on March 1, Bulgaria signed the Axis pact and German forces began immediately to occupy that country, and to move the Greek border.

24. *Ibid.*

25. *Ibid.,* p. 930.

26. *Keesing's Contemporary Archives,* Vol. No. IV, p. 4535.

27. *Ibid.*

28. Martin Kolinsky, *Britain's War in the Middle East,* (London: MacMillan Press Ltd., 1999), p. 150; "Minutes of a Conference on the Situation in Yugoslavia," March 27, 1941 and Führer's Directives No. 25, March 27, and 26; April 3: "Co-operation With Our Allies in the Balkans," in *Documents on German Foreign Policy,* Vol. XII, Doc. No. 217, pp. 372–375 and 440–442.

29. When Kinahan Cornwallis, the new British Ambassador to Baghdad, told Al-Gaylani towards the end of the month that more troops were being dispatched to Basra, the former insisted that those previously disembarked had

to leave. He, in fact, *"had already informed the Italian minister that they were going to challenge the British and requested Axis military and financial support."* Martin Kolinsky, *Britain's War.* . . , pp. 156-157.

30. *Ibid.,* p. 157.

31. Ş. Süreyya Aydemir, *İkinci Adam,* Vol. II., pp. 183-184.

32. Martin Kolinsky, *Britain's War.* . . , p. 160.

33. For the text of the treaty which was signed in Turkish and German languages, see, "Türkiye Cumhuriyeti ile Alman Reich'i Arasında Andlaşma," in İsmail Soysal, *Türkiye'nin Dış Münasebetleriyle İlgili Başlıca Siyasi Andlaşmaları,* (Ankara: Türkiye İş Bankası Kültür Yayınları, TTK Basımevi, 1965), pp. 293-294; Hüsrev Gerede, *Harb İçinde Almanya,* p. 212.

It is another fact that *"countries, like Czechoslovakia and Poland who refused to deal with Hitler and put their reliance solely on British power paid a heavy price in doing so. Turkey was very sensible in what it did."* The present writer thanks to Pat Walsh for his remarks.

34. Gül İnanç, "The Politics of 'Active Neutrality' on the Eve of a New World Order: The Case of Turkish Chrome Sales during the Second World War," in *Middle Eastern Studies,* Vol. 42, No.6, November 2006, pp. 908-909.

35. Johannes Glasneck, *Türkiye'de.* . . , pp. 156-157.

36. *Ibid.,* 158. The present writer thanks Pat Walsh who shared his view that *"this was a clear attempt to engage Turkey in the war through the fostering of irredentist designs in the Caucasus. Turkey sensibly ignored this attempt probably realising the disastrous effects it had had on countries that were lured into the first World War on this basis (Italy/Tyrol, Greece/Anatolia)."*

37. For an interesting account of Saraçoğlu-Knatchbull-Hugessen talks, see, Barry Rubin, *İstanbul Intrigues,* (NY: McGraw-Hill Publishing Co., 1989), pp. 45-47.

38. *Ibid.,* 159. Meanwhile, on August 10, 1941, Britain and the SU communicated to the Turkish Government that they never had claims on the Straits while the Kremlin further expressed that in view of the German propaganda, it saw a necessity to repeat its assurance which it had lastly expressed in the Communiqué dated March 24, 1941 that the SU had no claims on the Turkish territory and the Straits. Ernst Jack, P. Kuturman (trans.), *Yükselen Hilal* (Rising Crescent), (İstanbul: Cumhuriyet Matbaası, 1946), pp. 273-274; Yüksel İnan, *Türk Boğazlarının Siyasal ve Hukuksal Rejimi* (The Political and Legal Regime of the Turkish Straits), (Ankara: Turhan Kitabevi, 1995), p. 104.

39. From Prime Minister Şükrü Saraçoğlu's speech in TGNA on his Government's programme on July 9, 1942. http://www.tbmm.gov.tr/hukumetler/HP13.htm

40. *Ibid.*

41. Winston S. Churchill, *The Grand Alliance (The Second World War, Vol. III),* Boston: Houghton Mifflin Company, 1950), p. 444.

42. F. C. Jones, *Japan's New Order in Asia, 1937-1945*, (NY: Oxford University Press, 1954), pp. 242-246.

43. For the statement of the Japanese Government and a part of Secretary Hull's answer to Nomura, see, Michael H. Hunt, *Crises in U.S. Foreign Policy*, (NY: Yale University Press, 1996), pp. 109-110.

44. *Ibid.*, p. 111.

45. The signatories in order were the US, the UK, the USSR, China, Australia, Belgium, Canada, Costa Rica, Cuba, Czechoslovakia, Dominican Republic, El Salvador, Greece, Guatemala, Haiti, Honduras, India, Luxemburg, Netherlands, New Zealand, Nicaragua, Norway, Panama, Poland, Union of South Africa and Yugoslavia. Subsequent signatories were Bolivia, Brazil, Chile, Colombia, Ecuador, Egypt, Ethiopia, France, Iran, Iraq, Lebanon, Liberia, Mexico, Paraguay, Peru, Philippines, Saudi Arabia, Syria, Turkey, Uruguay and Venezuela. All of these governments declared war against one or more of the Axis powers.

46. Winston S. Churchill, *The Hinge of Fate (The Second World War)*, Vol. IV, (Boston: Houghton Mifflin Company, 1950), p. 327.

47. For an interesting account of this declared policy and its repercussions see, H.W. Baldwin, *Great Mistakes of the War*, (NY: Harper & Row Publishers, 1950), pp. 683-691; Anne Armstrong, *Unconditional Surrender: The Impact of the Casablanca Policy on World War II*, (New Brunswick: Rutgers University Press, 1961).

48. Chester Wilmot, *The Struggle For Europe*, (NY: Harper & Brothers, 1952), p. 714. See also, Captain Russell Grenfell, *Unconditional Hatred German War Guilt and the Future of Europe*, (NY: The Devin-Adair Company, 1958).

49. For this text and a further analysis of the issue, see, H.L. Stimson and McGeorge Bundy, *On Active Service in Peace and War* (NY: Harper & Row Publishers, 1948), pp. 569-582.

50. Roosevelt had also promised Chiang Kai-shek that an amphibious operation would be launched from India against southern Burma, to be synchronized with a land campaign from China. This plan, coded Operation ANAKIM, however was abandoned after Tehran because of the decision to shift the center of gravity of war to the cross-channel operation, named OVERLORD. Julius W. Pratt, *A History of United States Foreign Policy*, (NJ:Prentice-Hall Inc., 2nd ed. 1965), p. 426.

51. Yücel Güçlü, *"Eminence Grise of the. . . ,"* pp. 98; 100-101.

52. *Ibid.*, pp. 101-102.

53. F. Cemal Erkin, *Dışişlerinde 34 Yıl* (34 Years in the MFA), Vol. I., (Ankara: Türk Tarih Kurumu Yayınları, 1987), pp. 135-139 *passim*.

54. Cited in, Edward Weisband, *Turkish Foreign Policy 1943-1945*, 198-199, see note (23) on p. 199 as well.

55. Cited in *ibid*.

56. Valentin Berezhkov was a diplomat of the Soviet Delegation at Tehran Conference who had witnessed all sessions and other occasions of the leaders of the Big Three.

57. Valentin Berezhkov (Trans. Hasan Ali Ediz), *Tahran 1943*, (Ankara: Bilgi Yayınevi, 1970), p. 143.

58. *FRUS, The Conferences at Cairo and Tehran*, p. 505. On the contrary, Küçük argued that at Tehran, the Big Three had agreed that Turkey would enter the war, and delivered Churchill the mission of informing Allies' decision to İnönü. Along the lines of a study by A.I. Ganusets, named *Turyetskiy Vapros na Tegaranskoy Konferentsii*, Küçük stated that Stalin told his counterparts Turkish entry into war was a political and military question and that Turkey in alliance with Britain and continued friendly relations with the SU and the US, should stop changing sides between them and Germany. Yalçın Küçük, *Türkiye Üzerine Tezler* (Theses on Turkey) Cilt 2 (Vol. 2), (İstanbul: Tekin Yayınevi, 1989), pp. 273-276.

59. Edward Weisband, *Turkish Foreign Policy 1943-1945*, (NY: Princeton University Press, 1973), pp. 199-200. Stalin did not neglect to imply that he was merely interested to discuss the issue on general terms. In his turn, Churchill was still cautious while trying to bring Turkey into the war and at the same time was pleased to send a message to the Turks that their refusal to accept would have serious political and territorial consequences regarding the future status of the Straits after the war.

60. Arthur Bryant, *Triumph in the West*, (London: Collins, 1959), p. 294.

61. Explicitly, the timing of the conference was quite unfortunate for the Western Allies, coming as it did just after the set back they had suffered in the Ardennes, while the Red Army was winning continuous victories in Poland. See also, Chester Wilmot, *The Struggle. . .* , p. 12.

62. Kenneth W. Thomson, *Cold War Theories Vol. I: World Polarization 1943-1953*, (Baton Rouge: Louisiana State University Press, 1981), p. 29.

63. Fred W. Wellborn, *Diplomatic History of the United States*, (NJ: Littlefield, Adams & Co., 1961), pp. 359-360.

Evidently, discussions at Yalta were post-war oriented and to some extent, decisions were made in euphoria of the Big Three when V-E (Victory in Europe) Day was so close. For a study which admitted the criticisms directed at Yalta, but attempted to provide explanations, see, Julius W. Pratt, *A History of the United States Foreign Policy*, (NY: Prentice-Hall, 1955), pp. 428-432.

64. Graham Ross, *Great Powers and the Decline of the European States System 1914-1945*, (NY: Longman, 1991), p. 143.

65. Doğan Avcıoğlu, *Milli Kurtuluş Tarihi 1838'den 1995'e* (History of the National Liberation from 1838 to 1995), Cilt 4 (Vol. 4), (İstanbul: Tekin Yayınevi, 1997), pp. 1567-1568. For a similar hypothesis claiming that Soviet threats towards Turkey were merely designed stories by the Turkish officials who had deliberately chosen to incorporate Turkish politics into the US foreign

policy, see, Yalçın Küçük, *Türkiye Üzerine Tezler 1908-1998,* Vol. 2, pp. 280-286.

66. *Yalta Papers, Fifth Plenary Meeting, February 8, 1945, Bohlen Minutes,* Cited in, Weisband, Edward, *Turkish Foreign Policy 1943-1945,* pp. 299-300. See also, *FRUS, The Conferences at Malta and Yalta,* 1945, (Washington D.C.. USGPO, 1955), pp. 771-82.

67. Kamuran Gürün, *Türk-Sovyet İlişkileri,* pp. 276-277.

68. *Ibid.* See also, Hüsrev Gerede, *Harb İçinde Almanya 1939-1942,* pp. 347-348.

69. For this debate and telegram see, Attila İlhan, *O Karanlıkta Biz* (We, In That Darkness), (İstanbul: Bilgi Yayınevi, 1996), pp. 311-317; 331-332.

70. This treaty between Turkey and the SU, named as the Treaty of Friendship, Treaty of Friendship and Neutrality or the Treaty of Non-aggression and Neutrality throughout the relevant literature, referred to one single document which is the December, 17, 1925 Treaty between Turkey and the SU. For a detailed discussion of the issue, including the prior agreements of March, 16, 1921 Moscow and October, 13, 1921 Kars, between Turkey and the SU. See, Kamuran Gürün, *Türk-Sovyet İlişkileri (1920-1953)* (Turco-Soviet Relations 1920-1953), (Ankara: Türk Tarih Kurumu Basımevi, 1991), pp. 63-71; 109-118, respectively.

71. Uğur Mumcu, *40'ların Cadı* Kazanı (Witch's Cauldron of 40s), (Ankara: Um:ag Vakfı Yayınları, 1998), pp. 46-47. See this work for a detailed examination of the issue regarding the cases of both leftist and rightist extremists. See also, Günay Göksu Özdoğan, "II. Dünya Savaşı Yıllarındaki Türk-Alman İlişkilerinde İç ve Dış Politika Aracı Olarak Pan-Türkizm" (Pan-Turkism As An Instrument of Domestic and Foreign Policy in Turkish-German Relations During the Years of WW II), in Faruk Sönmezoğlu, 1st edt., *Türk Dış Politikasının Analizi* (Analysis of Turkish Foreign Policy), (İstanbul: Der Yayınları, 1994), pp. 357-372.

72. Kamuran Gürün, *Türk-Sovyet İlişkileri (1920-1953),* pp. 263-264. Molotov's statement included that the SU would not interfere in the domestic affairs of Roumania and not attempt to change its political and social regime. Besides, the SU had no claims of territory and the Soviet military presence in Roumania was merely for reasons of expelling German forces from this country.

73. The prolonged effects of this strong antipathy towards Russia should not be underestimated with a view to Turkish Cabinets formed under his Premiership between July 9, 1942- March 9, 1943 and March 9, 1943-August 7, 1946. For an interesting account of Saraçoğlu's visit, including top level bureaucrats of the Ministry of Foreign Affairs such as Assistant Secretary General Cevat Açıkalın, Director General of Political Affairs F. Cemal Erkin (later Ambassador to Washington), see, Mahmut Dikerdem, *Hariciye Çarkı* (Wheel of Ministry of Foreign Affairs), (İstanbul: Cem Yayınevi, 1989), pp. 37-43,

passim. For a detailed research on the governments of Turkey, see, Türker Sanal, *Türkiye'nin Hükümetleri* (Governments of Turkey), (Ankara: Sim Matbaacılık, 1997).

74. "Rus Elçisi Aralof'un Söylevine Cevap—Answer to the Speech of Russian Envoy Aralov, 3.3.1922," Sadi Borak, *Atatürk'ün Resmi Yayınlara Girmemiş Söylev, Demeç, Yazışma ve Söyleşileri* (Atatürk's Speeches, Statements, Correspondences and Interviews Which Were Not Officially Published)— (İstanbul: Kaynak Yayınları, 1997), p. 143.

75. For the telegram dated August 27, 1942, sent by F. Von Papen, the German Ambassador to Ankara, to Berlin see, Ö. Andaç Uğurlu, (ed.), *2. Dünya Savaşı'nda Türkiye Üzerine Gizli Pazarlıklar* (Secret Bargainings Over Turkey During the Second World War) (1939-1944), (İstanbul: Örgün Yayınevi, 2003), pp. 218-220, a book based on the Soviet sources—and as such, presumably including correspondence of the Nazis captured by the Soviets.

76. *Ibid.*, p. 262.

77. Mahmut Dikerdem, *Hariciye Çarkı*, p. 42.

78. F.O. 371 R9447/7/44. Knatchbull-Hugessen (Ankara) to F.O., 15 June 1944. Cited in, Yücel Güçlü, *Eminence Grise of the Turkish Foreign Service: Numan Menemencioğlu*, (Ankara: Ministry of Foreign Affairs, 2002), p. 104.

79. *Ibid.*

80. Kamuran Gürün, *Türk-Sovyet İlişkileri. . .*, pp. 264-265.

81. Edward Weisband, *Turkish Foreign Policy. . .*, p. 277.

82. *Ibid.*, p. 278. Interestingly, Necmettin Sadak, a journalist who would be appointed as the MFA a few years later in September 1947, showed a relative calmness in his column in *Akşam* explaining that the SU was acting in consonance with the British and the Americans and that the invasion merely suggested that the Kremlin intended to treat all defeated Axis countries alike. See, *Ayın Tarihi*, Vol. 130, September 1944, pp. 269-270. However, most of the voices in the press pronounced a heavy criticism of the Russian invasion of Bulgaria.

83. "Telegram of the Turkish Embassy in London to the MFA, February 23, 1945." *The MFA Archives.*

84. *Resmi Gazete* (Official Gazette), February 24, 1945, No: 5940, p. 1. Turkey joined the UN on October 24, 1945.

85. *Ibid.*

86. As told by George Harris in my interview with him.

87. "Telegram of the Turkish Embassy in Washington to the, MFA March 5, 1945." *The MFA Archives.*

88. Kamuran Gürün, *Savaşan Dünya ve Türkiye: 3, Savaş 1939-1945* (The World in Fight and Turkey: 3, War 1939-1945), (İstanbul: Tekin Yayınevi, 2000), p. 646.

89. İsmail Soysal, *Soğuk Savaş Kronolojisi ve Türkiye*, (İstanbul: İsis Yayımcılık, 1997), pp. 3-4.

90. *FRUS*, 1945, Vol. VIII, pp. 1221-1223.

91. Mahmut Dikerdem, *Hariciye Çarkı*, p. 80. Dikerdem argued that to complete his "stillborn plan," İnönü had chosen his "trustworthy man" S. Sarper. İnönü had quickly promoted Sarper to the General Directorate of Press post when he was Head of Department in the MFA and nominated him to Moscow as Ambassador In October, 1994. When İnönü Instructed Sarper without consulting the MFA to express Turkey's will to conclude an alliance with the SU, Minister of Foreign Affairs Hasan Saka was in San Francisco at the inauguration meeting of the United Nations while General Secretary Cevat Açıkalın was in London to attend another meeting, and the Minister of State, Nurullah Esat Sümer was the acting Minister of Foreign Affairs. *Ibid.*

92. Kamuran Gürün, *Savaşan Dünya.* . . , p. 649.

93. İlhan Akant, *Moskova Otel National 333 Numaralı Oda*, (Hotel National Moscow Room 333), (İstanbul: Milliyet Yayınları, 1990), pp.113-114. Gül İnanç uses the same quotation in her article "Bu Yazının Mahrem Tutulmasına İtina Edilecektir: US Missouri Zırhlısının İstanbul Ziyareti ve Soğuk Savaş Diplomasisinde Türkiye, 1946" (This is a Strictly Confidential Message: The Visit of USS Missouri Vessel to İstanbul and Turkey in Cold War Diplomacy, 1946) in *Toplumsal Tarih Dergisi*, Vol. 191, (İstanbul: Tarih Vakfı Yurt Yayınları, Kasım 2009), pp. 54-62.
İnanç also refers to the book of Feridun Cemal Erkin, *Türk- Sovyet İlişkileri ve Boğazlar Meselesi* (p. 255) where Erkin calls this encounter as the "Turco-Russian Duel."

94. Kamuran Gürün, *Türk-Sovyet İlişkileri 1920-1953*, p. 284.

95. *Ibid.*, p. 288.

96. Mahmut Dikerdem, *Hariciye Çarkı*, 81. See also, Joseph C. Grew. *Turbulent Era: A Diplomatic Record of Forty Years 1904-1945*, Vol. II, (Cambridge, Massachusetts: The Riverside Press, 1953), pp. 1468-1470.

97. Cited in, Kamuran Gürün, *Türk-Sovyet İlişkileri 1920-1953*, p. 289.

98. *Ibid.*

99. Cited in, *ibid.*, p. 290.

100. Mahmut Dikerdem, *Hariciye Çarkı*, p. 88. Before concluding this part of our discussion, it should be reiterated that Dikerdem was a declared socialist too. Thus, it would be right to approach his viewpoints with a view to this prism of his world view. As for his statements, one might accept that Dikerdem's statements should pertain to the year 1945 only, excluding the period of exchange of Notes between Ankara and Moscow which will be discussed later.

101. "Telegram of the Embassy in London to the MFA, February 23, 1945." *The MFA Archives*.

102. Doğan Avcıoğlu, *Milli Kurtuluş Tarihi,* Vol. IV, pp. 1578-1580.

103. It is simply because basing any statement on the knowledge of what happened in history is insufficient to reach an analytical explanation i.e. we know Sarper's nomination and further promotions so that direct relations can

be established between them and turned into statements. With these reservations, see, Yalçın Küçük, *Türkiye Üzerine Tezler*, Vol. 2, pp. 342–343. Two years later Sarper was appointed Ambassador to Rome. In 1947, Sarper was designated Ambassador and Permanent Representative of Turkey at the United Nations in New York. For ten years he remained in that post. Then he was transferred to the NATO HQ in Paris as Turkey's Permanent Representative. After serving two years in Paris, Sarper was appointed Secretary General of the MFA. Following the military takeover of May 27, 1960, he was appointed by General Cemal Gürsel as the MFA, a post which he held until his resignation on March 15, 1962. Sarper pursued a political career from then on. See. Metin Tamkoç, *The Warrior Diplomats*, (Utah: University of Utah Press, 1976), pp. 354–355.

104. *FRUS*, 1945, Vol. VIII, p. 1234.

105. *Ibid.*, pp. 1234–1235.

106. *Ibid.*, p. 1236.

107. *Ibid.* Bilal Şimşir, names Tevfik Rüştü Aras as the unchanging Minister of Foreign Affairs of the Atatürk era, who remained in charge of the Repuplic's diplomacy for over 13 years. Şimşir considers the term of Aras as period of consolidation of the foreign policy of the new Turkey, while going through various diplomatic incidents. Bilal Şimşir, *Bizim Diplomatlar* (Our Diplomats), p. 270. This expressions which we know now underscored that Aras who had assumed special responsibilities in perpetuating the Turco–Soviet relations was not regarded relevant any more in changing times, yet, he was then started to be perceived as "communist."

108. Joseph C. Grew, *Turbulent Era*, Vol. II, pp. 1469–1470.

109. Harry N. Howard, *Turkey, the Straits and U.S. Policy*, (Baltimore: The Johns Hopkins University, 1974), pp. 219–220.

110. Joseph C. Grew, *Turbulent Era*, Vol. II, p. 1471.

111. *Ibid.*

112. Grew stated that Baydur was clearly referring to the Grew–Balfour conversation in which the US Secretary of State had said that they would prefer to delay action on this matter until after the San Francisco Conference and that if action were to be taken there would be some time between the close of the conference and the meeting of the Big Three. Grew also stated that Balfour then called on him a few moments after his conversation with Ertegün and definitely corroborated his understanding of what he had said to him. Balfour told Grew that he had reported his position accurately to his government and that no indication had been given of any commitment whatever on Grew's part. *Ibid.*, p. 1472.

113. *Ibid.*, p. 1473.

114. Graham Ross, *The Great Powers and the Decline of the European States System 1914–1945*, p. 145.

115. James F. Byrnes, *Speaking Frankly*, (NY: Harper & Bros., 1947), pp. 77-78.

116. Harry N. Howard, *Turkey, the Straits and U.S. Policy*, 226; Michael Dockrill, *The Cold War 1945-1963*, (NJ: Humanities Press, 1988), p. 28.

117. Michael Dockrill, *The Cold War 1945-1963*, (NJ: Humanities Press, 1988), p. 28.

118. Graham Ross, *The Great Powers and . . .* , p. 46.

119. Zhadanov was a party activist and theoretician. See also, Michael Dockrill, *The Cold War 1945-1963*, p. 32.

120. The pressures of war had led to the rise of the Red Army, which had won much prestige in the SU as a result of its victories over Germany. Again, the rise of the heavy industry sector under G.M. Malenkov, which had been expanded enormously to meet the needs of the war, and of the political police (NKVD/KGB) under L. B. Beria, had accumulated vast powers during the war. See also, *ibid.*, pp. 31-32.

121. *Ibid.*, p. 32.

122. *Ibid.*, pp. 31-32.

123. George McGhee, *The US-Turkish-NATO Middle East Connection*, (London: The MacMillan Press, 1990), p. 14.

124. Martin Kolinsky, *Britain's War. . .* , p. 162.

Chapter 4

Tensions Revealed: Prelude to War Cold and Hot, and the Beginnings of the Turkish Quest for Security (1946)

Foreign influences at work would to most of Europe intensify the fact that the time for looking Turkey as the natural prey of the Powers is not passed.[1]

This chapter discusses the emergence of the crisis in Turkish Soviet relations in 1946 and Ankara's increasing security concerns throughout the same year. In this context, it is first explained that at a time when Turkey, Greece and Iran were under the pressure of Kremlin, ambivalence prevailed in Washington as to what extent and with which it could counterbalance the Soviet moves and which policy it should follow in regard to these countries. Subsequently, the chapter focuses on the main events of the period under review, the visit of *USS Missouri* and the Turkish–Soviet exchange of Notes (concerning the Soviet demands for a rearrangement of the Straits regime and Ankara's rejection of these demands), being the most important ones.

"In the Near East Things Are Not Always What They Seem"[2]

By the turn of 1946, the Soviet press and radios had intensified their broadcasting campaign against Turkey. The broadcasts propagandized that Turkey had served Axis interest during the war, that the Turkish government had fascist tendencies; and, in addition to Georgians, the Armenians had also legitimate rights over Turkey. Turkey's reply came on January 6, when Turkish Premiere Saraçoğlu explained in his statement to the press in Ankara that Soviet Russia had no rights over Kars and Ardahan. Those provinces had been ceded to Russia at the end of the 1878 Berlin Agreement, for the first time in history, in exchange for a huge war indemnity—an amount which couldn't be met—but were returned to Turkey following WW I through a plebiscite as well by the Brest–Litovsk (1918) Treaty, reiterated by the subsequent Moscow and Kars Agreements (1921).

Addressing the claims of the Georgian professors on the ownership of the Blacksea coastal strip till Giresun province and their demand for its returning to Georgia which was first published in a Georgian journal on December 20, 1945 and subsequently given place in Soviet radio and press,[3] Saraçoğlu pointed out that throughout those claimed areas Turks were in the majority and these claims resembled Hitler's well-known "living space" theory. In this context, Saraçoğlu also explained his gratitude to the world press that supported Turkey's rightful cause.

The Soviet pressure mounted when a few days later the Soviet Embassy in Ankara announced that those Armenians who wished to return Soviet Armenia could enroll in the list prepared by the Soviet General Consulate in İstanbul.[4]

As Davison pointed out:

> The eastern or "Armenian" provinces of Turkey since 1945 again the object of Russian claims, have long been one of the sensitive spots occupying the attention of European statesmen. In the two years before Sarajevo the question of the future of this region took on the proportions of a diplomatic crisis. When the question arose in serious form at the end of 1912, the Turks had just lost almost all their European territories in disastrous defeat at the hands of the Balkan states. Statesmen and journalists began to wonder whether Asiatic Turkey would hold together.[5]

Before ending the discussion here, it is interesting to note that in works as new as Hilmar Kaiser's *Regional Resistance to Central Government Policies*, the incidents of 1915 was not assessed as amounting to "genocide." Thus, "the notion of an empire-wide genocide of Ottoman Armenians perpetrated by a unified CUP (ruling Committee of Union and Progress government) is untenable" and "this kind of thinking needs to be revised and freed of claims that are based on imagination rather than evidence."[6] This being the case the introduction of this term in later decades to comment on this historical episode appears to have been made on dubious grounds while from the SU—again interestingly—to the US, the issue has been brought to agenda on different grounds to date.

Turning back to the situation in 1946, a few days before Saraçoğlu's press conference, the Turkish Minister of Foreign Affairs, H. Saka had arrived in London on January 3 to attend the first session of the UN General Assembly which was to be held on January 10. Saka interviewed allied and friendly statesmen for an entire week. While these deliberations were going on, Turkey's participation in the founding organizations of the West was increasing through its adherence to another major agreement. In this framework, on January 4, 1946, Turkey, Belgium, Denmark, France, Greece, Luxemburg, Netherlands, Norway, Britain and the US signed the Agreement of European Coal Organisation in London.[7] Subsequently, on his way back to Ankara, Saka paid a visit to Paris where he held similar talks with his interlocutors.

Meanwhile, the watershed in US–Soviet relations came on February 9, when Stalin delivered another major speech and described the causes of war. In this context, the war, he said, had been caused not by Hitler but by the workings of the Capitalist system: ". . . Marxists have declared more than once the capitalist system of world economy harbors elements of general crises and armed conflicts and that, hence, the development of world capitalism in our time proceeds not in the form of smooth and even progress but through crises and military catastrophes."[8] If Stalin's analysis was correct, there was no essential difference between Germany and the Soviet Union's allies in the war against Germany. A new war was inevitable sooner or later, "and the Soviet Union was experiencing armistice, not a true peace."[9]

On February 22, George Kennan sent his telegram to express his views that were already known and widely accepted within the US Government. Kennan's cable is regarded as one of the landmark documents of the early Cold War period.[10] As such, it mostly remained however, unchallenged too. In it, Kennan stated that:

. . . Wherever it is considered timely and promising, efforts will be made to advance official limits of Soviet power. For the moment, these efforts are restricted to certain neighboring points conceived of here as being of immediate strategic necessity, such as northern Iran,

Turkey, . . . a "friendly" Persian Government might be asked to grant
Russia a port on Persian Gulf. . .[11]

. . .Where individual governments stand in path of Soviet purposes
pressure will be brought for their removal from office. This can happen where governments directly oppose Soviet foreign policy aims
(Turkey, Iran), . . .[12]

Indeed, the crisis over Iran, indicated the way the Cold War was to
be conducted. The country had been occupied by Britain and the Soviets
since 1941 and both countries had agreed to withdraw by 2 March 1946.
However, even before the war ended, the Soviets tried to exact an oil
concession from the Iranian Government. Failing to realize this, the Soviets began to encourage the northern province of Azerbaijan to establish
its independence under their influence. The Soviets backed concurrently
the leftist Tudeh (Masses) party to spread its organization in the country.
However, the Soviet attempts reached a climax in January following the
establishment of a Soviet sponsored "Mahabad Republic" of Kurds. The
republic was headed by Ghazi Muhammad and Mullah Mustafa Barzani,
the leader of Barzani clan-led uprising, who had fled Iraq following his
rebellion. Barzani then undertook the defense ministry with his 3,000
militia.[13]

In its turn, the Truman administration aimed to counter the Soviet
aims. American support was given to the Shah's decision to send troops
to the northern border. The issue had come before the Security Council
between January 28–30, 1946, and the US Secretary of State, Byrnes,
had also seized the chance to publicly condemn the Kremlin since then.
After a deadline for the withdrawal of Soviet forces passed in March
1946, the US Embassy in Moscow issued Notes of protest to the Kremlin.

Explicitly, once Germany was defeated, the Soviets had shifted to
reevalaute their position over the lands they began to control in Europe
and ceased to cooperate with their former Allies. As a result of the war,
the SU had extensive territories under its sphere of influence. Equally
significant was the fact that the governments set up, after Poland,
Roumania, Bulgaria, Hungary and Czechoslovakia were liberated by the
Red Army were under the influence of the Soviets. It was in these circumstances that Winston Churchill, on a visit to America early on 5
March 1946 said: "From Stettin in the Baltic to Trieste in the Adriatic,
an Iron Curtain has descended. . . . Behind that line lie all the capitals of
the States of Central and Eastern Europe—all are subject in one form or

another not only to Soviet influence but to a very high and increasing measure of control from Moscow."[14]

Turning back to the Soviet onslaught in Iran, exchanges of grave Notes between Soviet Ambassador Andrei Gromyko and Byrnes regarding the situation in this country followed. Gromyko stated that "A murky wave of anti-Soviet feeling at once rose up and a question was tabled at the Security Council—which was what Washington wanted. I received the following instructions from Moscow: 'If this question is tabled, say that our troops are being kept in Iran because of unforeseeable circumstances.' When the initiators of the discussion heard our explanation, they asked 'would you mind telling us, please, just what these unforeseeable circumstances are?' I replied, 'Unforeseeable circumstances are unforeseeable precisely because you can't foresee them.'" Gromyko also explained the presence of Soviet troops in Iran in connection with the continued existence of British bases in Iraq and India, and the large number of US bases around the perimeter of Soviet frontier.[15]

On March 6, Washington issued a strong protest to Moscow on the basis of the US–UK–Soviet tripartite treaty of 1942. However, the situation continued to deteriorate. The US representative in Tabriz reported that by March 19, a minimum of 235 Soviet tanks and 3500 trucks had passed into Azerbaijan through the railhead in Tabriz. Concurrently, the Soviet troops appeared to be strategically heading in the direction of Turkey and Iraq. At this juncture, Iran called upon the UN for assistance and intense negotiations ensued, which shortly afterwards culminated in a worldwide support to Iran. Then the SU agreed to withdraw its forces, but quickly created a local militia "stiffened by a cadre of Soviet 'volunteers' numbering about 800"[16] as well. Following the Soviet withdrawal, the Tabriz government created in Iranian Azerbaijan and the Kurdish republic was completely dissolved. Ghazi Muhammad, the President of the Kurdish republic was executed on March 31, while Barzani passed to the SU.[17]

The Russian troops withdrew in April, but the Majlis (Iranian Parliament) repudiated the joint oil company. Tension increased again as the Tudeh Party demanded an election under its control. Acheson stated that in his talks with the Iranian Ambassador Hussein Ala—who wanted the US to take the initiative in reopening the Iranian case in the Security Council and in having it supervise elections in Azerbaijan—in October 1945, he had said to him and asked the US Ambassador George Allen in Tehran to tell the Iranian Prime Minister Qavam that the US would not act but only in support of the Iranian Government. He asserted that it seemed a mistake to hold elections until Iranian authority was established in the province and it was only then the UN observation could be useful.[18] Then, the US sent a favorable response to the Iranian Government's request for strong support should the SU object to Iranian forces entering Azerbaijan. When the troops arrived, the separatist regime collapsed and shortly afterwards the whole province was reacquired. In May of that year, when the Soviet forces completed their withdrawal from Iran, the crisis was over.

The Soviets' withdrawal from Azerbaijan, however, was not acclaimed as a signal that the Kremlin had accepted a more reasonable attitude towards Turkey or that it had abandoned its ambitions to encroach on Iranian and Turkish sovereignty.[19] W. Bedell Smith, the US Ambassador to Moscow, suggested that Russia's determination to gain a foothold in the region reflected the Soviets' conviction that their security interests were at stake and that they desired to gain independent access to the Mediterranean and the Arab world by severing the British Empire's "jugular" at Suez. Smith stressed that if the SU portrayed a friendly face to Turkey, it would be a purely tactical and temporary action, "as the Russians since the time of czars had linked advances in the Near East to their domination (or 'liberation,' in Soviet parlance) of Turkey."[20]

As for Turkey's foreign policy towards the Middle East, Ankara was interested in developing its relations with the countries of the region through completing a series of basic treaties. In this context, the Treaty of Friendship and Good Neighbourhood between Turkey and Iraq was signed on March 29, 1946 in Ankara by the MFA Saka and the Secretary General Erkin and the President of the Iraqi House of Representatives, Nuri As-Said, and the Iraqi Regent Prince Abdullah. In fact, the Turco–Iraqi treaty was more than an expression of a wish to perpetuate friendly relations between the two countries. The treaty was concluded to last for an indefinite period and included six additional protocols envisaging a broad range of cooperation which pertained to the following: a) the regulation of the waters of Euphrates and Tigris, b) mutual assistance on the issues of security, c) education, training and cultural affairs, mailing, cable and telephone services, d) economic affairs and border controls.[21]

Having concluded an important framework treaty with Iraq, in Ankara there was still a sense of urgency for assuring the security of the country. To justify these concerns, a few days before the US decision to send military advisers to Iran, the Soviets also tried to bring pressure to bear on Turkey to permit Soviet troops to have bases near the Straits. Together with this, the Turkish provinces of Kars and Ardahan were also demanded by the SU—in a way in which different interpretations prevailed as will be further discussed—within the context of restoring the pre-WW I status quo. This incident reinforced the already strong suspicions of Washington. A special report prepared for President Truman by his White House aide, Clark Clifford, stated that "compromise and concessions are considered by the Soviets, to be evidence of weakness."[22] Here, it was also underlined that the US must avoid the error of 'appeasement' and should even be prepared to go to war if necessary to resist Stalin's ambitions for world conquest.[23] As will be explained below, in his turn, Truman decided to give a decisive response to Soviet strategic maneuvers.

The US Gunboat Diplomacy in the Mediterranean and its Aftermath

On November 11, 1944, the Turkish Ambassador to Washington, Mehmet Münir Ertegün died in Washington, not a very important event at a time when Allied forces were sweeping across France and Eastern Europe towards Germany and Berlin and Tokyo were approaching the imminent end. Sixteen months later, however, the Ambassador's remains were the "focus of world attention as the curtain went up on a classic act in the use of armed forces as a political instrument."[24]

In fact, towards the end of 1945, the Turkish Ambassador to Washington, Hüseyin Ragıp Baydur, had held some talks with the Department of State regarding the sending of the remains of the late Ambassador Ertegün, his predecessor. As he was informed a few weeks ago that the ashes of Philip Kerr, the British Ambassador to Washington who had passed away in 1942 would be sent to Britain, Baydur had cabled Ankara to get a permission to ask the same for late Ambassador Münir Ertegün who was buried in Arlington Cemetery.

Expectedly, Baydur was told that Washington was ready to send the remains of Ambassador Ertegün in a glorious way. When Ertegün had passed away, his family had requested to receive his remains. However, Washington had informed Ankara that due to ongoing war effort a war vessel could not be given this mission but a bulk carrier which they did not want to. It was thus suggested to postpone it until the war was over

when this could be done accordingly and in a glorious war. This suggestion was accepted by Ertegün's family.

Against this background, a day later than Winston Churchill's famous "Iron Curtain speech" in Fulton, on March 6, 1946, the Department of State announced that the late Ambassador Ertegün's remains
would be sent to Turkey aboard the battleship *USS Missouri*, visibly the
most powerful warship in the US Navy and the ship on board which
General Douglas MacArthur had recently accepted Japan's surrender. It
was also decided that the *Missouri* would be accompanied by two cruisers, *USS Providence* and *USS Power* during its mission. Between the
Ambassador's death and this announcement, not only had WW II ended,
the Cold War—as yet untitled—had begun. In addition to conflicts between Washington and the Kremlin over Poland, Germany and other
areas, the Kremlin had demanded from Ankara the cession of two provinces in the east and in the west, a base in the Straits.

İsmail Soysal stated this incident briefly as "America's famous battleship Missouri, accompanied by two destroyers, brought the body of
Turkey's Ambassador Münir Ertegün who had died in Washington to
İstanbul and handed to Turkish authorities with a ceremony on April 5,
1946."[25] Around the same issue, Dean Acheson, then Undersecretary of
State, noted that ". . . The USS Missouri was already at İstanbul, where
it had been sent earlier with the ashes of a former Turkish Ambassador."[26] Whereas, Küçük argued that, the Truman administration used
this occasion for power projection against the Soviets at a time tensions
were increasing in the region. He stated that, although Ertegün had died
almost two years earlier and had been buried in Washington, upon the
suggestions of his advisors, Truman decided to send Ertegün's body to
Turkey with such an objective in his mind.[27] Interestingly, *Missouri*'s
sail to the Mediterranean followed by the dispatch of aircraft carrier
Franklin D. Roosevelt to the area in August.[28] A different account of the
incident explained the Turkish perception of this visit as an indication of
the US' emerging independent course of action in the Middle East which
might serve to Turkish interests.[29]

Another explanation underscored that

> However, today, there is no suspicion that this American action was a
> demonstration against the Soviet Union. . . . As early as the end of
> 1945, US Secretary of Navy Forrestal had demanded the dispatch of a
> considerable US naval force to the Mediterranean in view of the un-

compromising attitude of the Soviet Union on the issue of Iran. Although President Truman approved this suggestion, Secretary of State Byrnes did not like it as he was cautious on not to instigate the Soviets. It appears that the dispatch of *Missouri* with the pretext of taking the remains of the Turkish Ambassador was the middle way found between the US Naval and State Departments and since it was stated on the day US Note was given to the Soviet authorities, it was likely to be agreed upon at the March 4 meeting of the US Government.[30]

In any case, the US' interest in showing its concerns in the region and the acknowledgement of Turkey for this gesture was evident. Meanwhile, the US Government had opted for advising the US press to not to give a meaning to the allocation of *Missouri* for the sending of the remains of the late Turkish Ambassador to Turkey other than an act of courtesy. Same request was conveyed to Ankara through Ambassador Baydur to ensure taking of similar measures to properly channel the press in Turkey. According to İnanç, Truman was still looking for a way to reach a compromise with Stalin.[31]

The *USS Missouri* and the two cruisers left New York on March 22, and arrived in İstanbul on April 5. On the same day an extra-ordinary welcoming ceremony with dozens of gun salutes for the visit from Turkish battleships was made. The ceremony was attended by the personal representative of Truman, A. Veddell, representative of the State Department, George Allen, Admiral Henry Hewitt and Rear Admiral Jules Cames who were in the US delegation and Ambassador Wilson, and the representatives of the President of TGNA, Prime Ministry and the MFA, respectively, MP Halit Bayrak, Cemal Yeşil and Ambassador Şevki Berker, Governor of İstanbul, Lütfi Kırdar, General Cahit Toydemir and Asım Tınaztepe.

The next day, the US delegation paid a visit to Ankara where they were received by President İnönü. Prime Minister Saraçoğlu who had then strongly turned against the Soviets praised the visit with strong words and said that "the youngest and the most perfect child of our old world America and the Americans, the flags of humanity, justice, freedom and civilization in their hand, are marching onwards establishing a great world of humanity of the United Nations with strong and unwavered steps."[32] Saraçoğlu also expressed that Turkey would take its place in the frontiers the US would form and remain next to them [the Americans] "to serve the great cause."[33] The Turkish Chief of the General Staff, Kazım Orbay expressed similar views and said that Turkey was aware of the noble meaning in the demonstration of friendship through the assignment of *Missouri,* a historical and one of the mightiest ships of the US Navy, to the mission of returning the body of Ambassador Ertegün.

It was the first time since the end of the war that American vessels were in Turkish waters. This, to some extent, proved that the US was ready to face any danger, not only in the Pacific, but in the waters of the Mediterranean as well which dominated European affairs.[34] George Harris stated that to the man on the street here at last was tangible proof that Turkey did not stand alone, despite the refusal of the American visitors to confirm openly that their mission was more than a mere courtesy call. Regarding the Turkish press, it hailed the US as the defender of "peace, right, justice, progress and prosperity."[35]

As for the commentaries of the leading newspapers, repercussions of this incident were quite positive at large. N. Nadi wrote in *Cumhuriyet* that "the people of İstanbul joyfully welcome Missouri which visits the free and blue waters of the free Straits for a few days from across the Atlantic and see the idealism that works to realize tomorrow's peaceful world in the mighty features of this greatest American battleship."[36] Another comment was made in *Vakit* which pointed out that the visit of the US vessels to İstanbul coincided with a turn of events around the Iranian question towards acquiring a character in accordance with the UN Charter:

> It would be right to consider this coincidence as an auspicious sign . . . the US might assign another ship in order to send Ertegün's body to Turkey . . . the dispatch of *Missouri*, the symbol of American victory in the Far Eastern war is enough to express that a distinguished meaning other than a mere demonstration of friendship exists. . . . It is unnecessary to conceal this additional and distinguished meaning with any policy consideration. On the contrary, it is in the good of humanity and international peace if this is understood by the world. . . . We can now believe that the Russian occupation forces will move out of the territory of Iran until May 6. . . . We find a relationship between the coming of *Missouri* vessel to Turkish waters and the turn of events around the Iranian question towards acquiring a character in accordance with the Charter of the UN. We have an intuition that a meaning exists in the coincidence of these two incidents indicating the victory of human rights and international peace.[37]

Considerable evidence suggests that no one missed the meaning of this demonstration of serious concern of the US about Middle Eastern developments. Washington had not subtly reminded the Soviets that the US was a great power and that it could project this power abroad, even to shores far distant. Whether the visit of *USS Missouri* and subsequent US actions deterred the SU from implementing any planned or potential aggressive acts towards Turkey will probably never be known. "What is clear is that no forceful Soviet actions followed the visit."[38] Besides, as an illustration of American support for Turkey vis-à-vis the SU, the visit of *USS Missouri* was well received and appreciated by the Government of Turkey, the Turkish press and by the public opinion at large. The US Ambassador Wilson stated that to the Turks the visit indicated that "the United States has now decided that its own interests in this area require it to oppose any effort by the USSR to destroy Turkey's independence and integrity."[39]

According to Blechman and Kaplan, the 1946 visit to Turkey by the *Missouri* and further displays of US military support for Ankara which culminated in the decline of Soviet pressures on Turkey was an example to discrete political use of the armed forces which contributed to the establishment of new international relationships, such that US interests were protected for decades. They pointed out that generally, skilled US diplomacy during incidents has typically borne fruit only after ambiguous US military commitments have been clarified by the movement of major military units. Their conclusion however, included that demonstrative uses of the military in some cases with very special circumstances, were often effective political instruments in the short them, and that effectiveness declined when situations were re-examined after long periods of time had elapsed.

Similarly, Blechman and Kaplan argued that in the absence of a prior US commitment, as in Korea in 1950 for example, the US might surmise that not only would China and the SU have gone further in their initial actions, but also that diplomatic action, even if supported by a discrete political use of force, might have had a lesser effect. They suggested that the firmer the commitment implied by the military operation, the more often the outcome of the situation was favorable to the US. Thus, explaining one of the basic features of the US foreign policy, they said the US should (and could) not count on skilled diplomacy as being effective in controlling crises in the absence of prior commitments and reinforcing uses of the armed forces. Based on the past experiences, they asserted that the US "should however, aim to avoid such difficult tests in the first place by being quite clear as to what its commitments are."[40]

Undoubtedly, Turkish foreign policy makers were interested in to utilize this momentum in the economic field as well. In this context, Ankara's relations with the emerging Western Bloc was further developed when the TGNA approved Turkey's adherence to the United Nations Relief and Reconstruction Agency on May 8, 1946. According to Law No: 4881, the Government was authorized to adhere to this agency which was founded by the agreement signed by the UN in Washington on November 9, 1943 as member and pay for Turkey's contributions.[41]

Turning back to the crisis precipitated by the Kremlin's twisted vision of world domination, although the outcomes of the US gunboat diplomacy in the Dardanelles were favourable, evidence had been accumulating that Stalin's offensive had further aims. Acheson explained that geographically the Soviet offensive was concentrated along Russia's borders in Eastern Europe and the Middle East, where the Soviets' physical position was strongest and that of the US weakest. In a tour d'horizon he said:

> Politically, it [the Soviet offensive] centered against efforts to create a United Nations military force and the United States plan to put atomic energy under effective international control. Blocking tactics in the United Nations were made easy by Soviet possession of the veto. The creation of Soviet Satellites succeeded only where the Red Army was present to reinforce it. When the attempt moved beyond the Soviet occupied areas of Eastern Europe to West Germany, the Balkans, and the Middle East, the United States Government gave fair warning that, if necessary, it was prepared to meet Soviet force with American force, rather than with mere protests and resolutions in the United Nations. The first warning was given in August 1946 . . . but Stalin continued to probe cautiously and to receive firm but cautious responses until June 1950, when throwing off pretense, he made an attack in force through a satellite on the other side of the world in Korea. Here the American response was unequivocal.[42]

Indeed, in the August of 1946, the US Secretary of State, Byrnes found himself "enfiladed from three fields of fire."[43] The first question was the settlement of the Yugoslav–Italian border dispute. Since May, it had turned into a prestige battle between the Russian and the Anglo-American positions. On August 9, Yugoslavia forced down, and then on

August 19 shot down unarmed US Army transport planes. Simultaneously, the Kremlin which had backed Yugoslavia and Bulgaria to pressure Greece to detach its northern provinces, launched an all-out drive in the UN against Greece in support of an attempted communist takeover in Athens by the National Liberation Front (EAM).[44]

As for the general problem of the Soviets' independent course, the Soviet perception of post-war settlements was further complicating the process of negotiations. Given this, the Council of Foreign Ministers met in London (September 1945); Moscow (December 1945); Paris (April–May and June–July 1946) and New York (November–December 1946) to make prolonged and finally successful efforts to conclude treaties with the former Eastern European Axis satellites. In accordance with the agreement at the Potsdam Conference, the Council of Foreign Ministers drew up draft peace treaties with Italy, Bulgaria, Rumania, Hungary and Finland. It had been agreed at Potsdam that France should participate only in drawing up the treaty with Italy. The US which had not declared war upon Finland was not to be a party to the Finnish treaty.

The Peace Conference sat in Paris from July 29 to October 15, 1946. It could only recommend. All final decisions were made by the Council of Foreign Ministers. Then, the first meeting of the Foreign Ministers in London produced nothing but an unseemly wrangle. Though the agenda was limited to Europe, Molotov complained repeatedly of the exclusion of the Soviets from a share in the control of Japan. It was perhaps for these reasons that Molotov blocked all action by the Council. In Moscow, three months later, concessions were made on both sides and with reference to both Europe and the Far East. Partial agreement was realized on the question of satellite treaties as well. Ultimately, five treaties were agreed upon in New York and signed in Paris, in February 10, 1947. When the Council of Ministers next turned its attention to the treaties with Austria and Germany, the SU which was extensively exploiting Austria's resources, refused to negotiate the German and Austrian questions separately and no agreement could be attained. It was not before 1955 that, peace was signed with Austria alone upon condition that the SU received heavy reparations, and that Austria would be neutral.

In the meantime, the situation in the Balkans in general, and in Turkey and Greece in particular, could not be improved either. As will be discussed below, on August 7, the Soviet Government demanded that Turkey allow the SU to participate in what it called the defense of the Straits "but which meant the occupation of Turkey."[45]

Setting the Stage for Turco–Russian Cleavage

In the aftermath of the crisis in Iran and at a time Greece was still in serious turmoil, the Soviet Note of August 7 marked an ominous phase in the softening-up process of Turkey. Indeed, following the Soviet Note which Soviet Charge d'affaires conveyed to the MFA Saka, an atmosphere of extreme caution dominated in Ankara. A copy of the Note was given to the US and the British Governments in the guise of informing Washington and London of the Soviet wish to assume a greater responsibility in the defense of the Straits. Here, it was argued that some incidents of the last war had indicated that the Montreux Convention was no longer adequate to meet the security needs of the Black Sea states. The Soviet claims included that during the war, contrary to the convention, some battle and frigate ships had passed through the Straits. In particular, a demarché was made when German coast guard ship *Seafalke* had passed to the Black Sea on July 9, 1941. The Note expressed that in the same year, an Italian frigate ship, *Tarvisio*, was given permission to pass to the Black Sea and in October 1942, the SU had informed Turkey that German frigates each 140 tons were scheduled to pass through the Straits disguised as merchant ships. The SU had also protested the passage, in May and June of 1944, of eight *EMS* and five *Kriegstransport* type battle and frigate ships. Given these incidents, it was understood that the convention regarding the Straits could not prevent hostile states to use the Straits against the SU and other allied states for the purposes of war and "Turkey could not be held irresponsible in such a situation."[46] And for this reason the Soviet Government had proposed to discuss the question of the regime of the Straits. It was known that the Conference of Three States at Potsdam had agreed on the following:

a) the Three Governments recognized that the Convention regarding the Straits, concluded at Montreux, should be revised, failing to meet present-day conditions;

b) the Three Governments agreed that as the next step, this matter would be the subject of direct negotiations between each of the three states and the Turkish Government.

Howard pointed out to the existence of different texts regarding the phraseology here. He figured out that according to Anglo-American version as Foreign Secretary Bevin presented in an address to the House of

Commons on October 23, 1946: ". . . it was agreed that "as the next step" the matter "should be" the subject of "direct conversations" between each of the Three Governments and the Turkish Government." But, according to the Soviet version, the three governments agreed that "as the proper course" the problem of revision of the Montreux Convention "would be the subject of direct negotiations. . . ."[47]

Interestingly, as stated above, (my) direct translation from the Turkish version of this part of the Note emerged as a mixture of both versions. Since the Note was addressed to Turkey but circulated to both the US and the UK as well, it is very probable that either official or courtesy translations were added to the original Note. However, perhaps intentionally too, phrases and interpretations of the SU appeared differently. As Howard pointed out the US, Britain and Turkey in the period which followed the Potsdam Conference, looked upon the phrase "direct conversations" as being tantamount to an exchange of views prior to the calling of an international conference for the revision of the Montreux Convention, not as "direct negotiations" leading to a bilateral agreement between the SU and Turkey. It was also stated that the Note of the British Government which was given to the Turkish Government on November 21, 1945 was known to the Soviets.

In fact, this Note had followed the Note of the US Government dated November 2, 1945. Both Notes had similar departure points concerning the admittance of a need to revise the Montreux Convention. The Note of the UK, however, was different since it stated that negotiations towards this end was not an immediate question. Thus, the first three of these principles were in general consonance with the US and the British viewpoints. According to Howard, points 4 and 5 which outlined a new regime of the Straits by the Black Sea powers and the development of a joint Turco–Soviet system of defense for the Straits, were considerably identical with what Molotov had demanded of Nazi Germany during November 1940, and presented to the Turkish Ambassador in June 1945.[48]

Against this background, the Soviet demands were explained with brutal clarity:

1. The Straits should always be open to the passage of merchant ships of all countries.
2. The Straits should always be open to the passage of warships of the Black Sea powers.

3. Passage through the Straits for warships not belonging to the Black Sea powers shall not be permitted except in cases specially provided for.
4. The establishment of a regime of the Straits, as the sole sea passage, leading from the Black Sea and to the Black Sea, should come under the competence of Turkey and other Black Sea powers.
5. Turkey and the Soviet Union, as the powers most interested and capable of guaranteeing freedom to commercial navigation and security in the Straits, shall organize joint means of defense of the Straits by other countries for aims hostile to the Black Sea powers.[49]

The Soviet Note had been transmitted to the US and the UK as well and one of the first things done upon its receipt was to order a respectable naval task force to the Mediterranean, the *USS Missouri* arriving in the Bosphorus on April 5. The aircraft carrier, the *Franklin D. Roosevelt* and two destroyers, following a rendezvous off the Portuguese coast with two cruisers and three destroyers proceeded to the Mediterranean. The next step was to develop a firm position to stand resolutely by the Turkish Government. Truman asserted that this was an open bid to obtain control of Turkey. "To allow Russia to set up bases in the Dardanelles or to bring troops into Turkey, ostensibly for the defence of the Straits, would, in the natural course of events, result in Greece and the whole Near and Middle East falling under Soviet control."[50]

Then, as expected, the Turkish MFA which maintained exchange of views with the US Ambassador Wilson and the British Ambassador David Kelly, increased its efforts to draw Washington and London's attention to the threat posed by the Soviets. In his turn, Wilson informed Washington that the real objective of the Soviets was not to revise the Montreux Convention but to destroy Turkish independence by introducing to Turkey its armed forces with the ostensible aim of enforcing the joint control of the Straits and establishing a friendly regime and make Turkey its satellite. He pointed out that if Turkey fell under Soviet control, the last barrier would be removed before the Kremlin's advance to the Persian Gulf and Suez. Wilson concluded that the assets Turkey provided should not be allowed to fritter away.[51]

The developing crisis reached its climax when the news on an observable increase in the military activities of the Soviet troops were reported. McGhee underscored that in this context, reliable information indicated that the SU, as part of its continuing war of nerves against Turkey, also directed ground forces towards Turkish territory and held naval manoeuvres 45 miles off the Turkish coast. In its turn, Turkey, suspecting a real attack, mobilized its own forces under the guise of manoeuvres.[52]

Shortly afterwards, Truman instructed the Departments of State, War and Navy to study the situation and on August 15, at a meeting in the White House with Acheson, Secretary of War, Kenneth C. Royall, Secretary of Navy James Forrestal and the Chief of Staff, Dwight D. Eisenhower, where a report was discussed. Acheson stated that the report expressed the seriousness of the Russian moves against Turkey and Greece, which aimed at the domination of the Balkans and the eastern Mediterranean. He said the report asserted that they should be resisted at all costs and maintained, a Note to the Moscow "should by its studied restraint impress the Russians that we meant every word of it. Where they had valid criticisms of the Treaty of Montreux, we should say so, but be adamant against any interference with exclusive defense of the Straits. We recommend making very plain to the Russians, Turks, British and French that we were in deadly earnest."[53]

Here, it was also noted that if Turkey, under pressure, agreed to the Soviet proposal, any case which the US might later present in opposition to the Soviet designs before the UN or to the world public would be materially weakened. Besides, it was not realistic to count on Turkey's will to resist by force Soviet attempts to secure bases in Turkish territory even if it had to fight alone without assurance of support from the US. It was explained that the best hope of preserving peace was the conviction that the US would not hesitate to join other nations in meeting armed aggression by the force of American arms.[54] On August 16, in view of the delicacy of the situation, the Turkish Government was advised to assume a reasonable, but firm attitude and was told verbally that the American position of firm support had been formulated only after full consideration had been given to the matter at the highest levels.

Meanwhile, the *USS Missouri* was already in the Dardanelles and during this meeting it was also urged sending a powerful naval force, including the newly commissioned supercarrier *USS Franklin D. Roosevelt* to join the former vessel. Then, Acheson stated:

General Eisenhower asked me in whisper whether I had made it suffi-
ciently clear that the course we had recommended could lead to war.
Before I could answer, the President asked whether the General had
anything to add. I repeated his question to me. The President took . . .
a large map of the Middle East and eastern Mediterranean and asked
us to gather behind him. He then gave us a brief lecture on the strategic importance of the area and the extent to which we must be prepared to go to keep it free from Soviet domination. When he finished,
none of us doubted he understood fully all the implications of our
recommendations.[55]

On the following day, on August 19, Acheson delivered the US Note
to the Soviet Chargé d'Affaires, Fedor T. Orekhov and sent copies to
Ankara, Paris and London, urging their government to consider the issue. He told Orekhov that the fourth point in the Soviet Note did not
seem to require a revision of the Montreux Convention, but, devising a
new regime would in effect exclude all the non-Black Sea countries. The
US Government had already declared that the regime of the Straits was
an international question, the settlement of which required the contribution of all interested states including the US. As for the fifth point, the
US Government maintained its position that Turkey should be primarily
responsible for the defense of the Straits and warned: "Should the Straits
become the object of attack or threat of attack by an aggressor the resulting situation would constitute a threat to international security and would
clearly be a matter for action on the part of the Security Council of the
United Nations." The Note also declared that the regime of the Straits
"should be brought into appropriate relationship with the United Nations" while ensuring its "function in a manner entirely consistent with
the principles and aims of the United Nations."[56]

The US considered that the establishment of a regime in the Straits
was not the exclusive concern of the Black Sea Powers. The US view
was made public as well since two days before this interview Acheson
had briefed the press, stressing the seriousness of the situation, their
decision to stand firm against any outside military interference with the
defence of the Straits, and the undesirability of speculation upon possible
developments. McGhee explained that urging Turkey to reject these demands, after consulting with the British and Turks, Truman sent this
Note to the Soviet leadership. The US President had the opinion that this
incident had constituted a threat to international security and "would
clearly be a matter of action on the part of the Security Council."[57]

A few days later, in its Note of August 21, the British Government declared that it had long been internationally recognized that the regime of the Straits was the concern of other states besides the Black Sea powers. Thus, the British Government could not agree with the Soviet view that the future regime should be the concern of the Black Sea powers and Turkey alone. As regards the fifth proposal that Turkey and the SU should organize the defense of the Straits by joint means, it was considered that Turkey, as the territorial power concerned, should continue to be responsible for defense and control of the Straits.[58]

In view of these circumstances, the Turkish formal reply was given to the SU on August 22. It is interesting to note that the Turkish Note was not forwarded to the Soviets before the US and British Notes were sent. Moreover, on August 20, the US and British Governments informed Ankara that they had agreed with the "draft of the reply" to be forwarded to the SU.[59]

Given this premise, in its lengthy format, the Turkish Note addressed each of the Soviet claims concerning the passage of the Axis ships contrary to the convention, and emphasized that Turkey has strictly applied the rules pertaining to the passage of ships in concern. None of the Axis ships were in the list of frigate vessels except *Tarvisio*—petroleum ship—whose passage was allowed upon the statement of Italian Embassy, which declared that it was excluded from this list and it was cruising for purely commercial purposes. The passage of *Tarvisio* was not permitted for the second time and Turkey's determination in this regard was acknowledged by the Soviet Ambassador on August 25, 1941 in his interview with the Turkish MFA. The passage of *EMS* and *Kriegstransport* ships were also in conformity with the convention since the inspections had proved that the load of these ships were coal, timber and grass and they were not on the list of frigates either. Therefore, they could not be regarded under the IInd Annex of the Convention.

However, based on intelligence from the UK, forwarded to the Turkish MFA, which explained that these ships were employed in the navy and joined the activities of transport of troops, the first ship of this type was interrupted and from then on these grouping of ships were not permitted to pass through the Straits. It was also underlined that no breach of the convention was tolerated and the exploitation of Turkey's good intentions was not allowed to repeat. The Note stated that with the aim of obtaining a regime for the Straits, completely along the lines of its national interest, the Soviet Government was basing its evidence on the inadequacy of the regime established by the Montreux Convention to provide the conditions for the prevention of the hostile use of the Straits against the Black Sea states.[60]

In fact, except for a few incidents of fraudulent passage which were then followed by the demarchés of the Soviet Embassy, the Soviet Government had not appealed to the Turkish Government throughout the war for circumstances of passage endangering its security in the Black Sea. Besides, the SU had repeatedly observed that despite the facilities it provided vis-à-vis tactical and strategic targets, the Axis powers could not dare to force the Straits. It was emphasized that this was not an outcome of the underestimation of the use of the assets of the Straits, but an end-result of the power and honesty Turkey maintained, sometimes at its own expense, in this regard.[61]

The Note also pointed out that the objective of the Soviet Government was understood to have been the revision of the Convention in accordance with Article 29, which envisaged a term of 5 years after which requests for amendment might be directed. If this were the case, the SU would need at least one other signatory state to endorse its appeal which should be forwarded to other contracting parties with a minimum period of three months in advance. Given this, it was stated that the "Republican Government which took note of the wish expressed by the Soviet Government for revision, and on the other hand, desired to satisfy the wish of the American public opinion concerning the free use of the waterways"[62] did not intend to cause any difficulty in regard to the examination of any demand for revision in an international conference, following the approval of the contracting parties and the US.

Besides, the Turkish Government had favoured the first three articles of the Soviet Note in compliance with the suggestions of the Note of the US dated November 2, 1945. The reply of the Turkish Government to this note had included that Turkey would not hesitate to seriously examine the issue since it was informed about the viewpoints of the states present at Potsdam. The Turkish Government, however, had asserted that it had considered the suggestions of the US in the affirmative and found these proposals to plausibly constitute the basis for discussions under certain pre-conditions and reservations. As for the participation of the US in the proposed conference, the Turkish Government stated that it considered this "not just a realization of an ardent wish, but an international requirement."[63]

However, the 4th and the 5th points of the Note were found particularly inconvenient. In this framework, the 4th point appeared to be claiming the revision of the Straits regime through introducing new principles by the Black Sea countries and Turkey by excluding the other signatory states. Such a consideration was assessed as having inadmissible effects since it disregarded the coherence and the specific clauses pertaining to the revision of the convention which was agreed to last until 1956 in the first instance. Moreover, it did not leave room to the wishes of other states which had clearly expressed their will to take a part in the negotiations.

As for the 5th point put forward in the Soviet Note, the Turkish Government observed that it had "no other meaning but the arrangement of a joint Turco–Soviet defense for the security of the Straits against any violation originating from the Mediterranean."[64] Thus, the Soviet proposal was found against the sovereign rights and the security of Turkey. It was stated that the acceptance of this suggestion would result in ending Turkey's role of balance and communication and the establishment of the so called security of the Black Sea countries upon the destruction of Turkish security. Besides, the Note underlined that the Turkish Government had the conviction that wherever any danger might come from, the duty of defense belonged to Turkey alone. It was maintained that history had not recorded any example of war that Turkey participated in where Turkish nation did not perform its duties for the country. If Turkey had not the power to defend its sovereign rights over the Straits through its own instruments, it could not save itself from sharing the destiny of all its neighbours, which were subjected to violations or military invasion in the greatest war history registered.[65]

Lastly, it was emphasized that at a time in which all nations were endeavouring to establish peace and security, it would be a sign of mistrust to demand further reinforcement of a defense system which proved to be successful in the past. It was also pointed out that in addition to this strong assurance Turkey extended, in accordance with the new perception of war, Turkey had considered it rightful to conclude that the security of all states were primarily under the guarantee of joint forces that both Turkey and the SU allocated to the authority of the UN. Thus, in all circumstances, including the occurrence of an attack originating from the Mediterranean—which was stated as impossible—and passing through the Straits to the Soviet positions in the Black Sea, it was stated that "the Turkish Government is of the opinion that the Soviet Government should also trust to the effectiveness of the organization of the UN to which the Turkish Government is strongly attached."[66]

Meanwhile, on August 23, 1946, the US Joint Chiefs of Staff (JCS) reported that they viewed Kremlin's moves in the Middle East as "calculated Soviet policy of expanding de facto geographical control" and concluded that Turkey "was the most important factor in the Eastern Mediterranean and the Middle East."[67] Among other things, the JCS underscored that since Soviet military base rights in the Straits would not provide effective control of traffic unless such rights were extended to include military dominance of the area for several hundred miles in all directions. Given this, Soviet participation in the defense of the Straits would also tend to justify further military penetration through the Aegean. If the Soviets attained military dominance by political concessions in Turkey, there was grave doubt that in the event of a major world crisis, the Middle East and Eastern Mediterranean could be considered militarily tenable for the non-Soviet powers. In this context, it was recognized that an unwavering opposition to the SU rested essentially on the Turkish Government, that the security interests of Britain were more direct than those of the US, and that the American people were not well informed regarding problems in the region. On this premise, the JCS suggested encouragement of the Turkish purchase of both economic and military supplies from the US.[68] Thus, concurrently with the crisis in Turco–Russian relations, the rationale for US assistance to Turkey had been established, while in discussions with Britain the US gave assurances that it was prepared to assume greater responsibility in the region.

The SU did, however, continue its reckless policy towards Turkey. Following a short period of deceptive silence, the SU conveyed its second Note dated September 24, 1946 to Ankara. Although different in texture and intensity, the second Soviet Note was more or less a reshuffle of previous arguments and claims, but this time with a stronger phraseology. It was firstly stated that the Soviet Note of August 7 had not comprised all the incidents of violationary passages of German and Italian ships from and to the Black Sea. According to the Soviet Note, the Turkish Government's acceptance of the passage of hostile ships before the protest of the British Government confirmed the Soviet declaration that the Convention on the Straits was no longer adequate to prevent the use of the Straits for purposes of war. The overtones of intimidation were not confined to this. It was argued that Turkey had not raised the issue of revision of the related articles of the Convention during the war, and it had not accepted the need for revision before it became inevitable.

The Soviets also disagreed with the Turkish statement that the SU never applied to the Turkish Government claiming its security was endangered in the Black Sea as reflecting the truth. Besides, no correlation between Turkey's efficiency in regard to the performance of its duties in the Straits and the hesitation of Axis powers to dare any venture to violate the regime of the Straits could be made. In this context, it was argued that with a view to these free passage of enemy ships, the Soviets were compelled to move a significant number of their forces from the essential areas of the theater of war for the defense of the Black Sea region.[69]

Subsequently, it was put forward that the Black Sea was an inland sea and it was natural that the passage to this sea was regarded as a matter of greater concern for the Black Sea states since the positions of these countries could not be compared with other states. Besides, the case of the Straits differed in terms of the user nations and with a comparison of its characteristics to that of other waterways of global importance such as the Gibraltar and the Suez Canal.

To the astonishment of Turkish officials, the Soviet Note explained the Kremlin's perception that the special position of the "Black Sea Straits" was recognized through the Turco–Soviet agreement of March 16, 1921 where it was agreed to deliver the issue of determination of the definitive status of the Straits and the Black Sea to a conference composed of riparian states. Moreover, it was stated that a similar clause existed in the agreement between Turkey and the South Caucasian Soviet states dated October 13, 1921 and in the agreement of January 21, 1922 between Turkey and the Soviet Socialist Republic of Ukraine.

According to the Soviets, inclusion of the principle of determination of the Straits regime by the Black Sea riparian states was a clear indication of the degree of importance these countries and Turkey attributed to the matter. Given these, it was argued that the 4th point of the Soviet Note of August 7, was entirely in harmony with the previous agreements Turkey had signed since this proposal was designed to help the establishment of the conditions required for the maintenance of security in the Black Sea. Consequently, this would reinforce general peace. Moreover, both the experiences of the last war and the principle concerning the establishment of the Straits regime which was agreed to by the SU, corresponded to the rightful interests of the Black Sea states and these points did not contradict the "stability of the general peace and the interests of the other nations concerned with the security of nations."[70]

At this juncture, Soviet accusations of Axis ship appearances in the Black Sea during the war were combined with an historical example. This was the assault of the German cruisers *Göben* and *Breslau* on the Russian navy and some Russian harbors in the Black Sea in 1914. According to the Soviet Note, it was "very well remembered" that the two cruisers had inflicted serious unexpected damage, and regarding the proposal of the Soviet Union on the joint defense of the Straits, these were all considered. The reference of the SU to an obscure event in the Great War which had emerged as an outcome of the planning of the German Joint Staff and a small cliqué within the Ottoman Joint Staff, was regarded as quite disturbing in this regard.

There was further blame directed at Ankara with which the Note reached its abrupt ending. It was stated that the Soviet Government had felt it necessary to express that the Turkish Government seemed to have disregarded the decisions of the Big Three as stated in the Berlin Conference, and in this context, as for the preparations towards a conference on the regime of the Straits, the demand for an extensive negotiation of the issue through direct talks was repeated.

Interestingly, as it did in replying to the earlier Note, before Ankara's reply, on October 9, Washington again responded to the second Soviet Note although it was not addressed. This time, the Note had been handed by Lt.-Gen. Bedell Smith, US Ambassador in Moscow, to the Soviet Commissariat for Foreign Affairs. Here, the US, reiterating its previous position, recalled that in the protocol of the proceedings of the Potsdam Conference the three governments had recognized that the Straits Convention should be revised for failing to meet present-day conditions and it was further agreed that as the next step the matter should be the subject of direct pour-parlers between each of the three governments. Through this repetition it was aimed to underscore that the US Government did not believe that the Potsdam Agreement contemplated that direct conversations envisaged in the protocol should have the effect of prejudicing the participation of the other two signatory powers in the revision of the Straits regime. On the contrary, it was stated, the Potsdam Agreement had definitely contemplated only an exchange of views with the Turkish Government as a useful preliminary to a conference of all interested powers, including the US, to consider the revision of the Montreux Convention. It had also declared that in the US view Turkey should continue to be primarily responsible for the defence of the Straits and that should the Straits become the object of an attack or threat of an attack by an aggressor, the resulting situation would be a matter for action by the UN Security Council.

In its reply on the same day, like the US, the British Government laid down the same point that the Potsdam Agreement stated that as the next step, the problem should be subject of direct conversations between each of the three governments and the Turkish Government. But, differently, the British Note emphasized that the "next step" had already been completed by the exchange of views which had "now taken place between these Governments." As a result, it saw "no need for or purpose in the continuing direct correspondence on the subject."[71]

In other words, the future of the Straits regime between Turkey and Russia had now reached the limit which the British, US and Soviet representatives had in mind when they agreed at Potsdam that each should discuss the problem separately with the Turkish Government before moving towards the international conference necessary to revise the Montreux Convention. As for the points 4 and 5, it was stated that the British attitude towards these remained as it was indicated in the Note of August 21. Given this, the British Government was ready to attend a conference of the US, the SU, the UK, France and all other signatories of the Montreux Convention, with the exception of Japan, to consider a revision of that Convention.[72]

On October 15, Ankara Radio reported that representatives of the British and US Embassies had had long meetings with Turkish officials at the MFA and that Turkey "considering Britain and America party to all negotiations, is keeping them informed of all developments of the question of negotiations about the Straits," although the Soviet Government had failed to send a copy of its Note of Sept. 24 to London and Washington.[73]

The nature of the Turkish reply to the Soviet Note was indicated in a statement by Recep Peker, the Turkish Prime Minister, to the Ankara correspondent of the *Daily Telegraph*, on October 17. Peker said that there were no grounds for supposing that the Turkish reply would contain any modification of Turkey's position. He declared that Turkey could neither accept the 4th point of the Russian demands limiting discussions to the Black Sea Powers, which involved what would amount to bilateral conversations with the Soviet Government, nor the 5th point demanding the joint defence of the Straits by Turkey and the SU. He stated that

Turkey believed in the UN and said, "no one will admit the right of any Power to make demands on the territory and sovereignty of another, no matter what strategic convenience is at stake." Peker pointed out that it had always been the Turkish view that direct conversations regarding the provisions of the Montreux Convention could only usefully take place provided all interested parties were included, and that the conversations should only be preparatory to a general conference.

While the continued state of partial mobilisation of the country's armed forces was unquestionably accepted by the Turkish people, it hindered the realisation of government plans for economic development and the resumption of normal life in every direction. Schools, hospitals, clinics, and the building of 12,000 miles of highways, etc., were, Peker added, among the immediate needs of the country, as well as a great expansion of textile production, which was at present inadequate to clothe the population. Because of the present state of alertness however, he said, the Turkish Government could not make an effective start with its economic and social programme. Peker, expressing full satisfaction with the British and US attitude, concluded by stressing the five cardinal points of Turkish foreign policy as follows:

1. To maintain the sovereign rights of the Turkish nation and the territorial integrity of the Motherland.
2. Confidence in, and loyalty to, its friends and Allies, Britain and the United States.
3. Sincere attachment to the United Nations.
4. Within the framework of these conditions, friendship with its neighbours and especially the restoration of sincere friendship and reciprocal confidence with the SU in accordance with the tradition established after the Turkish War of Independence and developed between the two world wars.
5. Normal and reciprocal commercial relationships throughout the world.[74]

On October 18, a lengthy Note of the Turkish Government in reply was forwarded to Moscow. Here, it was reiterated that with a view to the concrete positions adopted by the both parties "it would be useful to consider that discussion in the field of diplomacy was exhausted"[75] and the Turkish Government would accept to go to international arbitration (as it was stated in its previous Note) if the Soviet Government wished to do so as well. As for the German ships which were the subject of Soviet claims once more, since these ships were built in the dockyards in the Danube, it was expressed that their presence in the Black Sea could not be related to the will of Turkey. Besides, if they had passed through the Straits this was because they had not carried any feature of battle or auxiliary support ships.

Regarding the Soviet statement on the Turkish Government's cession of the circulation of reports on the navigation in the Straits, it was explained that according to Article 24 of the Montreux Convention, Turkey was entitled to circulate the reports in concern to the contracting parties, but not to belligerent forces. Thus, it was explained that the Turkish Government had asserted that with a view to the interdiction of the passage of the warships through the Straits while the conflict was going on, and considering that no other war vessels from other countries were present in the Straits in this period, these reports which remained unrepresentative of regular peace time statistics were not conveyed to the Secretariat of the League of Nations or to the signatory states. These records were kept on a regular basis.

This being the case, it was assessed that the distribution of information concerning commercial navigation activities could have no use and in contrast, would have a negative effect on the Allied side since such reports would declare that these activities had considerably decreased as a result of the conflict. It was for this reason that though it had regularly prepared them, Turkey had dispatched annual reports pertaining to the years 1941–1944 following the end of the conflicts in 1945, on January 29, 1946. Besides, it was also worth noting that no signatory state to the Montreux Convention had raised an objection to Turkey's conduct. Meanwhile, the riparian states had not informed Turkey of the total tonnage of their ships in the Black Sea, as of January 1 and July 1 each year, during the period either, which would naturally be included in these reports. Given this, it was stated that Turkey had not considered to complain about this attitude of the SU.[76]

In sum, Turco–Soviet exchange of Notes in 1946 produced no outcome, but culminated in the strong suspicion at Ankara of the Kremlin's hostile intentions towards Turkey. As will be discussed under the subsequent title, from then on Ankara increased its efforts to side with the regimes of the Western camp. The Turkish policy makers asserted that the most direct way to achieve this objective was to shift to a multi-party parliamentary system at once. Their consideration would no doubt introduce a fundamental change in the country, but still a discreet one amidst the controversies of an unpredictable international political atmosphere.

Notes

1. "The Great Powers and Turkey," in *The Sun,* April 23, 1909, p. 6, img. 6, Library of Congress, http://chroniclingamerica.loc.gov/lccn/ sn83030272/1909-04-23/ed-1/seq-6/#date1 = 1836&sort = relevance&date2 = 1922&words = Empire + Ottoman&sequence = 0&lccn = &index = 16& state = &rows = 20&ortext = &proxtext = ottoman + empire&year = &phrase text = &andtext = &proxValue = &dateFilterType = yearRange &page = 386

2. Statement of Dean Acheson in his explaining of the events in Iran. Dean Acheson, *Present at the Creation,* p. 197.

3. Kamuran Gürün, *Savapan Dünya. . . ,* p. 661

4. Feridun Cemal Erkin, *Dışişlerinde. . . ,* p. 320.

5. Davison, Roderic H., "The Armenian Crisis, 1912–1914," in *The American Historical Review,* Vol. 53, No. 3, Apr., 1948, p. 481.

6. Hilmar Kaiser, "Regional Resistance to Central Government Policies: Ahmed Djemal Pasha, the Governors of Aleppo, and Armenian Deportees in the Spring and Summer of 1915" in, *Journal of Genocide Research,* September–December 2010, p. 210.

7. Law No. 4906, concerning the ratification of the Agreement of the European Coal Organisation by the TGNA was published in *Resmi Gazete* (Official Gazette) dated June 1, 1946, No: 6322. See also, *Düstur* (Laws), Vol. 27–3, (Ankara: Devlet Matbaası, 1947), p. 1171.

8. Cited in, Michael H. Hunt, *Crises in U.S. Foreign Policy,* p. 145. Stalin's address included further assessments such as: ". . . the unevenness of development of the capitalist countries usually leads in time to violent disturbance of equilibrium in the world system of capitalism, that group of capitalist countries which considers itself worse provided than others with raw materials and markets usually making attempts to alter the situation and repartition the 'spheres of influence' in its favor by armed force. The result is a splitting of the capitalist world into two hostile camps and war between them." *Ibid.*

9. Henry Kissinger, *Diplomacy,* p. 440.

10. Not surprisingly, it contained a persuasive analysis of the Soviet history, society, outlook, and intention that influenced US policy toward the SU for fifty years thereafter. As stated by Kennan, his telegram contained in five parts, the following subjects: I Basic features of postwar Soviet outlook, II Background of this outlook, III Its projection in practical policy on official level, IV Its projection on unofficial level and finally, V Practical deductions from stand point of US policy. See, *FRUS,* Vol. VI, 1946, 701–708. For a

detailed discussion of the subject, see, George Kennan, *Memoirs 1925–1950*, (NY: Pantheon Books, 1967), pp. 271–297 *passim*.

11. *Ibid.*, p. 702.

12. *Ibid.*, p. 705.

13. Barzani's feudal clan was said to have had 15.000 armed men engaged in fighting against the Iranian troops since March 23, 1947. *Ayın Tarihi*, No: 161, 1–30 Nisan 1947, p. 119.

14. Quoted, from the Winston S. Churchill's speech at Westminster College in Fulton, Missouri. See, *Winston S. Churchill His Complete Speeches 1897–1963*, Vol. VII, 1943–1949, Ed by. R. Rhodes James, (NY: Chelsea House Publishers, 1974). See, "The Sinews Of Peace," *passim*.

15. Andrei Gromyko (Trans. Harold Shukman), *Memories*, (London: Hutchinson (Arrow edition, 1989), p. 304.

16. George McGhee, *The US-Turkish-NATO Middle East Connection*, p. 16.

17. Having concentrated his forces in Ochnovick—his last resistance point, 12 km north of Iraq—Barzani continued his hopeless fight until this town fell to the Iranian forces on April 7. On April 15, he surrendered to the Iranian army, near Iranian–Iraqi border. *Ayın Tarihi*, No: 161, 1–30 Nisan 1947, p. 118.

18. Dean Acheson, *Present at the Creation*, p. 197.

19. As explained by Walter Bedell Smith, US Ambassador to Moscow. George McGhee, *The US-Turkish-NATO. . .*, p. 16.

20. *Ibid.*

21. "Treaty of Friendship and Good Neighbourhood Between the Republic of Turkey and the Kingdom of Iraq," in *Düstur* (Laws), Üçüncü Tertip, (Kasım 1946–Ekim 1947), (Ankara: Devlet Matbaası, 1947), pp. 1501–1502.

22. Cited in, Joseph Smith, *The Cold War 1945–1965,* (London: Basic Blackwell, 1986), p. 12.

23. *Ibid.*

24. Barry M. Blechman and Stephen S. Kaplan, "US Military Forces As A Political Instrument Since World War II," in *American Defense Policy*, Schuyler Foerster and Edward N. Wright (ed.), (Baltimore: Johns Hopkins University Press, 1990), p. 321.

25. İsmail Soysal, *Soğuk Savaş Dönemi ve Türkiye—Olaylar Kronolojisi (1945–1975)*, p. 23.

26. Dean Acheson, *Present at the Creation*, p. 195.

27. Yalçın Küçük, *Türkiye Üzerine Tezler*, p. 360. The terms of offices of the Turkish Ambassadors in Washington between 1934 and 1955 were as follows: September 1934 to November 11, 1944, Münir Ertegün; November, 11, 1944 to March, 15, 1945, Orhan Halit Erol (Charge d'affaires); March 16, 1945 to July 29, 1948, Hüseyin Ragıp Baydur; August, 11, 1948 to June, 18, 1955, Feridun Cemal Erkin. The MFA records.

28. Thomas G. Paterson, *On Every Front*, (NY: W.W. Norton Co., 1993), p. 65.

29. Cüneyt Arcayürek, *Bermuda Şeytan Üçgeninde Türkiye*, pp. 315–316.

30. Haluk Ülman, *Türk-Amerikan Diplomatik Münasebetleri 1939–1947 (Turkish-American Diplomatic Relations 1939–1947)*, (Ankara: A.Ü. Siyasal Dilgiler Fakültesi, 1961), pp. 73–74.

31. Gül İnanç, *Bu Yazının Mahrem Tutulmasına* . . . passim. İnanç discusses this flow of events, through her references to three telegrams of the Turkish Embassy in Washington to the MFA, two of which can be seen at the annex of her article and the *FRUS*, 1946, Vol VI *Eastern Europe, The Soviet Union*, p. 864, on the US Ambassador Walter Bedell Smith's conveying of the invitation of Stalin to the US.

32. *Ayın Tarihi (Chronicle of the Month)*, Ankara, Nisan 1946, 61–63; Bilal Şimşir, *Bizim Diplomatlar (Our Diplomats)*, p. 314.

33. *Ibid.*

34. Necmettin Sadak, "Aziz Dostlarımız Hoş Geldiniz" (Welcome Our Dear Friends), *Akşam*, March, 5, 1946. A year and a half later, Sadak was nominated as the MFA, in the government of Saka which remained in power from September 10, 1947 to June 10, 1948.

35. George Harris, *Troubled Alliance*, p. 20.

36. Nadir Nadi, "Dost Amerika'nın Denizcilerini Karşılarken," *Cumhuriyet*, March, 5, 1946.

37. Asım Us, "Missouri'nin Türk Sularını Ziyareti," *Vakit*, March 6, 1946.

38. Barry M. Blechman and Stephen S. Kaplan, "US Military Force As a Political Instrument Since World War II," p. 321.

39. Cited in, *ibid.*

40. *Ibid.*, pp. 321, 323 and 326, respectively.

41. "Birleşmiş Milletler Yardım ve Kalkındırma İdaresine Katılınması Hakkında Kanun" (Law Concerning the [Republic of Turkey's] Adherence to the United Nations Relief And Reconstruction Agency), 8 Mayıs 1946, in *Resmi Gazete* (Official Gazette), May 10, 1946, No: 6303.

42. Dean Acheson, *Present at the Creation*, p. 194.

43. *Ibid.*, p. 195.

44. *Ibid.*

45. *Ibid.*

46. From the Note of the Government of the Soviet Union to the Government of the Republic of Turkey, August, 7, 1946, para. 8, cited in, Feridun Cemal Erkin, *Türk-Sovyet İlişkileri ve Boğazlar Meselesi*, (Ankara: Başnur Matbaası, 1968), pp. 414–415.

47. *Ibid.*, 415; Harry N. Howard, *Turkey, the Straits and U.S. Policy*, p. 231. For various texts, see, US Department of State Press Release No: 238, March 24, 1947; United Kingdom, *Parliamentary Debates, House of Commons*, fifth series, p. 427, cols. 1500–02; Raymond Dennett and Robert K.

Turner, *Documents on American Foreign Relations, 1945-1946*, (NY:Harper, for the Council on Foreign Relations), 8: 936; and F. Cemal Erkin, *Türk-Sovyet İlişkileri ve Boğazlar Meselesi*, pp. 414-415.

48. Harry N. Howard, *Turkey, the Straits and U.S. Policy*, 244; and as for the US Note dated November 2, 1945, the principles of which was also accepted by Turkey as stated by the Turkish Note of December 6, and the Note of the UK, dated November 21, see, Yüksel İnan, *Türk Boğazlarının Siyasal ve Hukuksal Rejimi (The Political and Legal Regime of the Turkish Straits)*, (Ankara: Turhan Kitabevi, 1995), pp. 108-109; Kudret Özersay, *Türk Boğazlarından Geçiş Rejimi* (Transit Regime of the Turkish Straits), (Ankara: Mülkiyeliler Birliği Vakfı Yayınları, 1999), pp. 90-91 and *Ayın Tarihi*, (1945) Kasım, No. 144, 71; Aralık, No. 145, pp. 146-149, respectively.

49. *FRUS*, 1946, Vol. VII, (Washington, D.C.:USGPO, 1969), p. 829; Feridun Cemal Erkin, *Türk-Sovyet ilişkileri ve Boğazlar Meselesi*, p. 415.

50. Harry S. Truman, *Years of Trial and Hope*, (Garden City, NY: Doubleday, 1956), p. 97.

51. *FRUS*, 1946, Vol. VII, pp. 836-837.

52. As told by Retd. Col. şükrü Erkal, Research Specialist, in the TGS ATASE, Directorate for Military History and Strategic Research.

53. Dean Acheson, *Present at the Creation*, p. 195.

54. *FRUS*, 1946, Vol. VII, pp. 840-842.

55. Dean Acheson, *Present. . .*, pp. 195-196.

56. *FRUS*, 1946, Vol. VII., pp. 847-849; Harry Howard, *Turkey, the Straits. . .*, p. 246.

57. Dean Acheson, *Present. . .*, p. 196; *FRUS*, 1946, Vol. VIII, pp. 847-848; George McGhee, *The US-Turkish-NATO. . .*, p. 17.

58. *FRUS*, 1946, Vol. VII, 849-851; Harry Howard, *Turkey, the Straits and U.S. Policy*, p. 246.

59. F. Cemal Erkin, *Türk-Sovyet İlişkileri ve Boğazlar Meselesi*, pp. 296-297. Erkin stated that France had sent a Note on the same issue to the SU also at about the same time.

60. From the Note of the Government of the Republic of Turkey to the Government of the Soviet Union, August 22, 1946, para. 18, cited in, *ibid.*, p. 419.

61. *Ibid.*

62. *Ibid.*, p. 420.

63. *Ibid.*, p. 421.

64. *Ibid.*

65. *Ibid.*

66. *Ibid.*, p. 422.

67. *FRUS*, 1946, Vol. VII, 856-858; George McGhee, "*The US-Turkish-NATO. . .*," 17; Harry Howard, *Turkey, the Straits. . .*, pp. 248-249.

68. *Ibid.*

69. From the Note of the Government of the Soviet Union to the Government of the Republic of Turkey, September 24, 1946. Cited in, *ibid.*, p. 424.

70. *Ibid.*, pp. 426–427.

71. *FRUS*, 1946, Vol. VII., pp. 876–878; Harry Howard, *Turkey, the Straits.* . . , p. 251.

72. *Keesing's Contemporary Archives*, 1946–1948, Vol. VI, 8199. On October 10, the problem of the Straits came up indirectly this time at the Paris Peace Conference. The larger issues involved, of course, were those of the sovereign rights and the territorial integrity of Turkey. For a detailed account of the support of Russian thesis of the *mare clausum* in the Baltic and Black Sea Straits, and for some American perceptions of the regime of the Panama Canal which suggested settling of disputes in this area within the domestic jurisdiction of the US, see, Harry Howard, *Turkey, the Straits.* . . , footnote (77), p. 252.

73. *Keesing's Contemporary Archives*, 1946–1948, Vol. VI, p. 8199.

74. *Ibid.*

75. From the Note of the Government of the Republic of Turkey to the Government of the Soviet Union, dated October, 18, 1946, cited in *ibid.*, p. 429.

76. *Ibid.*, p. 430.

Chapter 5

Turkey's Transformation Amidst Forceful Change and Turkish Strategies in Adapting to a New Security Environment (1945–1947)

You will win the real victory by defeating the ignorance.
—Kemal Atatürk

This chapter discusses the Turkish transformation to a multi-party system and its foreign policy implications within the context of examining the course of events leading to the Truman Doctrine and the foundation of Economic Co-operation Administration (ECA) in Europe between 1945 and 1947. Here, the developments concerning the Turkish–US bilateral relations which culminated in the signing of principal agreements are also examined.

Evidently, following the end WW II, the idea of rejecting totalitarian regimes was increasingly gaining ground in Turkey and elsewhere. In his turn, İsmet İnönü, who had assumed the presidency and the leadership of the RPP after Kemal Atatürk in 1939 faced a conflict between attempting to protect the political status quo and devising a new one. Actually, this tension between the old and new lasted, perhaps, much shorter than expected. As a result of President İnönü's search for popular support of Western nations, fundamental changes were introduced, commencing with multi-party political life in the country. As will be first discussed below, external factors served as a catalyst towards this development.

The Turkish Transition to Multi-Party System and its Foreign Policy Implications

The history of multi-party politics in Turkey witnessed various difficulties one would rarely expect in an emerging democracy. Against all odds, Turkish democracy, however, had admittedly strong roots. The Turkish Grand National Assembly was established on April 23, 1920 and had assumed the control of the Turkish War of Liberation. As such, at the end of a period of three and a half years, on October 29, 1923, the country was brought to the day on which the Republic of Turkey was proclaimed. Having both a fighting and founding national assembly before the foundation of the Republic should not be overlooked as a factor which demonstrated that the desire for democratic advancement was previously in place.

Terakkiperver Cumhuriyet Fırkası (Progressive Republican Party—PRP) was the second political party after Republican People's Party in Turkey. It was established by Atatürk's comrades-in-arms, Ali Fuat Cebesoy, Kazım Karabekir, Refet Bele, Rauf Orbay and Adnan Adıvar on 17 October 1924. It remained however, a short lived attempt as it was abolished following an Islamic–Kurdish rebellion headed by Sheikh Sait in the East of Turkey with the purpose of establishing an independent Kurdistan which broke out on February 11, 1925 and which was soon quelled, while the insurgents and the supporters of the rebellion were found to have been connected with the PRP. Atatürk made some bitter remarks about the attempt of his former comrade-in-arms, General Kazım Karabekir, in his *Great Speech*:

> Gentlemen! Facts and events have proved that the programme of the Republican Progressive Party has been the work emanating from the brains of traitors. This Party became the refuge and the point of support for reactionary and rebellious elements.

> Gentlemen! The leaders of this party actually inspired the reactionaries with hope and strengthened them.

> Let me quote an example:

> In a letter written to Şeyh [Sheikh] Sait by Kadri (who was subsequently hanged), who the rebels of Ergani had recognised as Vali [Governor], he said: "Kazım Karabekir Paşa's party in the Assembly is

pious and respects religious rights. I do not doubt that they will give us their support."

At this time Şeyh [Sheikh] Eyüp declared: "The only party that could save religion is the one which Kazım Karabekir Paşa has formed; in the principles of this party it is mentioned that religious prescriptions will be esteemed."[1]

It is interesting to note that another founder of the PRP, a hero of the War of Liberation, Rauf Orbay, was an advocate of the continuation of Ottoman monarchy. To the disturbance of Atatürk, Orbay nurtured ideas unfit with the ideal of the new Republic. He had no hesitation to explain his loyalty to the Sultan either. Atatürk explained this as follows:

Rauf Bey did not confess his hostility against the Republic. But does not the fact of his speaking of the necessity for certain conditions for its maintenance on the very day of its proclamation clearly show that he did not believe that the happiness of the nation could be assured through the Republic?

He pretended that it was essentially a question of an alteration of the name and a modification of the form in the highest place, and endeavoured to inculcate the idea that the proclamation of the Republic had been a foolish and precipitate action. He finally said that it would be a grave error to believe that the republican form of government would satisfy the real needs. Does he not show thereby his complete indifference towards this form of government and how far he is away from it?[2]

Five years later, the establishment of *Serbest Fırka* (Liberal Party—LP) on August 12, 1930 by Fethi (Okyar) at the direct suggestion of Kemal Atatürk was the second experiment of Turkey in democracy. The LP had come about as a result of the desire of the government that a loyal party should fill the role of an opposition. The purpose in establishing this party, thus was to air the accumulated discontent by the domination of the RPP in a state owned economy and the personal advantages secured by some of its members through use of their position while the world economic crisis and bad harvests in 1928–1929 struck the economy. Given this, it was also aimed to correct the shortcomings of the government and to stimulate it to seek new ways of coping with the economic situation. However, tensions between the ruling RPP and the LP continuously increased and reached its peak when Fethi Bey asked Atatürk to remain neutral in the party disputes. Against this background, less than a month after the establishment of his party Fethi Bey was met in İzmir by thirty to forty thousand people who broke the windows of the newspaper *Anadolu* which had criticized the new party and held demonstrations against the RPP.

The Republicans finally persuaded Atatürk, "who initially had professed neutrality with respect to both parties, to change his position to support the Republican Party. Placed in the position of being forced to oppose Mustafa Kemal, the Liberal Party leaders decided to dissolve their party on November 17, 1930." The closure of other minor parties established during the same period i.e., *Ahali Cumhuriyet Fırkası* (Republican Public Party), followed.[3]

At the end of the war, challenged by the forces of change, the nationalist orientation of Turkish policy was experiencing sporadic and local political disturbances. The destruction of the one party regimes in Italy and Germany, the adherence of Turkey to the UN Declaration, and the closer relations with the West considerably weakened the foundations of one-party rule in Turkey. Accordingly, the political atmosphere abroad, especially in the US, made it apparent that without an opening-up in its political system Turkey would not be able to gain in the West the proper moral recognition it desired and needed. According to the advocates of this view, the strains of discontent at home, stemming from various economic social measures taken during the war had become "so serious that it was necessary to 'open a safety-vale' to prevent a general upheaval."[4]

At this juncture, divergences of opinion were embittering the defenders of the existing political structure based on the rule of RPP. The reasons behind this resistance to change had its roots in an understanding developed throughout the single party period. The RPP was formed of a socio-political coalition of two prominent classes in the country. According to the critics, this coalition consisted of the centralist elites and local notables in which the former exchanged recognition of local economic and social supremacy of the latter in return for the latter's political support "both for the republic and the cultural modernization policies it followed."[5] Not surprisingly, this coalition developed into a kind of symbiotic relationship. Those among the 'notables' who had identified with the RPP were awarded with the distribution rights of products both imported or produced by the state economic enterprises. In this respect, the rise in economic activity in the 1930s mostly served to boost their economic capabilities.

This mainstream did not change during the WW II, serving to create further economic opportunity for those who were already involved with it. Regarding this newly flourishing upper-middle class, which its members initially sought to find the ways they could enhance their ties with the central establishment, ". . . imports, due to unavailability, brought in high profits for those who could do the importing. The price of agricultural commodities also rose due to increasing world demand for them. The notables serving as intermediaries between the national markets and the peasants, enjoyed economic prosperity by purchasing products at moderate, but selling them at high prices. Thus an economic middle class having its origins in part in local notables and in part in urban commerce, began to take shape."6

Paradoxicaly, the members of this privileged group and owners of large lands would first rise to form the opposition to the RPP, creating an opposition while within the ranks of the RPP itself and asking for votes to offer democracy to the masses who were deprived of the wealth both generated and already available to the privileged. The voters would opt to believe in these promises at a time the RPP was seriously considering a land reform, which would clearly be an act directed to the wealth of the opponents of the party if the tides were not to have been reversed through this rare breed of ouverture.

Looking at other foras, i.e. world of thought in Turkey, even before the outbreak of the war, the tension between Ankara and the Kremlin (which continued in a controlled fashion) had its reflections in the formulation of Turkey's domestic politics and government–intelligentsia relations too. This included the unfortunate case of Nâzım Hikmet, a world wide known Turkish socialist poet, and many others. Hikmet was clearly purged as a communist/socialist and anti-imperialist poet. As his views were understood to be spreading among some groups which included some cadets and the students of military schools for non-commissioned officers too, he was given a 15 years sentence.

Although he resorted to write a letter to Atatürk to ask for help, it is commonly accepted that his plea did not reach Atatürk, whose illness was becoming severe. Nâzım Hikmet's letter was conveyed to *Dolmabahçe Palace* by his uncle Ali Fuat Cebesoy, a former General and Ambassador, then serving as a Member of Parliament, where Atatürk was coping with his illness. The letter was posted by Haluk Şahsuvaroğlu, Deputy

Prosecutor in Hikmet's case who had also copied the letter with a view to its historic value. The letter did reach Atatürk's private secretariat at *Dolmabahçe* and was received by Şükrü Kaya, Minister of Interior Affairs who were among the few who could see Atatürk, but it is understood to have never been brought to his attention. In his letter Hikmet underscored that he had believed in the Turkish Revolution and he was not guilty of the charges emphasizing that "the high military authorities, state and the justice are being deceived by the petité bureaucrats who are the enemies of the regimé.[7]

Turning back to the challenging needs of the Turkish Government during the war, it was forced to pursue ways in which it could simply increase its revenues to perform its role as a provider of welfare and to support an army which was kept fully mobilized for years throughout the war. Based on these assumptions as well as other issues, which will be discussed below, in 1942, the government shifted to other measures: the capital tax, and the compulsory sale of a part of the agricultural production to the state below the market price. Through the capital tax, it was intended to levy tax on war profits emerging out of commercial activities. However, it caused a serious burden on the weak middle class which started to believe that the small merchants and agricultural producers mistakenly devoted their efforts and capital for further production and investment. Besides, the compulsory sales which were expanded during the war damaged both the farmers and infant bourgeoisie.

In fact, in 1942, the German armies were concentrating their strongholds throughout Europe and being deployed in key areas. At a such a point in time, Ankara had shifted to implement the "capital tax" on the revenues of non-Muslims. Correspondingly, anti-semitic propaganda and the claims on the non-Muslims selfishness regardless of the countries domestic socio-economic problems were also increasingly tolerated in the press, radio and elsewhere and shortly afterwards, first group of indebted was sent to Ashkale in January 1943. Despite the fact that Ankara's measures against non-Muslims never acquired a wicked nature similar to that of Nazis, considerable evidence suggest that in this move, İnönü had planned to divert the attention of the Axis war machine to somewhere else and give a message that Turkey was considering to give credit to the new order envisaged by the revisionists.

But, İnönü was pursuing a meticulously calculated policy. Within a year, when he saw that the course of the global conflict was gradually removing Turkey out of the scope of belligerent powers, this time he decided to lift the pressures on non-Muslims in the country to the extent of abolishing the labour camps. It was also declared that the taxpayers would pay their debts without leaving their homes. Akar explained that as of September 1943, activities of the working camps were virtually terminated and for those serving in these camps, a waiting period for their return to home had started. It was stated that 1.229 indebted persons were sent to these camps and 21 people died—mostly as a result of age—during their stay in Ashkale. No torture or misbehaviour against these people were reported. However, the issue of working camps casted a shadow on the respectability of the Turkish Government.[8]

Apart from this discussion, the Turkish Government was criticized by some for its failure to host *Struma*, which was carrying 769 Jews who left from Roumania for Palestine. The ship which had spent 70 days in İstanbul between December 16, 1941 and February 23, 1942, until it was sunk by unidentified ships/submarines or sea mine, had caused pressure from Germany on Ankara, during its compulsory stay in the İstanbul harbor. When the British Government informed Ankara that it would not admit the passengers to Palestine, *Struma* left İstanbul to turn back to Romania, which resulted in the tragic end of its crew and 763 passengers. The increasing number of ships being organized by the Jewish groups to save the Jews in Europe from the Holocaust had met an unexpected response from London. In fact, as a result of the definite decision of the British Government on the "illegal" immigration of the Jewish refugees, and the recommendation of High Commissioner for Palestine, Harold MacMichael, right from the outset *Struma* was not allowed to sail to Palestine.[9]

The sea traffic between the Bulgarian and Romanian harbors—İstanbul Straits—Palestine which dramatically increased during the years of Holocaust caused some other disasters during the same period. These incidents which have been increasingly examined by contemporary historians nowadays are beyond the scope of the discussion at hand. Any specific study on Turkish policy towards the victims of the purges against the Jews, should also pay attention to other important aspects of the issue, i.e.: the numbers of Jews admitted to Turkey throughout these years, and the employment facilities offered to these people, many of whom served in the foundation years of basic institutions and universities in the country.[10]

Turning back to another foreign policy oriented decision of Ankara in domestic politics. In 1944, when the Red Army was gaining victories, the İnönü administration then turned against the Pan-Turanists, who were shortly after found guilty of racist actions. Explicitly, with these steps, İnönü was aiming at sending a message to the Soviets that Turkey would not allow the activities of the racists and those sympathetic to the crumbling Nazi empire.

At this juncture, by accepting the Charter of the UN, Turkey moved towards the democratization of its regime. It decidedly set the stage for the opposition to one-party rule, since it provided the dissidents with legal and moral arguments against the one-party system and encouraged them to bring their opposition into the open and to seek popular support. The Turkish delegation to San Francisco was instructed to declare that liberalization was under way in Turkey.

A few days later, İnönü declared on May 19, 1945:

> . . . the political régime and the government of the people established by the Republican régime shall develop in all aspects and in every way, and as the conditions imposed by war disappear, democratic principles will gradually acquire a larger place in the political and cultural life of the country. The Grand National Assembly, our greatest democratic institution, had the Government in its hand from the very beginning and constantly developed the country in the direction of democracy.[11]

International pressure embodied in the UN Charter made the RPP accept political liberalization, as in the past foreign pressure brought about the reform attempts of *Tanzimat* of 1839 and the Reform Edict of 1856. It was also explained that although the effect of indirect moral pressure for democratization from outside can not be minimized, it would be erroneous to consider it as the exclusive factor in the introduction of the multi-party regime in Turkey. "To do so would amount to the denial of the social and cultural forces within Turkish society, and would make the transition appear to be dictated only by opportunistic motives."[12] In this context, it was underlined that after the war every democratic tendency would be allowed to develop in the country.

The first opportunity to prove these liberal initiative came with the İstanbul by-elections on June 17, 1945. In these elections candidates were freely nominated, in contrast to the past when the RPP Central Committee had supreme control over nominations. The elected deputies, however, were the members of RPP.[13] In the meantime, martial law, enforced in İstanbul was extended for an additional six months. Since the most important part of the Turkish press was concentrated in İstanbul, such an over-all authority provided by this law, could be used, "as happened repeatedly, for political purposes."[14]

In fact, the opposition within the TGNA was gradually taking a more definite form. Opinion within the RPP had first polarised around the Land Reform Bill which came before the TGNA on May, 14 1945. Through this measure, "the hardline Kemalists wanted to break the political hold of the landlords and war profiteers by transforming Turkey into a republic of independent peasant proprietors."[15] The critics of the Bill in their turn, generally emphasized that their objection was for two reasons, one economic, the other constitutional. Land reform they argued, would lead to a decline in production which would have considerable adverse consequences; the principle of private property guaranteed by the constitution was also being violated. The debates around the Bill brought the cotton-growing landlord, Adnan Menderes, under the spot. Menderes, who appeared as the outspoken critic of one-party rule, succeeded to ensure the inclusion of certain limitations to the distribution of land to peasants which was envisaged by the Article 17. After weeks of debate, however, party discipline prevailed and the Bill was passed on June 11 heavily remaining along the existing lines.[16]

A severe criticism of the government voiced during the debate on the budget of the Ministry of Commerce in 1945 and the seven votes cast against it were the following steps of an ever increasing opposition to the government. Four votes belonged to the future founders of the main opposition Democrat Party (DP). From then on, four critics, the former Prime Minister Celal Bayar,[17] the bureaucrat Refik Koraltan, the historian Professor Fuat Köprülü and Adnan Menderes broadened the attack on the government. They demanded that the government implement fully the principle of national sovereignty as outlined in the constitution and that party administration be carried out in accordance with the principles of democracy.

Formal opposition developed with the submission to the RPP's Parliamentary Group of a proposal known as the *Dörtlü Takrir* (Proposal of the Four) of June 7, 1945. The signatories were Bayar, Menderes, Köprülü and Koraltan. They emphasized the democratic nature of the Turkish Constitution, the endeavours of Atatürk to give a more liberal character to the government, and the fact that the fear of reaction had necessitated the imposition of restrictions. Since the war was over and the Turkish intellectuals and peasants were ready for democracy, they proposed to restore to the Assembly effective powers of control over the government, grant to individuals the rights and freedoms which had been prescribed in the Constitution, and allow the development of a multi-party political life.[18] In an effort to arouse public backing, the signatories requested an open debate on the proposal as well. The RPP's Parliamentary Group met on June 12, 1945, and after a lengthy discussion rejected the proposal on the grounds that it aimed at certain amendments in the existing laws and regulations and that the Assembly and not the party group was the proper place to discuss these requests.

Meanwhile, the opposition's statements were reflected in the press and in the summer of 1945, a common opposition front was created around *Vatan* (Homeland) and *Tan* (Dawn). Shortly afterwards, a reckless political polemic between Ahmed Emin Yalman, the editor of *Vatan* and Falih Rıfkı Atay of *Ulus* (Nation), the official journal of the RPP, culminated in the *Ulus'* decision to adopt a strictly Republican Party line and give up its claims of general representation. Yalman was a pro-DP writer who later turned against it and was jailed for 15 months in 1959. He was released following the military takeover of May 27, 1960.

Surprisingly, against this political background, Nuri Demirağ, a rich İstanbul industrialist, requested on July 6, 1945 and obtained on July 18, permission to establish a new political party, forming the first opposition party in Turkey after WW II. Demirağ's *Milli Kalkınma Partisi* (National Resurgence Party) lacked an adequate program and limited its activities to the vision of its founder. It therefore played only a minor part in the political struggle. However, by allowing its foundation, the government expressed its decision to accept opposition parties.

As will also be discussed later, after the relatively stagnant first four months, contrary to the RPP's liberalization promises, a destructive action took place in İstanbul on December 5, 1945 and in a couple of hours crowds destroyed leftist journals and magazines as well as bookstores that were selling Soviet literature. This incident could be explained in part by the deterioration in Turco–Soviet relations prompted by the Soviet demands on Turkey. But undoubtedly, it once more covered the beginnings of democracy in Turkey with a cloud of fear and suspicion that force would eventually be used to silence all opposition to the government.[19]

Ş. Süreyya Aydemir pointed out that İnönü and the RPP Group had decided that under the existing laws an opposition could not flourish and it was an outstanding necessity to complete the legal framework before the general elections. Shortly afterwards, on April 29, 1946 a law concerning the modification of the clauses of the law of municipalities pertaining to elections was enacted. This was followed by the law of amendment of the elections law and the modification of the law on associations. Subsequently, on June 11, 1946, clauses of the law on the administration of provinces concerning elections were changed. Shortly afterwards, elections for the municipalities, provinces and the Assembly were scheduled.[20]

The municipal elections were held amidst this controversy on May 26, 1946. The Democrats decided to abstain in view of the existence of undemocratic laws. The date for general elections was set for July 21, 1946. The DP deemed the amendment of the election law insufficient to assure the secrecy and safety of the ballot. Besides, the elections were controlled by the government instead of the Judiciary, as demanded by the opposition. However, it was clear that "in a matter of months the Republicans abolished or greatly liberalized many of the restrictions that took them twenty-five years to impose" and with a certain degree of liberalization achieved the government decided to hold the general elections. In their turn, on the eve of elections the DP had already established party organizations in over forty-one provincial "seats" out of the existing sixty-three provinces, in 200 district "seats" and in a large number of villages.[21]

The DP had also a enjoyed a valuable support in the person of Marshal Fevzi Çakmak. Sent into retirement after 22 years of service in the capacity of Chief of the General Staff, Çakmak "had shown his antagonism to the Republicans" by refusing membership in the RPP and a seat in the Assembly. Thus, he had decided to enter the forthcoming elections as an independent candidate on the DP ticket.[22]

As a result of the control imposed on elections, the majority in the TGNA (396 seats) was easily attained by the RPP. In its turn, the DP won 65 seats in incoercible regions including İzmir and İstanbul. Having been ratherly discomforted since the notorious election results of 1946, when RPP rule experienced the very first challenge against its power, but managed to keep it in its hands in one way or another, the numbers suspicious of the honesty of the foundations of RPP rule were constantly rising. Indeed, 1946 elections where open voting and closed counting of votes system raised considerable criticisms. It was claimed that counting of votes and announced results were untrustworthy. Under these circumstances, on May 6, 1946, in a public speech, İnönü expressed that ". . . in this period it is required to make it clear as to which direction and understanding Turkey's policy would take. We saw the necessity in this regard with a view to the great interests of the country. . . ."[23] Thus, advised by President İnönü, the Turkish Government had clearly defined a direct relationship between the success of democratization process in the country and achieving a defensive partnership with the western grouping of states.

Undoubtedly, the first multi-party democracy experience of Turkey in the general elections of July 21, 1946 was marked by a great debate. From then on, both external and internal developments served to prepare the ground for political freedoms and necessitated the easing of the political restrictions. Thus, in the light of strong criticisms of the Ankara's regime, İnönü had gradually shifted to revise his attitude against his political opponents. Under such external and internal pressures, İnönü began to exhibit a conciliatory attitude towards his critics.

While maintaining a democratisation process in the country, there is ample evidence to believe that İnönü did not adopt a hasty anti-Soviet foreign policy. In contrast, he paid attention to the personal likes and dislikes between the Turkish statesmen and the Kremlin leaders. Erkin, however, related one of the strange episodes in regard to the Kremlin's indirect messages to İnönü to have Prime Minister Saraçoğlu removed and have him replaced by another person who would be amenable to wishes of the SU. He maintained that by January 1946, the Soviets began to implement tactics towards this end. The most direct attempt was made however, on an informal ground, during a reception by a foreign Ambassador in honour of the acting MFA, Nurullah Sümer. According to Erkin, the host had the audacity to approach Sümer and following a tour d'horizon on the reasons of the disturbing tension which poisoned the Turco–Soviet relations and had adverse effects on the political situation of Europe too, to tell him—as a very confidential secret—that the prevailing distrust that the Kremlin leaders felt towards Saraçoğlu and his cabinet was the major reason why the Turco–Soviet relations could not be improved.[24]

Erkin stated that having been told of such an undiplomatic and an discourteous act, he himself called in the foreign representative to the MFA and informed him in the strongest terms possible that the Turkish Government would not permit the foreign representatives to interfere in its domestic affairs and neither would it tolerate public statements by such envoys concerning their approval or disapproval of its conduct. However, as events unfolded, it was understood that Moscow's assertive policy towards Ankara would remain unaltered. Then, Secretary General of the MFA, disclosed the subsequent Soviet ouverture. Although he had not disclosed the details of the above-mentioned incident, he stated that this time at a reception held by the British Ambassador, Maurice Peterson, in mid-February, an unexpectedly lengthy discussion between the acting MFA Sümer and the Soviet Ambassador Vinogradov had taken place.[25]

At this stage, however, considerable evidence suggests that the "foreign envoy–Sümer" talk of January 1946 and "Vinogradov–Sümer" talk of mid-February should be examined separately. While Erkin's statements implied that the former talk was the first ouverture of the Soviets, based on the report of Wilson to the State Department dated January 22,[26] Küçük stated that the "foreign envoy" in concern who had hosted the dinner in honour of Sümer was not Vinogradov, but the Minister of the Bulgarian Embassy, Antonov. While separating the Antonov–Sümer and Vinogradov–Sümer talks, Küçük discussed the both episodes in his letter dated May 22, 1970 to the editor-in-chief of Turkish daily *Milliyet*, which he drafted after he read the concerned part of a serial *Milliyet* published in the same days. He argued that Erkin (who was still alive then), who could extend the first-hand information and correction and avoid associating Vinogradov with the first talks would not do so since he had preferred this to be known the way it was published.

Whereas, Küçük did not consider that the first of talks was very likely to be prompted by the Soviets as well. On the other hand, he quoted Antonov's statement to Erkin which the latter informed Wilson as the Bulgarian Minister said "he had done so only as expression of personal view because it was important to Bulgaria to see improvement in Turco–Soviet relations." As for the demand for the change of Saraçoğlu government, according to Küçük, it was normal that the SU would not trust Saraçoğlu since his statements to Papen on his wish to see the Soviets removed from the map was known by virtue of records. He, however overlooked the issue of Soviets' employing of seemingly irrelevant sources to deliver their messages as it happened when the two Georgian professors' claims on the rights of Georgia over the Turkish Blacksea coastal strip were made public on December 20, 1945.[27] Moreover, Bulgarian hostility towards Ankara was an issue crystallized around the unchanging issue of forced immigration of the Turks in Bulgaria. A few years later, the Bulgarian Note of August 10, 1950 with which Sofia demanded the acceptance of 250,000 Turks as immigrants to Turkey within three months underscored the seriousness of the hostile attitude of the Bulgarian regime.

It is however, a fact that around the issue of the first talk, to add to the uncertainty, Erkin referred to this foreign representative as, "foreign Ambassador," "foreign envoy," "foreign diplomat" and "foreign representative" in one single page.[28] In one way or another, despite the continuation of Turkey's firm stand against Soviet tactics, it is interesting to note that a few months after these episodes, on August 5, 1946, Premier Saraçoğlu resigned on the grounds of "ill health."[29]

Meanwhile, the small opposition group in the RPP was pressing for the establishment of a truly democratic regime and the elimination of restrictions over political freedoms. About this time, President İnönü was seeking economic and military assistance from the US. However, a considerable number of US Congressmen were strongly critical of the nature of the political regime in Turkey since the discussions on the Truman Doctrine. In fact, the Truman Doctrine was explained in the US Congress as an effort to save democracy and freedom in Turkey as well. "The views expressed in the U.S. Congress and the necessity of establishing closer relations with the West, may be assumed to have had some impact on political developments in Turkey."[30]

Against this background of events, early in March 1947, Bayar visited İstanbul where he sought the ways in which he could express his views to DP's İstanbul organization that the DP should not join the elections. However, the organization in İstanbul had already launched its propaganda campaign. Then, Bayar chose to remain neither in favour nor against the elections campaign. But, referring to the previous interim elections for sub-districts, he stated that "these elections were occurring as a forceful blow."[31] In his turn, Prime Minister Peker gave a strong reply to Bayar's accusations. Bayar's response followed, giving a start to a bitter discussion before public opinion.

On March 25, the RPP proclaimed its candidates for municipal elections while the DP was still keeping its silence. A few days later, this time Peker visited İstanbul and interviewed different occupational groups. Meanwhile, speculations about the DP's possible course of action continued. It was also speculated that Bayar might choose to gather the party's general administration board in İzmir. Peker himself, had also planned to visit İzmir where he intended to address Bayar's allegations on the spot. Peker arrived at İzmir on March 31. In his speech, he openly stated his rage at the strategy of the DP. He said "it will be a grave and a wrong move if the Democrats do not join the elections. I merely make them remember to avoid a mistake that will be regarded as a crime against the country throughout history."[32]

On the same day Bayar arrived at İzmir as well. The crowd gathered by the Democrats held demonstrations on this occasion equitably ostentatious to the welcoming of Peker by the RPP. The press was closely following these visits and a large group of journalists were invited to lunch by Peker, and to dinner by Bayar. Concurrently, as will be discussed below an inevitable tension was increasingly taking place soon to emerge as another danger to Turkey's efforts at democratization.

The dinner of Bayar became a scene of a brawl between the supporters of DP and the police. When their attempts to disperse the crowd failed, police forces opened fire to the air, leading to further chaos. Toker pointed out that, *Serbest Fırka* (Liberal Party), which was one of the two opposition parties formed in the Atatürk era as part of his attempts to start democratic life in Turkey, was shut down as a result of a similar incident which took place in İzmir as well. Thus, the leaders of the DP were excited. They all had in their mind the fear that this incident might be used to end the DP's political life. Indeed, Prime Minister Peker described the meeting as a "mob" and attempted to disperse it, but without much success.

The day after, with tactical considerations as well, Bayar informed his party organization that the DP would not participate in the by-elections for six seats which was scheduled to take place on April 6. Meanwhile, politically neutral groups and some businessmen attempted to find a rapprochement between the two parties. However, the prolongation of martial law for an additional six months, the rejection of a DP proposal for a new election law, the demand that A. Menderes be deprived of his deputy's immunity, and bitter editorials appearing in the RPP oriented journals and accusing the DP of revolutionary intentions kept the political atmosphere tense.

Interestingly, the important developments affecting party politics in Turkey were of interest in Britain, and London tried to improve the party relationships in Ankara. In April, a group of Turkish MPs visited Britain as the guests of the British Parliament. During this trip, Fuat Köprülü of the DP and Nihat Erim who shortly afterwards assumed the leadership of a group of moderates known as *Otuzbeşler* (Thirty-fives) in the RPP, both university professors and friends, discussed party politics in the country and reached a tacit understanding to the effect that the RPP would accept certain measures of democratization requested by the DP, which in turn would abstain from unorthodox means of propaganda.[34]

Concurrently, during the debates in the US Congress on the military aid to Turkey and Greece, the heated discussions on this aid focused on Turkey's political regime. On April 12, a US delegation headed by Congressman Barkley, visited Ankara. Under the pressure of international events as well, the aid bill which included a provision allowing American radio and newspapermen freely to transmit news concerning the implementation of the aid program was eventually accepted by Congress.

Undoubtedly, the Turkish Government followed the debates in the American Congress closely. Shortly after the decision of the Congress, President İnönü stated to a correspondent of the Associated Press that American aid was a step towards the defense of democracy and that closer relations between Turkey and the US would contribute to the firm establishment of democracy in Turkey.

Despite all optimism, the pressure on the DP continued while tension between Peker and Bayar and Peker and Köprülü persisted. Meanwhile, the former President of the TGNA, Halil Menteş, felt obliged to intervene in the process and invited İnönü to terminate the political rift. In his turn, İnönü conferred with Bayar.[35]

Turning back to post WW II politics in Turkey, since January 1947, the Turkish Government had been concentrated on a strong anti-communist policy. On January 29, in his speech in the TGNA, the Minister of Interior, Şükrü Sökmensüer, referred to the letters found in the house of Dr. Şefik Hüsnü, the leader of Turkish Socialist Party (TSP), which he implied, revealed a contact of the communists with the DP. According to Sökmensüer, the TSP was supporting the opposition which was increasing its strength around the DP. A leading leftist journalist, Zekeriya Sertel, explained that a relationship between the socialists and Bayar and Menderes existed in the beginning. Sertel stated that he and Tevfik Rüştü Aras, another disenchanted member of Turkish political life and a friend of Atatürk, held meetings with Bayar and Menderes in 1945 which laid the foundations of the DP. Sertel said they had hoped to work together until a democratic administration was established. However, he said "they" knew that Bayar and Menderes with whom they had limited common denominators would "sooner or later would escape to liberalism."[36]

Given this, Ankara's storming campaign against the leftist groups could inflict no damage to the increasing popularity of the DP but hit some important figures of the Turkish political life, Marshal Çakmak being the most important one. An indiscriminate sweep affected persons, such as Çakmak, who was among the founders of "*İnsan Hakları Derneği*—İHD" (Human Rights Association). Uğur Mumcu explained that İHD was founded by a group of leading figures from the Atatürk era, such as Dr. Tevfik Rüştü Aras (Former Minister of Foreign Affairs), Marshal Çakmak (Former Chief of General Staff), Zekeriya Sertel (Former General Director of Press House), Hasan Rıza Soyak (Private Secretary of Atatürk) and Cami Baykurt (Former Minister of Interior). Marshal Çakmak, who had enjoyed a great public sympathy in one of his domestic travels had accepted to lead this association. Later on, faced with severe attacks, he would feel obliged to express that he was not a communist and had no relationship with any of the communist parties. He said "Our nation is mature. These propagandas will result in the negative. . . . I have the opinion that a fire for freedom is in the hearts of the nation. And will not extinguish. Can the citizens whose troubles, compliances and wishes I have listened to in my various travels and contacts be called Communists?"[37]

Zekeriya Sertel also stated that, Aras who had worked as the MFA until the death of Atatürk was removed from office by İnönü as a result of İnönü's strategy of excluding the comrades of the Gazi (a salutation for Atatürk which means veteran) from his political order. Sertel argued that particularly daunting tactics of Turkish police culminated in Çakmak's decision to leave İHD. Sertel underscored that Çakmak was an important figure, pious and honest of character around whom a strong opposition could be gathered. According to him, the DP of Bayar and Menderes had lost its feature of being the hope for the people who longed for freedom and democracy. Therefore they had decided "to defend the freedom and democracy through another way"[38] and it was for this reason the İHD was founded. Similarly, Niyazi Berkes explained that in the beginning, the Republicans were extremely careful towards the Democrats since they thought the DP could be superior to them in terms of its program and ideology. The RPP was also propagandizing that the Democrats would confiscate the properties of the rich and establish public courts. The propaganda of the RPP when directed at the intelligentsia, explained Çakmak's siding with the Democrats as a threat to secularism. However, Berkes said, after a short period of time, differences between these two parties almost disappeared and they were seen as if they were in a competition to identify with each other.[39]

The debate around İHD, is indeed interesting in order to understand a significant endeavour of the socialist opponents of the regime in Ankara. Communism in Turkey, in fact, could hardly find mass public support. It was identified with atheism which was in severe contradiction to the dominant Muslim faith in the country. Additionally, Turkey was a largely classless society in the sense that large groups of industry workers and capitalists classes did not exist as they did in industrialized countries. For all these reasons, communist parties in Turkey which were established after WW II, such as *Türkiye Sosyalist İşçi Partisi* (Workers Socialist Party of Turkey) and *Türkiye Sosyalist Emekçi ve Köylü Partisi* (Socialist Labour and Peasants' Party of Turkey) could not enjoy substantial public support.

In the political atmosphere of the post WW, the age old Turkish dislike of Russia combined with the increasing sentiments of anti-communism was prevailing. Previously, towards the end of 1945, public discontent with the leftists had arisen when several magazines' and journals' suggestions for a reconciliation with the Soviets reached its peak. The mounting antagonism to *Tan* (Dawn) was increased further by its editors' (Sabiha and Zekeriya Sertel) publication of *Görüşler* (Views), a political magazine which openly attacked the RPP and İnönü and asked for a new orientation in internal and in external politics. On December 5, 1945, a crowd carrying anti-communist posters wrecked *Tan*, *Görüşler* and other publications of similar political orientation, namely, *La Turquie*, *Yeni Dünya* (New World) as well as bookstores, *ABC*, *Berrak* that were selling socialist and pro-Soviet publications.[40]

Despite such an atmosphere, the idea of Sertel and his friends to disseminate socialist principles through a relatively modest party program which would be canvassed by a respected military figure who enjoyed popularity among the young and the old, and also the religious groups, could have a chance to constitute a third alternative after the DP. There were indeed certain indications that under a political atmosphere in which the similarities between the RPP and the DP were increasingly defined, a conscious step to combine the reactionary political groups could well have a chance to succeed. In his turn, Sertel himself decided to voice these expectations, which would eventually be embodied in a political party, and then represent a genuine alternative to the existing parties. This attempt would no doubt endeavour to incorporate a mass public support into its organizational structure, around new political leadership.

Sertel said Marshal Çakmak had understood that Bayar and Menderes had politically used his name, and he had left the ranks of this party to spend his time in his house in İstanbul. Moreover, the Marshal's views pertaining to Turco–Soviet relations were of considerable importance for Sertel and his friends. Çakmak had told them that the Soviets had helped Turkey during the Independence War. Thus, he had underscored that the Soviets had not attempted to exploit Turkey's difficult moments, in contrast they had offered valuable help to Turkey. There were disagreements with the Soviets then as well. But these were all settled as a result of negotiations. Presently, they might have asked for three provinces the Marshal said, but the Soviets were understanding people and problems with them could be solved through discussions. They would also withdraw their demands when understood that they were wrong.

Sertel was no doubt delighted with the Marshal's statements. But, as mentioned above, he was frustrated shortly afterwards when Çakmak withdrew from the association. He explained the failure of this attempt along the lines of the Marshal's personality. He said, Çakmak was not of the same caliber as Atatürk. He did not have the necessary qualifications to lead a political party. Besides, he was surrounded by a group of retired officers who, in fact had a limited vision and in the end, Çakmak, wavered by the slashing attacks of the government, and turned his back to this group, eventually shelved himself until his death.[41] The less known short history of İHD underscored that political life in Turkey was destined to be dominated by the RPP and its sole opponent the DP for the following decades.

It is also interesting to note that Zekeriya Sertel, who was clearly on the side of the opponents of "pro-Americanism" was regarded to be as a figure who had turned against the revolutions of the Atatürk era as well. A Turkish Professor, Çetin Yetkin stated that looking at Sertel's opposition to changing of alphabet in Turkey and the introduction of Latin letters, it is unjust to place Sertel's name in history with an identity of an progressivist. Yetkin also argues that Sertel's wife, Sabiha Sertel's inclusion of Halide Edip Adıvar's writings to their political magazine *Views* (Görüşler) and naming this as a "gain" is a thought-provoking issue given Adıvar's opposition to Atatürk and her well-known "Americanist" ideas and as such considers Sertels contradictory.[42]

Against this background, on July 12, 1947, the Turkish President issued a long and formal statement known as the *12 Temmuz (Çok Partili) Beyannamesi (July 12 [Multi-Party] Declaration)*, promising to introduce a workable relationship between the government and opposition which indeed, paved the way to establishing the foundations of a democratic multi-party system. Here, İnönü said, "I consider myself, as the head of the state, equally responsible to both parties. . . . The responsibility of the government to maintain law and order is a fact, but its impartial attitude towards all the political parties established legally is the basic guarantee for political life."[43]

The date July 12, 1947, no doubt, marked a turning point in Turkish politics. It is worth noting that both the signing of the Aid to Turkey Agreement with the US and the Turkish President's Multi-Party Declaration took place on July 12, 1947.[44] Interestingly, the same day witnessed the resignation of Marshal Çakmak from the ranks of the DP.

Despite the controversial legal status and its debatable purpose, the declaration remains one of the major documents in the development of multi-party politics in Turkey. It brought peace and established normal relations between the political parties. Consecutively, opposition within the RPP began to organize itself in a more concrete manner as well. Different tendencies in the party paved the way to forming of two rival groups. The first group were the "extremists" headed by Premier Peker, who opposed any compromise and tried to give the opposition a subordinate role, while the second group, the *Otuzbeşler* (thirty-fives) emerged as moderate and younger Republicans. The position of *Otuzbeşler* became clear in the RPP Group's seven hour debate in August 1947 on the policies of the Peker government. At the conclusion, 303 deputies voted in Peker's favor and thirty-four against him. In the end, despite the great number of votes in his favor, Peker's position was shaken because the votes cast against him meant that the government did not have the confidence of the party hierarchy.

In an attempt to satisfy the critics, Peker changed six members of the cabinet, which, however, increased the disturbances within the RPP since they were not consulted prior to this. Meanwhile, Peker's disagreement with İnönü, who expressed that the approval of the the TGNA of the recent changes in the Cabinet should immediately be assured in order to comply with the Constitutional process, was mounting. Eventually the TGNA approved the changes, whereas three days later Peker resigned in view of the assessments in the party concerning the cabinet even after it received a vote of confidence. Shortly afterwards, the Hasan Saka Cabinet—the Turkish MFA who had signed the San Francisco Charter—was established on September 10, 1947.

The period in which the cabinets of H. Saka served was marked with an expectation that he would better the relations between the government and the opposition. It is also worth noting that since the beginning of the WW II, İnönü had adopted a particular strategy in regard to the changes of governments and this was greatly based on the nomination of MFAs as Prime Ministers. Thus, even the manner in which the changes came is reflective of the adaptive capabilities of the Turkish political system to maintain its permanent features. This being the case, upon Saraçoğlu's resignation, Hasan Saka was re-appointed as MFA in the Recep Peker Government which remained in office between August 7, 1946 and September 9, 1947. Aydemir stated that Peker was a man of the one-party regime and he could act as a strong administrator in a totalitarian rule. In fact, İnönü had first proposed the Premiership to Hilmi Uran. İnönü had appointed former Minister of Justice Uran as the Secretary-General of the RPP on October 15, 1945 in replacement of N. Atıf Kansu as a precaution to the extremists in the party. Since his nomination of Uran in December 1938 as the Minister of Justice in the IInd Cabinet of Bayar in which he had made important changes that were made necessary because of the "mismanagement of the of the domestic and external affairs of Turkey on the part of the responsible Ministers," Uran was the entrusted man of İnönü.[45]

However, Uran declined this offer, suggesting Peker to this post. With a view to these considerations, İnönü's nomination of Peker was a half-hearted decision. Shortly afterwards, the Turkish President's unwillingness surfaced in his decision to appoint Saraçoğlu as the Deputy Head of the Party.[46] Following the resignation of Peker, this time İnönü instructed Saka to form the new cabinet on September 10, 1947. On June 10, 1948, following a reshuffle by President İnönü, Hasan Saka formed his second cabinet in which Necmettin Sadak kept his position as MFA.[47] Despite the fact that Saka resigned on June 8, 1948 and reappointed as Prime Minister, the political situation in Turkey had been acquiring a relatively stable course while liberalization was showing rapid progress.

As for the democratization process in Turkey, the trial of the academics of Ankara University, Faculty of Language, History and Geography (Dil, Tarih ve Coğrafya Fakültesi—DTFC), Pertev Naili Boratav, Niyazi Berkes and Behice Boran, on the alleged grounds of their discouraging nationalism and indulging in leftist propaganda in their lectures was a serious blow to hopes for a pluralistic society. The "DTFC trial of 1948" raised significant issues regarding the political process in the post WW II Turkey. Trial transcripts have never been made fully public to leave Boratav's final defense which was not published until 1998, as the only comprehensive account of the overall event. In the end, these academics who have been found innocent of all accusations, lost their jobs in the DTFC. However, they continued to their prolific works, to leave numerous books to shape the intellectual life in Turkey and elsewhere.[48]

The murder of a long time regime opponent, a great writer and poet, Sabahattin Ali, in April 1948 represented another step backward. Ali was greatly disturbed by the attacks on *Tan* and other leftist press houses in December 1945 and was openly critical of RPP and President İnönü blaming them as being the perpetuators of these attacks.[49] Upon his release from one another term of imprisonment in 1948, he remained unemployed and denied of a passport to travel abroad. Ali attempted to go to Bulgaria through illegal ways and believed to be killed by a human trafficker/informant who cooperated with security forces.

Pro-western attitude of the Turkish Government quickly turned into strong anti-communism which claimed its toll in Turkey in various respects. Another example of this was the "Village Institutions." In 1930s, over 75 percent of population in Turkey lived in some 35,000 villages and over 80 percent of the villagers were illiterate. The Ottoman Empire, particularly under the orchestrated attacks of the Great Powers in its last decades, had left behind an education system which was mostly unworkable given its use of Arabic letters, the inadequate number of teachers and the resultant uneducated masses.

There were many Turkish intellectuals who had turned to educational solutions to address the problems of rural Anatolia since end of the War of Liberation. Şevket Süreyya Aydemir, a prolific political writer who had completed his education at the Moscow University and later combined his socialist leanings with the patriotism that the Republican regime endorsed, was among these firm advocates of bringing the inherent qualities of the Anatolian people under the sunlight.[50] Aydemir had the idea that a sound educational agenda to include productive skills as well as the literacy to help villagers see the exploitation they lived in were utterly needed. He also observed no religious fanaticism in the villages, but the existence of a wide spread illiteracy and naivety against the bitter problems they continued to encounter in their socio-economic life.

There were indeed serious steps to counter this fate before the observations of Aydemir took place. The new Turkish Republic had endeavoured to create a new system of education based on the Latin alphabet and a secular education. There weren't any schools in most of the villages and to achieve a reform in this field, the Village Institutes were introduced. The Village Institutes remained operational from 1940 to 1954. However, they became a subject of political criticism particularly in the first half of the 1950s.

It was said that they were merely another institution in the service of the ruling RPP. They were also accused of developing a revolutionary mentality among the students. The villagers criticised the new teachers, saying that they didn't show a good example from the religious standpoint. With the installation of a bipartisan regime, new ministers were appointed in the government, and the two who had inspired and created the Village Institutes were dismissed. In October 1947, the programs of the Institutes were fundamentally reformed: subjects like Psychology and Sociology were abolished, the class hours of most of the other subjects were diminished with the exception of Turkish language and Agriculture, the study of a foreign language became optional. At the same time, the Higher Institute for villages, was suppressed as were the "Houses of the People," which had been created by Atatürk for the diffusion of culture and to fight illiteracy among adults. With the coming to power of the new party of democrats in 1950, the Institutes were simply abolished; a period of two years was designated for their liquidation. As we have seen, the teacher's staffs of the Village Institutes in large part transferred to the ordinary Normal Schools and Teachers Institutions.[51]

Karpat pointed out that the political consciousness of the masses in Turkey developed regularly as they found their place in the various occupations. According to him, the main motive in all these activities was essentialy economic and among the working classes it emerged as a wish for material welfare. This process of growth from below, initiated by the Government,

seriously changed the country's social organization and the power relations within it. The bureaucracy, already affected by inflation, surrendered its political and social power to a new economic elite drawn from landed and business groups and their associates. Moreover, the intelligentsia, in the past strongly represented in the bureaucracy, saw the rise from its own ranks of professional groups either associated with the entrepreneurs as engineers and technicians, or finding lucrative employment in the service of private commercial and business enterprises. Earlier social values, based on education and dedication to state ideals, were undermined by an order based essentially on economic power. Socially and psychologically this was a far-reaching revolution. Materially and morally, it affected every section of the traditional ruling groups; the civil bureaucracy, the military, and all their affiliates. This social change occurred without benefit of intellectual justification or systematization. The automatic condemnation of all critical social ideas in the past as being conducive to socialism and communism greatly hindered the development of an adequate school of social thinking.[52]

Karpat emphasized that the intellectuals' reaction to these changes once more manifested itself in literature. According to him, various stories and novels with "social content" after 1950, reflected the trends of thought which eventually became the foundation of a new leftism. Authors such as Mahmut Makal, Yaşar Kemal, Orhan Kemal, Aziz Nesin, Kemal Tahir, Fakir Baykurt, Kemal Bilbaşar, Atilla İlhan, Necati Cumalı and others had their roots in villages and in the lower ranks of the urban intelligentsia. "They brought to public attention the unknown dimensions of Turkey's acute social problems, the widespread poverty, distress and injustice and under these influences, this type of writing found its way into the daily press."[53]

To conclude, Turkey's decision to ally itself with the Western grouping of states was not an easy one and required the country to make certain sacrifices from its regular course of development. This, however, remained as an issue which was interpreted differently in the ups and downs of 1950s, and was poorly perceived on the part of its Western Allies.

The Situation on Turkey's Western Flank Levels the US Aid

At this juncture, considerable evidence suggests that the US administration had left behind the times it was at odds between a confrontation or seeking peace with the SU and had decided to shift to a policy less tolerant of the Soviet ambitions. Indeed, the year following the end of WW II was marked by increasing tension between the US and the SU. The US and Soviet forces had confronted each other in Iran, with the Kremlin relinquishing claims to the northern portion of the country. Negotiations over the fate of Germany had faltered and the prospect of a permanently divided Germany seemed more and more likely. The gathering storms of Cold War were contributing to respond to such situations harsher than ever.

Against this background, the US Secretary of Commerce, Henry A. Wallace, became a leading figure for those who chose to pronounce that the US should seek peace with the SU. In his speech on September 12, Wallace stated that the US should recognize that it had no more business in the political affairs of eastern Europe than Russia had in the political affairs of Latin America, western Europe and the US. But, whether the US liked it or not, the Russians would try to socialize their sphere of influence just as the US tried to democratize its sphere of influence. He stated that Russia had to be convinced that the US was not planning for war against it, while the US had to be certain that Russia was not carrying on territorial expansion or world domination through native communists faithfully following every twist and turn in the Moscow party line. Besides, within this competition the US should insist on an open door for trade throughout the world. He said "there will always be an ideological conflict—but that is no reason why diplomats cannot work out a basis for both systems to live safely in the world side by side."[54]

In his turn, Truman registered deep disagreement with Wallace. He stated that Wallace was a pacifist one hundred percent who wanted to decommission American armed forces, give Russia atomic secrets and trust a bunch of adventurers in the Kremlin Politburo. He said "I do not understand a 'dreamer' like that. . . . The Reds, phonies and the 'parlor pinks' seem to be banded together and are becoming a national danger. I am afraid they are a sabotage front for Uncle Joe Stalin. . . ."[55]

Despite these developments, the Kremlin continued to maintain its foreign policy based upon expanding the territory under its control and weakening its potential opponents. No doubt, the crisis in Turco–Soviet relations was among the most significant trouble-spots which required diligent and considered effort on the part of the US if Soviet efforts for penetration were to be prevented. However, a scheme for the systematic support of regimes opposing the Soviet menace was still unorganized. A thoughtful observer then could see that the Soviets would not consider to hold back. As will be discussed below, shortly afterwards, the Kremlin did not hesitate to make another attempt to flow into the Straits.

In view of these circumstances, the primary Turkish effort went into strengthening its ties with the West to secure strong support for its territorial integrity and sovereignty in the face of Soviet irredentist claims. Towards the end of January 1947, the US Ambassador Wilson visited General Secretary of the MFA, Erkin. Erkin stated that it was usual for the British Ambassador to visit him once a week while Wilson made these kind of visits two to three times a week. This time Wilson was scheduled to leave for Washington shortly after his interview with Erkin. In his talk with the Turkish General Secretary, Wilson explained that Turkey's determined and calm resistance against the menacing attitude of the Soviets aroused great admiration in the US and with these bold efforts Turkey was not only defending itself, but was also undertaking a defensive role in the name of the Western Europe and the US.

In his turn, Erkin told Wilson that his assessments were entirely true, and in case of aggression Turkey was determined to defend itself whatever the cost and degree of pressure would be and the calm behaviors observed was the peace and the calm of people who had decided to perform their duties for the motherland. However, this will of Turkey compelled it to keep a large army in mobilization which brought the Turkish economy to the brink of collapse. Given this, Erkin inquired if the concerned countries which were the beneficiaries of Turkey's efforts might be urged to share the financial burden emerging from these defense expenditures. Then, Wilson, according to Erkin, remained silent as "Sphynx" for a while and continued his course of talk without addressing Erkin's statement.

Following the talks, as usual, Erkin sent a copy of his interview to the President, Prime Minister and the MFA. The day after, İnönü invited the General Secretary and congratulated him for his timely demarché he made in his talks with the US Ambassador. However, R. Peker who was nominated as Premier following the elections of July 1946 was critical of Erkin's statement. To the disturbance of Erkin, Peker argued that his demarché might have negative implications. Erkin explained to Peker that his reply was prompted by Wilson's speech and it was his duty to elaborate on this. The conversation ended in such an atmosphere after which Erkin decided to leave his office for a post in Rome.[56]

The following months would prove that Erkin's statement had prompted the inclusion of Turkey in the financial aid program for Greece which was launched following the British Government's informing of Washington that it desired to turn over its undertakings towards this country. Erkin pointed out that the Truman Doctrine was announced a few days after his talks with the US Ambassador. However, Erkin said, prior to this, his dramatic interview with Peker in which he was criticized of acting without an instruction of the government in his talks with the US Ambassador, had reached an unexpected and unpleasant ending. Erkin also felt it necessary to express that Wilson's informing of the Truman Doctrine which came shortly afterwards, made Peker regretful of his previous criticisms in regard to his demarché.[57]

Meanwhile, specific warnings concerning the situation in Greece had been cabled to Washington. As early as February 3, the US Ambassador in Athens, Lincoln MacVeigh, reported rumors that the British were pulling out of Greece, where, since 1945, their forces and finance had helped maintain a royalist government in a raging civil war with communist guerrillas. On February 12, another dispatch from MacVeigh urged immediate consideration of American aid to Greece. A few days later, Mark Ethridge, publisher of the Louisville *Courier-Journal* and a member of a UN investigating committee, cabled from Athens that Greece was a "ripe plum" ready to fall into Soviet hands.

In his consideration of the communist advance in Greece, Acheson pointed out that Ambassador Lincoln MacVeagh had informed in December, 1946 that the SU wanted complete control of Greece and would interfere with all positive steps by the Greeks to save themselves. Interestingly, in this context, Acheson discussed the outcomes of the mission of Paul Porter, former Administrator of the Office of Price Administration to Greece and his personal impression of Greek PM Constantine Tsaldaris. He said:

> Against this background the Porter mission set out for Greece in December, while Henderson and I listened for two hours to Tsaldaris [to whom he referred to as "a weak, pleasant, but silly man, obsessed by the idea, of which he talked incessantly, of solving Greek problems by obtaining from the peace conference, then meeting in Paris, cession of territory in the north and rivaling Venizelos, who at Versailles obtained Crete for Greece"] discuss a list of Greek demands given to Mr. Byrnes. When he became eloquent on Greek claims to northern Epirus, I quite lost patience with him and told him what sort of statesmanship it was that frittered away its time and energy on territorial claims, when not only northern Greece but all Greece was headed hell-for-leather toward total destruction.[58]

Meanwhile, similar warnings about Turkey had come even sooner, and Turkey had "little hope of independent survival unless it is assured of solid long-term American and British support," cabled Gen. Walter Bedell Smith, who had replaced Averell Harriman as the American Ambassador in Moscow.[59]

At this juncture, Secretary General of the Turkish MFA, Erkin's assessments were gaining the hands of those with this line of thinking in Washington through pointing out the accumulated evidence on the strong correlation between the course of events in Iran, Greece and Turkey. He put forward that the Soviet efforts aimed at the domination of the Mediterranean were not merely confined to the political and military pressure exercised on Turkey, but constantly supported by the plans applied in Greece and Iran as well.

Erkin explained that since the failure of the civil war in Greece, subversive activities of communism was provoking conflict between the communists and the non-communists on the one hand, and supporting the "Balkan insurgents" in their war of attrition against the Greek army and the public on the other. According to him, through this the SU aimed at destroying a British out-guard post in the Mediterranean and on the same occasion, obtaining the control of the Dodecanese Islands (Twelve Islands) which were "granted" to Greece in a hasty manner in the Italian Peace Conference through the support of the Soviet Government though they belonged to Turkey in historical and geographical terms in one way or another. Then, eventually, Turkey would suffer and the SU would use Greece to spread its influence to Italy and ultimately acquire the most convenient opportunity towards the establishment of communism in Europe with its all consequences.

Then, Erkin combined the cases of Greece and Iran and stated that the Soviet intervention had also caused a tragic crisis in Iran. Moscow had attempted to establish an obedient government in Tehran, annex Azerbaijan, terminate the British influence over this country and capture oil reserves both in the south and north of Iran. "It was not the product of an ordinary coincidence that all these plans were applied in a harmonious way in Greece, Turkey and Iran."[60] He further assessed that though in appearance, the campaign which was carried on in a balanced way in Greece and Iran had a local meaning, in reality, it had an extensive nature.

Turning back to discussions at Ankara, in late March, while Erkin was still in his office, Wilson paid another visit to him. He stated that he had explained the difficulties of Turkey regarding the large army it constantly maintained. And when he conveyed this message to Washington, concurrently, due to a serious lack of resources, the UK had stated its wish to transfer its undertakings towards Greece to the US. At this juncture, upon the statements of Wilson and the directive of the Secretary of State, it was decided to add Turkey to this aid program which was named the Truman Doctrine and would be announced in the near term.[61]

In fact, as explained by the Minister of Finance, N. Esat Sümer, on the occasion of his presentation of the programme pertaining to the 1946 fiscal year in the TGNA, the Turkish Government had already decided to obtain long-term credits and increase its internal debts in order to overcome the economic bottleneck. Correspondingly, Ankara had started receiving economic aid from Washington prior to the Truman Doctrine. In this framework, it was also pointed out that the issue of bilateral agreements had its roots in the year 1945, when an agreement between the Turkish Government and the US Government which envisaged Turkey's inclusion in the countries considered within the scope of the Lend and Lease Act of March 11, 1941, was signed on February 23, 1945—the same day with Turkey's declaration of war on the Axis. Through this agreement, it was decided that as authorized by the President, the US Government would continue to transfer defense items, defense information and services to the Turkish Government. In its turn, the Turkish Government would provide the items, services, facilities or information to the US.[62] It was also stipulated that the Turkish Government would return the undestroyed, unused and unlost items—in the conclusion of this extraordinary situation—which might be employed in the defense of the Western hemisphere, as determined by the US President.

Indeed, Turkey was faced with a dilemma of pursuing industrialization and maintaining a large armed force at the same time. To hamper the already crippled economy, the prices of Turkish export commodities which were high during the war, had fallen to a normal level with the end of the war. The transformation of Turkey from an agrarian to an industrialized country was one of the objectives of the government while agricultural production was conducted by primitive methods and poor transportation means. Thus, it was obvious that Turkey could not achieve the purpose of industrializing on its own. On the other hand, there were no signs of an economic collapse since Turkey had gold and foreign exchange reserves amounting to 245 million dollars which Turkey kept in case of a

Soviet attack. [63] Given this, Turkey sought foreign military and economic aid as a contingency measure.

In October 1945, Turkish–US talks had led to a Turkish request for a credit of $500 million from the Export–Import Bank. In April 1946, concurrently with the visit of *Missouri*, President İnönü had taken the opportunity to reveal Turkey's request of 500 million dollars credit for the realization of industrial development as well as infrastructure projects. At the same time, he had disclaimed any desire for American military equipment, saying that he "hoped it would not be needed."[64] However, only 25 million dollars were offered to Turkey despite the endeavours of Ambassador Wilson who argued that not to exceed Eximbank's 25 million dollars aid would be a severe shock the Turkish Government. In this context, he suggested that the State Department might take the following points into consideration before giving its final decision: first, since the Turkish position vis-à-vis the SU was critical, an unfavorable loan treatment could lead to misunderstandings in the Turkish Government; secondly, even though Turkey was not devastated by war, it was in need of financial aid in order to make certain economic readjustments; and lastly, Turkey was in need of modernizing its agriculture, minerals development, transportation and communications so as to bring its economy to a better situation, all of which necessitated more credits. At the same time, Ankara was informed that the stated amount far exceeded the total resources available to that lending agency and that much more detailed justification would be required in any event. Subsequently, in March, Washington sent word that Turkey was likely to receive no more than $23 million.

On May 23, 1946, the Director of Near Eastern and African Affairs, Loy Henderson, made clear to the Turkish Ambassador to Washington, H. R. Baydur, that because of the Banks' shortage of funds as well as its previous commitments, the chances of giving a 25 million dollars loan to Turkey was high but, increasing it to 50 million was not possible. Shortly afterwards, on July 3, 1946, Eximbank, with the approval of the National Advisory Council, gave 25 million dollars in exporter credits to Turkey for fiscal years 1946 and 1947. The term "exporter credit" meant that Eximbank would participate up to 25 million dollars in financing projects put forward jointly by the Turkish Government and the US suppliers, or put forward by the US suppliers and approved by the Turkish Government. In any event, Turkish Government's notes or Turkey's guarantee would be required, culminating in the effect that no advances would be made without the approval of the Turkish Government.[65]

Meanwhile, the first bilateral agreement between Turkey and the US in the aftermath of the WW II was signed in Cairo on, February 27, 1946. In this context, it was decided that a credit of 10 million dollars would be given to Turkey. Turkey would pay this credit back in 10 years in equal installments with an interest rate of 2, and in 3/8 ratio. Shortly afterwards, on May 7, 1946, another agreement between the two governments concerning the lend and lease requests was signed in Ankara. It was stated that through the credit agreements of 1946 and as will be discussed below, the agreement of July 12, 1947, Turkish statesmen sought the ways to increasingly obtain US economic aid beyond the military assistance provided by the Truman Doctrine.[66]

While these developments were taking place, within the framework of increasing Turkey's participation in the major organizations of the UN, Turkey adhered to United Nations Relief and Reconstruction Agency (UNRRA) on May 8, 1946.[67] On the same days, Turkish experts and commissions of Foreign Relations and Finance were working on the conditions for Turkey's adherence to the International Money Fund (IMF) and the International Bank for Reconstruction and Development (IBRD) as well. In the aftermath of the completion of these commissions, a justification of the law in regard to Turkey's accession to this organization signed by Prime Minister Peker was submitted to the TGNA for approval on November 30, 1946. Here, it was pointed out that Turkey's share in these organizations would amount to 43 million dollars for each. Finally the TGNA approved the Law No. 5016 on February 14, 1947.

Turning back to the crisis in the Mediterranean, evidently, the attention of the US foreign policy officials had already been drawn to the necessity of implementing a new strategy by the events in Iran and especially the Eastern Mediterranean. The real division between the SU and the US came in 1947, over Greece. Since its liberation by the British troops in 1944, Greece had been torn by a civil conflict between nationalists and a group of Soviet supported communist guerrillas. In 1946, as a result of elections, the Royalists formed a government and a plebiscite declared in favour of the return of the King. Civil war then broke out again. Greece took the case before the Security Council, and stated that the insurgent communists were receiving aid from Yugoslavia, Albania, and Bulgaria. The Soviets refused to accept the Greek appeal and attributed the disorders to the vindictive policies of the Greek government. On

24 February 1947, the British Ambassador to Washington, Sir Oliver Franks, told the Secretary of State that, Britain due to its financial problems, would no longer assist the Greek army in its conflict against the communists. The United Kingdom explained the necessity of the replacement of its aid with US subsidies. As will be discussed below, the response of the US was in launching the Truman Doctrine.

By articulating a greater concern and apprehension about the Soviet menace in the post-war era, the problem of assistance to Turkey and Greece was being studied by a special committee since February. Kennan, who was asked to participate in the deliberations of this committee was then in his tour of duty at the War College. Establishment of different structures within a short period of time was surprising to Kennan as well. Previously, he was informed by Under Secretary Acheson that General George Marshall, who had assumed the Office of the Secretary of State in January, had in mind the establishment within the Department of State of a planning unit—something to fill the place of the Divisions of Plans and Operations to which he was accustomed in the War Department— and Kennan himself would be asked to head this new unit.

When the special committee headed by Chief of the Division of Near Eastern Affairs, Loy Henderson—a colleague of Kennan from Moscow and Riga days[68]—met on February 24, Kennan asserted that, what they had before them, on that occasion, "was the task of recommending whether to respond affirmatively at all to the problem posed for us by the British withdrawal, or whether to leave the Greeks and Turks to their own devices."[69] Kennan stated that he had revealed that it was in fact had already been decided in principle and that the task of the committee was to outline in more detail the course of action that should be recommended to the President and Gen. Marshall. In his turn, Kennan gave it as his opinion that the US had no choice but to accept the challenge and to extend the requisite aid. This was the consensus of the group as a whole and subsequently, an appropriate recommendation was drawn up.

However, on the day before the State Department's final draft of this message went to the White House, when Kennan came over to the department to have a look at the paper, he figured out that the language to which he took "particular exception was not the product of Henderson's pen or of any of his associates in the geographic divisions."[70] It had been produced, at the initiative of the Department of State's public relations office, in a sub-committee of the State–War–Navy Coordinating Committee (SWNCC) which clearly felt itself under the necessity of clothing the announced rationale for Truman's decision in terms more sweeping than anything that Kennan envisaged. Kennan admitted that the reasons behind his unhappiness over the wording of Truman's message lied in the exclusion of conclusions he had obtained from the lengthy discussions of different working groups in the War College on the situation in Greece and Turkey, and the question of why it was desirable that the US Government should respond to the challenge of the British move which he later developed to lay down the basis of the text in concern.

Kennan asserted that in the words of the following War College presentation he had accepted the conclusion, to which many others in the government had arrived: "if nothing were done to stiffen the backs of the non-Communist elements in Greece at this juncture the Communist elements would soon succeed in seizing power and in establishing a totalitarian dictatorship along the lines already visible in Balkan countries." However, he considered that the Russians and their Eastern European associates were poorly set up to take responsibility either for the governing of Greece or for the support of the Greek economy. He said, "all this might boomerang on them in the form of serious economic difficulties and other problems, which the West might even ultimately exploit to good advantage." But, communist rule he asserted would probably be successfully consolidated in the long run and might some day have most unfortunate strategic consequences from the standpoint of any military adversary of the SU and more important were the probable repercussions which such a development would have on neighboring areas.[71]

On March 12, 1947, after the British Government formally informed Washington on February 24, through a note dated February 21 that as of March 31 the British Government could no longer shoulder the burden of militarily supporting Greece and Turkey and "would be obliged to discontinue the financial, economic and advisory assistance which it has been giving" to these countries, Truman informed Congress and the public of the situation and recommended that the US Government extend aid to Greece and Turkey. In his historic address to the Congress, the main points of which were to become known as the Truman Doctrine, the US President justified this request through describing a worldwide struggle between the free world and totalitarianism.

Regarding the crisis in Greece, he said, the existence of the Greek state was threatened by the terrorist activities of several thousand armed men, led by communists, who defied the government's authority particularly along the northern boundaries, while the Greek Government was unable to cope with the situation. Truman also pointed out that the Greek Government which had made mistakes had been operating in an atmosphere of chaos and extremism. Nevertheless, it represented 85 percent of the members of the Greek Parliament who were chosen in an election considered to be fair. It was then considered that the UN might assist in the crisis. He said, the situation was an urgent one requiring immediate action and the UN and its related organizations were not in a position to extend help of this kind that was needed.[72]

As for Turkey, Truman stated that the future of Turkey as an independent and economically sound state was clearly no less important to the freedom-loving peoples of the world than the future of Greece. Truly, the circumstances in which Turkey found itself were considerably different from those of Greece. Turkey had been spared the disasters that had beset Greece during the war and the United States and Britain had furnished Turkey with material aid. Since the war, Turkey had sought financial assistance from Britain and the US for the purpose of effecting that modernization necessary for the maintenance of its national integrity. "That integrity is essential to the preservation of order in the Middle East" Truman said.[73]

In this context, Truman further explained that it was in the US national interest to help free nations like Greece and Turkey become strong enough to resist communist aggression and he proposed an emergency military and economic aid program, which Congress finally approved on May 22, through the "Act to Provide for Assistance to Greece and Turkey." Truman in concluding his speech pointed out: "The seeds of totalitarian regimes are nurtured by misery and want. They spread and grow in the evil soil of poverty and strife. They reach their full growth when the hope of a people for a better life has died. We must keep that hope alive. The free peoples of the world look to us for support in maintaining their freedoms. If we falter in our leadership, we may endanger the peace of the world—and we shall surely endanger the welfare of our Nation."[74]

Among other things, the Act emphasized that "the President may from time to time when he deems it is in the interest of the United States furnish assistance to Greece and Turkey, upon request of their governments and upon terms and conditions determined by him. . . ."[75] It was enacted that the US President would implement the program by rendering financial aid in the form of loans, credits, grants, or otherwise to those countries; by detailing to assist those countries any persons in the employ of the Government of the US [Provided that no civilian person-nel would be assigned to Turkey and Greece to administer the purposes of this act until such personnel have been investigated by the FBI]; by detailing a limited number of members of the military services of the US to assist those countries, in an advisory capacity only; by providing for the transfer to, and the procurement for by manufacture or otherwise and the transfer to those countries of any articles, services and information and the instruction and training of personnel of those countries; and by incurring and defraying necessary expenses in connection with the carry-ing out out of the Act.

Thus, in parts, the Truman Doctrine comprised aid to Turkey, and large economic and military missions were established in Athens and small ones in Ankara to transfer $750 million worth of assistance. The initial amount was stated as $400 million appropriated to the US Presi-dent to carry out the provisions of the Act to Provide for Assistance to Greece and Turkey of May 22, 1947. In their turn, the Soviets had not viewed these developments without protest and countermoves. In fact, while the future of the US aid programme was back in the lap of the American Congress, the Kremlin was making clear to the world the hos-tile interpretation they had of it and the communist parties in Western Europe were trying to overthrow pro-Marshall Aid governments. Shortly afterwards, the Cominform was announced on 5 October and the autumn meeting of Council of Foreign Ministers in London, like all its predeces-sors stalled under Soviet intransigence. However, in the middle of De-cember the US gave interim aid to France, Italy and Austria and by a new agreement with the UK relieved its of all dollar expenditures in Germany, as well as assuming seventy-five percent of the cost of both zones.[76]

In his appraisal of the Truman Doctrine, Kennan pointed out that the situation of Turkey differed quite fundamentally from that of Greece. He evaluated that there was no serious communist penetration in Turkey and no comparable guerrilla movement. "The Turks had nothing to fear but fear."[77] He considered that if the Turks did not lose their nerves, if they kept their internal political life relatively clean and orderly and refused to get involved in negotiations with the Russians on a bilateral basis over complicated issues such as that of the Straits, they would probably con-tinue to enjoy a temporary and precarious immunity to Russian pressure. He said, should they be increasingly encircled by communist-dominated entities, it would plainly be harder for them to maintain this stance. Thus, aid to Greece was important as a support for stability in Turkey as well. However, Kennan concluded that this view of the problem of Turkey afforded no rationale for the mounting of a special aid program for Turkey itself.

According to him, the accent was put on international morale and on firmness of diplomatic stance, not on military preparations. Kennan stated that it was for this reason that he was not happy to find in the draft of the President's message to Congress a proposal for aid to Turkey as well as to Greece. He suspected that what was intended was primarily military aid, "and that what had really happened was that the Pentagon had exploited a favorable set of circumstances in order to infiltrate a military aid program for Turkey into what was supposed to be primarily a political and economic program for Greece."[78] Then, Kennan asserted that since it was important that the Soviet threat be recognized for what it was "primarily a political one and not a threat of military attack—it seemed unfortunate that the picture of what was needed in Greece should be confused by association with something that was not needed—or, if needed, was needed for entirely different purposes—in Turkey."[79]

In fact, the difference of the situation in Turkey was pointed by Acting Secretary Acheson as well. In his statement before the Committee on Foreign Relations on March 24, 1947, he explained that the Turkish Government had on various occasions applied to the United States for financial aid, but the US Government had not had the facilities for responding to those requests and since British aid was not available, the needs of Turkey for assistance were greatly increased. Subsequently, Acheson referred to both Turkey and Greece and said, "Greece and Turkey are in urgent need of aid and there is no other country to which they may turn."[80]

Following his explanation on the situation in Greece, Acheson underlined that the case of Turkey was substantially different, but Turkey needed this help. The Turkish Army had been mobilized since the beginning of WW II and this had put a severe strain upon the national economy. During the war, Turkey had received substantial assistance from Britain and the US, which had helped it carry this load. But, if these subsidies were no longer available, the Turkish economy would not be able to carry the full load required for its national defense and at the same time proceed with economic development which it needed to keep the country in sound condition.

Meanwhile, the Turkish Ambassador to Washington, R. Baydur, informed Ankara on June 25, 1947 that it was admitted in Washington circles that the US assistance prompted by the serious economic decline of France and Italy and consecutively extended to other countries, had been unfruitful. The amount of the US aid in credits and donations to Europe had reached 12 billion dollars, however it could accomplish very few tasks. It was also strongly advocated that anarchy and communism was gaining ground in Europe and the situation was likely to deteriorate further. Baydur also pointed out that the US–Europe trade balance was 15 billion dollars greater in favour of the former. The European countries could no longer sustain these commercial relations with the US due to their huge budget deficits and lack of finance in dollars. This would inevitably represent a 7.5 billion dollars decline per year in the trade volume with Europe.

In this context, Baydur underscored that when President Truman presented his aid plan to Greece and Turkey, despite the acknowledgement of the need for assistance to these countries, many congressmen had raised criticisms on the ill-defined scope of the programme and demanded a budgetary planning which would clearly state the boundaries of the job in hand. Consecutively, Secretary of State Marshall's speech at Harvard on June 5, was to the effect that it should be admitted that the assistance to Europe had remained in a particular disorder, weakening its effect, and the aid to Europe must be effectively coordinated and executed single handedly. He said, in its turn, Europe had to unite and the US should encourage its efforts in this direction.

As will be further discussed below, Baydur pointed out that following Marshall's speech, Britain and France had acted "at a speed which diplomacy did not witness before" to respond to the situation. According to Baydur, however, the US assistance programme was not ready even after the speech of Marshall. Baydur said, his encounters in the State Department had shown that the programme was mostly a projection aimed at preparing European public opinion and stimulating the European states to take necessary steps for unanimous action. Thus, the programme was expected to be substantialized at a later phase. In the meantime, Truman had decided to set up three commissions to examine the appropriation resources, to determine the positive and negative effects of the proposed assistance programme over the US economy, and the distribution of aids to the recipient countries.[81] In this context, Baydur stressed that the reactions of Congress might be seriously negative since Truman had vetoed the law which envisaged a tax reduction of 4.5 billion dollars in regard to the income revenues which was promised to the US voters by the Republicans.

Baydur's assessments concerning the possible course of action of the SU included: first, Moscow's satellites would request the permission of the SU to adhere to the US assistance scheme; secondly, the SU would desire not to stay out of the European integration which was under construction and would consent to an immediate ratification of the peace treaties and the settlement of the question of Germany; and lastly, a phase of exchange of views would be given its start between Moscow and its satellites, eventually half-removing the iron curtain. This would represent an ease for world peace. However, in case Russia declined the American proposal, the US would shift to an enforcement policy "which would mean the crystallization of the western bloc and the accomplishment of peace between the two blocs would get harder to achieve."[82]

As for the participation of Turkey in the programme for the reconstruction and economic development of Europe, through the Note of the British Embassy dated July 4, 1947, the MFA was informed that the British and French Governments had studied the suggestions contained in the speech of Secretary of State of the US, Marshall, at Harvard University on the 5th June, and the two governments had recognized that Europe had to take the initiative in the work of reconstruction, and that for this purpose it was essential to draw up as quickly as possible a programme covering both the resources and the needs of Europe. In this context, it was stated that "in the opinion of the two Governments a temporary organisation must be set up to bring together the data on which such a programme will be based."[83] Here, it was stressed that this organisation should consist of a "Committee of Co-operation" which would co-ordinate the work of special sub-committees to deal with certain products or branches of economic activity. The Committee of Co-operation would be set up with instructions to prepare a report on the available resources and needs of Europe during the next four years. It was stated that the Committee of Co-operation should, as the American Secretary of State himself suggested, seek the friendly aid of the US in drafting the programme. It would consist of representatives of the UK, France and certain other European states.

The text of the *Annex* [of this Note] *to the invitation to European Countries* further explained that the British and French Governments regarded it as all-important that swift action should be taken for the reconstruction and economic development of European countries which had suffered from the ravages of war. It was stated that the governments believed that this task would be made easier by economic aid from the US such as that suggested by Marshall in his speech of the 5th June. Thus, the first step should be for Europe to help itself by developing the production of its basic resources. "The support of the United States is essential to enable Europe to accomplish this by contributing resources which are lacking until this has been achieved. This is the best way to ensure the economic recovery of European countries and to safeguard their independence."[84] In regard to Germany, which was of course significant for Turkey as a trade partner, it was stated that information relating to resources and needs of Germany would be requested from Commanders-in-Chief, members of the Control Council.

In this framework, four sub-committees would be set up to assist the work of the Committee of Co-operation in regard to the following subjects; food and agriculture; fuel and power; iron and steel; and transport. British and French governments would invite representatives, appointed by countries which agreed to participate, to a meeting in Paris on the 12th July in order to settle the composition of the Committee of Co-operation and the special sub-committees which would begin their work on the 15th July. It was also decided that the report of the Committee of Cooperation should be drawn up in time to be presented to the US Government on the 1st of September, 1947, at the latest. As for the relations of this organization with other international bodies, the Economic Commission for Europe would be informed at its forthcoming session of the setting up of this organization. The Committee and sub-committees would be in contact with the UN Organization and its specialized agencies and services of inter-governmental organizations.

Given this, the Note concluded that:

> In the conviction that Mr. Marshall's suggestions are in the interests of Europe as a whole, that the task of European reconstruction would obtain essential help from the assistance of the United States of America, that this assistance is dependent on European nations making the effort to co-ordinate and to help each other, His Majesty's Government and the French Government have the honour to invite the Government of Turkey to take part in the administrative machinery which they desire to see set up.[85]

Interestingly, the Note Verbalé of the British Embassy discussed above was followed by a Note Signee dated July 5, in which Ambassador David Kelly explained that he was instructed to inform the MFA, Saka, that an important sentence was accidentally omitted from the preamble to the Annex attached to the invitation. After this sentence was inserted at the end of paragraph 2, it would read:

> 2. In order to collect quickly the information needed to draw up a programme covering the available resources and needs of Europe, a special organisation will be set up. All European states willing to do so will collaborate with this organisation. It will not interfere with the internal affairs of these states and no action will be taken by it which could be regarded as a violation of their sovereignty. [There will be no restraint placed upon desirable developments of European trade.][86]

The Note concluded that: "I am further instructed to inform Your Excellency that no significance should be attached to this omission and that the sentence is one to which both the United Kingdom and French Governments attach considerable importance."[87]

Despite the fact that the announcement of the Truman Doctrine paved the way to a greater collaboration in Europe, Kennan's unhappiness with the wording of Truman's message was evident. As he pointed out himself, this was mostly related with the inherent limits of the statement. He said, if he were reacting "today" to the Truman Doctrine, he would certainly have added to the list of specific requirements the willingness and ability of the threatened people to pick up and bear resolutely the overwhelming portion of the responsibility and effort in their own defense against both direct and indirect aggression. Kennan also expressed that what the US was concerned to defend in Greece was the democratic quality of the country's institutions. The US would find it necessary to give aid, over the ensuing years, to a number of regimes which could hardly qualify for it on the basis of their democratic character. Kennan admitted that it was unwise to suggest that this, too, was an essential criterion. "But these omissions, the recognition of which does indeed reflect the promptings of hindsight, only reinforce the validity of the objections to the language of the message that suggested themselves at the time."[88]

Almost three weeks before the announcement of the Public Law 75, it was decided to send a military mission to Turkey, whose work, later on would also serve the drafting of the Aid to Turkey Agreement signed on July 12, 1947, which provided the basis for carrying out the Turkish aid programme. The goal of the US military mission to Turkey, as directed by the SWNCC, was to assess the situation on the ground and recommend to the State Department how much of the $400 million authorised for Public Law 75, but not yet appropriated, was required that year by Turkey. The SWNCC group was also empowered to examine the needs of the Turkish armed forces for equipment and supplies and to suggest priorities; to evaluate the need for a reorganisation of the Turkish armed forces and for staff training by the US or Britain; to make suggestions as Britain's future role in aid to Turkey and how the two countries could work together if British aid were to continue; and finally, to make recommendations in concerning supervision of the use of US aid.

George Harris maintained that in its turn, the US Congress was suspicious of the Truman's decision to help Turkey. He stated that the Congressmen generally considered that the administration wanted to help Turkey, but since it could not do it on its own, it attempted to combine Turkey's case with Greece, where the problem was much more acute. The Truman Doctrine he said, finally marked a very sharp break because the British no longer had much of a role in "protecting" Turkey. Then the Turkish MFA and the military heavily focused on the US as the source of support.[89]

As McGhee put it, it was decided that the US aid mission to Turkey should work under the authority of Ambassador Wilson, since it was feared that the presence of an independent military mission might be construed as interference in Turkish domestic affairs. According to him, the Turkish Government had already expressed concern that Washington would try to exercise its "control" in Turkey. In his turn, Wilson assured the Turkish Government of the limited and cooperative nature of any such control. He said, the US Government "after consultation with Turkey, will determine what military equipment and other aid should be provided to Turkey. . . . All that will take place on Turkish territory will be 'observing' by US officials as to the manner in which Turkey utilizes assistance given."[90]

At this juncture, the question of the use of American advisers was discussed by Max Weston Thornburg in his work on the Turkish economy in the aftermath of the Truman Doctrine. Here, Thornburg pointed out that before WW II, Turkey had made extensive use of foreign advisers from Germany, Britain and Russia and since 1940, forced by circumstance, the government had relied on Turkish specialists, However, most of these technicians had not had the requisite experience to guide the economic development of the country and until this lack was supplied, the need for foreign advisers would continue. He argued that "since Turkey must in the next few years rely principally on the United States for resources previously supplied from Europe, there will be a need for American experts, who are familiar with American standards and practices."[91] According to him, the object was not to spread American influence but to offer the Turks whatever they were capable of making their own. It would not be in accord with "the American spirit to try to transplant a wholly alien system to Turkish soil, as the Russians and the Germans did during the thirties."[92] He explained that the governmental need for skilled advisers might be fulfilled through nominating:

1. General Consultants: Engineers with broad economic and industrial background to study the over-all needs and resources of the nation, its state of economic development and the priority which should be given to various fields of work;

2. Experts in Public Works: Engineers and other experts with appropriate specialized experience to work with the Ministries of Interior, Finance, Transportation and Communications and other agencies of government, to guide detailed studies of major projects;

3. Technical Specialists: Geologists, Mineralogists, Chemists, Architects, and other experienced specialists available in the US from the government and from private professional ranks whose selection could be made by a private consultant to Ankara. Close collaboration between Turkish and American technical colleges, interchange of ideas and publications with corresponding American organizations and formation of Turkish professional societies would offer a similar gain;

4. Agricultural Experts: Agricultural and livestock experts with long experience in American practices;

5. Public Health, Education, Economics Experts, who should be sent "especially to gain the benefits of American experience in vocational training, and to assist in adapting the technical programs in the higher schools to prepare students for work with Americans."[93]

In this context, Harris pointed out that in the long run, Turkish critics of the US would assail the Marshall Plan stress on agriculture in Turkey as a direct challenge to the philosophy of etatism the foundations of which were laid by Atatürk. Indeed, the idea that political independence required a self-sufficient industrial base had become widely accepted by the Turkish intelligentsia since the foundation of the Republic. Harris stated that according to the opponents of the assistance program, the American aid for development seemed to spurn industrial development. He explained that the program for aid to Turkey concentrated the limited available resources on agricultural and infrastructure projects. Of the some $300 million aid provided between 1948 and 1952, almost 60 percent appeared to have been invested in the agricultural sector. As a result, by 1953, Turkey had become one of the world's major wheat exporters and the Turkish national income grew nearly 45 percent during the five years following the start of the program. Besides the aid emphasis on agriculture encouraged the government's orientation towards the peasant masses. According to Harris, the operation of the Marshall Plan could be faulted for practices as encouraging diversity in the variety of agricultural equipment imported, thus excessively complicating the problem of spare parts. He stated that the mechanization of the Turkish farmer and of the military also paved the way to new demands for petroleum imports. However, he pointed out that the American aid "served to impart needed dynamism to the agricultural sector which faced the monumental challenge of a rapidly increasing population."[94]

In discussing the US aid, one is apt to overlook the fact that concurrently, the ground was being prepared for strong criticism of the actual reasons for receiving foreign aid. Yıldız Sertel asserted that throughout this period, as a result of its half-baked assessment of the foreign assistance, the RPP had concentrated its efforts on increasing the country's agricultural production. However, she said, in addition to its positioning as a base, Turkey's wheat production was regarded as another asset by the "imperialist" countries which supplied Turkey in material and credits. Referring to the statements of the IBRD officials, she argued that on paper, these officials maintained that their countries did not want Turkey quit its industrialization objective. Correspondingly, they were underlining that this objective could be reached through developing the country's agriculture which they said, would also pave the way to a balanced development.

Sertel argued that all the concessions made in this respect did not satisfy the imperialists who had the conviction that the statism of the Kemalist regime[95] was still the biggest handicap before the establishment of a liberal economy model. She also argued that despite the fact that the most significant difference between the RPP and the DP was around their interpretation of statism and liberalism while the latter was associated with the DP. Sertel put forward that the "liberal statism" as defined by the DP flourished in terms of both ideal and practice after its coming to power in 1950, however introducing another deviation from the Kemalist tradition and little difference from the previous administration in this respect. Sertel emphasized that even after 1950, the ruling big bourgeoisie and the land owners followed a fundamentally different strategy than that of the Kemalism, accepting to develop Turkey as an agricultural country. She maintained that this policy which was precipitated by US aid, through enveloping the credits, taxation and pricing, served to the accumulation of great wealth in the hands of the big land owners. Again in this period she said, part of the bourgeoisie made up considerable wealth through engaging in partnerships with foreign capital.[96]

Given these impressions, the US Embassy in Ankara also favoured the continuation of the assistance program in Turkey and advised that the time was right in order to increase the activities of the US military mission to Turkey. On June 6, Wilson reported to Washington that the Turkish Government and people welcomed US aid wholeheartedly, noting that a failure to produce the aid could be widely misunderstood. The investigations thus far, he stated, had revealed extensive need for equipment, supplies and training even greater than had been anticipated. Consecutively, as mentioned above, on July 12, Aid to Turkey Agreement was signed. In the preamble Article 1, the general framework for the agreement which had the Public Law 75 in its core, was explained and it was stated that aid was being supplied by the US at the request of Turkey to strengthen its security forces and maintain economic stability. The aid would further the basic objectives of the UN Charter and strengthen ties of Turkish–American friendship. Turkey would make effective use of the aid of the US Government as the President of the US might authorize in accordance with acts of Congress.

Article 2 of the agreement envisaged that information and technical assistance would be furnished as determined by the US Chief of Mission to Turkey in consultation with representatives of the Turkish Government, financial conditions being decided directly between the two governments. Accordingly, Turkey would send full reports, information and observations concerning use and progress of the aid program. The 3rd Article required that the aid program would be observed and reported by the representatives of the American press and radio. Importantly, Article 4 stipulated that both governments would take such measures for the security of articles, services and information furnished under the aid program "as the other judges necessary."[97] In this context, Turkey would not transfer title to the foregoing, permit use by anyone not official Turkish representative, nor use for any purpose other than that intended without the consent of the US.[98] By Article 5, it was secured that Turkey would not use any proceeds from aid to pay on a loan or interest to any other government.

Regarding the wording of the agreement, George Harris pointed out that the Turkish MFA had worked to soften the terms of the statutory requirements imposed by the US Congress. Concerning the 3rd Article he said, after considerable bargaining, the Turkish negotiators inserted phraseology making the freedom of reporters to gather news subject to "security" considerations. Besides, to remove the suggestion of foreign control, the term "aid administrator" was dropped in favor of the title "chief of mission." Washington also agreed to act discreetly in carrying out its supervisory functions. "As a further gesture to Turkish sensibilities, Ambassador Wilson was named chief of mission in an effort to submerge this function in his normal reporting responsibilities."[99]

In his speech made on the occasion of the approval of the agreement in the TGNA, the MFA, Sadak, explained the main features of the agreement. He maintained that the agreement provided a framework in which Turkey's use of the American aid was determined. Since the amount, application and duration of the agreement was not stated, these issues would be subjected to special agreements pertaining to its application. As a result, it would remain in force unless an action was taken on the contrary and would provide the necessary basis for a permanent and unilateral aid program.

On July 23, Wilson sent another report to Washington including the recommendations of the SWNCC team and in which he urged a five-year assistance programme be implemented in order to modernise the armed forces while at the same time reducing their size by two-thirds, at an estimated five-year cost of $500 million. Meanwhile, towards the end of September, the Turkish Government informed the US Embassy in Ankara that, due to budgetary reasons, it intended to demobilise a whole class of recruits, reducing the size of the army from 485,000 to 350,000. In this context, $100 million in US aid funds was requested to cover an anticipated deficit in the defense budget. Neither the State Department nor the British Foreign Office opposed the force reduction, "but Wilson and the department agreed that US aid should be limited to supplying military equipment and that funds should not be allocated for meeting the budget deficit, although US purchase of equipment should help to ease the deficit."[100]

Meanwhile, reactions of the Kremlin towards the US–Turkish collaboration were culminating in a stronger criticism. On August 17, 1947, E. Zhukov, writer of authoritative articles on international affairs and Soviet vision of world politics, alleged in *Pravda* that the US had finally replaced Britain as the world's imperialist power. He argued that one of the peculiarities of the postwar period was the increase of numbers of states that found themselves in a greater or lesser degree of dependency upon American imperialism. According to him, the expansion of the US directed itself primarily against sovereign states which were thus threatened with the danger of becoming semi-colonial. The same thing applied to Turkey "which lost its independence as a result of the the realization of the so-called 'Truman doctrine.'"[101]

Similarly, A. Zhdanov put forward the view that the strategic plans of the US envisaged the creation in peacetime of numerous bases and vantage grounds situated at great distances from the American continent and designed to be used for aggressive purposes against the SU and the countries of the "new democracy." Within a list of countries the US engaged in activities, Zhdanov mentioned Turkey, as "the US Government has officially declared that it has committed itself to assist in the modernization of the Turkish army."[102] According to him, the military was increasingly gaining strength in the US and the military circles were becoming an active political force in this country, supplying large numbers of government officials and diplomats who were directing the whole policy of the Washington into an aggressive military course.

In his speech in the organizing meeting of the Cominform held in Szklarska Poreba in southwestern Poland on September 22, Zhdanov commented on a broader picture of "imperialism" and stated that the principal driving force of the imperialist camp was the US and allied with it were Britain and France. He said, the imperialist camp was also supported by colony-owning countries, such as Belgium and Holland, by countries with reactionary anti-democratic regimes, such as Turkey and

Greece, and by countries politically and economically dependent on the US, such as the Near-Eastern and South-American countries and China. As for the US aid program, the expansionist ambitions of the US had found concrete expression in the Truman Doctrine and the Marshall Plan. He argued that the main features of the Truman Doctrine as applied to Europe envisaged the creation of American bases in the Eastern Mediterranean with the purpose of establishing American supremacy in that area and the demonstrative support of the reactionary regimes in Turkey and Greece as bastions of American imperialism against the new democracies in the Balkans. According to Zhdanov, "the vague and deliberately guarded formulations of the Marshall Plan amount in essence to a scheme to create a bloc of states bound by obligations to the United States, and to grant American credits to European countries as a recompense for their renunciation of economic, and then of political, independence."[103]

Against this background of events, on September 21, a US delegation headed by John Taber, the Chief of Committee on Appropriations of the US House of Representatives, arrived in Ankara on a mission to examine the use of US subsidies. Similar visits followed in the consecutive months including a visit of the members of the Committee on Foreign Relations who expressed their mission as preparing a report to the US Congress.[104] The visit of the Members of the US House of Representatives on October 31, 1947, had coincided with the visit of a parliamentary delegation from the British House of Commons and on November 1, both delegations were present in the inauguration ceremony of the 8th term, 3rd legislation year of the TGNA.

On the same occasion İnönü delivered a speech in which he underscored that the decision of the US, which acknowledged Turkey as a sincere and trustworthy element of peace in this part of the world and increasing its legitimate rights of defense as it would serve the world peace, to extend assistance to Turkey was a unique evidence of its efforts for peace. In its turn, the approval of the TGNA of the July 12 agreement was an expression of the appreciation of the Turkish nation. Here, İnönü stressed that Turkey was neither pursuing a policy of aggression nor would it tolerate any act of aggression against its territorial integrity. This was the straightforward and open policy of Turkey which had passed through an ordeal. He said, though it desired good relations with the Soviet Union, Turkey was subjected to the unrightful allusions of this country which promoted the events of the past as it perceived them and in a false manner. This being the case, Turkey wished the removal of these issues from the agenda.[105]

Given this background, through a series of steps explained above, in addition to this emergency assistance, the Marshall Plan, designed to reconstruct the war-ravaged economies of Western Europe, opened the door for large scale military and economic assistance to Turkey. On August 7, Major General Horace L. McBride was appointed Chief, US Army Group in Ankara. Later in 1947, separate Air Force and Navy Groups were also established. Subsequently, these programs paved the way for a greatly increased American presence in Turkey, but it is from the establishment of the Army Group that JUSMMAT traced its history.[106] The US aid mission to Turkey under the act in March 1948 comprised 182 personnel, including 51 civilians, 71 Army Group, 34 Air Force Group, and 13 Navy Group.[107]

At that moment, unquestionably, it was important for Ankara to ensure a partnership position with Washington to guarantee the flow of US subsidies in increasing amounts. An overwhelming majority of the Turkish military circles shared the contention that American war material would best suit the needs of the Turkish Army. There were, however, opposing views concerning the implications of Turkish–American military partnership. A retired Turkish Army officer, Orhan Erkanlı explained that through military aid, the US gave a vigorous start to reorganize the Turkish Armed Forces at American standards. He pointed out that under the umbrella of the US Military Mission for Aid to Turkey, the US military experts were assigned in smaller field teams which were designed to serve as advisory boards in the Turkish divisions. Correspondingly, courses were opened by these experts to introduce the Turkish officers and NCOs to the US war equipment. The Turkish Army personnel also attended programs in West Germany and in the US. Circumstances of the Turkish economy indeed further compelled Ankara to increasingly leave the control of its armed forces to the Americans as far as training, organization and logistic support activities were concerned. However, "since the US was carrying out a calculated and future oriented planning, as much as generously acting, together with its equipment, weaponry and knowledge, it brought its own military procedures into Turkey providing itself with a single handed supply of resources."[108]

It is indeed evident that the US military assistance eventually paved the way for a structural transformation of the Turkish Armed Forces. The US aid was broadened to include training, logistics as well as overall strategy and tactics. In a short period of time, books pertaining to all ranges of military activities were regularly translated into Turkish. Military schools were a part of this systematic change towards the American model. Most significantly, as will be discussed below, advanced training of the staff officers was attempted to be based on an entirely different system in the name of modernizing the army. In this framework, War Colleges were provided with a new curriculum which included a different understanding of strategy and tactical concept. "It was Americanized."[109]

As stated by another retired officer, Feridun Akkor, to *Cumhuriyet* in December 1967, American military experts were interested to introduce a fundamentally different model for the Turkish Army. In an attempt to limit the education period in War Colleges from three to one year, in 1950, the Chief of US Military Mission to Turkey communicated the Pentagon's decision that the staff training of Turkish officers should be limited to a year, otherwise the US aid would soon be terminated. Akkor evaluated that this dramatic incident underscored that the US military planners had decided that a battalion based Turkish land army would best suit their objectives. In their view, the Turkish Army would not be engaged in overseas battles and since it would conduct its land operations through the units formed in battalions, a three-years War College training for Turkish officers would be unnecessary. Facing the opposition of their Turkish counterparts, however, the US military experts ultimately gave up their insistence on the issue. However, their strict control on the flow of arms, equipment and related military know-how was increasingly felt.[110]

Concerning the US perception on the need of supporting the Turkish Land Forces, McGhee pointed out that when he came to Ankara as Ambassador in 1952, he figured out that the military had a call on the first 40,000 school graduates among those inducted into the Turkish Armed Forces each year—approximately 135,000, many of whom had not finished school—the Navy 16,000 and the Air Force 20,000 with the Army taking what was left. He underlined that this had created a great handicap for the Army in training those required as a result of the modernization of tanks, trucks and electronic communications equipment.[111]

Turning back to the economic aspects of the assistance, as Sander pointed out, it is almost impossible to figure out the total amount of US aid since these programs were widespread and outnumbered. It goes without saying that the debate around the issue of bilateral agreements rightfully underlines the existence of various joint activities of unrevealed nature, the scope and the financial dimensions of which are unknown even today.

The US Assistance Program and the Turkish Participation in the Committee of European Economic Co-Operation

Explicitly, US diplomacy favoured the continuation of the wartime collaboration and the fostering of international cooperation with the SU. However, the post WW II era proved to be too eventful to continue with this expectation. By the Summer of 1946, the dominant body of official opinion in Washington held that the very existence of the SU threatened American security. By March 1947, the idea that Soviet communism was bent on world conquest had been firmly implanted.[112] Michael MccGwire stated that even "the idea of preventive war was common currency and the option of bombing Moscow was openly discussed, to enforce compliance with US policies."[113]

With these considerations in Washington, the US Government sought the means to counterbalance the Soviet challenge without waging another war. Undoubtedly, the US assistance programme for Europe which was launched to draw the free countries of the region together served towards this objective. Although the recovery programme was intended to contain communist expansion, Marshall stated that it was open to all European countries, including those under communist regimes. He stated that, "Our policy is directed not against any country or doctrine but against hunger, poverty, desperation and chaos."[114] In this framework, after Marshall opened discussion of the the plan on June 5, 1947, Washington made it clear that the Europeans should take the initiative in drawing up the specifics of the program, that the SU and its allies were invited to participate, and that German recovery was necessary for the program to work.

On June 17–18, British Foreign Minister, Ernest Bevin and his French counterpart, Georges Bidault, met in Paris to discuss the speech of Marshall. Here, Bidault convinced Bevin that it was politically necessary for Paris to make a gesture to include the Kremlin.[115] Then they issued an invitation to Molotov to consult with them in Paris during the last days of June. In their turn, the Soviets accepted the invitation made by the

Foreign Ministers of Britain and France to attend a Three-power preliminary conference to discuss the American proposals.

On June 17, N. Menemencioğlu, then Turkish Ambassador to Paris, reported to the MFA that the grave consequences of the Moscow meeting of the Foreign Ministers of March 1947 had been followed by the widening of gap between the US and the SU. Menemencioğlu asserted that, having felt a necessity to enhance its sphere of influence, Russia had sponsored the coup in Hungary in May 1947, and had quickly begun to strengthen its position in the Balkans. It was eager to engage in activities even in Austria. Facing the Soviet threat, for the US, there could be no other option but to indicate a firm stand against the Kremlin. However, he said, this could not be in the form of an actual intervention. The fate of protests or resorting to the mechanisms of the UN could also hardly produce any positive outcome. Thus, it could be foreseen that the US would mobilize its powers other than arms to respond to the situation. This could be explained in terms of increasing the influence of the US on the satellites of Moscow too.

In this context, Menemencioğlu pointed out that Britain and France had taken action separately in the aftermath of Marshall's speech. However, they had acted together in order to ensure the US Secretary of State to announce that his speech had also meant an invitation to the SU and the eastern European states. Then, he said, France had assumed a special role in this regard. However, the officials of the French Ministry of Foreign Affairs saw little prospect for Moscow's wholehearted participation in the proposed assistance programme. According to them, the Soviets would either remain silent or accept the invitation, but if the latter option prevailed they would attempt to overthrow the organisation from inside. Thus, he said, with an objective analysis it could be perceived that the acceptance of the Marshall Plan by the Kremlin was out of question. Admittedly, within the framework of a general economic cooperation, the SU could hardly challenge Washington's leading position. In fact, if the Russians could admit this situation, the present impasse would not have been experienced. As a result, the SU would do everything in its power to ensure the failure of the US assistance plan.[116]

On the same day, the Turkish Embassy in Moscow informed the MFA that British diplomats in Moscow were emphasizing that Britain had an independent foreign policy from the US, and it was determined to protect this position. Similar statements were to the effect that the arguments on the American control of British foreign policy were pointless.

Particularly, with a view to tension between Washington and the Kremlin, they said, Britain could play a role of dispersing the causes of any actual or potential strife. With this objective in mind, the removal of reasons for the American intervention (which was prompted by a need for the reinforcement of British interests) in the Middle East and in the eastern Mediterranean, would serve the maintenance of peace as well as the Soviet interests. It was also stated that this status of Britain was significant in regard to the avoidance of any conflict which might break out between these two powers. Given this, the telegram stressed that the tones in these statements were worth noting especially on the eve of talks at Paris and since it had been understood that the British desired to communicate these issues to the Kremlin at a critical phase of the deliberations.[117]

Against this background, on June 27, 1947, Molotov arrived at Paris with a huge contingent of experts. In the talks, he raised mainly two issues. Claiming that the Marshall Plan would infringe on the sovereignty of recipient nations, he urged that European nations should individually calculate their needs and collectively submit their requirements to Washington. Secondly, he inquired how the European Recovery Program (ERP) would influence Germany's level of industry and reparation payments. Bevin and Bidault sought to avoid the German question and instead, they told the Soviet Commissar for Foreign Affairs that the US required a comprehensive plan, not a list of national requirements, "that American demands for statistics and cooperation were innocuous, and that European squabbling might mean the forfeiture of American generosity."[118] According to Molotov, however, the US aid was not without strings attached and the prospect of American supervision was unacceptable. After communicating with Moscow, he became more shrill and intimidated that unilateral Western action might lead to the division of Europe rather than to its rehabilitation. Then, he abruptly withdrew from the talks and accused the US of attempting "to rescue American capitalism by economically enslaving Europe."[119]

As the Soviets saw the Marshall Plan as a serious threat to their control of Eastern Europe, they applied pressure to persuade the governments of Poland, Hungary and Czechoslovakia which had expressed their intention to attend the conference to be held at Paris in late July. In the meantime, the Kremlin was perpetuating a systematic harassment of non-communist parties especially in Poland "but there was still no outright Soviet suppression of them."[120] However, the SU decided to reply to what it regarded as America's economic domination of Europe by calling a rival conference in which Cominform—Communist Information Bureau—to coordinate the activities of the communist parties of Bulgaria, Hungary, Poland, Czechoslovakia, Italy, France, Rumania, Yugoslavia and the SU was created.[121]

In fact, while Molotov was still in Paris, circles around the US Embassy in Moscow had started to express the sentiment that Molotov's participation in the Paris talks was aiming at creating an atmosphere of chaos rather than showing a real effort for the settlement of issues. On June 28, the Turkish Embassy in Moscow informed Ankara that through expressing similar views in the diplomatic circles of Moscow, the US officials were pointing out that the next couple of months would acquire a decisive character. Given this, the US was not expecting the Paris talks to produce any favourable outcome. Particularly, the word "decisive" would serve to the effect that the "Soviet satellites and the democrats" had moved into totally different camps in regard to the issues of international importance. As for the possibility of an armed conflict, based on his personal impressions of Ukraine and its vicinity, an American diplomat in Moscow had explained to his Turkish counterpart that with a view to its crippled economy, the Soviets could hardly dare a war with the West.[122]

Correspondingly, on July 1, 1947, Cevat Açıkalın, then the Turkish Ambassador in London, reported that in London the prevailing idea on the Russian participation in Paris talks was not in the affirmative either. However, the talks at Paris had been expected to have one of the two definite outcomes: agreement or break off. Here, Açıkalın asserted that the conclusion of the deliberations in the negative meant a reaffirmation of the tragic division of Europe.[123]

According to M. Leffler, the Soviet response to the Marshall Plan was harsh and calibrated but it was no declaration of war for the control of Europe as the US Ambassador in Moscow, B. Smith, said. He argued that the Soviet leadership saw its periphery being probed in Turkey and as well as in Eastern Europe, its fiercest enemy Germany revived and its foreign supporters imprisoned as in Greece, or excised from governments as in Italy and France. Thus, the Soviets had reacted defensively and their aim was to consolidate Kremlin's power within the orbit of Soviet influence rather than to seek new gains in the West.[124]

Having excluded the Soviets and their relentless delaying tactics, Western grouping of states in Europe gave fresh momentum to coordination and planning activities to create the conditions for a regular US assistance at once. Admittedly, the bulk of the work on the US assistance programme was being planned by the Committee of Co-operation to which Turkey was a party since its foundation at the Conference of Paris of July 12–15, 1947. N. Menemencioğlu, then the Turkish Ambassador to Paris, headed the Turkish delegation in the Conference. On July 15, Menemencioğlu informed Ankara that it was agreed that the conference mechanism would be replaced by the Committee of European Economic Cooperation. As another point of great importance, the talks in Paris had ended in a way in which the original the Anglo–French initiative aiming at confining the participation in the Committee of Co-operation to a limited number of European states and presenting the programme in concern to Washington along these lines had left its place to a greater scheme. In this regard, all nations present in Paris could have a seat in the Committee of Co-operation which would assume a representative role as well. Technical committees and sub-committees would also address their reports to the Committee of Co-operation which would have an executive board of five.[125] Menemencioğlu explained that within the organisational structure of the European Economic Cooperation Committee, the Committee of Cooperation was designed to assume a privileged role since it would be the executive branch of the organisation which would directly engage in deliberations with the US on behalf of the whole organisation. Despite Menemencioğlu's demarché, Britain and France favoured the inclusion of the Netherlands, Norway and Italy into this board while proposing Turkey a seat in the committees of iron-steel industry and transportation.

Interestingly, Menemencioğlu stated that prior to the talks on the establishment of the committees and the sub-committees, the Turkish and the Greek representatives had agreed to act as the representative of two states to optimize the benefits of their work. In this context, Greece was placed in the committees of energy and food and agriculture, while Turkey was given a seat in the sub-committee of agriculture. In its turn, Greece took a part in the sub-committee of naval transportation too. In the conclusion of his cable, Menemencioğlu also urged Ankara to send specialists to join the works of the relevant committees and the sub-committees.[126] This being the case, within ten weeks after the Paris Conference of July 1947, as will be discussed below, a comprehensive scheme was drawn up for the economic recovery of Western Europe.

As for the formulation of US policy towards the growing cleavage between the Western and Communists Blocs, in an article published in July 1947, Kennan, then Director of Planning at the State Department, stressed the need for "'a long-term, patient but firm and vigilant containment of Russian expansive tendencies.'"[127] He stated that the US should continue to regard the SU as a rival in the political arena. Subsequently, the term 'containment' was widely adopted to describe the aim of US policy in its dealings with the Soviets. Furthermore, Kennan stressed that the political personality of Soviet power was the product of ideology and circumstances: ideology inherited by the Soviet leaders from the movement in which they had their political origin, and circumstances of the power which they exercised for decades in Russia. Shortly afterwards, his telegram circulated in Washington's corridors of power and finally leaked to the press and definitively authored the US policy towards the SU. According to Alan Cassels, Kennan's strategy of containment had already been put into effect and "policy began to catch up with ideology" when the Truman Doctrine was enunciated before the US Congress.[128]

At this juncture, Walter Lippman, a journalist and political philosopher, published his book, *The Cold War,* which was a collection of related newspaper columns in which he criticized the ideas and recommendations expressed in the *Foreign Affairs* article by Kennan.[129] Lippman argued that the international behaviour of the SU was better explained by reasons of history and physical security than by Marxism. He criticized Kennan's arguments for containing the SU and questioned whether the US could afford a policy of confronting the Kremlin throughout the globe while, in fact, the primary threat to the US was not worldwide Soviet expansionism or communist ideology, but the military occupation of the Kremlin in eastern Europe. According to him, with its scope and aim, the containment policy would entangle Washington in many questionable alliances with other countries.

Lippman's explanations included that the natural allies of the US were the nations of the Atlantic community, in other words, the nations of Western Europe and of the Americas. The Atlantic Ocean and the Mediterranean Sea, which was an arm of the Atlantic Ocean, united them in a common strategic, economic and cultural system. The chief components of the Atlantic community, he said, were the British Commonwealth, the Latin states on both sides of the Atlantic, the Low Countries and Switzerland, Scandinavia and the US. The policy of containment, as described by Kennan, was an attempt to organize an anti-Soviet alliance composed in the first instance of peoples that were either on the shadowy extremity of the Atlantic, or were altogether outside it. Thus, he said, the active proponents of the policy "have been concerned immediately with the anti-Soviet parties and factions of eastern Europe, with the Greeks, the Turks, the Iranians, the Arabs and Afghans, and with the Chinese Nationalists."[130] He stated that the US, instead of concentrating its attention and its efforts upon the old allies of the Atlantic community, was aiming at reaching out to new allies on the perimeter of the SU. Given this, no doubt, Lippman's point of departure was totally different from what Kennan and his fellows were then planning in the State Department and the statesmen of the small powers in Europe, such as Turkish foreign policy makers, would want to hear.

Undoubtedly, in Turkey, there were certain groups who strongly opposed the US assistance program as well. According to M. Ali Aybar, the Soviets were also against American aid since they had the opinion that under this ostensible reason, Washington was carrying out the initial steps of a new war. He said, it was unthinkable that the Soviets were uninformed of the statements of some US senators and the writings of Walter Lippman. ". . . And again they know that the American forces which would launch an attack across the Turkish land can hit Russia at its most sensitive point. The Oil regions of Caucasia, regions of industry and metallurgy in the Urals, granaries of the black lands are accessed through the Black Sea coasts. And once these lands were captured, the European part of Russia is threatened by collapse. These are the reasons of Soviet opposition to American aid."[131] With reference to the statements of Lippman, Aybar stated that the US would launch a war against the SU in eight to ten years time, and the US foreign policy makers had designed Turkey as the center of gravity in their war plan. He said, Lippman was a journalist, but the statements of some US senators during the debates on the aid program had also underscored the same projection. Turkish journals had published the explanations of Sen. Edwin Johnson, who said it was an undeniable fact that the WW III would begin in the Middle East for the control of oil resources and the lines of battle was about to be established in Turkey. Then Aybar said, with a view to the discussions in the US Senate, at least as a contingency, Turkey was obliged to take into account that the aid program was designed as a prelude to war.[132]

Regarding the implementation of the US aid program, the Committee of 16 beneficiary nations of the Marshall Plan completed its report on September 22, in which the amount of aid required by these nations was stated as 22.5 billion dollars for the years 1948–1951. According to this report, Turkey's share would remain relatively small in the first years.[133] This report is also known as the Paris Report. In Paris, Turkey requested 615 million dollars for financing its projects. But, as will be further discussed below, in the beginning, the American experts were unwilling to meet this request while placing Turkey in a group of countries that had been considered capable of contributing to the development of war ravaged European economies with a view to its raw materials, gold and foreign currency reserves and foreign trade balance.

On September 27, members of the Committee of European Economic Co-operation[134] in Washington sent an Aide-Mémoire to the State Department, and explained that a large number of technical points which could not be clarified in the report of the 16 participating countries were then clarified. These particular points to which the attention of the State Department was drawn, consisted of the aid envisaged; its form and conditions; and the organisation which should be set up for its administration.

In this framework, it was pointed out that the figure for the dollar deficit in the balance of payments of the 16 participating countries during the next four years as shown by the Paris Report, constituted an order of magnitude below which the amount of aid should not be reduced without the risk of jeopardising the achievement of the programme that the participating countries had in view. It was also emphasized that it was not possible to calculate exactly the amount of this deficit which depended on the size of the harvests, on the movement of prices, on the development of dollar earnings, on the resumption of trade between Western and Eastern Europe, etc., while the uncertainty of the factors affecting the figure contained in the Paris Report might lead to revisions upwards as well as downwards. However, with a view to the consequences of insufficient availability of certain commodities necessary for the rehabilitation of the European economy, it was stated that "this factor, far from reducing the global amount of aid necessary, would tend to increase it."[135]

In regard to the form of proposed aid it was underscored that the American aid could be furnished either wholly in dollars or wholly in goods, or partly in dollars and partly in goods. It was preferred, however, that the greatest possible part of the external aid would be supplied in dollars. In carrying out the programme of imports, it was requested that so far as possible, the ordinary channels of trade should be used. Thus, this condition would be more difficult to fulfill if aid was furnished in commodities rather than in dollars. In addition, the possibility of receiving dollar rather than goods would permit each of the purchasing countries to procure the types and qualities of goods which were best suited to their needs. The Aide-Mémoire underscored that "there is no doubt that these dollars will for the most part be used directly in the U.S. themselves which are the principal suppliers of raw materials, foodstuffs and the necessary equipment."[136]

It was also expressed that the European nations would need to place contracts outside the US with producers who would demand payment in dollars. The participating countries would consequently have to rely on the dollar to enable them to pay for these supplies which were indispensable to the execution of the European programme. Additionally, it was recognized that all necessary steps should have to be taken to limit the inflationary pressure which might result from the purchases. Thus, the European Group was ready to examine with the US Government how it might best cooperate in this regard with the US administration in the common interest.

As for the conditions of the proposed aid, it was explained that the estimated requirements were so considerable that if the aid that was furnished should lead to Europe having to make large transfers, the participating countries would not be in a position at the end of the period in view to ensure a stable equilibrium in their balance of payments. At the same time, the charges to be paid to service an external debt that was too heavy would make it more difficult to obtain credits from the International Bank or private banks which would certainly be necessary to pay for long term capital equipments. The conditions under which these funds might be used would vary from country to country as well. Consequently, the arrangements governing the use of these funds would be different for each country and would lead to individual discussions. It was also considered important to note that these funds should be the property of the recipient countries.

Admittedly, the question of how these sums should be handled accoupled with a delicate political problem of Soviet propaganda warfare. Regarding the need for a political counter-offensive against the opponents of the Marshall Plan who had "announced their intention of using all means to block it," and who would "seek to show that the existence of these funds is capable of conferring upon the U.S. considerable powers infringing the independence of the European countries concerned," it was suggested that these governments have these funds in local currency at their disposal and employ them in accordance with whatever arrangements might be concluded.[137]

Lastly, as would also constitute the basis for an organisation of the 16 participant countries, it was reiterated that the concerned governments had declared in the Paris Report their readiness to set up a joint organisation with two functions; on the one hand to examine and report on the extent to which the programme was being realised; on the other hand to ensure by joint action, the realisation of the economic conditions necessary to enable the general objectives to which each country had pledged itself to be effectively achieved. Consecutively, the task which would be entrusted to this organisation would be elaborated. It was, however, evident that such an elaboration would depend on the character of the external aid and of the organisations "which on its side the American Government deems it useful to set up to ensure the execution of the programme."[138]

This being the case it was recognized that the problem of European recovery had both a commodity aspect and a financial aspect. Thus, a program of assistance from the US could be worked out when considered from either point of view, to a total program which would give real promise of success. However, the US State Department in its informal Aide-Mémoire dated November 4 to the European Group emphasized that "this could not be merely an American program."[139] Furthermore, the most intense efforts would be required on the part of the European countries, both individually and collectively which called for prompt and vigorous steps to restore internal monetary and budgetary stability. The participating countries were also expected to boost their production and their exports if sufficient means of payment were to be found to finance their other requirements. It was clearly basic to the whole program that exports from the European countries be rapidly developed and that these exports be of a character which could continue and expand after special US assistance to European recovery came to an end. Then, it was underlined that any conditions as to the use of materials supplied by the US in the export trade of the participating countries "had to be worked out with this basic objective in mind."

The Aide-Mémoire also stated that the US Government was in agreement with the point of the European Group that restrictions imposed on the use of local currency arising from US assistance should not interfere with or prejudice the economic and financial control of the economy that had to be exercised by the government of each country. Thus, it was desired that "a formulae can be mutually agreed upon between this government and the governments of the participating countries with respect to the use of these funds which will promote and not interfere with the over-all objectives of European economic recovery."[140] The Aide-Mémoire underscored that the US Congress had a controlling voice which it would exercise in these matters as well and this point was mentioned again to emphasize the present trend in formulating the recommendations of the State Department for presentation to the Congress.

In the Paris Report, the sixteen countries had declared their readiness to give, within the framework of the overall programme which they had in mind, a certain number of pledges concerning particularly their production targets, their foreign trade, European cooperation etc. As will be later discussed, in his explanations in the TGNA on Turkey's signing of the Agreement of European Economic Co-operation on April 16, 1948, and subsequently, the Turkish–US Economic Co-operation Agreement on July 4, 1948, the MFA, Sadak, stated that Turkey had submitted projects in the fields of agriculture and metallurgy.

Turning back to the above discussed Aide-Mémoire of the State Department, through this, the US informed the European Group that the US had to give careful thought to additional factors. The capacity of the US to continue to export far larger quantities of goods than it imports was strictly limited. Thus, the US could not assume unlimited obligations to meet the balance of payment deficits of other countries. It was stated that many of the commodities most essential to European recovery were in critically short supply, not only in Europe and in the US but in the entire world. In this context, if the US were to make more dollar assistance available than could be honored in the form of goods, the additional assistance would be purely illusory and would merely contribute to an undesirable inflationary spiral in world prices.

In their turn, the Republican majority hesitated to grant a huge amount to fund the programme to be spent by a Democratic administration. With a view to the deterioration of the international situation, however, in December 1947, the US Congress passed an interim aid program, with $552 million for Europe and $18 million for China. Doubts were quickly dispersed by the communist coup in Czechoslovakia in February 1948. On March 17, 1948, Truman stated in his Congressional speech that,

"We have learned that we must earn the peace we seek just as we earned victory in war, not by wishful thinking but by realistic effort."[141] With his heavy emphasis on Moscow's ruthless destruction of the independence of various Eastern European nations and its intent to sabotage the Marshall Plan, he asked that the Congress complete action on the Marshall Plan and provide for a general military training program. Fortunately for the Marshall Plan's chances of passage, as explained above, the SU and Moscow-oriented nations refused to participate, for Truman got it through the budget-conscious Eightieth Congress by presenting it in a crisis atmosphere. The Congress responded to his call and on April 3, 1948, he signed the Foreign Assistance Act, under which the US provided $12.4 billion to Europe over the next four years.[142]

Semih Günver who had served in Brussels as a Turkish diplomat in these years pointed out that particularly the deterioration in the French and Italian economies had prompted the regular American aid to Europe. He explained that despite the financial assistance provided by Washington in the aftermath of war, communism had advanced in Europe, necessitating a detailed aid project. He said, the US administration had come to the conclusion that no positive outcome could be expected from assistance packages made on an irregular basis, and a total action plan was required. Besides, it was agreed that Europe should be encouraged to unite and effectively cooperate in the administration of the aid. Interestingly, Günver said, in the beginning, it was evaluated by the US that the SU would also accept the assistance in line with its policy to remain in the negotiation table where the future of Europe was discussed. Thus, it was initially expected that through this move, the Kremlin would neither categorically reject the aid nor it would direct its satellites to do so. At this juncture, he said, launching of the assistance to Greece and Turkey was a serious decision which went through a process of long discussions in the US Congress since the US administration was already experiencing a considerable difficulty to explain about the future of the aid program to Europe. This period, he said then included a broader publicity of Soviets vicious goals and the Kremlin's assertiveness in different parts of the world, including the Mediterranean.[143]

It was asserted by some historians that fear of European collapse which prompted the ERP were exaggerated. In this counter-supposition it was put forward that similarly, a considerable economic recovery on the continent was already underway and the Europeans were never as psychologically demoralized as the Americans made them out to be. Others have added that the real crisis at the time was within the American economy that could hardly expect to function hegemonically if Europeans lacked the finance to purchase its products. At the same time, though it is difficult to see how a strategy of containment could have developed, with the Marshall Plan as its centerpiece, had there been nothing to contain. John L. Gaddis evaluated that Washington's wartime vision of a postwar international order had been premised on the concepts of political self-determination and economic integration. According to him, in this context, this was to work by assuming a set of *common* interests that would cause other countries to *want* to be affiliated with it rather than to resist it. He said, the Marshall Plan, to a considerable extent, met those criteria and although it operated on a regional rather than a global scale, it did seek to promote democracy through economic recovery that would proceed along international and not nationalist lines.

Given this premise:

Its purpose was to create an American sphere of influence, to be sure, but one that would allow those within it considerable freedom. The principles of democracy and open markets required nothing less, but there were two additional and more practical reasons for encouraging such autonomy. First, the United States itself lacked the capability to administer a large empire: the difficulties of running occupied Germany and Japan were proving daunting enough.[144] Second, the idea of autonomy was implicit in the task of restoring European self-confidence; for who, if not Europeans themselves, was to say when the self-confidence of Europeans had been restored?[145]

As will be discussed next, particularly in the aftermath of the Marshall Aid, Ankara's efforts to achieve a Mediterranean security organization took place. Meanwhile, Turkey's efforts to express its security concerns faced with setbacks since the US administration could hardly receive Congressional support to include Turkey in its further defense programmes and Britain could no longer be counted as provider of an offer in this direction with a view to its weak talks about revitalizing the 1939 Mutual Assistance Treaty.

Notes

1. Ghazi Mustafa Kemal Atatürk, *The Great Speech*, (Ankara: Atatük Research Center, 2008), pp. 710-711.
2. *Ibid*, p. 656.
3. See, Kemal Karpat, *Turkey's Politics*, pp. 45-47; 65-67. For *Ahali Cumhuriyet Fırkası* which was another short lived political party between September 24 and December 21, 1930, see, Meral Demirel, "Ahali Cumhuriyet Fırkası" in *Tarih ve Toplum*, Vol. 32, No. 192, (İstanbul: İletişim Yayınları, December, 1999), pp. 325-331.
4. Bernard Lewis, "Recent Developments in Turkey," in *International Affairs*, XXVIII (1952), p. 322. Cited in Kemal Karpat, *Turkey's Politics*, pp. 140-141. Karpat stated that he had also subscribed to Lewis' assessment which he attributed to the Democrats.
5. Ergun Özbudun, (ed.), *Perspectives on Democracy in Turkey*, (Ankara: Turkish Political Science Association, 1988), p. 69.
6. *Ibid.*, p. 70.
7. Yıldız Sertel, *Nâzım Hikmet ile Serteller,* (Nâzım Hikmet and Sertels), (İstanbul: Everest Yayınları, 2008), p. 44.
8. Rıdvan Akar, *Aşkale Yolcuları* (Passengers of Ashkale), (İstanbul: Belge Yayınları, 2nd impr., January 2000), p. 137. Ayhan Aktar, *Varlık Vergisi ve Türkleştirme Politikaları* (Capital Tax and the Turkification Policies), (İstanbul: İletişim Yayınları, 2000), pp. 197-198. For the Turkification policies, see, Rıfat N. Bali, *Cumhuriyet Yıllarında Türkiye Yahudileri, Bir Türkleştirme Serüveni* (Turkey's Jews During the Republican Years, An Adventure of Turkification), (İstanbul: İletişim Yayınları, 2nd impr., 2000).
9. Çetin Yetkin, *Struma*, (İstanbul: Gürer Yayınları, 2008), pp. 92-93.
10. *Popüler Tarih*, (Popular History), (İstanbul: NTV Medya Grubu, July 2000), pp. 58-65. *passim.*
11. Cited in, Kemal Karpat, *Turkey's Politics*, p. 141. For the declaration of İnönü, see also, *Ayın Tarihi*, May 1945, pp. 52-53.
12. Kemal Karpat, *Turkey's Politics*, p. 143.
13. *Ibid.*
14. *Ibid.,* See also, *Ayın Tarihi*, June 1945, p. 5.
15. Feroz Ahmad, *The Making of Modern Turkey*, p. 103.
16. *Ibid.;* Metin Toker, *Demokrasimizin* . . . , pp. 58-62.
17. Celal Bayar (or Mahmut Celal) joined the nationalist movement and served as deputy from Manisa in the TGNA from 1920 to 1923. On February 27, 1921 he was nominated as Minister of Economy and served until January 14, 1922. During the absence of the Minister of Foreign Affairs, Yusuf Kemal (Tengirşenk) he served as Acting Minister of Foreign Affairs between February 9, 1922 and April 3, 1922. He was a member of the Turkish Delegation to

Lausanne Conference from November 1922 to July 24, 1923. In August 1923 he was elected deputy of the RPP from İzmir. On March 6, 1924 Bayar was appointed Minister of Exchange of Population, Construction and Resettlement. He was asked by Atatürk to take charge of the founding and management of Turkey's first major bank, the *İş Bankası*. Then, he resigned from his post on July 7, 1924 and on August 26, 1924 he established this bank and served as its director general until November 10, 1932 at which time he was appointed Minister of Economy in İnönü's cabinet. Bayar served in that capacity until November 1, 1937. On that date Atatürk appointed him Prime Minister to succeed İnönü. Upon the death of Atatürk and the election of İnönü as President of the Republic on November 11, 1938, Bayar tendered his resignation but he was reappointed the same day.

Bayar served until January 25, 1939; he remained as deputy of the RPP until September 27, 1945. He resigned from the party on that date and on December 3, 1945, he resigned from his seat in the TGNA. Metin Tamkoç, *The Warrior Diplomats*, pp. 314–315.

18. Kemal Karpat, *Turkey's Politics*, p. 145. See, *Vatan*, September 22, 1945 for the declaration of Menderes.

19. *Ibid.*, p. 151. See also, *Vatan, Akşam*, December 5–7, 1945.

20. Ş. Süreyya Aydemir, *İkinci Adam,* Vol. II, 1938–1950, p. 446.

21. Kemal Karpat, *Turkey's Politics*, pp. 159–160.

22. *Ibid.*

23. From, Akşehir Söylevi (Speech at Akşehir), in *Ulus*, May 7, 1946.

24. F. Cemal Erkin, *Türk–Sovyet İlişkileri ve. . .* , pp. 275–277.

25. *Ibid.*, pp. 280–282.

26. *FRUS, Diplomatic Papers,* 1946, Vol. VII, pp. 810–811.

27. Yalçın Küçük, *Türkiye Üzerine. . .* , pp. 527–532.

28. F. Cemal Erkin, *Türk Sovyet İlişkileri. . .* , p. 276.

29. As Tamkoç put it, Saraçoğlu's long service was later rewarded by his election to the Presidency of the TGNA on November 1, 1948. He was re-elected to the same post the following year and served until May 14, 1950. Metin Tamkoç, *The Warrior Diplomats*, pp. 353–354.

30. Kemal Karpat, *Turkey's Politics*, p. 189.

31. Metin Toker, *Demokrasimizin . . .* , Vol. I, 1944–1950, p. 172.

32. *Ibid.*

33. *Ibid.*, pp. 187–188.

34. *Ibid.*, p. 188.

35. Necdet Ekinci, *Türkiye'de Çok Partili Düzene Geçişte Dış Etkenler* (External Factors in Transformation to Multi-Party Order in Turkey), (İstanbul: Toplumsal Dönüşüm Yayınları, 1997), pp. 333–334.

36. Zekeriya Sertel, *Hatırladıklarım* (Things I Remember), (İstanbul: Gözlem Yayınları, 1977), pp. 251–253; 265.

37. Uğur Mumcu, *40'ların* . . . , pp. 96–97.

38. Zekeriya Sertel, *Hatırladıklarım,* p. 266.

39. Niyazi Berkes, *Unutulan Yıllar* (Forgotten Years), (İstanbul: İletişim Yayınları, 1997), p. 362.

40. Altemur Kılıç, *Turkey and the World,* (Washington D.C.: Public Affairs Press, 1959); Kemal Karpat, *Turkey's Politics,* p. 150; Feroz ve Bedia Turgay Ahmad, *Türkiye'de* . . . , p. 16.

41. Zekeriya Sertel, *Hatırladıklarım,* pp. 266–273, *passim.*

42. Çetin Yetkin, *Karşı Devrim* (Counter Revolution) *1945–1950,* (Antalya: Yeniden Anadolu ve Rumeli Müdafaa-i Hukuk Yayınları, 2009), pp. 471–473.

43. From his July 12, Multi-Party Declaration in *Ulus.* Cited in, Kemal Karpat, *Turkey's Politics,* pp. 191–192. See, also, Metin Tamkoç, *The Warrior Diplomats,* p. 225.

44. Feroz and Bedia Turgay Ahmad, *Türkiye'de Çok Partili* . . . , p. 34. For a critical interpretation of this coincidence establishing a direct relationship between the Aid to Turkey Agreement and the July 12, Declaration, see, Yalçın Küçük, *Türkiye Üzerine Tezler, Vol. II,* pp. 457–460. Based on the memoirs of Turkish tycoon Vehbi Koç, Küçük also claimed that İnönü had shown the text of July 12 declaration to Koç—who was then the Chairman of the Ankara Chamber of Commerce—for *"approval."*

45. Feroz, Bedia Turgay Ahmad, *Türkiye'de.* . . , p. 26; Metin Tamkoç, *The Warrior Diplomats,* p. 221; Ş. Süreyya Aydemir, *İkinci Adam,* Vol. II, 26; Hikmet Bila, *CHP 1919–1999,* pp. 85–87.

46. Ş. Süreyya Aydemir, *İkinci Adam,* Vol. II, p. 456. Aydemir noted that since the Atatürk era, it was customary that the Prime Ministers assumed this title as well.

47. Saka remained in office until resigned once again on January 14, 1949, on account of strong differences of opinion between himself and the Parliamentary Group of the Republican People's Party and President İnönü.

48. See, Mete Çetik, *Üniversitede Cadı Avı* (Witch Hunt in the University), (Ankara: Dipnot Yayınları, 2008). This work also includes the complete text of Pertev Naili Boratav's final defense.

49. Yıldız Sertel, *Nâzım.* . . , pp. 89–90.

50. Şevket Süreyya Aydemir, *Suyu Arayan Adam* (The Man Searching for Water), (İstanbul: Remzi Kitabevi: 1959), p. 46.

51. Alexandre Vexliard and Kemal Aytaç, "The 'Village Institutes' in Turkey," in *Comparative Education Review,* Vol. 8, No.1 (June, 1964), p. 45. As different authors suggest, anti-communism in Turkey was an issue mixed with the manipulation of press. For a collection of news published in the Turkish newspapers particularly in the first half of 1950s which were later accepted as baseless if not ridiculous i.e. red beaked spy birds; communist symbols hidden handkerchiefs on which hammer and sickle appear once they are wet, etc., see,

Derya Çağlar, *Hayali Komünizm* (Imaginary Communism), (İstanbul: Berfin Yayınları, 2008).

52. Kemal Karpat, "The Turkish Left," in *Journal of Contemporary History, Vol. 1, No. 2*, (Sage Publications Ltd., 1966), p. 178.

53. *Ibid.*

54. Secretary of Commerce Henry A Wallace, Speech in New York, September 12, 1946, cited in, Michael H. Hunt, *Crises in U.S. Foreign* Policy, (NY: Yale University Press, 1996), p. 148. Wallace was vice president of the US under Roosevelt from 1941 to 1945. He previously served Roosevelt as Secretary of Agriculture. Wallace was replaced as vice president by Truman for Roosevelt's fourth election in 1944, and he became Secretary of Commerce shortly before Roosevelt's death and Truman's ascension to the presidency in April 1945. He differed with many in the Truman administration over US policies towards the SU. Wallace's speech angered many within the Truman administration and led to his resignation from government. In 1948, he ran for president under the newly formed Progressive Party, calling for disarmament and the end of the Cold War. Though he failed, he received more than one million votes. For the complete text of his speech, see William Dudley and Teresa O'Neill, *The Cold War Opposing Viewpoints,* (San Diego: Greenhaven Press, 1992), pp. 26-31.

55. President Truman, Memo of September 19, 1946, cited in, *ibid.*, p. 149.

56. Feridun Cemal Erkin, *Dışişlerinde 34 yıl* (34 Years in the MFA), Vol. I, (Ankara: Türk Tarih Kurumu Basımevi, 1987), pp. 184-185.

57. As stated by Wilson to Erkin towards the end of March. *Ibid.*, p. 188.

58. Dean Acheson, *Present at the Creation*, p. 198.

59. David McCullough, *Truman,* (NY: Touchstone, 1992), p. 540.

60. Feridun Cemal Erkin, *Türk-Sovyet İlişkileri ve Boğazlar Meselesi*, p. 342.

61. Feridun Cemal Erkin, *Dışişlerinde 34 Yıl* (34 Years in the MFA), Vol. I, p. 188.

62. Haydar Tunçkanat stated that particularly this clause had forced Turkey to assume broad undertakings since it had not prescribed the items, services or facilities in concern to have a "defensive" nature. Haydar Tunçkanat, *İkili Anlaşmaların İçyüzü* (The Inside of Bilateral Agreements), (Ankara: Ekim Yayınevi, 1970), pp. 23-26.

63. *Ibid.*, p. 28. According to George Harris the amount was $270 million in gold and foreign exchange. George Harris, *Troubled Alliance*, p. 24. Max W. Thornburg stated that when the Turkish Central Bank was established in 1931, paper money in circulation amounted to 158,748,563 Liras (about $75 million at the 1931 rate of 2,11 Liras to the Dollar). Concurrently, the government passed to the Central Bank the liability of redemption at some future time

when the currency should be stabilized. To cover the liability, the government paid to the bank 500,000 Turkish Liras in gold, and the balance in Treasury bonds, to be amortized at the rate of one percent of the credits provided each year in the ordinary and special budgets of the state. He also explained that in effect the gold standard had been abandoned except to a limited extent in international exchange, though the gold reserve was ample, amounting to 68 percent of the currency in circulation at the end of 1946 (931,444 Liras). As for the external debt, he explained, this was almost entirely funded and the doubling of this debt from 355 million Liras in 1945 to over 780 million Liras in 1946 was due not to new borrowings as much as to the devaluation of the Turkish Lira in September of that year. See, Max W. Thornburg, *Turkey An Economic Appraisal*, (NY: The Twentieth Century Fund, 1949), pp. 147–148; 155–157; 260, respectively.

64. *New York Times,* April 7, 1946. Cited in, George Harris, *Troubled Alliance,* p. 20.

65. *Ibid.,* 20–21; *FRUS,* 1946, Vol. VII, 902–904. *Ibid.,* pp. 907; 911.

66. Oral Sander, *Türk-Amerikan İlişkileri 1947-1964,* pp. 44–45.

67. *Birleşmiş Milletler Yardım ve Kalkındırma İdaresine Katılınması Hakkında Kanun,* in *Resmi Gazete* (Law on Turkey's Adherence to the UNRRA, the Official Gazette), 10 Mayıs (May) 1946, Vol. 6303.

68. Based on Daniel Yergin's "Riga and Yalta axioms," Arthur M. Schlesinger explained that one school of American policy-makers, guided by foreign service officers like Kennan and Charles E. Bohlen who had studied the SU from the Riga listening post in the years before American recognition, saw a revolutionary state committed by Leninist ideology to world conquest. The Yalta school, on the other hand, saw just another traditional great power. Arthur M. Schlesinger, *The Cycles of American History,* (Boston: Houghton Mifflin Co., 1986), p. 204.

69. George Kennan, *Memoirs 1925-1950,* p. 314.

70. *Ibid.,* p. 315.

71. *Ibid.,* pp. 315–316.

72. "Message from President Truman to the Congress on the Truman Doctrine," in, Arthur M. Schlesinger, *Dynamics of World Power,* pp. 111–115, *passim.*

73. *Ibid.*

74. Known as Public Law 75 (80th Cong., 1st. Session) too. From, "Act to Provide for Assistance to Greece and Turkey, May 22, 1947," in, Arthur M. Schlesinger, *The Dynamics of World Power,* pp. 122–125.

75. *Ibid.,* pp. 122–123.

76. George McGhee, *Envoy to the Middle World,* (NY: Harper & Row Publishers, 1983), p. 20.

77. George Kennan, *Memoirs 1925-1950,* p. 316.

78. *Ibid.,* p. 317.

79. *Ibid.*

80. "Statement by Acting Secretary of State Dean Acheson Before the Committee on Foreign Relations on an Explanation of the Truman Doctrine," in, Arthur M. Schlesinger, *Dynamics of World Power*, p. 115.

81. "Telegram of the Embassy in Washington to the MFA, June 25, 1947." *The MFA Archives.*

82. *Ibid.*

83. "The Note of the British Embassy in Ankara to the MFA, July 4, 1947." *The MFA Archives.*

84. *Ibid.*

85. *Ibid.*

86. "The Note of the British Embassy in Ankara to the MFA, July 5, 1947." *The MFA Archives.*

87. *Ibid.*

88. George Kennan, *Memoirs 1925-1950*, p. 321.

89. As told by George Harris in my interview with him.

90. Cited in, George McGhee, *The US-Turkish-NATO . . .* , p. 40.

91. Max Weston Thornburg, *Turkey An Economic Appraisal*, p. 212.

92. *Ibid.*, p. 216.

93. *Ibid.*, p. 215.

94. George Harris, *Troubled Alliance*, pp. 33-35.

95. In fact, a true definition of the Statism as part of the Kemalist ideology would require one to underscore that this approach had not envisaged a controlled economy. Partly corresponding to the statement above, Kemal Atatürk had made clear in his statements that Turkey's modernisation was dependent on economic and technological development. The principle of Statism was then interpreted to mean that the state was to engage in areas where private enterprise was not willing to invest or where private enterprise had proved to be inadequate although national interest required it. For a good deal of this debate see, Niyazi Berkes, *Türk Düşününde Batı Sorunu* (The Western Question in Turkish Thought), (Ankara: Bilgi Yayınevi, 1975), pp. 105-108; 109-115.

96. Yıldız Sertel, *Türkiye'de İlerici Akımlar* (The Progressive Movements in Turkey), (İstanbul: Ant Yayınları, 1969), pp. 75-77.

97. For the text of this agreement (signed in Ankara by the MFA Saka and the US Ambassador Wilson), see, *Resmi Gazete* (Official Gazette), September 5, 1947, No. 6699, pp. 1-2. See also McGhee's discussion of the Aid to Turkey Agreement, George McGhee, *The US-Turkish-NATO . . .* , pp. 41-42; and *FRUS*, 1947, Vol. V, pp. 190-192.

98. Years later, this point was raised in connection with the Cyprus crisis in the shocking letter of President Johnson dated June 5, 1964, which he sent following İnönü's informing him of the Turkish consideration of intervening in the island. See, *ibid.*, and Oral Sander, *Türk-Amerikan İlişkileri 1947-1964,*

(Ankara: Sevinç Matbaası, 1979), pp. 26–27; Melek M. Fırat, *1960–71 Arası Türk Dış Politikası ve Kıbrıs Sorunu*, (Ankara: Siyasal Kitabevi, 1997), pp. 130–133; Pierre Oberling, *The Road to Bellapais*, (NY: Columbia University Press, 1982), pp. 114–115.

99. George Harris, *Troubled Alliance*, p. 28.

100. George McGhee, *The US-Turkish-NATO . . .*, p. 43. As stated by a later State Department report, the breakdown of the $100 million furnished to Turkey were as follows: Ground Forces $48,500,000; Air Force $26,750,000; Naval Force $14,750,000; Arsenal Improvement $5,000,000; and Highway Improvement $5,000,000. *Ibid.*

101. E. Zhukov, "The Colonial Question After the Second World War" Trans., in, Arthur M. Schlesinger, *Dynamics of World Power,* p. 348.

102. A. Zhdanov, in "The International Situation," September 1947, in, *ibid.*, p. 356.

103. A. Zhdanov, "Speech at the Founding of the Cominform in Poland," September 22, 1947, in, Michael H. Hunt, *Crises in U.S. Foreign* Policy, pp. 159–160.

104. *Ayın Tarihi*, No. 166, Eylül 1947, pp. 13–15; No. 168, Kasım 1947, p. 1.

105. "Opening Speech of the President İnönü on the Occasion of the Inauguration of the TGNA'S 8th Term, 3rd Legislation Year," November 1, 1947, *İsmet İnönü'nün TBMM'deki Konuşmaları 1920–1073* (The Speeches of İsmet İnönü in the TGNA 1920–1973), İkinci Cilt (Vol. II) (1939–1960) (Ankara: TBMM Basımevi Müdürlüğü, 1993), pp. 71–72.

106. In 1949, MG McBride united the three groups to form the Joint American Military Mission for Aid to Turkey. This tri-service organization was one of the first of the military assistance and advisory groups (MAGGs) that the US was to organize in many countries to administer the distribution of American military equipment and to help train foreign military personnel. MG McBride served between August 10, 1947–June 30, 1950 and was replaced by MG William H. Arnold who served between June 30, 1950 and Jan 31, 1953. By 1951, JAMMAT had 1250 military and civilian personnel assigned and was the largest US MAGG. In 1958, JAMMAT was renamed JUSMMAT—the Joint United States Military Mission for Aid to Turkey. *40th Anniversary of Military Assistance to Turkey,* Commemorative Pamphlet, (Ankara: JUSMMAT, August 11, 1987).

107. Programmes conducted by US specialists included intensive training in the fields of supply, communications, ordnance, aircraft flight and maintenance, medical care, highway construction and machine operation and maintenance. George McGhee, *The US-Turkish-NATO . . .*, pp. 43–44.

108. Orhan Erkanlı, "Türk Ordusu Yeniden Düzenlenmelidir" (The Turkish Army Should Be Given A New Order), in *Milliyet*, February 19, 1968. For

further remarks and the opposite view on the subject, see, Doğan Avcıoğlu, *Türkiye'nin Düzeni* (The Order of Turkey), (Ankara: Bilgi Yayınevi, 1969), pp. 267–268.

109. *Ibid.*, p. 268.

110. *Ibid.*, pp. 268–269.

111. George McGhee, *"The–US–Turkish–NATO . . . ,"* p. 45.

112. Michael MccGwire, "Is There A Future For Nuclear Weapons?" *International Affairs*, 70:2, (April 1994), p. 216.

113. *Ibid.*

114. Cited in, *ibid.*, p. 15.

115. After having ousted the communists from his coalition, Socialist Prime Minister Paul Ramadier was governing with a precarious majority. If the Soviets were excluded, the communists would attack him that he was alienating the SU and dividing Europe. The Gaullist right as well, would denounce him for compromising French interests, sacrificing national well-being for Dollars etc. Bidault, however, assured Bevin that he would not tolerate Soviet delays or demands. Melvyn P. Leffler, *A Preponderance of Power*, p. 184.

116. "Telegram of the Embassy in Paris to the MFA, June 17, 1947." *The MFA Archives.*

117. *Ibid.*

118. *Ibid.*

119. Henry Kissinger, *Diplomacy,* (NY: Simon & Schuster, 1994), p. 443. In the first two years after the war, Stalin had been able to impose Eastern Europe's frontiers without undertaking an inordinate risk because the Red Army already occupied those areas. Until then, Albania and Yugoslavia had established communist regimes while Bulgaria, Czechoslovakia, Hungary, Poland and Romania had coalition governments in which the communists were the strongest but not yet the unchallenged political center of gravity. See also, George McGhee, *Envoy to the Middle World*, p. 20.

120. Czechoslovakia at first accepted the invitation to the second meeting but then withdrew under Soviet pressure together with other Eastern European states.

121. The Cominform's predecessor, the Communist International (Comintern), established in 1919 to unite world communist parties, was dissolved in 1943 in an attempt by Stalin to placate his Western Allies. By 1947, the growing division of Europe was coupled with the Soviet attempts to gain maximum control over Eastern Europe. The installation of a puppet government in Hungary a month before the meeting of Poland in September 1947 was one step in this direction. The Cominform was to increase the effectiveness of Soviet policy by organizing "interchange of experiment among the parties, and if needed be to coordinate their activities on the basis of mutual agreement." Commentary of Arthur M. Schlesinger, in, *Dynamics of . . . ,* Vol. II., p. 349. One of the results of this hard line was that when Tito endeavoured to create

national Communism in Yugoslavia, the Cominform declared him a heretic and expelled Yugoslavia from the Communist Bloc in 1948.

122. "Telegram of the Embassy in Moscow to the MFA, June 28, 1947." *The MFA Archives.*

123. "Telegram of the Embassy in London to the MFA, July 1, 1947." *Ibid.*

124. Melvyn P. Leffler, *A Preponderance of Power*, p. 186.

125. "Telegram of the Embassy in Paris to the MFA, July 15, 1947." *The MFA Archives.*

126. *Ibid.*

127. George Kennan (attributed to "X"), *The Sources of Soviet Conflict,* in Foreign Affairs, July, 1947, in William Dudley and Teresa O'Neill, *The Cold War Opposing Viewpoints,* p. 57.

128. Alan Cassels, *Ideology & International Relations in the Modern World,* (London: Routledge, 1996), p. 209.

129. Lippman is credited by some historians with creating the phrase "Cold War." See, Dudley and O'Neill, *The Cold War . . .* , p. 62. Walter Lippman, "Containment of the Soviet Union is Poor Policy," in, *ibid.,* pp. 63–72.

130. *Ibid., p. 69.*

131. Mehmet Ali Aybar, "Yardımın Aleyhinde Bulunmak Her Türk İçin Kutsal Bir Görevdir" (It's a Duty for Every Turk to Stand Against the Aid), in *Bağımsızlık Demokrasi Sosyalizm* (Independence Democracy Socialism), (İstanbul: Gerçek Yayınevi, 1968), pp. 104–105.

132. *Ibid.,* pp. 105–106.

133. İsmail Soysal, *Soğuk Savaş Dönemi ve Türkiye . . .* , pp. 44–46.

134. Within weeks after its foundation, this cooperation mechanism acquired different names such as, "The Committee of Co-operation; The Committee of European Economic Co-operation; or the European Group" which all referred to the same organization.

135. "Aide Memoire of the Committee of European Economic Co-operation to the State Department, October 27, 1947." *The MFA Archives.*

136. *Ibid.*

137. *Ibid.*

138. *Ibid.*

139. "Informal Aide-Mémoire of the State Department to the European Group, November 4, 1947." *The MFA Archives.*

140. *Ibid.*

141. From the "Message by President Truman to Congress on Western Reaction to the Soviet Coup in Czechoslovakia, March 17, 1948," Arthur M. Schlesinger (Gen. ed.), *Dynamics of World Power,* p. 129.

142. William E. Pemberton, *Harry S. Truman,* p. 100. An amount of $5.85 billion was the initial appropriation for the European Recovery Program, which between April 3, 1948 and June 30, 1952, was to cost over $13.3 billion. On

April 17, Truman drafted a speech which he did not deliver. Here he said "twice in a generation brave allies have kept the barbarian from our borders. It can't happen that way again." In this context he underscored the need for an immediate, balanced and a long range program which included calls for the return of selective service and a certain increase in the armed forces. He concluded, "Our friends the Ruskies understand only one language—how many divisions have you—actual or potential . . . ," "Draft Speech (Undelivered), April 17, 1948," in Robert E. Ferrell (ed.), *Off the Record*, (Missouri: University of Missouri Press, 1997), p. 133. See also note of the editor on p. 129.

143. As told by Retd. Ambassador Semih Günver in my interview with him.

144. Gaddis also stated that a related argument was laid by Hadley Arkes in *Bureaucracy, the Marshall Plan, and the National Interest*, (Princeton: Princeton University Press, 1972), p. 51.

145. Gaddis argued that the Marshall Plan was the means by which Washington sought to project overseas the mutually-beneficial relationship between business, labor and government they had worked out at home and the point was not to make Wilsonian values a model for the rest of the world, but rather the politics of productivity that had grown out of American corporate capitalism. John Lewis Gaddis, *We Now Know*, (Oxford: Clarendon Press, 1997), pp. 38–39, *passim*.

Chapter 6

War, Cold: Launching of the Western Security Pacts and a Re-Assessment of Turkish Role in the Middle East (1948–1949)

It is under internal conditions such as are suggested by the foregoing inadequate observations that the Turkish Empire is striving to maintain itself against the conflicting ambitions and jealousies of the Great Powers.[1]

Admittedly, from 1948 to 1950, the Turkish role in regional defense was a matter on which uncertainty prevailed. During this period, drawing on a variety of assumptions, Ankara produced a range of policy alternatives to associate its defense with that of the West. On this premise, this chapter explains that, as a result of the lack of an invitation to become a founding member first in the Brussels Pact in March 1948 and a year later in NATO in April 1949, Ankara increasingly needed to embark on developing its own projections, a Mediterranean security groupement offer being the most cited one. Here, it is also explained that, concurrently, increasing efforts to draw Middle Eastern states together under a new politico–military umbrella also raised the possibility of establishing a Middle East Defense Organization (MEDO) perhaps linked to NATO.

That was not what happened however. And, eventually, Anglo-American efforts to create a regional security grouping of states proved to be in vain. Given this, this chapter expresses that the conditions gradually

arose for Ankara—which was both trying to promote its Mediterranean
security pact proposal and contributing to the efforts around the establishment of MEDO—to renew its efforts for joining to the Western grouping of states, but this time in an entirely different region, in the Far East.

Progress Towards a Euro–Atlantic Pact Contains Turkish Participation in the Alliance

Evidently, the proclamation of the Truman Doctrine and the US aid program, addressed only in part, from Ankara's point of view, Turkish
security concerns since it did not provide Turkey with a permanent security mechanism. Thus, in the absence of an American commitment in the
Mediterranean and while the British maintained an essential strategic
interest in the area, inevitably, Turkey relied on its treaty of mutual
assistance with Britain and France of 1939 in its efforts to counter any
future Soviet pressure. Concurrently, Turkey had been hoping for some
security arrangement with the US since 1947, when the waning of British
power in the Eastern Mediterranean became apparent.

Meanwhile, according to McGhee, in a period of increasing demand
of the UK for US support "in other parts of the Middle East than Greece
and Turkey, as the military value of British treaty rights in Egypt, Iraq
and Jordan declined,"[2] the British whose objective was to hold on to
these rights for as long as possible, perceived the defence of the Middle
East as an instrument of continuing British influence in the region. Indeed, there were clear indications that Britain had shifted to formulate its
foreign and security policies on different grouping of states each led by
either itself or the US. McGhee pointed out that the main strategy of the
British was "Inner Defence" centred on the "Inner Ring" whose locus
was Suez. The US, however, saw Middle East defence as a way to defend the region as a whole from Soviet aggression by bolstering the
military strength of Turkey, Iran and Iraq—the "Outer Ring"—within an
"Outer Defence" strategy with "Inner Defence" as a backdrop.[3]

In a Memorandum dated January 5, 1948, Ernest Bevin presented
his account of Soviet policy according to which British and American
interests were undermined everywhere by growing Soviet ambitions. There
was a risk, he thought, that the communists would control Italy, France
and Greece. If Soviet plans in Greece succeeded Turkey also would collapse. Consequently, the success of Russian expansionist designs would
imperil the "three elements of Commonwealth defence, the security of

the UK, the control of the sea communications, and the defence of the Middle East." A few days later, on 8 January Bevin discussed with the Cabinet his idea of forming, with American backing, a Western democratic system which would include France, the Benelux countries and Britain and which would eventually extend to comprise Italy, Greece and possibly Portugal. At a later stage Spain and Germany could also be included. The Cabinet endorsed the proposal and on 13 January Washington was approached. Along the lines of the same policy, Ernest Bevin proposed a Western alliance against Moscow. When Truman responded positively, discussions quickened. At the same time, Bevin communicated the idea to his French counterpart as well, who agreed to co-operate. The exact nature of the alliance, and the American relationship to it, emerged slowly, and as will be further discussed below, on March 17, 1948, Britain, France and the Benelux countries signed the Brussels Pact, which provided for collective security.

On January 22, Bevin delivered to the House of Commons a message which underlined that the US and the UK were heading towards a western collective security arrangement. He said, "We are, indeed, at a critical moment in the organisation of the postwar world, and decisions we now take, I realise, will be vital to the future peace of the world. . . . I hope that treaties will thus be signed with our near neighbours, the Benelux countries, making with our treaty with France an important nucleus in Western Europe."[4]

Undoubtedly, Bevin's speech gave rise to mixed feelings in Ankara. On the one hand, the British initiative addressed what the Turks saw as a need for Western defence cooperation to counterbalance Soviet power. On the other hand, however, the proposed defence arrangement did not encompass the Eastern Mediterranean. Ankara became concerned over this exclusion. The world division into two blocs of power, which had become unmistakably clear by the end of 1947 certainly justified this concern.

In the meantime, a series of treaties of friendship and mutual assistance between the SU and Romania (February 4), Hungary (February 18), Bulgaria (March 18) and Finland (April 6) were concluded. The Eastern Bloc to which Poland and Chezchoslovakia also belonged, and from which Finland would gradually move out, started to take shape.

At this juncture, in the intensification of the Cold War in Europe two crises had the responsibility more than anything else for sharpening the acrimony: the communist assumption of power in Czechoslovakia in

February 1948, and the Berlin blockade, which lasted from June 1948 to May 1949. The Czechoslovakian coup surprised Washington precisely because it came against a backdrop of uncertainty about Soviet intentions. Hammond argued that before February 20, Czechoslovakia was a pluralistic democratic state supportive of Soviet foreign policy yet knitted to the West economically, by March 1, it had become a "communist dictatorship," a symbol of the fate that awaited any country that accepted communists into coalition governments.[5]

In Czechoslovakia, in the general election of May 1946 the Communist Party had secured approximately 40 percent of the votes in Bohemia and Moravia, emerging as the largest single party with 93 seats; the next largest, the National Socialists, which comprised supporters of moderate bourgeois, including Edvard Beneš, obtained around 24 percent and possessed 55 seats. The Government, thus, was a coalition comprising Communists, National Socialists, People's Party and the Social Democrats.[6] The government worked effectively until 1947. The communists held a number of leading posts, most significantly the Ministry of Interior, which controlled the police. Friction developed within the coalition in 1947 as a consequence of the problems encountered in the economy and of rivalry connected with the impending general election in May 1948. Rumours circulated that the communists might be forced out of the government or that Edvard Beneš might install a non-communist as Prime Minister in place of Klement Gottwald.[7] The crisis came to a head on February 13 when the members of the National Socialist, People's and Democratic parties tendered their resignations in protest of communist policy regarding the police.

In its turn, the Communist Party used its strength in the trade unions and associated bodies to rally support on the grounds of a bourgeois reactionary threat to the achievement of the state since 1945. No doubt, speculation in the West centred on the role in the crisis played by the Kremlin. Zorin, the deputy Soviet Commissar for Foreign Affairs was in Prague in February and was involved in consultations with Czechoslovak communist leaders. It was unlikely that, however, the Kremlin had masterminded the whole operation. Faced with mass demonstrations on February 24–25, Beneš accepted the composition of the government proposed by the communists. Jan Masaryk remained in the government as non-party Foreign Minister, in the hope that he could exert a moderating influence. On March 10, in talking to US Ambassador, Steinhardt, he described President Beneš who was indeed physically and psychologically exhausted, as a broken figure and he conceded that the communists dominated the government completely.[8] Two months later, on May 29, Beneš told Steinhardt that he condemned communist methods in seizing power and was determined to resign.[9] He resigned on June 7 and was replaced by Prime Minister Klement Gottwald, leader of the Communist Party.

Another importance of the Czech crisis in its wider effects was that it heightened tension in the Cold War and accentuated apprehension over a Soviet attempt to extend communism elsewhere. Shortly afterwards, the Kremlin designed its consecutive move towards the West Berlin. The Brussels Treaty was scarcely signed when the Soviets started the blockade of West Berlin (June, 1948). It was to last for 323 days, and was only countered by the organization of a costly air-lift by the Western Powers. The Berlin Blockade no doubt hastened the setting up of Western defence.

Having watched the events helplessly, the American and British Governments concluded that nothing could be done directly, but the "right lessons" should be drawn for other parts of Europe. Shortly afterwards, with Anglo–American encouragement and with the Czech crisis as a backdrop, Britain, France, Belgium, Luxemburg and the Netherlands increased their efforts to form a pact for collective defense.

From a Turkish point of view, however, the omission of Greece and Turkey as possible members of the Western bloc was deliberate. According to F. Cemal Erkin, at the time Ambassador in Rome, Bevin had in mind the creation of a bloc of states which would enable Britain to make some sort of a deal with the Soviet Union, possibly at the expense of certain small states such as Greece and Turkey. Besides, he had conceptualized an evolving western European security system to which Italy and Germany would eventually be restored. Under these circumstances, exclusion of Turkey and Greece—without an implication of the change in their status in the future—was not understandable.

Turning back to prevailing ambiguity about the Turkish situation in the aftermath of Britain's declared policy, the Turkish President asked urgently for an official summary of the speech and instructed the Anatolian News Agency to be instantly informed by telephone of world reactions as they came in. İnönü stated that the speech had impressed him more favourably because, it constituted a decision which meant that leaders in Western Europe were about to adopt to courageous activity in order to get organized.

As Erkin put it, Bevin's speech on January 22 was received with excitement in Ankara. He stated that the broadcasts of the radiohouse in Ankara included the statements of Turkish statesmen who expressed great satisfaction on the news concerning the political and military alliance, which was in fact, confined to West Europe. However, such positive reactions from Ankara would soon prove to be untimely. Erkin maintained that the attitude of West Europe lacked adequate attention to the fact that the Truman Doctrine had clearly underscored the existence of a threat against Turkey and Greece. Turkey had successfully repelled the Soviet threat directed at the Straits and its territorial integrity very recently. Given this, it was disregarded that the Soviets were aiming at settling the question of the Straits, while Greece was in a bitter civil conflict and Iran was under occupation[10] through placing Turkey in pincers. Furthermore, troop movements on the Bulgarian–Turkish border were taking place as part of Soviet designs aimed at increasing the pressure on Turkey.

When Erkin cabled his views to Ankara, the MFA Sadak, immediately invited him for consultations. In Ankara, Sadak told Erkin that a day before his statement, Bevin had informed Ambassador Açıkalın in London, and Kelly had visited him in Ankara concurrently, in order to explain the British initiative and the guarantee of Britain's uninterrupted interest and friendship, and stated that the British Government was convinced that this development would satisfy Ankara as well. Contrary to Erkin's expectations, Sadak also implied that Ankara was satisfied with these statements and the guarantee which Britain extended to Turkey. Subsequently, in Erkin's visit to Prime Minister Hasan Saka, Turkish Premiere expressed similar views too.

However, Erkin considered that Turkey had failed to take prompt action. He found a convenient ground when İnönü asked his assessments on the Brussels Treaty and its foreseeable outcomes. When Erkin explained his anxiety about the exclusion of Turkey, and the formulation of the new defensive scheme in Western Europe, İnönü agreed with Erkin's anxiety and asked him as to what could be done next. Erkin said that having failed to emphasize the imperative of Turkey's political and military presence immediately after Turkey was informed of the new formation, it was very unlikely that demarchés from then on could result in the affirmative. However, since the inclusion of Washington in this formation was nearer, it might be of use if Sadak was instructed to visit London, he told İnönü. Against these expectations, Sadak visited London.

But, deliberations in London were fruitless. Erkin maintained that Turkey's underestimation of Western efforts towards the conclusion of a defensive organization would repeat itself and cause considerable hardships in Turkey's application to NATO as well.[11]

As mentioned before, the coup in Czechoslovakia which took place on February 25, 1948 accelerated the discussions between the Western European States and the US regarding the establishment of a defensive alliance. In fact, the Prague Government which had favoured participation in the Marshall Plan was obliged to revise its views and reverse its decision after a hasty visit by the Czech Premier K. Gottwald, and the Foreign Minister Jan Masaryk to Moscow in July 1947. From then on, the communists, by means of a campaign of denunciation, secured the arrest and trial of many members of the People's National Socialist and Slovak Democratic Parties which held an absolute majority and finally in February 1948, Moscow's special envoy Zorin, engineered the resignation of President Beneš to pave the way to the formation of a Communist Government.

Under these circumstances, on March 4, 1948, negotiations were precipitated towards the conclusion of the Brussels Treaty which was proposed by Britain and France to Benelux countries, and within a fortnight's time on March 17, the treaty was signed. The Brussels Treaty had its roots in the Treaty of Dunkerque between Britain and France and came into being as an end-result of the extension of this formation. The Treaty of Dunkerque was signed by the UK and France on March 4, 1947 for a minimum of 50 years. This was an alliance treaty which included clauses explicitly directed against Germany, should it try to renew a policy of aggression and in certain aspects, it was regarded as an attempt at revitalising the "Entente Cordiale." Under its terms they were also bound, by means of continuing consultation on problems bearing on their economic relations, to take all measures necessary to increase their prosperity and economic stability and thus, enable them to make a more effective contribution to the economic and social aims of the United Nations.[12]

The Brussels Treaty was thus mainly directed against Germany and similar objectives were unavoidably transferred to it. This treaty was directed at different objectives afterwards. It represented the first step in the post-war reconstruction of Western European security and brought into being the Western Union and the Brussels Treaty Organization. The signatory countries pledged themselves to build up a common defence system and to strengthen their economic and cultural ties. This security mechanism was particularly endorsed by the willingness of the participant countries' expression of their readiness to come to the aid of any contracting party in case it became an object of an armed agreession "in Europe" as expressed in Article IV. This Article stated that in accordance with the provisions of Article 51 of the Charter of the United Nations, the other signatories to the treaty would afford the attacked party "all the military and other aid and assistance in their power." It was also stated in Article V of the treaty that all measures taken as a result of the preceding Article would be immediately reported to the Security Council, and they would be terminated as soon as the Security Council has taken the measures necessary to maintain or restore international peace and security.

Article VII of the treaty provided for the creation of a supreme body in Western Union, known as the Consultative Council, consisting of the five Foreign Ministers. Under it was a Western Defence Committee consisting of the Defence Ministers. Here, it was stated that at the request of any of the contracting parties, the council would be immediately convened in order to permit the contracting parties to consult with regard to any situation which might constitute a threat to peace, "in whatever area this threat should arise; with regard to the attitude to be adopted and the steps to be taken in case of a renewal by Germany of an aggressive policy; or with regard to any situation constituting a danger to economic stability."[13] It is interesting to note that towards the final articles of the agreement, the definition of threat was more clear and expressed merely as the "renewal by Germany of an aggressive policy" and "danger to economic stability." This, no doubt, was a clear indication of the decision of the participating countries to confine the scope of the agreement.

With a view to this fact, Turkish disenchantment with being left out of this agreement might be considered as untimely or as an exaggerated reaction. But as will be discussed below, the Brussels Treaty was designed to introduce a broader defense perspective which included cross-Atlantic partners, namely the US and Canada. In this context, it might be argued that the diversion of opinion between Ankara and the members of the Western Union had its roots in their perception of the Truman Doctrine and the Marshall Aid. According to Ankara, together with Greece, Turkey was unquestionably in the center of the Truman Doctrine and the American interest in Europe, while the others saw these two countries on the brink of Europe and whose defense had a minimum role for the security of the continent. Obviously, closer contacts of the WEU with Washington was shaping a similar idea in the minds of the US officials. This being the case, Ankara saw the danger of being excluded from this treaty which paved the way for a greater collaboration.

Meanwhile, economic aid to Ankara was no doubt on Washington's agenda. Marshall, in a letter to the Speaker of the House of Representatives on February 26, requested on behalf of the administration a further appropriation of $275 million so as to ensure continuing military aid to Greece and Turkey to June 30, 1949 as the next step. The Senate Foreign Relations Committee, on March 19, approved the administration's request and the Senate passed it on March 25.

The Foreign Assistance Bill in its final version was passed by the Senate on April 2, and by the House of Representatives the same day by 318 (167 Republicans and 151 Democrats) votes to 75 (62 Republicans, 11 Democrats, 2 American Labour) and on April 3, was signed by Truman, who declared that the act constituted an historic step in American foreign policy, that it was "America's answer to the challenge facing the free world," and that it was "a striking manifestation of the fact that a bi-partisan foreign policy can lead to effective action."[14]

Turning back to the cross-Atlantic reactions to this new treaty formation of states, the treaty was met with interest particularly by the Canadian Government. Subsequently, on April 28, 1948, the idea of a single mutual defence system, including and superseding the Brussels Treaty, was publicly put forward by St. Laurent in the Canadian House of Commons. A report of the Canadian Foreign Ministry on the international situation concluded on April 29, 1948 with a statement on possible intensification of cooperation between those free countries, which would assure mutual assistance and protection under the provisions of Article 51 of the UN Charter. On the other hand, despite his general support for the Brussels Treaty and his willingness, in principle, to grant assistance by appropriate means to the five signature states if necessary, the US President Truman did not express that Washington was ready to enter an alliance with those five states and to accept concrete obligations in the framework of a regional pact as Bevin had proposed. But it was essential that the US should be able, constitutionally, to join the alliance. The Vandenberg Resolution eventually brought out a break-through when it passed the US Senate on June 11, 1948.[15]

As for the reactions of Washington, contrary to Turkey's expectations, the US was not attempting to propose any modification in Britain's formulation of West European defense which would hamper the fulfillment of the European Recovery Programme originally prompted by assistance to Greece and Turkey. In an attempt to explain Turkey's case, on May 11, 1948, Turkish Ambassador to Washington, R. Baydur, criticized the US policy which envisaged to give certain guarantees to West European countries against aggression without any mention of Turkey.

Baydur emphasized the existence of a small minority who were pro-Soviet in Turkey, arguing that for such a small country like Turkey, it was in vain to resist the SU. Baydur stated that the present US policy which gave the impression that the security of Western Europe was more significant than Turkey's, would not only encourage the Kremlin to increase its pressure against Turkey, but also strengthen this minority group while undermining public morale. In this framework, he also pointed out the disappointment of Turks in regard to reduction of the ERP.[16]

Around the same issue, McGhee stated that both Greece and Turkey were included in the proposed ERP then before the Congress and it was assumed that any additional economic requirements of these countries would be met from that programme. If Turkey was required to spend considerable amounts on military equipment beyond the US aid programme, "a gold and dollar drain might be created that would prejudice its participation in the European Recovery Program on a cash basis."[17]

Another country which was interested in the developments around the Brussels Treaty was, of course, Italy. To share his concerns, on his return to Rome, Erkin visited the Italian Foreign Minister C. Sforza. Following an exchange of views on the foreseeable outcomes of the Brussels Treaty, Erkin underscored his assessment of the US' interest to adhere to this new grouping of states and this decisions' turning of this new defensive bloc in concern to a strong and large alliance, which would leave Turkey alone vis-à-vis Russia, eventually further weakening its position. In his report to Ankara dated May 8, 1948, Erkin asserted that Italy was then reluctant to appear attached to one of the emerging blocs. Though it was a natural member of the civilization and the corporate values of the West, he considered that this country would subject its accession to the WEU or the Mediterranean grouping of states, to the revisions in the Italian Peace Treaty pertaining to military issues and the future of its colonies. Thus, he pointed out that he couldn't avoid the exclusion of Turkey on these premises.[18]

Here, having combined his impressions of the talks he held in Rome and the experiences of years of service as Secretary General of the MFA,

Erkin expanded on the parameters of Turkey's Mediterranean policy, and the position of the regional countries towards a Mediterranean agreement. Firstly, he evaluated the Italian foreign policy towards participating in a regional agreement and partnership with Turkey within this "groupement." Erkin explained that the Italian Foreign Minister Sforza had made it clear that Italy had always felt itself sided with Turkey while always keeping itself as "far from any tumultuous and detrimental demonstrations."[19] However, Erkin had the impression that Italy had an objective of ensuring the revision of the clauses on its armed forces and the future of its colonies of the Italian peace treaty, in return for its accession to the Mediterranean groupement as well.

Regarding France, this country was unlikely to raise any objection to this "groupement" in the Mediterranean since previous deliberations in Paris were in the affirmative. However, he said, he could merely state his general impressions of the French attitude towards the groupement under discussion. In this framework, Erkin pointed out that based on the instructions of the Government, he had exchanged views with American, Greek, Italian and Egyptian Ambassadors on a theoretical basis. Then, referring to his talks with the Egyptian Ambassador in Ankara, Emin Fuad on the possibility of realizing a regional agreement, he said, this issue was discussed during a private visit of King Farouk to the Turkish coasts and Mersin as well. It was then decided that the conclusion of a Turco–Egyptian treaty could be announced on the occasion of an official visit of Farouk to be arranged accordingly. However, the deadlock in the Anglo–Egyptian dispute had handicapped this idea.

It is also interesting to note that on various occasions, Erkin implied that he was poorly informed of the talks held by the MFA Sadak and the officials of the Ministry, in Ankara and elsewhere. This being the case, while he was in Rome and subsequently in Washington (From June 1947 to August 1948 in Rome and Ambassador in Washington as of the latter date), he considered himself sometimes grooving in the darkness. He asserted that the way in which his personal relationships developed with Prime Minister Peker, the MFA Sadak and his successor in Ankara as General Secretary Fuat Carım had served to this effect. According to him, deterioration of his relations with the government was a result of Carım's ambitions who had constantly explained to Erkin, Saka's personal dislike of him while expressing similar views to Saka on behalf of Erkin. Interestingly, Erkin stated that he had not felt any negative vibes for a long time and on the contrary, he had suggested Carım as his replacement.[20]

Lastly, Spain might assume a place in this groupement, if it could remove the obstacles caused by its regime said Erkin. His report underlined that the natural members of the envisaged regional agreement would include these nations, whereas, the future this defense mechanism would certainly depend on the attitudes of Britain, France and particularly, of the US. As his personal opinion, he stated that the Americans would prefer to extend their guarantee to a political union of 16 nations that had already united around the Marshall Plan. Above all, this would serve to safeguard the future of the program and support the firm stand of the recipient nations against possible attacks. However, some small states were refraining from enlarging the term "region" while the British and the French had adopted a phase by phase enlargement policy for the union.[21]

Indeed, the Turkish Government was convinced that the emerging security grouping of the Western countries had reached a critical stage and it was the right time to voice Turkey's intention once more. As reflected in *The New York Times* of July 1, 1948, the Turkish Minister of Foreign Affairs Necmeddin Sadak stated that Turkey was already more than an ally of the United States and it was looking forward to crystallization of this relationship in an alliance. However, the tides were still not right. The US Secretary of State Marshall stated that such a move required the re-evaluation of American relations with practically every other country.[22]

Despite the fact that the way in which the Turkish involvement in a broader alliance was yet to be defined, on July 4, Turkey and the US concluded another major agreement in regard to the application of US assistance programmes to Turkey. The Economic Co-operation Agreement between Turkey and the US of July 4, was also significant since it underscored that Turkey had adhered to the Agreement of European Economic Co-operation signed in Paris on April 16.[23] Interestingly, both agreements were approved by the TGNA consecutively, allowing the Turkish–US economic cooperation agreement to state that Turkey was a participant country in the Organisation for European Economic Cooperation. In this framework, Ankara agreed to facilitate the activities of the press which would underscore the objectives and the progress achieved concerning the programs of the ERP, to further improve a sense of joint effort and mutual cooperation. Besides, Ankara would release information in regard to the use of finance, commodities and services received through this program every three months.[24] Article 8 of the agreement envisaged the establishment of a "Special Economic Co-operation Mission" of US experts, which would be considered as an integral part of the US diplomatic mission in Turkey.

Meanwhile, on June 10, 1948, following a reshuffle by President İnönü, Hasan Saka formed his second cabinet in which Necmettin Sadak kept his position as MFA. It is worth noting that since the beginning of the WW II, İnönü had adopted a particular strategy in regard to the changes of governments and this was greatly based on the nomination of MFAs as Prime Ministers. As mentioned above, on September 13, 1944, Saka was appointed as MFA in the 2nd Şükrü Saraçoğlu Government.[25] He had served as the chairman of the Turkish delegation in the United Nations Conference on International Organization in San Francisco. Upon Saraçoğlu's resignation, he was reappointed as MFA in the Recep Peker Government, which remained in office between August 7, 1946 and September 9, 1947. Following Peker's resignation, İnönü instructed Saka to form the new cabinet on September 10, 1947. Saka resigned on June 8, 1948, but he was reappointed as Prime Minister.[26]

The period in which the cabinets of H. Saka served was marked with an expectation that he would better the relations between the government and the opposition. Besides, the small opposition group in the RPP was pressing for the establishment of a truly democratic regime and the elimination of restrictions over political freedoms. About this time, President İnönü was seeking economic and military assistance from the US. However, a considerable number of US Congressmen were strongly critical of the nature of Turkey's political regime since the discussions on the Truman Doctrine. In fact, the Truman Doctrine was explained in the US Congress as an effort to save democracy and freedom in Turkey as well. "The views expressed in the U.S. Congress and the necessity of establishing closer relations with the West, may be assumed to have had some impact on political developments in Turkey."[27]

On July 8, 1948, Sadak explained in the TGNA that the Turkish–US agreement was made in accordance with the US Foreign Assistance Act, which envisaged the signing of separate agreements between the US Government and the recipient governments. He said the Turkish–US agreement was designed to serve to the effect that the US Congress would undertake to forward assistance to Turkey within the framework of the Aid Act, while Turkey would assume general responsibility in regard to the use of aid in concern effectively. He pointed out that in the beginning, as a result of the hasty assessments of the US specialists of the numbers and statistics submitted by the Turkish experts to the conference of the 16 in Paris, Turkey's dollar reserves were estimated greater than they were, eventually causing Turkey's replacement in a category which would purchase goods from the US through payment in cash. Following Turkey's explanations, this mistake was corrected, placing Ankara into the category of recipients of assistance. As a result, based upon the appropriations of the US Government, an amount of 10 million dollars would be transferred to Turkey for the first three months.

He further explained that Ankara had submitted projects in the fields of agriculture (6 million dollars) and metallurgy (3 million dollars) for financial consideration. He said, the Turkish Embassy in Washington was informed by the Economic Co-operation Administrator in charge of the ERP, Paul G. Hoffman, that following this period of three months, allocation of long-term credits of an uncertain amount would also be considered. In this framework, Turkey had submitted its projects, totalling 85 million dollars for a period of one year to the Committee of Co-operation and Washington.

Sadak also pointed out that in the letter of Ambassador Wilson dated July 4, the US Ambassador had stated that the Economic Co-operation Agreement between Turkey and the US was approved and through this Washington admitted that Turkey would enjoy the most favoured nation status in its commercial transactions in West Germany, Trieste, Japan and South Korea as long as the US maintained its controlling or occupying status in these countries. In this regard, the US Government would apply the related articles of the Trade Agreement between Turkey and the US dated April 1, 1939 or the General Agreement on Customs and Tariffs, dated October 30, 1947 and the latest agreement (July 4, 1948). As such, Sadak mentioned the emphasis he had made on the significance of the German market in Turkey's exports and Turkey's expectation that the American Government would not create a situation through closing Germany to Turkish goods which would have grave consequences.

Turning back to the issue of Turkey's participation in the Brussels Treaty, Ankara would soon have another try, following the nomination of Erkin to Washington. In fact, time was against Ankara, and there were no prospects of realizing a treaty relationship with the West. The US officials were finding it too hard even to try to explain Turkey's case given the poor public interest towards a country on the margins of the reach of the US assistance programs. Similar difficulties were experienced during the discussion on the extension of aid to Turkey in February 1947. Thus, Ankara could hardly expect to involve Washington in its active search for a security partnership with the West. However, the officials of the MFA strongly believed that they might convince all the concerned parties that Turkey's position was vital for an effective defensive grouping of the Western states since the basic idea had its roots in the Truman Doctrine, which focused on Turkish economic recovery as well as supporting the Greek Government in its fight against the communist insurgents. They considered that the ERP had a symbiotic relationship with the US aid to Greece and Turkey, just as the subsequent economic (Committee of Co-operation) and defensive (Brussels Treaty) grouping of the Western states had. Consecutive developments which culminated in Turkey's being left outside the Brussels Treaty, however, were both frustrating and inadmissible. Thus, Ankara launched an active foreign policy in order to "correct" a mistake. Washington was no doubt, a crucial place to pursue this objective since it was the center of Euro–Atlantic discussions aimed at transforming the Brussels Treaty into a major defense mechanism.

In August 1948, Erkin left his post in Rome and arrived in Washington in replacement of Baydur. Erkin stated that among the files he examined at the Washington Embassy, one single issue was of particular importance to him. This was a file on the demarchés of Turkey which would ultimately enable Turkey to adhere in the "Regional Agreement."[28] He noted that the MFA had instructed Baydur to approach the British and French Ambassadors in Washington in regard to Turkey's accession to the Brussels Pact. According to Erkin, this demarché was prompted by the Turkish Ambassador to Paris, Numan Menemencioğlu's interview with the French General Secretary in which, upon Menemencioğlu's suggestion on Turkey's joining the deliberations that concerned the "Western Regional Agreement" in Washington, his French interlocutor pledged to instruct French Ambassadors in various capitals to express Turkey's desire on the grounds this issue would be discussed.

Subsequently, Baydur had visited his French counterpart in Washington, but, he was told that no instruction had arrived from Paris towards this effect. In his turn, Baydur had cabled Ankara and explained the situation. The MFA had passed this information to Paris and following a renewed demarché, Menemencioğlu had informed Ankara that this time the French Minister of Foreign Affairs, himself, had told him that there might be a delay between Paris and Washington, and in any case the instruction would be renewed. The file he examined included that eventually it was decided that Erkin would relaunch the initiative as the new Ambassador.

Towards the end of August, Erkin interviewed his French counterpart, Henry Bonnet, and inquired if he was instructed to explain Turkey's wish during the deliberations between the US, Western European Union and Canada. Bonnet said that he was informed of the talks in Paris, which he assumed remained more along the lines of a friendly exchange of views. To the astonishment of Erkin, he added that he had expressed to the former Turkish Ambassador Baydur too that he was not particularly instructed to pronounce Turkey's wish in this regard in the Washington deliberations which was in an early phase.

In his turn, Erkin replied that with a view to the statement of Bonnet, it was understood the time for Turkey's formal application would have been too soon. However, if a defensive bloc were to be formed in Europe in association with the US, no other country's membership in it could be imagined as more natural than that of Turkey since it had launched resistance against the threat first time three years ago in its own capacity. Thus, he said Turkey would formally apply to the union from the moment the US partnership was incorporated into the WEU. Finally, in his conclusion, Bonnet told Erkin that the limited membership in the WEU was a result of the members' unwillingness to undertake military commitments outside their area. As for Turkey, however, this time he had stated unintentionally that deliberations in Paris were discussed in Washington within the framework of general exchanges of view.

At the end of the talks, Erkin had reached to the conclusion that Bonnet was instructed to make a demarché to point out the need for the willingness of the Mediterranean countries to assume their role within the West European security system. However, his efforts to invoke a response in this regard had remained futile. Thus, it was very likely that Bonnet had refrained from expressing the unfavourable responses of the countries in concern. Furthermore, Erkin criticized Bonnet's attitude when he explained the position of the US as too positivistic and rejected the US' call for an emphasis on the self-help of the Europeans before US subsidies were dispatched.

Shortly afterwards, on August 31, Erkin interviewed Undersecretary of State Robert A. Lovett, who had assumed the chairmanship of the Committee of the Six[29] as well. As Erkin stated, this Committee consisted of the Ambassadors of the WEU and Canada who participated in deliberations at Washington. To the disappointment of the Turkish Ambassador, Lovett made it clear that Washington would not intervene in the question of the enlargement of the Brussels Treaty. As set forth in the Vandenberg Resolution, Washington would only examine if the general requirements for the US participation in any defensive arrangements were met or not, and if these agreements were of interest to American national security. Regarding the term, "regional agreement," Lovett said, this would acquire the name North Atlantic Treaty Organization, and would include the countries along the east and west coasts of the North Atlantic Ocean which shared the seas, languages, cultures, civilizations and world views which had come together to defend themselves and their common values. He said, Turkey was, of course, a country whose importance was greatly acknowledged. But how one could incorporate this country which was on the eastern edge of the Mediterranean into this definition and the Atlantic world?

In his turn, Erkin strongly objected to Lovett's conceptualization of the Atlantic community and explained that the progress in the world civilization had reduced the continents to the size of cities in the sense that nations were brought closer and the solidarity among them were enhanced. Then, the term, "region" had lost its geographical meaning and acquired a definition pertaining to the common interests of the nations. To make this point another way, it was because of the same perception of the US administration that the threat against Turkey was considered as directed against the US as well. The Truman Doctrine and the aid act were accepted on the same premise and the mighty war vessel *Missouri* was dispatched to Turkey again with such an objective in mind. Thus, Erkin's interview with Lovett ended in a friendly atmosphere, however, producing little impetus. Subsequently, as will be discussed below, the Turkish Ambassador felt obliged to discuss the same issue, with Secretary of State Marshall.

In his talks with Marshall where Lovett was also present, Erkin reiterated Turkey's wish and need to accede to the most convenient regional agreement to be formed in Europe, and which would enjoy actual American military aid. Erkin stated that from his interview with Lovett, he had an impression that the time for Turkey's participation of Turkey in the deliberations of the Committee of the Six had not come yet. Then, Erkin inquired if in this interval President Truman or Secretary of State Marshall could publicly declare that with a view to the close relationship between peace and security in the Mediterranean region and that of the Atlantic, Turkey's territorial integrity, sovereignty and national existence, which was an indispensable component of peace and order in the Mediterranean, was of vital importance for the US. A declaration of this kind, would have significant effect on the morale of the Turkish public, and on Russia which was watching for an opportunity to hunt down Turkey with appealing suggestions. Erkin stated that a declaration of this kind would introduce an additional element of peace to the Near East too.

In Erkin's discussions with Secretary of State, Marshall and the Director of Near Eastern and African Affairs (NEA), Joseph C. Satterthwaite, referring to the Washington Security Talks, the Turkish Ambassador said that the completion of an adequate security mechanism undoubtedly required the inclusion of Turkey in the partnership of the West Europeans and the Americans. He underscored that options pertaining to the formation of one or more regional agreements should be revised as well. Erkin explained that for instance, Turkey, Greece, the UK and the US could form a groupement in the region. He maintained that while this and other similar options were being considered—as he repeated his projection on various grounds for a few times more from then on—it would be very useful if the US Presidency could declare the US "vital interest" in Turkey's integrity and sovereignty. He underscored as his personal view that the basis of such a declaration was included in the Greek–Turkish Aid Bill and what he suggested as a formula would represent a further step in this direction which will be in harmony with the constitutional requirements of the US.

The Turkish Ambassador emphasized that to respond to Turkey's needs would introduce additional components of peace to the Near East.[30] In his turn, Marshall questioned Erkin on the scope of his projection. However, he gave his interlocutor no sign of approval or decline. As for the Turkish exports to Germany, he explained that the decisions of the budgetary commissions of the Congress were heavily politicized, and suggested that Erkin could approach the Administrator of the ECA, Paul Hoffman.[31]

The report of the Director of NEA Satterthwaite revealed that the State Department initially refused the suggestion of Erkin on a US declaration for Turkey too. However, Erkin said, Satterthwaite shortly afterwards informed him that although it was not customary for the US administrations, President Truman had undertaken to deliver a message on the occasion of the celebration of the Day of Republic on October 29, in which he expressed his admiration of the Turkish Revolution and Republic and the importance he attributed to the Turkish–American cooperation.[32]

Subsequently, Erkin visited the Coordinator of Assistance to Greece and Turkey, Wilds. Here, he explained the crisis in Turkey's export items and its need to re-open trade relations with Germany. In his turn, Wilds, told Erkin that he had noted these points, however, he should like to make a "friendly suggestion." Turkey was not paying enough attention to the Marshall Plan and the preparations of its projects, which culminated in the delay of affairs in concern. According to him, Turkish balance of payments were totally imaginary and full of incoherent numbers.

Concurrently, the Turkish Ambassador in London, M. Cevat Açıkalın, held similar talks with his interlocutors. In the same days, he interviewed Bevin as well on the question of Turkish adherence to the WEU. The British Premiere considered the extension of the military guarantee of the WEU and of the US to Turkey, which was under discussion in Washington, as untimely. As for the Mediterranean Regional Agreement, with a view to the situation both in Italy and Spain, and the reactions of the Arab nations which might consider such an agreement against themselves as a result of their exclusion, planning for an organization to include a large number of countries was excluded from the current agenda too.

Around the same days, Erkin gave an interview to the Associated Press in which he explained that no statement was made to Ankara on the discussions pertaining to the "question of regional agreements." In this context he said, it was imperative that, either throughout entire Europe, or as a combination of separate systems in the northern, western and Mediterranean regions, unity be secured. Pan American unity he said, could be a model and in one way or another, Turkish participation in any security mechanism of the European states would be natural. His statements included that the Charter of the UN had envisaged the formation of regional agreements for the purpose of defense, and he was of the opinion that it would be preferable if the Asian countries in the southeast of Europe also conclude similar agreements and ultimately achieve solidarity among them. The next day, his statements were published in some US journals, which basically included that Turkey desired to take part in the Mediterranean sector of the security system as soon as the Western Unity actively started. Erkin noted that the correspondent informed that the interview was also cleared with the State Department. However, he said, the news also particularly emphasized an overwhelming superiority to the Mediterranean formula by his voice.

In discussing the approaches of various Western countries towards a regional agreement in the Mediterranean, Erkin stressed that the Greek Ambassador to Washington, Vassili Dendranis, told him that a competent official of the State Department had expressed that Washington desired the formation of a regional grouping in the Mediterranean. Erkin noted that in his interviews, the British Ambassador to Washington Sir Oliver Franks, had also pointed out that a separate formation of states in the Mediterranean would be good. The Ambassadors of Belgium and the Netherlands, however, had made it clear that their governments were against any enlargement of the Brussels Pact.

A few days later, to Erkin's big surprise, Ankara cabled him, and demanded an explanation of the news in regard to a statement of the spokesman of the State Department, declaring that the projections on a regional agreement in the Mediterranean were not approved by the US. Erkin stated that there were no news in the journals published in Washington to this effect. Having been disturbed by the news he had received from Ankara, in order to disperse the clouds of suspicion, Erkin asked for an urgent appointment with Satterthwaite. In their discussion, Satterthwaite told Erkin that although they had no fixed decision on the issue, the State Department was in fact, inclined to welcome a rapprochement among Turkey, Greece and Italy to this effect, hence, he assured Erkin that the State Department had not made and would not make a statement of this kind. The Director of NEA added that a statement on the issue might only be expected as a result of the meeting of the General Assembly of the WEU in Paris within three months.

Against this background, the Committee of Six, headed by Undersecretary of State Lovett, concluded the Washington Security Talks on September 9, 1948. The Washington Paper drafted by the Committee recognized the existence of a tie between European security and the US and denigrated the possibility of peaceful coexistence with Soviet communism and surveyed the practical problems of defining a North Atlantic security area.

In an attempt to explain their assessment of Turkey's possible course of action in view of these developments, the Turkish political leaders made it clear that Turkey could have a role to play in these new developments. According to the MFA Necmeddin Sadak, the speech of Bevin "held out the prospect of a system of political and economic collaboration from the Arab states through Turkey, Greece and Italy to the West which the Turkish Government would make every effort to help realise."[33] Turkish diplomatic efforts in the Middle East, he told Kelly, British Ambassador to Ankara, were directed towards this end, as Turkey's support for the Anglo-Iraqi Treaty had already indicated.

In late 1947, Bevin had launched a major initiative to negotiate mutual defense treaties with Egypt, Iraq and Jordan on the premise of recognizing the independence of those states, elicit their voluntary support of Western strategic needs in the region, and eventually perpetuate British influence in the region. Envisaged Anglo-Arab treaties promised to mitigate the political and strategic losses caused by the British withdrawal from Palestine and to "reconcile the Labour government's anti-imperial ideals with the realities of Cold War."[34] Correspondingly, on January 15, 1948, Bevin and Iraqi Prime Minister Saleh Jabr signed the Anglo-Iraqi Treaty (The Portsmouth Agreement) that Bevin hailed as the first in a new series of treaties regularizing and expressing the friendship between Britain and the Arab world. However, a shocking incident forced the British foreign policy makers to re-consider the threats towards Britain's position in the Middle East. In the aftermath of this agreement which sought to extend the 1930 Anglo-Iraqi Treaty in the guise of revising it, six days of mass demonstrations and some of the worst violence took place in Iraq. To ensure the extension of the 1930 Treaty had great importance for Britain. This treaty was drawn up to safeguard the essential features of the British order before the expiry of the mandate by October 1932 and would provide Britain a legal basis for its continuing presence in the country. To Britain's disappointment the Iraqi Government decided not to ratify it and with the resignation of Saleh Jabr's government, the treaty negotiations were suspended indefinitely.

At this juncture, Ankara's hope was to activate Britain's interest in including the Eastern Mediterranean in its security schemes by pointing out that "Turkey could become the bridge between London and the Arab states."

A Period of Redesign in the Middle East and the Anglo-American Perceptions of Turkish Regional Role

Having been excluded from the talks of the Western Union, it was imperative for the Turkish foreign policy makers to bring other alterna-

tives—which would connect Turkey to the Western strategic grouping—
under discussions at once. Against a background of the world's division
in two rival blocs, which had become unmistakably clear, dictated by the
circumstances, Ankara was concerned over two developments: first, the
Western Union which had addressed the need for a Western defense
cooperation, had excluded Turkey; and secondly, the proposed defence
arrangement had not introduced any prospect in regard to the inclusion
of the Eastern Mediterranean. Then, as will be discussed below, for
Turkey, the possibility of assuming a self-imposed role of leadership in
the Middle Eastern security grouping of states which would be in direct
connection with the West was increasingly brought under scope.

In their turn, the British and American Governments had shifted to
reorganize their defense positions in the region with a view to consolidate their stand against the Soviet threat through an ideological and actual penetration into this region. The Middle East was the pivot of security concerns of Britain, which was carrying out a regular withdrawal
from its global status, and its significance to the US was determined
mainly along the lines of replacing "Pax Britannica." At this juncture,
considerable evidence suggests that, Ankara ultimately concluded that—
through a partnership with the Anglo-Saxons—the making of a sound
foreign policy towards the region might culminate in two main outcomes:
first, Turkey's direct inclusion in the Western Union might be ensured;
or the complete integration of the defense grouping in the Middle East—
under the leadership of Turkey—to the Western Union might be realized, eventually bringing the Middle East and Europe under one single
security umbrella.

Around the same issue, a counter-argument pointed out that after the
Czech coup and the Berlin Blockade, Washington's primary concern
was the establishment of a formal security arrangement for Europe without mention of Turkey—and perhaps of Greece. Deliberations in regard
to the establishment of a Middle Eastern pact were already launched.
Correspondingly, on February 4, 1948, the Greek Ambassador to Washington, V. Dendranis, explained Athen's suggestion on the establishment
of forming an entente between Greece, Italy, Turkey and the Arab states
under the leadership of the US and Britain, which he said, could give the
necessary support and encouragement. While similar views were considered in Ankara, opponents of Turkey's active participation in defensive
grouping of states advocated that the Middle East entente or pact was
such a vast concept that could not be fulfilled and even if it was realized

on paper it would not have an operational value. In this context, it was also argued that a formal defense organization might provoke the Kremlin and the eastern bloc since it would be evaluated that it was established against them. This being the case, Turkey would remain weaker before such a danger since the extent of the US support to the Eastern Mediterranean and Middle Eastern countries was still unclear.[35]

To a certain extent, as will be discussed later, these doubts would prove to be right since the formation of such a pact—though still in vague and limited terms—would not be achieved before a series of attempts prompted by the Tripartite Declaration on May 25, 1950 by which the US, Britain and France recognized the existing Middle Eastern frontiers. In this framework, the creation of the Middle Eastern Defense Organization (MEDO), the Middle East Command (MEC) and the subsequent Four-Power proposals which Turkey, the US, Britain and France drafted for a MEC to Egypt, could be realized a year and a half later, in mid-1951, as part of a half-baked attempt towards the conclusion of the same issue.

In 1948, however, it was indeed an outstanding necessity for Ankara to assume the role of a reliable defense partner of the West, and the circumstances had laid the groundwork for Turkish contribution in the discussions around Middle Eastern security. While the Turkish interest in the Middle Eastern affairs were shaping along these lines, in July 1947, Egypt took its case against Britain, regarding the continuation of the August 26, 1936 Anglo–Egyptian Treaty and sovereignty over Sudan, to the United Nations Security Council. In fact, since 1946, the British Government had been negotiating with Egypt for the withdrawal of British troops from the Suez base stationed there according to the 1936 Anglo–Egyptian Treaty, which had given Egypt full recognition as an independent and sovereign state after fifty four years of British occupation. The question of Egypt's sovereignty over Sudan of which there had been no mention in the 1936 Treaty became also a matter of discussion. These two issues were seen by virtually every political circle in Egypt as matters of national pride and instigated nationalistic resentment against Britain.

In effect, the Anglo–Egyptian Treaty of 1936 formally recognized Egyptian sovereignty, ended the British occupation of Egypt, and granted the UK the right to deploy 10,000 soldiers, 400 pilots and an unspecified number of personnel in the Suez Canal and in Sinai and personnel to run naval bases in Alexandria. Both Cairo and London had gains from the 1936 Treaty. In this Treaty, Egypt had agreed to provide Britain with supplies and facilities and when war flared in Europe in 1939, Britain invoked the Anglo–Egyptian Treaty, and 55,000 British troops arrived in Egypt. British forces repelled the attacks of the Italians and Germans in the autumn of 1940 and in late 1941. However, despite the proximity of fighting, Egyptian authorities did not abandon their neutrality. Egyptian neutrality was disliked by the British and prompted a confrontation between Cairo and London when General Erwin Rommel repeated the German offensive in 1942, and captured El Alamein, just sixty miles from Alexandria. King Farouk, worried about German occupation, appointed Ali Maher as Prime Minister who was known for his sympathy towards the Germans. However, the British Ambassador, Miles Lampson, insisted that Nahas Pasha should be appointed in replacement of Ali Maher. In his turn, King Farouk resisted and on February 4, 1942, Lampson and General R.G. Stone surrounded the Abdin Palace with troops and tanks. Then, Lampson and Stone with a group of guards marched into the Palace and repeated their demands in Farouk's private study room. Here, Farouk was pressed to appoint Nahas or abdicate. Unable to raise any objection, Farouk appointed Nahas who stopped the activites of Axis sympathizers.

Following the parliamentary elections in which the Wafd won 231 of 264 seats, Egypt was kept on the Allies' side as a friendly neutral. In November 1942, General B. Montgomery defeated Rommel at El Alamein and drove the German forces out of Egypt. Then, Rommel was squeezed between the forces of Montgomery and Allied troops under General Dwight D. Eisenhower. Ultimately, the Axis forces surrendered on May 13 and Egypt remained out of the conflict for the rest of war. However, matters were still complicated in regard to the future of Nahas Government.

Given this background, since the 1936 Treaty was not due for revision before 1956, Britain was not obliged to enter into talks with Egypt. Nevertheless, when the Egyptians formally requested for a revision in 1945, Bevin agreed to negotiate on condition that the base would continue to operate under joint Anglo–Egyptian supervision and that British troops would be able to reoccupy the base in the event of a Soviet incursion in the Middle East. Discussions went through different stages, but by 1947 they reached a deadlock. The Egyptians inflamed by nationalistic feelings, demanded immediate and unconditional withdrawal of British troops and absolute sovereignty over the Sudan. In their report to the Security Council, they argued that the stationing of British troops was an offence to Egypt's dignity and an infringement of "fundamental principles of sovereign equality," and that the British had encouraged an artificial separatism in the Sudan, aiming to destroy the unity of the Nile Valley. Egypt failed to establish its contention that the 1936 Anglo–Egyptian Treaty was no longer valid, yet Britain won a modest victory. Although the Security Council did not present the British with an ultimatum to withdraw, it did not make a clear-cut decision in favour of the sanction of the Treaty as Britain had wished. Instead it called on Egypt and Britain to resume negotiations for a revision.[36]

Meanwhile, Britain's position in Iraq received a serious blow as well. The Anglo–Iraqi Treaty was signed on January 5, 1948 and it was a revision of the Anglo–Iraqi Treaty of Alliance of 1930, due to expire in 1958. The 1930 Treaty had terminated the British mandate and recognized Iraq's independence. It had also contained, like the 1936 Anglo–Egyptian Treaty, military clauses—Britain's acquisition of two air-bases and its right to transport forces across Iraq in the event of war—which were unacceptable to Iraqi nationalists. The new Treaty of 1948, which Bevin hoped would provide the model for defensive alliances with the other Arab states too, was signed as a first step towards relinquishing British military presence in Iraq. For the time being, however, Britain was again granted the right to use Iraqi territory in case of war, and to maintain the bases in Iraq, but by 'sharing responsibility' with the Iraqis.

The Treaty gave rise to serious opposition in Iraq and it was never ratified. Iraqi nationalists maintained that it was even worse than the old treaty on the grounds that while Britain enjoyed basically the same rights as before, it was no longer committed to defend Iraq in case of war. On January 21, (before Sadak's conversation with Kelly on the same issue in which the former expressed Turkey's support for the British endeavour to renew the treaty in concern), the Iraqi Regent who had signed the new agreement had stated that he was not going to ratify it.

Under these circumstances, King Abdullah of Jordan, who had a long friendly relationship with Britain, asked in early 1948 for a revision of the 1946 Treaty with London. Abdullah's aim was more to silence Arab accusations that he was a British stooge rather than seriously challenge the British military presence in Jordan. Thus, in the revised treaty, the essential military clauses remained unaltered. Nevertheless, his move did not help to alleviate the fact that British influence in the area was collapsing.

Ankara's foreign policy towards the region throughout 1949 and then on, had also been shaped with a view to its relations with Israel. Considerable evidence suggests that Ankara had included Israel in its policy plannings and had been approaching this country in a cautious way. Explicitly, formulation of the Turkish foreign policy towards the developments in Palestine and the Arab–Jewish conflict were under the strains of Turkey's historical ties with the region as well. Turkey and previously, the Ottoman Empire had no "Jewish problem" or anti-semitic feelings in the past. As for the Arabs, despite sharing the Islamic faith and again a long common past, emotionally, the Turks had perhaps, a bewildering feeling that the entire region, including the Holy Lands and Palestine were lost to the Arabs—operating under British command—in the Great War who had betrayed the Ottoman Empire.

Indeed, after the British occupied the southern part of Palestine, local Arabs joined the Army of the Arab Revolt led by Amir Faisal, son of Sharif Hussein of Mecca. Some of them participated in the conquest of Syria in 1918. Some remained in Faisal's Syrian army until its destruction by the French in July 1920.[37] As a result of these dictating perceptions, as will be discussed below, beyond any binding moral obligations towards the region—except viewing the developments from the perspective of international law and the decisions of the UN—Ankara eventually felt comfortable in adopting a similar policy to those of the Big Three towards the State of Israel. In fact, soon after the proclamation of the State of Israel, Turkish foreign policy makers had asserted that, it would be a lasting entity in the region. This early decision to recognize Israel then provided the Turkish and the Israeli statesmen with extra time in establishing bilateral relations.

Undoubtedly, since the beginning of the British Mandatory rule by the decision of the League of Nations in July 1922, the issue of Palestine had been pursued by Ankara with close interest. Correspondingly, in the first years of the Republic, Ankara showed an interest towards Palestine and a group of people to include the members of the Jewish community from Palestine were invited to join in the economic and cultural activities, the first İzmir Exhibition of Commerce and Industry which was, and has been held annually to this day. In the meantime, Ghazi Mustafa Kemal also dispatched experts to examine the situation in Palestine. In November 1938, the leader of the Jewish community, Chaim Weizmann (later the first President of Israel) visited Turkey and held conferences with his interlocutors.

As for the establishment of Israel, particularly in the first months of 1947, Britain's inability to reconcile the conflicting demands of the Jewish and Arab communities led the British Government to request that the question of Palestine be placed on the agenda of the United Nations General Assembly in April 1947. Shortly afterwards, a special committee was constituted to draft proposals concerning the country's future. On November 29, 1947, the Assembly voted to adopt the committee's recommendation to partition the land into two states, one Jewish and one Arab. The Jewish community accepted the plan, while the Arabs rejected it. Turkey voted along with Arab countries against the UN Resolution. Following the UN vote, local Arab militants, supported by irregular volunteers from Arab countries, launched attacks against the incoming Jews in an effort to prevent the establishment of a Jewish State. The Jewish organizations routed most of the attacking forces, taking hold of the entire area which had been allocated for the Jewish state.

The UN vote for partition of Palestine essentially enhanced the same impression while simultaneously making it obviously more difficult for London to appease Arab nationalists, who viewed "Zionism" and "British Imperialism" as complementary, if not identical forces. On May 14, 1948, the day Britain withdraw from Palestine, the State of Israel was proclaimed according to the UN partition plan. Less than 24 hours later, war erupted between Israel and the Arab states which refused to recognize this new entity. The regular armies of Egypt, Jordan, Syria, Lebanon and Iraq invaded the country. The war lasted some 15 months. Between the years 1948 and 1950, during which heated discussions took place over the question of Palestine, Ankara closely watched the developments in the region and nominated the journalist Hüseyin Cahit Yalçın as one of the three members in the Palestine Conciliation Commission (PCC) who would also serve as the Chairman in this body—although the Arab countries were against the formation of this commission—established in December 1948 by the General Assembly.[38] In the aftermath of his visit to Israel, in his report to the President İnönü, Yalçın pointed out that it was very unlikely that Israel would emerge as a communist state in the region and it would be a right decision for Ankara to extend its recognition of this new state at once.[39]

During the first months of 1949, direct negotiations were conducted under UN's auspices between the conflicting parties. Ultimately, Israel concluded armistice talks with Egypt, Syria, Lebanon and Jordan[40] resulting in armistice agreements which reflected the situation at the end of the fighting.[41] Subsequently, on May 11 1949, Israel took its seat as the 59th member of the UN.[42]

With a view to the emergence in the region of Israel as a state, and its recognition by its neighbours through armistice agreements and the prompt extension of *de jure* recognition of various states—including the US and the SU—of Israel, Ankara's *de facto* recognition of this new entity came on March 28, 1949. Towards the end of the year, Turkey's first representative to Israel, Seyfullah Esin was dispatched to Tel-Aviv as Charge d'affaires. Shortly afterwards, Turkey elevated its emissary in Tel-Aviv to Minister Plenipotentiary.Undoubtedly, the year 1949—particularly in the aftermath of Ankara's recognition of Tel-Aviv—marked a turning point in the making of Turkish foreign policy towards the Middle East. Under the pressure of dictating circumstances, Turkish foreign policy towards the region envisaged a categorical denial of the Soviet influence from the region. Thus, the foreign policy makers in Ankara calculated that Turkey could assume a leadership role in a military and economic alliance of the Arab and other countries in the Middle East. In this context, Ankara followed a policy of improving its technical and economical relations with Israel, which it assessed, was a country with Western norms, while maintaining its relations with this country in the military and economic fields in a discreet manner to avoid the sensitiveness of the Arab states.

Admittedly, Turkish–Israeli relations were essentially based on an acknowledgement of the mutual needs of both countries. There were however, some suspicions in Ankara in regard to the future of the regime in Israel. The position of the leftist parties and labour unions in Israel had prompted certain anxieties both in the RPP and in the DP, which came to power in May 1950.[43] Following the outbreak of the crisis in Korea, when the Arab states remained impartial towards the conflict, while Israel supported the UN decisions, Ankara's remaining suspicions were quickly dispersed.[44] On July 4, 1950, a modus vivendi regarding economic and commercial relations was reached, and technical and cultural relations were provided with a regular fora. Military attaches were also nominated in each capital.[45]

Turning back to the British considerations on the establishment of a regional organization, at this stage, the Foreign Office had been increasingly felt that they had to pull back since the over-extended use of their resources had caused serious strains for the British economy. In the eastern Mediterranean, this situation had first culminated in Britain's withdrawal from its status as the main supporter of Greece and Turkey in the aftermath of the war. Ankara was also informed of the UK's difficulty to continue as the main supplier of countries in this region. Britain's war ravaged economy "was the reason they came to the US and said, we can no longer help the Turks, we don't have the resources and if you don't do it, nobody could."[46] The deterioration in Britain's ability to take the lead in regional affairs was also apparent in London's weak attempts to create a defensive grouping in the Middle East.

Under these circumstances, Anglo–American officials agreed that "it did not seem wise to consider evacuating British troops from Egypt . . . , Russian aggression in the Near East was entirely possible and it would be essential to our common strategic plan to have the British on the spot."[47] But clearly, there were strong differences of opinion on the need for a regional pact. In May 1950, Foreign Office Under Secretary, Michael Wright draw attention to the possibility of making a Middle Eastern defence pact, probably to be linked to NATO. He asserted that this would also remove the deadlock in the Anglo–Egyptian talks. However, the Near Eastern Affairs officials of the State Department declined this project, which would force to extend the obligations of the US under NATO to the Middle East and expressed their view that the area lacked a "power center on the basis of which a pact could be built."[48] In their turn, the officials at Pentagon opposed the idea either, because it might represent an undertaking of the US to use force against aggression in the Middle East.

Despite these reservations, the State Department officials drafted the declaration in May. Subsequently, on May 25, 1950, the Tripartite Declaration by which the US, Britain and France recognized the existing Middle Eastern frontiers came into the scene. The Tripartite Declaration was defined as the expression of these powers of their determination to lean on their security interests in the area. Besides, through the Tripartite Declaration these countries aimed to coordinate the supply of arms to regional states which were under an embargo imposed by the UN after the May 1948 Arab–Israeli war.

In fact, Britain was at odds between continuing its supply of arms to the countries of the Middle East which were polarized around the Arab–Israeli dispute and making an implausible suggestion for leaving their deep disagreements behind and unite under a defense organization in the region, the latter no doubt constituting an unconvincing option. Besides, controversially, more these countries were armed, their inclination towards an armed struggle would increase and in case the British rejected their demands for the supply of war material, they (particularly the Arab states, except Jordan with which Britain maintained the strongest relations in the region) could gradually move to the Soviet orbit. Indeed, in February, 1950, to convince Egypt to join a defense body, Britain agreed to sell this country arms and munitions including jet-fighters. As expected, Israel asked for similar war equipment from the US. Regarding the Israeli demands for military assistance, although the US had initially chosen to avoid any commitments in the region, domestic pressures were forcing the US to change this policy. Given this, Anglo–American understanding around the question of the Middle Eastern security was handicapped by the intricacies of the inter-state tensions in the region. In the end having regarded the weak possibility of forming a joint defense body in the Middle East, the US, Britain and France launched a project to limit the flow of arms to the region. This was the Tripartite Declaration. Similarly, the British Minister of State for Foreign Affairs, Anthony Nutting held the view that under the Tripartite Declaration of 1950 three powers were alone responsible for preventing another round in the Arab–Israeli struggle and there was every reason to demand this responsibility be more widely shared.[49]

Attempts to achieve a reliable defense organization in the region, thus had these limitations in their origin. From then, following the talks in the second US Chiefs of Mission Conference in İstanbul in February 14–21, 1951 the considerations for the formation of a regional defence organization continued in some vague forms. At this stage—and as will be further discussed in the subsequent chapter—in an atmosphere dominated by the success of Turkish Brigade in Korea, on July 18, the new British Foreign Secretary, Herbert Morrison publicly announced Britain's support for the admittance of Turkey and Greece to NATO.

The North Atlantic Treaty Takes to the Stage

One year after the proclamation of the Truman Doctrine, and in the absence of a formalized relationship with Washington, Turkey continued to rely on its alliance with Britain in its search for security. In Açıkalın's words, Britain was Turkey's closest friend and ally and an important link with the West. The prevailing understanding between the two countries accommodated Ankara's perception of regional power politics and the reasons behind Turkey's siding with the West. Britain had historically

played a predominant role in the Middle East and Ankara remained interested in maintaining close and firm co-operation with London in the
[obviously, so shaped, one can add] post-war period. In its turn, Britain
regarded the Middle East, including Turkey, as key to overall struggle
between the West and the SU. The removal of Western influence from
the Middle East, London feared, would create a vacuum into which the
Kremlin would immediately advance and a move towards communism in
the region would pave the way for communism in Africa as well and
would negatively affect British interests in Asia. Moreover, the loss of
the Middle East to communism would prejudice the recovery effort in
Britain, depriving the economy of oil and cotton.[50]

Thus, despite its obvious weakness, Britain was still the only power
heavily involved in the region and with long established interests there.
As İnönü put it in July 1948 to an American journalist, he would very
much like an alliance with the United States, but he was of the opinion
that American interest in Turkey was not a permanent factor.[51] Truly,
İnönü's doubts were confirmed previously on April 23, 1948 when the
US Undersecretary of State, Robert Lovett, stated that the US was not
against proposals towards this effect, but it was neither prepared to make
any promises nor take any initiative about the proposed pact of the Middle
Eastern or Eastern Mediterranean states. The US Department of State
regarded the prospect of including Arab states dubious, hence, suggested
a Turkish–Italian–Greek trilateral declaration which seemed more advantageous.[52]

At this juncture, alternative bases in the Mediterranean were appealing to Washington because, if war should erupt suddenly, the US would
have a greater capability to defend this area. This being the case, attention focused increasingly on the Wheelus field in Tripoli, still under
British control pending UN resolution of its status and in January 1948,
the US and Britain struck a deal providing for American access to Wheelus
which envisaged its use by transport airplanes while military aircrafts
had the right to land there as well. Lovett's suggestion for a trilateral
declaration which would also include Turkey was reasonable with a view
to fact that in late 1948, the Americans started to refurbish the housing
and petroleum facilities and planned to lengthen the runways so that the
Air Force could use Wheelus for strategic operations in case of war.[53]
For Ankara, however, an Italian–Greek–Turkish trilateral declaration or
pact with military bases in Libya as its center, was outside the reach of
Turkish interests. It was plausibly calculated that any concentration of

power in this defensive scheme, might weaken the defense ability of Turkey rather than enhance it.

In its turn, for the US, the Middle East was still a peripheral area of secondary importance and had an auxiliary relationship to Western Europe by holding the largest oil resources and potential bases for airfields on which the US and British strategic plans depended. Indeed, the Marshall Plan had accentuated US economic interests in this region. There was a shortage of Western Hemisphere oil and the US was becoming a net importer of oil. The Middle Eastern petroleum was easy to get out of the ground and could be transported to Europe cheaper than Western Hemisphere oil. Section 112 of the Economic Cooperation Act of 1948 mandated that European petroleum requirements should be fulfilled as much as possible from repositories outside the US.[54] Besides, studies suggested that in wars that might break out in the mid-1950s, petroleum of the Middle East would be vital to the West and the Soviets would be forced to wage an oil-starved war if they could be denied entry into this region.[55] Equally important for the US and Britain were the use of airfields in the region. However, as will be discussed below, the safeguarding of air operations depended on the active defense of the area by the Turkish Army.

In the fall of 1947, war plan BROILER had assumed that within fifteen days after the eruption of hostilities, the US would launch the air offensive from bases in the Middle East, Britain and Okinawa. The base at Cairo–Suez was particularly important since a major target was the Soviet oil-refining facilities. Almost 84 percent of this refining industry was thought to be within the radius of B-29s operating out of Egypt. In the spring of 1948, the JCS adopted war plan HALFMOON which incorporated much of the Middle East strategy initially outlined in BROILER. It was estimated that Soviet radar nets and air defenses in the south were weak and that launchings from Egypt might be possible up to six months before Soviet forces seized the area.

As for the coordination of the American and British strategic planning, British war plan SPEEDWAY of December 1948 called for the defense of Egypt—despite continuing Anglo–Egyptian dispute—by British Commonwealth forces while the US Air Force utilized Cairo–Suez to launch a nuclear offensive with scores of heavy bombers. Admiral Richard Connolly, Commander of the US forces in the Eastern Atlantic and Mediterranean, was headquartered in London as well and coordinated Middle East strategy with his British counterparts.[56]

At this juncture, the US officials intensified their military aid programs in Turkey. This was no doubt, an urgent requirement in order to complement the Middle East Strategy envisioned in BROLIER and HALFMOON. The US Army Group in Ankara sought to reorganize and modernize the Turkish Army, augment its mobility and firepower, improve its command, control and communication skills, its transportation infrastructure and logistical capabilities. The US advisers wanted the Turkish Army to retard the Soviet land offensive, thereby affording time for the US and Britain to launch the strategic air campaign from Egyptian bases. "The Turkish army was given equipment to blunt a three-pronged Soviet attack across the Bosphorus, the Black Sea, and the Caucasus, to fallback gradually, and to mount a final, large-scale stand in southern Turkey in the Iskenderun pocket."[57]

Throughout 1948, Washington also transferred over 180 F-47s, 30 B-26s, and 86 C-47s to the Turkish Air Force which would assist Turkish Land Forces and help interdict Soviet troops moving toward Persian Gulf oil or sweeping toward Cairo–Suez. The Pentagon placed ever greater stress on reconstructing and resurfacing airfields in Turkey at such places as Bandırma (west) and Diyarbakır (south). Concurrently, training of the Turkish Air Forces was increasingly supported. On July 11, 1948, on the occasion of the visit of US Undersecretary of the Army General William H. Draper, the head of Air Group in Ankara, Major Gen. Earl S. Hoag expressed to Turkish press that, supported by the assistance material and the expertise of the technical advisers, over 40 specialized training courses were continuing its activities in Turkey. It was stated that the objective of the courses was to train the trainers. The training comprised A-26 Invader and P-47 Thunderbolt fighters, C-47 Dakota planes and related command, control and communication systems. Besides, 45 Turkish officers had attended further training programs in the US.

In his statement to the Turkish press, Undersecretary of the Army, Draper, underscored that an answer to the question whether the US would come to the aid of Turkey or not in case Turkey was attacked could be given by the State Department. He stated that he believed no one desired a war and no prospect of war in the near future could be mentioned. Gen. Draper also explained that the US had understood the importance of restoring Turkish foreign trade with Europe and providing a greater flow of Turkish export items, tobacco being in the first place. The US policy in this regard he said, was to support trade activities in Europe to reach the pre-war numbers without any barrier. But, particularly for Germany, priorities were food items and wheat.[58]

In fact, top level visits of US officials frequently took place in mid-1948. Previously, on July 1, Admiral Forrest Sherman had visited İstanbul with three cruisers, each carrying two sea-planes and equipped with lethal weapons which, no doubt, further impressed his Turkish counterparts. Admiral Sherman was the former vice chief of naval operations and a member of a sub-committee of SWNCC with an exclusive focus on the SU. In this post, he was the subordinate of Secretary of Defense, James V. Forrestal. In the same sub-committee, Secretary of War, Robert Patterson had designated General John R. Deane, while Secretary of State Byrnes appointed his adviser Charles E. Bohlen. Since then, Sherman was known as a strong defender of Turkey's strategic position. During the discussions on assistance to Turkey, when the Director of Policy Planning, George Kennan, claimed that the Pentagon deftly inserted military aid for Turkey into legislation originally designed as a political and economic program for Greece, Sherman had conceded that Greece was on the flank, but if Turkey fell into the Soviet orbit, the US would have an impossible situation. According to him, the Mediterranean strategy of the US was of vital importance, and it should be conceived as a highway for the projection of military power "deep into the heart of the land mass of Eurasia and Africa."[59] Secretary of Air Force, W. Stuart Symington, and Secretary of Defense, James V. Forrestal wanted some of the airstrips designed to handle B-29s which, if wartime circumstances allowed, US forces would fly in. Moreover, by the end of 1948, officials in the State Department endorsed the idea of constructing medium bomber bases in Turkey. Consequently, "Turkey began to develop the ability to attack vital Soviet petroleum resources in Romania and the Caucasus."[60]

As the Director of NEA in the State Department, on December 17, 1948, McGhee recommended $300 million in aid for fiscal year 1950, including $200 million to Greece and $100 million to Turkey. Three weeks later, in early January 1949, Ambassador Averell Harriman, the US Special Representative in Europe for the ECA, met with President İnönü, most of the members of government and a number of senior governmental departmental administrators.[61] Shortly afterwards, on January 6, 1949, Harriman cabled the ECA Administrator, Hoffman, explaining that after his conversations he had a renewed confidence in determination of the Turks and in their effective use of American aid under the direction of the US. Harriman said, İnönü stated that he believed that war could be avoided if the US could develop unity among the free countries of Europe, which required determination and maximum effort by each country, and that Turkey would do its part. He underlined that the Turkish President emphasized that firm American moral support was of even greater value than material aid. He urged that the US supply Turkey as a matter of urgency on the recommendations of Russell H. Dorr, Chief of ECA Mission in Turkey, in consultation with Ambassador George Wadsworth and General McBride. Harriman concluded that "with our assistance, and only with our assistance, can Turkey become an increasingly effective deterrent to Soviet aggression and a contributor to economic developments in Eastern Mediterranean and Europe."[62]

In the meantime, in the aftermath of Anglo–Turkish financial talks in Ankara which was concluded on January 23, 1949, the British Government announced that agreement had been reached with the Turkish Government on the question of drawing rights under the Intra-European Payments and Compensation Agreement of October 16, 1948, and that subject to approval by the OEEC, the UK Government proposed to grant such rights in sterling in favour of Turkey to the equivalent of $8,000,000 (£2,000,000). The statement added that it was expected that Turkish exports to Britain in 1949 would be larger than ever.[63]

The continuation of US financial aid was also of great importance for Ankara. However, contrary to the ECA Administrator Harriman's initial considerations, the aid was being reduced. On February 19, during a general discussion in Paris, the MFA Sadak told Harriman that his government was disappointed at the reduction which had been made in aid for Turkey in ECA's recent submissions to the Congress. Harriman said that he explained to Sadak that these submissions were purely of an illustrative nature and they were "in no sense designed by ECA to prejudge the recommendations which might be made by OEEC in connection with the division of whatever American aid might be available."[64]

Harriman also expressed that parts of this program which had been included in Turkey's estimates were probably beyond the scope of ECA financing. He suggested that Turkey should push the negotiation to obtain World Bank funds in order to finance some its projects. In his turn, Sadak recalled Turkey's need for the continuation of foreign assistance. Because, 48% of the Turkish budget was devoted to defense expenditures which drained sources to be spent for local investment objectives.[65]

Meanwhile, negotiations of the Brussels Pact powers with the US and Canada towards the creation of a single North Atlantic Alliance based on security guarantees and mutual commitments between Europe and North America intensified. They were concluded in September 1948 with a report to the various governments. The report was accepted by all governments in concern, thus enabling the Consultative Council of the Brussels Treaty to announce complete identity of views on the principle of a defensive pact for the North Atlantic area in October 1948.

The text of the Treaty was published on March 18, 1949 and three days after Denmark, Iceland, Italy, Norway and Portugal were invited by the Brussels Pact states to become participants in this new formation. Undoubtedly, the Kremlin made its last attempts to change the course of events. Being extremely suspicious of the nature of conversations between Turkey and the US, the Soviet Ambassador to Ankara Lavrishchov told the Turkish Minister of Foreign Affairs that the Soviets, in one day had captured from the Germans double the number of military equipment that the Washington was prepared to give to Turkey.[66]

In spite of the efforts of the SU to prevent the formation of the alliance by a memorandum addressed to the twelve original signatories alleging the hostile nature of their action, the talks followed the signature of the Treaty of Washington on April 4, 1949, bringing into being a common security mechanism among these 12 countries. The parliaments of the member countries ratified the Treaty within five months thereafter.

The Article 3 of NAT treats the means of maintaining and increasing the individual and collective capacity of NATO member countries to resist and to act jointly through the medium of mutual assistance. Such joint action might be achieved by a gradual integration of armed forces and coordination of instruction and training which has been an essential function of Supreme Headquarters Allied Powers Europe to this date. It was explained that "mutual aid" also meant the assistance of any kind. In this respect, the Treaty allowed that the military assistance provided by the US might take the form of end-items (delivery of a wide variety of military items ranging from ammunition to ships and airplanes) or to offshore orders (which was designed as a system whereby the US bought in various European countries with funds from its Military Assistance Program and gave equipment to one of the Allied countries for equipping its armed forces).[67]

Article 4 pertains to a threat to one of the NATO countries. The only obligation stated in this Article is for signatory countries to consult together if the territorial integrity or political independence of one of them is endangered. Such consultation may be requested by a country other than the one threatened and this consultation would take place within the framework of the North Atlantic Council meetings. As stated in Article 7, which expresses the compatibility of the Treaty with the Charter of the UN, the primary responsibility of the UN Security Council is in no way affected. Thus, in the event of threat, when a consultation of member countries of NAT reveal that enforcement action should be taken, the only competent body to authorize such action would be the Security Council or in case of default, the General Assembly of the UN.

Article 5 contains one of the essential provisions: "The Parties agree that an armed attack against one or more of them in Europe or North America shall be considered an attack against them all. . . ." This commitment, introduced a crucial measure, because the resulting accord created a situation against any possible aggression. The Article then goes on to define the obligations of countries in the event of armed attack. These obligations consist in taking forthwith individually and in concert with the other member countries to the Treaty, such action, including the use of armed force, as is deemed necessary by each Party. Significantly, joint action is justified by the exercise of the natural right of self-defence, individual or collective, as provided for in Article 51 of the UN Charter. It was, therefore, admitted that the right of self-defense is a legitimate right, the exercise of which in no way affects the primary competence of the Security Council in matters relating to the maintenance and restoration of peace. The final provisions of the Article include that the measures so taken shall be reported to the Security Council and shall be terminated when that body has taken the necessary measures.

Article 6 defines the area in which the provisions of the Article 5 are applicable.[68] In this context, it is emphasized that the NATO was not established to defend a geographically homogenous territory, but was created to defend a way of life. Significantly, the definition of the area in no way implied that political and military events occurring outside it can not be the subject of consultations within the Council. It is believed that the overall international situation is liable to affect the preservation of peace and security in the area in question, and it is to consider this situation that the Council must and does devote its attention as a matter of course.

Article 7 expresses the compatibility of the Treaty with the Charter of the United Nations and in Article 8, the Parties confirm compatibility of the Treaty with their other international obligations and undertake not to enter into any international engagements in the future in conflict with the Treaty.

Article 9 makes provision for the creation of bodies to implement the Treaty. It is these bodies which constitute the "Organization" as such within the meaning of the NAT.

Article 10 states that the Parties may, by unanimous agreement, invite any other European State in a position to further the principles of the Treaty to accede to it. In this brief examination of the Text of the Treaty, it should also be noted that the NAT Organization has no supranational character. All decisions must be taken by national representatives unanimously.[69]

Turning back to the Turkey's exclusion from this formation of states, evidently, the political and military circles in Ankara were greatly disturbed by the course of developments. Until then, Ankara had repeatedly expressed its willingness to incorporate its defense scheme to that of the West. Towards this end, Turkish policy makers had made endeavours to create a Mediterranean pact including the West European countries and the scope of which included the defense of the Middle East. Despite their optimism, neither the plans around a Mediterranean pact nor the projects aiming at realizing a defensive grouping of states in the Middle East were fulfilled. Italy's inclusion to NAT was another surprising development. Although the US and British Ambassadors communicated their governments' view to Ankara that the NAT was based on certain geographic boundaries which contained only countries of the North Atlantic region, Ankara, soon realized that Italy which was regarded as a Mediterranean country in previous security plannings, as well as territory in North Africa comprising the Algerian departments of France, would be included in this formation. Ankara, then considered that its exclusion might indicate the reduction of US strategic interest coupled with an imminent reduction of US aid.

The Turkish Government thought that they should not lose further time to launch a diplomatic campaign to seize an opportunity to incorporate Ankara to the emerging defense scheme. The Turkish MFA Sadak, despite the suggestions of some officials in the MFA to postpone his demarché, decided to beat the iron when it was still hot and traveled to New York in early April on the occasion of the opening of the Second Part of the Third Session of the UN General Assembly which was scheduled to meet between April 5–May 18. As will be discussed below, Sadak, who was the first Turkish Minister of Foreign Affairs to visit the US, visited Washington from April 12 to 15 and held conversations with his counterpart and the officials of the State Department.

In his meeting with Acheson on April 12, Sadak communicated the views of the Turkish Government on the present circumstance that Turkey felt itself deprived of the US guarantee offered to Europe. In the beginning of their conversation, Sadak told his counterpart that he would review the position in which Turkey found itself as a result of the recent signature of the NAT. He said, in March 1947, the US Government had announced its program in support of the independence and security of Turkey. Subsequent to that time Acheson told Sadak that this support was confirmed through the effective military assistance which Turkey received from the US and later the formation of the WEU took place and the talks were directed at a security arrangement with the US for the North Atlantic area. Acheson recalled that in the autumn of 1948, conversations took place at Ankara with the US and UK Ambassadors in which Turkey raised the question of Turkey's position in the contemplated security arrangement. The US Secretary of State reminded Sadak that the Turkish Government was informed in reply by written memoranda that while details of the proposed arrangement had not yet been formulated the conception was clearly a geographical one, restricted geographically in scope to countries of the North Atlantic region.

Concerning Italy, the Turkish Government having been previously informed that the contemplated pact would be limited geographically and that Italy would not be included, had so informed the TGNA. Ankara was satisfied with this situation since the geographical conception of NAT was clear and understandable while this left the door open for later consideration of a Mediterranean defense arrangement within which Turkey might consider to find an adequate place together with other Mediterranean countries. Acheson said, despite the fact that the Turkish Government was informed that Italy would not be included, "subsequently, however, it was learned that Italy and the territory in North Africa comprising the Algerian departments of France would in fact be brought within the scope of the North Atlantic Pact."[70] Then, he admitted that the inclusion of Italy completely upset the situation so far as the views and perceptions of the Turkish Government were concerned.

Subsequently, Acheson underlined that the overall situation seemed all the more incomprehensible to the Turkish Government and people in as much as Turkey had been undergoing constant Soviet pressure and threats since the spring of 1945. He pointed out that since that time

Turkey had been making great sacrifices by maintaining a large armed force to withstand Soviet threats, at the cost of what was becoming an unbearable burden upon Turkey's economy and finances. He said, the fear had begun to creep into Turkish minds that with the negotiation of the Atlantic Pact the US had altered its position concerning Turkey and that it no longer maintained the powerful interest in the maintenance of Turkey's independence and integrity which had characterized the attitude of the US Government since 1946 and added that the Soviet propaganda had not been slow to make the most of this situation. Then, he expressed that Sadak said that he was frankly at a loss to know what explanations he could give to the Turkish Parliament and public.

However, in certain respects the US Government was still lacking a firm conception of Turkey's role in any given defense mechanism. Correspondingly, in reply to Sadak, in addition to his previous perception of Turkey's role in regional defence within a Mediterranean security arrangement, this time Acheson said that the security of the Middle East was one of the most important problems with which the Department was confronted soon after he had become Under Secretary in 1945. This time in this context he explained that facing Soviet demands over Turkey, the President and the Department took a serious view of this challenge and the conclusion was reached that the Soviet aspirations of dominating Turkey would be contrary to the vital interests of the US. "As a result a strong position was taken by the US Government in support of Turkish independence with the full knowledge of the possible consequences. The President considered this the most important decision he had made subsequent to the Bombing of Hiroshima."[71] Indeed, as discussed before, the first action taken by the US Government was the dispatch of *USS Missouri* accompanied by the *USS Providence* and *USS Power*, the prolonged effects of which continued in the following decades.[72] Then Acheson went on to summarize the incidents until the making of NAT and assured Sadak that in the US President's thinking and in his, the vital importance to the US of Turkey's independence and integrity was in no way diminished as a result of these developments.

In his turn, Sadak told Acheson that two years ago Turkey had stood in the very forefront of US preoccupations concerning security questions. However, recently, the US had transferred its interests to the West European countries, and had now gone further in guaranteeing their security than it had in the case of Turkey. As regards the West European countries, the US pledged to come immediately to their aid if they were attacked; no such pledge existed concerning Turkey. "If there were any consistency or logic in international relations, then it would seem that Turkey, the first object of US solicitude in security matters, would have been the first to be given, the protective cover of a guarantee."[73] However, Sadak said, this had not proved to be the case. If, as stated, the US position towards Turkey had not changed, why had it been impossible for the US to extend the Atlantic Pact to include Turkey, or for Ankara at least to consider the extension of a similar guarantee to an Eastern Mediterranean Pact?

Acheson replied that first, there was the series of statements by Truman and himself already referred to beginning in 1946 at the time of the Soviet demands on the Turkish Straits up to those made in connection with the signing of the Atlantic Pact. Secondly, there was the important military assistance rendered to the Turkish Government by the US. In a matter of days a new military assistance bill would be presented to the Congress. From the hearings in Congress on this bill, it would be made clear that a substantial amount of this assistance was intended for Turkey. This would he said, give evidence of continuing US interest in Turkey. Thirdly, in Truman's thinking the economic development of the Middle East, particularly of Turkey, Greece, Iran and the Arab states, complemented the ERP. US assistance in this respect also would make evident US interest in that region.

As for the invitation extended to Italy to become one of the North Atlantic Treaty countries. Acheson pointed out that:

> this had been done not merely to please that country or France, but was a logical development. France had argued that Italy has been the backdoor into France through which throughout history attacks had been made upon it. It was only after this backdoor had been closed through the decision to include Italy that France's attitude had changed with reference to its own security problems and that it had been found possible to reach a settlement in West Germany.[74]

Before parting, when Sadak asked to whom Acheson could recommend him to discuss economic issues, Acheson suggested that he discuss these problems with Assistant Secretary of State for Economic Affairs, Williard L. Thorp and the Director of NEA Satterthwaite. The day after Sadak held a conference with Thorp. In their talks, Sadak requested increased US financial aid, citing the serious financial position of the Turkish Government as a result of its continuing defense burden which was making most difficult financing ECA and anticipated IBRD projects. He requested a US grant of additional $30 million under the military aid program to finance current consumption items. Acheson stated that Thorp had informed him that Sadak also requested US support in anticipated approach by Turkish Government to US private money market for a loan probably less than $70 million with the principal objective of providing dollar exchange for imports by Turkish private enterprise.

Meanwhile, on April 13, 1949, Sadak conveyed the message of İnönü to Truman in which the Turkish President expressed that he should like to lay particular stress on the precious military aid which had been given to Turkey by the US in one the most critical periods which the world was going through. At this juncture, the makers of US strategic military planning were increasingly concerned with strengthening US strongholds in the Eastern Mediterranean. In a policy paper approved by the Foreign Assistance Correlation Committee on May 25, it was pointed out that it was the long-range US military objective to be able to prevent the loss or destruction of Western European and Middle East nations and by securing the natural approaches to the enemy sources of power to facilitate conduct of offensive operations. It was explained that the short-range military objective was to improve to the maximum extent practicable, and at the earliest day possible, the capability of Western European nations to provide for their own defense and to increase the capabilities of the Middle Eastern countries to impose a delay on enemy operations directed towards their areas. In this context, it was pointed out that Italy and Turkey were important for their strategic locations astride a natural sea approach to areas from which air power may be projected towards an important segment of the industrial capacity of Soviet areas.[75]

The US NSC, was however, in favour of adopting a careful policy concerning the issue of including Turkey to the Western defence scheme. The NSC asserted that it would be unwise for the time being to seek an arrangement with the Turkish Government for the construction of airfields or for the stockpiling of aviation gasoline. The reason for this decision was that these efforts would be regarded by the Kremlin as a threat to its security and would stimulate further pressure on Turkey and perhaps on Iran. It was pointed out that the SU was watching carefully any development which could be exploited to support the Soviet thesis that the NAT was aggressive in intent and operation.[76]

As for Ankara's foreign policy towards Europe, after much effort, finally on August 8, 1949, Turkey and Greece were invited to be members of the Council of Europe. Although Turkey was admitted into the Council of Europe, Turkish foreign policy makers were of the opinion that this could not constitute an alternative to the commitment of the US within a formal alliance or through NATO. Under these circumstances, Ankara could not help seeking Turkey's security under the defensive shield of the Western camp. But, as will be discussed next, there was a price which Turkey was required to pay for admittance into the Western security system.

Notes

1. "After the Turk, Who?" in *The Sun,* May 17, 1903, p. 2, img. 34, Library of Congress, http://chroniclingamerica.loc.gov/lccn/sn83030272/1903-05-17/ed-1/seq-34/#date1 = 1836&sort = &date2 = 1922&words = Empire +Ottoman&sequence = 0&lccn = &index = 8&state = &rows = 20&ortext = & proxtext = ottoman +empire&year = &phrasetext = &and text = &proxValue = &dateFilterType = yearRange&page = 378

2. George McGhee, *The US-Turkish-NATO Middle East Connection*, p. 54.

3. *Ibid.* As McGhee put it, these defensive strategies were extensively discussed during US-UK talks in 1950 in order to determine the ways in which the two allies could co-operate in defence matters.

4. CAB129/23 C.P,(48)7, 5 Jan. 1948; CAB128/12C.M.2(48), January 8, 1948; see also, Harry Truman, *The Memoirs of Harry Truman: Years of Trial and Hope 1946-1951*, p. 257; 13 January 1948. *FRUS*, Vol. III, 4-5; William E. Pemberton, *Harry S. Truman*, p. 103.

5. Thomas Hammond, *The Anatomy of Communist Takeovers*, (New Haven, Conn.: Yale Univ. Press, 1989), pp. 398-432. Prior to the Czech crisis, there were asserted signs that the Kremlin encouraged the communist leaders in West Europe to revert to electoral process. Kennan had taken note of Soviet ouvertures in Berlin for a possible summit meeting between Truman and Stalin. The CIA had also stressed the failure of Soviet satellite governments to recognize the Markos Vafiades regime in northern Greece, the substantial concessions in Soviet proposals on Austria, the Polish Government's announcement that the bulk of increased coal production would go to the West, and *Pravda's* opposition to a Balkan-Danubian Federation. Melvyn. P. Leffler, *A Preponderance. . . ,* pp. 204-205; John H. Bruins to Marshal, December, 22, 1947, in *FRUS*, 1947, IV, p. 255.

6. Martin Myant, *Socialism and Democracy in Czechoslovakia*, (Cambridge: University of Cambridge Press, 1981), pp. 106; 125-129. In Slovakia, the Democratic Party was the strongest with about 61 percent of the votes and

43 seats, while the Communist Party obtained about 30 percent and 21 seats. The Communist Party gained appreciably from the Russian role in liberating the country and from the prominent communist participation in the resistance movement. Within a short time, party membership increased dramatically from approximately 50,000 in 1945 to 1 million in the spring of 1946. The communists enjoyed a strong power base among the working class while trade unions were powerful and party members were active with them.

7. "Bruins to Marshall, January 28, 1948," in *FRUS*, 1948, IV, p. 734

8. "Steinhardt to Marshall, February, 25, 1948," in *ibid.*, pp. 741–742.

9. "Steinhardt to Marshall, May 29, 1948," in *ibid.*, pp. 754–755.

10. F. Cemal Erkin, *Dışişlerinde. . .* , Vol. I, p. 267. Erkin considered this country then still under Soviet influence.

11. *Ibid.*, p. 269.

12. *Ibid.*, p. 270. It is worth noting that this was done a month after the signing of peace treaties with Finland, Italy, Hungary and Bulgaria (February 10, 1947) and in expectation of the Conference of Foreign Ministers in Moscow (March 3–April 24, 1947) where problems with Germany were to be further discussed. Dankward Gerhold, "Armament Controls of Germany: Protocol III of the Modified Brussels Treaty" in, Fred Tanner (ed.), *From Versailles to Baghdad: Post-War Armament Control of Defeated States*, (NY: United Nations Publications, 1992), p. 72. See also footnote (1) on the same page. Although the idea of the Dunkerque Treaty was warmly welcomed, it might be preferable to take the Rio Treaty as a model. On September 2, 1947, in a conference in Brazil, twenty-one Western Hemisphere countries produced a mutual assistance pact with the exception of Nicaragua and Ecuador, the Rio Treaty, the first of five such regional pacts (Brussels Pact, NATO, SEATO, and the Baghdad Pact which was later on known as the Central Treaty Organization (CENTO) were the others). The signatories agreed that aggression against an American nation, whether by an outside power or by signatories, required joint action against the aggressor. It was essentially a collective defensive alliance and provided an example of regional grouping within the framework of the UN Charter.

13. "Brussels Treaty," in, *The North Atlantic Treaty Organization Facts and Figures*, (Brussels: NATO Information Service, October 1971), pp. 266–268.

14. As finally approved, the Foreign Assistance Act of 1948 therefore provided for expenditure on foreign relief and rehabilitation as follows: ERP (first 12 months) $5,300,000,000; China $463,000,000; Greece and Turkey $275,000,000; UN Children's Fund $60,000,000. *Keesing's Contemporary Archives*, Vol. No. VI, 1946–1948, p. 9252.

15. The Vanderberg Resolution included that within the UN Charter, the US Government should particularly pursue ". . . progressive development of regional and other collective arrangements for individual and collective self-

defense . . . association of the United States, by constitutional process, with such regional and other collective arrangements as are based on continuous and effective self-help and mutual aid, and as affect its national security. . . ." "The Vanderberg Resolution, June 11, 1948" in, Arthur M. Schlesinger, *The Dynamics of.* . . , p. 133. In the meantime, alarmed by the crisis of the Berlin Blockade, common consultations on military questions within the Western Union were held, which led to the establishment of a permanent defence staff under Marshal B.L. Montgomery in August 27–28, p. 1948.

16. *FRUS*, 1948, Vol. IV, pp. 83–85.
17. George McGhee, *The US–Turkish–NATO.* . . , p. 48.
18. F. Cemal Erkin, *Dışişlerinde.* . . , Vol. 1, pp. 270; 278–279.
19. *Ibid.,* p. 278.
20. *Ibid.,* pp. 142–143; 157; 175–177; 183–193, respectively.

Obviously, this represents an ample example of the debate on the role of "agent(s)" in foreign policy/decision-making. Although familiar throughout the discipline of international relations, the agent-structure debate has been brought under discussion of international politics increasingly. It is now widely accepted that any analysis of events must be able to generate explanations that take account of both structure and agency. The problem arises because explanations so frequently operate at one of two extremes. At one extreme, human beings (actors–agents) are seen to be free agents with the power to maintain or transform the systems in which they operate. At the other extreme, it is assumed that actors are caught in the grip of structures which they did not create and over which they do not exercise control. Then the problem of structure and agency surfaces because of the failure to find a way of synthesizing these two extreme positions. The debate is admittedly too large to reach a conclusion here since both old and new approaches (i.e., structuralistm, opposing a unit actor-agent-based explanation, etc.) of the behaviour of states in terms of their internal properties and advocating that in social systems agents are constrained by the structure of the systems in which they operate; scientific realism explaining that invisible structures have just as tangible an existence as the individual agents constrained by them) introduced a variety of analysis around the question. The problem still persists apparently in democracies. For a general explanation, see, Barry Buzan, (1st edt.), *The Logic of Anarchy Neorealism to Structural Realism*, (NY: Columbia University Press, 1993), pp. 102–113, *passim.*

21. F. Cemal Erkin, *Dışişlerinde* . . . , Vol. I, pp. 277–281, *passim.*
22. *The New York Times*, July 1 and 3, 1948.
23. Sixteen signatories of this agreement were Turkey, Austria, Belgium, Denmark, France, Greece, Ireland, Iceland, Luxemburg, Norway, Netherlands, Italy, Portugal, United Kingdom, Sweden, Switzerland and the commanders of the US, the UK and France of Germany under occupation. *Resmi Gazete*, July 13, 1948, No: 6956, p. 14393. The TGNA approved this agreement with Law No: 5252 and the Economic Co-operation with Law No: 5253 consecutively on

July 8, 1948. For the texts of the agreements see, *ibid.*, pp. 14393–14398; 14398–14401 respectively.

24. *Ibid.*, Article 7, pp. 14399–14400.

25. The Saraçoğlu Governments served between July 9, 1942–March 9, 1943 and March 9, 1943 to August 7, 1946 consecutively. In the cabinets of Saraçoğlu, Numan Menemencioğlu (until June 15, 1944) and subsequently, Hasan Saka were nominated as MFA. Previously Dr. Refik Saydam had formed two cabinets consecutively, between April 3, 1939 and July 9, 1942 in which Saraçoğlu had served as MFA. Kemal Girgin, *T.C. Hükümetleri Programında Dış Politikamız 1923–1993*, (Ankara: Dışişleri Bakanlığı Yayınları, 1993), pp. 19–21.

26. As mentioned earlier, Saka remained in office until he had to resign Premiership on account of differences of opinion with President İnönü. On January 16, 1949 Şemsettin Günaltay succeeded him and served until the defeat of RPP in the general elections of May 14, 1950 (formally, until May 22) which brought the Democrat Party and Adnan Menderes to power. Meanwhile, in the both cabinets of Saka and in the subsequent Günaltay Government, Necmettin Sadak served as MFA. Metin Tamkoç, *The Warrior Diplomats*, (Salt Lake City: University of Utah Press, 1976), pp. 315, 328, 341, 344, 352; Kemal Girgin, *T.C. Hükümetleri. . .* , pp. 21–26.

27. Kemal Karpat, *Turkey's Politics*, p. 189.

28. Erkin used the terms "Regional Agreement" and "Western Regional Agreement" to refer to an agreement which was being planned between the US and the countries of Western Europe (which emerged as the North Atlantic Treaty) throughout his work.

29. F. Cemal Erkin, *Dışişlerinde. . .* , Vol. II, p. 12.

30. *Ibid.* pp. 15–16.

31. *FRUS*, 1948, Vol. IV, p. 173.

32. F. Cemal Erkin, *Dışişlerinde*, Vol. II, p. 17.

33. As stated in the reports of Ambassador David Kelly to London (FO, 26 Jan. 1948, FO371/72534 R1203/114/44 and FO, 28 Jan. 1948, FO371/72534 R1270/114/44), cited in, E. Athanassopoulou, "Western Defence Developments and Turkey's Search for Security in 1948," in, Sylvia Kedourie (ed.), *Turkey, Identity, Democracy, Politics*, (London: Frank Cass, 1996), p. 79.

34. For a discussion of the subject, see Peter L. Hahn, *The United States, Great Britain and Egypt, 1945–1956*, (North Carolina: The University of North Carolina Press, Chapel Hill, 1991).

35. *FRUS*, 1948, Vol. IV, pp. 71–72.

36. Peter L. Hahn, *The United States, Great Britain and Egypt, 1945–1956*, 11–12,30.

37. Joseph Nevo, "Palestinian–Arab Violent Activity during the 1930s" in Michael J. Cohen and Martin Kolinsky (eds.), *Britain and the Middle East in*

the 1930s, (NY: St. Martin's Press, 1992), p. 170. Al-Hajj Amin al-Husyni, the future Mufti of Jerusalem had helped to mobilise 2000 persons. Philip Mattar, *The Mufti of Jerusalem, Al-Hajj Amin al-Husayni and the Palestinian National Movement*, (NY: Columbia University Press, 1988), p. 12. Another source stated that the number amounted to several thousands throughout the country. Bayan Nuyhad al-Hut, *Leadership and Political Institutions in Palestine 1917-1948*, (Beirut: Institute of Palestine Studies, 1981), p. 56.

38. "Note on the Turco-Israeli Relations." *The MFA Archives.*

39. Gencer Özcan, "50. Yılı Biterken Türk-İsrail İlişkileri" (Turco-Israeli Relations Towards the End of Its 50th Year), in *Çağdaş Türk Diplomasisi: 200 Yıllık Süreç* (Contemporary Turkish Diplomacy: A Process of 200 Years), Symposium Papers, Ankara, October 15-17, 1997, (Ankara: TTK, 1999), p. 538. See also, George G. Gruen, "Dynamic Progress in Turkish-Israeli Relations," in *Israel Affairs*, (Vol. I, No. 4, Summer, 1995), p. 44.

40. Except Iraq which refused to negotiate with Israel. *Facts About Israel*, Israel Information Center, 1996, pp. 31-32.

41. Accordingly, the coastal plain, Galilee and the entire Negev remained within Israel's sovereignty, Judea and Samaria (the West Bank) came under Jordanian rule, the Gaza Strip came under Egyptian administration, and the city of Jerusalem was divided, with Jordan controlling the eastern part, including the Old City, and Israel the western sector. As for the partition plan of 1947 (UN Resolution 181) and 1949-1967 armistice lines, *ibid.*

42. The first 120-seat *Knesset* went into session following the elections on January 25, 1949. As mentioned above, Chaim Weizmann, head of the World Zionist Organization, was elected as the first President and David Ben-Gurion, head of the Jewish Agency was chosen as the first Prime Minister.

43. Amicam Nachmani, "*Israel, Turkey and Greece—Uneasy Relations in the East Mediterranean*," (London: Frank Cass, 1987), pp. 44-49.

44. Gencer Özcan, "50. Yılı Biterken. . . ," p. 538.

45. Subsequently, in 1951, an air transport agreement was signed, which gave a start to the flights of the Israeli airways, El Al to both Ankara and İstanbul. In 1953, Israel dispatched aid to the earthquake struck regions in Turkey and Israeli war vessels visited İstanbul in the same year.

46. As told by George Harris in my interview with him.

47. Sayed-Ahmed, Muhammed Abd el-Wahab, *Nasser and American Foreign Policy 1952-1956*, (Surrey: Laam Ltd., 1989), p. 23.

48. Peter L. Hahn, *The United States, Great Britain and Egypt, 1945-1956*, p. 97.

49. Nutting also had in mid a form of a permanent police force stationed on Israel's borders. He said, "this would relieve us of the obligation—which could all too easily arise in the inflamed state of Arab-Israeli relations—of having to fight against an Arab state, such as Jordan, with whom we had a treaty of

alliance. It would also enable us to reduce or withdraw our forces from Jordan or elsewhere in the Middle East if either political or military requirements demanded it." Anthony Nutting, *No End of A Lesson*, (London: Constable & Co.Ltd, 1967), pp. 33–34.

50. F.O. 371 R3379/114/44, "Record of Conversation between Bevin and the Turkish Ambassador Açıkalın," F.O. Minute, 9 March 1948, Cited in, Yücel Güçlü, *The Life And Career of A Turkish Diplomat: Açıkalın,* (Ankara: MFA Publications, 2002), p. 73.

51. C.L. Sulzberger, *A Long Row of Candles, 1934–1954,* (London: Macmillan, 1969), p. 356.

52. *FRUS,* 1948, Vol. IV, p. 79.

53. Melvyn P. Leffler, *A Preponderance of Power*, p. 289; see also notes (87) and (88) on the same page and *FRUS,* 1949, Vol. IV, pp. 526–613.

54. *FRUS,* 1948, Vol. V, pp. 550–51.

55. Melvyn P. Leffler, *A Preponderance of Power,* pp. 237–238.

56. *Ibid.,* p. 238.

57. *Ibid.,* p. 238–239.

58. *Ayın Tarihi,* Vol. 176, July 1–31, 1948, pp. 25–26; 43–45.

59. Melvyn P. Leffler, *A Preponderence of Power,* 144. For Sherman's visit to stanbul, see, *Ayın Tarihi, ibid.,* p. 1.

60. Leffler also pointed out that when Tito suspended aid to the Greek insurgents and guerrilla activity waned, it was agreed to transfer aid under the Greece-Turkey program to the latter nation where the money could be used to bolster overall strategy for the Middle East. *Ibid.,* p. 239.

61. George McGhee, *"The US-Turkish-NATO . . . ,"* p. 57.

62. *FRUS,* 1949, Vol. VI, pp. 1640–1641.

63. *Keesing's Contemporary Archives,* Vol. No. VII, 1948–1950, p. 9769.

64. *FRUS,* 1949, Vol. VI, p. 1643.

65. *Ibid.,* pp. 1643–1644.

66. *Ulus,* Ankara, March 26, 1949.

67. Monroe MacCloskey, *North Atlantic Treaty Organization,* (NY: Richard Rosen Press, Military Research Series, 1966), pp. 25–26.

68. It was amended after the accession of Turkey and Greece to the Treaty through the Protocol dated October 22, 1951 the ratification procedures of which were finally completed on February 18, 1952.

69. Undoubtedly, throughout the years of the Alliance common sense was applied in this regard. The unanimity requirement in actual usage leads to what is tantamount to a veto, however, it reflects motives opposed to those which underlie the right of veto. The latter is essentially negative. It confers on certain members the definite right, by casting a negative vote, to nullify a majority decision without even giving reasons for doing so. The unanimity requirement, on the contrary, constitutes a pressing invitation to reach agreement.

70. *FRUS*, 1949, Vol. VI.

71. *Ibid.*, p. 1649.

72. Interestingly, it is still explained commonly by the Turkish and American officials that the foundation of the 6th US Fleet had its roots in this incident. Referring to the statements of high level US officials, a similar assessment was made by Kamran İnan on May 24, 2000, then the Head of Foreign Relations Committee of the TGNA, during his explanations to the Committee concerning his visit to the Washington in May, 2000. *Personal diary note.*

73. *FRUS*, 1949, Vol. VI, p. 1650.

74. *Ibid.*, p. 1651.

75. *FRUS*, 1949, Vol. I, pp. 314–315.

76. *Ibid.*, p. 324.

Chapter 7

War, Hot: The Test of Wills in the Korean War and the Turkish Involvement in the Conflict (1950–1952)

I can say we are going to be much more sympathetic in helping those who helped most in Korea, we want all of our friends tied together as free nations militarily, economically and politically.[1]

This chapter will discuss the development of a local dispute in Korea between 1950 and 1952 into the biggest international conflict since the WW II. Here, the emphasis will be on the Turkish participation in this conflict and the background of events which shaped the decision of Ankara. In this context, it will be first explained that the crisis over Korea embodied and epitomised the global conlict of the Cold War era. It was the Korean war that first brought communist China into the international arena as well. Indeed, Korea, the place where the world peace was broken, not five years after the end of WW II, was fated to be the battleground of contesting ideologies and interests. At this stage, having withdrawn its troops in 1949 in line with a policy of disengagement, the US was unprepared for involvement in the war that began with a massive attack on South Korea by the North Koreans on June 24, 1950 and which lasted three years at a cost of more than 150,000 US casualties.

Consecutively, the making of Turkish foreign policy leading to Ankara's decision to assign a combat force under the UN Command in Korea will be examined. In this framework, Turkey's participation in the

Korean War will be explained as a crucial point in recent Turkish history which remarked an important test case for Ankara's re-evaluation of Turkey's place in international politics. Here, it will be underscored that participation in the war ended nearly 30 years of a policy of non-involvement in international conflicts as well. Given this, Turkish entry into the Korean War, especially after maintaining a strict policy of avoiding involvement in international conflicts since the founding of the Republic will be explained through a critical approach to Ankara's efforts to tie Turkey's defense with that of the US and the NATO. The impact of Turkish involvement in the conflict in its foreign and domestic policies will also be discussed in this context.

Conflicting Strategies Lay Out Options from Total to Limited War

As for the agreements of the victors of WW II on the future of Korea, it was decided by the US, Britain, and China at the Cairo Conference of 1943 that once the Japanese had capitulated, Korea was again to become a free and independent nation. At the Potsdam Conference of 1945 these same powers reaffirmed this pledge. In its turn, when the SU declared war against Japan in August of 1945, it formally agreed to stand by these pledges.

At Yalta, Roosevelt had been urged by his military planners to seek a definite commitment for intervention of the SU in the Pacific struggle. The US President also sought Stalin's agreement to giving China a significant place in the UN and allowing it to gain back its lost territories. Shortly afterwards, the US received guarantees of Soviet entry into the Pacific war. In effect, outer Mongolia and strategic assets were conceded to the Soviet Union following the defeat of Japan with the concurrence of Generalissimo Chiang Kai-shek, which Roosevelt agreed to obtain. Eventually, the SU agreed to conclude with the Nationalist government of China a pact of friendship and alliance. It was also agreed that the part of the agreement on Far East would remain secret because Russia had a treaty of neutrality with Japan, and information largely leaked from the Nationalists to the Japanese and an immediate announcement might jeopardize negotiation on differences between Chinese Nationalists and Communists, which the US Ambassador to China, Major Gen. Patrick J. Hurley, evaluated were close to success. At this juncture, the terms agreed at Yalta were not officially disclosed to Chiang Kai-Shek until June 15, 1945.

It was in September of 1945 that Japan's unconditional surrender in the aftermath of the atomic bombing of Hiroshima and Nagasaki brought World War II to its formal ending. Liberated from Japan in 1945 only to become a hostage to the Cold War, Korea remained divided at the 38th parallel, its two halves occupied by US and Russian troops until 1948 when communist refusal to accept UN-supervised elections led to establishment of rival regimes: the US backed Republic of Korea (ROK) in South, and the SU sponsored People's Republic in North. Countries who sent their troops to Korea could hardly dream that the two leading communist powers, SU and China would blatantly combine in rallying against them.

The Kremlin, in fact, had made preparations for the occupation of North Korea in August 1945 where People's Committees operated extensively. While it is true that in the same month a line was drawn across Korea at the 38th parallel, this was done to facilitate the arrangements made for the surrender of Japanese forces in the area. Russia would accept the surrender of Japanese troops north of this line, while the US would handle those troops surrendering south of the line.[2] Thus, the 38th parallel was the result of a temporary expediency, having nothing to do with natural boundaries, politics or the history of the country.

At the end of 1945 a big-power conference at Moscow called for a five-year period of trusteeship by Britain, the United States, the Soviet Union and China, and the establishment of a provisional democratic government. But, when the executive agency of the trustees, the Soviet Union and the United States met in Seoul in March of the new year, it was obvious that it would not work. All the Korean political parties except the communists demanded immediate and complete independence and refused to cooperate. The Soviets then insisted that the communists were the only legitimate party in Korea, and that it form the government, but the United States was equally insistent. Ultimately, both sides set up their own governments in their own zones. The Soviets passed control over to a Provisional People's Committee, and in the summer all of the parties of the north coalesced into the Korean National Democratic Front; then the northern part of the peninsula made a predictable transition into the People's Democratic Republic, the standard Marxist–Leninst one-party state modeled itself after the Soviet Union, while in December 1946, in the south, a legislative assembly was set up, half of it elected and half of it nominated. However, the country was in near chaos, hundreds of thousands were hungry, unemployed and homeless, while they wanted their independence.

In May 1947, the Joint Commission of the trustee powers had one more try. The Americans proposed free elections throughout the entire peninsula; the Russians rejected the idea. They countered by proposing a meeting of equal numbers of representatives of all the parties of the south, and all the parties of the north, which would have meant the communists, since they were the only one. Washington declined this suggestion on the grounds that the representatives of the communist party of the north would be controlled by the Russians.

As for the reasons behind China's increasing attention towards Korea, it can be stated that developments in China in the first half of the 1940s were of crucial importance for the sequence of events in 1950, culminating in the Chinese intervention in Korea in October 1950. During the WW II, the Kuomintang, under the leadership of Chiang Kai-shek, was regarded favourably by the US administration as a result of the Chinese resistance to Japanese aggression. However, the US Government's disillusionment with China developed from the negative contribution made by Kuomintang in the Pacific War. Instead of playing a vigorous part in the defeat of Japan in the Pacific, the top Kuomintang officials and generals were interested in exploiting large-scale American aid for their own benefit while Chiang Kai-shek was pre-occupied with his long-term feud with the Chinese communists. Indeed, numerically, the Kuomintang forces were superior to the communists, but in morale, commitment and leadership the communists were far ahead of the Kuomintang as the civil war was to reveal. The Chinese Communist leader Mao Tse-tung had managed to transform the Chinese Communist Party (CCP) into a powerful platform to attract the Chinese masses.

In fact, the Japanese aggression of 1937 had first created the conditions for a communist leadership in China and for spreading the conflict to most of the neighbouring countries. At this juncture, Stalin surprised the Chinese communist rebels after having forced them into a reconciliation with the nationalist leader Chiang Kai-shek against the invader, when he concluded a non-aggression treaty with Japan in August 1941 that implied among other things, the end of Soviet assistance to China and the recognition of Manchukuo and hence of the seizure of China's richest province by the Japanese imperialists.

After the Japanese surrender in August 1945, the Kremlin followed a cautious policy towards China "and one less sympathetic to Chinese communism than might have been expected.[3] Stalin was considerably dubious about the character of the CCP and the prospects for the CCP taking power throughout China. It is argued that the Soviet leader anticipated a slow decline of the Kuomitang balanced by a gradual growth of the CCP which could point towards a division of China. This also explains the Kremlin's preservation of diplomatic relations with the Kuomintang until a surprisingly late stage in April 1949, by which time it was obvious that the CCP would succeed on the mainland within the near future.

Meanwhile, speculation grew at the end of 1948 and beginning of 1949 as to whether Chiang Kai-shek might stand down tactically or because he had wearied of the setbacks that had occurred. In October 1948, in his statement to the *New York Tribune,* Chiang spoke of the world menace of communism and of the need to support nationalists' resistance to it. In this context, he linked his message with communist activities in Korea and Japan. "A feature of the decline of the Kuomintang was Chiang's interest in forging links with [the designated South Korean President] Syngman Rhee and his reference to Korea was one first signs of this trend. Chiang and the clique surrounding him had reached the conclusion that the only hope for the salvation of the Kuomintang lay in the third world war; this, too, was a consistent outbreak of the war in Korea and after."[4]

In October 1949, following a decisive victory over Chiang Kai-shek's Nationalists, the CCP formally proclaimed the People's Republic of China (PRC). In the months following, the socialist-bloc states, joined by some Asian neutrals i.e., Burma, India and Indonesia as well as Britain, Switzerland, and Scandinavian states offered diplomatic recognition to the new Chinese regime. The US held aloof, and the doors to the UN closed shut.

The PRC had an immediate agenda for regulating its international affairs based on its ideological vision. At the top was the conquest of Tibet, preparations were taking place for Taiwan and the conclusion of an alliance with the SU. Beijing did also quickly change diplomatic recognition with P'yongyang, the North Korean capital. By then, Mao had already begun to repatriate Koreans who had fought in the Chinese civil war, and by June 1950 some fifty thousand to seventy thousand had crossed the Yalu River into Korea to strengthen the North Korean leader Kim Il Sung's army.[5]

Turning back to the efforts for a settlement of the Korean question in the UN, in September 1947, the US took the problem to the United Nations. Two months later the United Nations agreed that Korea ought to be independent, and voted to set up a temporary commission to bring that about. The members from eastern Europe boycotted the vote, and when a UN commission reached Korea early in 1948, with the task of supervising elections, it was refused admission to North Korea. With no recourse, it then recommended free elections in the south; these were held on May 10, and the conservative rightist parties gained a large majority. On August 15, 1948, Syngman Rheee became the first President of the Republic of Korea.

Four months later the republic was recognized by the UN as the only free state in Korea. But it was given diplomatic recognition just by the western powers, as the People's Democratic Republic received recognition solely from the eastern bloc. The UN then set up a permanent commission to try to unify the country. The Americans ended their military government of the south and agreed to provide advisers and training for defense forces. The Russian occupation forces left the north. Both countries left behind a government which the other denounced as illegitimate and which claimed to represent all of Korea. Within six months there was occasional raiding across the 38th parallel, and major exchanges of gunfire. Both sides were calling each other "reactionary imperialist traitor" or "communist terrorist revolutionary."

In fact, Truman's policy on Korea at the United Nations experienced a significant success during the last month of 1948. On December 6, the Political and Security Committee voted by a large margin to reject the Democratic Peoples' Republic of Korea (DPRK)'s claim to legitimacy and instead to invite the ROK to send representatives to the UN. It then paid attention to Washington's proposal calling for international involvement in Korean affairs. John Foster Dulles, then the US Representative to the UN delivered a speech appealing for UN approval of the resolution. American diplomatic pressure proved to be effective and two days later, the Committee overwhelmingly voted to recommend that the General Assembly adopt the American resolution. It amended the proposal to provide for withdrawal of foreign troops from Korea "as soon as practicable" rather than ninety days, after adoption. At the same time, however, the Committee refused to recognize the ROK as Korea's national government, observing that it controlled only half of the peninsula.[6]

Four days later, on December 12, the General Assembly approved the American resolution despite sharp criticism from Soviet delegation. After rejecting the Soviet proposal to disband the planned commission on Korea by a wide margin, the General Assembly voted to create a new commission that would be smaller than its predecessor United Nations Temporary Commission on Korea (UNTCOK), excluding both Canada and Ukraine. It was decided that within thirty days, the United Nations Commission on Korea (UNCOK) would arrive in Korea and begin to cooperate with the ROK for the achievement of reunification.

Often mentioned is the fact that the US Administration withdrew its troops too quickly from South Korea, thereby failing to provide a military establishment which could match the one that the SU had set up in the northern part of the peninsula. Previously, in September 1947, the US JCS had made the decision to withdraw the US troops from South Korea on the basis of two military considerations: that the area was not of sufficient military importance to warrant the US presence there; and that in the light of the US' general manpower shortage, the troops stationed in Korea might be more useful elsewhere. These opinions of the JCS, taken together with the Kremlin's announcement that it was withdrawing its forces from North Korea, led Truman to decide in the spring of 1949 that Americans should leave Korea.[7]

South Korean resources underscore that meanwhile, in April–May 1949, the secret consultations between communist China and North Korea with regard to the invasion of South Korea were given a start, one year before the outbreak of the war, with the visit to China by Kim Il, Chief of the Political Department of the North Korean Army. The Kremlin was a part of the process as well, since prior to his visit to China, Kim Il had held a meeting with Stalin in Moscow. In Moscow, as proposed by Kim Il Sung, Chief of the Political Department Kim Il and his Soviet counterparts initially agreed that the war should begin in the form of North Korea's counterattack against South Korea's provocation. They also agreed that China's role in connection with the invasion plan and the Chinese–Korean relationship would be settled through consultation with Mao Tse-tung. It was in compliance with these agreements that Kim Il Sung dispatched Kim Il to Beijing.[8]

In December, this time Mao visited Moscow and stayed there for around two months, holding extensive meetings to discuss with Stalin the expansion of communism throughout Asia and the rest of the world and other pending issues between the two countries. On January 2, 1950,

Mao cabled his Foreign Minister Zhou Enlai and informed him that Stalin had agreed to Zhou's and other necessary aides' arrival to Moscow and to the signing of a new Sino–Soviet Treaty of Friendship and Alliance, as well as agreements on credit, trade, civil aviation, and others.[9]

In the Republic of Korea, as the breadth of the North Korean attack became apparent, there was dismayed alarm. The frontier was fully breached, the capital threatened, refugees thronged the roads. According to Washington then, what was important in this situation was therefore not what the North Koreans intended to do, which was clear enough, or what the South Koreans could do, which was little enough, but rather what the US and the UN could do.

The Democrat Party's Redefinition of Turkish Foreign Policy and Turkey's Participation in the Korean War

Against this background, on March 30, 1949, the US Embassy in Ankara conveyed a Memorandum to the MFA expressing the views and expectations of the US Government with regard to the problem of Korea. The US Memorandum underscored that it was the US view that the UN had made substantial progress toward restoring the freedom and independence of the Korean people and that in the General Assembly Resolution of December 12 it had a "formula for pursuing that progress to fruition."[10] Here, it was stated that the US believed that consolidation of existing gains and the success of further UN efforts in Korea would depend in large measure on the firm and unwavering support by the UN member states of the December 12 Resolution and the endorsement of the Government of the Republic of Korea contained therein. In this context, it was emphasized that the US felt that every assistance and facility should be afforded the UNCOK in its efforts to help the Korean Government and their lawful government to achieve the objective of a free and united Korea, "a goal to which the United States is convinced an overwhelming majority of Koreans of both north and south wholeheartedly aspire."[11]

The Memorandum also explained the US position on troop withdrawal as based on the view that to withdraw its occupation forces prematurely or to permit their retention on Korean soil for any longer than necessary would in either case jeopardize attainment of UN objectives in

Korea. It was stated that it was the intention of the US to continue to provide limited amount of economic, technical, military and other assistance regarded as essential to the economic and political stability of the newborn Republic. Lastly, it was underscored that the main burden of responsibility for the failure of UN efforts "must be placed on the Soviet Union and its evident determination to subordinate legitimate aspirations and the welfare of the Korean people to its own objective of communist domination of the entire Korean peninsula." [12]

The US point of view was clear to Ankara as the Turco–Soviet relations were already in a state of distrust and unpredictability. To add to the disturbance of Ankara of Kremlin's wicked attempts, the third week of June 1949 witnessed a disgusting incident. Turkish diplomatic courier Army Captain Fuat Güzaltan was found shot in his head in the Moscow train where he had started his journey back to Turkey. Soviet authorities claimed that the incident was a suicide while the foreign press reported the murder of Güzaltan as an assassination by the Soviet agents who suspected the Turkish courier in possession of top secret documents which would be handed over the US agents in Ankara. [13]

Turning back to the boiling waters in Northeast Asia, by the beginning of 1950, in Ankara, there were however no signs of relating the Turkish wish for joining NATO and supporting the US efforts in Korea. Thus, the US position in Korea was still a matter of less interest for Turkey, as Ankara was still concentrating on its Mediterranean security groupement offer. But, it would soon prove that Ankara would be obliged to shift to participate in the US sponsored discussions on the future of Korea to perpetuate its policy of drawing together with Washington.

As part of Ankara's last effort on its usual line of policy, on February 15, 1950, Turkish Ambassador in Washington, Erkin renewed Turkey's suggestion for a Near Eastern Pact with the support of the US. However, Erkin tried in vain to assure some sort of a US assurance to Turkey and explained that such an assurance could be in the form of a declaration by the US President which would announce Turkey in the same category as members of the NAT. Erkin also proposed, while awaiting the decision for a US political commitment, that the General Staffs of the two countries could undertake discussions of common defense and assistance plans. Although this suggestion was declined by the US on the ground that such planning could not be undertaken without a political agreement first, The US Chief of Military Mission in Ankara, Gen. McBridge, continued to extend strategic military advice—which he said, would not mean that the US would directly or indirectly commit itself to any future course of action—to his Turkish counterparts.[14]

Grooving in the darkness, on April 27, Erkin this time pointing to the possibility of the Soviet Union to create a crisis in order to alter the Montreux Convention in 1951, suggested that the establishment of Mediterranean pact would increase the confidence of Turkey as well as serve as a warning to the Kremlin. He requested his suggestions to be discussed in the London meetings. To his disappointment however, in London, NATO's enlargement was not on the agenda. In bilateral terms, however, in order to compensate Turkey's disappointment, jet aircraft and rehabilitation of air strips at Diyarbakır, Kayseri and Eskişehir were added to the US aid program in the same days.[15]

At this juncture, few words needs to be said on the US–Bulgarian and Turco–Bulgarian relations which prove to be the litmus paper of political atmosphere between the emerging rival blocs. On February 21, diplomatic relations between Washington and Sofia were cut. The event was triggered by the Bulgarian Administration's demand for the recalling of American Ambassador on the alleged grounds of his spying activities. Washington's reply to this clearly stated that Sofia's insistence on this decision would result in the cutting of political relations. As Bulgaria did not change its position, the US Embassy personnel left Bulgaria on February 24 and so did the Bulgarian Embassy personnel in Washington.

Less than three weeks later, on March 13, the Bulgarian Ministry of Foreign Affairs "decided" to reply to the Note of Turkish Embassy in Sofia which protested the explosion of a bomb before the Turkish General Consulate in Filibe on September 10, 1949. The Bulgarian Note in reply worded in brusque language rejected the Turkish Note of protest and stated that the perpetrators of the attack were caught and sentenced on February 2, whereas the peace and the security of the Bulgarian representations in Turkey were under constant violation. The Turkish Embassy in Sofia returned this Note as its ways of expression were not found in conformity with the international customs and politeness. As the unfolding events prove that the Bulgarians were reckless to strain their relations with US and Turkey, it was obvious that the Kremlin and Sofia were in joint terms vis-à-vis the Western grouping of states.[16] Correspondingly, this no doubt weakens the arguments of Turkish socialist critics of those i.e. Secretary General of MFA Erkin who—still with a question mark of why—did not separate the Kremlin and Sofia from each other in their actions as previously discussed.

On May 11, 1950, while İnönü was still President, Turkey first applied for admission to NATO. However, at that time the Atlantic Pact members declined Turkey's application. Admittedly, there were various reasons behind the Council's denial of Turkey's request. Firstly, the European members of NATO regarded that the membership of Turkey and Greece would be disadvantageous for their short and long term interests since it would represent an extension of their own financial commitments and increase their risk of involvement in a possible conflict. Secondly, as mentioned earlier, London was supporting the idea of establishment of a Middle East Command under MEDO, consisting of Britain, Turkey, Israel, Egypt, Iran, Greece and the Arab League countries.[17]

Socialists in Turkey, now and then approached the matter from another perspective. It has been suggested that the third reason for declining Turkey's application was cultural. According to this view, an overwhelming consideration of the European members of the Atlantic Pact was to the effect that NATO was an instrument of the Western civilization and Turkey was not a part of this. It was also argued that in addition to this factor, it was the smaller members of the organization i.e. Norway and Denmark which considered that, with regard to its geographical location, Turkey's inclusion in the alliance would introduce additional security risks.[18]

At this juncture, the Democrat Party's success in May 14, 1950 elections in Turkey remarked a turning point in Turkish politics. Out of 8.905.576 eligible voters, 7.953.055, or 89.3% of registered voters joined elections. The candidates of the DP received 4.242.831 votes and the Republican candidates received 3.165.096 votes. Since the majority system is accepted in Turkey, out of the total of 487 seats in the Assembly, 396 went to the DP and 68 to the Republicans. Since the foundation of the Republic, the RPP rule had dominated in Turkish politics and as far as official efforts for modernizing the Turkish nation are concerned, in all aspects of social life. It had undoubtedly controlled the destiny of the country, always maintaining its Kemalist revolutionary character. With a view to this past, the result was more than surprising for President İnönü, who had assumed the title of "the National Chief," and controlled the regime's destiny after Gazi Mustafa Kemal Atatürk and the sole political party organization until then, namely the RPP.

The DP's election victory can be explained in various ways. Among these, the RPP's overconfidence of its power and its control over the establishment and the basic structure of the country should be stated first. As expected by the RPP officials, even under a pressing international political atmosphere for the democratization of the regime in Turkey, the opposition could only be flourished within the RPP. Subsequently, the short process of searching for the new leader paved the way to a race between several aspirants and their groupings. According to Ergun Özbudun, it was some of these factions within the RPP "which eventually provided the cadres who led the movement to establish opposition parties or to join the opposition movement after its successful commencement in 1945."[19]

Another factor which served to the DP's coming to power was a genuine wish of the voters to enjoy the liberalism of another political party. "The average citizen thought that a real political liberalization could not be achieved except by sending the Republican Party into opposition."[20] Besides, the DP propaganda successfully exploited the similarities of single party rule in the country with those of totalitarian regimes. Meanwhile, there were almost no attempts on the side of RPP to introduce at least some kind of transparency to its capitulation of the rule of country, nor any insignia of will to improve democratic skills in Turkish political life. Having rather been discomforted since the notorious election results of 1946, when RPP rule experienced the very first challenge against its power, but managed to keep it in its hands in one way or another, the numbers suspicious of the honesty of the foundations of RPP rule were constantly rising. Again, 1946 elections where open voting and closed counting of votes system applied raised considerable criticisms. It was claimed that counting of votes and announced results were untrustworthy. Under these circumstances, a discomfort in the country strengthened the feeling of revanchism and ultimately paved the way to the DP's winning of the election.

On May 22, Celal Bayar was elected as the 3rd President of the Republic of Turkey. İnönü issued a declaration a day later and announced that following the end of his term of office he would actively undertake the Chairmanship of the RPP.[21] The Günaltay government, the fourth since the 1946 elections, was replaced by the government of Adnan Menderes. Fuat Köprülü was designated as the MFA.[22] As will be discussed below, the change in the Turkish leadership introduced an imminent deviation from the cautious policy of İnönü administration.

Turning back to the situation in Korea, on June 25, 1950, the Secretary General of the United Nations Tyrgve Lie was informed by the

United States and the United Nations Commission on Korea that North Korean forces had invaded Korea that morning. On the same day the Security Council determined by 9 votes to non, with 1 abstention of Yugoslavia and one member absent (the SU), that the armed attack was a breach of peace, called for immediate cessation of hostilities, withdrawal of North Korean forces to the thirtyeighth parallel, and the assistance of members in carrying out the Resolution. The USSR had not participated in the Council's work since January 13, 1950, explaining that it would not recognize as legal any decision of the Council until the representative of the Kuomintang Group had been removed. It resumed, however, attendance at the meetings on August 1, 1950, when the Presidency of the Council again devolved upon it under the system of monthly rotation.

On June 27, the Security Council adopted a United States draft resolution noting that the authorities in North Korea had neither ceased hostilities nor withdrawn their armed forces, and recommending that members furnish such assistance to the Republic of Korea as might be necessary to repel the armed attack and restore international peace and security in the area. The vote was 7 to 1 (Yugoslavia), with the SU absent and with Egypt and India not voting but later indicating their positions as abstention from and acceptance of the Resolution, respectively.

Also on June 27, the United States announced that it had ordered its air and sea forces to give cover and support to the troops of the Korean Government. On June 30 it informed the Council that it had ordered a naval blockade of the Korean coast and authorized the use of ground forces as a further response to the June 27 Resolution. Fifty one member states expressed support for the stand taken by the Security Council, while five, including the SU, together with the PRC and the Democratic People's Republic of Korea, shared the view that the June 27 Resolution was illegal because it had been adopted in the absence of two permanent members of the Security Council, the PRC and the SU. The SU also declared that the events in Korea were the result of an unprovoked attack by South Korean troops and demanded the cessation of the United States intervention.

Turkey was a member of the UNCOK which made the recommendation that the Security Council take military action against North Korea. From the beginning the Menderes Government supported the Security Council decision. Thus, the leaders of the DP believed that Turkey's participation in the UN effort in Korea would enhance its international standing.

Turkey's position concerning the Security Council Resolution of 27 June was stated in a cable dated June 29, 1950, from the MFA Fuat Köprülü, addressed to the Secretary General of the United Nations as follows:

> With reference to your telegram number 8755 of 28 June, I have the honour to inform you that the Government of the Turkish Republic regards the steps taken by the United Nations Council with a view to putting an end to the tragic situation existing in Korea as the proper expression of a salutary decision to restore peace and to safeguard the sovereign rights of a State which has just been the object of an unprovoked attack. Such a decision, constituting the most certain guarantee of independence the peaceful nations will certainly have the effect of strengthening the confidence of anxious people in world security. It is with conviction that, in reply to the recommendation you communicated to it on behalf of the Council, my Government declares that it is ready to execute loyally and in complete conformity with the provisions of the Charter the undertakings which Turkey assumed as a member of the United Nations.[23]

Two days later, on July 1, the UN Secretary General Lie communicated the Resolution adopted by the Security Council at its 474th meeting on June 27 which recommended that the members of the United Nations furnish such assistance to the Republic of Korea as might be necessary to repel the armed attack and to restore international peace and security in the area. The message of Lie also included that in the event that the Turkish Government was in a position to provide assistance, it would facilitate the implementation of the Resolution. Lie said, the UN expected to receive an early reply which he would transmit to the Security Council and to the Government of Korea.[24] On the same day, Köprülü cabled Lie expressing that:

> Reply to your telegram dated 1 July, as I had the honour to inform your excellency on 29 June last, the Government of the Republic of Turkey is faithful to its undertakings arising out of the Charter of the United Nations. It is consequently ready to comply with any decision taken by the Security Council on this subject and to enter into contact with the Council.[25]

On July 7, the Security Council, by 7 votes to none, with abstentions (Egypt, India, Yugoslavia), and 1 member absent (USSR), requested all member states providing military forces in pursuance of the Council's resolutions to make them available to a unified command under the United States. Subsequently, combatant units were provided by the following sixteen member states: Australia, Belgium, Canada, Colombia, Ethiopia, France, Greece, Luxembourg, the Netherlands, New Zealand, the Philippines, Thailand, Turkey, the Union of South Africa, the UK and the US. In addition, five nations—Denmark, India, Italy, Norway, and Sweden—supplied medical units. The Republic of Korea also placed all its military forces under the Unified Command.

Following the Resolution of July 7, recommending that all assistance should be made to the Unified Command under the United States and authorizing the Unified Command at its discretion to use the United Nations flag in the course of operations against North Korean forces concurrently with the flags of the various nations participating, responsibility for deciding what specific measures would be taken to assist the Republic of Korea rested upon the Members of the United Nations.

On July, 18, following a meeting of Council of Ministers convened far from Ankara at Yalova it was agreed to send a combatant force to Korea. In fact, endorsed by the MFA Köprülü, Prime Minister Menderes had made up his mind much before this meeting. Under these circumstances, discussions could hardly produce a different outcome other than approving Premier Menderes. Following a hasty discussion, the Council of Ministers decided to send a 4.500-man unit to join the US troops in Korea.

Not surprisingly, in the same days, the Menderes Government was paying a special attention to frequently discuss the issue of Turkish participation in the Korean War with the US Government. On July 20, at a private talk with Ambassador Wadsworth, Köprülü said he wished particularly to orient the US Ambassador in relation to major matters discussed at Yalova conference. Köprülü then informed Wadsworth that the conference discussed and decided that there was pressing need to strengthen existing Turkish Armed Forces; immediate action would be taken in cooperation with aid mission to implement the recommendations which were explained by the Head of US Military Aid Mission, General McBride to Turkish Chief of General Staff, Nuri Yamut, in the letter of the former dated, June 30; and finally Menderes should invite Köprülü and Wadsworth to confer "to review entire field US–Turkish cooperation from economic as well as military aspects." Besides, Köprülü explained that the conference "took position that in event third world war, defense through neutrality would be illusory for any nation and for Turkey."26

On July 22, this time, Köprülü told Wadsworth that he would discuss with him the Turkish reply to the UN Secretary General Lie's circular to 50 UN member nations urging that they consider offering effective assistance—including ground forces—to resist North Korean aggression. The Turkish MFA went on to explain that the Turkish Government wished its reply "bear witness to its sincere desire manifest by practical action its loyalty to UN and Turk–US collaboration" and added that "we wish particularly that our reply conform with US policy and public opinion."27 In his turn, Wadsworth noted that his immediate reaction was that he should urge prompt dispatch of ground forces. Bu he said, "I refrained from so replying except in general appreciative terms pending consultation with General McBride."28

A day later, on July 23, after consultation with General McBride and Senator Harry P. Cain—who arrived from Athens—Wadsworth decided to reply that in his personal view the Turkish Government could best manifest its support of UN policies by prompt dispatch of fully equipped regimental combat team. Wadsworth noted that McBride described this force as consisting of infantry regiment, artillery battalion and appropriate headquarters, anti-tank, anti-aircraft, engineer, motor transport, signal, ordnance and medical units and normal loads of ammunition, spare parts, mines, wire, etc; a fully self-contained combat unit of between 4,000 and 4,500 officers and men approximately 10 percent above war strength. Wadsworth said, McBride gave further details as to such a unit could be assembled for embarkation at a Turkish port within one month. If sent, it would after arrival have to maintained by UN Commander. Its artillery, trucks and general services equipment would conform to US Standards.

Wadsworth stated that on July 24, he had presented this strictly personal suggestion of McBride to the Secretary General of the MFA, Faik Zihni Akdur. The US Ambassador said, Akdur told him that he "trust this decision will be taken promptly by Cabinet and will render even more effective our collaboration in political as well as military fields."29

In the same cable to Washington, Wadsworth explained more than that. He stated that on the same day afternoon, Senator Cain, General MacBride and himself had prearranged conference with Turkish MFA, Minister of National Defense, Chief of TGS and Commanding General of Turkish Ground Forces. According to Wadsworth, here, Köprülü said, "personally I am wholeheartedly in favor of sending ground forces promptly and will present your suggestion to Cabinet at earliest opportunity, if possible tomorrow." In his turn, Minister of National Defense said "I share my colleague's view." Wadsworth noted that the TGS was also wholly favorably disposed. He knew that the G-3 of General Staff, Maj. Gen. Yusuf A. Egeli wrote a memorandum to the Chief of TGS, Yamut expressing that "it will be the greatest crime in Turkish history if we fail to take advantage of this opportunity."[30]

On the same day at dinner, Köprülü informed Wadsworth that he had telephoned President Bayar, Prime Minister Menderes and three other Ministers due return Ankara the next day from Bairam holiday to arrange Cabinet meeting that afternoon. Wadsworth said, Köprülü expressed that "he hoped sincerely and believed favorable decision could then be taken. If so, he would at once telegraph Secretary General Lie and instruct Turkish Embassy at Washington to inform the Department."[31]

A day later, on July 25, the Council of Ministers met in Ankara under the Chairmanship of President Bayar to determine the details of the decision at hand and the wording of the press statement. After the meeting in Yalova, the President of the TGNA, Refik Koraltan, the Minister of National Defence, R. Şevket İnce and the Chief of General Staff, General Nuri Yamut were again present in the meeting. Shortly afterwards a text was finalized which included that the Council of Ministers had realized exchange of views on the text prepared by the Turkish MFA and considered the subject in full details. On the same day, in accordance with the decisions taken in the Council, a telegram signed by the MFA Köprülü was sent to Secretary General Lie expressing that:

> In reply to your cable of 15 July; the Government of the Republic of Turkey, believing it to be its duty to comply with the obligations arising from the Charter of the United Nations as well as with the decisions of the Security Council, has examined carefully and in this spirit your aforementioned cable. As a result of this consideration, and realizing, in the present world conditions and in the interest of general peace, the necessity and the importance of the effective implementation of the aforementioned decisions, the Government of the Republic of Turkey had decided to place at the disposal of the United Nations a Turkish combat force of 4500 men to serve in Korea.[32]

Menderes Government's announcement of the decision to send troops to Korea remains a controversial issue to date. The RPP and the whole opposition put forward that the capacity to send armed forces abroad was strictly in the power of the Assembly and no decision was obtained from the TGNA to this end. Their point of departure was from the Constitution which stipulated that the making of agreements and peace with other countries or to declare war on any state was in the jurisdiction of the Assembly. In his turn, Menderes argued that the sending of the troops to Korea did not mean to declare war on this country and the decision of the government was entirely in conformity with the Charter of the UN; a document which was previously approved by the TGNA and acquired the force of a law for the Republic of Turkey.[33]

George Harris maintained that the decision of the Turkish Government had emerged from the approach of Menderes and Bayar. He stated that the decision of the DP was well calculated in the sense that it had not taken too long for the DP administration to see the importance and the opportunity it provided. According to Harris, the reason that they could take such a quick decision was that Bayar and Menderes were also very strongly in control of their party. He pointed out that at a time of uncertainty when the orientation of the new deputies was not certain, both Menderes and Bayar had managed to overcome the difficulties in this regard. Harris also asserted that the control they could exercise over the DP was quite unusual since they did even not know all the deputies. In contrast to the DP's case, in previous years, İnönü had known all the deputies and he had put them on the list himself because he knew them.

However, Harris explained that the problems of the speed with which the DP regime had taken the decision to send troops to Korea could not be confined to the reactions of the opposition. He said, when Bayar and Menderes had taken this decision, they had realized that they had to leave out the Minister of National Defense İnce, and one other Minister (of Health and Social Assistance) Nihat Reşat Belger, whom they thought would vote against them on sending troops to Korea. Thus they had not created a unified cabinet on this one question either.[34]

Around the same issue, R. Salim Burçak, a member of the TGNA from the DP pointed out that in certain respects, it was indeed hard to explain the decision of the Menderes Government that it took after one and a half months of its coming to power on Turkey's "entry into the war" and sending a force of 4,500 to a country which the Turkish people had not even heard of its name. He said, while the RPP had based its domestic propaganda on its success of Turkey's remaining outside of the WW II, the DP was following an entirely different policy and involving Turkey into a war. This situation however, was constituting a negative propaganda subject which could be used against the DP.[35]

Kasım Gülek, then the Secretary General of the RPP stated that upon the news on the Menderes Government's consideration of a decision to enter in the Korean conflict, he had visited İnönü to express his view that such a decision should be the outcome of a united national will and it ought to be unanimously made by both the government and the opposition. However, Gülek said, İnönü replied him as "You can not explain this." Gülek stated that, consecutively he had visited Menderes as well who was a very close friend of him since the years of the single party rule in Turkey. Gülek said, he had told Menderes that "You won a great victory. A Historical one. There is now again a historical matter. Turkey will enter into war. Make it with the opposition as a joint national decision." Then, Gülek explained that Menderes replied him that "It is difficult to decide on these matters. If I go and propose this to İsmet Pasha, people will hear about this. And then, people will say, 'they are unexperienced, they felt obliged to go and consult the old experienced ones', this will not be good for us." Gülek commented that perhaps Menderes was right in his suspicions. But, in one way another, this opportunity was lost.[36]

As a matter of fact, there were different reactions in the Turkish press and civilian organizations on the Government's decision. On August 28, Abidin Daver of Cumhuriyet wrote that if Soviets had an intention to attack Turkey, they would not have a difficulty to find a reason other than Turkey's sending troops to the Korean War. Meanwhile, the Friends of Peace Association led by the former Associate Prof. Behice Boran who was a suspended member of Ankara University, protested Turkey's participation in the Korean War and some of its members including Boran, were arrested and condemned to various prison terms. Friends of Peace Association's famous Declaration, known as *Kore Nere?* *(Where is Korea?)* remains as a landmark document of brutally oppressed civil disobedience of the era to date.[37]

Turning back to the discussions in UN, the June Resolutions of the Security Council were the first occasions in history when an international organization as such used force to stop aggression. The prompt action of the Council and of certain Members of the United Nations, which included Turkey, acting in accordance with the Security Council's recommendations not only served to throw back the armed attack but, in addition, greatly enhanced the security of all people living under the fear of aggression that the assistance would be forthcoming when needed. In particular, it increased the feeling of security of those people, like the people of Turkey who at the time enjoyed no other protection than that provided by the guarantees of the United Nations and their own ability to resist. Despite these developments in the General Assembly, the progress on the ground was not favourable for the UN forces. Korea's capital, Seoul, fell on June 28, 1950, and in August the United Nations forces were confined within a small area in southeast Korea.

Meanwhile, the situation in Korea had been brought to the agenda of the TGNA. On July 30, Minister of Foreign Affairs Fuat Köprülü, following his announcement of UN Secretary General's telegram on the aggression in Korea before the members of the TGNA stated that:

Esteemed friends,

It is of your knowledge that in our foreign policy, to participate in the Charter of the UN with full strength and sincerity constitutes an unwavering principle for us. In actual and spiritual capacity of this charter, to protect peace and security on earth, to resist aggression, and respect the territorial integrity and independence of all nations, to ensure the welfare and well-being of humanity is the basis of our foreign policy. . . . Along the line of these tenets, our close and sincere cooperation with US, our present alliance with England and France are the requirements of our open, explicit and correct policy. Facing this last situation, had the UN not taken action immediately and accept this fait accompli, this would be a source of insecurity for all the regions of the world and global peace would suffer. Therefore, it is the duty of all peace-loving and democratic nations who believe that aggression is completely illegal, to welcome the US who took prompt action and mobilized its forces to implement the UN decision to protect the world peace.[38]

Köprülü also stated that he had informed UN Secretary General Lie that he was prepared to carry out his undertakings in the capacity of a member of the TGNA. Following Köprülü's words, the statement of Dr. Hayri Üstündağ and his five colleagues expressing their praise for the government's peace understanding under the principles of UN was endorsed by the TGNA.

From then on, as the TGNA was not functioning between the 7th and 10th months of each year, and no special session or gathering was asked from the TGNA, the criticisms of opposition could be voiced—of course in limited ways under the threat of censorship—in other fora, which were mainly the press statements of the MPs from the opposition.

As for the international repercussions of Ankara's decision, the picture so far presented of the Turkey's willingness to cooperate with the countries of the West in general and the US in particular reaching a postwar peak in the Korean War. Turkey, although thousands of miles away from Korea, and although it strived for years under considerable economic strain, demonstrated an impressive example of the sense of responsibility to the Charter provisions for enforcement measures against an aggressor when it contributed forces for Korean action. During the general debate in the Fifth Assembly in September, Sarper stated in connection with the Korean action that:

Aggressive elements in Korea have, by an actual breach of the peace, threatened the peace and security of the world, and challenged not only the decisions and actions of this august Assembly, but also the very principles of our Charter. In the face of this challenge, the high sense of responsibility and solidarity demonstrated to the world by the overwhelming majority of the Members of the United Nations was an expression of the high responsibility of the United Nations, and a living proof of the reality of a fundamental principle of this Organization, that is, that the peace and security of the world is one and indivisible and that all should join hands in co-operation and devotion in order to safeguard this sacred treasure. The action taken in Korea clearly showed that this principle was not only a theory destined to remain in the pages of the Charter, but the expression of a living spirit.[39]

The attitude of the DP Government, leaving the TGNA aside throughout the process of its crucial decision to assign a combat force in Korea remains controversial to date. Undoubtedly, the DP Government had tied its commitment to the UN effort in Korea to entry into NATO. It could also be recalled that the Turkish Ambassador in Washington, Erkin had told Acheson on August 25 that the commitment to send troops to Korea intensified among Turkish leaders and the people of the notion that Turkey should be included in the European collective security arrangement. Erkin said "today there are three important organizations: the OEEC, the Council of Europe, and the North Atlantic Treaty. Turkey is included in the first two, and her exclusion from the latter on a geographical basis would, in his opinion, be inconsistent."[40]

Similarly, on September 12, President Bayar told Wasdworth of his concerns about Washington's reluctance to extend formal support for Turkey's entry into NATO. Here, Bayar straightforwardly asked Wadsworth if the Government of the US did not realize that Ankara would consider further deferment of favorable action on its request by the Atlantic Pact powers as a refusal and as unwillingness to accept Turkey as an equal partner in meeting jointly any threat of aggression. Bayar said, "we have shown our good faith by forthright action towards meeting the Korean crisis. I fear frankly that, if Atlantic Pact Council of Foreign Ministers turns down our request, our morale will be seriously affected."[41]

August 10-30, 1950, however, prove to be a profoundly significant period the role of TGNA was also endorsed in the eyes of many. On August 10, Bulgaria gave a Note to the Turkish Embassy in Sofia precipitating an issue the discussion of which can hardly be confined to a few paragraphs in here. With the Note of August 10, Bulgaria demanded in bitter language the admission to Turkey as immigrants of 250,000 Turks in Bulgaria within the next three months. It was an announcement of an intention to send a quarter of a million of Turks living in the country before November 10.[42]

Emigrations from Bulgaria to Turkey were not a not a novel issue. As Bilal Şimşir put it,

> Emigrations from Bulgaria to Turkey were continuous during the nearly 35 years that passed between the establishment of the Bulgarian Principality and the 1912-13 Balkan War. . . . The 1912-13 Balkan war was a rout for the Turks in Roumelia just like the 1877-8 Turco-Russian war. . . . According to a report published in the 7 February 1913 issue of a Hungarian newspaper called *Anap*, 60,000 Albanians and 40,000 Turks were killed in Macedonia. . . . It is reasonable to assume that at least that many Turkish Muslims may have been killed in Eastern and Western Thrace, because the Bulgarian armies went through regions in Thrace which were heavily populated by Turks and they did not abide by the rules of war. In short, estimating that about 200,000 Turks-Muslims must have been killed during the Balkan War would not be a gross mistake.[43]

If the Turco–Bulgarian border had always been kept open for emigrations, an orderly emigration for 15,000 to 20,000 immigrants annually could be achieved. However, the border was kept closed to emigrations for nearly ten years as the IInd WW and the Bulgarian regime did not allow this. "A potential of about 200,000 emigrants had accumulated like the waters behind a dam and had begun to force the barriers by 1950. Furthermore, the establishment of a communist regime in Bulgaria under the name of 'Fatherland Front' also swelled the desire for emigration among the Turks."[44] Until then, obtaining a visa from Turkey took really some time. Between 1947–1949, Turkey shifted to demand financial guarantee from the relatives of those applying for a visa to avoid any burden on its budget. Obtaining a passport and an exit visa from the Bulgarian authorities equally demanded a lot of time and patience. The Bulgarian Government changed its attitude as of September 1949 and began to issue passports more rapidly to Turks. This was reflected on the number of visas being issued.

Having seen the course of events, in 1950, Turkey prepared a visa regime and planned to accept 25,000 to 30,000 immigrants, with a decision to increase the number in the years to follow. "However, if 30,000 immigrants were to be admitted annually, the process of bringing the Turks in Bulgaria to Turkey would be completed by 1980. The period of admitting immigrants could be shortened by increasing the annual quota."[45] The Bulgarian Note of August 10 arrived in this atmosphere. Not only announcing the Bulgarian Government's decision to begin a forced emigration, the Note claimed that "the Turkish authorities are using unfounded rumours to create anti-Bulgarian sentiments in public opinion, and especially among the Turks in Bulgaria in an effort to cover their own errors . . . fooled by the Turkish propaganda, the Turkish people in Bulgaria leave their jobs, sell their property, and find themselves in serious difficulty"[46] According to the claim of Sofia, the Turks in Bulgaria were determined to emigrate to Turkey because of Ankara's anti-Bulgarian propaganda. The Turkish Government did not accept the Bulgarian Note.

Şimşir underscores that dispatching 250,000 Turkish immigrants in a period of three months was, in effect, a clear act of mass deportation. He also stresses the possibility of Moscow's instigation of Sofia which aimed at crippling the Turkish economy at a time the Korean War broke out and the Turkish Government decided to send a brigade to Korea. The migration crisis continued while a total of 212,150 entry visas to Turkey were issued to the Turks in Bulgaria between January 1, 1950 and September 30, 1951.

Amidst these developments of disturbing nature, on October 7, the General Assembly adopted a Resolution which recommended that all appropriate steps be taken to ensure conditions of stability throughout Korea; established the United Nations Commission for the Unification and Rehabilitation of Korea (UNCURK) of seven member states to represent the United Nations in bringing about the establishment of a unified, independent, and democratic government of all Korea; and recommended that the United Nations forces should not remain in Korea other than for the objectives stated, and that all necessary measures be taken to accomplish the economic rehabilitation of Korea. Meanwhile, in mid-October, following an amphibious landing at Inchon, the UN forces regained almost all the territory of the Republic of Korea and were advancing far into North Korea.

The first Turkish Brigade, led by Brigadier General Tahsin Yazıcı arrived at Pusan in October 1950. The Brigade did not arrive with its own weapons, and had to be trained to use new American weaponry which was in fact, an effort begun during its long sea journey. An intensive training period then immediately started for the Brigade. Colonel Celal Dora uses a bitter language to tell that as a result of the hasty composition of the brigade, most of the soldiers had not completed their training and had not even seen the new American war equipment, including infantry rifles and other small arms. Referring to the Chief of TGS Yamut's not joining to the farewell ceremonies held in İskenderun port on September 25, Dora said, unable to hide his anxieties on the dispatch of the half-trained Turkish Brigade to Korea, Yamut had chosen to watch the departure of the Brigade's ship from his hotel room.[47]

If a few words could be said on General Yamut, though it was most likely in his promotion line, he was promoted to this post by the newly elected DP Government which associated him with the fate of this party following the May 27, 1960 military takeover in Turkey. A Turkish columnist narrates a memory of Retd. Col. Mehmet Çatalkaya concerning İnönü's request for support from the high level officers just three months before the 1950 elections while naming those who established the DP as "marauders." According to him, when all the officers replied İnönü "we are at your service" with loud voice, only Nuri Yamut, the Commander of the First Army (in fact, the correct title should be, the Commander of Turkish Land Forces) told İnönü before this group that he would not allow this to happen and stood against him. His remark dead silenced the room.[48]

On November 6, 1950, a special report of the United Nations Command informed the Security Council that United Nations forces were in contact in North Korea with military units of the PRC. A representative of the PRC participated in the Security Council's subsequent combined discussion of complaints of aggression upon the Republic of Korea and of armed invasion of Taiwan (Formosa). On November 30, because of the negative vote of the SU, the Council could not adopt a resolution calling, among other things, on all states and authorities to refrain from assisting the North Korean authorities, and affirming that it was United Nations policy to hold the Korean frontier with China. The Council rejected by a vote of 1 (the SU) to 9, with India not participating, a draft resolution condemning the United States for armed aggression against Chinese territory and armed intervention in Korea, and demanding withdrawal of US forces.

Meanwhile, Brig. Gen. Yazıcı informed his American counterparts that it was for almost two months that his brigade was not given a duty. Yazıcı said, the Brigade had completed its training and was in Korea to fight, not to parade. Subsequently, towards the end of November the Turkish Brigade was moved to north to front just as the Chinese launched a massive counterattack that drove the UN forces out of north Korea. Following its battles in Wawon (November, 28) and Sinnim-ni (November 28–29), the Brigade saw its first great action in the battle of Kunu Ri and in the Sunchon Passage (November 29–December 1).

The mission of the Brigade required it to support the regular retreat of the 8th Army, a duty which was left to it when the 9th Corps, concerned with the ROK collapse, sent the Brigade up the Kunu Ri road to Tokch-on to guard 2nd Division's flank. Shortly afterwards, however, the Turks understood that the main strength of the Chinese burst over them. At a point when completely surrounded by the Chinese forces, the Brigade stormed the Chinese position with hand-to-hand combat. The Brigade engaged in an uninterrupted fighting for two days in minus 15 C, low in ammunition and supplies and finally arrived in P'yongyang on December 1. Evidently, the repercussions of this success immensely contributed to Turkey's image throughout the Western world. A few days later, the General Assembly on December 12, 1950, requested the Secretary General to arrange with the Unified Command for the design and award of a distinguishing ribbon or other insignia for personnel who had participated in Korea in the defense of the principles of the Charter of the United Nations.[49]

On December 6, 1950, the General Assembly included the item "Intervention of the Central People's Government of the People's Republic of China in Korea" in its agenda. On December 14, it established a three-man Cease-Fire Group—the President of the Assembly, Canada, and India—to recommend satisfactory cease-fire arrangements in Korea. The Group's program, aimed at achieving a cease-fire by successive stages, was transmitted to the PRC on January 13, 1951.

After discussing the Chinese reply to the Cease-Fire Group's program, the Assembly adopted a Resolution in February which noted that the People's Republic of China had not accepted the United Nations proposals to end hostilities and found that it had engaged in aggression in Korea. The Assembly called on it to withdraw its forces and nationals from Korea, requested a committee—the Additional Measures Committee—to consider measures for meeting the aggression, reaffirmed the policy of achieving United Nations objectives in Korea by peaceful means, and created a Good Offices Committee (the President of the Assembly, Sweden, and Mexico) to further those ends.

During the same weeks, the Turkish Brigade was adding to its reputation in Korea. Between January 25–27, 1951, the Brigade won another astonishing offensive battle in Kumiangjang-ni against the Chinese forces. The reports soon arrived that the American troops had counted 1734 bayoneted Chinese soldiers around the trenches in Kumiangjang-ni. The reports on this battle underscored that most of the enemy soldiers were eliminated in their foxholes which prove that they were fully trained and ready to fight to death. This indicated that they belonged to the combat ready Chinese troops while there were tens of thousands of "voluntary" and irregular Chinese soldiers who were used to test the opponents fire power etc. and killed in non-combatant duties or trying to escape from the battle. Upon the news on this fascinating fighting power, the Turkish Brigade was awarded the American Distinguished Unit Citation; the South Korean Presidential Unit Citation; and the South Korean Order of Military Merit Taeguk with Gold Star.[50]

The Final Steps Towards the NATO

On May 18, 1951, the General Assembly, in the absence of a satisfactory progress report from the Good Offices Committee, recommended that every state apply an embargo on the shipment to areas under the control of the Chinese Central People's Government and of the North Korean authorities of arms, ammunition, and implements of war, items useful in their production, petroleum, and transportation materials. The SU and four other members did not participate in the voting on the ground that the matter was exclusively within the jurisdiction of the Security Council.

Meanwhile, Turkey's significance as an ally was explained by Truman in his message to Congress, dated May 24. He said, he had transmitted in the first week of May a request for 60 billion dollars for the US defense establishment during the fiscal year ending June 30, 1952, and this time he was recommending for the same year a Mutual Security Program.[51] As explained by Truman, the bulk of the assistance was allocated to the members of the NAT, but, in addition, substantial quantities would be supplied to nations in the Middle East and Asia.

As for the US aid to the Middle East, Truman pointed out that no part of the world was more directly exposed to Soviet pressure. Truman stated that until then the Kremlin had lost no opportunity to stir these troubled waters, as the post-war record amply demonstrated. He said, "civil war in Greece; pressure for Turkish concessions on the Dardanelles; sponsorship of the rebellious Tudeh party in Iran; furthering a fractional strife in the Arab states and Israel—all reflect a concerted design for the extension of Soviet domination to this vital area."[52] The US President put forward that the pressure on the nations of the Middle East could only be overcome by a continued build-up of armed defenses and the fostering of economic development. Thus, to this end, he said he was recommending 415 million dollars in military aid, for Greece, Turkey and Iran. He underscored that continuing military aid for Greece and Turkey would make the further strengthening of these countries' large and well-trained armed forces possible, "which have already displayed their valiant resolution in the fight for freedom in Korea."[53]

In the meantime, armistice negotiations between the military commanders of the opposing sides began in Korea on July 10, 1951. On October 8, 1952, the negotiations were recessed indefinitely because of differences over whether all prisoners of war should be returned, by force if necessary. The United Nations Command was willing to return all except those who would resist repatriation. The other side, however, insisted on the return of all prisoners.

The Armistice Agreement was signed on July 27, 1953, by the Commanders of the United Nations Command, the Korean People's Army, and the Chinese People's Volunteers, and hostilities ceased. The Agreement established a demarcation line and demilitarized zone; provided that no reinforcing personnel or combat equipment be introduced except on a replacement basis; set up a Military Armistice Commission of representatives from the two sides to supervise and settle any violations of the Agreement; set up a Neutral Nations Supervisory Commission of four—Sweden and Switzerland appointed by the United Nations Command, and Czechoslovakia and Poland by the other side to observe and investigate troop withdrawals and weapons replacement. It also recommended to the Governments of the countries concerned a political conference within three months to settle through negotiation the question of the withdrawal of all foreign forces from Korea and the peaceful settlement of the Korean question; and declared that the Agreement would remain in effect until superseded by mutually acceptable changes or by provision in an agreement for a peaceful settlement at a political level between both sides. Shortly thereafter, the sixteen powers contributing forces to United Nations action in Korea affirmed their determination to carry out the Armistice Agreement and to resist promptly in case of renewal of armed attack.

On August 28, 1953, the General Assembly reaffirmed United Nations objectives of the achievement by peaceful means of a unified, independent, and democratic Korea under a representative form of government and the full restoration of peace in the area, and recommended that those member states contributing armed forces under the Unified Command should participate in the political conference envisaged in the Armistice Agreement. The participation of the SU in the conference was also provided for. The PRC and North Korea, however, rejected the Assembly's proposal. Subsequent negotiations on the conference between the two sides at Panmunjom broke down. On February 23, 1954, however, following a meeting in Berlin, the Foreign Ministers of France, the SU, the United Kingdom, and the United States announced that they would convene a conference at Geneva for the purpose of reaching a peaceful settlement of the Korean question.

The conference would be composed of representatives of their Governments, the PRC, South and North Korea, and other countries whose armed forces had participated in the Korean hostilities. The conference failed to find an agreed solution to the Korean question. On November

11, 1954, fifteen of the sixteen members of the United Nations which had participated in the Korean action and had been present at Geneva—the Union of South Africa was absent—underlined that the failure of the conference did not prejudice the armistice, which remained in effect.[54]

Turning back to the discussion on NATO's enlargement in the Mediterranean, in the spring of 1951, the US Joint Chiefs of Staff agreed that it was in their strategic interest that full membership in NATO be accorded to Greece and Turkey.[55] They would provide a bulwark for General Eisenhower's southeastern flank.[56] On May 15, the US formally suggested the membership of Turkey and Greece to Britain and France. Few weeks later, the British Under Secretary of State for Foreign Affairs said that Britain had not opposed Turkish and Greek membership and this question was still being discussed with the Allies.[57]

Two weeks later, the British Foreign Secretary Morrison said in the House of Commons that the British Government was ready to support the inclusion of Greece and Turkey in NATO. Concerning Turkey he said, the main difficulty was to reconcile Turkey's desire to join the NATO with its position in relation to the general defence of the Middle East. But having examined the matter fully, the British Government "have come to the conclusion that Turkish and Greek membership of the North Atlantic Treaty Organization is in fact the best solution. At the same time, they are most anxious that Turkey shall play her appropriate part in the defence of the Middle East."[58]

At this stage, on June 8, 1951, the British Chief of Staff, William Slim, and the Chairman of the US JCS, Omar Bradley met in London to discuss the British proposal that Turkey should be a part of a Middle Eastern Command, which would be linked to NATO. In this context, the British Government accepted Turkey's entrance to NATO if it would be part of the Middle Eastern theatre of operations under an integrated command, "and provided that theatre, which would include Egypt and certain members of the Commonwealth in addition to Turkey and the three great Western Powers, be placed under a special military organism that assures its high level strategic direction." Interestingly for Greece, it was considered that this country should be attached to theatre operations of SACEUR.[59]

On 18 July, the British Foreign Secretary, Herbert Morrison publicly announced UK's support for the admittance of Greece and Turkey to NATO.[60] It was concurrently believed in the Foreign Office that Turkey's presence in the envisaged Middle Eastern Defense Organization (MEDO) would be of considerable value. In this context, at the State Department, the idea of creating a common Middle Eastern Defense Board including US, UK, France and Turkey was welcomed. Shortly afterwards, the Ambassadors of the US, Britain, France and Turkey drafted the Four-Power proposals for a MEC to Egypt. With these proposals it was aimed to stress that "Egypt belonged to the free world and in consequence, her defense and that of the Middle East in General is equally vital to other democratic nations."[61] However, the dominant opinion in the Foreign Office was that the Egyptian Government would not show any marked friendliness towards these suggestions.

This was the second major document since the Tripartite Declaration of May 25, 1950 by the US Britain and France which recognized the existing Middle Eastern frontiers. Undoubtedly, Britain's center of gravity in the Middle East was around Cairo and the Suez. To the disappointment of the Foreign Office however, before the Four-Power Treaty was concluded, due to the increasing anti-British sentiment in Egypt, a British effort in April 1951, to realize joint defense arrangements and British retention of the military base at Suez had failed. Subsequently, the policy planning staff developed another plan. This was based on a Supreme Allied Commandment with its headquarters in Cairo. The base at Suez would be turned over to Egypt, and all British forces not allocated to the Supreme Commandment would be withdrawn. By such clauses, it was hoped to transform the character of remaining British forces from "occupiers" to "defenders."[62]

Turning back to the repercussions of the British support for Turkey's membership in NATO, the Turkish Minister of Foreign Affairs, speaking at the Grand National Assembly on July 20, 1951 stated that the people of Turkey had received the announcement of the British Government with great satisfaction. He added that as soon as Turkey had been admitted to the NATO, it would be ready to play its part in defense of the Middle East and to enter into negotiations with other countries to ensure the strategic and economic safety of that area.[63]

Two months later, on September 21, 1951, the North Atlantic Treaty Council recommend at Ottawa the inclusion of Turkey and Greece in NATO. "The Protocol to the North Atlantic Treaty on the Accession of Greece and Turkey" was finally completed in London, on October 22. As the Article III of the protocol stipulated that "the present Protocol shall enter into force when each of the Parties to the North Atlantic Treaty has notified the Government of the United States of America of its acceptance thereof," it was opened-up to the approval of the member countries.

As mentioned earlier, when Turkey became a member in NATO, Article 6 of the Treaty was amended to comprise the Turkish territories as follows:

> For the purpose of Article 5, an armed attack on one or more of the Parties is deemed to include an armed attack—
>
> (i) on the territory of any of the parties in Europe or North America, on the Algerian Departments of France, on the territory of Turkey or on the islands under the jurisdiction of any of the Parties in the North Atlantic area north of the Tropic of Cancer;
> (ii) on the forces, vessels or aircraft of any of the Parties, when in or over these territories or any other area in Europe in which occupation forces of any of the Parties were stationed on the date when the Treaty entered into force or the Mediterranean Sea or the North Atlantic area north of the Tropic of Cancer.[64]

Not surprisingly, the Soviet Embassy in Ankara delivered a Note to the Turkish Government a few days later, on November 3, protesting the participation of Turkey in NATO.[65] Concurrently a *Tass* statement stated that the Turkish Government should be aware of "the responsibility it has assumed by joining the aggressive Atlantic bloc and allowing Turkish territory to be used for the establishment of foreign military bases on Soviet frontiers."[66] Washington's reply to the Soviet statements came first. A Spokesman of the US State Department said in Washington on November 5 that the Soviet Note was apparently a further effort to misrepresent the objectives of the NAT and "to frighten a prospective new member out of adhering to the Treaty."[67]

While these steps were taken, Ankara was taking its part in the negotiations concerning the Middle East. On November 10, 1951, the US, Britain, France, and Turkey issued a declaration expressing their intention to establish the MEC. Here, among other things, it was decided that the Supreme Allied Commander Middle East would command forces placed at his disposal and would develop plans for the operations of all within the area or to be introduced into the area in time of war or international emergency. Leaving the door open to other states in the region (and perhaps the US, which insistingly stayed out of military arrangements in the region), it was stated that the sponsoring states of the MEC did not regard the initial form in which the MEC would be organized as unchangeable.[68] In this framework, combined with its support for Ankara's entry into NAT, it can also be evaluated that through these steps, Britain was considering to place Turkey "into the Middle Eastern picture as a firm ally"[69] despite the fact that its proposal of MEC would come to nothing.

Meanwhile, on November 12, Ankara replied to the Soviet Note of November 3 too. The Note underlined that Turkey had only one objective in joining the NATO and this was to assure its own security within the framework of common security. It reiterated that all military measures that the Turkish Government had taken were defensive ones, and that the SU should know that there were good reasons for Turkey to be anxious about its territorial integrity.[70] The Kremlin reiterated its claims once again on November 30 when it handed the Turkish Ambassador a second Note stating that Turkey was participating in "aggressive plans of the Atlantic bloc, directed against the U.S.S.R."[71]

On January 15, 1952, in a statement to the Foreign Relations Committee of the US Senate when it considered the "Protocol to the North Atlantic Treaty on the Accession of Greece and Turkey" the Chief of US JCS remarked that from the military view point, it was impossible to overstate the importance of Greece and Turkey. Bradley said, "located as they are—and allied with the free nations—they serve as powerful deterrents to any aggression directed toward Southern Europe, the Middle East, or North Africa . . . Turkey, astride the Bosphorus and Dardanelles, guards the approach by water from the Black Sea to the Mediterranean and to the Suez Canal and Egypt farther south." Bradley also underscored that "Turkey, too, flanks the land routes from the North to the strategically important oil fields of the Middle East."[72]

Subsequently, the Foreign Relations Committee stated the following reasons for inviting Turkey and Greece to accede to the North Atlantic Treaty:

a) The protection of their territory will serve to insure the benefits which our economic and military aid has brought these countries.

b) Their accession will also add to the security of the Eastern Mediterranean and the Middle East, which are strategically important to the defense of the free of world.

c) The southeastern flank of General Eisenhower's NATO army
    will be greatly strengthened.
d) Greece and Turkey have sizeable forces in good state of readi-
    ness and of tested valor.
e) The two nations have been strengthening their democratic
    institutions and have actively cooperated with the West for
    many years.
f) They are devoted to the cause of peace and collective secu-
    rity.[73]

On January 18, 1952, the Council of the NATO invited the Governments of Turkey and Greece to consider with appropriate NATO bodies
the applicability of the findings and recommendations of the Temporary
Council Committee of North Atlantic Council to them, and "it opened
the way for the participation of Greece and Turkey on a full and equal
basis in the annual review to be undertaken beginning next summer."[74]
Shortly afterwards, the US Senate approved without objection the participation of Turkey and Greece in NATO. Finally, the "Protocol to the
North Atlantic Treaty on the Accession of Greece and Turkey" went into
effect following the completion of the NAT members' notification of the
Government of the US of their acceptance on February 15, 1952. A few
days later, on February 18, the Turkish and the Greek Parliaments approved adherence of their Governments to the North Atlantic Treaty.[75]
Upon deposit of its instrument of accession to the North Atlantic Treaty
on the same day, Turkey emerged as a full member of NATO. At the
ninth session of the Council of NATO which was held in Lisbon between
February 20–25, Turkey and Greece were present as the newest members.

Before concluding the discussion here, few words needs to be said
on the emerging rapprochement between Turkey and Greece. Sharing
the same goals and a common defense strategy, the two countries were
closer than ever when their accession to the NATO was completed. This
was illustrated by the exchange of high level visits between the two countries in the same year and the momentum was thoroughly maintained
until the end of 1952. However, Greece had its own agenda concerning
serious issues, Cyprus being in the first place. These second thoughts
were also nurtured by the positive remarks of the Turkish statesmen. It
was first Fuat Köprülü who, on his plane's transit passage in Athens had
stated to Greek journalists that "There is no issue called Cyprus between
Turkey and Greece."[76] In the visit of Sophocles Venizelos, the Greek

Deputy Prime Minister and Minister of Foreign Affairs to Turkey in February 1952, Turkish Prime Minister Adnan Menderes also shared his wish to solve the Cyprus question between the two countries in a friendly manner.

Despite the fact that Venizelos made a statement to the press a few months later that Cyprus was an issue to be solved between Greece and the UK, Ankara's hopes were not affected. As the Cyprus issue was brought before the UN General Assembly at the initiative of Greece in 1954 and the emergence of EOKA, an ultra rightist armed Greek–Cypriot organization following the objective of union of Cyprus with Greece—ENOSIS—came on the scene in 1955, Ankara was caught unprepared. EOKA's attacks were against the British, Turks and even the Greek Cypriots when they stood in its way. Pressed hard by the public opinion concerned by the situation of fellow Turks living in Cyprus, Ankara's wavering caused a moment of domestic turmoil. The September 6–7, 1955 incident, which was a divisive attack against non-Muslims particularly Greeks living in İstanbul, was the climax of this domestic unrest.[77]

On September 6, state radio announced a bomb-attack on Mustafa Kemal Atatürk's birthplace in Thessalonica. Simultaneously, the popular evening paper *İstanbul Ekspres* announced the incident in two separate editions. On the night of September 5, a bomb was set off in the courtyard of the Turkish Consulate in Thessalonica, adjacent to the house where Mustafa Kemal was born. The damage was understood to be minimal with some broken windows. The Greek authorities arrested and prosecuted Oktay Engin, a Turkish law student of Western Thrace origin who was seen as the prime suspect—and who fled the country after a few months of imprisonment. Engin, despite his acceptance that he was a sometimes informant of the Turkish National Intelligence Organization, never accepted that he did or did not know about the bombing which precipitated the September 6–7 incident.

In the afternoon of September 6, The Association of Turkish Cyprus (Kıbrıs Türk Cemiyeti—KTC), arguing that defending the Turkish minority in Cyprus against the United Nations and EOKA, required launching of country-wide protests, along with some student organizations, started a protest rally in Taksim, İstanbul. Following the rally, attacks began in various neighbourhoods in the city. It was only with the declaration of martial law that order could be restored, on the second day of the civil chaos.

Although the limits of this book do not allow to discuss this incident in detail, September 6–7 needs to be considered a relevant issue in understanding the shaping of Turkish foreign policy in the second half of the 1950s. It remains a controversial issue up to the present day as some scholars, columnists and people from various walks of life bring it under the spotlight from time to time. The controversial aspects of this episode included question marks as to who were behind it. The Government of Menderes was blamed with planning and then inadequately responding to the attacks. Those who were blamed included many, from the clandestine communists and the Soviets to the Special Operations Department (known as *Seferberlik Tetkik Kurulu—Mobilization Inspection Board*) of the Turkish Armed Forces acting under the false or desired influence of its US counterpart which is known to have stimulated and experimental chaos plans aiming at first sorting out the dissident groups and then crushing them. According to the last theory, there was no anxiety on the part of Washington, which saw both countries having no chance of escaping from the alliance. Claims abound on this organisation getting out of control and making the environment susceptible to the menacing actions of the Soviets. The analysis of 6–7 September, is still being carried out within conflicting assumptions and ideologies due to the absence of proper documentation.[78]

The 6–7 September incident proved to be fairly divisive in the sense that following the attacks many citizens of Greek, Christian and some Jewish origin in Turkey opted for leaving Turkey, the Turkish society was divided between those finding what had happened understandable or overlooking it; and those who considered it inexcusable as well as some who stood against it during and after the 48 hours of chaos. In fact, the mounting crisis represented a serious blow to the Western alliance as it brought out the destruction of confidence in the Mediterranean—the restoration of which would take decades.

Notes

1. From the statement of the US Senator Harry P. Cain at a news conference in Ankara on July 25, 1950. *FRUS*, 1950, Vol. V, p. 1286.

2. Harry S. Truman, *Memoirs, II*, p. 317.

3. Peter Lowe, *The Origins of the Korean War*, 2nd ed., (London: Longman, 1997), p. 112.

4. *Ibid*, p. 116.

5. Michael H. Hunt, *Crises in . . .*, p. 172.

6. James Irving Matray, *The Reluctant Crusade,* (Hawaii: University of Hawaii Press, 1985), pp. 177–178; *FRUS*, 1948, VI, p. 1335.

7. Robert E. Osgood, *Limited War: The Challenge to American Strategy*, (Chicago: University of Chicago Press, 1957), pp. 167–168.

8. *The Korean War*, Korea Institute of Military History, (Seoul: The Military Mutual Aid Association, 1998), pp. 5–6.

9. "Mao Cables from Moscow," in the appendix of, Sergei N. Goncharov, John W. Lewis, Xue Litai, *Uncertain Partners Stalin, Mao and the Korean War*, (Stanford: Stanford University Press, 1995), 242. In its appendix, (229–291), this book includes a selection of translated documents from Mao Tsetung's manuscripts in the period of September 1949–December 1950, which introduce an interesting account of negotiations regarding Sino–Soviet Alliance and the Korean War. For the record of conversations between Mao, Zhou Enlai and Stalin, see, *The Cold War in Asia*, Cold War International History Project, Issues 6–7, (Washington: Woodrow Wilson International Center for Scholars, Winter 1995/1996).

10. "Memorandum by the US Embassy in Ankara to the MFA, March 30, 1949." *The MFA Archives*.

11. *Ibid.*

12. *Ibid.*

13. İsmail Soysal, *Soğuk Savaş Dönemi ve Türkiye Olaylar Kronolojisi* (The Cold War Era And Turkey Chronology of Events) *1945–1975*, (İstanbul: İsis Yayımcılık Ltd., 1997), p. 79. For an account of Soviets' daunting tactics towards Turkish officials in these years, see, Memduh Tezel, *Moskova'dan Geliyorum* (I am Coming From Moscow), Güven Basımevi, İstanbul, p. 1950.

14. *FRUS*, 1950, Vol. V., pp. 1232; 1236–1238; 1239–1240.

15. *Ibid.*, pp. 1252–1253; 1264–1265.

16. İsmail Soysal, *Soğuk Savaş Dönemi ve Türkiye Olaylar Kronolojisi,* (İstanbul: İsis Yayımcılık, 1997), pp. 90–91.

17. Wm. Roger Louis, *The British Empire in the Middle East 1945–1991*, (Oxford: Clarendon Press, 1985), p. 583.

18. For a strong criticism of the Western countries' perception and Turkey's Western oriented foreign policy, see, Haluk Gerger, *Türk Dış Politikasının Ekonomi Politiği* (Politico-Economy of Turkish Foreign Policy), (İstanbul: Belge Uluslararası Yayıncılık, 1998), pp. 67–68.

19. Ergun Özbudun, (ed.), *Perspectives on Democracy in Turkey*, p. 69.

20. Kemal Karpat, *Turkey's Politics*, 243; *Vatan* (editorial), 7 June, 1949.

21. Metin Toker, *Demokrasimizin . . .* Vol. II, 1950–1954, pp. 30–32.

22. Fuat Köprülü served as the MFA in the 1st (May 22, 1950–March 9, 1951) and 2nd (March 9, 1951–May 17, 1954) Menderes Governments. Türker Sanal, *Türkiye'nin Hükümetleri*, pp. 130–131.

23. "Telegram of Fuat Köprülü to the UN Secretary General Trygve Lie, June 29, 1950." *The MFA Archives.*

24. "Telegram of the UN Secretary General Trygve Lie to the Turkish MFA Fuat Köprülü, July 1, 1950." *The MFA Archives.*

25. "Telegram of Fuat Köprülü to the UN Secretary General Trygve Lie, July 1, 1950." *The MFA Archives.*

26. "Wadsworth to the Secretary of State," in *FRUS*, 1950, Vol. V., 1950, p. 1280.

27. *Ibid.*, p. 1281.

28. *Ibid.*

29. *Ibid.*, p. 1282.

30. *Ibid.*

31. *Ibid.*

32. "Telegram of Fuat Köprülü to the UN Secretary-General Tyrgve Lie, July 25, 1950," *The MFA Archives.* For the Turkish text of the telegram, see, Metin Toker, *Demokrasimizin . . .*, p. 80.

33. Metin Toker, *Demokrasimizin . . .*, Vol. II, pp. 82–83.

34. As told by George Harris in my interview with him.

35. From the interview with former Member of Parliament, Rıfkı Salim Burçak, cited in M. Ali Birand, Can Dündar, Bülent Çaplı, *Demirkırat*, (İstanbul: Doğan Kitapçılık A.Ş., 1999), pp. 78–79.

36. From the interview with the former Secretary General of the RPP, Kasım Gülek, cited in, *ibid.*, p. 79.

37. The text of the Declaration (in Turkish) is available at the following website dedicated to Boran, http://www.behiceboran.org/index.php?option=com_content&view=article&id=23:60-ylnda-barseverler-bildirisi&catid=8:aforizmalar&Itemid=8

38. *TBMM Tutanak Dergisi* (TGNA Journal of Records), Vol. IX, (Ankara: 1950, Devlet Matbaası), p. 313.

39. "The Text of the Speech by Ambassador Selim Sarper Delivered in the UN, September 1950." *The MFA Archives.*

40. *FRUS*, 1950, Vol. V., p. 1301.

41. *Ibid.*, p. 1312.

42. Bilal Şimşir, *The Turks of Bulgaria*, (London: K. Rustem & Brother, 1988), p. 167.

43. *Ibid.*, p. 162.

44. *Ibid.*, p. 168.

45. *Ibid.*, p. 173.

46. *Ibid.*, p. 173.

47. Celal Dora, *Kore Savaşında Türkler* (Turks in the Korean War), (İstanbul: İsmail Akgün Matbaası, 1963), pp. 27; 32, respectively.

48. Abdullah Aymaz, "Obama'ya Kitap" (A Book to Obama), in *Zaman*, December 6, 2009. We, however, maintain our reservations over the issue in

the absence of verification of this statement through further elaborations of eye witnesses. In one way or another, General Yamut was part of the polarization in Turkey, surrounded by likes and dislikes towards his decisions. He died tragically in *Yassıada* where he was held for trials in the aftermath of the overthrow of the DP Government. Another talismanic figure of the episode, Major General Tahsin Yazıcı, Commander of the Turkish Forces in Korea, was also not spared and subjected to *Yassıada* trials.

As for the May 27, 1960 military takeover, this incident was a reckoning with Turkey's domestic and foreign politics in the period of 1950 to 1960, admittedly, in a traumatic way. However, there are only a few more episodes in the history of the Republic of Turkey over which diversions of opinion so widely persist. From ultra leftists to leftist, center to right and ultra right, "May 27" has been regarded utterly different. Mehmet Perinçek, a contemporary Turkish political scientist, known with his socialist and patriotic views explains that a military intervention made together with people should be considered a "revolution" while any military intervention supported by "the US" is merely a "coup d'etat." This, as such, rules out the potential danger and the difficulty of any attempt of differentiating the military takeovers on the basis they were made, and remains controversial in the final analysis. To give a contrary example, Altemur Kılıç, a rightist and nationalist writer and columnist gives a fairly negative account of May 27, by naming the military takeover as "the beginning of disasters" since he says it triggered the other coups to follow. It is another fact that the ousted leaders of the DP government were exposed to defamatory propaganda. For an account of dreadful events which includes key person interviews, documents and other first-hand accounts of this period, see, Nazlı Ilıcak, *27 Mayıs Yargılanıyor* (May 27 on Trial), (İstanbul: Kervan Yayınları, 1975); Nilüfer Bayar Gürsoy, *27 Mayıs Darbesi ve Bizler* (The Coup of May 27 and We), (İstanbul: Timaş Yayınları, 2014).

In terms of foreign policy, on June 28, 1960, Nikita Khrushchev, First Secretary of the Central Committee of the Communist Party wrote to General Cemal Gürsel, the head of then military rule in Turkey and proposed that Ankara could consider neutrality. This was a change in Kremlin's policy towards Turkey "which was now demanding the neutralisation (sometimes referred to as the 'Finlandisation') of Turkey rather than its effective conversion into a satellite." Whereas General Gürsel, acting in a spirit to convince Ankara's Western allies that Turkey had no intention to leave its alliance failed to respond this. Correspondingly, both the military government and the civilian administration under İsmet İnönü which took over in November 1961 later declined a 500 million USD aid programme from the SU with suspicions that political demands of the Kremlin would be next to come. See, William Hale, *Turkish Foreign Policy, 1774–2000*, (London: Frank Cass Publishers, 2000), p. 122; and the footnotes no, 41 and 42. In one way or another, in view of the controversies at hand, many admit that the revelation of the real story of "May 27" may lead to the re-writing of Turkey's near history.

49. For a detailed discussion of the battles of the Turkish Brigade in Korea see, Celal Dora, *Kore'de* . . . ; Ali Denizli, *Kore Harbi'nde Türk Tugayları* (Turkish Brigades in the Korean War), (Ankara: Genelkurmay Basımevi, 1994).

50. It was explained that particularly the psychological effects of the Turkish Brigade's strong unyielding fighting will was used against the Chinese forces by the Americans. From then on, illustrations of a Turkish soldier bayoneting a Chinese soldier shot between their eyebrows were dropped on the Chinese positions. See, Ali Denizli, *Kore Harbi'nde* . . . , p. 131; 136; 207; 209.

51. See, "Extracts From President Truman's Message to Congress Containing His Recommendation For A Mutual Security Programme, 24 May 1951," in *Documents on International Affairs*, 1951, (London: Oxford University Press, 1954), pp. 32–33.

The Mutual Security Program envisaged: (1) military assistance to other free nations in the amount of 6.25 billion dollars; (2) economic assistance to other free nations in the amount of 2.25 billion dollars, primarily to support expanded defense abroad. These amounts were compared with 5.3 billion dollars appropriated for military assistance, and 3 billion dollars for economic assistance in 1951.

52. *Ibid.,* p. 38.

53. *Ibid.,* p. 39.

54. The report included a declaration, to which the Republic of Korea was an additional signatory, of two principles: (1) the United Nations, under its Charter, is fully and rightfully empowered to take collective action to repel aggression, to restore peace and security, and to extend its good offices in seeking a peaceful settlement in Korea; (2) in order to establish a unified, independent and democratic Korea, genuinely free elections under United Nations supervision, should be held to constitute the Korean National Assembly in which representations should be in direct proportion to the indigenous population in Korea. See, Chi Young Pak, *Korea and the United Nations*, (The Hague: Kluwer Law International, 2000), Ch. 6.

55. *U.S. Senate,* 82nd Congress, 2nd Session, S. Exec. E. Cited in, Türkkaya Ataöv, *NATO and Turkey*, (Ankara: Sevinç Printing House, 1970), p. 112.

56. *Ibid.*

57. *Ibid.,* 113. See also, Great Britain, *Hansard's Parliamentary Debates (Commons)*, Vol. 489, Col. 217.

58. *Ibid.,* See also, *Hansard's Parliamentary Debates (Commons)*, Vol. 490, Cols, 1227–1228.

59. *FRUS*, 1951, Vol. III, pp. 530–531; 556.

60. George McGhee, *Envoy to the Middle World*, p. 273.

61. See, "Proposals on Defence Presented to the Egyptian Government by the Governments of the United Kingdom, the US, France and Turkey, 13 October 1951," in *Documents on International Affairs*, 1951, p. 425.

62. *Ibid.*

63. Türkkaya Ataöv, *Turkey and NATO*, p. 113.

64. *United States Treaties and Other International Agreements: 1952*, Vol. III, Part I, (Washington, D.C.: US Department of State, US Government Printing Office, 1954), pp. 43–51.

65. "Soviet News, October 22, 1951," in *Documents on International Affairs*, 1951, Royal Institute of International Affairs, (London: Oxford University Press, 1956), pp. 68–69.

66. "Soviet Protest Against Proposed Membership of Turkey" in *Current Developments in US Foreign Policy*, Vol. IV (November 1951), (Washington D.C.: The Brookings Institution), p. 19. Cited in, Türkkaya Ataöv, *Turkey and NATO*, p. 114.

67. *Ibid.*

68. "Declaration by the Governments of the U.S.A., the United Kingdom, France and Turkey on Their Intention to Establish A Middle East Command, November 10, 1951," in *Documents on International Affairs*, 1951, p. 427.

69. Anthony Eden, *The Memoirs of Sir Anthony Eden Full Circle*, (London: Cassell & Co.,1960), p. 244.

70. Türkkaya Ataöv, *Turkey and NATO*, p. 114.

71. "Soviet News, December 4, 1951," in *Documents on International Affairs*, 1951, pp. 70–71.

72. Cited in, George McGhee, *The US-Turkish . . .* , pp. 88–89. McGhee stated that by a vote of 73 to 2, with 21 members not voting, the Senate approved ratification of the protocol on February 7, 1952.

73. *US Senate*, 82nd Congress, 2nd Session, S. Exec. E. Cited in Türkkaya Ataöv, *Turkey . . .* , p. 115.

74. See, "Communiqué on the Agreement Reached Between President Truman and the British Prime Minister, Mr. Winston Churchill, on the Appointment of A Supreme Commander for the Atlantic, Washington, January 18, 1952," in *Documents on International Affairs*, 1952, p. 4.

75. Türkkaya Ataöv, *Turkey . . .* , p. 115.

76. Semih Günver, *Fatin Rüştü Zorlu'nun Öyküsü*, (The Story of Fatin Rüştü Zorlu), (İstanbul: Bilgi Yayınevi, 2005), p. 47.

77. Works as, *6-7 Eylül Olayları, Fotoğraflar—Belgeler (September 6-7 Incidents, Photographs—Documents), Fahri Çoker Arşivi*, (İstanbul: Tarih Vakfı Yurt Yayınları, 2005), compiling photographs and interviews scholars discussing the issue introduced not only further arguments but new evidence to debate as well.

78. Şükrü Sina Gürel, *Türk-Yunan İlişkileri* (Turco-Greek Relations) *1821-1993*, Ankara: Ümit Yayıncılık, 1993), p. 56.

Chapter 8

The Northern Tier Arrangements and the Prelude to Regional Divergences (1953–1958)

We are to-day turning over a leaf in history which for these peoples of the Near East is momentous. For them the pages of the past have been written letters of blood. Now we turn for them and for the whole world to a much fairer and a brighter page, the one whereon will be inscribed the victories of peace and the triumphs of the right—the right for which those people in that far off land have looked for so far in vain. It may be, it is to be hope, that this time it is not to be in vain.[1]

The Middle East, with its own internal deep seated problems and conflicts represented a source of instability where a power vacuum could never be tolerated within the Cold War rivalry. This instability attracted the intervention of both Cold War super-powers, but in different ways and on different premises. By their nature, the Northern Tier and the Baghdad Pact were designed to entrench the Western position against the Soviets in the Middle East, through establishing a collective security system in the region, obviously, along these lines. A military–political organization to include Iraq, Turkey, Pakistan, Iran and probably Syria was the "American promotion of the 'Northern Tier' concept during the period 1953–54,"[2] at a time when British presence had mostly focused on the Suez Canal Zone in Egypt.

At this juncture, considerable evidence suggests that there were some differences between the American strategic interests in the Middle East and those of Britain. For the former, the containment of any Soviet influ-

ence in the "outer-ring" area which had become known as the Northern
Tier (and later known as the Baghdad Pact) was the main priority, whilst
the British were mainly concentrated upon consolidating their own position in the "inner-ring" of the area, most notably Egypt.[3] The Baghdad
Pact eventually represented an adaptation of the Northern Tier scheme in
which "Britain was glad to take the lead."[4]

When the British and American governments attempted to reorganise
their positions in the Middle East, they did so with the intention of consolidating their stand against the Soviets through an ideological and actual penetration into this region. Given this, it will also be discussed if
the policies of the UK and US in the Middle East were the outcome of an
intricate pattern of relationships between the American and British administrations which were not necessarily at harmony at all times.

The Middle Eastern defense organisation that Britain was canvassing
was seen as an instrument to prolong Western influence in the Middle
East. It was asserted that it would strengthen Western positions and act
as a major deterrent to Soviet influence. With these prospects the Baghdad
Pact came and was promoted as opening the real possibility of a political
and military alliance, sympathetic to the West and protective of its interests, specifically of oil and the Suez Canal. The first step towards the
forming of a group of Northern Tier states was a treaty of friendship and
cooperation signed on April 3, 1954, between Turkey and Pakistan. But
the difficulties were not resolved.

Not surprisingly, the Indian resentment of the Turco–Pakistani Agreement came first. The Kashmir question, the division of the canal waters,
and compensation for refugee properties were still the sources of dispute
between India and Pakistan, leading to the objections of the former. At
the time of the announcement of the extension of the US military aid to
Pakistan, the objection of India to Pakistan's inclusion in this Pact was at
its peak. A remark expressed by an Indian right-wing journal, *Capital*,
claimed that, as long as India and Pakistan were carrying on a cold war
of their own, any military assistance by a third power to Pakistan would
be an act of hostility to India. Moreover, Nehru stated that the Pact
would enlarge the area of the Cold War, make actual war likelier and
threaten India with involvement if war came. In his turn, the Pakistani
Prime Minister, Muhammad Ali Bogra charged Nehru that he was endeavouring to hold the balance of power between the two blocs and feared
weakening of his bargaining power. In addition to hostile Indian state-

ments against the Pakistani inclusion in this new organisation, when it came to the formation of the Pact (as this chapter concentrates on) explosive developments took place. Egypt and Israel blatantly objected to Iraq's membership, clearly for very different reasons.

In the course of a series of developments, one cardinal difference emerged between the Anglo–American outlooks. Oddly, the United States, despite its major leading role in launching the project, held back while Britain joined it. Besides, it "tried to take credit for this attitude in capitals like Cairo which were hostile to the pact."[5] At this stage, Gamal Abd-el Nasser, an Egyptian nationalist, and a Pan-Arabist who wished to eliminate foreign influence not just in Egypt, but throughout the Middle East, became the central figure of resistance to the Baghdad Pact. Being backed in his course by the Soviet Union, which was taking care to avoid any overt interference in Arab affairs, Nasser gradually moved into the Soviet sphere. Further events as it happened in the negotiations for the construction of a High Dam at Aswan which resulted in the US withdrawal of aid, embittered Nasser. Thereafter, the region became a scene of the escalating tensions to the extent of precipitating the war over Suez.

In other words, Egypt's nationalisation of the Suez Canal marked a turning point in Middle Eastern history. For Britain, to abandon control of the Suez Canal was a risk hardly to be contemplated. The experience of the two world wars "had confirmed the importance of the waterway to British trade and security in the Middle East and North Africa."[6] But the crisis itself, and the aftermath, were rather a political discord between the US and the UK. As a result, the US refused to support Britain and France in the war over Suez. Besides, the UN condemned France and Israel together with Britain with bringing about the crisis.

Certainly, it is worth pointing out that the attention of the Anglo-American foreign policy makers had already been drawn to the necessity of implementing a new strategy in the Middle East by the end of the WW II. At this juncture, having regarded the emerging tensions, the British, who were yet to consent to the abandonment of their global status in favour of the US, wished to perpetuate their influence in the region by means of a collective political–military organization. Given this, this chapter begins with discussing the post-war political environment in the Middle East.

The Cold War and the Anglo–American Attitudes to Middle Eastern Security

Following the end of the Second World War, it was an immediate necessity for Britain to concentrate on its Middle Eastern strongholds. For its oil supplies it was a crucial area for British economic recovery and the military bases in the region were indispensable to safeguard Britain's position as a global power. The dual question of how to preserve the oil supplies in the area and the military bases were first to be addressed by the post-war Labour Government headed by Clement Attlee, and the Foreign Secretary, Ernest Bevin. Bevin and the Chiefs of Staff regarded the Middle East as acquired a significant role in peace time and emphasized the strategic importance of the region in time of antagonisms.

In a period of growing resentment towards the British in Egypt and Palestine, London continued to seek ways of maintaining its facilities in the Middle East. To overcome the disturbances of these countries, Bevin tried to pursue a strategy of maintaining Britain's political and economic interests in the area with the renewal of bilateral treaties. Bevin's efforts to realize long-term treaties with the Middle Eastern states were mostly hampered by the growing disturbances of the Arab nationalists in these countries of the British influence.

Against this background, the Egyptian nationalists complicated the Anglo–Egyptian negotiations. Towards the end of 1945, the Wafd party led by Mustapha Nahas emerged as the leading organisation of the nationalists. Wafdists demanded that Prime Minister Ismail Sidky agree to nothing except unconditional British withdrawal from Egypt. In the meantime, Wafdist journals maintained that a defense partnership would also mean prolonged British occupation of the country. When talks started in April 1946, Ismail Sidky acquiesced to Wafdist policies. He stated that the presence of British under any agreement undermined the Egyptian sovereignty, and interfere the Egyptian internal affairs and violate the UN Charter.[7]

In order to control Egyptian nationalism, Bevin reassigned Ambassador Lord Killearn (formerly Miles Lampson), the man responsible for the February 4, 1942 incident.[8] He also sent Secretary of State for Air, Lord Stansgate who was known with his sympathy for Egyptian demands to proceed with the talks in Cairo. But, the domestic pressures caused Sidky to oppose British proposals. At this stage, Bevin faced with a dilemma. Anything less than unconditional withdrawal from the Canal

Zone might cause nationalistic violence against the British troops and oblige Egypt to seek a United Nations censure of the British occupation. Yet maintenance of the British presence in Egypt seemed essential on strategic grounds. Bevin explained to the Defence Committee, "If we move out of the Mediterranean, Russia will move in, and the Mediterranean countries, from the point of view of commerce and trade, economy and democracy, will be finished."[9] Bevin and Attlee also reviewed the option of agreeing to withdraw troops and count on the Egyptian Government. They thought that such an attitude would lead to voluntarily invitation of the Egypt of the British for a joint defense arrangement. The Chiefs of Staff explained that, "it would be better . . . to make a bold gesture at the outset . . . and thus hope to gain the willing cooperation of the Egyptian Government in negotiating the base and other requirements in Egypt which are essential to us both in war and also in peace."[10] On May 7, 1946, Attlee publicly announced the concessions to the Egyptian Government for the aim of ensuring a more favourable atmosphere for negotiations. But this did not lead to desired effects. Besides, domestic opposition which culminated in Conservative Party's complaints took place.

In October 1946, at the renewal of 1936 Anglo–Egyptian Treaty which had provided the basis for formal independence of Egypt in return for British entitlement to defend the Suez Canal, differences arose in relation to the control of Sudan. The country had been administered under Anglo–Egyptian dual control since the 1899 Condominium agreement and the tension emergent over Sudan was in relation with Egypt's desire to unite this country with itself. Although Egypt enthusiastically wanted to restore its rule over Sudan, Britain opposed Egyptian domination of this country. Following this dispute, there was no further talks over Sudan for British fear that it would bring the negotiations on Suez base to an impasse. In their turn, the Americans were continuing their efforts to persuade Egypt not to abrogate its treaty with the UK.

The bottleneck was left behind in the same month when Sidky arrived in London. Bevin agreed to withdraw the British troops from Cairo and Alexandria by March 31, 1947 and all of Egypt by September 1, 1949. In return, Sidky stated that Egypt would take part in a joint defense board to consult in the event of war in the Middle East. Over Sudan, parties reached to an ambiguous settlement recognizing "'the framework of unity between the Sudan and Egypt under the common crown of Egypt'"[11] but explaining their aim to be Sudanese well-being, independence, and self-government. Not surprisingly, Britain was not considering a complete withdrawal from Sudan. The main British political course was to maintain the British presence in Sudan whilst making some concessions to Egypt.

As a result of the differing interpretations of the clause for Sudan, the Sidky–Bevin treaty was short lived. Following his return to Cairo, Sidky announced that he had secured unity with Sudan. Shortly after, uprisings broke out in Khartoum organised by the members of the pro-independence Umma party. Bevin publicy repudiated Sidky's statements and Attlee invited the leaders of Umma party to London. Two days later Sidky resigned in protest and Mahmoud Nokrashy returned to office for the second time. On January 27, 1947, Nokrashy declared that Egypt would appeal to the UN to order Britain to evacuate Egypt and Sudan.[12]

At this crucial moment, Bevin considered that, the decline in Britain's economic power and the increasing difficulties to revert the Arab nationalism required the involvement of the US in Middle Eastern affairs. Though some officials of the State Department would choose to support the Egyptian struggle for independence and urge London to make concessions to Cairo, in a period of increasing tensions US decided to not risk alienating the British. To the disappointment of a group of Egyptians who desired American backing for their sovereignty, soon after the Security Council hearings, the US gave its full support to the United Kingdom. In replacement of the commercial and ideological interests, strategic concerns were shaping American policy making.

As previously discussed the initial major dispute however, broke out over Iran. The situation in Iran came before the Security Council in January 1946. The US strongly supported Iran's appeal to the United Nations for Soviet withdrawal and the US Secretary of State James Byrnes also seized the chance to publicly condemn the Soviet menace. After a deadline for the withdrawal of Soviet forces passed in March 1946, the US Embassy in Moscow issued notes of protest to the Soviet Government. At this stage, the US Government dispatched the battleship *Missouri* to İstanbul to return the body of the Turkish Ambassador to the United States, who had died in Washington. Meanwhile, heated exchanges concerning the situation in Iran occured in the United Nations between Byrnes and Soviet Ambassador Andrei Gromyko.[13] Finally, in May of that year, Soviet forces withdrew from Iran.

Again, as mentioned before, a few days before the US' decision to send military advisers to Iran, the Kremlin also tried to get Ankara's approval for bases near the Straits for Soviet troops. Furthermore, the SU pronounced its intention of restoring the pre–Great War status quo, bringing the case of Turkish eastern provinces of Kars and Ardahan to mind. This ouverture of the Soviets alarmed the US and Britain in many respects. A special report prepared for President to Truman underscored that compromise and concessions would be interpreted by the Soviets as the evidence of weakness.[14] In this context, it was also stressed that the US had to avoid the error of appeasement and should even be prepared to go to war if necessary to take stand against Stalin's ambitions for world conquest.

As it was anticipated, the increasing involvement of the United States in Middle Eastern politics paved the way for a new Anglo–American cooperation. The US interest was focused on a Graeco–Turkish–Iranian tier to contain the Soviet Union. Indeed, the US was highly engaged in Western Europe, Greece, and Turkey and in the Middle East, where its policy was to support Britain to exert its influence in the region as long as possible. Assistant Secretary of State for Near Eastern Affairs, George McGhee stated: "The US Joint Chiefs of Staff had in 1947, recognized officially that the security of the Eastern Mediterranean and Middle East was vital to our security. It also became US policy that we should be prepared to make full use of our political, economic, and if necessary, military power to defend this area."[15] Significantly, another fundamental concept was concurrently introduced to describe the purpose of US policy against the Soviets. In his article published in July 1947, George Kennan emphasized the need for "a long term, patient but firm containment of Russian expansive tendencies."[16] Subsequently, the term 'containment' was adopted to describe the aim of US policy in its dealings with the Soviets.

Apparently, an important division between the West and Soviets came in 1947, over Greece. Following the end of the WW II, Greece, on the fringes of the Middle East, emerged as an important country in this area. Since its liberation by the British forces in 1944, Greece had been torn by a civil war between nationalists and communist guerrillas. In 1946, as a result of elections, the Royalists formed a government and a plebiscite favoured the return of the King. Civil war then broke out again. On February 24, 1947, the British Ambassador to Washington, Sir Oliver Franks told the Secretary of State that, Britain due to its financial problems would no longer assist Greek army in civil war against the communists. The United Kingdom explained the necessity for the replacement of its aid with that of the US. In effect, Britain was obliged to pursue a policy of systemic withdrawal from its global status. Don Peretz argued that as Britain was forced to abandon its "self imposed role as arbiter" in the region, the US "felt obliged to return and assume" many British commitments lest the region fall under Soviet influence.[17]

The British appeal for US contribution to the Middle Eastern position precipitated a comprehensive policy to be initiated by the United States. This was the Truman Doctrine and large economic and military missions were established in Athens and smaller ones in Ankara to transfer 750 million worth of military and economic assistance. In other words, with its part concerning the aid to Turkey, the Truman Doctrine became the first direct involvement of the US in Middle East.

In January 1948, a shocking incident forced the British foreign policy makers to re-consider the threats towards Britain's position in the Middle East. This was the failure of the Anglo–Iraqi Treaty (Portsmouth agreement). Following the mass demonstrations in Iraq, violence took place in the aftermath of this agreement between the British and Iraqi governments which sought to extend the 1930 Anglo–Iraqi Treaty in the guise of revising it. To ensure the extension of the 1930 Treaty had a great importance for Britain. This treaty was drawn up to safeguard the essential features of the British order before the expiry of the mandate by October 1932, and was providing Britain a "legal" basis for its continuing presence in the country. However, to Britain's disappointment, with the resignation of the Saleh Jabr's government, the treaty negotiations were suspended indefinitely. To add to the instability of the region, in May 1948 shortly after the British withdrawal, the war in Palestine erupted. At this juncture, Britain precipitated its policy of forming an organisation to safeguard its position in the region. As will be discussed under the subsequent title, this military body was to include the US, France and Turkey.

The Tripartite Declaration, The Four Power Treaty, and the Formation of the Middle Eastern Defense Organization

Much due to the historical evaluation, the importance of the Middle East to the US was determined to a large extent by its importance to the United Kingdom. Apparently, the US held no colonies in Africa and in Asia compared to those held by the British. But, the US interest in the region was great because of its strategic position and control of air routes. Moreover, both the US and UK were interested in to control the Middle Eastern oil. As another essential point, the US found it advantageous to support nationalism in the region against the spread of communism, although this was not always friendly to British and American interests. At that time, this view was also shared by Britain. Superintending Under Secretary of State for Foreign Affairs, Michael Wright, in his talks to the US officials approved that it should be the joint objective of the US and UK to convert the nationalism of the Middle Eastern countries into a friendly force.

Washington was quick to act in its foreign policy calculations. In November 1949, at the meeting of US Chiefs of Diplomatic Missions of the Middle East in İstanbul, the major issues were; Soviet propaganda activities, Arab–Israeli conflict (with a US emphasis on remaining impartial between Arabs and the Israelis), two recent Syrian coups and the prospects of a Syrian–Iraqi union. At the same time, the implications of the Point Four program in Iran on the nationalisation of the Iranian oil was also discussed. Here, the Soviet pressure on Iran and the future of Iranian oil and in a broader sense, the oil reserves in the Middle East were discussed with regard to how much US aid would be adequate to the Middle Eastern countries against the Soviets.

In his expression of reasons for the calling of the conference, the Under-Secretary for Near Eastern Affairs, George McGhee pointed out the emergence of the Middle East as a key area in the world which became subject to a wide struggle between the West and the Soviet Union. He argued the US as a latecomer in the area, needed to coordinate its efforts with those of British to prevent the creation of a vacuum which could be exploited by the communists (which obviously, always referred to the SU without pronouncing it).[18]

Accordingly, it was decided to entrench a strong and popular resistance to communism. At the same meeting, concerning the initial steps to build a regional bulwark against the communism, the resolution adopted in the same meeting on October 22, 1949, called for a collective security pact among the Arab states. With regard to Western position in the pact, it was also concluded that, "the proposed pact would not likely to have any significant effect, and did not require a definite position by the US."[19] Besides, the conference did not recommend the extension of military assistance to Middle Eastern states outside of the present military assistance program, except aid to Saudi Arabia, to a certain extent with the authorisation of the U.S. Congress. With its overall features, this conference was an introductory phase of Western policy making in the Middle East. As McGhee stated, "The Conference did not result in any startling policy recommendations. It is included mainly as a point of reference to our changing attitudes toward the Middle East."[20]

Another consideration of the Anglo–American officials was the preservation of the British presence in Egypt. In January 1950, George McGhee expressed his British counterpart the view that: "It did not seem wise to consider evacuating British troops from Egypt under present circumstances, Russian aggression in the Near East was entirely possible and it would be essential to our common strategic plan to have the British on the spot."[21]

When Wafd assumed power again in Egypt in the same month, trying to assure the American support on the Wafd regime, the new Egyptian Foreign Minister, Muhammad Salaheddin told the American Ambassador that Egypt had no intention of attacking Israel.[22] To stabilize the region through accommodating an adequate truce between Israel and Egypt and to perpetuate the Western strategic interests in the region, the British and the Americans sought the ways to embrace Egypt into a joint body. In February 1950, to convince Egypt to join a defense body, Britain agreed to sell this country arms and munitions including jet-fighters. As expected, Israel asked for similar war equipment from the US. Although the US had initially chosen to act carefully in terms of any commitments in the region, since the UN embargo ended, domestic pressures were forcing the US to change this policy.

In May 1950, Foreign Office Under Secretary Michael Wright drew the attention to the possibility of making a Middle Eastern defense pact, probably to be linked to NATO. He considered that this would also remove the deadlock in the Anglo–Egyptian talks. Whereas the Near Eastern Affairs officials of the State Department declined this project which would force to extend the obligations of the US under NATO to the Middle East and stated that the area lacked a "power center on the basis of which a pact could be built."[23]

Having regarded the weak possibility of forming a joint military body in the Middle East, the US and Britain together with France launched a project to effectively control the flow of arms to the countries in region. On the other hand, the officials at Pentagon initially opposed the declaration because it might represent an undertaking of the US to use force against the aggression in the Middle East. Secretary of Defense Louis

Johnson "implored" Under Secretary of State Dean Acheson to refrain from any declaration that might "have adverse military implications for the United States."[24] Not surprisingly, however, State Department officials drafted the declaration in May, converging the interests of Washington and London in the Middle East. On May 12, Assistant Secretary of State for Near Eastern, South Asian and African Affairs, Raymond A. Hare expressed the British Officials that US considered the declaration as an important development presenting advantages at a critical time."[25]

On May 25, 1950, the Tripartite Declaration by the US, Britain and France recognized the existing Middle Eastern frontiers. The Tripartite Declaration by the principal Western powers involved in the Middle East was a clear expression of these powers of their determination to hold on their strategic interests in the area. In essence, through the Tripartite Agreement these countries aimed to coordinate the supply of arms to regional states which were under an embargo imposed by the UN after the May 1948 Arab–Israeli war. British Minister of State for Foreign Affairs Anthony Nutting himself had the view that:

> Under the Tripartite Declaration of 1950, . . . three powers were alone responsible for preventing either side from starting another 'round' in the Arab–Israeli struggle, and there was every reason why this responsibility should be more widely shared. I had in mind a form of permanent U.N. police force stationed on Israel's borders. This would relieve us of the obligation—which could all too easily arise in the inflamed state of Arab–Israeli relations—of having to fight against an Arab state, such as Jordan, with whom we had a treaty of alliance. It would also enable us to reduce or withdraw our forces from Jordan or elsewhere in the Middle East if either political or military requirements demanded it.[26]

US assurance for the implementation of the tenets of the Declaration was also significant. The New York Times described the Declaration as: "A great and welcome step in the 'total diplomacy' which must be the goal of the west. . . . The lack of a unified Western policy on the Middle East has been one of the worst gaps in the battle lines of the Cold War. . . . this new move is just and wise and it will strength the West in the global struggle."[27]

As for the repercussions of the Declaration, Israeli Foreign Office expressed its satisfaction by the Western pledge to oppose Arab aggression against Israel. Lebanese deemed it 'a freeze' in the status quo. Egyptian nationalists condemned the declaration because it realized the foreign control of Egyptian arms acquisition, however, King Farouk and the Foreign Minister Muhammad Salaheddin stated their approval and most press commentary were supportive. The Syrian Prime Minister considered it primarily good. Significantly, initial reactions of the Arab League were moderate.[28]

In October 1950, with the launch of the US' "Outer Ring" strategy concerning Greece, Turkey, Iran and Pakistan, joint Anglo–American efforts to coordinate their policies were accelerated. The US Chief of Staff, Omar Bradley stated that, in war time Britain would be in a position to hold the area without American assistance. This was a clear indication of US comprehension of Britain significance in the Middle East and the appreciation of collaborating with it in the region. Subsequently, in the second US Chiefs of Mission Conference in İstanbul on February 14–21, 1951, a Middle Eastern Defence Pact was rejected. But, the considerations continued for the formation of a regional organisation of this kind.

At this stage, on July 18, the new British Foreign Secretary, Herbert Morrison, publicly announced UK's support for the admittance of Greece and Turkey to NATO.[29] In addition, at the State Department, the idea of creating a common Middle Eastern Defence Board including US, UK, France and Turkey was approved. Consequently, the Middle Eastern Defence Organisation (MEDO) and the Middle Eastern Command (MEC) were established. Shortly afterwards, the Ambassadors of the United States, Britain, France and Turkey drafted the Four-Power proposals for a Middle Eastern Command to Egypt. These proposals centered around the "problem" and stressed that "Egypt belonged to the free world and in consequence, her defense and that of the Middle East in general is equally vital to other democratic nations."[30]

Therefore, the proposal was designed to invite Egypt to participate in the Allied Middle East Command on the basis of "equality and partnership." The US strongly supported the proposals because "the proposals offer the best prospect of relieving the present tension in Egypt." Furthermore, the US Secretary of State, Dean Acheson stated that "[MEDO] will give Egypt and other Arab states something more productive to think about than their feud with Israel and thus pave the way for an eventual peace settlement."[31]

Before the Four-Power Treaty was concluded, however, a British effort in April 1951 to realize joint military arrangements and British retention of the military base at Suez had failed due to the increasing anti-British sentiment in Egypt. Subsequently, the policy planning staff developed another plan. This was centered on a Supreme Allied Command with its headquarters in Cairo. The base at Suez would be turned over to Egypt, and all British forces not allocated to the Supreme Command would be withdrawn. By such clauses, it was hoped to transform the character of remaining British forces from "occupiers" to "defenders."

Concerning the integration of British policy to that of US, some low-points were appearing. In fact, beneath the surface of a cordial relationship, there still remained some differences between the American and British outlooks. The American view was that the British should sacrifice Sudan in return for the Egyptian participation in the Middle East Defense Organisation.[32] In other words, the US policy was based on the satisfaction of both Western military needs and Egyptian aspirations. On the contrary, the British view was that, the American appeals were undermining British interests in the Middle East, particularly in Egypt and the Sudan. It was further argued that by establishing the Middle East Defense Organisation, the US aimed to change Britain's position in Egypt "from that of an imperial power to that of a surrogate for America, and the British military presence in Egypt would become an integral part of American global strategy."[33]

On the British side, it was a fact that, despite the State Department's suggestion for the recognition of King Farouk as King of Sudan as well, the oppositionary Conservative party's leader Winston Churchill, in conformity with the backbench Conservatives, was emphasizing the necessity of maintaining British position in Egypt and in the Sudan. Churchill evaluated this as a must in Britain's Middle Eastern position. In his turn, although it continued to support British position in Suez, the US did not believe that the Suez Canal base agreement should be linked to the Sudan at the same time.

Given this fact, the Americans were also continuing their efforts to persuade Egypt not to abrogate its treaty with the UK. Regardless of the Anglo–American efforts, Anglo–Egyptian relations were further complicated when the Egyptian Prime Minister Nahas Pasha rejected the British suggestions for Egypt's agreement with the Four-Power statements. On October 13, 1951, as the Commander of the Arab Legion, John Bagot Glubb stated, "aware of the proposals about to be submitted to it," Wafd government's Prime Minister Nahas Pasha rejected the British led proposals. On October 15, the Egyptian Parliament adopted decrees unilaterally abrogating both the 1936 Treaty and the Anglo–Sudan Condominium, and Farouk was declared King of Egypt and the Sudan. This was later remarked by US Secretary of State, Dean Acheson, as: "if there was a political stillbirth, this was it."[34]

Not surprisingly, Britain refused to accept these developments. The situation continued to deteriorate with the increasing guerrilla attacks in the Canal Zone. On January 18, 1952, the State Department urged King Ibn Saud of Saudi Arabia to precipitate mediatory efforts between Britain and Egypt. On the same day, in a Cabinet meeting, Dean Acheson stated that, "the US is backing the British position in the Egyptian crisis."[35] The forthcoming events were to show that all the mediatory actions were in vain. On January 25, a battalion of an Egyptian force at Ismailia was surrounded by British troops and were called upon to surrender. The Egyptian Minister of the Interior ordered them to resist. Within a couple of hours, fifty Egyptians were killed. News of the event in Cairo, caused a wave of violence.[36] The massacre of several dozen Europeans and nine Englishmen on January 26, 1952 (Black Saturday),[37] led to Churchill, who succeeded the Premiership after the Labour government's fall in October 1951 elections, to warn King Farouk that, British forces would move out from their Suez Base to reoccupy Cairo and Alexandria if Egypt did not protect British lives and property. Farouk guaranteed this, just six months before the outbreak of the Revolution.

With the dismissal of the Wafd on January 28, 1952, the last phase of the old political course in Egypt was opened. In effect, the removal of the Wafd did not relieve the tension between Egypt and Britain. Prime Minister Nahas Pasha's successors proved to be unable to conduct a social programme in the country to restore the deteriorated Anglo–Egyptian relations. From January to June 1952, the US government acted as an honest broker and asked the Egyptian government not to break its diplomatic relations with Britain. In the same period it focused its attention on persuading Britain to adopt a more conciliatory attitude towards Egypt. On July 16, 1952, a week before the military takeover, US Ambassador in Cairo, Henry Byroade told his British counterpart that, "the British must understand that we can not blindly support them."[38] On July 21, Byroade saw the danger that uprisings and disorder would escalate to the extent which the Egyptian authorities might not be able to control. Forty-eight hours later, the Free Officers overthrew King Farouk's monarchy and grasped power.

As the dynamics which channeled the developments towards 23rd of July were noticed by both the US and UK, the military takeover itself was nearly expected. Interestingly, a scholar argued that, Americans had considered the chance of a peaceful revolution under King Farouk, "in the hope of forestalling a more extreme popular uprising of uncertain orientation and direction."[39] Justifying this, early in 1952, a CIA official, Kermit Roosevelt, was assigned the duty of planning and executing a secret project to accomplish, in a sense, a preemptive coup. Roosevelt soon reported that, this policy would not be feasible. He was more convinced that, the Free Officers could make a coup with consequences not detrimental to American or Western interests in Egypt and the Middle East; "that the officer corps represented the only credible alternative to the Farouq regime."[40]

The American decision, in certain respects, was a kind of reaction to Wafdist neutrality during the 1951 Korean War. A view expressed by George McGhee, in one of his articles in 1951, explains the foundations of the American foreign policy towards Egypt in that decade. He stated that; "The events of the Middle East are moving rapidly. The US cannot afford to allow the force of neutralism and anti-Western sentiment to gain any further ground."[41] Having considered the American attitude, the Free Officers wanted to maintain US' benevolent neutrality towards their coup plan.[42]

With the departure of the king, three major problems faced Nasser and his friends. First, they had either to try to improve the old structure or devise a new one. Second, the British still had 75,000 troops and £500 million worth of installations in the Canal Zone, and as for Sudan, they were working to divide the country apart from Egypt forever. Finally, the economy was stagnant, the conditions of poverty, disease, illiteracy and exploitation especially among the peasants who formed the two-thirds of the population were among the worst in the world.[43]

Again, differences between the US and UK with regard to the new Egyptian administration's programmes were surfacing as it happened in evaluating the land reform. In general terms, the main difference of opinion here was that, while Britain was giving support to the status quo, the American approach was to encourage nationalist movements and to cultivate the new leaders to collaborate with the US. The US was also trying to distance itself from the impressions of British colonialism. However, a cautious policy was pursued by the US, as Britain's collaboration was essential for the Truman administration when the Cold war and the war in Korea were at their peak. Therefore, the steps taken by the Soviet Union, and communist China alarmed the West in the Middle East. Given these, to a certain extent, the threat perception of the US about the communist designs worked to Britain's advantage. As a result, the Anglo-American cooperation in the region continued for the time being. Washington became convinced that the British military presence at the Suez base was vital to Western global strategy.[44]

Another unpleasant development for the Nasser's new regime occurred when he failed to secure the support of Ankara. As will be discussed below, indeed, the years 1952–1958 witnessed a serious freze in Turco–Egyptian relations which inevitably had negative effects on the general attempts of the US and the UK. Nasser recalled the background of this episode first in 1958 on the occasion of the visit of a Turkish delagation headed by Turkish Minister of Commerce Abdullah Aker to a commerce fair in Cairo. Prior to the departure of Turkish delegation, Prime Minister Menderes had instructed diplomat Oğuz Gökmen to convey his greetings to Nasser while expressing his remarks in an attempt to mend relations between the countries He said:

> You know that in the past days we used to have different customs, when families were greater, living in the same home and the children of brothers came to earth under the same roof and raised. We and the Egypt are the members of a great family living in a mansion, like the children of brothers. . . . Later on when we were grown we found different friends and companion outside our mansion and in different neighbourhoods. . . . While joning them we had forgotten that we were the children of a family living in the same home and we are brothers. In my view, this is what should be regretted.

> We found the assurance of our security against the Soviet threat in joining the NATO . . . proceeded to become close friends and integrate with the West. Whereas Egypt became a friend of the Soviets, to start playing tip-cat with Syria over us. . . . We forgot that we are brothers. . . . Now, I think its time and turn. Turkey and Egypt may wish to keep the friends and companions they later made. But they should never forget that they are the brothers of the same big family and the noble members of the Islamic community. . . . If you find the ground and time right, convey Nasser my greetings and respect and talk to him in this way.

Though Turkish delegation was well received in Cairo, Nasser's invitation came only in the last minute when the delegation was about to leave for airport. However, this gave Oğuz Gökmen the opportunity to convey the message of Menderes to Nasser. Nasser, with a small smile on his face replied that:

> I am very grateful to Menderes, and for these words. We have never forgotten that we are brothers with Turks especially brothers of the same faith. Our generation raised with the ideals of Atatürk. Life of Atatürk and all those books on what he did were under our pillow. When we were in our school benches we used to ask ourselves how and when we could do what Atatürk did. And the day we waited for arrived, and after we sent Farouk off from Alexandria on his yacht *Mahrousa* with Naguib, we were on a jeep returning to Cairo and dead tired. We had not slept for the past three days. In this time we had even forgotten to eat and drink. While dreaming of having a shower and some rest, we said lets go to the Turkish Embassy. Have a cup of Turkish coffee to get refreshed and tell that after all these years, we did what Atatürk did at last. Whereas, what we had from the Turkish Ambassador was not the coffee but almost a slap on our face to bring us back to ourselves. The man received us as if we were bandits. We left the place hopeless and broken. We had failed to consider the Ambassador's closeness to the overthrown king, to make this point clearer, as to how this relativity could be employed to justify his manners. . . .

> We hoped that the Republic of Turkey would recall or change its Ambassador who is a relative to the former king, even your Ambassador who continued to act as an opponent to us would demand to leave the country himself and go. We waited for so long and neither this nor that happened. Whatever took place among us happened all due to this. However,now esteemed Menderes sent a distinguished delegation like yours to our fair, furthermore said "it is time to remember that we are brothers." Please tell him that I sincerely share the same views.[45]

Turkey's invitation for an Egyptian delegation headed by the Egyptian Minister of Commerce to İzmir International Fair was also accepted by Nasser. In August 1958, the Egyptian Minister of Commerce arrived in Turkey and because of the Turkish Minister of Foreign Affairs' being out of the country and the inadequacy of the Prime Minister's program, accepted by Celal Bayar, the President of the Republic of Turkey first. However, against a background of hopes vested in a chance of rapprochement between the two countries Bayar opened up a discussion with over-looking tones. As Gökmen stated:

> Celal Bayar was addressing to his interlocutor not as a particular Arab country but as 'you all Arabs' and adding that 'you are an ungrateful nation . . . despite all the service Turks did to the Islamic world Arabs always looked for an opportunity to betray. In their weak and busy moments they have always tried to hit them from the back. You are used to follow the order of whoever strong, whoever holds a whip in his hand' and so on and forth . . . it was a monologue getting extended and as such, getting tougher, giving his counterpart cold sweats visible on his temples. The Egyptian Minister of Commerce, having believed that no self-defence would have any use, was seeing that nothing could be done except waiting for this extremely painstaking visit end at once.

> Celal Bayar was telling historical incidents, mentioning Atatürk and through narrating the similar views and statements of the past and historic famous personalities, was wishing to strengthen and improve his anti-Arab thesis. At last, this long and heavyhearted interview came to an end without causing another sad circumstance.[46]

While the visiting Minister was still in Ankara, in a last attempt to prevent another crisis, he was also brought together with the Turkish Prime Minister and the Minister of Foreign Affairs, but to no avail. The thaw in the Turco–Eygptian relations in 1958 was destined to short live.

It appears that the crisis in Turco–Egyptian relations had unfolded with events following the very first encounter of Nasser, Naguib and the Turkish Ambassador in the aftermath of the military takeover of July 23, 1952. Dikerdem maintains that thanks to the efforts of the Military Attaché of the Egyptian Embassy in Ankara who had close friends in the Egyptian Revolutionary Council and who expressed the Turkish Ambassador in Cairo, Hulusi Fuat Tugay that he could bring along the members of the Revolutionary Council to the Embassy,Tugay hosted a dinner for the Council. The dinner was the first invitation extended by an embassy and accepted by Nasser. It was a time, the Revolutionary Council was carrying on tough negotiations with the London Government with the aim of ensuring the British withdrawal from the Suez Canal and the full sovereignty of Egypt.

However, the dinner would not be a quiet occasion. Following the dinner, the guests were taken to the terrace of the Embassy and conversations on political issues started. Then:

The Ambassador Tugay was suggesting the revolutionary officers to compromise with the English: the English had mighty forces at the Suez Canal, they could completely destroy Cairo the moment they wished. Besides, without the help of the English and its allies, the new regime would be unable to find remedies to its economic difficulties. In short, it was required to act wisely and not to enrage the English. This words were like a cold shower for the young officers. They were advancing that they knew the strength and weaknesses of the English better as a result of their experiences of long years of occupation, and they would fight till the last drop of their blood if it takes. In short both parties left that night utterly discontent with each other. The most interesting aspect of this unfortunate occasion was Ankara's approval of our Ambassador's harsh démarches to Nasser. I remember Ankara's message of congratulation to Tugay who, as being customary to do so, cabled his interview with the new leader of the Egypt without hiding anything. In return, the revolutionary government would give its first bad mark to our Ambassador on that night. Later on, this mark would get worse and every action of Tugay would be monitored by the Egyptian officers. Finally, on the day of ceremony for the proclamation of the Repuplic, when Tugay replied to the question of 'How did you find our new Republic?' by Hussein el-Shafei, a member of the Revolutionary Council who had approached him, 'Let me respond to you by the words of the mother of Napoleon: *Pourvu que cela dure—hopefully it will prevail*', the Turkish Ambassador would start turning into persona non grata.[47]

Indeed, there is evidence to suggest that Ambassador Tugay who was married to Princess Amina, (Amina was daughter of Princess Nimet who was sister of the former king Fuad, father of deported king Farouk) was embittered by the military takeover of young officers.

In one way or the other, the accumulation of incidents culminated in the increasing of negative publications in Egyptian press on Turkey and its Embassy. The news were alleging that Ambassador Tugay was interfering with the internal affairs of Egypt and the Embassy of the Republic of Turkey had become a niché for those conspiring against the regimé in Egypt. Meanwhile, things were going from bad to worse for the members of the Egyptian dynasty following the enactment of a new law concerning the confiscation of their properties which had not spared the wife of Ambassador Tugay.

As a result of the mounting crisis between Nasser and Tugay, the inevitable occured on the night of January 2, 1954 at the Opera House of

Cairo. As Dikerdem, who was then the First Secretary of the Turkish Embassy in Cairo stated, on that night "when Nasser, shaking hands with Ambassadors approached Ambassador Tugay and said 'hello,' Tugay, without extending his hand that he was keeping behind him, shook his finger towards the face of Nasser and told him, 'You didn't behave like a gentleman with your press attacks,' his words audible to other Ambassadors. Nasser, who was about to slap our Ambassador, preferred to turn his back and leave the room and unable to stay in the Opera house any longer with his furiousness, returned to his Office and convened the Revolutionary Council on that night immediately."[48]

Resultantly, Ambassador Tugay was declared persona non grata. However, neither Cairo, nor Ankara considered this unpleasant development as a stalemate. On the contrary, following the signing of the Suez Canal Base Agreement between the UK and Egypt on October 19, Menderes sent a message of congratulation to Nasser. Nasser's message in reply carried warm tones. When an assassination attempt made on Nasser in the same month, Menderes sent another message of sympathy to Nasser. Shortly afterwards, when Nasser's article name "Brother Turkey" was published in a journal published in Cairo, Menderes decided to send his personal message of invitation to Nasser conveyed by Kemal Aygün, the Governor of Ankara. In his message Menderes also mentioned his readiness to visit Cairo or meet in an impartial and friendly third country.

Nasser, caught by surprise with the ouverture of the Turkish Prime Minister, declined the invitation, however felt obliged to furnish Menderes with his reasons. He explained that the Egyptian public opinion was not ready for his meeting with the Turkish Prime Minister; two factors were labeling Turkey unsympathetic before the Egyptian public opinion, one of them was Turco–Israeli relations and the other was UK's, US', France's and Turkey's leading of the Middle Eastern Defence Pact and through paying no attention to these, his attempt to meet Menderes would draw a harsh reaction from the Egyptian nation. Thus, it was first required to prepare the public opinion for Turco–Egyptian friendship and towards this objective, instead of mutual visits of the statesmen, exchange of delegations of friendship and good intentions would be more right.[49]

It may be stated that behind the tension of Turco–Egyptian relations, although no reference was made then, surfacing bitter memories of "the fez incident" of October, 29, 1932 should have contributed to the political atmosphere of unrest in part. At the reception given on the occasion of the proclamation of the Republic on October 29, 1932, the fez of the Egyptian Ambassador was requested to be taken off by Atatürk. While the President of the Republic was extremely kind and tender to express his request after caressing the face of Ambassador like a father as he approached him, he was exceptionally determined in his words too.

The steps of the inevitable were in fact loud and clear. Prior to this incident, the Egyptian Ambassador, no doubt instructed by his king Fuad, descendant of the Egyptian Khedive who had semi-separated the country from the Ottoman Empire with his vicious tactics which employed European imperial powers too, was carrying his fez recklessly in various occasions. With these disturbing advances, Egypt was searching for a ground to declare its interest to occupy the power vacuum created by the retreat and the eventual fall of the Ottoman Empire.

The series of civic revolutions of Mustafa Kemal Atatürk had started with the revolution of dress code on November 25, 1925. Atatürk and his comrades, no doubt had seen the need for introducing western standards in place of existing confusion in the way in which masses are dressed. In the end, when the revolution was fully achieved in an amazingly fast period of time, it introduced a clear demarcation line between the Republic of Turkey and the former lands of the Ottoman Empire. Perhaps, contrary to Atatürk's expectations, conservative forces in the Middle Eastern countries developed a debate around the issue, though Ankara had not made an attempt "to export its revolution" to the region.

This being the case, importance of the issue of "headdress" should not be overlooked either. Throughout the history of Islamic societies the "headdress" acquired different statuses and shapes from a mere piece of dress safeguarding the head from sunlight to a symbol used by the Christians to render themselves unnoticeable within the larger society. The headdresses originated in one geography or a society and as such or with adoptions used in there and/or elsewhere. The fez was no different. The Khedive of Egypt had adopted it from Tunisia, while it was used in North Africa and seen even in Venice. Against this mixed background, towards the last quarter of the 19th century, facing the advances of colonialism, the fez emerged as the symbol of Muslims. Its this status was taken seriously and subjected to attacks of European imperial powers too. Meanwhile, from diplomats to others, those who used it in their countries opted for not using the fez in order not to make themselves subject to attacks.[50] Though, Atatürk's revolution of dress code of 1925 landed in such a controversy, its presentation as an instrument of reform for those who opted for it was unwaveringly continued.

Interestingly, Nasser's Arab socialism and the Turkish left had important commonalities without coming into direct contact. According to a view, the large-scale conversion of the Turkish bureaucracy and the intelligentsia to the left occurred gradually after 1954. In 1954, Democrats won a victory at the elections, and

> decided to speed up their development drive, based chiefly on an inflationary unplanned economic policy. Capital accumulation in private hands increased and inflation mounted, while salaries remained relatively stagnant. The dissatisfaction aroused provided the foundations of a new leftist movement not associated directly with marxism, as was the case for most earlier leftist endeavours. Furthermore, the new leftism was a response to domestic conditions, not a replica of a foreign ideology. As such it held the promise of taking shape in economic and social policies designed to broaden and modernize the Republic from within.[51]

Turning back to the US perception of regional events, in this transitional phase, the US government believed that the British presence in the Middle East had a stabilizing influence, avoiding a need of intervention by the US. The US would continue to be a strong supporter of any defence organization rather than becoming a direct participant in any emerging defence organization. This was in conformity with the fact that "it was still assumed that Britain would bear the burden of direct involvement."[52] However, the US Interdepartmental Committee on the Middle East took a more radical approach. On June 17, 1953, John Jernegan of the State Department noted that:

> To tie ourselves to the tail of the British kite in the Middle East . . . would be to abandon all hope of a peaceful alignment of that area with the West. Unless there is marked change in British Policy . . . the British and ourselves would be driven out completely or . . . we would have to maintain ourselves in the area by force at heavy material cost and even greater cost in terms of moral standing throughout the non-European world.[53]

Indeed, these words underlined the dual nature of US policy. Despite its references to the existence of cordial relations with Britain, the US had been accommodating a critical approach in its attitudes towards the

UK. The Eisenhower administration was clearly taking this line. The new US government fostered its Northern Tier project which had a principal concept that "the Middle Eastern defence would be assured by indigenous forces." Thus, as it will be discussed in the following section, at the beginning, the Americans rejected to commit themselves to form an organisation with the British.

This being the case, the beginning of the Eisenhower period did not introduce new policies regarding anti-communism. However, "in rhetoric more than in action, the new administration was obsessed with the need to prove how its policy differed from that of Truman."[54] Eisenhower and the new Secretary of State John Foster Dulles defined their approach to the Middle East as "friendly impartiality" towards both Israel and the Arab states, as distinct from the Truman's presidency. US policy, in their view should not be influenced by the pressures of the Zionists and personal preferences. In contrast, to maintain a balanced policy "the Arab interest would be upgraded, Israel would be looked after but downgraded."[55] Besides, the role of the US outside the Atlantic Alliance was revised. This introduced a US policy of evaluating the Alliance in areas outside the NATO on a "case by case" basis. Additionally, Dulles classically stated his notions against the spread of communism and also emphasized that the peace and the security of the free world would be ensured by the United States leadership.

As another feature of the American strategy, Eisenhower and Dulles still aimed to realize MEDO. Eisenhower and British Foreign Secretary Eden, agreed in March that MEDO remained a key objective. But, shortly afterwards, Dulles decided that MEDO could not be achieved. He considered that states north of Egypt would provide a more reliable basis for action. Since Turkey joined NATO in March 1952, "Pentagon officials had been considering the merits of a forward defense along the Turkish–Iranian–Pakistani frontier, but their ideas remained undeveloped until Dulles shifted the State Department's attention to the north in early 1953."[56]

In the spring of 1953, Dulles made his historical visits to six Arab countries in addition to Israel, Turkey and Pakistan. Prior to Dulles' expedition, on May 6, 1953, the Arab Foreign Ministers, following a meeting, had stated their support for Egypt, and called upon Britain to withdraw its forces from Egypt without any precondition.[57] On May 11, Dulles arrived in Cairo. Four days before his arrival in Cairo, he had received a confidential message from Winston Churchill, requesting the

US to suspend its military assistance to Egypt. Given this fact, Dulles had three fundamental purposes in his mind: first, the settlement of the Anglo–Egyptian dispute, second, the "Containment" of Soviet penetration to the region through a security pact, and thirdly, to realize an effective balance in US foreign policy in mediating the Arab–Israeli conflict. Whereas, Dulles had the impression that, many of the Arab peoples "are more fearful of Zionism than communism"[58] and "they were so enfulged in their quarrels with Great Britain and France that they paid little heed to the Soviet threat."[59]

Moreover, Dulles had reached the conclusion that "the heartland" of the Middle East was not ready for a military alliance centered on Egypt. Particularly in Egypt, he realized a strong opposition to foreign involvement. Previously, on January 16, 1953, the Egyptian President General Mohammad Naguib, had repeated the Egyptian aim of "driving foreign troops out of the Nile Valley unconditionally, and to liberate it from any kind of political, economic or social colonization."[60] What Dulles was faced was not different from these. The Egyptian statements included messages which required the US to revise its policies.

At the end of May 1953, having switched his attention on the Northern Tier project, Dulles returned from his mission.[61] He had also concluded that, an Arab–Israeli peace settlement was not possible in the existing conditions either. He stated the necessity of improving relations with Syria and Saudi Arabia and recommended Britain to conciliate with Egypt regarding the Suez Canal Base. He submitted a comprehensive report to Eisenhower, assessing the Anglo–Egyptian dispute and his personal analysis of it. He suggested that, "the United States must convince the British to relax their position."[62] His conclusion included some negative assertions as well, such as, "the days when the Middle East used to relax under the presence of British protection are gone" and "such British troops as are left in the area more a factor of instability rather than stability."[63] He recommended that US should act independently of British policies as well. The US had started to pursue a different pattern in relations with the Middle Eastern countries, specifically with Egypt.

Regarding Britain, "Churchill and Eden sought to stress their hand by bringing the United states directly into negotiations, but Nasser stubbornly resisted this, and both Eisenhower and Dulles refused to join the talks without Egyptian consent."[64] Indeed, there were outstanding differences of opinion between the British Foreign Minister, Eden and his American counterpart Dulles which surfaced with the latter's report. On a broader perspective, after his return to the US, Dulles wanted to re-solve the problems which prevented the realization of a Middle Eastern security pact. According to him, it had become evident that, rather than concentration on the Suez base, the defense of the area called for several bases in the Northern Tier. The Anglo–American political outlooks with their contradicting assumptions, thus, remained unchanged. In June 1954, Churchill and Eden visited Washington D.C. The talks held in Washing-ton were successful regarding Indochina and the latest Anglo–Egyptian negotiations. For the time being, the Anglo–American policies were once more coordinated in the Middle East.

By then, the Northern Tier defence grouping to include Iran, Iraq, Turkey, Pakistan and perhaps Syria appeared to be possible in the views of US policy makers, while, "the rest of the Middle East presented a pact-maker's nightmare."[65] Subsequently, it was announced that, an amount of $50 million would be allocated to Northern Tier states. Turkey's agreement to the Turco–Pakistani Pact, proposed by the US followed this. The US also considered the British position in enforcing the North-ern Tier plan to be significant. Correspondingly, British policies were also related to the renewal of existing Anglo–Iraqi Treaty due to expire in 1957. Therefore, the Northern Tier, linking the British presence in Iraq to the new US policy, presented a significance for Britain in this sense too.

In its turn, the Egyptian Revolutionary Command Council felt un-able to firmly stand against the new joint Anglo–American policy. In some respects, the time had come by February 1954 for the Egyptian military to pronounce its further political intentions. However, General Naguib's resignation on February 25, following his disagreement with RCC members over matters of policy and the allocation of authority alarmed some of the army officers and indicated that the ranks of the RCC were divided. The Cavalry Corps officers commanded by Major Khaled Muhieddin led a demonstration in favour of Naguib and subse-quently Nasser himself, held a talk with those officers. As a result, Naguib was brought back to the Premiership three days later.

The incident encouraged disaffected political groups (primarily the Wafdists, socialists, communists, Muslim Brotherhood) to increase their courting of General Naguib. In the meantime, the RCC appointed Nasser Military Governor of Egypt. Facing such attempts, Nasser gradually employed tactics to disarm his enemies. By March of that year, he an-nounced a decision to restore the parliamentary formations, and ordered the release of certain political prisoners. Lured by the RCC's relaxation of suppressive measures, the civilian political forces together with the loyal Free Officers, launched the Liberation Rally, controlled by Secretary-General Nasser. The demonstrations of March 25–27 in Cairo and Alexandria and the ensuing general strike in some public services, combined with the protest of Free Officers against the proposed relinquishing of authority by the RCC. On March 28, the RCC announced the indefinite cancellation of the proposed June elections for a constituent assembly, and ousted General Naguib from the Premiership. On the other hand, the removal of Naguib and the victory of Nasser did not lead to a more stable political atmosphere in Egypt in the short run.

While the RCC retained Naguib as symbolic President of the Republic to placate public sentiment as well as Sudanese feelings (Naguib was half Sudanese) it tried to restore its influence in the country. However, Nasser was determined to gain the absolute control and on April 15, issued a decree in the name of the RCC depriving all those Wafdists, Liberal Constitutionalists, and Saadists who held various cabinet posts between 1942 and 1952, of their political rights for ten years. His cabinet of April 18 featured most of the Free Officers loyal to him.[66]

Turning back to discussion around the Northern Tier, Nasser was alarmed with the Turco–Iraqi rapprochement as he perceived it to be against his own interest. Hence, he had every reason to oppose the Northern Tier's transformation into the Baghdad Pact. Nasser did not share Dulles' anti-communism nor see the Soviets as a threat to his people or the rest of the Arab world. He was primarily preoccupied with the Israeli reprisal raids, "and the Zionist enemy just across the Canal."[67] Moreover, the Americans had rejected the requests of Nasser to purchase weaponry for his forces because Churchill had intervened personally with Eisenhower. At Dulles' mediatory attempts, the British had delivered sixteen Centurion tanks to Cairo as part of a shipment the Egyptians had already paid for, "but were holding back the rest as a carrot with which to tempt Nasser into the Baghdad Pact."[68] But, this strategy never worked to desired ends. Instead, Nasser choose to sent out negotiators to buy arms in Belgium, Switzerland, and Holland, with meager results.

When the British approach to Iraq became apparent, Nasser launched his counter diplomacy. First, he sent his Minister of Guidance, Salah Salem, on a tour of Arab states in the summer of 1954. At this stage, rather than trying to overthrow his opponent, Iraqi Premier, Nuri As-Said, Nasser was looking for ways to improve Egypt's relations with

Iraq which had been unfriendly since As-Said's, "Fertile Crescent" scheme had been ditched in the early 1940s in favour of an Arab League centered on Cairo. In his negotiations with Nuri As-Said, King Feisal and the Crown Prince Abdullah, at Sarsank, Salem before all emphasized Egypt's opposition to Iraq's getting involved with NATO. He stated Egyptian Government's anxieties concerning the promotion of a common Arab League policy. In reality, he insisted that it would be advisable not to get "entangled in any foreign commitments."[69] He put forward that this would also prevent the West from playing one Arab state against another.

As-Said's objection was based on his perception of the communist threat. In his turn, Salem replied that engaging in foreign pacts would be the strongest invitation to communism. He further argued that should Iraq be engaged in such pacts, nationalists would also resent this "subservience to imperialism."[70] Facing the determination of As-Said, Salem raised another issue. He stated that as the proposed pact would link Iraq with NATO and since Iraq was a member of the Arab League, it was the assumption of Nasser that this would put the League's neutrality at risk. He made his point that such an irresponsible engagement, in any unpredictable circumstance could involve the League's members in NATO's disputes should Iraq get involved.

On the contrary, Iraqi Premier saw every reason to join this British initiative. Certainly, by consenting to Britain's proposal, Iraq would obtain large quantities of arms supplies. Apparently, this embittered Nasser even more. He was rather disturbed that Iraq, which strengthened its military arsenal, added to its rich oil reserves, "would become the predominant Arab power and in consequence the center of political gravity in the Middle East would shift from Cairo to Baghdad."[71]

Nasser considered that Britain, having been forced to abandon its bases in Egypt was trying "to stage a re-entry on the Arab scene via Iraq."[72] In contrast to Nasser's expectations, when it came to a joint statement, Nuri As-Said outwitted Salem. Salem returned to Cairo with a statement expressing that Egypt and Iraq would examine the ways of strengthening the Arab League and would hold talks with the US and Britain to this end. However, Nasser was even more disturbed that Salem should have given his acknowledgement to the idea that Iraq and Egypt should consult the West about the Arab League. He further argued that such an approach would further weaken the League by "encouraging the imperialists to prolong and strengthen their grip on the Arabs to play them off against each other."[73]

Despite the fact that British considerations on the Suez Canal Base to be held as the pivot of Britain's Middle Eastern position had been its main strategy for more than a half century, on an account of recent developments in Egypt, British Foreign Minister, Eden, decided to shift Britain's strategic Middle Eastern center from Cairo to Baghdad and Amman. Hence, forces were deployed to Libya, Jordan, Cyprus and Aden.[74] Meanwhile, the US enlarged its already outstanding nuclear arsenal with the inclusion of the Hydrogen Bomb. When the deployment of allied forces in Cyprus, Libya, the Persian Gulf and in Jordan was negotiated in Washington in December 1953, this had also comprised the stocking of military equipment in southern Turkey to support Middle Eastern defence. Following the changes in war technology, the positioning of nuclear weaponry was also planned.

Against this background, the Anglo–Egyptian Treaty, regulating the maintenance of Suez Canal Base with civilian technicians was ratified on July 27, 1954. When the UK agreed, through the mediatory efforts of the US, to start withdrawing its garrison of eighty thousand troops from the Suez Canal Base, Churchill asked Dulles why he was so interested in to ensure such an agreement in favour of the RCC of Egypt. Dulles told Churchill that, "it will restore Egyptian pride and strengthen the Egyptian position, so that she can in future play a leading role in the Middle East."[75] Churchill replied that, "Anything in which Egypt plays a leading role, means trouble."[76] From the statement of Dulles, it can be understood that, the US Secretary of State was still considering to include Egypt in the new security organisation in one way or another. But, the US' rejection of Egyptian arms requests, combined with Nasser's increasing anxieties that the Zionist enemy just across the Canal might endanger his regime, were the essential factors which remained unchanged leading to Egypt's opposition against the new military formation.

In the meantime, the US had extended its military aid to Iraq by April 1954. Surprisingly, about the US military aid to Pakistan within the Middle Eastern Defense scheme, a Memorandum dated January 5, 1954 by the British Foreign Secretary stated that

> The US Ambassador in Ankara has told the Turkish Government of the proposed military aid for Pakistan and suggested that the Turks should propose military conversations to Pakistan. What is suggested is not a treaty of alliance, but some form of joint planning in which other Middle Eastern states particularly Iraq and eventually Persia,

might later take part but from which the United states and other Western powers would be excluded. . . . The Turkish Prime Minister's initial reaction to this suggestion is understood to have been favourable.[77]

Interestingly, at first the British Foreign Secretary was doubtful whether the State Department's project would have useful or practical results, given the Middle Eastern countries' perception of the role of Western states in the defense of the area.[78] In fact, this was related to the British efforts for the renewal of the Anglo–Egyptian Suez Canal Agreement. Having granted the top priority to accomplish this, British policy makers would not welcome any other option to divert the attention from their desire for a lasting presence over the Suez.

In this forum, although the Northern Tier was basically the creation of Dulles, oddly, when Turkey and Pakistan (which were the countries receiving US aid) stated their plan to form a pact, the US decided not to join the new alliance for the time being. In another perspective, the US was already committed to the security of Turkey through NATO.[79] Additionally, it continued to provide support for the enhancement of Britain's regional role. On April 2, 1954, Turkey and Pakistan signed the above mentioned military pact. In September, Pakistan joined the the Southeast Asia Collective Defense Treaty, playing another role in the military umbrella that the US created from Europe to the Far East.[80]

As for Iran, after the assassination of Prime Minister Razmara by Fada'iyan-i Islam, a religious extremist group which aimed at nationalizing the Anglo–Iranian Oil Company (AIOC), peaceful settlement of the dispute between Britain and this country was jeopardized. The Four Point introduced by Razmara comprised a ten-year Iranization program for the AIOC, and his moderation was favourable to the US. However, the open support that Razmara had given the company had discredited him in the public eye, and he was accused by the press of being a "British stooge."[81] The Shah, also could not prevent the failure of the AIOC, which came upon the assassination of Razmara. With Razmara's death, resistance to Dr. Mohammad Mosaddeq and the National Front collapsed. In expressing the common points with Britain, the US found the nationalization of oil concessions as distasteful as Britain had. As the US had experienced this in Mexico, its companies had much suffered from the nationalization of its companies.

Britain had agreed with the US suggestion of a fifty–fifty profit sharing model, but did not leave any room for nationalization. The basic difference between the policies of the US and UK over nationalization prevailed here. The US notion had been based on the acceptance of the UK for greater control of Iran in the AIOC, which would allow Iran to obtain increased benefits from its petroleum. Looking back to the period 1951–53, in the years when Mosaddeq was in power, US had pursued a policy without any close interaction as well. However, the US policy which kept itself distant from the Anglo–Iranian dispute failed. In the next three years, the nationalist government attacked the AIOC, and eventually the Shah was forced to leave the country. A senior State Department official reminisced:

> our lack of trust both in motives and abilities, and fear of offending the British who considered him [Mosaddeq] an enemy kept us from any close association. . . . Unable to perceive any alternative to the Shah, whether we wanted or not, we seemed destined to support him—blindly and on his terms—until we both went down in Iran together.[82]

In view of a stalemate on negotiations, the Iranian Prime Minister, Mohammad Mosaddeq had led the Iranian nationalists and nationalized the Anglo–Iranian Oil Company. In 1953, the overthrown of Mosaddeq by the CIA, can be evaluated as the first significant incident that indicated the Anglo–American sensitivity against the violation of joint assets.

However, when an Anglo–American Agreement was reached on the proposals to President Naguib of Egypt on the Suez Canal base, despite the still fresh memory of Britain's disputes with Mosaddeq, again some differences in policies pursued by the US and UK surfaced as:

> The US Embassy in Cairo, supported by the State Department, now argued that the points of package agreed in January between Byroade and British officials were not interdependent. The US might push Britain into a settlement on the Suez Canal, this without ensuring Egypt's commitment to the Middle Eastern Defense Organization.[83]

The British, once they concluded the Canal Zone Agreement with Nasser in October 1954, "hoped to be friends with everyone in a westward facing Middle East."[84] In part, due to Eden's evaluations of the half-hearted Egyptian approval for an agreement over the Suez Canal was followed by Eden's two initiatives. One of them was based on the Northern Tier idea presented by Dulles. Considering this, Foreign Office planned that, Egypt's self-exclusion would be based on the Northern Tier plan.[85] Secondly, it was aimed to reach a solution to the "Palestine problem." This was built on the talks of the British Minister of State for Foreign Affairs, Anthony Nutting with Nasser at the Nile Dam concerning future bilateral relations in the context of NECMU—The New Era of Cooperation and Mutual Understanding.[86]

The first initiative was evolved in the Baghdad Pact, and the second became to be known as ALPHA project, which was a secret plan.[87] At this juncture, these policies appeared to be contrary to each other. Truly, the Baghdad Pact as will be further discussed, in effect excluded Egypt, whereas ALPHA was concerned with ensuring Egyptian involvement in seeking a solution to the Arab–Israeli problem. Others, however, argue to the contrary, and correlate the ALPHA Project with the Baghdad Pact. For instance, Nigel Ashton stated that, if Arab–Israeli tensions could be defused, the Arab states might be prepared to turn their attention outwards and join "a renewed Nothern Tier Pact."[88] Eventually, by the beginning of 1955, Henry Byroade was appointed Ambassador to the American Embassy in Cairo (replacing Jefferson Caffery), along with launching the ALPHA project.

Regarding Egypt, when a member of the Muslim Brotherhood tried to assassinate Nasser in Alexandria on October 26, 1954, Nasser moved to mollify the organisation completely. The trial of the assassins in November implicated Naguib. He was removed from his office and placed under house arrest. Having crushed the influence of the Muslim Brotherhood and with the elimination of Naguib, Nasser became able to appoint trusted officers in key positions. "Within the RCC and the Free Officers group, personal loyalty to Nasser soon became the criterion for political longevity."[89]

Dulles' expectation that he might succeed to establish stronger links between the Northern Tier and the Arab League led to him to take another step. To this end, he decided that the US should promote the Military Defence Assistance Act (MDAA). In the beginning, within the context of MDAA, Americans indicated an enthusiasm to send military advisers and an uncertain number of troops. Nasser stressed that this was not acceptable after the agreement that brought an end to British occupation. It can be stated that the practical situation was against his assumptions, regarding the fact that, Egypt was receiving US aid and the CIA was training Egyptian officers.

With regard to Anglo–Egyptian relations, despite the renewed Anglo–Egyptian Treaty, British relations with Egypt were deteriorating. The reason behind this was Nasser's principal rejection of the presence of foreign troops in Egypt. In response to US pressure for military cooperation, Nasser stated the pre-condition of an Arab–Israeli settlement. He also stressed his view that the Unified Arab Command should be established without any foreign influence. Given these, it can be concluded that at this juncture, Nasser intensified his opposition to eradicate Western influence in the region and Iraq's inclination to the Baghdad Pact under the Anglophile As-Said's regime against the joint Anglo–American initiatives.

The Establishment of the Baghdad Pact: "An Illustration of Collaborative Policy at Its Best"[90]

The September 1954 elections in Iraq had brought back to power the Anglophile Nuri As-Said. Iraqi Prime Minister's first aim was to renew the Anglo–Iraqi Treaty. This was rather favourable to Britain as it was in search of an agreement to replace the existing treaty due to expire in 1957. With this in mind, the Turkish–Iraqi Defence Pact, going beyond the formal general staff conversations and the decision to provide free transit of military equipment was of significance for the British and American policy makers. In early January 1955, the Turkish Prime Minister Adnan Menderes arrived in Baghdad with a large group of delegation which included his Foreign and Communications Ministers and nine members of the Turkish Grand National Assembly. A couple of days later, on 13 January, a Communiqué was issued which proclaimed that Iraq and Turkey had agreed to sign a mutual defense pact and they hoped "other like-minded states" in the area would join them and they would also make "every endeavour to persuade the states to sign the treaty simultaneously with them."[91]

While the Turkish Prime Minister was in Baghdad, pan-Arab newspapers[92] in other Arab countries tried to hamper the talks, this time, truly from a very unconstructive point, urging that the precondition of any understanding with Turkey should be a settlement of the question of the Sanjak of Alexandretta—İskenderun—and of the Hatay province which were annexed by Turkey from Syria in 1939 through a plebiscite. On the Sanjak of Hatay (where the main city and bay is İskenderun) which had acquired a special regime of local autonomy under the French Mandate for Syria, various agreements between Turkey and France had previously been made, the most recent being in July 1938, with the Franco–Turkish Treaty of Friendship. Additionally, the breaking of economic relations between Turkey and Israel was demanded.

When, on January 13, the above mentioned Turco–Iraqi Communiqué announced the two governments' proceeding towards a defense pact, there was an immediate reaction in Egypt. The Egyptian Foreign Minister protested that the Egyptian government had not been informed and that Iraq's action violated the "spirit" of the Arab League. Besides, the Egyptian government controlled journal *Al-Gumhuriyya* began a series of personal attacks on Nuri As-Said. Replying to this, the Iraqi Ambassadors in Egypt and Lebanon expressed to the correspondents that, the pact with Turkey would not be brought to existence without consulting the other Arab countries.

Certainly, for Iraq, it was gaining importance to justify to the Arab states that its recent actions were not in violation of the interests of the Arab League. In this framework, some cynically, but not convincingly, the Iraqi Director-General of National Orientation, tried to make a point that Egypt had not kept the other Arab states informed on its recent negotiations with Britain.

In this context, severe radio attacks from Radio Cairo increased. Subsequently, an Egyptian official of the Radio Cairo was expelled from Iraq and tensions remained high. In effect, the Egyptian campaign was counter-productive and in consequence, As-Said's policy gained additional support within the Iraqi and Syrian political circles. A respected, elder statesman, Tawfiq As-Suwaidi and As-Said's long standing political opponent Saleh Jabr supported the Iraqi Prime Minister.[93] As for the Turkish efforts to include other regional countries in their initiative with Iraq, on January 14, Turkish Prime Minister Adnan Menderes and his delegation visited Damascus to draw Syria into the Pact. But, the talks were fruitless.

Against a background of Egyptian generated opposition, the British view was highly in favour of the Turkish–Iraqi Pact. On January 14, 1955, Eden wrote As-Said that he was "much encouraged" by the Turkish–Iraqi announcement. This left little doubt at Baghdad that Eden expected an Anglo–Iraqi arrangement to follow the Turkish–Iraqi agreement. Michael Wright, the British Ambassador in Baghdad, also advised Eden that an Anglo–Iraqi treaty under cover of the Turkish–Iraqi Pact was possible to secure.[94]

Nutting stated that this was even worse than Nasser had feared. The reasons for Nasser's disturbance were because, "not only Iraq was to form with Turkey the nucleus of a multilateral alliance with Britain which would link her with NATO; she was also going to canvass other Arab states to join as well."[95] On February 20, 1955, Eden visiting Cairo, met Nasser for the first and only time. Following the exchanges of congratulations over the new Anglo–Egyptian Treaty, Eden shifted to discuss Egyptian–Iraqi relations and the Turkish–Iraqi Pact. Eden's impressions of Nasser (which he reported to Churchill on his arrival in London) can also explain some of the reasons behind Nasser's disturbance of the Turkish–Iraqi Pact: "I was impressed by Nasser, who seemed forthright and friendly although not open to conviction on the Turkish–Iraqi Pact. No doubt jealousy plays a part in this, and a frustrated desire to lead the Arab world."[96]

The other fundamental cause for Nasser's resentment was explained as related to his humiliation by the Western powers. Indeed, "the West was anchoring its Middle Eastern Policy in Nuri-el Said and the Hashemite rulers of Iraq, who were rivals of him for Arab leadership."[97] It was also underlined that the Arab dimension of Nasser's policy emerged after the Baghdad Pact.[98]

In his statement to the UN Chamber of Deputies on February 6, 1955, the Iraqi representative Dr. Fadhil Jamali clarified the legal aspects of the Baghdad Pact which he had also previously expressed in his talks in Cairo. Jamali stated that any Arab country might conclude a treaty in accordance with Article II of the Arab Collective Security Pact, and Article VII and paragraph 2 of Article X of the Arab League Charter stipulated that any country might conclude a special agreement without committing the other countries.[99]

On February 15, the Foreign Office without waiting for Cabinet's authorisation, informed Iraq and Turkey that Britain was prepared to accede to the Pact. When Eden stopped off in Cairo on the same day on his way to a conference in Bangkok of the South-East Asia Treaty Organisation, Nasser made his ambitions for the leadership of the Arab world explicit. Eden stated in his memoirs that Nasser was not open to conviction on the Turco–Iraqi enterprise. He indicated that Nasser considered the pact ill-timed and one which would seriously impair effective cooperation between the West and the Arab world. Concerning his attacks on Nuri As-Said, Nasser, "rather naively asserted that, they were an internal Arab affair and needed therefore be no concern of the British."[100]

With this confirmation of the adverse Egyptian attitude, Britain decided to extend its full support to the Iraqi Government. Eden stated that Nuri As-Said was Britain's ally and attacks on him could not be ignored as a mere internecine quarrel between Arabs. He further emphasized that, although the timing of the new pact might be unfortunate for Egypt, it was essential for Britain. It was no surprise that this was followed by Eden's unavoidable obligation to leave Egypt out of the proposed pact.

A few days after Eden's talks with Nasser in Cairo, Anglo–Iraqi military talks on British requirements in Iraq were concluded with success, on February 22, two days before the finalization of the Turco–Iraqi Pact. In its talks with Britain, Iraq aimed to get the British to terminate the 1930 Anglo–Iraqi Treaty. This was agreed by Britain, if Iraq joined an open-ended collective security pact with Turkey.[101]

On the same day, the Egyptian government convened an extraordinary meeting of the Arab League Prime Ministers in Cairo. The Prime Ministers of Syria, Lebanon, Saudi Arabia, Jordan, Yemen and Libya were assembled without Nuri As-Said and his Foreign Minister, both of whom pleaded illness, but were refused a postponement by Nasser. Here, Nasser had Saudi Arabia, a rich and influential ally, that had currently engaged in a dispute with Britain over the possession of the Buraimi Oasis, on the fringes of the British-protected Trucial Sheikhdoms. Basically, since King Saud's father, Abdulaziz Ibn Saud, the founder of the kingdom had evicted Sharif Hussein from the Hejaz in 1924 and annexed this territory to Saudi Arabia, he and his dynasty were the enemies of the Hashemites. Thirty years later, Ibn Saud's successors had been still carrying on the vendetta against the grandson of Sharif, Feisal of Iraq and Hussein of Jordan.

This time, backed by the Saudis, in the first days of the meeting Nasser managed to control the reactions of League's members. Therefore, the Iraqi action was generally blamed. In the meantime, *Al-Gumhuriyya* continued its attacks on the Iraqi government for having become the "ally of Israel."[102] The Iraqis were not represented for the first five days and when they finally appeared on the scene they were led by a former Prime Minister, Fadhil Jamali, "who was pathologically anti-Egyptian."[103]

At the meeting, certain divisions of opinion among the League members surfaced as well. Syrian representative Fares el-Khoury had opened the meeting with a "pedantic" statement that whilst they would not join any foreign alliance, it would be pointless for them to oppose the Iraqi government for doing so, since such a decision would not bind any future Syrian government.[104] In Syria, there was an apparent tension between the conservatist People's Party who favoured a union with Iraq and the Baath Party's adherents who desired a broad Arab union. Therefore, Fares el-Khoury felt obliged to disclaim any intention of joining As-Said's alliance and in order not to frustrate the People's party he rejected to condemn Iraq. It was clear that, Nasser's efforts were not adequate to influence Syrian public opinion. Besides, his regime was disgraced in socio-political circles dominated by the Muslim Brotherhood by his Arab socialist standpoint which was further fueled by the execution of the Brotherhood leaders associated with the Alexandria assassination attempt.

To the disappointment of Nasser, the Jordanians also advanced the view that though they disliked the pacts with the foreigners, they were placed in difficulty to condemn Nuri As-Said's alliance since they depended on Britain's subsidies regarding the needs of the Arab Legion. Moreover, just a few weeks ago, a Jordanian delegation had held discussions in London about the revision of the Anglo–Jordanian treaty. Here, the British had set a condition that any changes in the treaty could only be considered as part of a new defense system in the Middle East. In other words, in return for British subsidies, Jordan would have to join the Turco–Iraqi Pact.

Nor were Syria and Jordan alone in their ambivalences. Lebanon too was under some pressure to join the Turco–Iraqi Pact. The Lebanese delegation to the Cairo pointed out that the Turkish Prime Minister Menderes had, on leaving Baghdad, called in at Beirut "to dangle before them the considerable advantages which Lebanon would enjoy if she joined the Turco–Iraqi alliance."[105] Turkey, so Menderes had said, had an army of ten divisions with the newest equipment and there were now 50,000 tractors working on the land, all provided by the US. Menderes had also stated that Turkey would support the Arabs against Israel if they agreed to sign up with him and Nuri As-Said. Certainly, the Lebanese pro-Western President Camille Chamoun was impressed by these statements. Perhaps, as a result of his political convictions, Chamoun also considered that Turkey should be encouraged to side with the Arabs in their conflict with Israel and this emerging scheme of pro-Western grouping of states could allow this to happen.

Though the arguments of the Syrians, Jordanians and the Lebanese mentioned above made a considerable impact on the meeting as a whole, "they failed to convert those who had already spoken against condemning Nuri who, they believed, had special problems arising from Iraq's more exposed situation and who should therefore be allowed to make whatever arrangements he thought necessary for his security."[106] Whereas, in the end, Nasser succeeded in fostering his idea that Nuri As-Said had rejected suspension of his talks with the Turks to enable any alternative to be worked out which would strengthen the Arabs. To his disappointment, the Lebanese joined the Syrians and the Jordanians in declining to censure the Iraqi initiative. Then, Nasser had no other alternative policy to offer. In one of the last moments he suggested that Arab League security arrangements should be strengthened through forming a joint military command which could coordinate training and manufacture of arms and supplies.

When Fadhıl Jamali stated that Iraq might join in these arrangements, but it must still retain its right to enter into whatever foreign alliances it deemed necessary, Nasser withdrew his proposal, "acidly remarking that if the Iraqi reservation were accepted, the joint command would extend the Arab League's commitments further than ever. . . ." Eventually, at the request of the Premiers of the Arab League, Nasser consented to receive an Iraqi delegation deputizing for Nuri, which took its seat on January 27, whereas, it was argued that there was still a good deal of doubt and hesitation prevailing at the Conference.[107] Regarding the Turkish Government which urged Egypt to put considerations of regional defence in the Cold War before national "amour-propre," Ankara was constrained to deny reports emanating from Cairo that it would conclude a military pact with Israel.

On February 24, 1955, Turkey and Iraq signed the Mutual Cooperation Pact which was opened to all members of the Arab League and states "concerned with peace and stability in the Middle East."[108] The United Kingdom adhered to this agreement on April 4, 1955 and terminated the Anglo–Iraqi Treaty of 1930. On April 5, 1955, Britain's formal accession turned the Turco–Iraqi Pact into the Baghdad Pact.

Iraq's inclusion in this pact as the only Arab country increased the verbal attacks of Nasser. The Egyptian President blamed Iraq of betraying Arab unity.[109] Nasser's Egypt and Nuri As-Said's Iraq, with the former standing against the Baghdad Pact and with the latter's commitment to join the Baghdad Pact and to draw other Arab countries into it, became the orbits of intra-Arab rival policies. Iraq had been generally opposing the alleged Egyptian domination of the Arab League. This being the case, Iraq's participation in the Baghdad Pact was explained as the illustration of differences between the two countries.[110] The League's policy assiduously promoted by Egypt, as one of non-cooperation with the West until the Arab national objectives had been realised, placed Iraq and Egypt in opposite camps.

It was explained that though the principal objective of the Baghdad Pact was to include all the Middle Eastern countries, in all reality, the pact divided the region into three groups of states in which, Iraq, Pakistan and Iran formed the first group as the Baghdad Pact states. The opponents of the Pact; Egypt, Syria, Yemen and Saudi Arabia formed a second grouping of states, and Jordan together with Lebanon, remained in a third group which was excluded from these two.[111] Actually, when Britain and United States shifted their emphasis to the Northern Tier project and subsequently "fathered" the Baghdad Pact, in its turn, the Arab League Council took the official stand that the Arab Collective Security Pact was adequate for Arab policy and no member of the Arab League should become a party to an agreement with a Western state that was likely to affect the sovereignty and independence of Arab League member states.

In fact, Nasser's strong arguments had affected the anti-Hashemite Saudis and their Yemeni neighbours. He had also suggested that the Arab League security arrangements should be strengthened by the creation of a joint military command. Vaguely, it was put forward that, this structure would coordinate training, communication and the manufacture of weapons. It would also decide members' peace-time contribution to socio-economic projects and the extent of their commitment in time of war. But, as it was mentioned before, Iraqi representative Jamali had wrecked this proposal by insisting that the Iraqi Government would reserve its right to conclude foreign alliances even it might join an Arab Unified Command. Ultimately, Nasser had withdrawn his proposal, and no binding decision was taken.

As regards the Soviets, at this time Nikita Khrushchev had just emerged as the Premier of the Soviet collective leadership. His attention was diverted to West Germany which had been rearmed—adding to the strength of NATO. Therefore, he had no time for concentrating on what had been taking place in the Middle East. In this context, Dulles and Eden could comfortably contemplate the prospect of Middle Eastern countries, in due course, subscribing to the Baghdad Pact. But only four days after signing of the Baghdad Pact, an event occurred that could shatter all the hopes invested in this new organisation.

On February 28, Israeli and Egyptian forces clashed in Gaza. This changed the priorities of Nasser's regime, reminding the Arab world of the case of Palestinian refugees. This was a significant issue to chew over regarding his ambitions for the leadership of the Arab world. Moreover, his fears of military weakness surfaced with this incident.[112] In fact, while the Israelis claimed that they had been attacked first, and this was the latest of a series of clashes in this area, it was difficult not to connect the incident to the Egyptian hanging of the two Jews a month before.[113]

Nasser and Israeli Foreign Minister, Moshe Sharett, had held covert negotiations between 1952 and 1955. These included talks with third parties. But, the tension always remained and sometimes increased, due to the Israeli reprisals. Major raids of varying intensity throughout 1954, weakened the chance for peaceful settlement. And finally, Ben Gurion's succession to the Ministry of Defence broke the talks with Egypt. Nasser also shifted his policies by supporting the "fedayeen" attacks against Israel. In analysing the outcomes of the attacks of February 1955 on the Gaza Strip, it can be stated that, regardless of the reasons behind them, Israeli attacks which were launched a few days after the signing of the Turco–Iraqi Pact, seriously jeopardized the stability of the Middle East. Moreover, the Egyptian propaganda hastened to argue that the Israeli attack had been encouraged by the disunity "caused" by the Turco–Iraqi Pact, or was even instigated by the US and Britain as they pressed the Arab States to accede to that pact.[114]

Explicitly, Nasser's defeat in Gaza led him to assume that he was under Western pressure forcing Egypt to participate in the Baghdad Pact contrary to his desire for an Egypt free from any foreign interference especially that of British. In any terms, his scepticism dramatically increased. In addition to this, his rivalry with Iraq drove him to determine that he must not appear weak, nor submit to any Israeli threat.[115] Nasser considered that, his prestige as the leading figure in the Arab world against Nuri As-Said would be damaged if he showed compromise after this destructive raid. To make the situation more serious for the Anglo–American policy makers, a rather complicated behaviour was to be adopted by Nasser. "Nasser was now bent upon using Arab unity under his leadership as leverage to gain more concessions from the West and Israel."[116]

In fact, for its own reasons, Israel as well as Egypt was opposing the Baghdad Pact. Based on risks involved, Israel apparently feared that if British efforts succeeded in turning the pact into a Middle Eastern asset controlled by Britain, traditionally no friend of Israel's, then the Jewish state would be surrounded by a unified enemy.[117] In the comment by the Israeli Foreign Ministry dated on February 26, 1955 on the signature of the Turco-Iraqi Pact, it was stated that:

> the letter signed by the Iraqi Premier, and endorsed by the Turkish Premier, states that this new pact is designed to meet aggression from any direction. The letter also says, continuing the same passage, that, in order to protect peace and security in the Middle East, the two parties agree to co-operate to ensure the implementation of the UN resolutions. This letter's hostility towards Israel, which is an integral aspect of the alliance, is obvious to anybody. This new alliance must encourage aggressive ideas and tendencies of hostility to Israel, and, in this way will serve to undermine stability and internal security in the Middle East.[118]

Eventually, the Israeli opposition would drag the US into a dilemma, as it would see the urgent need of backing the Baghdad Pact against Soviet expansion into the Middle East, whilst it wanted to maintain its friendly relations with Israel. Another reason for the Israeli disturbance was the transfer of weapons to Iraq within the framework of the Baghdad Pact. Admittedly, a far-sighted evaluation had been made on a probable change in the Iraqi administration which could result in Iraq's leaving collaboration with the West, since armaments might be used against Israel. Lastly, with the Israeli impressions of the Baghdad Pact being committed to the Arab point of view, it was regarded as a serious failure. Evron took a more radical approach. He stated that, "The Baghdad Pact, instead of creating a barrier against Soviet penetration and aggression 'invited' such penetration and precipitated the intra-Arab conflict and competition for power while as a result the Arab–Israeli conflict entered a new and more critical phase. Ultimately, it completed the erosion of British power in the Middle East and was among the causes of the revolution in Iraq in July 1958."[119]

Turning back to Egyptian opposition, the unacceptable thing for Nasser was the prominent role of Iraq in the Baghdad Pact. This precipitated his challenges against the pact, its participants and its promoters to curb their interests by any means in the region, including an arms deal with the Soviets. Additionally, as it will be discussed in the next section, it was a fact that Nasser's action was a risk taking which could not be enframed with Egypt itself. In certain respects, it imperiled regional stability and security in an era which was dominated by the Cold War hostilities as well. As will be further analyzed, an ostensible reason for his resort to Soviet supplies, was the condescending Anglo–American attitude towards self-assertiveness in the Middle East and their disregard for the Egyptian needs for its security.

Whereas, London considered that as a pretext to his arms deal, although he could control it, Nasser abused the tension with Israel, probably to ensure military supremacy. It was argued that the West was convinced that an adequate quantity of arms which would be allocated to the Middle Eastern states were needed as these regimes were in need of arms to protect their internal stability. In this context, in conformity with the Anglo–American Middle Eastern policies, there was already a flow of arms, supporting the maintenance of stable regimes in the Middle East which would be open to collaborate with the West. However, Egyptian demand for arms was considered to be destabilizing for the region and not regarded as an act associated with Egypt's search for enhancing its security. The arms deal was construed as a "source of deep anxiety," by Foreign Secretary Harold Macmillan, because it signaled the "opening of a new offensive in the Middle East."[120]

Nasser, pre-occupied with the situation on Gaza and the discussion of the Turco–Iraqi Pact, openly asked Britain for the present membership of Baghdad Pact to be frozen. The British responded that this should be consulted with other Pact members. In evaluating the overall position of Egypt, Eden worried about the defeats which Nasser's regime experienced and approved the transfer of arms supplies to Egypt. With American interference, decreased quantity of weaponry was allocated to Egypt.

As regards British politics, in April 1955, a change in the British Cabinet took place. On April 6, 1955, Winston Churchill retired for the last time, and Anthony Eden took his place as Prime Minister. The new British Foreign Secretary with whom Dulles now had to deal directly with was Harold Macmillan who remained at the Foreign Office for almost a year, that is until December 22nd, when he became Chancellor of Exchequer and was succeeded by Selwyn Lloyd.[121]

At the end of April 1955, Nasser left Egypt for the Conference of Afro-Asian states at Bandung. There, he found himself seated with Nehru, Zhou Enlai, and Sukarno. Having failed to ameliorate his relations with the West, Nasser sought support from the Asian states. In the Bandung Conference, Nasser was informed by the Chinese Premiere Zhou Enlai that Soviet supplies were attainable.

In the meantime, Israel was becoming increasingly disturbed with the recent developments. In May 1955, the Israeli Prime Minister Moshe Sharett asked the US for a guarantee of Israel's borders. The "legal-minded" Dulles took the line that it was not possible to guarantee frontiers which had not been agreed on between the various parties. It was noted in Harold Macmillan's diary that, "It is clear that the Americans are becoming as worried as we are about the situation in the Middle East. The difficulty is to get them to act with any speed. Yet, without them, with our slender resources, there is little that we can do."[122]

Henry Byroade, who succeeded Caffery as the US Ambassador to Cairo in February 1995, was primarily assigned with the mission to make progress in talks with the Egyptians. At that time, Egypt's concern with receiving arms that its regime needed was faced with British and French cuts that indicated an influence on Washington's arms supply decisions.[123] The Tripartite Agreement signed between US, Britain and France in 1950, was designed among other things, to prevent an arms race among the major powers of the Middle East, in particular, Egypt, Iraq and Israel.́ In June 1955, this time, the Egyptian demand for $27 million worth of arms met with procrastination by the US State Department and Pentagon not to mention the Congress. Concerning US aid, Egypt had rejected a US military mission and in response to this the US argued that, it had a cotton surplus, therefore could not afford to purchase the Egyptian cotton. Thus, Egyptian demands for trade exchange were rejected. Additionally, Dulles stated that they would sell weapons to both Israel and Egypt since the US was impartial.

Then, Nasser turned to the Soviets. He first accepted a request from the editor of *Pravda*, Dimitri Shepilov, who in the following year was to become Soviet Commissar for Foreign Affairs, to visit Cairo. Consecutively, the Soviet Ambassador to Cairo, Daniel Solod, told Nasser that the Soviet Union would accept supplying Egyptian Army with weaponry in exchange for cotton and rice. In the same month, the Egyptian President told Byroade that, on May 23, the Soviet Union had offered to supply Egypt with arms, and an Egyptian mission would leave for Moscow in the following week.[124] Facing the Soviet penetration into the region, the US stated that, the acceptance of Soviet arms, "would be considered a very serious act."[125] Besides, Dulles sent a letter to Nasser that amounted to a virtual ultimatum about the question of the continuation of Washington's good will, which had no effect on Nasser. "These events amounted to a humiliation for the United States, joyfully reported on Radio Cairo and in Al Ahram."[126]

Replying to this, Nasser stated that the US had not met Egypt's demands. Concerning the Soviets, Eden thought to send a personal message to the Soviet Premier Nikolai Bulganin to show his concern about compromising with the Soviets. But, the State Department indicated an opposite reaction, because this would create a precedent of consulting the Soviets on Middle Eastern issues. As regards coming to an understanding with Egypt, although, some foreign officials recommended a limited arms supply to Egypt, Eden had also turned against Nasser. Then, the US and British officials produced policies, concerning a variety of approaches from coercing measures to bribing or overthrowing Nasser. At the same time, it was decided to demonstrate to other Arab countries that Egypt would not benefit from this policy. Whereas, no effort would be able to reverse the course of the developments proceeding in domino effect. It was argued that the arms transfers from the Soviets were introduced in a way in which Nasser's image was supported. Nasser, hitherto, an unfavoured ruler by the large groups which disliked him due to his overthrow of General Naguib and the oppression of him on the Muslim Brotherhood, turned into an Arab hero overnight.

On September 7, 1955, Nasser publicly referred to the existence of secret Franco–Israeli arms which he stated, included one hundred French tanks and Mystere jet fighters to Israel.[127] A CIA report dated 19th September warning of Nasser's agreement with Soviets, was followed by Nasser's sensational announcement of receiving $80 million worth of aid in arms from the Soviets, consisting of 200 tanks and 100 MIGs and jet bombers. Nasser stated that, having failed to secure arms from the West, and facing a secretly arming Israel, Egypt had contracted to buy arms through Czechoslovakia in barter for cotton and rice.[128] This specifically changed the mode of interactions between Egypt and the super powers. On September 30, 1955, Deputy Under Secretary Harold Caccia, cabled British Foreign Secretary Harold Macmillan, discussing probable policies. "Caccia argued that a comprehensive programme against Egypt 'might even discredit Nasser to the point where he was removed by Egyptian processes alone. . . . If this came about, it would have happened without our direct interference in Egyptian politics.'"[129]

On the other hand, to the Eisenhower administration, it was explained by CIA in Cairo and State Department officials that Nasser did not plan to join the communist side. Humphrey Trevelyan, now the British Ambassador in Cairo, also commented that Nasser's receiving of Soviet supplies were due to internal pressure and the immediate threat following the increasing tension in Gaza. In contrast, P. J. Vatikiotis argued that Nasser's and the Soviets' interests in opposing Western policy converged. This asserted Nasser the power of opposing Western engagements in the Middle East with Soviet support, whilst the Soviet Union thought this to be an opportunity to "break up the strategic–political monopoly of the West in the region."[130] In an effort to get Nasser to reverse his policy, Byroade warned him about the outcomes of communism. But, Nasser assured Byroade of being able to handle the communist fractions in Egypt. In reality, communism in Egypt was not unified. The largest group was the Democratic Movement for National Liberation (DMNL). DMNL was in support of Free Officers, and during the first half of 1955, Nasser had put nearly 750 communist members behind the bars.[131]

According to some analysts, the Soviets used the singularly unmenacing Baghdad Pact "as a pretext to press the arms deal still harder with the Egyptians."[132] In every aspect, the Soviet–Egyptian arms deal in September 1955 was regarded at the time as a great turning point in the Middle East, the end of an era, and the beginning of another.[133] As for Egypt, the arms deal enabled it to strengthen its position in the Arab political circles, whilst fostering Nasser's popularity and image in the Arab world. This allowed Nasser "to assume the role of the defiant hero; in contrast to the Iraqi leadership, which had bowed to Western demands."[134]

Further against the plans of the Anglo–American policy makers, the Council of the Arab League supported Nasser's stand in buying arms through the communist countries. Moreover, the Saudi Arabian Ambassador in the Arab League told reporters that he saw no reason why all other Arab states should not follow Egypt's example.[135] The Syrian, Lebanese and Jordanian Chamber of Deputies enacted a resolution of congratulations to Nasser. Even Nuri As-Said, feeling constrained to do so, sent a message of congratulation to Nasser. Then, Nasser was more encouraged to think that Egypt under his rule and his ruling elite would become "the new protagonists of the Arab world, and not Iraq under Nuri As-Said and the old politicians."[136]

Lastly, the Egyptian policy was adjusted by considering Mosaddeq's mistake in Iran of trying to improve his relations with the Soviet Union in order to force the US to adopt a more cautious policy. Nasser realized that a similar approach would only antagonize the US. Despite an account of mutual dislike, eventually, ensuring the friendlier-line policy of the US was important to Nasser especially during his rivalry with the British sponsored Nuri As-Said. Besides, Nasser had still been aspiring to receive US aid to build the Aswan High-Dam which had become the vital aspect of Egypt's ten-year economic plan. "Egyptian policy makers thus tried to avoid total dependence upon the support of one bloc, as this would put an end to their ability to manoeuvre between the two blocs, and thus achieve their aims more easily."[137]

Meanwhile, the Baghdad Pact had been gaining strength. Pakistan was included in the Baghdad Pact on September 23, 1955. Since this meant that on paper the southwestern border had been secured by the US, Dulles was gratified. "He had always placed reliance in such pieces of paper, representing, as he hoped they would, the pledge of the governments subscribing."[138] Having accomplished the Pakistani adherence to the Pact, Britain further pressed the US to join the Baghdad Pact. However, the Eisenhower administration's Middle Eastern policy had been shaped by its New Look strategy. Set forth in the October 1953, National Security decision, NSC-162/2, the New Look was a major effort to regain the initiative in the global confrontation with the Soviet Union whilst reducing the US defense expenditures. The fundamental purpose of the New Look was to accomplish this through scaling back the conventional forces on the ground while strengthening the pro-Western countries along the entire Soviet sphere of influence. Therefore, the Eisenhower administration had begun to establish cliency relationships along the Sino–Soviet periphery in order to extend security assistance and economic aid to those countries.[139]

Although Iran was to play a key role in the US strategy in view of its location on the Northern Tier, the Secretary of State, Dulles had not included Iran in his Middle East trip in 1953, because in his own words, "it is now preoccupied with its oil dispute with Britain. But still the people and the Government do not want this quarrel to expose them to Communist subversion."[140] Indeed, for the last two years, President Eisenhower had been told that the Shah of Iran believed that, Iran could link itself in the "Free World's defense."[141] But, no public statement of such an intention could be made before the Zahedi Government was able to establish itself firmly in power. On July 26, 1954, Premier Zahedi made the most candid statement of his Government about Iran's desire to move closer to the West. In his talk with a group of Iranian editors, he stated, "we have witnessed how aggressors have wantonly occupied neutral countries in defiance of international law and their own undertakings. Therefore, it is certain in this turbulent world that a government can preserve itself only if it has the power of resistance against an aggressor."[142] Thus, the Iran's decision to join the Baghdad Pact was known before October 1955, but the announcement of its intention was being delayed in view of Soviet opposition. Late in the previous month, Egypt's arms deal with Czechoslovakia was announced. This incident, increasing Iran's security anxieties, had a catalyst effect in Iran's statement of intention to accede to the Baghdad Pact.

In October 1955, British Foreign Secretary, Harold Macmillan, obtained the approval of the Cabinet on the requests of transferring arms to Iran, to ensure Iran's inclusion in Baghdad Pact. Following the Turkish State visit to Teheran, Iran stated its request to join the Baghdad Pact. Although J. F. Dulles had complained to the Secretary of Defense, Charles Wilson, about the cost of re-arming Iran, when Iran was at the brink of adherence to the Baghdad Pact, both the US and Britain highly favoured this. On October 12, 1955, the State Department declared that drawing together of the Northern Tier nations of the Middle East is a normal development which should promote peace, stability, and well-being in the area. It was stressed that "In no respect can this natural association be deemed hostile or threatening or directed against any other nation."[143] The Foreign Office on October 13, 1955, stated that it was "a step that would increase security and help the cause of peace in the area."[144] Not surprisingly, the US' remaining outside the pact frustrated the Iranian Government. The Iranian administration thought that, without the formal presence of the US, the Baghdad Pact might fail to provide a strong defense against the Soviets. Iranians also considered that this was likely to bring about limitations in military and economic aid. Again, the prevailing thinking considered the decline of British influence without a substituent American presence, might lead to a favourable situation to Soviets and the radical regimes of the Middle East.[145]

As expected, the Soviet Union vigorously opposed Iran's adherence to the Baghdad Pact. Soviet opposition was also based on the fear of being encircled by an Islamic crescent. Laqueur states that ". . . all Islamic experts were urged to realize the very complex character of the problem,"[146] since in Soviets' consideration, "the aggressive Baghdad Pact exploited the slogan of 'unity of Islam,'"[147] Iraq had cut off diplomatic ties with the Soviet Union a few months before, and the Iranian Government "being last to join the Pact, had obviously anticipated the Soviet reaction."[148] Soviet Note to Iran on October 12, 1955 stating, "Iran's accession to this military alignment is in contradiction with Iran's good-neighbourly relations with the Soviet Union and the known treaty obligations of Iran,"[149] was coupled with *Pravda* reminding the Iranian Government that, it did not have to join any "anti-Soviet" pact, according to the treaties of 1921 and 1927.[150]

As for the US and Britain, having achieved Iranian adherence to the Baghdad Pact, Anglo–American policy makers fostered their efforts to bring additional partners into the pact. Whereas, the forthcoming incidents would prove that the pact itself was orbit of the escalating tensions.

An Unstable Environment Around the Baghdad Pact and the Showdown in Baghdad: 1955–1958

Cleavages over the possession of the Buraimi Oasis between Saudi Arabia and the Trucial Sheikhdoms of Abu Dhabi, Muscat and Oman, including the disputes on the control of oil reserves, had been created some tensions to occupy the agenda next. The course of events would evoke greater US' involvement in the region as well. On October 18, 1955, British officers led troops of the Trucial Sheikhdoms had taken control of the Oasis. Shortly after, the King of Saudi Arabia expressed his expectation of US assistance against the British led occupation. Not surprisingly, Nasser's regime sided with King Saud. Egyptian propaganda especially through the 'Voice of Arabs,' Cairo's Radio, targeted Britain's relations with the Gulf Sheikhdoms. "The Saudis, fearful of the Hashemites, sided with Egypt as did Yemen. Lebanon stood neutral, whilst Syria and Jordan remained undecided but under the pressure of two parties."[151]

On October 26, Macmillan met with Dulles to negotiate reports on Egypt's signing a defence pact with Saudi Arabia and Syria. At the time, Dulles believed that Syria was the nearest entity in the Middle East to a Soviet satellite, and he was ready for counteraction in Syria. Dulles and Macmillan also agreed that the Baghdad Pact should be consolidated through convincing some other countries to join it. Regarding his talks with the US Secretary of State, Macmillan stated "Mr. Dulles asked me whether we could not bring pressure upon Jordan to join the Baghdad Pact. He thought it would be a fine thing if they did."[152]

Increasing tension in the region, and the colonialism charges, added to the increasing anti-Westernism "rang a bell with Americans."[153] But, obviously, the British opposition to Saudi actions was the main cause of diversity between the US and British policies since the relations with this country had a particular importance to the US. Whilst Britain had retained the impulses and character of a colonial power wishing for continued influence in the region on this basis, the US, having an anti-colonial outlook, desired to accommodate the former victims of colonisation within an anti-Soviet bloc as its major objective. This was a grit in the gears of the Anglo–American alliance and other signs of fraction were working their way to surface. Around the same issue, in November 1955, the Iraqi Premier Nuri As-Said suggested that "the US withhold Saudi royalties for six months to prevent Saudi funding of 'anti-Western' and 'anti-Iraqi' forces in Syria and Egypt."[154] Having also considered the Iraqi Premier's request, British Foreign Minister, Macmillan proposed to take joint steps by the US and British governments in order to impose sanctions on the petro-dollar income of the Saudi oil companies. Whereas, this met with the response of Dulles expressing the US' difficulties on controlling Saudi revenues.

In November, Macmillan went to Baghdad to attend the first meeting of the Baghdad Pact powers. There, desiring to keep the faith in the Pact, he advocated that the Egyptian arms deal had been planned long before the Pact. Moreover, he insisted that the economic aspect of it was much more important than the military. Back in London, he explained "the Pact is not intended to split the Arab World. . . . I believe in the long run it will unite it."[155] Indeed, Macmillan was remarkably content with the Pact, but, was rather alarmed by the opponents' activities as well. He had also decided that Jordanian adherence to the Pact should be realized as soon as possible.

Concerning Jordan, a proposal by the British Defence Coordinating Committee for the Middle East (BDCC) suggested that Jordan could only be defended by British troops. To conduct this, the CORDAGE plan was approved by the British Chiefs of Staff. Indeed, previously, on February 15, 1955, Jordan had requested British support against a possible Israeli attack. The British Chiefs of Staff had not informed King Hussein of the CORDAGE plan. A formal reply to the Jordanian request expressed that, ". . . . Tripartite Declaration would bring Britain 'side by side with Jordan to resist Israeli aggression, provided Jordan did not take precipitate action against Israel."[156]

In addition to the above mentioned Jordanian–Israeli tension, this country had various threat perceptions. Obviously, one threat was perceived from the traditional rival of the Hashemite Kingdoms, Saudi Arabia. To a certain extent, Jordan was anxious of Iraqi regime as well, in case of Iraqi monarchy's attempt to unite the two Hashemite monarchies. Until the outbreak of the Second World War, the Hashemite dynasty had a significant role in the modern history of Arab nationalism. Arabism and its followers had gravitated towards Hashemite leadership concentrated in the Fertile Crescent lands. The downfall of the Hashemites had actually followed Iraq's efforts to incorporate Jordan into an Arab Union. It is not difficult to assess that from time to time, through referring to the existence of tribal–religious relationships among themselves, the sons of Sharif Hussein, ruling in Hejaz and Iraq, had pressed young Jordanian King Hussein to subordinate their authority.

In the light of a series of developments taking place in the Middle East, clearly, Jordan and King Hussein personally occupied a great place in Anthony Eden's mind in order to consolidate the Baghdad Pact. His interest in Jordanian membership to the Pact pushed him to the extent of instructing the Chiefs of Staff to prepare plans for limited military actions against Israel, which, according to some, included seaborne invasion, if Israel attacked Jordan. In their turn the Chiefs of Staff concluded that Jordan's Arab Legion commanded by John Glubb, popularly known as "Glubb Pasha," a Scottish General, working with Arabs for many years, was not an adequate force to meet serious threats.[157] Regarding this, the British offered tangible military assistance and equipment to Jordan to counter clandestine Saudi finance and influence—which were also sedulously undermining the position of the Hashemite Monarchy in Iraq—that had ambitions for change in the Hashemite monarchy in Jordan. King Hussein was faced with the Egyptian–Saudi–Syrian defense offer at the same time. Should the Jordanian Government accepted this offer, the contracting parties were to consider any armed attack on the territory or forces of Jordan as an attack on themselves. But, King Hussein had no intention to accept these proposals.

As regards Syria's position, having noticed the Syrian Government's collaboration with Egypt to harm the British interests and weaken the authority of the British protected Jordanian king, Britain decided to back Iraqi efforts to gain influence over Syria at the expense of further destabilizing the region. This was favoured by the Foreign Office, because it was considered that such an action would decrease the threat from Egypt as well. In addition to this, an enlargement in Iraqi–Jordanian axis, perhaps, to include Syria in the future, was targeted.

Meanwhile, King Hussein was now coming under intense pressure in Amman from anti-colonialists loudly encouraged by the 'Voice of Arabs' and financed by both Egypt and Saudi Arabia. As the situation was found disturbing and the Arab Legion was considered weak, London took some more measures to hold its troops ready in Cyprus to go to King Hussein's assistance in case of emergency. Saudi Arabia was also warned that in the event of a Saudi attack on Jordan, Britain would fulfill its undertakings in the 1948 Treaty to go to Jordan's help. Although this worked and the Saudis drew back their forces from the Jordanian border, they drastically increased their backing of oppositionary activities in Jordan. Nasser was also told that he should stop his policy of inciting the people of Jordan to civil war and his attacks on King Hussein. Nasser told the British Ambassador in Cairo, Humphrey Trevelyan that broadcasting against Jordan and Britain would be stopped. However, there was no lessening of the events, but even more attacks on Iraq, and an increasing criticism against Hussein and Glubb.

Under these pressures, King Hussein told British Ambassador in Amman, Charles Duke, on 9 November that Jordan was ready to join the Baghdad Pact "given the necessary backing."[158] On the other hand, there was no agreement in the House of Commons as regards the arms deliveries to the Middle East. Obviously, the Jordanian arms requests were cautiously handled because of the Arab–Israeli tension at hand. There were even questions directed to the government as to why it could not talk over the issue with the Russians, making the debates more complicated. On November 12, in his speech in the House of Commons, Eden stated his views on the arms transfers to the Middle East that:

> This is one of the most difficult topics to handle from the point of view of the Government. . . . At the present time, of course, the House is apt to look at this matter as though the arms deliveries were only coming from ourselves, France and the United States who are signatories to the Tripartite Agreement and perhaps from Russia as well.

> That is not true. They are coming from all parts of the world to Israel and to the Arab States on a very large scale. We have done what we could ourselves during this period, and when it was my responsibility

at the Foreign Office we spent a great many hours trying as far as we could to see that the balance of deliveries was kept fairly as we could contrive, not only by ourselves, but together with the United States and France, our principal Allies.

Now, of course, a new element has been injected into this situation. The right hon. Gentleman asked, "Why cannot you talk over this new situation with the Russians?" . . . We have made a number of approaches to try to see whether anything of this kind was possible, but I am bound to say, to put it mildly, that the replies have not been encouraging. . . . We asked, as we hoped, for a hopeful answer, but we did not get it.[159]

Facing a strong domestic opposition, Eden sought the ways to receive a definite US commitment to the Baghdad Pact. The expectations of the British Government from the US in ensuring this backing to Jordan was also explicit in the Memorandum dated December 9, 1955, from the Director of the Office of Near Eastern Affairs to the Assistant Secretary of State George Allen. Here, this was clearly stated as:

we asked Ambassador Mallory to keep us informed and also to comment on the British view that United States support for the U.K. in its efforts to get Jordanian adherence would be of particular significance. The British have said that a U.S. promise of additional economic aid to Jordan would be very helpful.

Ambassador Mallory has replied . . . giving his view that a mere verbal assurance of U.S. support for Jordan's adherence or even an undertaking to provide additional economic aid would have limited effect on the Jordanians. He feels that the strongest effect could be gained through commitments to furnish military aid.[160]

But, the demonstrations held in December increased bitterness, challenging the pro-Western government and the Baghdad Pact. The message from the British Commander in Chief of the Arab Legion in Jordan, General John Glubb, also warned that increasing Egyptian pressure, supported by the Saudi finances was an irritant. One ambition of the Egyptians he argued was "to dominate the Middle East and to this purpose it is essential for them to get rid of British and American influence,"[161] and, as it was mentioned before, the Saudis had already taken a stand against the British in the Buraimi Oasis dispute. In response to this, the

Jordanian Kingdom repeated its need for a greater army which would be financed by Britain.

Subsequently, at Macmillan's suggestion, the Chief of the Imperial General Staff, General Gerald Templer, was sent to Amman to make a proposal on behalf of the UK. General Templer said that if Jordan would not cooperate with its real friends, the Jordan would be risking its very regime and its very existence as an independent state. He further emphasized that the Jordanian decision to take sides with Britain would be followed by an offer of military supplies and the establishment of the Jordanian air force by sending Jordan ten Vampire fighters.[162] At the same time, Jordanian accession would be supported by doubling the British aid of £10 million. But, as will be discussed below, Templer's mission was a failure. Behind the unexpected rejection of the Jordanian Government of the British proposals, there were primarily the fear of Nasser and the popular case of the Palestinian refugees. Given this analysis, in the context of rising pro-Nasserist sentiment, the overwhelming majority of King Hussein's ministers rejected signing a letter of intent to collaborate with Britain.

As regards Turkey, the Turkish Government favoured the inclusion of Jordan and Lebanon in the Baghdad Pact. According to the Menderes Government, this would create a positive example to all the countries of the Middle East and consolidate the popular opposition against Soviet menace. Turkey was among the countries which were principal recipients of the US aid. As was mentioned previously, following the end of the Second World War, increasing Soviet territorial demands were seriously felt too. Turkey had enthusiastically desired NATO membership and had achieved this concomitant following its involvement in the Korean War which would last nearly three years, thus, in a sense, at the expense of having dramatic casualties.

   Having provided a considerable contribution to Iran's inclusion in the Baghdad Pact, the second destination of the Turkish delegation was Amman. When they came back from their visit to Amman, Turkish President Celal Bayar and the Minister of Foreign Affairs Fatin Rüştü Zorlu, had the impression that they had brought King Hussein to the verge of membership. In reality, anti-Westernism was winning over Jordan. In the week General Templer visited Amman, between December 7th and 14th, four ministers of Palestinian origin from the West Bank resigned in protest. This led to a change in the Cabinet. Hazza Majali headed the new Government. Wheras, as he was pro-Pact, the opposition continued unabated. Increasing pressure upon Majali, aimed to obtain a statement from him against the Baghdad Pact.

Meanwhile, another dispute was surfacing on the part of North Africa, a region in close proximity to the Middle East and the political developments of which had considerable impact in the general plannings of the Western grouping of states. As the spotlights were turning to Tunisia and Morocco which were about to accede to independence, partly as a result of UN Resolutions adopted in the early 1950s, France was extremely cautious to set back the emergence of an international opinion in favour of an independent Algeria. As of 1955, the French Government was anxious to underscore that the administrative organisation of Algeria was the same as that of the rest of France on the continent while other French colonies in North Africa remained as protectorates. From the 1871 uprising, which had only been crushed after one year of military repression to the Sétif massacre of May 8, 1945, when the French army had killed—according to different sources tens of thousands of Algerians in a campaign of reprisals against the killing of a hundred Europeans that had followed a nationalist demonstration, the Europeans and North Africans in Algeria had existed as members of parallel societies. In this atmosphere, the Front of National Liberation (FLN) which had formed itself into the lead of Algerian nationalism sent its representatives to the Bandung Conference of April 1955. Expectedly the report of the emerging Movement of Neutral and Non-Aligned Countries made reference to the question of Algeria, which the Afro–Asian group raised at the UN shortly after.

Despite these gathering storms of serious discontent, Anthony Eden's visit to Washington late in January 1956, did not resolve a serious difference of opinion between the Americans and the British at this juncture. Interestingly, Sherman Adams stated that "our firm opposition to colonialism made us sympathetic to the struggle which Egypt and the other Arab states were making to free themselves from the political and economic control that the British felt they had to maintain in the Middle East in their own self-interest."[163] In a sense, Britain was left a maverick in pursuance of its policy in the Middle East.

It was on March 1, 1956, the Jordanian Prime Minister Samir Rifai, with the direction of King Hussein who was under increasing pressure, asked General Glubb to leave the country in two hours. When King Hussein dismissed his long time British adviser, and commander of the Arab Legion, Eden was infuriated. Anthony Nutting, who was then the

Undersecretary of State for Foreign Affairs, recalled how Eden shouted in anger: "What's all this nonsense about isolating Nasser or neutralizing him, as you call it? I want him destroyed, can't you understand?"[164] When Nutting urged that Eden, before overthrowing Nasser, should have thought of an alternative, a more amenable man to succeed him, so as to avoid turmoil in Egypt, Eden decidedly replied: "But I don't want an alternative, and I don't give a damn if there's anarchy and chaos in Egypt."[165]

Against this background, the new British Foreign Minister (after Eden's reshuffle in the Cabinet at the end of December 1955), Selwyn Lloyd arrived in Cairo on the day of Glubb's dismissal. Lloyd was determined to make progress in his talks with Nasser who was causing his government various difficulties with his opposition against the Baghdad Pact and his advance of Arab Nationalism. At the peak of tension, Nasser proposed to Lloyd that he would stop the anti-British and anti-Pact propaganda, if Britain would "freeze" its active role in the Baghdad Pact.[166] Besides, as Lloyd learned that the dismissal of Glubb was conducted upon Nasser's inducement, he stated the adverse effect of this on bilateral relations. In the end, Lloyd did not get any better with Nasser than had Eden the year before.

Actually, nothing in the past year had contributed more to the growing friction between these countries than "Britain's reckless determination to enlist Arab nations in the Pact, and Egypt's unyielding opposition."[167] Lloyd tried to persuade Nasser that the British had no interest in old-fashioned domination and the Baghdad Pact looked north, not south. It was to prevent Soviet infiltration and to protect the oil.[168] Whereas, Lloyd failed to assure Nasser of Britain's benign intentions.

Anglo–Egyptian relations worsened within this context. This was also due to Eden's growing anti-Nasser policy which had increased to the extent of comparing Nasser with Mussolini and Hitler.[169] On March 10, 1956, Britain realized more the necessity of updating its policies towards Jordan, when Egypt, Saudi Arabia and Syria repeated their proposals to replace British assistance to Jordan. This led to considerations of bringing Iraq and Jordan closer in bilateral treaties, subsequently to encompass the conclusion of trilateral treaties including Britain. However, further events were yet to unfold and prove that all the efforts were futile to halt the escalating tension. Reports continued to flood London and Washington about the deteriorating stability. The region was on the verge of a major crisis.

Against the background of prevailing differences of opinion with Britain, a decision to support the Baghdad Pact, and the policies specifically directed to Egypt and other countries were expressed by Dulles to Eisenhower on March 28, 1956. The US administration, in conformity with British foreign policy officials, decided to damage Nasser's prestige and provide support to the oppositionary Arab elements.

The first pressure was put on Egypt's Aswan Dam project. The projected High Dam on Aswan was a gigantic undertaking in the land of the Nile. It was the most cherished project of Gamal Abd-el Nasser and his Revolutionary Council of young army officers. The first Aswan Dam was completed in 1902 and heightened in 1912 and 1933. Egypt had been faced with a rapid population growth which was greater than the amount of cultivable land added by the dam enlargements. Only the fertile delta and the narrow strip of land near Nile were under irrigation, equal to a mere three percent of Egypt's land, beyond lay the sere Sahara. The country was in a bitter race between people and hunger thus the water of the Nile had to be captured and adequately distributed to begin to catch up its agricultural wealth of a century earlier.[170] Under these circumstances, it had been considered by Washington that the time for ignoring Egyptian need for a High Dam on Aswan had passed and the entry of Russia into the Middle East was the act that finally pushed Washington into backing the Aswan Dam.

However, Israel's increasing influence and the growing Soviet activities in Egypt, which was spreading to some other regional countries changed the policy of the State Department that they had to act together with UK to warn Nasser. The UK and US, by demonstrating that they could withdraw their financial and technical contribution from the project aimed to show their determination to resist communist infiltrations and their intolerance towards the regimes receiving aid from the Soviets. Subsequently, Egypt's talks with the World Bank was broken. However, the success of the Anglo–American strategy was jeopardized by the Soviet threat to finance the Aswan Dam. The Anglo–American policy makers regarded the Soviet attempt as a serious communist penetration into the Middle East and shifted to a hard-line policy, especially the British. Macdonald argued that the withdrawal of the American aid "not only led to the Suez Crisis and the punitive expeditions staged by Israel, France and Britain, but also opened the door for the unrestrained development of Soviet bloc influence in the area and thereby destroyed the utility of the Baghdad Pact."[171] Indeed, falsifying the Western powers' anxiety,

Nasser rejected $400 million by the Soviets for fear of being dragged into a long-term dependence on Moscow.[172]

In the meantime, a threat to Western position in Syria emerged when the Government of Said Ghazzi resigned on June 2 because of increased student demonstrations opposing Syria's economic interaction with France and to protest French policy in Algeria. Sabri Asali, who was Prime Minister between 1954–55, formed a Cabinet including two ministers of Ba'ath. Salah Bitar became Minister of Foreign Affairs. Asali and Ba'ath leader, Akram Hourani were close to each other and they agreed on the proclamation of an Egyptian–Syrian Union, open to all Arabs who have no defence treaties with foreign powers. In addition, left-wing Army officers were insistent on such a statement. Britain opposed prevalence of Ba'athist policies which were against Western influence. Therefore, Anglo–American officials unanimously aimed to build opposition to this.

Discussions around the operation STRAGGLE were designed to intervene in the elections or to sponsor a coup in Syria. The Anti-Leftist Arab Liberation Party formed by a group of officers was led by an important figure, Michel Ilyan, who was assisted to overcome Leftists. Ilyan tried to control Aleppo and Damascus. He was also supported by the media from Egypt, and by the Saudis, who were enjoying the flow of Western finance. Muslim Brotherhood and the tribes on the Iraqi–Syrian border were on Ilyan's side. In addition, when Iraqi pressure increased, the former President, Hashim Atassi came back from Rome to establish a right-wing coalition.

As for Jordan, on June 26, 1956, King Hussein dissolved the Chamber of Deputies because of the loss of cooperation between the Chamber and the Executive.[173] King Hussein's care-taker appointment was this time the elderly Ibrahim Hashim. Pro-Nasser Samir Rifai was the deputy Prime Minister. As the new Government under Hashim could not settle the riots, Samir Rifai was appointed Prime Minister of Jordan in January 1956. He stated that his Government would not participate or link-up with any new alliances. Suleiman Nabulsi, who had been Minister of Finance and Ambassador to London, was offered a portfolio position in Rifai's Cabinet. He was among the admirers of Nasser as well. On this case, Eisenhower noted the following in his diary, "We tried to make the British see the danger of pressuring Jordan to join the Northern Tier Pact. They went blindly ahead and only recently have been suffering one of the most severe diplomatic defeats Britain has taken in many years."[174]

Turning back to the cleavages around the financing of the Aswan Dam, it can be stated that in part, the withdrawal of financial aid by the US was a result of the decision of the Senate Appropriations Committee for the fiscal year of 1957. However, this action prompted Nasser to reevaluate his policies, including the potential nationalisation of the Suez Canal Company. In reality, the reasons which temporarily stopped Nasser from going ahead with the nationalisation project were the poor foreign exchange reserves of Egypt, not knowing how to compensate Suez Canal share holders, and the lack of technical ability to construct the Aswan Dam. Additionally, Moscow was not a reliable ally to substitute for the Western aid. Corresponding to this, Dimitri Shepilov expressed that, the Soviet Union was not interested in financing Egypt in its Aswan Dam project, as Egypt was considered to be in need of a more general economic development.[175] Then, Nasser choose to take the US withdrawal of aid as a personal affront and emphasized Egypt's determination to meet its own needs.

On July 26, seven days after the American announcement of the withdrawal of financial support for the construction of the Aswan Dam, Nasser, who meanwhile returned from his visit to Yugoslavia, proclaimed in a mass meeting at Alexandria that, "We shall eliminate the past by regaining our right to the Suez Canal."[176] On the same day the Egyptian Government declared that "the Suez Canal Maritime Company, S.A.E., is nationalized. All money, rights and obligations of the company are transferred to the State. All organisaions and committees now operating the company are dissolved."[177]

In the same speech by Nasser, it was also stated that, imperialism had annihilated Palestine and supported Israel in converting the Arabs into a mass of refugees. In explaining the international support of his decision, Nasser emphasized that the statements of the Brioni conference in Yugoslavia endorsed the principles of Bandung and added that, the resolution issued in Brioni by the heads of states of Yugoslavia, India and Egypt stated that the cooperation among them contributed to develop relations among nations on the basis of equality. He also expressed that all nations should have the right to choose freely their political and economic systems, and their mode of life in accordance with the purposes and principles of the UN Charter.[178]

The British and French reactions to the Egyptian decision were severe. In the House of Commons, Eden declared that Nasser's action was in breach of the Concession Agreements and he referred to it as an arbitrary action which would affect both the operation of the Canal and wider questions.[179] He also stated that the British Government were consulting other governments immediately concerned with regard to the serious situation created. On July 30, Eden declared that, "no arrangements for the future of this great waterway could be acceptable to Her Majesty's Government which would leave it in the unfettered control of a single Power which could, as recent events have shown, exploit it purely for purposes of national policy."[180] By that time, the Egyptian Sterling balances had been frozen. On August 2, Eden informed the House of Commons that certain precautionary measures of a military nature were being taken. Here, Eden emphasized his view of the outstanding necessity to implement different measures other than economic sanctions.

In France, the reaction was more vigorous. M. Pineau handed the Egyptian Ambassador such a strongly worded note that there was a talk of a break of diplomatic relations. The reaction of the US was less severe. It stated that, the matter was one of concern mainly to the principal users of Canal. On July 28, the Acting Secretary of State, Herbert Hoover, protested to the Egyptian Ambassador in Washington, only about the "intemperate, inaccurate and misleading statements" which President Nasser made at Alexandria on July 26. In general terms, the US firmly disassociated itself from the challenge to the Egyptian Government which had been launched by the reactions of the British and French Governments.

In his turn, Eden continued to press for implementing heavy sanctions to Egypt. Following Dulles' visit to London, at a meeting between Dulles, Lloyd and Pineau, Eden stated that Nasser's action was a breach of the Constantinople Convention on transit through the Canal. Dulles consented to the tripartite members making a strong condemnation of Egypt's action and affirmation of the need to place the Canal under international control. As a result, a tripartite Anglo–French–US statement was made on August 2. It was proposed to hold a conference of the signatories of the 1888 Convention and its beneficiaries[181] to consider the establishment of an operating arrangement for the Canal under an international system.

Contrary to the British anxiety for direct action to keep Nasser in line and protecting the Suez Canal and Western Europe's supply of oil,[182] the US indicated its reluctance to use of force. "It was the reverse of the Indo–China situation, where Dulles had been unable to persuade the British to join the United States in direct military action to keep the Communists out of Vietnam. Now the shoe was on the other foot and it did not fit well."[183] "Dulles, the brinksman whom Europeans for years had criticized as being bellicose, was now preaching peace and patience; Eden the compromiser wanted war."[184] In the meantime, in order to attain a quick resolution, the Egypt Committee in the Foreign Office planned for military involvement even without waiting for Eden's order.

As regards Israel, since its dependence on outside Western powers was evident for its survival in the region, the Israeli Government decided to join the Western alliance, which was mustering to remove Nasser. First, Ben Gurion removed a major obstacle in collaborating with France by pressing the Foreign Minister Moshe Sharett who advocated cooperation with the US. Sharett was against the British, French and Israeli involvement in Suez. Thus, he had sided with the US which was against military option. Director General of the Israeli Ministry of Defence, Shimon Peres, Chief of the General Staff, General Moshe Dayan, and the Chief of Army intelligence, General Yehoshafat Harkabi met with French officials of the corresponding services to coordinate the proposed operation. The details of the assault plan were concluded through intergovernmental talks. The primary goal was the overthrow of Nasser. The approved route was from Alexandria to the Canal and Cairo. The operation was codenamed: MUSKETEER.

In reality, planning for the invasion had started on July 28. France sent its highest ranking military officials to London on that date to meet with their counterparts, and during the weekend a secret joint military command was formed. Meanwhile, Dulles decided to leave for London. On Wednesday, the day Dulles arrived in London, the War Office reported that "precautionary military measures were being taken."[185]

The US, which remained outside the operation, was also seeking alternative schemes to prevent an Anglo–Egyptian confrontation. Indeed, Washington was trying to develop alternative policies to enhance its free hand in the region. Previously, Robert Anderson whose mediatory mission took place in the early months of 1956, had suggested Dulles on April 4 that NATO work out a military plan to protect the assets in the Middle East. But, Dulles had rejected Anderson's plan. The Eisenhower administration had been loosely associating itself with the Northern Tier Pact and aiming to build up confidence in its policies. Thus, facing the crisis over Suez, the US again tried to avoid conflict in the region at any expense. Eisenhower stated that the use of force could be necessary only under extreme circumstances. Meanwhile, Nasser made his view contrary to the internationalisation of the Suez Canal explicit to Washington, London and Paris. In this context, Eden's determination to suppress or overthrow Nasser was publicized during his speech, broadcasted on Radio and television on August 8.

On August 12, the Egyptian Government issued a statement in which it declined to attend the London Conference. In London, a Suez committee chaired by Australian Prime Minister, Robert Menzies was appointed by the eighteen powers among the participant countries. Not surprisingly, Shepilov, on behalf of the Soviet Union criticized the American proposals and stated that, the only legitimate owner of the Canal was the Egyptian state. Despite the Soviet efforts, the idea promoted by the US to bring Nasser to the negotiation table found a stronger basis with the initialization of the tripartite proposal for the international control of the Canal. However, Nasser expressed that Egypt would be the decision-maker to allow the Canal's international use, and that he would not consent to the idea of a multilateral agreement. Besides, Nasser blamed the proposal as a "restoration of collective colonialism."[186] In the end, the talks between Menzies and Nasser were fruitless. Thus, the conference approach failed.

There are some grounds for believing that the independent action which Britain undertook in the Suez dispute, was intended to be an assertion of Britain's independence in its policy from the US in the region. The issue had been turned into something that would show Washington what London could do. Anthony Nutting noted that:

> Nobody was kept more completely in the dark than the President of the United States. After Eden's initial confession that he wanted war had provoked Eisenhower to indignant protests, the President was treated as unreliable ally. The more he warned Eden that American and world opinion would not support him if he appeared to be trying to browbeat a smaller nation into submission, the more determined Eden became to conceal his hand from the Americans.[187]

It was a matter of reinforcing Britain's status in the Middle East as well. On the other hand, any successful prospect of the operation launched by London and Paris could hardly please the US, "since it would have meant a radical strengthening of British positions in the Middle East."[188] From the outset, Eisenhower evaluated the Suez Canal dispute and the influence of Nasser in the Arab world as two separate issues neither of which could be solved by war. Truly, Eden's panic about the action of

Nasser was not shared by the US. For the US, the Canal was less important economically than for Britain and Europe.

In the eyes of the US policy makers, the Canal was an inconvenient issue to try to bring down Nasser because of its colonialist associations. Besides, "Egypt could count on widespread Arab and Afro–Asian sympathy as it faced the two old imperial Powers, Britain and France."[189] Thus, dealing with Nasser was seen in Washington as a long-term process. Again, the US Government had no wish to quarrel with the Arabs, therefore, the British could hardly expect any American support in their war against Nasser. Bearing this in his mind, Eden merely informed Eisenhower of decisions after they were taken, and then in very general terms. These contributed to an emerging US interest which was implicitly interested in the failure of Eden's initiative.

Dulles, among his conference making policies, introduced the Suez Canal Users Plan, which basically proposed to pay off Nasser while running the Canal pilots employed by the US. However, Britain was revising the plans of invasion. General Keightly, who was the Commander in Chief of MUSKETEER, brought out a MUSKETEER revise, which concentrated upon the material devastation of Egypt by aerial and naval bombing. Additionally, Operation REVISE was approved and complimentary operations PICK UP and CONVOY were proceeded to hinder Egyptian supervision of Canal Transit. Besides, directly targeting the overthrow of Nasser, MI6 operated in Egypt with the opponents of the regime as well. Egypt Committee was the center where intelligence gathered by MI6 was analyzed.

In Eden's and Lloyd's discussions with Mollet and Pineau, the British commitment to Jordan under CORDAGE re-surfaced. The tension at the Israeli–Jordanian border was compounded by the shaky political situation in Jordan, while King Hussein's authority was continuously challenged by the clandestine activities backed by Nasser. Moreover, the Soviet Union was aiming to topple Hussein in order to bring the Kingdom under Nasser's influence. The British had also planned Jordan to receive Iraqi troops in case of an urgency. Whereas, Israel's rejection to countenance the deployment of the Iraqi military units further strained the Israeli–British relations. Having considered the significance of Jordan, Eden said, "if Israel attacked Jordan, we are bound to go to Jordan's help."[190] Certainly, legal grounds had been existing for this. In the event that Israel took military action, Britain would be obliged to come to Jordan's help under both the Anglo–Jordanian Treaty of 1948 and the

Tripartite Declaration of 1950. Thus, a supplementary policy was designed in case of an outbreak of an Arab–Israeli war. Looking at the political atmosphere in the region, obviously, the hopes invested on the infant Baghdad Pact were already shadowed with the war plans.

The second (mid September 1956) and the third (October 1–5) international conferences met in London could not overcome the existing impasse. As for the super powers, the Soviets, occupied with the revolution in Hungary, and the US engaged in Presidential elections, had moved their focus away from the Middle East. In appearance, the timing for an opportunistic military intervention in Suez was appropriate. In addition, during the last week of October, intelligence reports received by the US indicated that Israel was mobilizing its forces and on October 29, Israeli troops invaded the Sinai Peninsula and advanced rapidly both in the direction of the Straits of Tiran and Canal. On October 30, the US sponsored a resolution which called upon the withdrawal of Israel behind the armistice lines. However, the Anglo–French vetoes started to paralyse the UN. Anglo–French Naval action begun on the evening of October 31. On November 1, air-raids were launched, on November 5–6, paratroopers were dropped and bombardment and invasion continued. By November 7, following the US' attempts the cease-fire was declared.

Referring to the Anglo–French invasion, President Eisenhower said in a broadcast that "the United States was not consulted in any way about any phase of these actions. Nor were we informed of them in advance. . . . We believe these actions have been taken in error."[191] Indeed, the US administration evaluated the armed intervention of Britain and France as actions which could lead to actual involvement of the SU into the region through Egypt and the Suez affair. The Anglo–French decision to resort the use of force, thus was rejected in favour of the promulgation of the Eisenhower Doctrine, a presidential commitment "to assist any state in the Middle East threatened by the communism."

Nasser's action was criticized in the West for not having concentrated on internal affairs and precipitating "adventurist actions." In the war, Egypt suffered an estimated 3,000 dead and lost large amounts of equipment. But, with start for the evacuation of the Suez Canal, ports and other invaded areas, the outcome of the Suez affair turned into a political and, to a certain extent, economic victory for Nasser. It remarkably consolidated his position inside Egypt and encouraged him to more enthusiastically pursue the Arab revolution against Western Imperialism. Besides, "it ended the period of British paramountcy in the central area of the Arab Middle East and brought the United States and Russia face to face in that region where the Arabs themselves sought to 'fill the vacuum' between them."[192] The progress of events in the Suez conflict in 1956 are outside the focus of discussion in here. However, as Devereux stated, "they happened against a background of the substantial rethinking and reorganization taking place in the British defence establishment during late 1955 and early 1956."[193]

With the Middle Eastern countries possession of much of the world's oil reserves and with the shortest sea and air routes to Asia and East Africa, the danger felt by the West of leaving a power vacuum in the area for the Soviet Union to fill was explicit. On the other hand, the years 1950 to 1954 were in a messy confusion and proved to be difficult ones for US–British relations in the Middle East. France had already been expelled from the Middle East, and now Britain's withdrawal from its Empire was taking place.[194] Facing the decline of British influence in the Middle East, the US got more actively involved in the region. By the time that the Eisenhower administration took office in January 1953, American foreign policy makers had made a judgment that the US might soon have to take over the British position in the Middle East. Actually, Britain seemed to accept a larger US role in the area. The forthcoming Northern Tier Project initially offered a collaborative policy which would be promoted under the title of the Baghdad Pact by the UK.

For Britain, the Suez Canal area had long been the vital centre of the British defense system in the Middle East. But, no formula could be found for the conciliation of Britain's strategic interests with Egyptian nationalism and Nasser's will for an undebatable leadership position in the Arab World. In this context, Britain agreed to evacuate the Canal Zone, and it absolutely failed to secure Egypt as the hinge upon which a new political/military organisation might turn. Subsequently, the Pact between Turkey and Iraq which was signed in Baghdad on February 24, 1955 was adopted as a substitute. However, Egypt accused Iraq of bowing to the will of Western imperialism.

Nasser's attitude certainly evoked a considerable popular reaction throughout the Middle East. Ultimately, none of the Arab states joined Iraq in the Baghdad Pact. Moreover, with Egyptian–Syrian Mutual Defense Pact on October 20, 1955 and with a similar pact between Egypt and Saudi Arabia signed on October 27, 1955, Egypt managed to draw Syria and Saudi Arabia into what amounted to a counter alliance directed to the Baghdad Pact. The adherence to this arrangement of Saudi Arabia, which had significant ties with the United States, was another of the obstacles which hindered a common Anglo–American approach vis-à-vis their respective calculations in the Middle East.

At the beginning of 1956, British policy-makers' projects reached a phase in which the attitude of Jordan was critical. Britain had bases in Jordan and the country was in receipt of British military and financial support. Jordan's Arab Legion was commanded by General Glubb and the defense of the country was almost entirely dependent on this force. However, Jordan had not joined the Baghdad Pact. The British Government had sent General Templer to Amman in order to draw Jordan into the Baghdad Pact. But, the riots broke out and the Government resigned. Chaotic developments and the changes of Government followed. Early on the morning of March 2 the dismissal of General Glubb was announced by Jordan radio. The dismissal of General Glubb was a heavy blow to Britain's position. And, as expected, Jordan showed no more inclination to join the Baghdad Pact.

The formation of the Baghdad Pact coincided with rapid international changes comprising the other states in the Middle East. The continued opposition of Egypt and finally the Egyptian nationalization of the Suez Canal Company on July 26, 1956, moved the focus away from the Baghdad Pact. Shortly afterwards, war over Suez broke out. The war in Suez had the worse effect on Anglo–American relations. In Britain, anti-American feelings as Ambassador Winthrop W. Aldrich warned Washington, were at a post-war high.[195] On 17 January 1957, on a television broadcast, Macmillan, having succeeded Eden following his leave of Premiership due to ill-health early in the same month, said of restoring the amity with the United States:

> The life of the free world depends upon the partnership between us. Any partners are bound to have their differences now and then. I've always found it so. . . . But true partnership is based on respect. We don't intend to part from the Americans, and we don't intend to be satellites.[196]

Another factor which handicapped the development of the "infant" Baghdad Pact into a reliable military asset, was the US' decision not to join it. In the beginning, within the framework of establishing a Northern Tier, the Eisenhower administration had pressed the Pakistani Government to make a Pact with Turkey. Besides, the US, in conjunction with

Britain, had launched the ALPHA project to settle the Arab–Israeli dispute through secret negotiations. Whereas, the dramatic events of 1955, especially the Egyptian arms deal with the Soviets in his mind, Dulles appeared to be unconcerned about the Baghdad Pact. He concluded that, "If they had not moved to join and promote the Baghdad Pact, then Nasser might not have turn hostile and taken Soviet arms."[197] On the other hand, contrary to the expectation of the British and in spite of the part it played in bringing the Pact about, the United States remained outside of it. As was mentioned above, this was a veiled aspect of the divergence between British and American policies in the Middle East.

The fundamental problem faced by the Baghdad Pact was the lack of any reliable unanimity in the actions of all its members and concerned major powers. On November 21, 1956, Eisenhower told a meeting of advisors "if the British get us into the Baghdad Pact—as the matter would appear to the Arabs—we would lose our influence with the Arabs."[198] Consequently, as Ashton stated, the Baghdad Pact was rejected in favour of the Eisenhower Doctrine; a presidential commitment to assist any state in the Middle East, threatened by "communist menace." Paradoxically in appearance, the regimes inclined towards Moscow in the region was mostly nationalist and this was an ideology the US supported against socialism. In essence however, Arab nationalisms were gaining ground on anti-imperialism championed by the Soviets and this was where the menace Eisenhower concerned with was emanating from. Regarding Britain, Devereux stated that "By 1956, Britain was rethinking her global defense position, and the Baghdad Pact was in effect eliminated as a defense priority."[199]

Had the Suez Debate ended, another threat to Western positions emerged, precipitated by the Soviets' gaining further influence over Syria. Moreover, in Lebanon, there were the signs of confrontation between Muslim and Christian communities, and between pro-Western and pan-Arab fractions which were to prove lethal in the distant years to come.

The US decision to join the Military Committee of the Baghdad Pact, announced at the Bermuda Conference of March 1957, as Foreign Secretary Selwyn Lloyd stated to Harold Caccia, the British Ambassador in Washington, was "very much second the best and no substitute for full accession to the pact."[200]

Under these circumstances, the fourth session of the Council of the Baghdad Pact was convened in Ankara, from January 27 to 30, 1958, under the chairmanship of Adnan Menderes, Prime Minister of Turkey and was attended by delegations from Iraq, Iran, Pakistan and the United Kingdom, as well as the US Secretary of State John Foster Dulles, representing the nonmember US as an observer. British Foreign Secretary Selwyn Lloyd was also present. At the opening meeting the delegates from Iran, Iraq, Turkey, and Pakistan stressed the need for more economic aid to the pact area, while the speakers of United Kingdom and United States expressed the belief that member nations should concentrate on completing economic projects already under way. Dulles, in his opening address pointed out that Congress had authorized the President to use armed forces to assist any nation or group of nations in the Middle East, including the Baghdad Pact nations, that requested assistance against armed aggression by any communist-controlled country.

On the second day of the session the Council approved reports of the military, liaison, and countersubversion committees. The report of the military committee recommended a long term defense building project, which would include a communications system from west Turkey to Pakistan with trunk and lateral highways, harbor and storage facilities at seaports on the Mediterranean, Persian Gulf, and the Arabian Sea, and civil airports that could be readily converted for military use. In the meeting on January 29, Dulles announced that, subject to funds being made available by Congress, $10 million would be provided by the US for the improvement of telephone and radiotelephone links between the capitals of Pakistan, Iran, Iraq, and Turkey, in addition to $8 million already provided for surveys being carried out.

The following months witnessed no increase in efficiency of the Baghdad Pact. In fact, the developments in the region were heading towards another direction. On the 14th of July 1958, Iraqi officers, adhered to the Nasserist pan-Arabism and the *qawmiyya* (historic Arab unity) overthrew the Hashemite monarchy of Iraq established by the support of Britain. During the 14th of July Revolution, the twenty-three-year-old king Faisal II who was educated in Britain (together with his cousin, King Hussein of Jordan), his wife and some of his relatives were killed. Nuri As-Said escaped, but was caught the day after, and was also killed. "Iraq had left the ranks of the Western Alliance. The Baghdad Pact was no more."[201]

The tragedy of Faisal II was another episode which emphasized the fact that the interventions of Britain could no longer be accommodated in the Arabian Peninsula. Faisal IInd's grandfather Faisal, who was the younger son of Sharif Hussein of Mecca, the leader of British instigated

Arab Revolt, was enthroned by Churchill first in Syria in 1920 and after his pressing hard to leave by France, in Iraq in 1921. Churchill noted on this operation of him by saying that "The Sharif's son Faisal offered hope of best and cheapest solution."[202]

The 14th of July Revolution was just 11 months later than the *TIME* magazine had put As-Said on his cover, quoting a senior U.S. diplomat: "We feel Iraq is potentially if not right now the brightest spot in the area. There's hope here to build something solid, and with Nuri in power we can work and build. He has our complete support, and we do not mind the rest of the world knowing it."[203]

Unwavering in its attitude, on February 3, 1958, what *TIME* was reflecting in its cover story allocated to the Turkish Premiere Menderes was, "where a plank bridge spans a small brook that runs into the Black Sea, two Turkish infantrymen stood guard this week. . . . They were two of the thousands of 12¢-a-month Turkish mehmetciks who keep sleepless vigil over the 367-mile border which is the only frontier between Russia and the rest of the world (save for a small, frozen strip of Norway) that the U.S. is committed to defend."[204]

The analysis of *TIME* included that "with his every year in office, Menderes has become more autocratic, more sensitive to criticism. Striking out in fury at anyone questioning his policies, he has half smothered both the press and opposition political parties under a blanket of repressive legislation. Today, only seven years after Turkey won its graduation certificate as a democracy by peacefully voting out of office a regime of a quarter of a century's standing, the Turks again live in a society characterized by the over-the-shoulder glance to see who may be listening."[205] And despite positive reflections as well of Menderes as fairly as possible like his insistence on enhancing Turkey's infrastructure and strengthening national economy, the bright image of the Turkish Premier put forward by *TIME* would dramatically shatter by the military takeover of May 27, 1960 in Turkey, and his bitter fate following Nuri As-Said's destiny.

Interestingly, Vander Lippe argued that during the 1950s the military became a more important political actor in Turkey "because the bulk of American assistance and investment went into military related projects. The increasing status of the military created tensions between civilian and military authority which were manifested in the military coup of 27 May 1960 which overthrew the Democrat Party government."[206]

The emergence of a popular front against the DP Government in Turkey led by—even if this could be true only in part—"American aid destabilized" armed forces and socialists, resented by various measures of the government including the widespread arrests of the protesters of the involvement of US in Turkish politics was a clear paradox. This, therefore requires a wider explanation to give room to the statements on the contrary that mention, in essence, the lowering of the status of the Turkish intelligentsia, meritocrats and military vis-à-vis the *nouveau riche* and *parvenu* who grew rich on lucrative government contracts.

All these contradictions perhaps could lead to nothing else but to the inevitable. In one way or another, the image of "12¢-a-month" Turkish foot soldier presented by *TIME* and once also heard from Dulles when he said that "a Turkish soldier costed 23¢-a-month" created an issue of deep resentment among the Turkish intelligentsia. When the famous socialist poet, Nâzım Hikmet replied to this with his poem "23 Sentlik Askere Dair" (About the Soldier of 23¢)[207] anti-Americanism, no doubt backed by the Soviets, took a giant leap towards becoming a dominant social force in Turkey.

Notes

1. "Americas's Duty in Near East Problem," in *The Sun and the New York Herald*, March 21, 1920, Section 7, Magazine Section, p. 2, img. 88, Library of Congress, http://chroniclingamerica.loc.gov/lccn/sn83030273/1920-03-21/ed-1/seq-88/#date1 = 1836&sort = relevance&rows = 20&words = Empire + Ottoman&searchType = basic&sequence = 0&index = 18&state = &date2 = 1922&proxtext = ottoman + empire&y = 0&x = 0&dateFilterType = year Range&page = 4

2. Nigel John Ashton, "The Hijacking of A Pact: The Formation of the Baghdad Pact and Anglo–American Tensions in the Middle East 1955–58," in *Review of International Studies*, 19, 1993, p. 123.

3. Muhammed Abd el-Wahab Sayed-Ahmed, *Nasser and American Foreign Policy 1952–1956*, (Surrey: Laam Ltd., 1989), p. 26.

4. Elie Kedourie, "Quest for Stability," in *Soviet–American Rivalry in the Middle East*, ed. by J. C. Hurewitz, (New York: Praeger Publishers, 1969), p. 194.

5. Anthony Eden, *Memoirs: Full Circle*, (London: Cassel & Co. Ltd., 1989), p. 331.

6. Roy Fullick and Geoffrey Powel, *Suez: The Double War*, (London: Hamish Hamilton Ltd., 1979), p. 1.

7. Peter L. Hahn, *The United States, Great Britain, and Egypt, 1945–1956*, (North Carolina: University of North Carolina Press, 1991), p. 30.

8. *Ibid.*, pp. 11, 12, 30.

9. Cited in, *ibid.*, p. 30.

10. *Ibid.*

11. *Ibid.*, p. 34.

12. *Ibid.*, pp. 34–35.

13. Mark J. Gasiorowski, *U.S. Foreign Policy and the Shah*, (New York: Cornell University Press, 1991), p. 51.

14. Cited in, Joseph Smith, *The Cold War 1945–1965*, (London: Basic Blackwell Ltd., 1986), p. 12.

15. Cited in, George McGhee, *Envoy to the Middle World: Adventures in Diplomacy*, (New York: Harper & Row Publishers, 1993), p. 20.

16. Cited in, Smith, *The Cold War 1945–1956*, p. 12.

17. Don Peretz, *The Middle East Today*, (New York: Praeger, 1983), p. 124.

18. McGhee, *Envoy to the Middle World*, p. 84.

19. Cited in, *ibid.*, p. 85.

20. *Ibid.*, pp. 86–87.

21. Cited in, Sayed-Ahmed, *Nasser and . . .* , p. 23.

22. *Ibid.*, p. 23.

23. Cited in, Hahn, *The United States . . .* , p. 97.

24. Cited in, *ibid.*, p. 100.

25. *Ibid.*, p. 101.

26. Anthony Nutting, *No End of A Lesson*, (London: Constable & Co.Ltd.,1967), pp. 33–34.

27. Cited in, McGhee, *Envoy to the Middle World*, p. 211.

28. The Tripartite Declaration continued to be cited as a basis for various actions in the Middle East by every American President up to Carter. *Ibid.*, p. 212.

29. *Ibid.*, p. 273.

30. Sayed-Ahmed, *Nasser and . . .* , p. 28.

31. *Ibid.,* pp. 28–29.

32. *Ibid.*, p. 30.

33. *Ibid.*

34. Townsend Hoopes, *The Devil and John Foster Dulles*, (Canada:Little,Brown & Co., 1973), pp. 180–181.

35. Cited in, Sayed-Ahmed, *Nasser and . . .* , p. 30.

36. *Ibid.*, pp. 31–32.

37. Hoopes, *The Devil and . . .* , p. 181.

38. Cited in, Sayed-Ahmed, *Nasser and* . . . , p. 32.

39. P. J. Vatikiotis, *Nasser and His Generation*, (London: Croom Helm Ltd., 1978), p. 108.

40. *Ibid.*

41. Cited in, Sayed-Ahmed, *Nasser and* . . . , p. 58.

42. Vatikiotis, *Nasser and His Generation*, p. 108.

43. Robert Stephens, *Nasser*, (Aylesbury, Bucks: Pelican Books, 1973), p. 109.

44. Sayed-Ahmed, *Nasser and* . . . , p. 24.

45. Oğuz Gökmen, *Bir Zamanlar Hariciye Eski Bir Diplomatın Hatıraları* (Once Upon A Time The Ministry of Foreign Affairs Memoirs of A Former Diplomat), (İstanbul: self publication), pp. 1999; 344–349, respectively.

46. *Ibid.*, pp. 350–353.

47. Mahmut Dikerdem, *Orta Doğu'da Devrim Yılları, Bir Büyükelçi'nin Anıları* (Years of Revolution in the Middle East, An Ambassador's Memoirs), (İstanbul: İstanbul Matbaası, 1977), pp. 68–69.

48. *Ibid.*, p. 77.

49. *Ibid.*, 99–103, *passim.* For the "fez incident," *see,* Bilal Şimşir, *Bizim Diplomatlar (Our Diplomats)*, pp. 270–276.

50. Orhan Koloğlu, *Cumhuriyet'in İlk Onbeş Yılı (1923–1938)* (The First Fifteen Years of the Republic 1923–1938), (İstanbul: Boyut Kitapları, 1999), pp. 303–323, *passim.*

51. Kemal Karpat, "The Turkish Left," in *Journal of Contemporary History, Vol. 1, No. 2*, 1966, p. 179.

52. Cited in, David Devereux, *The Formulation of British Defense Policy Towards the Middle East 1948-56*, (Canada: Macmillan Ltd., 1990), p. 156.

53. Cited in, *ibid.*, pp. 156–157.

54. Isaac Alteras, *Eisenhower and Israel: U.S.-Israeli Relations, 1953–1960*, (Gainesville: The University Press of Florida, 1993), p. 21.

55. *Ibid.*

56. Hahn, *The United States,* . . . , p. 158.

57. Sayed-Ahmed, *Nasser and* . . . , pp. 80–81.

58. *Ibid.*, p. 83.

59. *Ibid.*

60. Folliot, Denise, ed., "Manifesto of the Egyptian Liberation Rally," published on 16 January 1953 in, *Documents on International Affairs 1953,* (London: Royal Institute of International Affairs, Oxford University Press, 1956), p. 308.

61. Yair Evron, *The Middle East: Nations, Super-powers and Wars*, (London: Elek Books Ltd., 1973), p. 132.

62. Sayed-Ahmed, *Nasser and American Foreign Policy 1952-1956*, p. 83.

63. *Ibid.*

64. Hoopes, *The Devil and . . .* , p. 182.

65. William R. Polk, *The Arab World Today*, (Massachusets: Harvard University Press, 1991), p. 390.

66. P. J. Vatikiotis, *The Egyptian Army in Politics,* (Bloomington: Indiana University Press, 1961), pp. 90–92, *passim*.

67. Leonard Mosley, *Dulles: A Biography of Eleanor, Allen, and John Foster Dulles and Their Family Network*, (London: Hodder and Stoughton Ltd., 1978), p. 384.

68. *Ibid.*

69. Anthony Nutting, *Nasser*, (London: Constable and Co. Ltd., 1972), p. 78.

70. *Ibid.,* p. 79.

71. *Ibid.*, p. 77.

72. *Ibid.*

73. *Ibid.*, p. 80.

74. "Middle East Defence, Memorandum by the Chiefs of Staff, on 9th January 1954" in, *Cabinet Papers, CAB. 129/65, C.(54) 9.*

75. Cited in, Mosley, *Dulles: A Biography of . . .* , pp. 383–384.

76. *Ibid.*, p. 384.

77. "United States Project to Associate Military Aid To Pakistan With Middle East Defence, Memorandum by the Secretary of State for Foreign Affairs, on 5th January 1954" in, *Cabinet Papers, CAB. 129/65, C.(54) 4.*

78. *Ibid.*, Article 3.

79. Evron, *The Middle East*, p. 133.

80. SEATO was another anti-communist military pact made up of the US, Britain, France, Australia, New Zealand, The Philippines, Thailand and Pakistan and was formed in September 1954 to counter the communism in the south-west Pacific area below the latitude, 21–31, Polk, *The Arab World Today*, p. 392.

81. Mark J. Gasiorowski, *U.S. Foreign Policy and the Shah*, p. 49.

82. Cited in, McGhee, *Envoy to the Middle World*, p. 79.

83. Scott Lucas, *Divided We Stand: The US and the Suez Crisis*, (London: Hodder and Stoughton, 1991), p. 25.

84. Elisabeth Monroe, *Britain's Moment in the Middle East 1914–1971*, (London: Chatto & Windus Ltd., 1981), p. 180.

85. Keith Kyle, *Suez*, (London: Weidenfeld and Nicolson Ltd., 1991), p. 56.

86. *Ibid.* p. 54.

87. The US in conjunction with Britain, aimed to seek a solution to the Arab–Israeli dispute through covert negotiations as well. Ashton, *Hijacking of A Pact*, p. 131.

88. *Ibid.*

89. Vatikiotis, *The Egyptian Army in Politics*, p. 94.

90. Another perspective on the Baghdad Pact, linking the American promotion of such an organisation with the Britain's decision to join it in April 1955, considered the pact as such. Ashton, *Hijacking of A Pact*, p. 123.

91. Nutting, *Nasser*, p. 81.

92. The Press in Iraq was strictly controlled by the government and the situation was not different from this in throughout the almost entire Middle East. Chatham House Review, *The World Today 1955*, (London: Chatham House, 1955), p. 147.

93. *Ibid.*, pp. 147–148.

94. Cited in, Lucas, *Divided We Stand*, pp. 41–42.

95. Nutting, *Nasser*, p. 81.

96. Cited in, Lucas, *Divided We Stand*, 41. See also, Nutting, *Nasser*, p. 89.

97. Vatikiotis, *Nasser and His Generation*, p. 230.

98. *Ibid.*

99. Noble Frankland, ed., "Statement by Dr. Fadhil Jamali, Iraqi Representative to the United Nations, to the Charter of Deputies, on 6 February 1955," in *Documents on International Affairs 1955*, (London: Royal Institute of International Affairs, Oxford University Press,1958), pp. 320–321.

100. Nutting, *Nasser*, p. 89.

101. William R. Polk, *The US and the Arab World*, (Massachusets: Harvard University Press, 1991), p. 202.

102. Chatham House Review, *The World Today*, p. 148.

103. Nutting, *Nasser*, p. 82.

104. *Ibid.*

105. *Ibid.*, p. 83.

106. *Ibid.*, p. 85.

107. Chatham House Review, *The World Today 1955*, pp. 148–149.

108. Polk, *The Arab World Today*, pp. 392.

109. Polk, *The US and the Arab World*, pp. 230.

110. Robert W. Macdonald, *The League of Arab States*, (Princeton: Princeton University Press, 1965), pp. 77–78.

111. Fahir Armaoğlu, *XX. Yüzyıl Siyasi Tarihi* (XXth Century Political History) *1914–1980 Vol. I*, (Ankara: T.C. İş Bankası Yayınları Kültür Yayınları, 1991), p. 492.

112. The Israeli doctrine of inflicting military reprisal for a string chain of border incidents first applied against Jordan in October 1953. Kylie, *Suez*, p. 62.

113. Chatham House Review, *The World Today 1955*, p. 150.

114. *Ibid.*, pp. 150–151.

115. Sayed-Ahmed, *Nasser and . . .* , p. 107.

116. *Ibid.*, p. 108.

117. Donald Neff, *Warriors at Suez*, (Vermont: Amana Books, 1988), p. 152.

118. Frankland, ed., "Comment by the Israeli Foreign Ministry on the Signature of the Turkish–Iraqi Pact," in *Documents on International Affairs 1955*, p. 289.

119. Evron, *The Middle East*, p. 133.

120. Cited in, Hahn, *The United States . . .* , p. 192.

121. Richard Goold-Adams, *The Time of Power*, (London: Weidenfeld and Nicolson, 1962), p. 79.

122. Alistair Horne, *Harold Macmillan Vol I. of the Official Bibliography*, (London: Macmillan London Ltd., 1988), p. 378.

123. Geoffrey Kemp, "The Military Build-up: Arms Control or Arms Trade?" in *Crisis Management and the Super-powers in the Middle East*, ed. by Gregory Trevarton, (London: The International Institute for Strategic Studies, Gower Publishing Ltd., 1981), p. 31.

124. Nadav Safran, *From War to War*, (Indianapolis: Bobbs-Merril Educational Publishing, 1977), p. 51.

125. Cited in, Lucas, *Divided We Stand*, p. 48.

126. Robert Rhodes James, *Anthony Eden*, p. 444.

127. Erskine B. Childers, *The Road to Suez*, (London: Bobbs-Merril Educational Publishing, 1977), pp. 133–134.

128. *Ibid.*

129. Cited in, Lucas, *Divided We Stand*, p. 59.

130. Vatikiotis, *Nasser and His Generation*, p. 232.

131. Joel Beinan, "The Communist Movement and Nationalist Political Discourse in Nasserist Egypt," in *The Middle East Studies*, (Autumn, 1987), pp. 568–584, *passim*.

132. Horne, *Harold Macmillan Vol. I . . .* , p. 378.

133. Walter Z. Laqueur, *The Soviet Union and the Middle East*, (London: Routledge & Kegan Paul Ltd., 1959), p. 211.

134. Sayed-Ahmed, *Nasser and . . .* , p. 111.

135. *Ibid.*

136. *Ibid.*, p. 112.

137. *Ibid.*

138. Peter Lyon, *Eisenhower Portrait of the Hero*, (Boston: Little, Brown, 1974), p. 685.

139. The project of strengthening the pro-Western countries along the borders of the SU had begun in 1950 under the Truman administration but, stalled by the reconstruction of Europe and the outbreak of the war in Korea. Following the shift in US' military and economic aid programs from Europe towards countries in the Middle East and east Asia, the US concentrated its efforts on regaining the initiative against the SU. Gasiorowski, *U.S. Foreign Policy and the Shah*, p. 93.

140. Rouhollah K. Ramazani, *Iran's Foreign Policy 1941–1973: A Study of Foreign Policy in Modernizing Nations*, (Virginia: The University Press of Virginia, 1975), p. 276.

141. Eisenhower, *Mandate for Change 1953–1956*, p. 165.

142. Cited in, Ramazani, *Iran's Foreign Policy 1941–1973*, p. 277.

143. Noble Frankland, ed., "US State Department's Statement on Persian Adherence to the Baghdad Pact, 12 October 1955," in *Documents on International Affairs*, (London: Royal Institute for International Affairs, Oxford University Press, 1958), p. 304.

144. Cited in, Ramazani, *Iran's Foreign Policy 1941–1973*, p. 278.

145. *Ibid.*, p. 279.

146. Laqueur, *The Soviet Union and the Middle East*, p. 178.

147. *Ibid.*

148. *Ibid.*, p. 193.

149. Noble Frankland, ed., "Soviet Note to Persia, 12 October 1955," in *Documents on International Affairs 1955*, p. 305.

150. *Ibid.*, p. 208.

151. Safran, *From War to War*, p. 69.

152. Cited in, Lucas, *Divided We Stand*, p. 68.

153. Certainly, the most apparent signal that Nasser was getting entangled with anti-Western sentiments was his recognition of communist China and breaking off relations with Formosa on 16 May 1955. To Western diplomats, Nasser tried to explain that he had fears that the Soviets might agree to Western proposals for an arms embargo to the Middle East. He said, in case of an embargo, he might be able to find another source in China. In reality, a Chinese mission was established in a large villa in Cairo and Egypt had sold £10 million worth of cotton to China. Stephens, *Nasser*, pp. 183–184.

154. Lucas, *Divided We Stand*, p. 79.

155. Cited in, Anthony Sampson, *Macmillan A Study of Ambiguity*, (London: Allen Lane The Penguin Press, 1967), p. 104.

156. Cited in, Lucas, *Divided We Stand*, p. 91.

157. James, *Anthony Eden*, p. 429.

158. Lucas, *Divided We Stand*, p. 75.

159. Frankland, "Speech by Anthony Eden in the House of Commons, on 12 November 1955," in *Documents on International Affairs*, 1955, pp. 394–395.

160. *FRUS*, 1955–1957, Vol. XIII, p. 8.

161. Cited in, Kylie, *Suez*, p. 90.

162. *Ibid.*

163. Sherman Adams, *First-hand Report The Inside Story of the Eisenhower Administration*, (London: Hutchinson & Co. Ltd., 1962), p. 196.

164. Cited in, Lyon, *Eisenhower Portrait of the Hero*, p. 686.

165. *Ibid.*, pp. 686–687.

166. Lucas, *Divided We Stand*, pp. 129.

167. Neff, *Warriors at Suez*, p. 174.

168. *Ibid.*, pp. 174–175.

169. James, *Anthony Eden*, p. 433.

170. Neff, *Warriors at Suez*, pp. 124–125.

171. Macdonald, *The League of Arab States*, p. 293.

172. Lucas, *Divided We Stand*, p. 129.

173. Uriel Dann, *King Hussein and the Challenge of Arab Radicalism Jordan 1955–1967*, (London: Oxford University Press, 1989), p. 36.

174. Cited in, Kyle, *Suez*, p. 90.

175. Lucas, *Divided We Stand*, p. 138.

176. Cited in, Noble Frankland, Vera King eds., in "Introduction to the Suez Crisis," in *Documents on International Affairs 1956*, (London: Royal Institute of International Affairs, 1959), p. 73.

177. "Speech by President Nasser at Alexandria, 27 July 1956," in *ibid.*, pp. 80–81.

178. *Ibid.*

179. "Answer by Sir Anthony Eden to Questions in the House of Commons on the Nationalization of the Suez Canal Company, 27 July 1956," *ibid.*, p. 115.

180. Cited in, "Introduction to the Suez Crisis," *ibid.*, pp. 73–74.

181. As a result of the disintegration of the Ottoman, Habsburg, Hohenzollern and Romanov Empires and the changes in the British which had been occurred since 1888, the operative word was in essence "beneficiaries." The signatories to the 1888 Convention were the representatives of Britain, France, Turkey, Russia, Germany, Austria, Hungary, Italy, Spain and Netherlands.

182. Lucas, *Divided We Stand*, p. 155.

183. Adams, *First-hand Report*, p. 105.

184. Neff, *Warrior at Suez*, p. 290.

185. *Ibid.*, p. 289.

186. Lucas, *Divided We Stand*, p. 186.

187. Nutting, *No End of A Lesson*, p. 110.

188. Stephens, *Nasser*, pp. 204–205.

189. *Ibid.*

190. Cited in, Lucas, *Divided We Stand*, p. 239.

191. Frankland, *Documents on International Affairs 1956*, p. 244.

192. Stephens, *Nasser*, pp. 246–247. Evidently, Nasser's daring attitudes had a "dark" side. Whilst it fostered the self-confidence of the Arab countries, it increased the risk takings in the foreign policy decisions makings. Almost a decade later, Nasser hoped in June 1967—the Six-Day War—to emerge as political and diplomatic victor without having to wage war, as he had succeeded in doing after Suez in 1956. However, Nasserism became the principal victim of the Six Day War which seriously challenged the room for huge risk-taking in foreign policy formulation emergent from the Suez experience. Bassam Tibi,

Conflict and War in the Middle East 1967–91, (New York: St. Martin's Press, 1993), pp. 82; 92–93.

193. David R. Devereux, *The Formulation of British Defence Policy Towards the Middle East 1948–56*, (Canada:MacMillan Academic and Professional Ltd., 1990), p. 184.

194. Fullick, *Suez: The Double War*, p. 5.

195. Horne, *Macmillan*, p. 21.

196. *Ibid.*, p. 16.

197. Ashton, *Hijacking of A Pact*, p. 131.

198. Cited in, *ibid.*, p. 136.

199. Devereux, *The Formulation of British* . . . , p. 184.

200. Cited in, Ashton, *HiJacking of A Pact*, p. 136.

201. Horne, *Macmillan*, p. 93.

202. Janet Wallach, *Desert Queen*, (London: Weidenfeld & Nicolson, 1996), p. 297.

203. "Iraq: The Pasha," in *TIME*, June 17, 1957, http://www.time.com/time/magazine/article/0,9171,867710-9,00.html

204. "Turkey: The Impatient Builder," in *TIME*, February 3, 1958, http://www.time.com/time/magazine/article/0,9171,865731,00.html

205. *Ibid.*

206. John M. Vander Lippe, "Forgotten Brigade of the Forgotten War: Turkey's Participation in the Korean War," in *Middle Eastern Studies*, Vol. 36, No. 1, Jan. 2000, p. 100.

207. Sertel, *Nâzım Hikmet ile* . . . , p. 172.

Chapter 9

Conclusion

A great noise has been produced by the so-called change of policy of the United States toward European affairs. The topic of the day, here and all over the East, as you may well believe, is the alleged demand of the Cabinet of Washington to the Porte of a spot where to harbor, under an American flag, an American fleet, with the right of property on it. True or not, the matter is fully discussed, and I may say admitted.[1]

International relations of the immediate aftermath of WW II were dominated by chaotic changes. There is a strong argument that Churchill miscalculated the Kremlin's ability to turn around the situation against the Germans and he expected a deadlock which would greatly weaken both Bolshevism and Nazism. That is why the Soviet Army appeared unexpectedly in Berlin and the Russians had such bargaining power. Admittedly, from then on the Soviets' increased assertiveness in global affairs prompted a rivalry between the Kremlin and Washington. Unlike any other Allied country, the SU had reached the end of the war with its forces deployed in critical parts of Europe. The vigilance of Soviet military machine had paved the way to assure Kremlin's seat in the negotiation table of the Big Three. Soviet assertiveness, thus was perceived as a potential threat by many countries, particularly by those bordering the SU.

As for Turkey, the prelude to the post WW II period was marked by its suspicions of the Kremlin's intentions. At this juncture, the Soviet demands on Turkish territories and over the Turkish Straits in 1945 accelerated Ankara's search for a definitive alliance with the West. Despite the fact that some Turkish statesmen and ex-military officials i.e. the former MFA Tevfik Rüştü Aras, and Marshal Fevzi Çakmak advocated that an understanding between Ankara and the Kremlin could be reached—similar to the first Turco–Soviet rapprochement which took place during the Turkish War of Liberation—events proved that the conditions in 1917 and in 1945 were dramatically different making any agreement hardly possible.

Turkey's quest for a Western Alliance in the aftermath of WW II was a natural end-result of the experiences inherited from wartime diplomacy, however, with hasty attempts some times. According to Turkish foreign policy makers, the years of WW II had proved that aggression could emerge from the side of totalitarian regimes which had combined their forces or by one of them acting alone. It was also evaluated in Ankara that it was the rising aggression itself on the part of these regimes which prompted their revisionist attempts; a fact which could not be reasoned by their wish for the correction of the misgivings of the previous world order imposed by the great powers.

While Turkey's sensitivity against the bloc strategy of world powers was increasing, the Nazi–Soviet pact of 1939 demonstrated that the danger could emerge as a collective movement. Subsequently, it was understood that the threat would continue to exist even in the aftermath of the split in this bloc. Thus, the threat itself was asserted as being in the very existence of undemocratic and totalitarian powers. Given this, forced by the conditions of an unpredictable international environment, Turkey constantly sought the ways to enhance its security; an effort which eventually paved the way to building a peculiar sui-generis crisis management/prevention system. This was a complex system which could not be simply explained in terms of classical neutrality or an evasive foreign policy.

Undoubtedly, Ankara was a center where the Allied and Axis diplomacy was trying to counter-balance each other, which brought Turkey to the edge of belligerency on the Allied side some times. Indeed, prior to 1944, neither the victories nor the threats of the Axis could produce a desired outcome for Berlin. İnönü firmly believed that the Western nations would sooner or later win the war and it was merely a matter of time to save Turkey from the destruction of the global conflict. When it came to 1944, admittedly, efforts to drag Turkey in the conflict had come to an end. In this regard, particularly the Soviets were uneager to accept Turkish belligerency which would legitimize Turkey's position on the side of the Allies and provide it with a say-so on the post-war order.

As generally agreed upon, Turkish foreign policy was oriented towards the Allied side during these years. Ankara's balancing attitude was also being shaped by the course of international affairs. In many respects, however, Ankara's increasing responsiveness to the fluctuations in international politics was a deviation from the foreign policy of Atatürk. Instructed by Atatürk in January 1938, Bayar, who was Prime Minister then, had no hesitation to clearly express in his press statement that it was unthinkable that any other political system of foreign origin could ever be imported into Turkey and there was no anti-Jewish feeling in Turkey. Following the death of Atatürk in November 1938, as the Provisional President, İnönü had made a statement which indicated that Turkish policy would follow the Kemalist heritage and remain in the existing line. The—frequently referred—Treaty of Mutual Assistance Between Turkey, Britain and France on October, 19, 1939 was concluded by the Turkish Government in this spirit.

However, in comparison to the Atatürk era, İnönü administration was in favour of maintaining a more flexible foreign policy. Correspondingly, in 1942 when the German armies were concentrating their strongholds throughout Europe and being deployed in key areas, Ankara had shifted to implement the "capital tax" on the revenues of non-muslims. Consecutively, an undiscriminatory sweep affected the Turkish citizens of Christian and Jewish origin—some of whom were sentenced to serve years in working camps—who could not meet the enormous amounts of tax arbitrarily assessed and imposed by the Turkish authorities. Antisemitist propaganda and the claims on the non-Muslims "selfish money making efforts" regardless of the country's domestic socio-economic problems were also increasingly promoted in the press, radio and elsewhere. With a view to the fact that, however, Ankara's measures against non-Muslims never acquired a wicked nature similar to that of Nazis, there is every reason to assert that in this move, İnönü had planned to divert the attention of the Axis war machine to somewhere else and give the message that Turkey was seriously considering to give credit to the new order envisaged by the revisionists.

Within a year, having seen that the course of the global conflict was gradually removing Turkey out of the scope of belligerent powers, İnönü decided to lift the pressures on non-Muslims in the country and quickly abolished the working camps. Subsequently, it was announced that the taxpayers would pay their debts without leaving their homes.

In 1944, when the Red Army was gaining victories, İnönü then turned against the Turkish nationalists (Pan-Turanists), who were trialed and found guilty of racist activities. This was clearly a message to the Kremlin which underscored that Turkey would not allow the ultra nationalists to act freely in the country.

Under these circumstances, the development of Turkish democracy, basically had its roots in Ankara's wish for joining the Western camp. While the difference between the Western grouping of states and the Eastern bloc was crystallizing, Ankara moved quickly to put in order its domestic affairs. The first elections in 1946 were not a successful attempt in this respect since the rumours of Ankara's reckless manipulation of elections were widespread in the country.

Apparently, the post-election government was at odds between pursuing a more liberal attitude towards the opponents of the regime in Turkey and closing of ranks against the external danger. Initially, it was aimed to develop a middle-way approach to conciliate these policies, which soon proved to be in vain. Again, İnönü felt a necessity to shape Ankara's foreign policy in line with the basic trends in the Western grouping of the states and a strong anti-communist policy adopted by the government became dominant. From then on, this closing of ranks against the SU affected particularly the left wing of the political spectrum. There had been a strong upsurge of socialist activity in the period immediately following the war. In December 1945, the Turkish socialists' attempts for a greater freedom of political expression for the left had been decisively set back by the violent demonstrations and a year later in December 1946 the small bodies of the leftist opposition were dissolved by the martial law that had been maintained in Thrace and the İstanbul region since the war.

This policy choice of İnönü was criticized especially by those who believed that Turkey's relations with the SU had some basic features which separated it with those of the West in general and the US in particular. As for the democratization efforts of Turkey, it was also asserted by various scholars that İnönü's moving towards a liberal system in Turkey was not basically an outcome of his close watch of possibilities as he had realized that this was the only way to lead the country into the future. However, WW II and the extreme measures arising out of these extraordinary times had interrupted Turkey's development in this regard.

In the aftermath of the war, İnönü was determined to act quickly to embark on democracy. This was not in order to please the West, but as a result of his careful study of democratic literature and his apprehension that modernizing character of the Republic could only be maintained through achieving a multi-party political life in the country. This was undoubtedly, aimed at by Atatürk as well, although the attempts in this direction in his time were unfruitful. Looking at these, it was also evaluated that İnönü was predominantly acting for domestic reasons, because he had begun this process before WW II and then he had returned to it afterwards. On this premise, he was determined to achieve a greater democracy standard in Turkey regardless of the course of international events.[2]

By the turn of 1945, Turkey was indeed at a turning point. It was increasingly felt in the power corridors of Ankara that maintaining an alliance with Britain and the US was of utmost importance. Meanwhile, in 1945, in line with the opinion of some British statesmen and officials, the British Minister for Board of Trade, Harold Wilson, pointed out in his speech in the House Commons that the 1939 Mutual Assistance Treaty between Britain, France and Turkey was still in force and could be utilized as a proper basis to strengthen relations with Ankara. Britain's acknowledgement of the 1939 Treaty was an encouragement to the Turks. It was, however, soon understood by İnönü that British efforts were overwhelmingly focused on the Middle East. Concurrently, there was every reason to believe that London was pursuing a regular withdrawal strategy from its global status. In this case, the pro-Western explanation of the Turkish perception of regional developments included that the Turks "began after WW II to look to the United states more and more. They saw that Britain was not going to be able to continue to be the protector of small countries around the world as it had been in the inter-war period."[3]

In its turn, the US was not in favor of expanding the scope of 1939 Treaty either. Until the Truman Doctrine Washington had thought that Turkey was in Britain's "area of responsibility." It was the Truman Doctrine that marked a complete change in the US perception of Turkey. With a view to the attempts of the Kremlin in the region, in fact, Washington was mainly interested in Greece and Turkey and to some extent in Iran. First of all, it was considered that Greece was the country that was under siege while Turkey was relatively quiet. In view of this circumstance, the Truman Doctrine was more about Greece rather than Turkey.

In fact, some of the Congressmen then said, linking Turkey with Greece was the only way that the administration could get a program for Turkey, "because on its own merits it did not require one. In one way or another, the Truman Doctrine in 1947 marks a very sharp break. Because no longer did the British have much of a role in protecting Turkey."[4]

Particularly in the aftermath of the Marshall Aid, Ankara's efforts to achieve a Mediterranean/Middle Eastern security organization either as proposed by London along the lines of 1939 Treaty or in another form, proved to be unfruitful. Because, the US neither dealt with the 1939 Treaty nor it reacted to suggestions for a Mediterranean pact. As mentioned above, since the Truman administration could hardly convince the Congress on the necessity of including Turkey in the assistance program, Ankara was experiencing a serious difficulty to express its security anxieties and its wish to incorporate its defense to that of the West. Besides, the optimism in some US circles about continued cooperation with the SU following the defeat of the Axis, was no doubt increasing Turkey's difficulties to express its need for Western support to stand against the claims of the Kremlin.

Throughout the WW II, Turkey had kept its army mobilized and its determination to resist strong. The Turkish forces were also increasingly deployed against a threat which might possibly be generated from the SU. Even after 1944, when the SU preferred the preservation of Turkey's non-belligerent status and tried to give assurances of its good intentions, alarmed by the vigilance and assertiveness the Soviets demonstrated, military exercises were regularly held in the Eastern Anatolia. Here, the troop movements in big scales were a clear indication of Ankara's threat perception from the Red Army which the Turkish General Staff considered that might attempt to exploit the chaotic international situation to grasp the long disputed provinces in this region.[5]

Meanwhile, despite the fact that the Soviet ambitions for an extensive sphere of influence was apparent, among the Turkish intellectuals, there were strong opponents of the pro-American attitude of the Turkish Government. In its turn, the İnönü administration was not tolerant against such an opposition, particularly at a time when he was in search of a definitive alliance with the West in general and the US in particular.

The DP's election victory in May 1950 was a hope for those who assumed that Bayar and Menderes would take greater steps towards democratization in the country. To the disappointment of those optimist about this new regime, the DP administration soon proved that the time was still not ripe to voice such expectations. From then on, the Turkish socialists' and communists'—although they were few in a comparison to the former—attempts to explain their views were frequently hampered and brought about disastrous consequences for themselves.

Similar to the RPP administration and many times more severely, the DP Government chose to suppress the opposition, especially the "communists" through relentless measures. In this context, regardless of their statements explaining that they were not communists, the socialist opponents were all considered as ideologically associated with the SU. Meanwhile, a group of socialist figures explained their view that they desired neither an American nor a Soviet model for the country. M. Ali Aybar wrote in April 1947 that "we are obliged to be the friends of the Americans, the English, and the Soviets. . . . In this understanding and sincerity, we can make an alliance with America and England which will not be directed against the Soviets on the one hand, and conclude an alliance with the Soviets which will not be directed against America and England on the other." In an attempt to explain that better relations between Turkey and the SU were in the interest of both countries—and also agreeing with the reactions of the Turkish Government, Aybar stated that it might be found reasonable to resort to other measures when the Soviet claims of territory and bases were faced. However, he said, "we do not believe that a friendship established in the first days of the War of Liberation and continued until the last years may be replaced by an enmity for a non-apparent reason. Of course, there will be some reasons for this. It was necessary to find out these reasons and remove them, and to work for revitalizing this old friendship. It was natural that this could be done mutually. But we had to and must do it in our share without fail. It should not be forgotten that Russia is very close to us, while the US is very far."[6]

Clearly, this was a generally acknowledged idea among the socialists in Turkey, since many of them believed in the virtue of following an independent course of action in international affairs. The advocates of this view put forward that Turkey should follow an independent policy which would guarantee its impartiality in any possible conflict. Again, it was pointed out that, through bilateral agreements—the number and scope of most of which kept secret to date—Ankara's granting of rights to the US to control the usage of American aid was irreconcilable with Turkey's sovereignty.[7]

It was also argued that Turkey's traditional relations with the SU which went back to the foundation years of both countries were providing them with further means of understanding. This historical ground—which was not shared with the US for instance—could be developed to overcome the crisis between the Kremlin and Ankara.

Similarly, Z. Sertel, another writer of socialist origin, who had also served as the General Director of Press during the Atatürk era, explained that friendship with the Soviets was one of the pillars of Atatürk's foreign policy. According to him, even in his last moments, Atatürk had reiterated that Turkey should not follow an offensive policy against the Soviets. Besides, he had stated that Turkey should not participate in any agreement targeting the Soviets either directly or indirectly. Sertel stated that Bayar—then, the Prime Minister—had told him this wish of Atatürk in one of their conversations, which was later on approved by the former MFA, T. Rüştü Aras as well. Sertel argued that İnönü's first act after coming to power, however, was to remove Bayar from the office—to whom he felt a personal dislike as a result of Atatürk's nomination of Bayar in replacement of him as the Prime Minister—instead of dealing with substantial issues, such as trying to enhance this understanding of Kemalist heritage on the making of foreign policy.[8]

As for the Turkish participation in the Korean War, even after then, Washington had not decided to give its support to Turkey's adherence to NATO. In September 1950, the US JCS was still arguing that the inclusion of Greece and Turkey to NATO could adversely affect the progress achieved. Corresponding to the analysis above, the JCS asserted that the inclusion of these states would cause a problem in concerting military planning and actions in the Middle East and the Mediterranean with those in progress in Western Europe. Therefore, the JCS offered to give these countries associate status by which their representatives would participate in coordinated planning against any Soviet attack.

In this context, the JCS envisaged a series of alternatives. The first alternative was granting Greece and Turkey a consultative status in NAT, the consequences of which the JCS asserted that, would be mostly on the extent and nature of the consultations which would be held. The second alternative was to concentrate on the option of creating a regional pact in the Eastern Mediterranean and the Middle Eastern area. Whereas, with the exception of Turkey, the countries in the Near and Middle East were militarily weak, making such an arrangement unsound. Of course, political difficulties in drawing these countries together was another handicap.

The last alternative was a unilateral declaration by the US, or a multilateral declaration with Britain and France to express that aggression against Greece, Turkey and Iran would not be tolerated. However, again the JCS did not recommend this option since the US had made an extensive military commitment and it could not provide more military aid in the near future. In its report, the JCS formulated this last alternative along the lines of communicating an informal guarantee to Turkey by these three states. It was asserted that since the defensive strength of NATO had not achieved the necessary improvement which would permit Turkey's membership, such assurances would dispel the Turkish feeling of insecurity and compensate to some extent the possible disappointment in Turkey's failure to achieve full membership in NATO. Here, it was stated that Greece and Turkey could be offered membership as soon as the defense of the members of NATO were reasonably guaranteed.[9]

All of these perhaps, served to build a repulsive attitude in the making of Turkish foreign policy the effects of which was felt in many years to come. Meanwhile, the strategies of socio-economic development could hardly be improved and the country's resources were unsystematically used, and its dependency constantly increased, making it almost unavoidable to tie its fate to a Western alliance.

Undoubtedly, Ankara's exclusion from the NATO as a founding member and consecutively, the rejection of its two formal applications caused both anxiety and disturbance in the Turkish Government. The second application of the Turkish Government was made in August 1950, following the Menderes Government's decision of contributing troops to the UN Command in Korea. However, to the astonishment of Ankara, the Council of NATO declined this application on the grounds of its smaller members' unwillingness to make commitments for the defense of Turkey.

However, the conditions of the Cold War soon dictated its own requirements in Turkish–NATO relations. Through its participation in the Korean War and in the military/diplomatic efforts aiming at forming a politico–military grouping in the Middle East, Ankara had demonstrated that it had all the assets to be placed in this scheme. Ultimately, backed by the US' evaluation that Turkey's geostrategic position was of tremendous value for the alliance, the difficulties caused by the resistance of the European members of the NAT were gradually overcome. In fact, this time, the US' leading role in the alliance was forcing the American military planners to make recommendations for the inclusion of Turkey in the NAT. Even the listening stations in Turkey and the intelligence gathered by the U-2s based on the Turkish territory would soon provide the US with an efficient system of monitoring the Soviets; a regular reconnaissance activity which would otherwise cost tens of million dollars to the US.[10]

Finally, when a comparison between the outcomes of the futile efforts around the MEDO and the concurrent hot conflict over Korea was made, it can be concluded that between 1950 and 1952, the continuation of politics by war, and the continuation of war by politics, perhaps acquired one of its most interesting examples in the making of Turkish foreign policy. The first enlargement of NATO by the inclusion of Turkey and Greece coincided with this period. The Soviets' and the US' moves towards escalating the Cold War continued in the same interval and a bipolar search for balance of power ensued which in fact, was a contradiction in the original concept of balance.

The Middle East was not spared from various ups and downs either. In Iraq, Nuri As-Said and the old nationalists around him had believed that Arab aspirations could and should be achieved and reconciled with the Western powers. Whereas, the young nationalists led by Egypt had put forward that the Arab lands divided up after the first World War to give the West, specifically to Britain, were the instruments of "divide and rule." As-Said and his Government had only one chance. It was that the West should extend them military and political backing. He was in a desperate need of a strong military–political support because his friendship with Britain and the West had laid the ill-conceived Iraqi monarchy wide open to attacks. This help never came and unfolding events prove that As-Said had, in fact, a poor reading of the events surrounding Iraq.

At a National Security Council Meeting on 24 July 1958, US Secretary of State, John Foster Dulles commented that, "the Iraqi Government fell because Iraq was in an unnatural association with Turkey and the United Kingdom in the Baghdad Pact."[11] While, according to some, however, it was clear that the long-standing misgivings of the US Government about the Baghdad Pact worked to the disadvantage of this formation, and as regards the coup in Iraq, the US attitude did not resist the military conspirators in their action to tear Iraq apart from the Western camp. The advocates of this view suggested that another consequence of the Middle East Crisis in 1958, had been "to create an apparent threat to Turkey by allowing Russia to establish herself on Turkey's southern flank."[12]

In the end, many of the results of the Anglo–American policies around the Northern Tier project, were far from the predicted and were at least dramatic. The Baghdad Pact which became subjected to various challenges, with the shift of the policies mainly pursued by the UK and US, was left out of strategic planning by the late 1956s. However, a quest for "Northern Tier defense" remained but, could hardly be achieved. The Baghdad Pact, renamed the Central Treaty Organisation (CENTO) after Iraq's defection, was not attempted to bring into life again.

Turkey's decision to ally itself with the Cold War Western grouping of states and ruling out the existence of reliable possibility of distancing itself from the bipolar conflict required it to make a fundamental decision that shaped its *weltanschauung* and its course of action in country's all areas of development. This, however, remained as an issue which was neither adequately perceived nor fully appreciated in the volatile atmosphere of 1950s and onwards and went largely unnoticed on the part of Western grouping of states.

For Turkey, the years 1952 to 1958 marked the end of an era and the beginning of another. The Turkish position in the Cold War was first consolidated in the same period. Eventually, Turkey placed itself in the Western camp, no doubt, with accompanying duties arising thereof.

Notes

1. "Excitement About the United States' Policy on European Affairs", in *New-York Tribune*, November 12, 1866, img. 1, Library of Congress, http://chroniclingamerica.loc.gov/lccn/sn83030214/1866-11-12/ed-1/seq-1/#date1=1836&sort=&date2=1922&words=Empire+Ottoman&sequence=0&lccn=&index=5&state=&rows=20&ortext=&proxtext=ottoman+empire&year=&phrasetext=&andtext=&proxValue=&dateFilterType=yearRange&page=377

2. These views were expressed by George Harris in my interview with him.

3. *Ibid.*

4. *Ibid.*

5. As told by, Retd. Col. Þükrü Erkal, Research Specialist in TGS, Directorate of Military History and Strategic Research, in my interview with him.

6. M. Ali Aybar, "Her Şeyden Evvel ve Herşeyin Üstünde İstiklal," (Above All and Before All Independence), in *Bağımsızlık Demokrasi Sosyalizm* (Independence Democracy Socialism), (İstanbul: Gerçek Yayınevi, 1968), p. 100.

7. M. Ali Aybar, "Dosta Düşmana Beyanname" (Declaration to the Friend and Foe) in, *Bağımsızlık Demokrasi* . . . , p. 118.

8. Zekeriya Sertel, *Hatırladıklarım*, p. 216.

9. *FRUS*, 1950, *Vol. V.*, pp. 1306–1309.

10. As told by George Harris in my interview with him.

11. Ashton, *HiJacking of A Pact*, p. 136.

12. Horne, *Macmillan*, p. 99.

Bibliography

Primary Sources: Published Official Documents

Turkey

Düstur (Laws), C. 27, 28, 29, 30, 31, Ankara: Devlet Matbaası.

Genelkurmay Harp Tarihi Başkanlığı, Kore Harbinde Türk Silahlı Kuvvetlerinin Muharebeleri (Battles of Turkish Armed Forces in the Korean War) (1950–1953), Ankara: Gnkur. Basımevi, 1975.

İsmet İnönü'nün TBMM'deki Konuşmaları (Speeches Delivered by İsmet İnönü in the TGNA, C. 2, (1939–1960), Ankara: TBMM Basımevi Müdürlüğü, 1993.

Resmi Gazete (Official Gazette), Years, 1946–1950.

TBMM Tutanak Dergisi (TGNA Journal of Records), 1946–1952.

United States of America

China and U.S. Far East Policy 1945–1966, Washington D.C.: Congressional Quarterly Service, 1967.

Current Developments in US Foreign Policy, Volumes, I–IV, Washington D.C.: The Brookings Institute.

Foreign Relations of the United States, Washington, D.C.: USGPO.

    i.   1945, The Potsdam Conference, Vols. I, II.

    ii. 1945, Conferences at Malta and Yalta.

    iii. 1945, Vol. VIII.

    iv. 1946, Eastern Europe, The Soviet Union, Vol. VI.

    v.   1946, The Near East and Africa, Vol. VII.

    vi. 1947, The Near East and Africa, Vol. V.

    vii. 1948, Eastern Europe; The Soviet Union, Vol. IV.

    viii. 1949, Western Europe, Vol. IV.

ix. 1949, Eastern Europe; The Soviet Union, Vol. V.
x. 1950, The Near East, South Asia, and Africa, Vol. V.
xi. 1951, The Near East and Africa, Vol. V.
xii. 1952–1954, The Near and Middle East (in two parts), Vol. IX.
xiii. 1955–1957, Near East: Jordan–Yemen, Vol. XIII.
United States Treaties and Other International Agreements: 1952. Volumes I–II–III, Washington, D.C: USGPO.

United Kingdom

Cabinet Papers, CAB. 66/3, 66/4. Public Record Office.
Cabinet Papers, (5th January 1954) CAB. 129/65, C.(54) 4.
Cabinet Papers, (9th January 1954) CAB. 129/65, C.(54) 9.
Command Papers, Cmd. 5755.
Command Papers, 1950, Cmd. 8078.
Command Papers, October 1950 to May 1951, Cmd. 8366.
Command Papers, 1953, Cmd. 8793.
Command Papers, Session 1955–56 (9531–9558), Cmd. 9544.
Documents on International Affairs, Royal Institute of International Affairs,
   i. 1937, ed. by, Stephen Heald, London: Oxford University Press, 1939.
   ii. 1938 Vol. I, ed. by, Monica Curtis, London: Oxford University Press, 1942.
   iii. 1939–1946 Vol. I (March–September 1939), ed. by,Arnold J. Toynbee, London: Oxford University Press, 1951.
   iv. 1953, ed., by Denise Folliot, London: Oxford University Press, 1956.
   v. 1955, ed., by Noble Frankland, London: Oxford University Press, 1958.
   vi. 1956, ed., by Noble Frankland, Vera King, London: Oxford University Press, 1959.
Documents on British Foreign Policy, Third Series Vol. V (April 4–June 7, 1939), ed. by, E. L. Woodward, London: HMSO, 1952.
Documents on German Foreign Policy, Series D,
   i. Vol. V (June 1937–March 1939), London: HMSO, 1953.
   ii. Vol. VI (March–August 1939), London: HMSO, 1953.
   iii. Vol.VIII (September 4, 1939–March 18, 1940), London: HMSO, 1954.

iv. Vol. X (June 23–August 31, 1940), London: HMSO, 1957.
v. Vol. XI (September 1, 1940–January 31, 1941), London: HMSO, 1961.

Hansard: The Official Record of House of Commons Debates, Fifth Series,
i. Vol. 336, London: HMSO, 1938.
ii. Vol. 347, London: HMSO, 1939.
iii. Vol. 355, London: HMSO, 1939.

Royal Institute of International Affairs, Documents on International Affairs,
i. 1937, ed. by, Stephen Heald, London: Oxford University Press, 1939.
ii. 1938 Vol. I, ed. by, Monica Curtis, London: Oxford University Press, 1942.
iii. 1939–1946 Vol. I (March–September 1939), ed. by,Arnold J. Toynbee, London: Oxford University Press, 1951.
iv. 1953, ed., by Denise Folliot, London: Oxford University Press, 1956.
v. 1955, ed., by Noble Frankland, London: Oxford University Press, 1958.
vi. 1956, ed., by Noble Frankland, Vera King, London: Oxford University Press, 1959.

Memoirs and Other Published Primary Sources

Acheson, Dean, *Present at the Creation*, NY: W.W. Norton & Co., 1987.

Adams, Sherman, *First-hand Report: The Inside Story of the Eisenhower Administration*, London: Hutchinson & Co. Ltd., 1962.

Akant, İlhan, *Moskova Otel National 333 Numaralı Oda* (Hotel National Moscow Room 333), İstanbul: Milliyet Yayınları, 1990.

Aydemir, Şevket Süreyya, *Suyu Arayan Adam* (The Man Searching for Water), İstanbul: Remzi Kitabevi: 1959.

Cordier, Andrew W. and Foote Wilder (edts.), *Public Papers of the Secretaries-General of the United Nations Vol. I, Trygve Lie 1946–1953*, NY: Columbia University Press, 1969.

Craster, H. H. E., (Ed.), *Speeches By Viscount Halifax*, London: Royal Institute of International Affairs, Oxford University Press, 1940.

Danışman, H. Basri, *Situation Negative!*, Bangkok: SEATO, 1969.
Dikerdem, Mahmut, *Hariciye Çarkı* (The Wheel of Ministry of Foreign Affairs), İstanbul: Cem Yayınevi, 1989.
———, *Orta Doğu'da Devrim Yılları, Bir Büyükelçi'nin Anıları* (Years of Revolution in the Middle East, An Ambassador's Memoirs), İstanbul: İstanbul Matbaası, 1977.
Dora, Celal, *Kore'de Türkler* (Turks in Korea), İstanbul: İsmail Akgün Matbaası, 1963.
Eden, Anthony, *Full Circle: The Memoirs of the Rt. Hon. Sir Anthony Eden*, London: Cassel & Co. Ltd., 1960.
Eisenhower, Dwight D., *The White House Years*, New York: Garden City, Doubleday Co., 1963.
Erkin, Feridun Cemal, *Dışişlerinde 34 Yıl* (34 Years in the MFA), Vols. I-II-III, Ankara: Türk Tarih Kurumu Basımevi, 1992.
Glubb, John, *Britain and the Arabs: A Study of Fifty Years 1908 to 1958*, London: Hudder & Stoughton Ltd., 1959.
Gökmen, Oğuz, *Bir Zamanlar Hariciye Eski Bir Diplomatın Hatıraları* (Once Upon A Time The Ministry of Foreign Affairs Memoirs of A Former Diplomat), İstanbul: Self publication, 1999.
Grew, Joseph C., Turbulent Era: *A Diplomatic Record of Forty Years 1904-1945*, Volumes. I-II, Cambridge, Massachusetts: The Riverside Press, 1953.
Gromyko, Andrei, *Memoirs*, NY: Doubleday, 1989.
Günver, Semih, *Fatin Rüştü Zorlu'nun Öyküsü* (The Story of Fatin Rüştü Zorlu), İstanbul: Bilgi Yayınevi, 2005.
Gürsoy, Nilüfer Bayar, *27 Mayıs Darbesi ve Bizler* (The Coup of May 27 and We), İstanbul: Timaş Yayınları, 2014.
Harvey, John, (Ed.), *The Diplomatic Diaries of Oliver Harvey 1937-1940*, London: Collins Clear-Type Press, 1970.
Hunt, Michael H, *Crises in U.S. Foreign Policy*, New Haven: Yale University Press, 1996.
Ilıcak, Nazlı, *27 Mayıs Yargılanıyor* (May 27 on Trial), İstanbul: Kervan Yayınları, 1975.
Karabekir, Kazım, *Ankara'da Savaş Rüzgarları* (The Winds of War in Ankara), İstanbul: Emre Yayınları, 1994.
Kennan, George F., *Memoirs, 1925-1950*, New York: Bantam, 1967.
———, *Memoirs: 1950-1963*, Boston: Little, Brown, 1972.
Knatchbull-Hugessen, H.M., *Diplomat in Peace and War*, London: Murray, 1949.

Langworth, Richard M. (ed.), *Churchill by Himself: The Definitive Collection of Quotations*, London: Public Affairs, 2008.

Madanoğlu, Cemal, *Anılar* (Memoirs), İstanbul: Evrim Yayınevi, 1982.

McGhee, George, *Envoy to the Middle World: Adventures in Diplomacy*, New York: Harper & Row Publishers, 1983.

Muggeridge, Malcolm, (Ed.), *Ciano's Diplomatic Papers*, (Trans. by Stuart Hood), London: Long Acre, Odhams Press Ltd., 1948.

Nutting, Anthony, *Nasser*, London: Constable & Co. Ltd., 1972.

——, *No End of A Lesson*, London: Constable & Co. Ltd., 1967.

Ridgway, Matthew B., *The Korean War*, NY: Doubleday, 1967.

Sertel, Zekeriya, *Hatırladıklarım* (Things I Remembered), İstanbul: Gözlem Yayınları, 1977.

Tezel, Memduh, *Moskova'dan Geliyorum* I am Coming From Moscow), İstanbul: Güven Basımevi, 1950.

Truman, Harry S., *Memoirs: 1945, Year of Decisions*, NY: Signet, 1955.

——, *Memoirs: 1946-1952, Years of Trial and Hope*, NY: Signet, 1956.

Iatrides, John O., (Ed.), *Ambassador MacVeagh Reports Greece, 1933-1947*, Princeton: Princeton University Press, 1980.

Weizsäcker, Ernst, *Memoirs*, London: Victor Gollanz, 1951.

Interviews

Retd. Ambassador Semih Günver, (Ankara, 11/5/1998).

Former Undersecretary of Turkish Ministry of Foreign Affairs, Retd. Ambassador Namık Yolga, (Ankara, 16/9/1998).

Hasan Basri Danışman, Retd. UN Official, Aide and Personal Interpreter of Brigadier Gen. Sırrı Acar, Commander of Turkish Brigade to Korea, (İstanbul, 8/5/1999).

Şükrü Erkal, Retd. Col., Research Specialist, Directorate of Military History and Strategic Research, (TGS, ATASE, Ankara, 20/7/1999).

Prof. George Harris, Author of Troubled Alliance and Turkey Coping with Crisis, (Ankara, 26/8/1999).

Documentary Collections

Ayın Tarihi (Chronicle of the Month), Ankara: Başbakanlık Matbaası, Years, 1946-1950.

Keesing's Contemporary Archives, London:
i.　Vol. No. IV, 1940-1943

ii. Vol. No. V, 1944–1945

iii. Vol. No. VI, 1946–1948

Royal Institute of International Affairs, Documents on International Affairs, Oxford: Oxford University Press, Years, 1949–1952.

The World Today, Iraq, Egypt and the Arab League, London: Chatham House, 1955.

Other Published Materials

The Cold War in Asia, Cold War International History Project Bulletin, Washington D.C.: Woodrow Wilson International Center for Scholars, Issues 6–7, Winter 1995/1996.

History of Soviet Foreign Policy 1945–1970, (translated), Moscow: Progress Publishers, 1974.

The Korean War, Korea Institute of Military History, Seoul: The Military Mutual Aid Association, 1998.

Kore Nere? (Where is Korea?), http://www.behiceboran.org.

Milestones of Soviet Foreign Policy 1917–1967, (translated), Moscow: Progress Publishers, 1967.

Mao Zedong's Manuscripts Since the Founding of the Republic, Vol. I, Jianguo Yilai Mao Zedong Wengao, Beijing: The Central Press of Historical Documents, 1987.

Stalin's Dialogue with Mao Zedong, in the Appendix of, Goncharov, Sergei N., Lewis, John W., and Litai, Xue, Uncertain Partners: Stalin Mao and the Korean War, Stanford: Stanford University Press, pp 227–300, 1995.

Note of the Government of the Soviet Union to the Government of the Republic of Turkey, August 7, 1946;

Note of the Government of the Republic of Turkey to the Government of the Soviet Union, August 22, 1946;

Note of the Government of the Soviet Union to the Government of the Republic of Turkey, September 24, 1946;

Note of the Government of the Republic of Turkey to the Government of the Soviet Union, October 18, 1946, in the Appendix of, Erkin, F. Cemal, Türk–Sovyet İlişkileri ve Boğazlar Meselesi, Ankara: Başnur Matbaası, 1968.

Survey of Attitudes of Arab States Toward Turkey by US Diplomats, in the Appendix of, McGhee, George, The US–Turkish–NATO Middle East Connection, London: Macmillan, 1990.

Survey of International Affairs The Eve of War 1939, edited by Arnold J. Toynbee and Veronica Toynbee, London: Royal Institut of International Affairs, Oxford University Press, 1958.

Treaty of Mutual Assistance Between His Majesty in Respect of the United Kingdom, the President of the French Republic, and the President of the Turkish Republic, on 19 October, 1939, in the Appendix of, Deringil, Selim, Turkish Foreign Policy During the Second World War, Cambridge: Cambridge University Press, 1989.

Türkiye Cumhuriyeti ile Alman Reich'ı Arasında Andlaşma (Agreement Between the Republic of Turkey and the German Reich), in Türkiye'nin Dış Münasebetleriyle İlgili Başlıca Siyasi Andlaşmalar (Major Political Agreements of Turkey Regarding its Foreign Affairs), Soysal, İsmail, Ankara: Türkiye İş Bankası Kültür Yayınları, TTK Basımevi, 1965.

Unpublished Materials

Archives of the Turkish Ministry of Foreign Affairs; Years, 1945–1952; Sections: US, UK, Middle and Far East, Yalta Conference and San Francisco Conference which include the following in chronological order:

Telegram of Chungqing (China) Embassy dated January,24,1946, to the MFA Concerning the Manifesto of Provisional Korean Government in Chungqing.

Telegram of the Turkish Embassy in London to the MFA, dated February 23, 1945.

Telegram of the Turkish Embassy in Washington to the MFA, dated March 3, 1945.

Telegram of the Turkish Embassy in Washington to the MFA, dated June 25, 1947.

Note of the British Embassy in Ankara to the MFA, dated July 4, 1947.

Note of the British Embassy in Ankara to the MFA, dated July 5, 1947.

Telegram of Charge d'Affaires in Moscow to the MFA (undated, unsigned), on News Published in Pravda (issues October, 13–14, 1948).

Letter dated December, 9, 1948, by Ambassador John M. Chang, Chief Delegate of the Republic of Korea to the United Nations, to the Minister of Foreign Affairs Necmettin Sadak.

Telegram of Ambassador Selim Sarper, to the MFA, on the Note by UN General Secretariat Concerning General Assembly's Decision dated January 10, 1949.

Memorandum of the US Embassy in Ankara, dated March 30, 1949 to the MFA: The Present Views of the United States Government with Regard to the Problem of Korea.

Letter(s) dated May 23, 1949, July 21, 1949, by Ambassador Chough, Fyung Ok, Chief Delegate of the Republic of Korea to the United Nations, to Ambassador Selim Sarper, Permanent Representative of Turkey to the United Nations.

Note (MFA) dated September, 1949, Concerning the Chronology of Events in Korea.

Note (MFA) dated October, 1949, Concerning the Letter dated September, 1949 of the Korean Minister of Foreign Affairs.

Telegram dated June 29, 1950, from the Press Attaché in Washington to the General Directorate of Press.

Note (undated, unsigned) by the Embassy in Rome to the MFA, Concerning the Press Releases Between June 29, July, 6, 1950 on Korea.

Note dated November, 25, 1950, by the Embassy in Brussels to the MFA, Concerning the Press Releases on Korea.

Secondary Sources

Books

Ahmad, Feroz, *The Making of Modern Turkey*, London: Routledge, 1994.

——, *The Turkish Experiment in Democracy*, Colorado: Westview Press, Boulder, 1977.

Ahmad, Bedia Turgay, Feroz, *Türkiye'de Çok Partili Politikanın Açıklamalı Kronolojisi 1945–1971* (Chronology of Multiparty Politics in Turkey with Explanations 1945–1971), Ankara: Bilgi Yayınevi, 1976.

Akar, Rıdvan, *Aşkale Yolcuları* (The Passengers of Ashkale), İstanbul: Belge Yayınları, 2000.

Aktar, Ayhan, *Varlık Vergisi ve Türkleştirme Politikaları* (Capital Tax and the Policies of Turkification), İstanbul: İletişim Yayınları, 2000.

Alistair, Horne, *Macmillan 1894–1956, Vol. I of the Official Bibliography*, London: Macmillan Ltd., 1988.

Alteras, Isaac, *Eisenhower and Israel U.S.-Israeli Relations 1953-1960*, Gainesville: The University Press of Florida, 1993.

Arcayürek, Cüneyt, *Şeytan Üçgeninde Türkiye* (Turkey in the Bermuda Triangle), Ankara: Bilgi Yayınevi, 1987.

Armaoğlu, Fahir, *XX. Yüz Yıl Siyasi Tarihi 1914-1980*, Vol. I, Ankara: T.C. İş Bankası Kültür Yayınları, 1991.

Ataöv, Türkkaya, *NATO and Turkey*, Ankara: Sevinç Printing House, 1970.

Avcıoğlu, Doğan, *Milli Kurtuluş Tarihi* (History of National Liberation) Vol. IV, Ankara: Tekin Yayınevi, 1997.

——, *Türkiye'nin Düzeni* (The Order of Turkey), Ankara: Bilgi Yayınevi, 1969.

Aybar, Mehmet Ali, *Bağımsızlık Demokrasi Sosyalizm* (Independence Democracy Socialism), İstanbul: Gerçek Yayınevi, 1968.

Bağcı, Hüseyin, *Demokrat Parti Dönemi Dış Politikası* (Foreign Policy of the Democrat Party Era), Ankara: İmge Kitabevi, 1990.

Bali, Rıfat N., *Bir Türkleştirme Serüveni* (An Adventure of Turkification) (1923-1945), İstanbul: İletişim Yayınları, 2000.

Barlas, Dilek, *Etatism & Diplomacy in Turkey*, NY: Brill,1998.

Berkes, Niyazi, *Türkiye'de Çağdaşlaşma* (Westernization in Turkey), İstanbul: Doğu-Batı Yayınları, Undated.

——, *Türk Düşününde Batı Sorunu* (The Western Question in Turkish Thought), Ankara: Bilgi Yayınevi, 1975.

——, *Unutulan Yıllar* (The Forgotten Years), İstanbul: İletişim Yayınları, 1997.

Beugel, Ernst H. Van Der, *From Marshall Aid to Atlantic Partnership*, NY: American Elsevier Publishing Co. Inc., 1966.

Bilge, Suat, *Güç Komşuluk* (Neighbourhood of Hardship), Ankara: İş Bankası Kültür Yayınları, 1992.

Blake, Robert, *The Decline of Power 1915-1964*, London: Granada, 1985.

Bozdağ, İsmet, *Menderes . . . Menderes*, İstanbul: Emre Yayınları, 1997.

Broad, Lewis, *Sir Anthony Eden The Chronicles of A Career*, London: Hutchinson, 1955.

Bryant, Arthur, *Triumph in the West*, London: Collins, 1959.

Childres, Erskine B., *The Road to Suez: A Study of Western-Arab Relations*, London: MacGibbon & Kee Ltd., 1962.

Çağlar, Derya, *Hayali Komünizm* (Imaginary Communism), İstanbul: Berfin Yayınları, 2008.

Çetik, Mete, *Üniversitede Cadı Avı* (Witch Hunt in the University), Ankara: Dipnot Yayınları, 2008.

Dallin, David, *Soviet Russia's Foreign Policy During The Second World War*, New Haven: Yale University Press, 3rd Printing, 1944.

Dann, Uriel, *King Hussein and the Challenge of Arab Radicalism Jordan 1955-1957*, London: Oxford University Press, 1989.

Denizli, Ali, *Kore Harbi'nde Türk Tugayları* (The Turkish Brigades in the Korean War), Ankara: Gnkur. Basımevi, 1994.

Dennett, Raymond and Turner, Robert K., *Documents on American Foreign Relations, 1945-1946*, NY: Harper, for the Council on Foreign Relations, 1971.

Deringil, Selim, *Turkish Foreign Policy During the Second World War*, Cambridge: Cambridge University Press, 1989.

Deutscher, Isaac, *Stalin*, Middlesex: Penguin Books, 1996.

Devereux, David R., *The Formulation of British Defence Policy Towards the Middle East 1948-1956*, Canada: Macmillan Academic and Professional Ltd., 1990.

Dockrill, Michael L., *The Cold War 1945-1963*, NJ: Humanities Press, 1988.

Dudley, William (ed.), *The Cold War Opposing Viewpoints*, San Diego: Greenhaven Press, 1992.

Erkin, F. Cemal, *Türk-Sovyet İlişkileri ve Boğazlar Meselesi* (Turkish-Soviet Relations and the Straits Question), Ankara: Başnur Matbaası, 1968.

Eroğul, Cem, *Demokrat Parti Tarihi ve İdeolojisi* (Democrat Party Its History and Ideology), Ankara: İmge Kitabevi, 1990.

Evron, Yair, *The Middle East: Nations, Super-powers and Wars*, London: Elek Books, 1973.

Faik Ökte, *Varlık Vergisi Faciası* (The Disaster of Capital Tax), İstanbul: Nebioğlu Yayınevi, Undated.

Ferrell, Robert H., (ed.), *Off the Record: The Private Papers of Harry S. Truman*, NY: Harper & Row, 1980.

Fehrenbach T.R., *This Kind of War*, Washington: Brassey's, 1998.

Fox, Annette Baker, *The Power of Small States*, Chicago: University of Chicago Press, 1959.

Fraser, Harbutt, *The Iron Curtain: Churchill, America and the Origins of the Cold War*, NY: Oxford University Press, 1986.

Fullick, Roy and Geoffrey Powel, *Suez: The Double War*, London: Hamish Hamilton Ltd., 1979.

Gaddis, John Lewis, *We Now Know*, Oxford: Oxford University Press, 1997.

Gasiorowski, Mark J., *U.S. Foreign Policy and the Shah*, NY: Cornell University Press, 1991.

Gerger, Haluk, *Türk Dış Politikasının Ekonomi Politiği* (The Politico-economy of Turkish Foreign Policy), İstanbul: Belge Yayınları, 1998.

Glubb, John B., *Britain and the Arabs: A Study of Fifty Years 1908 to 1958*, London: Hudder & Stoughton Ltd., 1959.

Goncharov, Sergei N., Lewis, John W., and Litai, Xue, *Uncertain Partners: Stalin, Mao, and the Korean War*, Stanford: Stanford University Press, 1995.

Goold-Adams, Richard, *The Time of Power A Reappraisal of John Foster Dulles*, London: Weidenfeld and Nicolson, 1962.

Grenfell, Captain Russell, *Unconditional Hatred German War Guilt and the Future of Europe*, NY: The Devin-Adair Company, 1958.

Güçlü, Yücel, *Eminence Grise of the Turkish Foreign Service: Numan Menemencioğlu*, Ankara: MFA Publications, 2002.

———, *The Life And Career of A Turkish Diplomat: Açıkalın*, Ankara: MFA Publications, 2002.

Günver, Semih, *Fatin Rüştü Zorlu'nun Öyküsü* (The Story of Fatin Rüştü Zorlu), İstanbul: Bilgi Yayınevi, 2005.

Gürel, Şükrü Sina, *Türk Yunan İlişkileri 1821–1993* (Turco–Greek Relations 1821–1993), Ankara: Ümit Yayıncılık, 1993.

Gürün, Kamuran, *Türk–Sovyet İlişkileri 1920–1953* (Turkish–Soviet Relations 1920–1953), Ankara: Türk Tarih Kurumu, 1991.

———, *Savaşan Dünya ve Türkiye: 3, Savaş 1939–1945* (The World in Fight and Turkey:3, War 1939–1945), İstanbul: Tekin Yayınevi, 2000.

Hahn, Peter L. *The United States, Great Britain, and Egypt, 1945–1956*, North Carolina: The University of North Carolina Press, 1991.

Harris, George S., *Troubled Alliance*, Washington: American Enterprise For Public Policy Research, 1972.

Hastings, Max, *The Korean War*, NY: Touchstone, 1998.

Haydar Tunçkanat, *İkili Anlaşmaların İçyüzü* (The Inside of Bilateral Agreements), Ankara: Ekim Yayınları, 1970.

Hoopes, Townsend, *The Devil and John Foster Dulles: The Diplomacy of Eisenhower Era*, Canada: Little, Brown Co., 1973.

Howard, Harry N., *Turkey, the Straits and U.S. Policy*, Baltimore: Johns Hopkins University Press, 1974.

Hurewitz, J.C., (ed.), *Soviet-American Rivalry in the Middle East*, NY: Praeger Publishers, 1969.

İlhan, Attila, *O Karanlıkta Biz* (We, In That Darkness), İstanbul: Bilgi Yayınevi, 1996.

İnan, Yüksel, *Türk Boğazlarının Siyasal ve Hukuksal Rejimi* (The Political and Legal Regime of the Turish Straits), Ankara: Turhan Kitabevi, 1995.

Inglis, Fred, *The Cruel Peace*, NY: Aurum Press, 1992.

Jack, Ernst, Kuturman P. (trans.), *Yükselen Hilal* (The Rising Crescent), İstanbul: Cumhuriyet Matbaası, 1946.

James, Robert R., Editor, *Winston S. Churchill His Complete Speeches 1897-1963* Volume VII 1943-1949, 5 March 1946, "The Sinews of Peace," NY: Chelsea House Publishers, 1974.

Karpat, Kemal H., *Turkey's Politics: The Transition to a Multi-Party System*, Princeton, N. J.: Princeton University Press, 1959.

Kılıç, Selami, *Türk-Sovyet İlişkilerinin Doğuşu* (The Birth of Turkish-Soviet Relations), İstanbul: Dergah Yayınları, 1998.

Koçak, Cemil, *Türk-Alman İlişkileri 1923-1939* (Turco-German Relations 1923-1939), Ankara: Atatürk Supreme Council For Culture Language And History, Publications of Turkish Historical Society, Serial XVI, No. 66, 1991.

Koloğlu, Orhan, *Cumhuriyet'in İlk Onbeş Yılı (1923-1938)* (The First Fifteen Years of the Republic 1923-1938), İstanbul: Boyut Kitapları, 1999.

Kissinger, Henry, *Diplomacy*, NY: Simon & Schuster, 1994.

Kuniholm, Bruce R., *The Origins of the Cold War in the Near East: Great Power Conflict and Diplomacy in Iran, Turkey and Greece*, NJ: Princeton University Press, 1980.

Küçük, Yalçın, *Türkiye Üzerine Tezler 1908-1998* (Theses on Turkey 1908-1998), İkinci Basım, İstanbul: Tekin Yayınevi, 1998.

Kylie, Keith, *Suez*, London: Weidenfeld and Nicholson Ltd., 1991.

Laqueur, Walter Z., *The Soviet Union and the Middle East*, London: Routledge & Kegan Paul Ltd., 1959.

Leckie, Robert, Conflict, *The History of the Korean War*, NY: Da Capo Press, 1990.

Loewenheim, Francis L., (ed.), *Roosevelt and Churchill: Their Secret Wartime Correspondence*, NY: Dutton, 1975.

Lowe, Peter, *The Origins of the Korean War*, (sec. ed.), NY: Longman, 1997.

Leffler, Melvyn P., *A Preponderance of Power*, Stanford: Stanford University Press, 1993.

Lucas, Scott, *Divided We Stand: The US and the Suez Crisis*, London: Hodder & Stoughton, 1991.

Lyon, Peter, *Eisenhower Portrait of the Hero*, Boston: Little, Brown, 1974.

Macdonald, Robert W., *The League of Arab States: A Study in the Dynamics of Regional Organization*, Princeton: Princeton University Press, 1965.

McCarthy, Justin, *The Ottoman Peoples and the End of Empire*, NY: Oxford University Press, 2001.

McCullough, David, *Truman*, NY: Touchstone, 1993.

McGhee, George, *Envoy to the Middle World: Adventures in Diplomacy*, NY: Harper & Row Publishers, 1983.

——, *The US-Turkish-NATO Middle East Connection*, London: Macmillan Press Ltd, 1990.

Monro MacCloskey, *North Atlantic Treaty Organization*, NY: Richard Rosen Press, 1966.

Monroe, Elisabeth, *Britain's Moment in the Middle East 1914-1971*, (secd. edt.), London: Chatto & Windus Ltd., 1981.

Mosley, Leonard, *Dulles: A Biography of Eleanor, Allen and John Foster Dulles and Their Family Network*, London: Hodder and Stoughton Ltd., 1978.

Milner, Helen and Ruggie, John Gerard, (edts.), *The Logic of Anarchy*, NY: Columbia University Press, 1993.

Neff, Donald, *Warriors at Suez Eisenhower Takes America into the Middle East in 1956*, Vermont: Amana Books, 1988.

Nye, Joseph S. (ed.), *The Making of America's Soviet Policy*, New Haven: Yale University Press, 1984.

Orkunt, Sezai, *Türkiye–ABD Askeri İlişkileri* (Turkey–US Military Relations), İstanbul: Milliyet Yayınları, 1978.

Özersay, Kudret, *Türk Boğazlarından Geçiş Rejimi*, Ankara: Mülkiyeliler Birliği Vakfı Yayınları, 1999.

Pak, Chi Young, *Korea and the United Nations*, The Hague: Kluwer Law International, 2000.

Peretz, Don, *The Middle East Today*, fourth ed., London: Praeger Publishers, 1983.

Plischke, Elmer, (ed.), *Contemporary U.S. Foreign Policy: Documents and Commentary*, Connecticut: Greenwood Press, 1991.

Polk, William R., *The US and the Arab World*, second printing, Massachusetts: Harvard, University Press, 1976.

——, William R., *The Arab World Today*, fifth ed., Massachusets: Harvard University Press, 1991.

Ramazani, Rouhollah K., *Iran's Foreign Policy 1941-1973: A Study of Foreign Policy in Modernizing Nations*, Virginia: The University Press of Virginia, 1975.

Pratt, Julius W., *A History of the United States Foreign Policy*, NY: Prentice-Hall, 1955.

Reed, John, *Ten Days that Shook the World*, NY: Vintage Books, 1960.

Rhodes, Robert James, *Anthony Eden*, London: Weidenfeld and Nicolson, 1986.

Roberts, Andrew, *The Holy Fox A Biography of Lord Halifax*, London: Weidenfeld and Nicolson, 1991.

Ross, Graham, *The Great Powers and the Decline of the European States System 1914-1945*, (ninth impression), NY: Longman, 1991.

Rubin, Barry, *Istanbul Intrigues*, NY: McGraw-Hill, Publishing Co, 1989.

Safran, Nadav, *From War to War: The Arab-Israeli Confrontation 1948-1967*, first ed., Indianapolis: Bobbs-Merril Educational Publishing, 1977.

Sanal, Türker, *Türkiye'nin Hükümetleri* (Governments of Turkey). Ankara: Sim Matbaacılık, 1997.

Sampson, Anthony, *Macmillan A Study in Ambiguity*, London: Allen Lane the Penguin Press, 1967.

Sander, Oral, *Türk-Amerikan İlişkileri 1947-1964* (Turkish-American Relations 1947-1964), Ankara: SBF Yayınları, 1979.

Sayed-Ahmed, Muhammad Abd el-Wahab, *Nasser and American Foreign Policy 1952-195*, Surrey: Laam Ltd., 1989.

Schlesinger, Arthur M., *The Cycles of American History*, Boston: Houghton Mifflin Co., 1986.

Sencer, Muammer; Yalçın Mehmet Ali, *Gizli Belgeler* (Secret Documents), İstanbul: May Yayınları, 1968.

Sertel, Yıldız, *Nâzım Hikmet ile Serteller*, (Nâzım Hikmet and Sertels), İstanbul: Everest Yayınları, 2008, 44.

——, *Türkiye'de İlerici Akımlar* (The Progressive Movements in Turkey), İstanbul: Ant Yayınları, 1969.

Smith, Joseph, *The Cold War 1945-1965*, London: Published by the Basic Blackwell Ltd. for the Historical Association Studies, 1986.

Sonyel, Salahi R., *Atatürk—The Founder of Modern Turkey*, Ankara: Atatürk Supreme Council For Culture Language And History, Publications of Turkish Historical Society, Serial XVI, No. 55, 1989.

Soysal, İsmail, *Soğuk Savaş Dönemi ve Türkiye Olaylar Kronolojsi* (The Cold War Era And Turkey Chronology of Events) 1945–1975, İstanbul: İsis Yayımcılık Ltd, 1997.

Spanier, John W., *American Foreign Policy Since World War II*, NY: Praeger Publishers, 1973.

——, *The Truman-MacArthur Controversy and the Korean War*, NY: Norton Co., 1965.

Stephens, Robert, *Nasser*, Aylesbury: Pelican Books, 1973.

Şimşir, Bilal N., *The Turks of Bulgaria (1878–1985)*, London: K. Rustem & Brother, 1988.

——, *Bizim Diplomatlar* (Our Diplomats), Ankara: Bilgi Yayınevi, 1996.

Tamkoç, Metin, *The Warrior Diplomats: Guardians of the National Security and Modernization of Turkey*, Utah: University of Utah Press, 1976.

Thomson, Kenneth W., *Cold War Theories Volume I: World Polarization 1943–1953*, Baton Rouge: Louisiana State University Press, 1981.

Toker, Metin, *Tek Partiden Çok Partiye 1944–1950* (From Single Party to Multi Party 1944–1950), Ankara: Bilgi Yayınevi, 1998.

Tibi, Bassam, *Conflict and War in the Middle East 1967–91*, NY: St. Martin's Press, 1993.

——, *DP'nin Altın Yılları 1950–1954*, Ankara: Bilgi Yayınevi, 1991.

Toland, John, *In Mortal Combat Korea, 1950–1953*, NY: William Morrow, 1991.

Vali, Frenc A., *Bridge Across the Bosporus: The Foreign Policy of Turkey*, Baltimore: The Johns Hopkins Press, 1971.

Vatikiotis, P. J., *The Egyptian Army in Politics*, Bloomington: Indiana University Press, 1961.

——, *The History of Egypt*, second ed., London: Weidenfeld and Nicolson, 1980.

——, *Nasser and His Generation*, London: Croom Held Ltd., 1978.

Wallach, Janet, *Desert Queen*, London: Weidenfeld & Nicolson, 1996.

Walsh, Pat, *Britain's Great War on Turkey*, Belfast: Athol Books, 2009.

Waterfield , Gordon, *Sir Percy Loraine Professional Diplomat*, London: Murray, 1973.

Weber, Frank G., *The Evasive Neutral*, Missouri: University of Missouri Press, 1979.

Weisband, Edward, *Turkish Foreign Policy 1943-1945*, Princeton: Princeton University Press, 1973.

Wellborn, Fred W., *Diplomatic History of the United States*, New Jersey: Littlefield, Adams & Co., 1961.

Wilmot, Chester, *The Struggle for Europe*, New York: Harper & Brothers,1952,

Woodward, Sir Llewllyn, *British Foreign Policy in the Second World War*, London: Her Majesty's Stationery Office, 1962.

Yetkin, Çetin, *Karşı Devrim* (Counter Revolution) 1945-1950, Antalya: Yeniden Anadolu ve Rumeli Müdafaa-i Hukuk Yayınları, 2009.

———, *Struma*, İstanbul: Gürer Yayınları, 2008.

Zhivkova, Ludmilla, *Anglo-Turkish Relations 1933-1939*, London: Secker & Warburg, 1976.

Articles

Ashton, Nigel John, "The Hijacking of A Pact: The Formation of the Baghdad Pact and Anglo-American Tensions in the Middle East 1955-1958," in *Review of International Studies*, 19, 1993.

Aymaz, Abdullah, "Obama'ya Kitap" (A Book to Obama), in *Zaman*, December 6, 2009.

Beinan, Joel, "The Communist Movement and Nationalist Political Discourse in Nasserist Egypt," in *The Middle East Studies*, Autumn, 1987.

Brown, Robin, "Towards A New Synthesis of International Relations," in *From Cold War To Collapse Theory and World Politics in the 1980s*, ed. by, Mike Bowker and Robin Brown, Cambridge: Cambridge University Press, 1993.

Davison, Roderic H., "The Armenian Crisis, 1912-1914," in *The American Historical Review*, Vol. 53, No. 3, Apr., 1948.

Demirel, Meral, "Ahali Cumhuriyet Fırkası," in *Tarih ve Toplum*, Vol. 32, No. 192, İstanbul: İletişim Yayınları, December, 1999.

Dilks, David, "The Twilight War And The Fall of France: Chamberlain And Churchill in 1940," in *Retreat From Power*, Vol. Two, edited by David Dilks, London: Macmillan Press, 1981.

İnanç, Gül, "The Politics of 'Active Neutrality' on the Eve of a New World Order: The Case of Turkish Chrome Sales during the Second World War," in *Middle Eastern Studies*, Vol. 42, No.6, November 2006,

———, "Bu Yazının Mahrem Tutulmasına İtina Edilecektir: US Missouri Zırhlısının İstanbul Ziyareti ve Soğuk Savaş Diplomasisinde Türkiye, 1946" (This is a Strictly Confidential Message: The Visit of USS Missouri Vessel to İstanbul and Turkey in Cold War Diplomacy, 1946), in *Toplumsal Tarih Dergisi* (Journal of Social History), Vol. 191, İstanbul: Tarih Vakfı Yurt Yayınları, November 2009.

Kaiser, Hilmar, "Regional Resistance to Central Government Policies: Ahmed Djemal Pasha, the Governors of Aleppo, and Armenian Deportees in the Spring and Summer of 1915," in *Journal of Genocide Research*, September–December 2010.

Karpat, Kemal, "The Turkish Left," in *Journal of Contemporary History*, Vol. 1, No. 2, Sage Publications Ltd., 1966.

Kedourie, Elie, "Quest for Stability," in *Soviet–American Rivalry in the Middle East*, ed. by J. C. Hurewitz, NY: Published for the Academy of Political Science Columbia University by Frederick A. Praeger Publishers, 1969.

Kemp, Geoffrey, "The Military Build-up: Arms Control or Arms Trade?" in *Crisis Management and the Super-powers in the Middle East*, ed. by Gregory Trevarton, The International Institute for Strategic Studies, Gower Publishing Ltd., 1981.

Kürkçüoğlu, Ömer, "Türk–İngiliz İlişkileri (1920'lerden, 1950'lere)" (Anglo–Turkish Relations From 1920s to 1950s), in, *Türk–İngiliz İlişkileri 1583-1984, 400. Yıldönümü* (Anglo–Turkish Relations 1583–1984, 400th Anniversary), Ankara: Başbakanlık Basın Yayın Ve Enformasyon Genel Müdürlüğü, 1985.

Lippe, John M. Vander, "Forgotten Brigade of the Forgotten War: Turkey's Participation in the Korean War," in *Middle Eastern Studies*, Vol. 36, No:1, January 2000.

Okyar, Osman, "Fethi Okyar'ın 1922 Ve 1934–1939 Yıllarında Londra'da İlk Kez Görevlendirilmesinin Işığında, Türk–İngiliz Ticaret İlişkilerinin Savaş Arası Dönemdeki Gelişimi" (The Development of Anglo–Turkish Commercial Relations in Interwar Period in the Light of the First Nomination of Fethi Okyar in London in 1922, and in the Years 1934–1939), in, *Türk–İngiliz İlişkileri 1583-1984, 400. Yıldönümü* (Anglo–Turkish Relations 1583–1984, 400th Anniversary), Ankara: Başbakanlık Basın Yayın Ve Enformasyon Genel Müdürlüğü, 1985.

Sadak, Necmeddin, "Turkey Faces the Soviets," in *Foreign Affairs*, 27, No. 2, April 1949.

Vexliard, Alexandre and Aytaç, Kemal, "The 'Village Institutes' in Turkey," in *Comparative Education Review*, Vol. 8, No.1, June, 1964.

Periodicals, Newspapers

Ayın Tarihi
Foreign Affairs
The New York Times
Cumhuriyet
Milliyet
Ulus
Vatan

Index of Names and Subjects

About the Author

Yusuf Turan Çetiner is a career diplomat in the Turkish MFA since 1995. His posts include three Embassies and a General Consulate stretching from far East to Europe, namely Singapore, Albania, Germany and Ireland. He was a former Head of Department at the MFA, Archives and Communication. Çetiner has a PhD (2001, Bilkent University, Ankara) and has two masters degrees (University of Birmingham, Bilkent University). His works and various articles concentrate on the topics of XXth Century diplomatic history and problems of reinterpreting major foreign policy issues. *Turkey and the West: From Neutrality to Commitment* is his first book and a major work completed in the span of a decade.